FAUNA BRITANNICA

FAUNA BRITANNICA

THE PRACTICAL GUIDE
TO WILD & DOMESTIC
CREATURES OF BRITAIN

DUFF HART-DAVIS

WEIDENFELD & NICOLSON

Contents

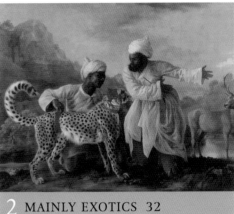

Introduction

This book is essentially a practical guide, describing the creatures, wild and domesticated, that now live in the British Isles or have lived here in the past. It does not claim to be by any means exhaustive, or to cover every species. Rather, it concentrates on the mammals, birds, fish, reptiles, amphibians and insects which people are most likely to come across or to have read about. Selection has been an invidious task, particularly with insects, of which there exist at least a million known species, 100,000 of them in Britain alone.

The book also aims to show how attitudes to animals have changed over the centuries, and to demonstrate how our exploitation of them has had a far-reaching influence on the environment. By no means all the species that feature here are indigenous, for the fauna of Britain has been evolving throughout history. During repeated ice ages the slate was several times swept almost clean as wildlife, driven southwards by advancing cold, abandoned the country for more tolerable climes. When warmer weather returned, animals came back with it, but in different combinations. In historical times some species have been deliberately and accidently imported and others have gone extinct. The result is the unique mixture that we have today; but so long as a creature is well established in the United Kingdom or Ireland, it can fairly be called British.

Man has lived among animals for the whole of his existence on Earth, first competing with them, then dominating, using and all too often abusing them. But in the past 50 years or so the people of Britain have become overwhelmingly urban, and in consequence have lost contact with nature and the country. Most children have little direct experience of animals and birds: they see them on television, but rarely meet them in the flesh. Yet the growing popularity of farms open to the public, and the striking success of projects like Farms for City Children, which takes whole classes of inner-city schoolchildren to live and work on farms, demonstrate the atavistic affection that people have for animals, and also the beneficial effects that contact with animals can produce. My hope is that this book will be useful as a reference for people whose interest in animals has been awakened by passing acquaintance.

It was only in the twentieth century that the idea of conserving our wildlife took root. The pace at which ideas changed is illustrated by the growth of the Royal Society for the Protection of Birds (RSPB), which, after a slow start, accelerated phenomenally as the last century ran out. The Society, founded in 1889, was incorporated by Royal Charter in 1904, and acquired its first reserve in 1928. Yet it was not until 1960 that membership reached the 10,000 mark. Then, with growing anxiety about toxic agricultural chemicals acting as a spur, it began to climb rapidly – to 50,000 in 1969, 100,000 in 1972 and 200,000 in 1976. Even that spurt was nothing compared with what followed: after breaking the 500,000 barrier in 1989, the Society took only nine years to reach the magic figure of a million.

Similarly, the Society for the Promotion of Nature Reserves – forerunner of the Wildlife Trusts – was founded in 1912, and the first of the Trusts (Norfolk) was created in 1926. At the end of the year 2000 the group had a network of 46 independent wildlife charities, over 100 urban wildlife groups and 325,000 members. Few single events gave the conservation movement greater impetus than the publication, in 1962, of Rachel Carson's ground-breaking book *Silent Spring*, which revealed the damage being done to birds and animals by agricultural chemicals.

Concern over the welfare of animals, both wild and domestic, has also increased enormously. The Royal Society for the Prevention of Cruelty to Animals is the oldest animal welfare organisation the world, and now one of the largest. It was founded in 1824 as simply the SPCA, and received its royal charter from Queen Victoria in 1840. Today its annual income (all from voluntary donations) is £60 million; its hospitals and clinics in England and Wales treat over 270,000 creatures every year, and its 320-odd inspectors investigate 100,000 complaints of cruelty.

Today the drive for conservation of the environment and its creatures is omnipresent. In 1991 the government body English Nature began its Species Recovery Programme, designed to halt the decline of creatures that were under threat. Having originally included only 13 species, the programme has expanded so much that it now aims to protect over 400 species, of flora as well as fauna, and has identified another 250 that need help. The word on everybody's lips is 'biodiversity' – a shorthand expression meaning that man should encourage and preserve as many species as possible, of plants and trees as well as of wildlife. In 1994, as a follow-up to the 1992 Earth Summit in Rio de Janeiro, English Nature launched the UK Biodiversity Action Plan, which aimed to coordinate the efforts of national conservation bodies, and, at local level, to protect the characteristic wildlife and habitat that make particular areas unique. The initiative set in train more than 100 local action plans, designed to benefit 400 species and 45 priority habitats.

We have come a long way since wheatears, 'dressed to perfection', were on the menu at the Castle Inn in Brighton, and a local historian in Bedfordshire, writing in 1820, described how 'Dunstable larks are served up in great perfection at some of the inns in this town (owing to a peculiar and secret method in the process of cooking them); they are admired as a luxury by the nobility and gentry who travel through Dunstable in the lark season.'

A few words of background may help explain my own position. I was lucky enough to grow up on a remote farm tucked away in one corner of a 2500-acre estate in the Chiltern Hills. With its deep, brick-lined cisterns for storing rainwater, its spacious wood-framed barns with their lofts and dark corners, its antique implements rusting under layers of dust, the farmyard itself made a thrilling play-ground for a boy with country leanings. Yet for me the real magic of the place lay in its isolation. Below the garden and orchard a secret, wooded valley swung round in a right-angle bend, cutting the house off from the rest of the world. Beyond the valley farmland rolled on to the horizon.

I have often wondered how I would have turned out if I had been brought up in a town. There was nothing in my immediate ancestry to give me rustic longings. My father, the ultimate bookworm, never shot, fished or hunted in his life, and he rented the farmhouse only because it was standing empty, and a friend besought him to take it. My mother was equally unversed in rural pursuits.

All the same, I took to the country with unquestioning delight. From someone, or somewhere, I had inherited the hunting instinct, and this was fanned into flame by the enthusiasm of the estate owner, who was also my god-father. The gift of an airgun at the age of ten meant that I could engage the rats and (I am afraid) the sparrows in the farmyard. Soon, armed with a single-barrelled 28-bore, I began to prowl the hedgerows and woodland edges in search of rabbits.

My godfather encouraged me to go out with the game-keeper, Harry Brown, a tall, slow-spoken man from Dorset, on his daily round of traps and snares; the squire must have given instructions that I was to be looked after, because the keeper tolerated my presence and answered my questions with unfaltering patience. From him I learnt how to build tunnel traps for rats and stoats; how to spot the points at which rabbits touched down in their runs across the field, and there to set snares; how to handle ferrets; where to stand and flight pigeons on winter evenings. I became so keen that, the moment I came home from prep school for the holidays, I would rush out into the woods and stay there for every daylight hour – to the growing chagrin of my mother, who began to feel that I preferred the locals' company to hers. In the evenings, I was riveted by Richard Jefferies' classic evocations of the Victorian countryside, *The Gamekeeper at Home* and *The Amateur Poacher*.

In my teens I started to help on the farm, not least as stand-in milkman – and I am still haunted by the dreadful morning on which a cow fell dead in the dairy. Surely nothing that I had done could have killed her? Nevertheless, there she lay, an immense black-and-white hulk, blocking the passage along the middle of the shed.

Harvest was a time of blistering hard work but also of high excitement, for as the binder clattered round and round, and the patch of standing corn grew ever smaller, the rabbits trapped in it would rush madly about: you could see lines of disturbance rippling through the ears, until suddenly a desperate fugitive would burst into the open, and everyone would try to whack it with a stick or drop on it before it could escape to safety. Then came the marathon task of building the sheaves into stooks, six or eight in each little assembly: a job which left the insides of forearms raw from wrist to bicep.

In winter one of the great thrills was thrashing: the bulky machine, driven by a canvas belt linked to a tractor or steam-engine, was parked alongside the rick, and as the man on top of the stack lifted each sheaf with a pitchfork, to toss it into the maw of the rumbling, rattling giant, rats and mice would erupt from their nests, slither desperately to the edges and leap into space, falling like manna among the terriers waiting below.

Yet it was always the open country that drew me most powerfully. The result was that I came to know one stretch of the Chilterns in intimate detail. I learned the names not just of every wood and copse, but of every field as well – Blackbirds, Amos, Marlins, Searchlight. I knew the wood-land rides, the foxes' earths, the dew-ponds hidden among the trees, the mossy banks that marked the lines of ancient pathways, the hollow trunks in which one could shelter from the rain. From all my lurking and prowling came a life-long love of that rolling landscape, in which flints burst from the chalky soil by the million and autumn beechwoods cloak the hills in folds of copper.

As I grew older, I gradually realised how important it is that man should manage his surroundings. At home the most obvious illustration of this principle was our system of storing water. On those chalk hills there are no springs or streams; so the builders of house and barns had made elaborate arrangements for catching rain off the roofs. Their subterranean cisterns were works of art, and without them, before the days of piped supplies, the place would have been uninhabitable. Men, women, the dairy herd, the working horses – all depended on the underground tanks for drinking water, which came up into our kitchen through a hand-worked pump.

The need for control of the environment was equally evident in the woods. During the Second World War large areas of beech had been felled in an all-out drive for timber production. The new plantations that took their place were a mixture of hard and soft wood: among the larch and spruce, every seventh row was of beech saplings. The idea was that the quick-growing soft wood should nurse the hard: that beech would be the final crop. Alas for human plans! The beech grew well until they were 10 or 12 years old and had a diameter of three or four inches: then, almost without exception, they were maimed or killed by the voracious bark-gnawing of grey squirrels. We realised what was happening, and did our best to destroy the pests; but the survivors continued their deadly work, and whole generations of beech trees were wiped out.

In the same way, I saw that if crows and magpies were allowed to flourish unchecked, they ate the eggs and young of game and songbirds. If plantations were not fenced against rabbits, the seedling trees were soon destroyed. Later, if not regularly cleared of scrub, the new woods turned into jungle, which suffocated any trees that survived. If fields were left uncut or untilled, they were soon over-run by pernicious weeds. Cattle not confined by sound fences would trample crops and trees alike. In the farmyard, rats would kill chicks, steal food and eat away the very foundations of the barns with their endless tunnelling and boring.

Again and again I saw creatures living on each other: badgers eating earthworms, birds devouring caterpillars, owls catching mice, sparrowhawks downing blue tits, foxes killing rabbits or snatching our chickens from the farm. I realised that in the country death is an inescapable part of everyday life. Whenever I watched a thrush smashing open a snail's shell, or heard a rabbit squealing with terror in the lethal grip of a stoat, I was fascinated but not upset, because I knew all this was part of nature. In the same way, I felt that shooting was a natural activity. I never had the slightest wish to inflict pain on any bird or animal, but I did want to shoot rabbits and pigeons for the pot, and to kill animals like squirrels or rats which were deemed a menace. I was brought up to look on game as a crop, which, if properly cared for, produces an annual surplus, and can be harvested just like wheat – not merely without detriment to the countryside, but with positive benefits to the land.

So I grew up a hunter, imbued with the belief that man should actively manage his environment, controlling wildlife in the same way as he controls farm animals, so as to produce a reasonable balance. When I was a boy, the concept of conservation had not been invented. Now it is the watchword everywhere, and management of nature has become immensely more professional – a development entirely for the good.

During the twentieth century attitudes to animals changed radically – and the main reason, undoubtedly, was the huge shift in the human population. The first census, taken in in 1801, showed that 30 per cent of British people lived in towns or cities. By 2000 the figure had grown to 90 per cent. The vast majority of our people are now cut off from the land, and many of those who have moved out into country villages take no part in rural activities. This mass withdrawal from the soil has induced entirely new perceptions. In the words of the distinguished biologist Dr William Stanton:

> Thanks to Beatrix Potter, Kenneth Grahame, Walt Disney and others, the wild animals most familiar to man (i.e. species with which he was [once] constantly at war) are perceived to have human characteristics. Rabbits are jolly but a bit dim, foxes are clever rogues, badgers wise and kind, otters heroic, squirrels delightful, hedgehogs and moles worthy, water voles clever, rats evil, and deer sweet and cruelly persecuted. Consequently, pressure groups protest loudly and sometimes violently when man lays hands on these animals.

The drive for conservation reached a peak – though whether of excellence or absurdity depends on your viewpoint – with the construction of bungalows designed entirely for bats. One such went up in the winter of 2000 at Over, on the western outskirts of Gloucester, where the development company Swan Hill Homes acquired the site of a former isolation hospital and set about building 30-odd executive-style houses. At an early stage of the proceedings they found that they would have to rehouse, besides executives, a colony of 50 lesser horseshoe bats which had been living for years in a disused subterranean boiler-room. Because the species is classed as endangered, and is fully protected by law, the colony could not legally be evicted.

The developers' (perfectly correct) response was to engage a leading environmental consultant to design a bat bungalow, with an open-plan ground floor, a cellar for hibernation in winter, and a steeply pitched roof of black tiles which would attract heat in summer and build up a comfortable temperature for nursing mothers inside. The building was allocated a garden of its own, to give the occupants some privacy, and had only one small window at the back, facing a hedge (used by the bats as a flight-line) and open fields. When the bungalow was finished, a large-diameter, subterranean concrete pipe, leading from the old boiler-room, was opened up to give access to the cellar, and the bats moved in.

The cost of the bungalow was £30,000; but if one takes into consideration the fact that its site could have been occupied by one more £300,000 house, it is clear that the expenditure per bat was phenomenal. If the old boiler-room had simply been opened up on a warm summer evening, would the tiny mammals not have found other quarters in some nearby barn? Is this not conservation gone mad? 'Not at all,' said Glyn Mabey, nanaging director of Swan Hill Homes. 'We were very glad to do something positive for the environment.'

NATIVE PINEWOOD: DAWN MIST
RISES THROUGH THE PINES IN
STRATHSPEY, SCOTLAND.

1 IN THE BEGINNING

Small as it is, the land that

is now Britain has given sanctuary to an amazing variety of creatures over the vast expanse of time. Dozens of species have evolved, and dozens have gone extinct. Written accounts of animals go back barely more than a thousand years; primitive pictures, sculptures and ornaments take us further, but the fossil record reaches out into the deep space of the distant past to reveal the wealth of wildlife that once flourished here.

Until about 8500 years ago animals could come and go at will, for this country was joined to the mainland of Europe; then, with the melting of the northern ice, the sealevel rose, cutting us off and creating what John O'Gaunt, in Shakespeare's *Richard II*, called 'this little world, this precious stone set in the silver sea'. Once Britain had become an archipelago, birds and marine creatures could still migrate over or through the water; but land-living creatures were confined, and their future depended largely on the degree to which human beings managed or harassed them.

The balance of nature in these islands has constantly changed over the centuries, and it is still changing today, as conservationists strive to support species that are faltering, enthusiasts press for the reintroduction of animals like the wolf, the brown bear and the lynx which have long since gone extinct, and powerful survivors such as the North American mink establish themselves in the wild after escaping from captivity. Considering how crowded our land space has become, with almost 60 million human inhabitants in Britain and Northern Ireland, and nearly four million in the Irish Republic, the wealth of our fauna remains astonishing.

ANCIENT DORSET (previous pages)
ENGRAVING BY GEORGE SCHARF
(1820–95) DEPICTING THE TEEMING
LIFE OF THE JURASSIC SEAS.

GEOLOGY AND PALAEONTOLOGY (right)
NINETEENTH-CENTURY ILLUSTRATION
SHOWING FORMATION OF ROCKS AND
EVOLUTION OF LIFE ON EARTH.

Dinosaurs

Because *Homo sapiens* has so firmly taken control of the animal kingdom, it is tempting to introduce humans first, as the planet's leading mammal. Yet to give humans such priority might be confusing, for in terms of living creatures we came on the scene relatively late.

Fans of Steven Spielberg's *Jurassic Park* films may have gained the notion that early humans were a contemporary of the dinosaurs. Any such idea is a very long way wide off the mark – for although the great reptiles inhabited the Earth for millions of years, they disappeared 65 million years ago – at least 40 million years before primates began evolving in Africa. After the dinosaurs' demise, 60 million years passed before chimpanzees – man's closest living relatives – went their separate evolutionary way, and the hominid *Australopithecus*, which walked upright, came on the scene. At least 64 million summers and winters came and went before the tall *Homo erectus* (1.9 metres tall) wandered across the Earth. Nevertheless, dinosaurs did once live in the land we now call Britain, and traces of them abound beneath our feet.

Imagine an environment almost entirely green, brown and grey-blue, the ground carpeted not with grass, but with moss and fern-like plants, interspersed by shallow lagoons fringed with trees more akin to giant ferns than any of the species we know today. On still days the hot, steamy air must have been very quiet, for it was a world without birds, and only the occasional scream or roar of a reptile tore the silence. Such were the surroundings in which the dinosaurs existed. The landmass of the Earth was all in one piece – a single, huge continent stretching from pole to pole, which scientists now call Pangaea – 'Whole Earth' – with a vast, dry desert at its centre.

That time now seems unimaginably remote. Yet we have clear evidence that dinosaurs and pterosaurs (winged reptiles) evolved in the Late Triassic age, some 230 million years ago. With them developed primitive forms of turtles, crocodiles and the earliest

mammals: fossils of a tiny animal called *Morganucodon* have been found in caves in South Wales. This was a shrew-sized creature, and the many small openings in the bones of its pointed snout suggest that it had long, sensory whiskers, like its modern counterparts. The animal's small stature and the nature of its teeth indicate that it ate insects and other small invertebrates, and its relatively large eye-sockets may mean that it was nocturnal.

To our eyes the dinosaurs were grotesquely misshapen and alarming: the two Greek words that make up the name, *deinos* and *sauros*, mean 'terrible lizard'. They were also the biggest creatures (apart from the blue whale) the world has ever known, and among the longest survivors, existing for 165 million years. Scientists remain divided on the question of whether they were warm or cold-blooded: some palaeontologists believe that all dinosaurs had rapid metabolic rates, like modern mammals and birds, and so were warm-blooded; but others doubt it. There is no definite evidence either way. Nor is anyone sure what colour they were, but various combinations of grey, green and brown have been suggested: maybe some creatures developed stripes or blotches for purposes of camouflage, like latter-day tigers.

Dinosaurs reached their greatest dimensions in the Jurassic period. The largest so far discovered, *Brachiosaurus*, probably weighed 70 tons – as much as a dozen elephants – and its head waved around on the end of an elongated neck 12 or 13 metres above the ground – as high as a three-storey house. Chisel-like teeth enabled it to nip leaves and branches from all but the highest trees. Less massive, but at 35 metres even longer, was another herbivore, *Apatosaurus*, formerly known as *Brontosaurus*, which weighed about 35 tons. Longer still was the *Diplodocus*, with a tiny brain, the size of a human fist, boosted by a concentration of nerves at the base of the spine, which helped control its hind legs and long, whip-like tail. The large olfactory lobes in its brain suggest that it had well-developed senses of taste and smell, and may have depended to some extent on scent to warn of approaching danger. Because its teeth were too simple for it to chew, it swallowed stones, which

Geological Periods

	Million Years Ago
TRIASSIC	235
JURASSIC	194
CRETACEOUS	135
PALEOCENE	65
EOCENE	54
OLIGOCENE	38
MIOCENE	23
PLIOCENE	5
PLEISTOCENE	1.7

Archaeological periods

	Dates BC–AD
LATE PALAEOLITHIC	11,000–9000
MESOLITHIC	9000–3000
NEOLITHIC	4000–2500
BRONZE AGE	2400–700
IRON AGE	700–0
ROMAN	43–450 AD
ANGLO-SAXON	500–1000

GEOLOGY AND PALÆONTOLOGY.

1

In the Beginning

Dinosaurs

remained in its stomach, grinding up ingested vegetation.

Such monsters must have needed huge amounts of fresh food to fuel their systems: considering that a modern elephant needs to eat up to 150 kg of green fodder a day, it is astonishing that they did not strip their environment bare. How did each one manage to find and swallow a ton or more of leaves, branches and bark every day? Perhaps they were forever moving on, eating out one patch of greenery and leaving it, with the light let in, to regenerate. The evidence of growth rings and bone textures suggests that these dinosaurs grew to full size in fewer than 20 years, and had a life expectation of 70–130 years.

None of these giants has been found in Britain; but numerous fossilised remains of other types have been discovered here, not least in the Wealden Formation, which extends from under the Weald of Surrey, Sussex and Kent to the Isle of Wight and on beneath France and Belgium. Here, in the Cretaceous period, sand and clay were deposited on low-lying flood-plains and in coastal lagoons which were repeatedly flooded by the sea; and it was here in the 1820s that the doctor and geologist Gideon Mantell became the first Briton to discover the remains of a dinosaur, the *Iguanodon*.

This was a creature from the late Jurassic and early Cretaceous periods, 10 metres long, 5 metres high when upright, and weighing 4 or 5 tons, with strange, 5-fingered hands on its forelimbs, each of which had a rigid thumb projecting upwards in the form of a spike. Mantell named the animal after iguana lizards, because its teeth were of a similar shape – and it was this likeness that gave him the first clue to the fact that dinosaurs were reptiles. Groups of remains found together suggest that the animals moved around in herds: several of their well-used, fossilised trackways have come to light.

Another rich source of finds has been the substratum known as the Oxford Clay which lies beneath much of southern England, coming to the surface in a band that slants up across the country from

Weymouth to the Yorkshire coast. The most prolific sites have been near Oxford and Peterborough, in quarries where clay is dug for brick-making. In the late Jurassic period the clay lay deep under the sea, and – apart from fossils of land-based dinosaurs, whose carcasses must have drifted out to sea from the shore – it contains several species of marine ichthyosaurs and plesiosaurs.

One was *Cryptoclidus*, a very large fish-eating creature about 8 metres long and weighing 8 tons, with pointed teeth, a long, straight neck, a bulbous body and four paddle-shaped limbs amidships. Another was *Ophthalmosaurus*, a sea-dwelling reptile armed with a sharply pointed jaw, which fed on shellfish: curious rings of bone inside its eye sockets may have helped it focus in murky waters. The most celebrated discoverer of such sea dragons was Mary Anning – the Fossil Lady of Lyme Regis – who came on her

MEGALOSAURUS, (top): REMAINS OF THIS LARGE CARNIVORE HAVE BEEN FOUND IN THE MIDLANDS AND SOUTHERN ENGLAND.

POLACANTHUS (bottom): THIS SQUAT, SPIKY HERBIVORE LIVED IN SOUTHERN ENGLAND IN THE EARLY CRETACEOUS PERIOD.

first ichthyosaur in 1812, at the age of only 13, and devoted much of her life to combing the Dorset beaches.

Another early find in Britain was that of *Megalosaurus*, a carnivore with long, serrated teeth, short forelegs and clawed hands that could grasp prey. The first fossil remains of this ugly customer were discovered by the Reverend William Buckland, an Anglican priest and fellow of Corpus Christi College at Oxford, who became the first Reader in Mineralogy and Geology at the University. Rev. Buckland struggled to reconcile the evidence of his own finds with his belief that all erosion and sedimentation on the Earth had been caused by the biblical flood, and when he found a Palaeolithic human skeleton, stained with red ochre, in the Goat's Hole Cave at Paviland, in the Gower Peninsula, South Wales, he suggested that the remains must be from the time of the Roman occupation of Britain.

Yet another grotesque creature that lived in what is now southern England in the early Cretaceous period was *Polacanthus* (literally 'many spikes'), a squat, four-legged herbivore up to 4 metres long and 1.5 metres tall, weighing perhaps a ton, covered with a thick coat of plates that sprouted rows of ferocious-looking spikes. No sprinter, it must have depended on its heavy armour for defence against carnivorous predators. Only a few fragments of skeletons have come to light, but many skin-plates have been found, especially in the Isle of Wight.

Airborne over southern England at much the same time was *Ornithocheirus* ('bird hand'), a pterosaur with a wingspan up to 12 metres – as big as many light aircraft. Its wings were made of skin stretched between its elongated finger and its ankles, and the dispersal of remains over a wide area suggests that it could fly long distances, its capacity increased by the fact that it had hollow bones, which made the whole creature light for its size. Teeth in its long, pointed jaw enabled it to catch fish.

During the dinosaurs' reign the super continent Pangaea broke apart, and by the process known as plate

tectonics its pieces drifted off into their present positions round the globe, carrying the great reptiles into all the new continents. Sharing their world were primitive, shrew-like creatures, parts of which – mainly fossilised jaws – have been found in the carboniferous limestone of the Mendips in Somerset and South Wales. Remains from the sea cliffs in the Isle of Purbeck, in Dorset, dated to 135 million years ago, include other small mammals, with strong incisor teeth at the front of their jaws, showing that they were herbivorous – a form of rodent, although true rodents did not appear until much later.

At the end of the Cretaceous period, 65 million years ago, the dinosaurs died out. Did they all go at once, and, if so, what finished them off? Nobody is certain what happened, but there are two main theories to account for their extinction. One is that their habitat gradually deteriorated, and they ran out of food; the other, which now has most credence, is that the impact of an asteroid or comet

In the Beginning
Dinosaurs

on what is now the Yucatan peninsula of Mexico caused a lethal change in climate.

Experts have calculated that the celestial body, 10 km wide, seared into the Earth's atmosphere at a devastating speed of 25 km per second and struck the shallow Bearpaw Sea that then lay between the eastern and western halves of the North American continent. Such was its explosive impact that it blew a hole 5 km deep into the Earth's crust, created colossal tidal waves, and sent millions of tons of debris flying into the atmosphere. All life in the immediate vicinity must have been instantly wiped out by blasts of shock and heat; but the effects went right round the world, as airborne dust blotted out the sun and precipitated violent falls in temperature. Immense volcanic eruptions set off by the impact may have intensified the destructive process. Plants deprived of sunlight died away, and, with their source of food gone, night fell on the dinosaurs' long ascendancy on Earth.

After that catastrophe, it took millions of years for creatures to develop again – and their return and spread are poorly recorded in Britain, because successive ice ages ground away most of the fossil-bearing rock that would have told their story. The fossil record is better preserved in North America.

Turtles and terrapins came through the cataclysm apparently unscathed, as did several species of alligator and crocodile, along with some frogs and toads. Very few mammals survived, and it took aeons for new ones to evolve. Then, perhaps 80 million years ago, there appeared the **condylarths**, carnivorous creatures with hooves, ranging in size from rat to bear, which diversified into the **mesonychids**, carnivores the size of leopards and the **phenacodonts**, which were herbivores or omnivores, ranging from rabbit-size to an animal weighing 90 kg. From the phenacodonts descended the **perissodactyls**, which included horses, rhinos and tapirs. Yet another branch of the condylarths gave rise to the **arctocyonids**, which in turn produced the **artiodactyls**, among them sheep, pigs and cattle.

Specialists are still divided about where all these creatures originated – whether in Asia, America or Europe. In the early Eocene period, 55–50 million years ago, land bridges between North America and Asia (across what is now the Bering Strait) and between America and Europe (one via Greenland and the Faroes, another via Scandinavia), made it possible for animals to migrate in any direction; yet it seems fairly certain that the ancestors of most of our mammals trudged down from the far north-west.

One of the most curious was *Eohippus*, or Dawn Horse, later renamed *Hyracotherium*, whose remains were found in the London clays of the Thames Basin, dating from between 50 and 40 million years ago. A small animal the size of a fox terrier, with five toes on its front feet and four on the back, it had a definitely equine-shaped head, and teeth that showed that it browsed on leaves and twigs, rather than eating grass. A reconstruction of this early horse in the Natural History Museum in London gives it a buff colour, with darker stripes running horizontally along its body, although there is no evidence to support this one way or the other. When first discovered, it was not recognised as a horse at all; but finds of other extinct equines made its relationship to them clear. Not long after that (in the geological timescale) there appeared the first dormice, hamsters, beavers, hedgehogs, moles and bats, besides primitive forms of camels, hippopotamuses, pigs and horses, all of which seem to have flourished in the tropical conditions then prevailing.

By the end of the Pliocene period, 2.5 million years ago, with the climate in what we call Britain still warm, the British fauna included a striking range of animals, including a large deer, a gazelle, mastodons, elephants, a tapir, a rhinoceros, a panda, a clawless otter and a sabre-toothed cat. An abundance of fossils from the Freshwater Bed in the cliffs at West Runton, in Norfolk, has revealed the presence (among many other mammals) of red, roe and fallow deer, wild boar, bison, hyena, wolf, cave bear, common hamster, wood mouse, hedgehog and many others.

The Ice Ages

Global warming is no new phenomenon. In the distant past it came and went several times, with a violence far greater than anything the Earth is experiencing today; and whatever caused the wide fluctuations in temperature, it was not the influence or activities of humans, who, if they existed at all, were far too few to have any effect on the climate. For so long as temperatures remained high in northern latitudes, a wide variety of mammals could flourish. But at the beginning of the Pleistocene — estimated at about two million years ago — there set in a series of severe glaciations, during which ice sheets moved down from the north and temperatures fell drastically.

Between great freezes lasting thousands of years came interglacial periods of warmer weather in which mammals increased again and developed: there were at least two such milder periods, possibly three, and during one of them there lived the animals whose remains were found under the site of Trafalgar Square – lion, straight-tusked elephant, hippopotamus, giant Irish elk and aurochs. In their book *Prehistoric Britain*, Jacquetta and Christopher Hawkes painted a graphic picture of the ebb and flow of the ice ages:

> When the sun was triumphant, Britain became a land attractive to life of all kinds, rich vegetation clothed the countryside, elephants and rhinoceroses roved from the Thames Valley to East Anglia, hippopotami floated in the rivers and wallowed in the swamps; when the ice had the victory, southern England alone remained habitable, and there vegetation was reduced to a low scrub, rivers froze and valleys were blocked by snow for many months, and only such hardy animals as mammoth, bison and reindeer could endure even the summer weather.

Humans

Homa sapiens

During the seventeenth century the cleric and scholar Dr John Lightfoot, who became Vice-Chancellor of Cambridge University, proved to his satisfaction that 'man was created by the Trinity on 23 October 4004 BC, at nine o'clock in the morning'. Alas for religious conviction! Far from being born in an instant, human beings evolved so slowly, over such an inconceivably long period, that the precise timing of our origins is impossible to determine.

Recent research, carried out as part of the Natural History Museum's Ancient Human Occupation of Britain project, suggests that the earliest evidence of hominid settlement in Britain dates from 700,000 BC. Until these finds of animal bones and teeth were analysed, the oldest known British human remains were those of Boxgrove Man (*Homo heidelbergensis*) – a tibia and two teeth discovered in Sussex in 1993 and thought to be 500,000 years old. The size of the leg bone shows that its owner was a robust individual, 1.8 metres tall and weighing 90 kg. Flint hand-axes found on the site, together with the bones of rhinoceros and wild horse, reveal that Boxgrove men hunted animals and butchered them for food . The next-oldest British human remains are those of Swanscombe Man, found in river gravel at Swanscombe in Kent, and dating from about 300,000 BC. In fact the three pieces of skull belonged to a young woman, and with them were found fragments of elephant bones, as well as red deer antlers.

From *Homo heidelbergensis* evolved Neanderthal Man (*Homo neanderthalensis*), whose place in evolution has been the subject of extensive debate. Was he a direct ancestor of *Homo sapiens*? The general verdict is now 'Probably not'. The only remains of a Neanderthal so far discovered in Britain were found in Pontnewydd Cave in Wales; but because the flake flint tools typical of those creatures have come to light at sites all over England and Wales, it seems that they must have lived in many parts of the country.

Primitive humans presumably migrated in much the same pattern as the animals, moving north and south on the fringes of the habitable world as changes in climate dictated, following the herds on which they depended for food. Yet anthropologists are puzzled by the fact that the human habitation of Britain seems to have been more intermittent than can be accounted for simply in terms of ice ages: for 100,000 years, between 170,000 and 70,000 BC, hominids appear to have been absent, and they seem to have established a permanent presence in Britain only about 12,000 years ago.

Whatever movements were forced upon them by the climate, Neanderthals survived in Europe until about 40,000 years ago. They were gradually replaced by *Homo sapiens*, who may have migrated from the Middle East, bringing with them superior tools made of flint, ivory and bone. The earliest remains of modern man, found in Kent's Cavern, Devon, date from 31,000 years ago. Did *Homo sapiens* exterminate the Neanderthals, or did they die out naturally? We will probably never know.

Those ancient Britons were not what we tend to think

of as cave-men, slouching and shambling: rather, remains suggest that they were tall, long-legged and broad-shouldered, with long, narrow heads. Hunter-gatherers, they lived off the land in family groups. While the men pursued wild animals, women collected fruit, nuts, roots and grubs. During the summers they lived in the open or built rough shelters, and in winter they withdrew into the shelter and safety of caves.

The final ice age, known as the Devensian Glaciation, lasted from roughly 120,000 to 8000 BC. Analysis of deep-sea cores has shown that at the extremity of the cold, between 23,000 and 12,000 BC, the polar front reached as far south as the latitude of Lisbon. The ice mass covered a third of the Earth's surface (compared with one-tenth today): the whole of Scotland and the northern half of England, as well as almost all of Wales and Ireland, lay beneath a sheet hundreds of metres thick, and even on open land arctic conditions prevailed. So much water was locked up in the ice that the sea level was at least 100 metres lower than it is today. South of the ice stretched sparsely vegetated tundra, and experts believe that only animals adapted to extreme cold could have tolerated such an environment: woolly mammoth, woolly rhinoceros, reindeer, bison, wild horse, arctic fox and lemming.

Mammals now extinct

Aurochs *or* Urus

Bos taurus primigenius

The great wild ox – the ancestor of all modern cattle – stood 2 metres at the shoulder, and even if it did not quite live up to Julius Caesar's description as 'slightly smaller than an elephant', it was clearly a substantial beast. The shape and detail of bones found in peat bogs and marl deposits indicate that its conformation was much the same as that of a modern ox; but the huge, heavy skulls are a third larger, and the size of the horn-cores suggests that the horns were of splendid length.

Experts differ on the question of colour, but most believe that the bulls were very dark reddish-brown or even reddish-black, with a white stripe along the back and curly white hair between the horns, and the cows brownish-red. According to Caesar, they were not only quick on their feet but also aggressive towards man and other beasts.

Skeletal remains show that the auroch spread through northern Europe and Britain during the last ice age. In the earliest British deposits, dated to about 10,500 BC, their bones are associated with those of the giant Irish elk or

fallow deer, but they survived the primeval deer by many thousands of years, and, although hunted and driven northwards by Neolithic man into the wilder extremities of Scotland, they lived on until almost 1000 BC. It is not clear to what extent they were ever domesticated, if at all, but they must have cross-bred with the smaller and more amenable short-horned cattle, *Bos taurus longifrons*, favoured by Celts, and it seems likely that all modern cattle are descended from this mixture.

Cave Bear

Ursus spelaeus

A larger relative of the modern brown bear, this powerful scavenger, mainly vegetarian, was common in southern Europe during the late Pleistocene era. Most of its remains have been found in the caves in which it hibernated. At one stage it certainly existed in central England, but traces of it are so few that little can be inferred about its distribution.

Giant Irish Elk

Megaloceros giganteus

Another large mammal that survived the fierce ice ages – probably migrating northwards during interglacial periods – was the giant Irish elk, the most impressive deer ever to have lived in Britain. It stood 2 metres tall at the shoulder (nearly twice as tall as a modern red deer) and weighed perhaps 700 kg, and the males' palmate antlers – the biggest ever grown by any deer, extinct or extant – were more than 3 metres wide. Since the antlers themselves weighed up to 45 kg, the owners developed powerful neck vertebrae (and no doubt muscles) to carry them.

Remains of this huge creature have been found in many English counties, from Kent and Essex in the east to Somerset and Devon in the west, and as far north as southern Scotland and the Isle of Man; but hundreds of skulls, and all the finest specimens, have come from Ireland, the earliest dating from 35,200 BC, the latest from 8960 BC. Although most of the remains have been discovered in deposits that once were the beds of lakes beneath the peat bogs, the best-preserved specimens have come from the peat itself, usually from 2 to 3 metres beneath present ground level. The first complete skeleton was found in the Isle of Man early in the nineteenth century, and it is thought that there are several hundred sets of antlers in various museums and private collections.

Megaloceros is the Greek for 'big horn'; and the sheer spread of the giant's antlers must mean that it lived mainly in the open – for an animal with that headgear would have found it impossible to move around freely in the dense

forest which then covered much of the land. It seems more likely to have inhabited the kind of relatively barren terrain favoured by reindeer; but as no remains have been found in any of the mountainous regions of Ireland, the evidence suggests that it was a creature of the low ground.

One puzzle is that the number of male heads and bones greatly exceeds that of females, whereas in a living population the ratio would normally be the other way round. From the fact that numerous stags' heads and skeletons were found close together in what had obviously been a shallow lake or bog at Ballybetagh, County Dublin, it was at one time inferred that primitive man must have driven the animals over a cliff and clubbed them to death at the bottom; but later commentators have pointed out that the deer may simply have fallen through ice. The American expert Dr Valerius Geist reckons that in winter *Megaloceros giganteus* 'would have chosen the snow-covered surfaces of frozen lakes as escape terrain, just as caribou do today. The big stags would have "camped out" on lake ice during diurnal rest periods, ruminating and sparring, as expected

of antlered wintering males.' He also suggests that some of the antlers could have been cast in the annual spring cycle as stags grazed on pond weed along the shore of the lake.

Many features of the giant deer remain mysterious. Why, for instance, did they develop such vast heads? To have cast such a weight of antlers every spring, and grown a fresh set, must have used up a huge amount of energy. And why did the species become extinct? It was the view of the Edwardian naturalist Sir Harry Johnston that these two puzzles may be connected. In his *British Mammals*, published in 1903, he suggested that 'over-specialisation' was the basic cause of decline, and that some sort of hormonal imbalance may have led to sterility: 'The extravagance of antler growth...may actually have reacted unfavourably on the generative powers.'

Judging by its relatively light skeleton, it seems that the giant deer was a fast-moving animal. Dr Geist believes 'It was a specialist in speed and stamina, able to extricate itself quickly and unpredictably, leaving culling predators behind.' One can imagine that its antlers, with their long tines, were effective weapons against any attacker that came at it head on, but that it must have been vulnerable to wolves hunting in packs, which run prey animals down over long distances and grab them from behind, and to bears, which hunt at night.

Not to be confused with the giant Irish elk is the primitive form of fallow deer known as *Dama dama clactoniana*, whose antlers, found at Clacton, Essex and Swanscombe, Kent are larger than those of modern fallow, and differ in that the spellers, or points, grow from the leading edge of the palmated antlers as well as from the rear. Clacton fallow appear to have died out during the final glaciation.

Scimitar-toothed Cat

Homotherium latidens

Although often referred to as a sabre-toothed tiger, this animal was not closely related to tigers, but evolved as an independent line for at least 20 million years, before going extinct about 40,000 years ago. Only a few fossilised teeth have been found in Britain; but it is known that the scimitar-tooth was a powerful hyena-shaped animal about the size of a lion, equipped with two very long, curved canines, sweeping down 20 cm from the front of its upper jaw. With these it could slash and disable prey as large as mammoths, which are beyond the capabilities of modern lions and tigers, by inflicting such deep, fatal wounds that the victims bled to death.

MAMMOTHS

'Until a few centuries ago, any large bones discovered in the fields or caves of Europe were usually assumed to be the remains of giants, and were often displayed as curiosities in castles, palaces, town halls, churches and monasteries...In 1577 a collection of mammoth bones sparked a heated theological debate in Switzerland. When it was proposed that they should be given a Christian burial in a cemetery, a doctor studied them closely and declared them to be the bones of a giant, 18 ft (5.5 metres) tall, who deserved no such courtesy, being a heathen.'
From *Mammoths: Giants of the Ice Age*
by Adrian Lister and Paul Bahn.

Ancestral Mammoth

Mammuthus meridionalis

These huge animals – 4 metres at the shoulder, and weighing 10 tons – appeared in Europe between 3 and 2.5 million years ago, having gradually worked their way up from Africa, either by a land bridge over what is now the Strait of Gibraltar, or via the Middle East and Turkey. In many ways they probably looked like modern elephants, having smooth skins, rather than the shaggy coats later developed by woolly mammoths, but already their curving tusks and pointed foreheads indicated their true lineage.

Forest dwellers, they lived mainly on the leaves and bark of trees. Remains have been found in the Red Crag deposits in Suffolk, and in the nineteenth century hundreds of molars were dredged from the sea off the Norfolk coast. The creatures survived for about two million years, but then major changes in climate hastened their evolution towards mammals better able to deal with the cold.

Steppe Mammoth

Mammuthus trogontherii

Next in line after the ancestral mammoth came the steppe mammoth, another colossal creature, perhaps even larger, and standing over 4 metres at the shoulder, which evolved about one million years ago. It had twice the mass of a modern African elephant, and its enormous tusks – up to 2.5 metres long – curved upwards and inwards at the front. Its name derives from its habitat, which included large, grassy plains, and its main food was grass, along with the leaves, branches and fruit of trees and shrubs.

During the 1990s an almost complete skeleton was recovered from the Freshwater Bed in the cliffs at West Runton, Norfolk, 20 metres below ground level. The animal, a male, had died in its forties some 600,000 years ago; hyenas had fed on the body and left tooth-marks on some of the bones, along with their own droppings, and other mammoths appear to have trampled on the carcass, drawn – as modern elephants are – by the remains of one of their kind. The animal had damaged its right knee, and, perhaps weakened by the injury, it apparently sank down on to its front to die in the shallows at the edge of a river.

When conservation work is complete, the skeleton will go on display in the Norwich Castle Museum. This thrilling discovery is yielding a mass of information about the environment at that time, when Britain was still joined to Europe, and the climate was similar to that of today.

Woolly Mammoth

Elephas primigenius

Many whole carcasses of woolly mammoths have been discovered frozen in the permafrost of the northern Russian tundra, some almost perfectly preserved, with not only hair, skin and flesh intact, but also internal organs and the contents of stomachs. As a result, much has been learned and is now known about the physiology of these shaggy monsters, which were perfectly adapted to life in a cold climate.

The size of a modern African elephant, they stood about 3 metres at the shoulder and were equipped with immensely thick coats, their dense under-fur being 10 cm deep and their guard-hairs 25 cm long. Further insulation came from a 10-cm layer of subcutaneous fat; and, as yet another means of conserving heat, the animal had a shorter trunk and smaller ears than modern elephants that live in hot countries.

The woolly mammoths were creatures of open grassland: they are thought to have evolved some 250,000 years ago, and by 100,000 years ago they had spread across the vast, treeless plains that stretched from Britain to eastern Siberia. Fossil remains have been found at several sites in Britain, most spectacularly at Ilford in Essex, where an almost-intact skull with tusks attached, was dug out of a gravel deposit beside the River Rochford in 1864. Another striking find was made at Condover in Shropshire, where five woolly mammoths became trapped in the clay of a kettle-hole in about 10,800 BC. One was a 30-year-old adult, the others juveniles aged between 3 and 5. Further remains have come from caves in Derbyshire, Somerset and Devon. In the lands that are now Poland, the Czech Republic, Slovakia and the Ukraine, early man used their bones for building huts. The species survived until a few thousand years BC, and there is no clear indication of why the woolly mammoth then went extinct, when others, like the reindeer and bison, kept going; a warmer, wetter climate, with consequent changes in vegetation – particularly the reduction of grassland and the spread of forest – may have contributed to its decline, along with increased hunting pressure from humans.

RHINOCEROS

Woolly Rhinoceros
Coelodonta antiquitatis

This was a massive animal, higher in the shoulders than a modern rhino, with two horns on the front of its skull. The long, leading horn was flattened at the sides, suggesting that its owner used it as a plough for digging through snow to get at vegetation underneath. Frozen carcasses found in Siberia show that the animals had enormously thick coats, like those of the woolly mammoth, and were well adapted to live in a very cold climate. The earliest remains found in the Pin Hole cave in Derbyshire date from 39,400 BC, the latest from 22,350 BC.

Man Makes His Mark

By 8300 BC, as the glaciers of the last ice age retreated, humans beings were migrating northwards out of Europe. These Mesolithic wanderers came on their feet, for the area we now know as Britain was still part of the mainland, and they were still hunter-gatherers who led nomadic lives, sometimes settling, but often moving on in search of food, leaving practically no mark on the landscape. They ate snails, fish of many kinds, including molluscs, gathered fruit and nuts in season, caught ground-nesting seabirds on the coasts, and hunted animals with bows and arrows or spears tipped with flint or sharpened bone.

They also used slings to propel pebbles (found embedded in shoulder blades of deer), and caught animals in camouflaged pits or by driving them over cliffs. Red and roe deer, bears, wild boar, otters, beavers and hares provided much of their meat, and they depended on the animals also for their clothes, made of fur, skins and sinews. They were a good deal shorter and more spare than the people of today: an average man was probably 1.6 metres tall, and an average woman just over 1.5 metres. Their active, strenuous lives kept them fit and gave them great endurance; but, with their primitive weapons, they must have lived in constant fear of predators.

About 6500 BC Britain became an island when the Channel was formed, principally because the ice caps melted and released colossal quantities of water, so that the sea level rose. Most of the land that remained above water level was covered in dense, trackless forest, except for the coastal flood-plains and the tops of the highest mountains. With many inland valleys rendered impassable by marshes, human beings naturally settled on chalk and limestone uplands, where the soil was (in modern terms) poor.

Gradually they evolved from hunter-gathers into farmers. Having discovered how to grow crops, they started to create clear land by setting fire to areas of forest or ring-barking trees so that these died and became easier to burn. They probably began quite high up the hills, where trees were sparse, and gradually the forest was pushed back – although experts today find it hard to distinguish between what was done by humans and what by the climate, which in about 6000 BC turned wetter and colder. The destruction of the forest was not a continuous process: whenever disease or famine wiped out the local population, trees would invade cleared ground for a few generations, until humans recovered.

Finds of bones show that people were keeping dogs by 6000 BC, and suggest that domestication of farm animals began about 5000 BC, towards the end of the Mesolithic Age. By 3000 BC life had become altogether more static. The early farmers built hill-top enclosures like the one at Windmill Hill in Wiltshire, and raised more children. It is impossible to tell how they spoke, but it seems unlikely that there was any common tongue: language probably varied from one tribe to the next. The population was still small and scattered.

Stonehenge became an important cult or religious centre very early: the first Mesolithic activity detected on the site dates from between 8000 and 7000 BC. But it is estimated that the main ring ditch round the monument was excavated between 3020 and 2910 BC, and the tools used to dig it were deer antlers. The great ring of sarsen stones was erected during the next few centuries.

The building of monuments like Stonehenge continued for another 1500 years, and represented colossal physical effort. It is estimated, for instance, that excavation of the main ring ditch at Avebury involved the removal of 200,000 tons of chalk and soil; the outer of the three circles of sarsen stones originally consisted of 98 monoliths, some of which weighed 60 tons, and are thought to have been dragged from the neighouring Fyfield Down.

But during that time mankind took a huge step forward by learning to make and use bronze, an alloy of copper and tin. For many years archaeologists believed that the skill was spread through Europe and imported to Britain by people known as the Beaker folk, so called from their use of bell-shaped pottery drinking vessels, who migrated northwards from the Iberian peninsula. Now, however, it is thought that bronze may simply have acted as its own ambassador, and that word of its qualities travelled ahead of it. In any case, the new material created a demand for tin and copper, both of which were available in Britain: tin was mined in Cornwall, copper in Cornwall, Wales and southwest Ireland. By about 1500 BC humans were living in settlements and growing cereals in small fields delineated by banks, walls or ditches, and they stored grain in pits or silos hacked out of rock.

During the Iron Age (800–100 BC) Celtic tribes raised husbandry to new levels. They grew cereal and garden crops, and kept cattle, sheep, pigs and horses; they also had goats, and ranched semi-wild deer. People who farmed on chalk downland tended to have more sheep, those on lower land more cattle. The cattle were smaller and lighter than those of today – progenitors of the modern Welsh Black and Irish Kerry – but they were highly valued, especially in Ireland, where they became the main measure of wealth. There, at the beginning of May, in the festival of Beltane, cattle and sheep were driven between banks of fire to purify them before being moved up to high pastures for the summer.

Milk was an important element in the early farmers' diet, and they almost certainly made some of it into yoghurt or cheese. Dogs of various types guarded their flocks, cleaned up edible rubbish round encampments, and helped keep vermin like rats in check. Cats did the same, and were perhaps also kept as pets. Horses, which were small, and resembled today's Exmoor ponies, were sometimes eaten, but mainly they were used as pack and draught animals, or ridden for rounding up other stock, and also for pulling chariots in battle.

Some of the British hill forts were probably built partly or wholly as enclosures to protect animals and keep them together: archaeologists believe that the middle earthwork at Danebury, added between 400 and 100 BC, may have been designed as a stock enclosure. For much of the year pigs were allowed to forage in woodland, feeding themselves; and although the Celts also hunted wild boar, bone deposits show that most of the pork they ate came from domesticated animals. These were killed at about two years old, when they were full-grown and still tender, but many other domestic animals were kept alive well beyond optimum slaughter age, indicating that sheep were valued more for wool than for meat, and cattle more for their pulling power than as beef.

Some historians have surmised that the Celts must have killed all their animals every autumn, because they could not feed them through the winter; but this idea has now been discredited by evidence that the early farmers understood how to make hay, and also had dried leaves, barley-chaff and straw as winter forage. Altogether, the Celts were famous as keepers of farm animals, and when a group of them went to live on the island of St Kilda, off the west coast of Scotland, they took their sheep with them – ancestors of the Soay sheep which are there to this day. The skeletons of modern Soays are very similar to those of Iron Age sheep, and it is reasonable to suppose that their goat-like appearance – brown and white, and both sexes with horns – also resembles that of their progenitors.

The Celts were ardent hunters, and apparently went after wild animals as much for sport as for more practical reasons. They attached importance to the ritual sacrifice of animals, not just in sacred centres, but in and around the places where they lived. Numerous skeletons have been found buried in pits dug out of the chalk and formerly used for grain storage, often in puzzling combinations: two pigs and a dog buried together at Twywell, in Northamptonshire, dogs and horses together in a pit at Danebury, a cat with a sheep elsewhere. Experts surmise that the animals were killed as special offerings to the gods, and that by eating part of them, humans shared the sacrifices with their deities.

Animals featured strongly in Celtic art, often in naturalistic forms, but also in abstract or stylised designs, as in the marvellous bronze horse-mask from the first century BC found at Melsonby in Yorkshire. (The Celtic goddess Epona looked after horses and ponies, and sometimes appeared in their form.) Sometimes human and animal features are merged together, so that a human head, for instance, has hare's ears. Weapons – swords, scabbards, shields, armour – were decorated with representations of animals such as deer or wild boar, perhaps to invoke an element of magic and increase their efficacy by harnessing some of the attributes of the creatures portrayed. One of the most striking British finds has been that of a bronze trumpet-mouth in the form of a boar's head, discovered at Deskford, in Scotland, dating from the first century AD. This has a palate like that of a pig, and was fitted with an articulated wooden tongue which would have vibrated when blown, adding an extra, unnerving note to the cacophony of battle.

Mammals no longer wild in Britain

Arctic Fox

Alopex lagopus

Distinctly smaller than its red counterpart, the Arctic fox has shorter ears and muzzle, and is a different colour – fairly dark grey-brown or blue-brown in summer, and pure white in winter. The winter coat is immensely thick and provides such remarkable insulation that an animal does not even start shivering until the temperature drops to

−40˚C. Females are highly prolific, and can give birth to as many as 18 cubs in one litter, although the usual number is about 6. Arctic foxes were once common in Britain, but the European population is now restricted to the far north of Scandinavia.

Beaver

Castor fiber

Although beavers existed in Britain from early times, the first historical reference to them occurs in the code of laws drawn up in the middle of the tenth century AD by the Welsh King Hywel Dda, who laid down that he was to receive the skins of all martens, ermines and beavers killed, so that they could be used for the borders of his ceremonial garments. The high price of a beaver's pelt – 5 times that of a marten, 15 times that of a wolf, fox or otter – may not only reflect the superiority of the fur; but it also suggests that beavers were already fairly rare. They were also much valued for the substance now known as *castoreum* which they secrete from eating willow bark, and which acts as a naturally medicinal form of aspirin.

The historian Giraldus Cambrensis, writing of his journey through Wales in 1188, reported that there were still beavers in the River Teifi in Cardiganshire: often this author was wildly credulous and fanciful, but it sounds as if in this instance he was correct, for he described how the creatures cut down trees and built them into what he called castles – now known as lodges. Similar uncertainty bedevils accounts of beavers in Scotland. Hector Boece, writing in 1526, confidently included them among the denizens of Loch Ness, but others have doubted his accuracy on the point. Certainly the Highlanders had their own name for the amphibian rodent – *Dobhran losleathan* or the broad-tailed otter – but there is no certainty that the beaver lasted beyond the beginning of the fifteenth century.

For England, historical references are few, but fossils and bones show that beavers existed in good numbers, especially in eastern counties. The Fens of East Anglia appear to have been one stronghold, Lincolnshire another; and many towns and villages have names that seem to derive from association with the dam-builders, from Beverley in Yorkshire to Beverstone in Gloucestershire and Beverege in Worcestershire. Again, it is not clear when the last of the beavers died out, but there is no evidence that they survived beyond the fifteenth century. There is currently a move to reintroduce the European Beaver to Britain, with schemes proposed for both England and Scotland (*see page 394*).

Bison

Bison priscus

This ancestor of the European bison was numerous in England around 70,000 years ago: remains discovered at Wretton and Coston in Norfolk outnumber those of any other contemporary species. Finds at Upton Warren in Worcestershire show that the animals were still present in 40,000 BC, and remains from another Worcestershire site, Beckford, have been radiocarbon-dated to 25,650 BC. Since there is no evidence to show that bison remained in Britain after the coldest phase of the Devensian glaciation (between 23,000 and 13,000 BC), it must be presumed that the animals migrated south, never to return.

Brown Bear

Ursus arctos

Bones found mainly in caves show that brown bears once lived in many parts of Britain, from Devonshire to northern Scotland, and that the animals were killed and eaten by early man. They are formidably large creatures, capable of killing cows, sheep, elk and reindeer. They stand over 2 metres tall and weigh up to 300 kg, and for animals of such bulk, have a surprising turn of speed, able to outrun a horse over short distances. Especially to men equipped with primitive weapons, brown bears must have seemed terrifying monsters.

At first they were hunted purely for food and their skins, but in the first century AD the Romans brought with them their predilection for baiting wild animals, and at some stage the natives began catching wild cubs which could be reared in captivity. The main stronghold of brown bears was the Great Caledonian Forest that covered much of Scotland, and at the end of the first century AD, the Greek historian Plutarch recorded that brown bears were transported from Britain to Rome, 'where they hold them in great admiration'.

A reference in the *Penitentiale* of Archbishop Egbert, dated about 750 AD, suggests that wild bears still existed in Britain in the eighth century; and then in the Domesday Book of 1086, there is a reference to the time of Edward the Confessor (earlier in the eleventh century), when the town of Norwich annually provided the king with one bear and six dogs for the baiting of it. Historians, however, are sceptical about these literary records, believing that they refer to domesticated animals rather than to wild ones, and that the wild strain had probably died out by the beginning of the Christian era.

Common Hamster

Cricetus cricetus

A larger relative of the household pet – brown and white, about the size of a rat, with a short, furry tail – this rodent of steppe grassland lived in Britain during early glacial times, between five and three million years ago, but then disappeared. It is still abundant in eastern Europe, but because it is an agricultural pest, it has been persecuted and become rare in western areas. It is mainly nocturnal, carries food in its cheek pouches and hibernates in winter, living on the large stores of potatoes and grain which it has cached.

Elk

Alces alces

Numerous remains of elk found in peat bogs show that this large deer was once common in England and Scotland, and that it was similar in size and appearance to the elk which inhabit Scandinavia today – that is, a bull stood just under 2 metres at the shoulder. Almost certainly it had the same ungainly appearance, with uneven antlers and swift but shambling gait.

One bull, found near Blackpool, was radiocarbon-dated to 10,400 BC, and what fascinated archaeologists especially about it was the fact that two barbed arrow- or spearpoints made of bone were discovered with its skeleton, one in the ribs and one in a hind foot. Numerous scars on the ribs, shoulder blade and leg bones suggested that the animal had been attacked by hunters using flint-tipped weapons.

Unlike the giant fallow deer, elk are essentially forest-dwellers, and it seems that they survived until the ninth or tenth century AD. Southern Scotland, Northumberland and Yorkshire were among their strongholds; but they also lived along the Thames, near what is now Walthamstow. It was apparently the destruction of woodland that hastened their extinction. A few elk have been reintroduced to Britain for commercial purposes (see page 401).

Lynx

Lynx lynx

This powerful, long-legged big cat, with its characteristic tufted ears and short, black-tipped tail, was once native to most of Britain; bones found in a cave near Inchnadamph in Scotland, were among the blackened hearth-stones of Neolithic fires. Standing up to 75 cm at the shoulder, and weighing 25 kg, the lynx is well able to kill sheep and medium-sized cattle, besides roe deer and smaller wild animals. It must have been a much-detested enemy of Neolithic and later herdsmen, feared for its favourite method of attack – a careful stalk or ambush, followed by an explosive rush.

Experts long believed that the lynx went extinct at an early date, its demise hastened by humans defending their herds and flocks. But radiocarbon-dating of the remains found at Inchnadamph produced a big surprise, showing that the animal was still present in about 180 AD.

Norway Lemming *and* Arctic Lemming

Lemmus lemmus and *Dicrostonyx torquatus*

These small rodents were present in prehistoric Britain and Ireland, but dating of their fossil remains is uncertain. Today *Lemmus* lives only in Scandinavia, and *Dicrostonyx*, which turns white in winter, occurs farther north. It is thought that both species became extinct in the British Isles when the climate began to warm up at the end of the last ice age, about 8000 BC.

Reindeer

Rangifer tarandus

Ungainly reindeer, with the tines of their lop-sided antlers pointing forwards, are known to have existed for at least 750,000 years, and they once migrated in thousands across Britain as they do across Lapland and Russia to this day. Tremendous numbers of bones found in caves and river gravel deposits show that they were among the earliest animals to arrive in this country towards the end of the last ice age, being among the best able to withstand the rigours of the post-glacial climate. At some stage they also crossed the Bering Strait into North America, where they still exist but are called caribou.

At first in Britain they were far more numerous than red deer; but as the climate warmed up, the proportions changed. The gravel beneath Oxford is particularly rich in reindeer fossils, and among the animals' contemporaries in the south of England were hippopotamuses, hyenas and cave lions, besides marmots and lemmings. Scotland has also yielded numerous remains, including large antlers discovered more than 10 metres beneath the surface of the ground near Kilmaurs in Ayrshire. Bones found in the deposits of human settlements show that men either kept domesticated reindeer or hunted them, or both. Local tradition holds that in the twelfth century AD the *jarls* (or earls) of Orkney used to cross the Pentland Firth to hunt red deer and reindeer in the wilds of Caithness, but how long the herds survived is not known. During the 1950s a small herd of reindeer was reintroduced to the Cairngorm mountains in Scotland (see page 400).

Saiga

Saiga tatarica

This strange-looking antelope survives today in the dry grasslands of Kazakhstan and Mongolia. A few finds show that during the final glaciation it spread out across Europe and into Britain: representations of it are included in the cave paintings and carvings of southern Europe. In deserts its bulbous nose appears to act as a dust-filter, but the biological function of the organ in cooler, wetter climates is not clear.

Spotted Hyena

Crocuta crocuta

Remains have been found at many sites in England, the earliest radiocarbon-dated to 40,200 BC and the latest to 30,200 BC. These carnivorous scavengers lived on wild horse, bison, reindeer and woolly rhinoceros, and carried back enormous numbers of bones to their cave dens. It seems that they were eventually driven southward, into Europe and then into Africa, by the increasing cold of the final glaciation.

Tarpan (Wild Horse)

Equus equus

From the number of specimens found in Gough's Cave in Somerset, dating from 10,530 to 10,260 BC, and at numerous other sites, it is clear that wild horse was a frequent prey of Upper Palaeolithic hunters, second only to reindeer. The gradual fade-out of remains indicates that it disappeared from Britain when the last of the ice ages ended and a more temperate climate came in. Some experts, however, believe that it may have hung on in higher, open areas such as the Peak District, and indeed that it survived right

through into comparatively recent times, the ancestor of domestic horses.

This theory appears to be validated by the fact that there is very little difference between ancient tarpan skeletons and those of modern animals. Colour also casts a vote on the issue: one feature of wild horses depicted in cave paintings, and found in latter-day survivors such as Przewalski's Horse, is that they have 'mealy noses', or pale muzzles, like those of modern Exmoor ponies, which are thought to be descended from tarpans. Yet against any direct relationship is a clear difference in the appearance of the mane: whereas all wild horses and zebras have short, upstanding manes, the manes of breeds such as Exmoor are long and hang down.

Wild Boar

Sus scrofa

From the enormous number of remains found all over Britain, it is clear that wild boar once flourished in all the great forests of antiquity, living on acorns, beechmast, roots and so on. In England many a placename carries their echo – Boar's Hill, Boarstall, Boarsford, to say nothing of the Boar's Head tavern in Eastcheap, rendezvous of Shakespeare's Sir John Falstaff and his merry crew. In the Scottish Highlands the name occurs frequently in its Gaelic form, 'tuirc' – *Slochd-tuirc* (the boar's den), *Beannan Tuirc* (the boar's mountain) – as it does also in Ireland.

Men hunted the animals with spears, dogs and nets for their meat, but also because they were pests, causing enormous damage to crops, and potentially dangerous to humans: old records are peppered with references to boars that terrorised particular districts. A Roman altar found in Weardale, County Durham, for instance, carried an inscription dedicating it to the god Sylvanus, in gratitude for the capture of a boar which many earlier hunters had tried in vain to destroy. Hunting was a dangerous business, for with one upward sweep of its tusks a big boar could disembowel a mastiff. In his *Booke of Hunting*, published in 1575, George Turbervile of Dorset described how he once saw a boar chased:

> by fiftie good houndes at the least, and when he saw they were all in full crie, and helde in round together, he turned heade upon them and thrust amiddst the thickest of them in such sorte that he slew sometime six or seaven...in the twinkling of an eye; and of the fiftie houndes there went not twelve sounde and alive to their masters' houses.

Wild boar escaping from farms have established a feral population in the woods of southeast England.

Wolf

Canis lupus

> *The lean and hungry wolf,*
> *With his fangs so sharp and white,*
> *His starvling body pinched*
> *By the frost of a northern night,*
> *And his pitiless eyes that scare the dark*
> *With their green and threatening light.*

ELIZA HARRIS, *Book of Highland Minstrelsy*

Stories like that of Little Red Riding Hood echo the fear of wolves that prevailed in Britain from time immemorial until the Middle Ages. Ancient anxieties are manifest also in the legend of the werewolf, a man-turned-wolf, or creature half-man-half-wolf, that prowls about devouring babies. 'Lycanthropy' was supposed to be a state of madness in which men or women, imagining themselves to be wolves, walked on all fours, howled, dug up graves and attacked innocent passers-by.

Remains found all over England, Wales, Scotland and Ireland show that the wolves of antiquity were much the same size as those of today; and their ferocity, together with their habit of hunting in packs, made them a serious threat to livestock. So long as the country remained heavily forested, they had impenetrable retreats from which to launch raids on domestic animals, and even though handsome rewards were offered for their deaths, they could never be suppressed. This meant that every night, sheep and cattle had to be brought into a fold or shelter, and fed and watered – all time-consuming operations. William Taplin, writing in 1803, described how in Yorkshire wolves used to breed in the carrs, or bogs, among the gorse and rushes, and come up into the towns at night, killing any sheep that had not been properly folded.

Whether or not wolves were normally a threat to human beings is another question. Modern records of the animals attacking humans are extremely rare, and latter-day evidence shows that they avoid people whenever they can. The idea that wolves crave human flesh is largely a myth, and people's exaggerated dread of them perhaps derived from occasional assaults by animals suffering from rabies. The fact that one might die, raving horribly, from a single wolf-bite was itself enough to engender dread.

The earliest record of a bounty being paid for the destruction of a wolf comes from the time of Dorvadilla, the legendary fourth king of the Scots, who reigned in the second century BC, when anyone who slew a wolf was rewarded with an ox. Among ancient Britons wolf-hunting seems to have been a favourite sport, as exciting and dangerous as it was necessary. Because the animals were most likely to attack at the time of greatest hunger, in the depths of winter, the Saxons called January 'Wolf month', and an outlaw was known as a 'wolf's head', since he was beyond the protection of the law, and as fair game as any wild beast.

A charming story was related by James Howell in his *Familiar Letters*, published in 1624, of a Scottish soldier in Ireland, on his way back to England, who sat down under a tree for a rest, opened his knapsack and began to eat some food he had brought with him.

> On a sudden he was surprised with two or three wolves, who coming towards him, he threw them some scraps of bread and cheese, till all was gone; then, the wolves making a nearer approach to him, he knew not what shift to make, but by taking a pair of bagpipes which he had, and as soone as he began to play upon them, the wolves ran all away as if they had been scared out of their wits: whereupon the soldier said, 'A pox take you all, if I had known you had loved music so well, you should have had it before dinner.'

John Dunton, travelling through Ireland perhaps half a century later, left a revealing glimpse of the problems wolves caused when he spent a night at an inn in Connaught:

> I had just compos'd my selfe to sleep when I was strangely surprised to heare the cows and sheep all comeing into my bed chamber. I enquired the meaning and was told it was to preserve them from the wolfe which everie night was rambling about for prey. I founde the beasts lay down soone after they had enter'd, and soe my feares of being trodden upon by them were over, and truly if the nastines of their excrements did not cause an aversion hereto, the sweetness of theire breath, which I was never sensible of before, and the pleasing noyse they made in ruminating or chawing the cudd, would lull a body to sleep as soon as the noys of a murmuring brook and the fragrancy of a bed of roses.

Wolverine

Gulo gulo

This heavily built, low-slung carnivore is a member of the weasel family, but looks and moves like a small bear. It grows to a length of about 80 cm, including its tail, and weighs up to 30 kg. In Alaska and northern Scandinavia it is still trapped and shot as a pest and for its fur. A few fossil remains, mostly from Somerset and Devon, reveal that wolverines once lived in Britain, probably preying on reindeer. One specimen from Devon has been radio-carbon-dated to 20,160 BC, but it is not known when the animals disappeared.

AN EXTRAORDINARY GLIMPSE of Neolithic man was afforded by the discovery in 1991 of a body which emerged from a glacier high in the Alps on the border between Austria and Italy. The corpse was so well preserved that the walkers who found him thought that they had come across the remains of some relatively recent casualty; but specialists immediately realised that this find was one in a million. Promptly christened 'the Iceman', the body was 5000 years old, but in such an intact state that scientists could infer a great deal about the life and times of the dead man.

As specialists studied his remains, they came to call him Ötzi, after the Ötztal, the valley above which he was found. In life he stood 1.6 metres tall and weighed about 50 kg. His back, legs and feet bore many blue tattoos, mostly linear, some in the form of crosses. His teeth had been worn down by chewing coarse food, but were entirely free of caries, the decay caused by modern diets. He had died between the ages of 45 and 50, and his demise had been precipitated, if not directly caused, by a bronze arrow-head which had penetrated deep into one shoulder. An injury on the back of his skull suggested that he had also been bludgeoned.

All his equipment was home-made and derived directly from natural materials. His clothes were made from square patches of deer-hide neatly stitched together with twisted animal sinews. He wore a cone-shaped fur cap with a chin-strap, a cape that reached to his knees, and leggings like cowboys' chaps. His garments were well worn, and splits had been crudely cobbled together with grass thread. On top of the cape he wore a grass cloak plaited from stems more than a metre long, which may have acted as a thatch, keeping off snow and rain; it may also have served as a portable hide, making the hunter almost invisible in any scrub or woodland. His shoes had leather soles and uppers made of grass cords.

On his back he carried a pannier with a frame made from a U-shaped hazel rod braced by cross-boards of larch. He also had two cylindrical containers fashioned from birch bark, one of which he had lined with green maple leaves and used for transporting live embers. A body-belt and pouch, both made of leather, gave him further secure carrying capacity, and the pouch contained his vital equipment for making fire: three flint implements and a piece of tinder. His tools included an axe with a copper blade and a yew shaft, beautifully fitted together, glued with birch tar and bound with leather thongs. He also had a net made from woven grass: at first it was thought that this had been designed for fishing, but later, because of its wide mesh – about 2.5 cm – researchers decided that its purpose was to catch birds. A small knife, with oak handle and flint blade, was housed in a sheath on his belt; but for some reason his bow – made of yew and nearly 2 metres long – had never been finished: it had no notches or holes to hold a string, and could not have been used to shoot the 14 arrows found in his quiver. Among his possessions were two small pieces of birch fungus, each with a hole drilled through the middle and threaded on to a strip of fur. Since the fungus contains a natural antibiotic, it has been assumed that the pieces were some kind of medicine kit.

Microscopic study of material recovered from his colon revealed that he had eaten meat (probably from an ibex) and einkorn, the form of wheat grown by Neolithic farmers, but that he had not had a meal for about 8 hours before his death. Where was he going when he struggled up to that desolate pass more than 3000 metres above sea level?

It is true that this lone wayfarer lived in central Europe – but would not the people of Britain in 3000 BC have dressed and been equipped much the same? By the time he lived and died, Stonehenge had been an important cult or religious centre for several

Although 5000 years old, the body of the Iceman was so well preserved that the walkers who found him thought they had come upon the remains of some more recent casualty

Ötzi the Iceman

thousand years: the earliest Mesolithic activity detected on the site dates from between 8000 and 7000 BC. But it is estimated that the main ring ditch round the monument was excavated between 3020 and 2910 BC – exactly the date ascribed to the Iceman – and the tools used to dig it were deer antlers, with which, as a hunter, he must have been familiar. It is tempting to think of the world at that time as some sort of Arcadia, in which machines, pollution, taxes, bureaucrats and politicians were unknown; yet common sense suggests that life was tough and short. The Iceman and his fellows must have lived in constant fear of hunger, of the big animals around them, and of the violent forces of nature whose causes they did not understand.

Considering the fragility of Neolithic clothes and equipment, it is hardly surprising that men made such colossal efforts to keep the gods – or whatever supernatural powers they worshipped – on their side. By hauling vast lumps of stone across the country, and building them into rings, Ötzi's British contemporaries did what they could to insure their lives.

In the Beginning
Ötzi the Iceman

31

2 MAINLY EXOTICS

Since time immemorial potentates have kept wild animals as pets or status symbols. It may well be that the very first menageries were established in China, but no nation embraced exotic species more enthusiastically than the ancient Egyptians. Many of the pharoahs kept lions, and the displays organised under the Ptolemies – the line of Macedonian kings who ruled Egypt during the last three centuries BC – were occasions of fantastic extravagance. In one spring festival dedicated to Dionysus the procession was led by 84 chariots drawn by elephants; next came 60 chariots pulled by he-goats, 12 drawn by lions, 15 by buffaloes, 4 by wild asses, 8 by ostriches, 7 by stags, and sundry more drawn by camels and mules, with various other wild creatures, among them a giraffe, a rhinoceros and a 'great white bear'.

In terms of sheer cruelty to animals and people, the Romans were unrivalled. To entertain the public, they set lions, bulls and bears to fight each other, or to do battle with human gladiators. They used elephants to trample recaptured deserters to death, or to tear them limb from limb. When the first giraffe reached Rome in 43 AD the Emperor Claudius had it slaughtered, along with 400 lions, as a sacrifice at the consecration of his new forum – whereas his predecessor Caligula had merely fed criminals to his carnivores.

Compared with such extravagant brutality, the British treatment of animals has always been relatively restrained. Nevertheless, for hundreds of years our ancestors treated animals as inferior beings, to be used or abused at will, with no apparent care or thought for the cruelty and suffering involved.

The Norman kings were fanatical hunters, who set aside for the chase, or afforested large areas of the countryside in which they alone had the right to pursue game, and

**CHEETAH AND STAG WITH TWO
INDIANS** (previous pages) BY GEORGE
STUBBS, OIL ON CANVAS (DETAIL)
PAINTED c.1765.

EXOTIC BEASTS (below) TWELFTH-
CENTURY ENGLISH BESTIARY
ILLUSTRATING A VARIETY OF REAL
AND FANTASTICAL BEASTS.

THE LADY AND THE UNICORN
(right) FIFETEENTH-CENTURY FRENCH
TAPESTRY, PART OF AN ALLEGORICAL
SERIES IN THE 'MILLE-FEUILLE' STYLE.

established barbaric penalties for anyone who broke the forest laws. A man convicted of killing a boar, a stag or a roebuck, for instance, was punished by having his eyes gouged out. William Rufus, second son of the Conqueror, was driven by a passion for the chase, and was killed by an arrow while hunting in the New Forest. His brother Henry I was equally fascinated by animals, and apart from hunting, established the first English royal menagerie at Woodstock near Oxford.

According to Dr William Plot, in his seventeenth-century history of Oxford, it was Henry who enclosed the park at Woodstock with a stone wall 'for all foreign beasts, such as lions, leopards, camels, lynxes, which he procured abroad of other Princes; amongst which...he kept a porcupine...covered over with sharp-pointed quills, which they naturally shoot at the dogs which hunt them'. Some sources record that the king himself engaged in hand-to-hand combat with the denizens of his park. The monarch took a selection of his rare creatures with him when he travelled about his kingdom, even when he went to war, as proof of his pre-eminence.

Henry II and John both preserved wild animals, the better to hunt them, and because they monopo-lised large tracts of country, they in effect gave protection to predators like wolves and bears, which their subjects were not allowed to kill, and which therefore survived for longer than they would have if persecuted by all and sundry. Not until the signature of the Charter of the Forests, at the same time as the Magna Carta in 1215, were the extreme wildlife laws repealed.

DENIZENS OF THE TOWER

In 1235 Henry II moved the royal collection of beasts to the Tower of London, where it remained for 600 years, fluctuating in the number and variety of inmates, but almost always including lions, and always acting as a magnet to the people of

the capital. Entrance fees – modest in any case – were waived when visitors brought along unwanted dogs or cats as supplementary rations for the big carnivores. At least such items of prey were live and fresh – more than could be said of the remains of human bodies, which were taken to the Tower when surgeons had finished dissecting them.

Fascinated though they were by strange animals, people were stupendously ignorant about them. A lynx, for instance, was thought to have such piercing eyes that it

could see through stone walls – and this because its staple prey was cats, which themselves are very keen-sighted. Knowledge had not advanced much since Julius Caesar, writing in the first century BC, had described the elk of the Hercynian Forest in Gaul as:

> entirely lacking in joints in its legs, for which reason it is unable to lie down to sleep. Instead, it is obliged to lean against a suitable tree trunk when it wants to rest. The wily Germanic hunters take advantage of this fact by cutting through the roots of suitable sleeping trees without allowing them to fall. When presently an elk leans against one of these trees, both the tree and the animal crash to the ground, and the hunter has only to go up to the helpless quarry and kill it.

The first comprehensive account of exotic creatures in English was compiled by Edward Topsell and published as his *Historie of Four-footed Beastes* in 1601. In many of his ideas the author was little more advanced than the Greek historian Herodotus, who, writing in the fifth century BC, recorded that once in every 500 years the bird known as the phoenix flew from Arabia to the temple of the sun at Heliopolis in Egypt to sit beside its father's remains. Drawing heavily on the earlier *Historia Animalium* by the Swiss naturalist Conrad Gesner, Topsell did his best to distinguish between myth and reality, and he was well aware that his account might be met with scepticism. Thus, when he came to the rhinoceros – which, at that date, no one in England had seen – he went out of his way to emphasise that the creature actually existed. Gesner, he wrote, had seen one alive in Lisbon, and 'that there is such a beast in the world both Pliny, Solinus, Diodorus, Aelianus, Lampridius and others do yield erefrigable [sic] testimony'. Yet Topsell was handicapped by having to rely mostly on other people's accounts, rather than on personal knowledge, and as a result his book was an extraordinary mixture of fairly accurate fact and total fantasy.

Much of what he wrote about the elephant, for instance, was sound enough, but then he said: 'Many times upon the leaves of trees he devoureth chameleons, whereby he is poisoned and dieth if he eat not immediately a wild olive'. Female elephants, he reckoned, went into water to calve, for fear of the 'subtil dragons', 30 paces long, which otherwise would strangle them.

Unicorns, for him, were entirely real: they lived in the deserts and on the mountain tops of Ethiopia, and were preyed upon by lions, which had a singular method of catching them. When a lion saw a unicorn, Topsell reported, the carnivore quickly positioned itself behind a tree, and the unicorn, charging, would impale its horn in the trunk, thus immobilising itself. On the other hand the unicorn itself, though swift and strong, was easily caught by hunters, for it was irresistibly fascinated by human virgins, and if a comely girl was stationed out in the wilderness, the animal would come and lie down beside her.

As for the rhino: 'He is taken by the same means as the *Unicorn* is taken, for it is said...that above all creatures they love virgins, and that unto them will they come, be they never so wild, and fall asleep before them, so being asleep they are easily taken and carried away.' Sexual allure was the weapon also of the Lamia, a kind of terrestrial mermaid, with scaly body, claws on front feet, cloven hoofs behind, and 'no other voice but hissing like dragons', who lured men into range by exposing her comely breasts, then pouncing on her victims and devouring them.

Topsell, it must be remembered, was an expert: ordinary people were even more ignorant than he. Perhaps this was one reason why they had no sympathy for the suffering of animals. Just as they threw coins and iron nails to captive ostriches, having been told that the birds could digest anything, so they were thrilled by the spectacle of one beast tearing another to pieces. Blood-lust was rampant in every level of society, from the monarchs down. When Mary I visited her sister Princess Elizabeth, during her confinement at Hatfield House, a grand exhibition of bear-baiting was laid on for the royal ladies, much to their satisfaction, and on 25 May 1559, not long after her accession to the throne, Elizabeth I entertained the French ambassadors to dinner, followed by the baiting of bulls and bears.

BEARS AND BULLS
In her great speech at Tilbury in August 1588, at the approach of the Spanish Armada, the Virgin Queen famously declared, 'I know I have the body of a weak and feeble woman; but I have the heart and stomach of a king' – and many a time did she prove that this was no idle boast. Three years later, at the age of 57, she rode into Cowdray Park, took up position in a specially prepared bower under which musicians were playing, and with a cross-bow shot three deer as they were driven past her – after which she rode to Cowdray for dinner, 'and about six o'clock in the evening, from a turret in the house, she saw 16 bucks, all having a fair start, pulled down by greyhounds on the lawn'.

If the head of state was a born hunter, and enjoyed watching animals destroy each other, how can one blame her subjects for sharing her enthusiasms? During her reign the office of Chief Master of the Bears was a Crown appointment, and it was the holder's duty to provide bears and dogs whenever called for. The royal bears – some brown and some white (genuine polar bears, caught as cubs) – were kept at the Paris Garden in Southwark, an amphitheatre ringed by tiers of wooden platforms capable of holding more than a thousand spectators. Members of the public were admitted for a small charge, and there, on Sunday 13 January 1583, a scaffolding or stand collapsed in the middle of a fight between a dog and a bear, killing five men and two women and maiming many others – an accident which the Puritans lost no time in attributing to divine intervention. (It was on arenas like the Paris Garden that the design of new, circular theatres like the Globe was based.)

At that time bear-baiting was rife all over the country. Every town of consequence had its own bear, bear-ward and set of dogs, as did individual noblemen, who employed bear-wards in the same way as they did gamekeepers. Scandal long clung to Congleton in Cheshire, after an incident said to have taken place in 1620. The Bible in the church was falling apart, and a new one was needed; but instead of buying a new holy book, the corporation gave the money collected for the purpose to the bear-ward, to acquire a new town bear, the old one having died. For centuries afterwards the people of the town could be provoked by quoting the rhyme:

> Congleton rare, Congleton rare,
> Sold the Bible to pay for a bear.

Sometimes half a dozen bears were brought into an arena to fight at the same time, all anchored by long ropes or chains, and four or five savage dogs would be set on them. A bear's tactics were to seize hold of a dog, if it could, and bite or claw or squeeze it to death; but generally the battles consisted of a series of rushes and retreats, and bears survived dozens of fights to become popular heroes with well-known names: Sackerson, Don John, Tom of Lincoln. Occasionally a bear broke loose, to the terror of the spectators. The noise was phenomenal – and to this day people speak of a place in which pandemonium reigns as a bear-garden. Bull-baiting followed the same pattern: the bull was tethered to a stake and did its best to gore attacking dogs, which tried to rip off its nose and ears.

King James I of England (and VI of Scotland) set no better an example than his predecessor Elizabeth. A fanatic for the chase, he revolutionised British deer-hunting by having the whole field of mounted followers gallop after the hounds flat out, thereby greatly increasing the danger to themselves; and at the Tower he gloated over bloody combats – between dogs and a lion, dogs and a bear, a lion and a bull. Once at the Paris Garden he arranged for three ferocious mastiffs to be let loose on a lion, one by one. The first two died, but the third dealt the lion such a bite that it retired to its den – and thereafter the dog was fêted. His subjects followed suit whenever they had the chance, even if lowly bear-, dog- and cock-fights were the worst form of

sadistic entertainment that most of them could afford. An advertisement from the reign of Queen Anne (1665–1714) shows that in these grisly entertainments there was something for everyone, and plenty of chances to lay bets:

> At the Bear Garden at Hockley-in-the-Hole, near Clerkenwell Green, this present Monday, there is a great match to be fought by two dogs of Smithfield Bars against two dogs of Hampstead, at the Reading Bull, for one guinea to be spent; five let-goes out of hand; which goes fairest and furthest in wins all. Likewise there are two bear-dogs to jump three jumps apiece at the Bear, which jumps highest for ten shillings to be spent. Also a variety of Bull-baiting and Bear-baiting; it being a day of general sport by all the old gamesters; and a bulldog to be drawn up with fireworks. Beginning at three o'clock.

In 1764 George II's son, the gross Duke of Cumberland, the Butcher of Culloden, commissioned the East India Company to send him some beasts that would entertain him and his cronies by fighting each other or hunting lesser species in the Great Park at Windsor. The Company obliged with a brace of big cats, officially described as tigers, but almost certainly cheetahs, one of which was let loose in a canvas-walled arena to fight a stag. After a few clashes the cheetah bolted under the canvas and ran out into the park, where it found, killed and began to eat a hind. The big cat must have been fairly tame, for its two Indian keepers soon recaptured it; as for the stag – the duke was so delighted by its fortitude that he had a silver collar made for it, engraved with a brief account of its triumph, and turned it loose, thus decorated, into his park.

A Cool Cheetah

A year later another hunting cheetah was immortalised by the painter George Stubbs (see page 33). This animal was sent as a gift to George III by the Governor of Madras, and, once again, two Indian keepers came with it. Notice was given that it would be let loose in Windsor Great Park to run down a stag, and a large crowd assembled to witness the chase – but alas, as Stubbs's marvellous painting shows, no hunt took place. Even with the stag standing not far off, and the keepers doing their best to launch the pursuit, the cheetah declined to move.

At the end of the eighteenth century casual cruelty to animals was the rule in every level of society. At country fairs contests were held at biting off the heads of live birds – chickens or sparrows – and rural gentlemen entertained visitors by throwing a goose or chicken into a pond full of pike, to see how quickly, and by what degrees, it would be ripped to pieces.

Cock-fighting was one of the chief sports of the rural aristocracy, whose game-cock caravans travelled about the country from match to match. As in bull-baiting and prize-fighting, the principal attraction was the fact that fights gave owners and spectators the chance to gamble, and matches were regular features of race-meetings and fairs. Birds were specially reared and trained for battle: they fought with their wings clipped, their wattles and combs cut off, and their feet fitted with metal spurs.

Most matches were 'mains', contests between teams, often from different counties or districts, with a member of one side paired off against an opposite number from the other. Meetings often went on for several days, and the wagering was intense. Bird-to-bird single combats were the usual order of the day, but the most spectacular event was a 'battle royal', for which several birds were let loose in a pit at the same time. Not surprisingly, even the strongest and most ferocious cocks did not last long: if one got through a dozen fights, it was exceptional.

A fighting cock at least had some chance of survival: a bird condemned to the even more despicable sport of cock-throwing had none, for it was tethered to a stake or buried in the ground up to its neck, and bombarded with missiles until it died. In the seventeenth century the sport was highly regarded, and practised especially as a ritual on Shrove Tuesday in grammar schools throughout Britain. Out of school, boys naturally tortured and killed any small animal they could lay hands on.

Another widespread country amusement was badger-digging and baiting, whose horrors stand starkly revealed in the poem by John Clare.

THE BADGER
When midnight comes a host of dogs and men
Go out and track the badger to his den,
And put a sack within the hole and lye
Till the old grunting badger passes by...

They get a forkéd stick to bear him down
And clapt the dogs and bore him to the town.
And bait him all the day with many dogs,
And laugh and shout and fright the scampering hogs

He runs along and bites at all he meets
They shout and hollo down the noisey streets.
He turns about to face the loud uproar
And drives the rebels to their very doors

The frequent stone is hurled where'er they go;
When badgers fight, then every one's a foe
The dogs are clapt and urged to join the fray
The badger turns and drives them all away.
Though scarcely half as big, demure and small,
He fights with dogs for hours and beats them all.
The heavy mastiff savage in the fray
Lies down and licks his feet and turns away.

The bulldog knows his match and waxes cold,
The badger grins and never leaves his hold.
He drives the crowd and follows at their heels
And bites them through the drunkard swears and reels.

The frighted women take the boys away,
The blackguard laughs and hurries on the fray.
He tries to reach the woods, an awkward race
But sticks and cudgels quickly stop the chase

He turns agen and drives the noisy crowd
And beats the many dogs in noises loud
He drives away and beats them every one
And then they loose them all and set them on

He falls as dead and kicked by boys and men
Then starts and grins and drives the crowd agen
Till kicked and torn and beaten out he lies
And leaves his hold and cackles groans and dies.

Gradually public opinion turned against cruel sports: people came to believe that although it was morally acceptable to keep animals, and kill them for their meat or their skins, it was not acceptable to cause them unnecessary suffering. Wild animals, similarly, could be killed for food or if they were causing a nuisance, but not simply for pleasure. Little by little the realisation dawned that animals were intelligent creatures, even if their brain-power and range of emotions were smaller than those of humans, and that all members of God's creation – not merely men – were entitled to be treated humanely.

In 1833 cockpits were made illegal in London, and two years later they were banned throughout the country. Cockfighting was finally prohibited in 1849 – although of course it survived clandestinely. Yet interest in exotic species remained intense, and any private menagerie which could exhibit a lion or an elephant attracted flocks of visitors.

DEATH OF A GIANT

For years the best-known menagerie was the Exeter 'Change, which opened in the Strand in the eighteenth century, and was later taken over by Edward Cross; its most celebrated inmate was Chunee, an Indian elephant who arrived in England in 1810 and became a star when he performed in *Blue Beard* at the Covent Garden Theatre, and became a favourite of the actor Edmund Keane.

In 1826, however, Chunee met a dreadful end. His death was one of the most traumatic events in the annals of Victorian zoo-keeping, and illustrates all too well the amateurish level at which even an experienced man like Cross operated. A startlingly vivid account of the disaster was left by William Hone in his *Every-Day Book or Everlasting Calendar of Popular Amusements* for the year 1826.

Inappropriate as it sounds, Chunee was by then housed on the first floor of the Exeter 'Change, above an arcade of shops, flanked by lions in separate cages. His 'den' was stoutly built of wood and iron, and had a reinforced floor made of wood and brick. Some six years before the disaster, Hone explained, Chunee had started to 'indicate an excitement which is natural to the species...the first appearance of those annual paroxysms wherein the elephant, whether wild or confined, becomes infuriated'. In other words, he was regularly coming into musth, the state of sexual excitement which makes bull elephants dangerous.

In India the animal would have been turned loose into the jungle until the phase wore off. Hone continued:

> But, such an experiment being impossible for Mr Cross, he resorted to pharmacy, and in the course of 52 hours succeeded in deceiving his patient into taking 24 lbs of salts, 6 ounces of calomel, one and a half ounces of tartar emetic and 6 drams of powder of gamboge. To this he added a bottle of croton oil, perhaps the most potent cathartic in existence.

Such terrific purges seemed to have little effect, but after periods of great violence the elephant had always returned to normal. Not so on 25 March 1826, when he launched such furious charges at the gates of his cage that they began to come away from their hinges. The danger of his escaping became acute: had he broken out of his den, his five-ton weight would have sent him crashing through the ceilings of the shops below, and if he had gained access to the Strand, it was 'impossible to imagine the mischief that might have ensued in that crowded thoroughfare'.

To prevent loss of human life, Cross decided he must destroy the animal immediately. But how? First he tried poison, running to Mr Gifford, a chemist in the Strand, who reluctantly supplied him with 110 g of arsenic. This he mixed with oats, but Chunee was too crafty to touch it, or the tinctured rose jam which was offered him next. Cross then despatched a messenger to his brother-in-law, Mr Herring, in Paddington – 'a man of determined resolution and an excellent shot' – asking him to come at once, which he did. The pair hastened to Mr Stevens, a gunsmith in High Holborn, who lent them three rifles.

Back at the 'Change, Cross left Stevens in charge, with instructions to shoot immediately if Chunee precipitated a crisis, while he himself sped off to Great Marlborough Street, seeking advice from the eminent anatomist Mr Joshua Brookes about where best to shoot an elephant. Brookes was in the middle of delivering a lecture, but broke off to discuss the emergency, and lent one of his students as a helper. Hurrying back towards the Strand, Cross was met by some of his own people, who told him that shooting had already started. He therefore ran to the soldiers guarding the entrance to Somerset House, in search of more fire-power.

In his absence Chunee's aggression had increased to such a degree that Mrs Cross, 'who had the highest regard for the animal', agreed to his immediate execution. Marksmen opened up on him from point-blank range, the first two bullets entering behind the shoulder-blade:

> The moment the balls had perforated his body, he made a fierce and heavy rush at the front, which further weak-ened the gates ... The fury of the animal's assault was terrific, the crash of the timbers, the hallooing of the keepers in their retreat, the calls for 'Rifles! Rifles!' and the confusion and noise incident to the scene rendered it indescribably terrific ... [Had he burst through the gate] and descended on the floor, his weight must inevitably have carried it, together with himself, his assailants and the greater part of the lions, and other animals, into the 'Change below, and by possibility have buried the entire menagerie in ruins. 'Rifles! Rifles!' were again called for ... The elephant flew round the den with the speed of a race-horse, uttering frightful yells and screams, and stop-ping at intervals to bound from the back against the front. The force of these rushes shook the entire building

Under a hail of more than 150 bullets, speared from every side by pikes and swords lashed to poles, Chunee twice went down, only to struggle up again and make one last frantic charge. In the end he astonished his attackers by sinking down on all fours and dying in the posture in which he had habitually slept – an end which seemed so remarkable to William Hone that he commemorated it with a little poem:

> In the position he liked best
> He seemed to drop, to sudden rest;
> Nor bowed his neck, but still a sense
> Retain'd of his magnificence;
> For as he fell, he raised his head
> And held it, as in life, when dead.

It is clear that Chunee's death severely shook all those concerned – but whether it improved the lot of Cross's other animals, it is impossible to know.

The ambivalent attitude of keepers towards their animals was exemplified by George Wombwell, whose travelling menagerie was so successful that at one time he owned 20 lions and 40 caravans. He seems to have loved his animals and looked after them well; when he died, *The Times*

DESTRUCTION OF THE FURIOUS ELEPHANT AT EXETER CHANGE

OBAYSCH (below) THE FIRST HIPPO
SEEN IN EUROPE SINCE ROMAN TIMES,
OBAYSCH DREW A RECORD CROWD
WHEN HE REACHED REGENT'S PARK.

JENNY AND JANE, FIRST ORANG-
UTANS AT ZOOLOGICAL SOCIETY
LONDON (right)
BY G. SCHARF, 1837.

recorded in its obituary that 'No one probably did more to forward practically the study of natural history among the masses'. Yet Wombwell's most notorious achievement was his attempt to stage a fight at Warwick between his most ferocious lion, Nero, and six mastiffs. The project ended in fiasco, for Nero refused to do battle, and when another lion was substituted, the dogs turned tail. Yet the showman was prepared to risk the lives of his most valuable creatures purely to cause excitement and earn money.

Another arena to which wild animals drew the crowds was the circus, in which clans like the Chipperfields founded and maintained a tradition that lasted hundreds of years. The first recorded member of the family took a performing bear on to the ice when the Thames froze over in the bitter winter of 1684, and although at first the show was very small – just the bear, a couple of baboons, a pony, a few jugglers and a clown – it flourished, and dangerous animals, lions particularly, became its strongest suit. No doubt the cramped wagons in which the animals lived would be condemned today; but the owners looked after their performers as well as they could, for the creatures were their life.

Of all the Chipperfields' old-fashioned circus acts, for sheer excitement none could match that of the Untameable Lion. As the finale of his performance the trainer would announce that one lioness – she in the travelling cage – had proved impossible to train, but that, as a special favour to the audience he would go into the cage with her and come out again: that was all he could promise. As he talked, the lioness would be snarling, growling and striking out at the bars behind him, showing every symptom of ferocity, and by the time he moved towards the door, the audience was at a high pitch of tension.

One assistant wielded a pole to keep the animal at bay. Another stood by to open and shut the barred steel door. At a signal the door was flung open. The trainer stepped inside. With a roar the lion sprang. Inside the bars there was a blur of man, lion, man, almost too fast to follow, as the huge animal flew round the walls of her enclosure, first in front of the intruder, then behind him. Seconds later the door opened again, the man popped out and the lion hit the bars with a tremendous clang. By then half the women in the audience had fainted from fright – but, miraculously, the trainer was unharmed. What none of the spectators realised was that, after years of practice, the lion was

playing to the gallery as surely as the humans, and that the whole thing was a put-up job.

THE ARK IN THE PARK

In 1826 – the year that Chunee met his end – the advocacy of Sir Stamford Raffles, the founder of Singapore and a formidable animal collector in his own right, led to the creation of the Zoological Society of London, whose purpose would be to form a collection of living animals and a museum of preserved speciments. A site was found in Regent's Park, and on 27 April 1828 the Society opened its gate to members (known as 'Fellows') and their friends. The charter granted by King George IV laid down that the Society's aims were 'the advancement of zoology and animal physiology and the introduction of new and curious subjects of the animal kingdom'.

'The advancement of zoology' was badly needed, for prevailing ignorance was still enormous, not just among poorly educated members of the public, but among the keepers and allegedly learned fellows of the Society as well. The transport of wild animals was erratic, to say the least. In 1835 the Society's first chimpanzee, Tommy, arrived by stage coach, but a year later the first four giraffes had to walk the last stretch of their journey from the dock where their ship had berthed, and could hardly be induced to go past a cow grazing in a field beside Commercial Road.

Lack of experience inevitably meant that the care of animals was amateurish, and many died prematurely as a result of unsuitable diets. The first orang-utan offered to the zoo was a young male sent from Calcutta in 1830, who reached London alive but expired before he could be put on show. His successor, Jenny, survived for eighteen months, and her successor, another Jenny, lasted four years. The reaction to this ape of Queen Victoria, who visited her in

YOUNG HIPPOPOTAMUS
Presented to the Zoological Society by H H Abbas Pasha.

Chimpanzee or African Orang-Utan.
ZOOLOGICAL GARDENS.
Regent's Park.

May 1842, misreading her gender, would probably have been echoed by many of her subjects: 'The Orang-Outang is too wonderful, preparing and drinking his tea, doing everything by word of command. He is frightful & painfully & disagreeably human.'

At its inception the Society had had no plan to admit members of the public; but by 1847 its finances were in such a state that it was obliged to do so, charging one shilling (5p) per head – a fee that remained constant for nearly a century. The gardens in Regent's Park rapidly became popular, and every new arrival in the country created a wave of excellent publicity – none more so than that, in 1850, of Obaysch the young hippopotamus, the first of his kind seen in Europe since Roman times. Captured as a baby on the Nile, brought to London by ship and train in the care of an Arab attendant, Obaysch instantly hit the headlines

of the popular press, which christened him HRH – His Rolling Hulk – and wrote him up so extravagantly that the number of visitors to the gardens shot up to double that of the previous year.

Victorian naturalists were perplexed by many questions. 'What do we know of Man from the dissecting room? Of Man the warrior, the statesman, the poet or the saint?' asked the Reverend J. G. Wood in his *Natural History of Mammals*, published in 1865. 'In the lifeless corpse there are no records of burning thoughts, the hopes, loves and fears that once animated the now passive form.' Wood knew a lot about British mammals, but admitted that his knowledge of what he called 'quadrumana' – four-handed animals, including apes, baboons and monkeys – was slender. Such creatures, he thought, were 'not very pleasing animals in aspect or habits, while the larger apes and baboons are positively disgusting'. As for the gorilla – 'there is a treacherous and cruel aspect about his hind foot, with its enormous thumb' with which (Wood maintained) the creature reached down out of trees to snatch up any man who passed underneath.

Of the various private animal dealers who flourished in London during the second half of the nineteenth century, the most celebrated was Charles Jamrach, a German who took British nationality and had his premises in the notorious Ratcliff Highway, opposite the entrance to London Docks. He was well known to the officials of Regent's Park, for he often gave them first refusal of any unusual creature that came into his hands. Because he had agents in foreign parts, and runners who met ships as they arrived in London, he monopolised the trade in exotic animals, and probably knew more about how to look after them than most of the zoo-keepers. A brave and exceptionally powerful man, he became famous for his single-handed recapture of a tigress – an incident which he himself described to the naturalist William Buckland.

The animal had recently arrived on a ship, but during the voyage the boards of its cage had rotted, with the result that it had hardly come ashore before it escaped and set off down the street. A boy about nine years old, thinking the animal was a big dog, went up and patted it, whereupon the tigress seized him by the shoulder and started to drag him away:

> Jamrach immediately running up grasped the tiger by the loose skin of her neck, but, although a very strong and powerfully built man, he could not hold the beast, who immediately started off down the street at a gallop, carrying the boy in her mouth as a cat would a mouse, Jamrach holding on tight all the time to the tiger's neck, and keeping up long strides by her side ...

Finding that his hold was giving way, he managed to slip the tiger's hind leg from under her, and she fell to the ground. Jamrach instantly threw his whole weight down on her, and letting go the skin of her neck, fastened his two thumbs behind her ears with a firm grip. There tiger, man and boy lay many minutes altogether in a heap, the man gripping the tiger, the tiger (still holding the boy in her fangs) all the while suffering great pain from the pressure of Jamrach's hands, and from impeded respiration.

Relief came when one of Jamrach's men appeared and, in response to an urgent order, brought a crowbar, with which he hit the tigress 'three severe blows on the nose'. The animal released the child, and, after escaping its master's grip, rushed back to take refuge in its cage. Miraculously, the boy was not much hurt, but he was so shocked that for four hours he could not speak. Jamrach,

in contrast, got very much the worst of the affair, since, in Buckland's words, 'having had to fight the tiger, he then had to fight the lawyers, and the whole business cost him, in damages and law expenses, over £300'.

Knowledge spread slowly. Not only had most supposed experts no experience of exotic animals: they buttressed their ignorance with unshakeable bigotry. When Charles Darwin published *The Origin of Species* in 1859, with its outrageous suggestion that humans had evolved from apes, men of learning condemned the book as disgusting and unworthy of serious consideration. Similar scepticism greeted Paul du Chaillu, a young American of French extraction, who in 1861 came to London for the publication of *Explorations and Adventures in Equatorial Africa*, his highly coloured account of how he had shot gorillas and other creatures in the Congo.

With him he brought a collection of skins and stuffed specimens, including the remains of more than 20 gorillas – and yet members of the scientific establishment derided him viciously, claiming that he had never travelled through the regions he said he had explored, and that his accounts of gorillas' behaviour – roaring and chest-beating – were 'a disgrace to zoology'. Their attacks were based entirely on ignorance and jealousy: at that date nobody in England had seen a live male gorilla, and only one or possibly two young females had reached Britain. Admittedly du Chaillu's descriptions were melodramatic – 'With a groan which had something terribly human about it, and yet was full of brutishness, he [the ape] fell forward on his face' – yet he had undoubtedly had more experience of Africa than most of his critics, and they did not like it.

Only in 1867 was the cumbersome title 'Zoological Gardens' abbreviated to 'Zoo', but the word was swiftly taken into everyday use, and as the organisation in Regent's Park expanded, one first followed another: the first reptile house in 1849, the first public aquarium in 1853, the first insect house in 1881, the first children's zoo in 1938. Yet it has always been individual animals that have commanded the keenest interest.

The entire country loved Jumbo the African elephant, the Zoo's star for 17 years, and in 1882 thousands of people were outraged when, because he was becoming fractious, the authorities sold him to the American showman Phineas Barnum, of Barnum and Bailey's Circus. From the 1950s to the 1970s Guy the mighty gorilla exercised a tremendous fascination, drawing enormous crowds who sympathised with his lonely situation, incarcerated as he was without companions or mate; and during the same period Chi-Chi the panda became an international symbol of political goodwill between Britain and China, when these two countries attempted a captive breeding programme.

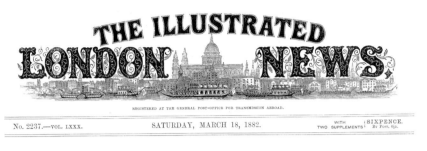

A FAREWELL RIDE ON JUMBO.—SEE PAGE 254.

WHIPSNADE WILD ANIMAL PARK

During the 1920s Sir Patrick Chalmers Mitchell, Secretary of the Zoological Society of London, decided that the establishment needed a larger, open-plan park in order to study wild animals and their behaviour adequately. At the time the idea of a zoo without bars was revolutionary, and a complete departure from the urban jungles to which people were accustomed: what emerged was in fact a prototype of the safari parks developed in the 1960s. In 1926 a perfect site was found in the form of 600 acres of derelict farmland near the village of Whipsnade, on the Chiltern Hills in Bedfordshire. Conversion work started at once: the project was so large that workmen had to be drafted in from all over the country to build fences and animal enclosures. The perimeter fence was originally tilted inwards, but later had to be slanted the other way, to stop foxes climbing in.

The first few birds and animals started to arrive in 1928, and when the park opened to the public in May 1931, it was an immediate success, even though the weather was atrocious and many of the paddocks were still empty. Major reinforcements arrived in January 1932, when London Zoo took over a number of animals from Bostock & Wombwell's Circus and Menagerie, which had been based in Scotland and was closing down after 126 years on the road. The newcomers included 11 lions, 5 leopards, 2 brown bears, a polar bear, 2 elephants, 2 camels, 2 wolves, a spotted hyena, a sea lion, a red kangaroo and a black-necked crowned crane. They all travelled from Scotland to Dunstable by train, and the elephants and camels walked on over the Downs, while lesser fry finished their journey in wagons and lorries. Since then the park has been continually developed. In 1970 a narrow-gauge railway was opened, running through the rhino paddock, and in 1973 the line was extended to take in the paddocks holding deer, camels, rhinos, elephants and yaks. The original farmhouse was first converted into a restaurant; now it has become the Discovery Centre, but still it is reputed to be haunted by at least one ghost. At the millennium the park had over 2500 animals of 200 species, and was attracting 450,000 visitors a year. Apart from showing wildlife to the public, Whipsnade plays an important role in the breeding of rare and endangered species, and animals are often transferred from other countries to achieve the best results: the park's two

Siberian Tigers, for instance, came from zoos in Moscow and Prague. Its staff is, or has been working on conservation projects in other countries including Saudi Arabia, Nepal, Ghana and Kenya.

The white lion cut in the turf of the chalk downland outside the park was begun in 1932 and completed 18 months later. It is 140 metres long, and has become a familiar landmark to air travellers flying over Luton airport.

Safari Parks

Another revolution in animal-keeping was born in 1966, when the former circus man Jimmy Chipperfield joined forces with the Marquess of Bath to create the Lions of Longleat, the first safari park. Having grown up in his family's travelling circus, and himself trained wild animals, Chipperfield realised what a powerful attraction it would be if lions were released in an extensive park, and members of the public were able to drive through the enclosures in their cars.

The plan nearly foundered, because Lord Bath did not at first grasp what Chipperfield had visualised; but later he embraced the idea enthusiastically, and construction of 4-metre-high fences went ahead in the autumn of 1965. Representatives of London Zoo refused an invitation to come and inspect the site, on the grounds that they could not be associated with so controversial a project; and in September *The Times* inadvertently gave the undertaking an immense boost by condemning it as dangerous and calling for it to be suppressed.

Chipperfield collected his pride from zoos and circuses in many countries – Germany, Spain, Holland, Denmark and Israel – and included ten animals which had starred in the film *Born Free*. But even he, with all his experience, was not sure what the lions would do when let loose in ancient parkland. In the event some of them instantly began fighting, then raced wildly about and hid under trees or bushes, apparently disconcerted by the huge, open space of the sky above their heads – a phenomenon they had never known. Gradually, however, they settled down.

Lions of Longleat

By the time the Lions of Longleat opened at Easter 1966, expectation had reached fever pitch, and every road round the park was jammed with traffic throughout the weekend. The Chipperfields took so much money that they immediately set about building a second safari park, in partnership with the Duke of Bedford at Woburn Abbey; this one was on a grander scale, and cost much more to install, because by then the organisers had expanded their original idea to include many species besides lions: elephants, rhinos, giraffes, antelopes, chimpanzees, monkeys and so on.

When Woburn's safari park opened, two years after Longleat, business was at first inexplicably slow. Then a single incident transformed the situation: in spite of all the notices telling drivers to keep their car windows shut, and rangers reinforcing the message verbally, one family persisted in opening the windows of their Mini, and allowed a young girl to struggle about so much that her behind stuck out. In an instant a lioness called Twiggy (named after the skinny model, because she was so thin) darted at the car and took a swipe at the wriggling target.

The girl was severely mauled, and next day the accident hit the headlines of national newspapers. For the Chipperfields, the result was magic. Attendances rocketed, and the park never looked back. It said a good deal about people's appetite for scandal and danger that hundreds of visitors wanted to see the lion that had injured the child. In fact the lioness had been quickly moved elsewhere, and was not on hand to satisfy their morbid curiosity.

Numerous other safari parks followed, and the new style of zoo quickly became established. Its success led to bitter rows between Chipperfield and the zoo establishment, for the former circus man pointed out, with some truth, that once people had seen lions running free in fine parkland, they would never again want to watch them pacing a small concrete enclosure behind bars. When traditional zoos condemned the safari parks as commercial gimmicks, and said that animals were being exploited for financial gain, the Chipperfields retorted that they were valuable sanctuaries in which breeding groups of endangered species such as tigers could be established – in fact both lions and tigers bred so successfully that birth control had to be instituted.

As the twentieth century progressed, all zoos gave more and more attention to the captive breeding of threatened species, the aim being to establish reservoirs of endangered animals, in case those in the wild die out. Among the leaders of the movement were the naturalist and author Gerald Durrell, who in 1959 opened his own zoo on the Channel Island of Jersey, and the millionaire gambler John Aspinall, who established two outstanding zoos in Kent, Howlett's and Port Lympne.

Durrell chose as his emblem the dodo, which went extinct on Mauritius in the 1660s, and declared that the purpose of his zoo was 'to prevent other species becoming as dead as the dodo'. The Jersey Zoological Park is now an world class centre for breeding and research, and describes itself as 'a safe haven for the world's rarest animals'.

The outstanding feature of Howlett's is its captive-breeding colony of Western Lowland gorillas – the largest in the world – which has recorded over 60 births. The zoo's purpose is to breed rare and endangered species, with the ultimate aim of returning them to the wild when or if it is safe to do so. The park has already sent a number of Przewalski's horses to Mongolia, Burmese pythons to Indonesia, ocelots to Mexico, a black rhino to South Africa, and nine gorillas to the Lefini reserve in the Congo.

John Aspinall, who died in 1998, always pursued an unconventional policy of encouraging his keepers to bond with their charges by going into their enclosures and spending time with them. Several keepers were killed by tigers, which led to some controversy and criticism, but Aspinall maintained that the close association between man and animal made a major contribution to the success of his breeding programmes. He himself frequently spent time in the gorillas' enclosure, bonding especially with an immense silverback called Djoum (see picture opposite).

In spite of intense competition from wildlife films on television, people have retained their appetite for seeing exotic animals in the flesh. The extensive improvements in animals' living conditions and general display, made in all major zoos over the past 20 years, have kept crowds coming. The pace has been

set by Chester Zoo, which which is home to more than 500 species, and in 2000 became the most popular wildlife centre in Britain with 1.2 million visitors, surpassing even Regent's Park, which had about a million. Chester has achieved notable breeding success with many endangered species, particularly chimpanzees, orang-utans, black rhinos and Asiatic elephants, and it supports parallel breeding programmes in more than 20 countries overseas, doing its best to encourage the conservation of natural habitats in those places.

3 WILD MAMMALS

Mammals are warm-blooded, vertebrate animals that suckle their babies: the name derives from the Latin *mamma*, a breast or teat, and was coined by the eighteenth-century Swedish botanist Linnaeus. All British mammals – from bats turning the scales at a few grammes to whales weighing several tons – give birth to well-developed young after relatively long periods of gestation: a leveret, for instance, is fully furred and able to run from the moment it is born. Most mammals live on land, and all breathe air, even if their home is in the sea: the only ones that can fly are bats.

A survey conducted by the Mammal Society in 2001 revealed that people have definite favourites in each group of animals. Among bats, for instance, the little pipistrelle won 34 per cent of votes and left all rivals standing. Of the carnivores, the red fox was the winner, with 27 per cent, just beating the otter (25 per cent), and leaving the badger (16 per cent) trailing in its wake. The fact that stoats, polecats and mink each rated only 2 per cent probably reflected the fact that they are rarely seen. Among insectivores, the hedgehog (58 per cent) was way out in front, as was the red deer (29 per cent) among herbivores. But the fact that 34 per cent of votes for cetaceans (whales, dolphins and porpoises) went to the blue whale – far ahead of any rival – can only be a tribute to the creature's size, and to nature programmes on television, since few, if any, of the voters can have seen one in the flesh.

Carnivores

Carnivores — literally 'meat-eaters' — are distinguished by the possession of pairs of carnassial teeth, one set on the upper jaw and one set on the lower jaw, with a shearing edge for cutting flesh. Some animals, like cats, are almost exclusively carnivorous, but others, like badgers and foxes, also eat fruit, grain and a wide range of other foods.

Badger

Meles meles

Black and white facial markings make Brock the Badger one of our most instantly recognisable wild animals, and one of the best loved. Unfortunately the species has also become surrounded by controversy, because it suffers from bovine tuberculosis and can apparently transmit the disease to cattle, with the result that thousands of cows have had to be put down, and whole milking herds have been destroyed. This susceptibility to infection has made badgers direly unpopular with farmers.

Various Acts of Parliament, passed between 1973 and 1992, have given the species complete immunity from persecution. Not only is it illegal to kill a badger without special licence: it is also against the law to damage or alter a sett. Even if a colony undermines a field by extending its tunnels beyond the edge of a wood, a farmer may not do anything to curb its excavations. In spite of appalling slaughter on the roads – badgers are run over at the rate of 50,000 a year, or 140 every night, or one every five minutes – the population has reached about 250,000. As numbers have rocketed, so too have the totals of cattle compulsorily slaughtered by the Department for Environment, Food and Rural Affairs because of TB outbreaks – from 942 in 1980 to 1570 in 1990 and 6890 in 1999. Many observers, including dedicated conservationists, feel that protection has gone too far, and that some form of licenced culling of badgers should be introduced. Yet total preservation is fervently championed by the National Federation of Badger Groups (NFBG), which has 80,000 members.

It seems bad luck on badgers that they should harbour contagious disease, for they are essentially clean-living animals, and excellent housekeepers: they live in social groups and maintain their setts in pristine order, raking out old bedding and depositing their droppings in specially dug pits which serve as communal latrines. Most of these are sited some distance from base, and often mark the boundaries of a territory. Setts, which remain in use for generations, gradually become impressive feats of natural architecture as the networks of tunnels grow: the largest ever recorded had 1.3 km of tunnels, 180 entrances and more than 50 sleeping chambers. A sett is recognised from the large diameter of the tunnels – about 30 cm – and from the huge mounds of sand and earth that pile up outside.

Because badgers are almost entirely nocturnal, they are rarely seen except by dedicated watchers; but their presence can always be detected, both from the fresh spoil at the entrance to setts, and from the clearly defined paths which radiate from the site out into the surrounding countryside.

Emerging at last light, the inmates trundle off in search of food, which consists largely of earthworms: the enormous numbers eaten – maybe 250 a night by a single animal – give droppings a sludgy texture. Other food includes fruit, nuts, beetles, baby rabbits, voles, slugs, frogs, grass snakes, wheat, cattle-feed such as maize, birds' eggs, fungi and even the nests of bumblebees and wasps, which badgers somehow tackle without getting seriously stung. Some individual badgers are reputed to specialise in catching hedgehogs, leaving cleaned-out skins as evidence. Research conducted in the Woodchester Valley near Stroud in Gloucestershire, has revealed that they are much more athletic than people imagine, and can climb into cattle feeding troughs more than a metre off the ground.

In winter they do not hibernate, but their body temperature falls and they become dormant for days and nights on end, as they sleep cold weather away, comfortably rolled up in their nests of dried grass and leaves. Mating can take place at different times of the year, as sows share with roe deer and other animals the biological phenomenon known as delayed implantation, in which eggs, though fertilised, do not start to develop for several weeks or months after copulation. When gestation starts, it takes only seven weeks, and up to five cubs are born in February, underground. At first they are blind and hairless except for a little thin, silver-grey fur, but they grow quickly, and start coming into the open at about eight weeks. After three months their mother begins to wean them, regurgitating half-digested food.

Even after many years' research, scientists have not been able to determine exactly how bovine tuberculosis passes from cattle to badgers and vice-versa. One theory is that the bacilli are transmitted in urine deposited on grass fields where cows are feeding; another, that they are airborne, and carried on the animals' breath. Past attempts to control the disease have consisted mainly in eliminating all badgers from infected areas, and these have been successful, especially at Thornbury near Bristol, during the 1970s,

BADGER (previous pages)
BY FRANCIS BARLOW (1626–1702)
DETAIL

BADGER, *MELES MELES* (below)
YOUNG BADGER FORAGING. CUBS
START TO COME INTO THE OPEN AT
ABOUT 8 WEEKS OLD.

and in County Offaly in Ireland, during the 1990s. But in 1997, because the problem was still so poorly understood, the government set up a new body, the Independent Scientific Group, and this in turn devised a large-scale trial, to find out what would happen if badgers were systematically culled in ten experimental areas. The work was fiercely opposed by pro-badger activists, who cut up cage traps, threw them into rivers, and released animals that had been caught. Nevertheless, the operation went ahead until it was interrupted by the foot-and-mouth epidemic of 2001.

The best long-term prospect for control of bovine tuberculosis is to develop a vaccine which will immunise both cattle and badgers. The government is now spending £1.5 million a year on research in this area, but describes the work as 'at the frontiers of science,' and reckons it will

take between 10 and 15 years to achieve a breakthrough. Nobody still believes – as many people did in the Middle Ages – that badgers' right legs are longer than their left, so that they can travel easily round hill-sides; but the species still holds many secrets.

Meanwhile many farmers are taking the law into their own hands and shooting badgers which threaten their dairy herds or damage their cereal crops. Illegal badger-digging and baiting are also, regrettably, still rife: the National Federation of Badger Groups claims that 10,000 animals are killed in this way every year.

At the other end of the scale, in 2001 Aberdeenshire County Council sanctioned the construction of an artificial sett as a new home for a colony of badgers which had undermined the main road between Huntly and Banff. A radar survey convinced the council that the animals'

ever-extending excavations were threatening the carriage-way with collapse, and it was decided to move the badgers some 30 metres to new premises comprising nine sleeping chambers approached by wood-lined tunnels at a cost of around £30,000.

Countless enthusiasts have become fascinated by badgers – and few more so than the Hertfordshire wildlife artist Eileen Soper, who painted birds and animals in watercolours between 1950 and 1970. So captivated was she by a colony near her home outside Welwyn that she often spent most of the night sitting above a sett in a wooded dell, observing and sketching the occupants as they went about their business. In due course she won their trust so completely that they would come up to her and lick the syrup which she smeared over her boots.

Every year about 40 homeless badger cubs are brought to the RSPCA's hospitals, and a similar number are taken to the NFBG. The orphans are reared and, as soon as possible, put back into the wild, even though, because of anxiety about bovine TB, sites are not easy to find. In 2001, however, the Woodland Trust (see page 404) formed a new partnership with the RSPCA, and offered to help provide release areas.

So Brock remains the rope in a tug-of-war between the men who manage the countryside on one hand, and emotional preservationists on the other. In the words of the distinguished research scientist Dr Humphrey Kay, 'What we need is a population of healthy badgers, but not too many of them. The key word is "balance".'

Ferret

Mustela putorius furo

A domesticated variety of the polecat, ferrets are usually pale lemon yellow or white, but some throw back to the wild strain and are dark brown. Their traditional role has always been to bolt rabbits and rats from their burrows, and many gamekeepers still keep them in hutches for this purpose. Properly trained and handled, they are usually quite docile, and travel happily in their owner's jacket pocket; but if frightened or alarmed they can bite savagely, fastening their teeth onto a hand or finger.

Man's use of ferrets is age-old. The geographer Strabo, writing towards the end of the first century BC, recorded that a plague of rabbits in Iberia (modern Spain and Portugal) and the Balearic Islands became so severe that

the inhabitants petitioned the Roman emperor Augustus for help; and Pliny, in his *Natural History*, published soon after the start of the Christian era, confirms the story, adding that ferrets (*viverrae*) were much in demand because they were so good at driving rabbits into the open.

The ferret population of Britain is now thought to be between 800,000 and one million, and a glance at the Internet confirms that interest in the animal is growing rapidly in America as well as in Europe. Many ferrets are kept as pets: to take one random example, the Essex Ferret Welfare Society promotes the creatures at country fairs and fêtes in the east of England, and on its website offers micro-chipped and neutered animals for rehoming.

Yet most of those in Britain are still working at their traditional task of bolting rabbits from their burrows. In recent years modern technology has greatly improved their efficiency. In the old days, if a ferret made a kill or went to sleep underground, the handler's only recourse was to a 'liner', a hob (male) ferret trained to wear a collar with a long cord attached. With luck, by energetic digging, one could follow the cord to the scene of action (or inaction); but today electronic bleepers worn on ferrets' collars provide quicker and surer guides. Animals lost underground can usually survive in the wild, as their dormant hunting instincts reassert themselves and they start to catch their own prey.

Ferret racing has become a popular hobby. Because the creatures' natural curiosity makes them keen to explore any tunnel they come across, they need no persuading to enter drainpipes laid out across a yard or lawn. Races are scarcely exacting, for courses are normally no more than 10 metres long, with wire-mesh sections in the centre so that punters can see what progress, if any, their entries are making; but results are unpredictable, for although some runners charge straight through, others turn back or doss down for a nap in the middle. Many races are organised by International Ferret Welfare of Great Britain, a body which rescues and rehabilitates animals lost or abandoned by unscrupulous owners. Race meetings are held in order to promote the image of the ferret, and to raise money for rescue work.

Red Fox

Vulpes vulpes

The red fox is lithe, agile, graceful – and an exceptionally good survivor. Persecuted by hunts, heavily culled by gamekeepers, massacred by motor traffic, it nevertheless flourishes throughout Britain. The adult population in winter is thought to number 240,000; in early summer, after cubs have been born, it rises to about 650,000, but

then quickly falls back again. A survey completed by the Game Conservancy Trust in 2000 recorded that some 16,000 foxes are killed every year by the hunts, and some 80,000 by gamekeepers, but conjectured that a maybe 300,000 die of natural causes or in road accidents.

A big dog-fox has a body up to 90 cm long, and a thick tail, or brush, half as long again, often with a white tip, or tag, on the end. Vixens are smaller and more lightly built. Both sexes are mainly rich red-brown, with white on chin and chest, and black socks on all four feet – although in hill areas such as the Scottish Highlands they tend to be longer-legged and more grey than red.

These powerful predators excite strong emotions in human beings. Sheep-farmers, gamekeepers, poultry-keepers and the wardens of bird reserves all hate them because they are such efficient killers. Hunting people are ambivalent: they love foxes and preserve them, yet chase them to death. Volunteer bodies like the National Fox Welfare Society spend enormous amounts of energy, and all the cash they can muster on rehabilitating casualties. Even birds on which foxes do not normally prey fear them: if a fox appears in daylight, it is instantly mobbed by jays, magpies, crows and songbirds.

Foxes are indigenous to the whole of Britain, and ancient records show that man has regarded them as a pest for centuries. In Tudor times bounty schemes administered by individual parishes paid 12 times as much for a fox as for any other proscribed creature. The animal's destructive powers are certainly formidable: farmers often find the remains of two or three newborn lambs in a single vixen's belly, and one gamekeeper in County Durham, opening up a fox he had shot, discovered 13 recently devoured grouse chicks in its stomach. Sometimes the excitement of killing seems to go to the predator's head: if one gains access to a hen-house or a pen full of pheasants, it may slaughter 50 or 60 birds – far more than it can possibly eat or carry away – in a murderous frenzy, apparently brought on by the commotion of fluttering wings and the inability of the victims to escape.

At other times a fox carefully buries spare items of food in caches for future reference. Its diet includes a wide variety: rabbits, young hares, rats, mice, birds and their eggs, earthworms, beetles, frogs, and carrion of various kinds. Another favourite is fruit, and in autumn droppings often turn purple from consumption of plums, black-berries and elderberries. Foxes are highly opportunistic, ready to take advantage of any sudden offering: they have even been seen leaping into the air to snatch down low-flying pheasants.

Few animals advertise their mating rituals more loudly. Starting in December, dog-foxes make their rounds of the woods, letting off short bursts of dry, staccato barks, two or three at a time – *roff, roff, roff* – which enable a listener to chart their progress, even in the dark. Sometimes one will answer another, setting up an antiphonal duet. When a vixen is in season, and allows a prospective mate to come to close quarters, she looses off hair-raising screams which echo through the night so wildly that they give the impression she is being murdered. At close quarters both sexes make a mechanical, clicking noise known as geckering.

For much of the time foxes live above ground, lying up during the day in thick cover, in the roots of trees or under heaps of brushwood; but cubs are generally born, between March and May, underground in an earth – often a former rabbit burrow, taken over and enlarged. At birth they are blind and deaf, and covered in dark-brown fur. When their eyes open, at about ten days, they are blue at first, but later turn amber. Both parents bring food to the earth to feed their young, which grow rapidly and play enchanting games around the entrance to the den.

At the age of six months juveniles start to disperse in search of new territories, which they mark by urinating and depositing droppings on prominent points like mole-hills or tussocks of grass. There is one record from America of a young male travelling some 400 km from his birthplace. Mortality is extremely high during the first year, and the annual diaspora ensures that the population is evenly spread.

Like other members of the dog family, foxes cannot sweat: the only way they can discharge heat is by panting, or through the soles of their feet. In hot weather they are thus liable to lie about on their side, breathing heavily, with their feet turned outwards.

Most country people accept the fact that foxes are a pest, and that they should be culled; but argument rages over the most humane method of keeping numbers down. Traditionalists maintain that hunting with hounds is the least cruel and most efficient, because if a fox is killed, its death is instantaneous, and if it escapes, it gets away uninjured. Also, hounds are most likely to catch old or sick foxes, so ensuring the survival of the fittest. Others claim that lamping – shooting at night with high-velocity rifles – is more humane. Snares and poison are both increasingly seen as unacceptable.

The attempts made by recent Labour governments to ban hunting with hounds drove fox-hunting men and women to unite in stating their case. In 2000 the general debate led to the appointment of an official inquiry under Lord Burns, who concluded that hunting with hounds was no more cruel than any other method of control. In spite of this verdict, the House of Commons twice voted for a ban on hunting with dogs by a large majority, and in February 2002 the Scottish Parliament voted in similarly decisive fashion. These reverses notwithstanding, pro-hunting activists remained determined to preserve their freedom of action, if necessary by having recourse to the European Court of Human Rights.

One relatively recent development has been the appearance of foxes in towns and cities. Some 25 years ago an urban fox was a rare creature: now, with the proliferation of fast food and the increase of slovenly habits among humans, thousands of the predators have adapted to city living, lured by casually discarded leftovers and easy pickings from overflowing dustbins. Many animals take up residence under garden sheds and raise cubs there, and foxes are so frequently seen in central London that they excite little comment. Occasionally, however, nature strikes back. During the 1980s Bristol acquired the highest urban fox population of any city in Britain; but then in the 1990s virulent mange came up out of the Somerset Levels, the low-lying land to the southwest, and killed 90 per cent of the invaders. Another unfortunate consequence of the drift into towns is the dumping of urban foxes in the countryside. If a householder wants to get rid of a fox, he or she sometimes specifies that the animal must be taken away but not put down – and there is always somebody who will oblige. Most

pest control agencies deny all knowledge of such operations, but a few admit that, for £50 or so, they will get rid of a troublesome squatter. Such evictions by no means benefit the foxes: having grown up in an urban jungle, they have never learnt to hunt, and when turned out in open country wander about bewildered and starving. The fact that the practice goes on is confirmed by a few honest operators, and by reports from gamekeepers who can scarcely believe their eyes – as when one man saw 13 foxes sitting around in broad daylight in a field at Aberedw in Radnorshire.

Perhaps because they hunt mainly at night, and are rarely seen in daytime, foxes have the slightly sinister reputation of harbouring supernatural powers. Many a spooky story is told of their strange behaviour – as of the occasion when friends of a well-known hunting man, who had just died, were on their way to his funeral, and were astonished to see a fox sitting by the road at the end of his drive, eating a rat in broad daylight. Similarly, for the Gormanston family of County Meath, foxes have long been associated with death. One night in October 1907 a whole pack of them came to besiege the chapel in which Colonel the Hon. Richard Preston was keeping vigil over the body of his father. When Preston heard a scrabbling at the door and opened it, so that candlelight fell on the assembled

throng, he was 'very conscious of the golden-yellow stare'.

Who can forget the experience of the tenth Duke of Beaufort, one of the most dedicated hunting men of the twentieth century, who went out for his usual walk before breakfast one Sunday morning at Badminton, his home in Gloucestershire, at the age of 85? There in the churchyard he saw three foxes, one sitting on the grave of his grandfather, one on his father's, and the third on open ground. The Duke himself thought nothing of the phenomenon, but when he reported it to a friend, Daphne Moore, who lived in the village, she knew at once what it portended. 'The third fox was for him, of course,' she said – and sure enough, he died the following Sunday.

Mink

Mustela vison

There are no European mink (*Mustela lutreola*) in Britain. The feral population are all American mink (*Mustela vison*), descendants of animals brought from the United States to be farmed for their fur. The first escapes were made in the late 1930s, but it was not until the 1950s that mink were found breeding in the wild, on the River Teign in Devon. After a slow start, the colony suddenly expanded, and by 1970 the species had spread out along watercourses and

AMERICAN MINK, *MUSTELA VISON*
(below): THIS YOUNG MINK WILL GROW
TO BE A HIGHLY EFFICIENT PREDATOR
ON NATIVE FAUNA.

BRITISH OTTER, *LUTRA LUTRA* (right):
THE OTTER IS MAKING A VIGOROUS
COMEBACK IN SOME PARTS OF THE
BRITISH ISLES.

rocky coastlines into most of lowland Britain.

Like grey squirrels, mink have proved most unwelcome aliens, for they are highly efficient and opportunistic predators, and in the absence of muskrats – their staple prey in the United States – they make severe inroads into native fauna. They eat fish, frogs and nesting birds, and are a menace to fisheries, to bird reserves and to estates or farms rearing game: in one recorded massacre, a single mink killed 180 pheasant poults in a pen containing 400. But a particular victim has been the water vole, which rapidly disappears from any area in which mink take up residence.

Because they are predominantly nocturnal, mink often infiltrate new territories without being noticed, and the first signs of their presence are discarded crayfish claws or the eaten-out shells of molluscs left on the banks of rivers. Once spotted, the animals are easily recognised, from their dark pelts, which look black at a distance (although they contain some brown) and slender, streamlined bodies on short legs. Males are longer than females – up to 45 cm, including the tail – and more heavily built.

For dens, both sexes use natural cavities in roots, hollow trees and rocks, lining nests with fur, dry grass, feathers and so on. In the mating season, between February and April, males become very aggressive and fight. Litters of up to seven young are born in April or May, and only the mother feeds her kits; if she is disturbed, she may shift them to another den. After being taught to hunt, juveniles disperse when only about 14 weeks old.

It will never be possible to eliminate mink from mainland Britain; but in 1998 a group of landowners and conservationists called MESH (Mink Eradication Scheme

Hebrides) laid plans for a determined counterattack on the islands of Harris and Lewis (which are joined together). There, captive mink escaped from a fur farm 30 years ago and bred so vigorously that they made it impossible for anyone to keep poultry. They also killed thousands of nesting ducks, moorhens, waders and other seabirds, and altogether they are thought to have cost the local economy some £10 million.

In 2002 there were 19 packs of mink hounds in Britain (most of them converted from otter hunting) and two in Ireland, which between them kill some 750 mink a year – but far more are caught by trapping.

Otter

Lutra lutra

There is something very appealing about otters: whether it is their broad muzzles and small ears, the sleekness of their long, sinuous, beautifully streamlined bodies, or the fact that they are easily tamed and have a playful nature, they have a special place in many people's affections. Medieval commentators wrestled with the conundrum that although they were obviously animals, they lived on fish and spent much of their time in the water. Were they, then, fish or flesh? Many people, unworried by the distinction, kept tame otters, and sometimes used them instead of dogs to turn roasting spits at the fireside.

The fact that in the twentieth century otters almost went extinct, and are now making a strong comeback in many parts of Britain, increases sympathy for them. During the 1960s the author Gavin Maxwell scored a huge success with *Ring of Bright Water*, his account of living with otters on the west coast of Scotland, and in the 1990s Daphne Neville's small Asian otter Bee became a television star.

Otters have existed in Britain at least since late glacial times – that is, for 12,000 years or more – inhabiting the banks of rivers, lake shores and rocky coasts, where they live mainly on fish, worms, insects and occasional waterbirds. Because they are largely nocturnal, they often occupy a stretch of water without being seen,

the only signs of their presence being pathways worn where they enter and leave the water, remains of fish they have eaten, and their tarry, black droppings known as spraints deposited on prominent rocks or mounds. They spend much of the day in holts, or dens, in cavities in river banks or hollow trees, but they also have daytime lying-up places in stands of reeds or other tall vegetation. In the water they float with only nose and eyes above the surface, watching their surroundings until, with a quick heave of the back, they dive. Wonderful swimmers, they use body, thick tail and all four webbed feet for propulsion.

From a distance they look slim and slight, but in fact they are substantial creatures. A typical male is up to 90 cm long, with tail half as much again (although it is hard to tell where body stops and tail begins), and weighs 10 or 12 kg. Females are about two-thirds that size and weight. All otters have extremely sharp canine teeth, but their cheek-teeth are broad and flattened so that they can crunch bones and the shells of crayfish. If attacked, they defend themselves ferociously, and can give vicious bites. They can close their nostrils at will, for diving, and when they go under water, air forced out of their coat by the pressure leaves a trail of bubbles rising to the surface.

Both sexes establish extensive linear territories along the banks of rivers and lakes, marking their ground with a powerful-smelling substance secreted by two scent glands under the tail. A male's range may extend to 20 km, and a female about half that. To avoid over-fishing any one area, the creatures are constantly on the move at night, hunting up and down, their favourite food being eels. Adults are solitary, coming together only to mate (which they do at any time of year), but several females with cubs may live together in family groups. Litters are usually of two or three cubs, which are blind until the age of five weeks; at about three months their mother takes them to the water and encourages them to swim. A month later she weans them, but they stay with her, learning to hunt, for nearly a year.

Although shy and elusive, otters are great opportunists. Many an unwary fisherman has left a fine salmon or trout lying on the river bank while he goes to fish another pool, only to find, on his return, that an invisible thief with very sharp teeth has taken a chunk out of his catch.

From time immemorial otters have been killed for their pelts, and in the Middle Ages they fell victim to the general campaign against predators because they raided fish-ponds. Game fishermen also waged war on them to protect river stocks.

Then at the end of the eighteenth century the first specialised packs of otter-hounds were formed. Probably because it lacked the excitement and danger that gave fox-hunting such a wide following, otter-hunting never achieved the same popularity; yet it continued to flourish, and by the 1930s there were 23 otter hunts, killing 400 or so animals every year. Paradoxically, this organised persecution probably did the species more good than harm, for the hunts not only prevented gamekeepers and others from killing otters in their countries, but also took steps to maintain the habitat.

Until the 1950s numbers of otters remained steady. It was aggressive farming – the excessive use of pesticides, destruction of suitable habitat by the removal of cover from river banks, new drainage schemes – combined with pollution of the waterways, that drove otters to their lowest point and banished them from former haunts. Many were slowly poisoned by the toxins that accumulated in their bodies, especially when stored fat was broken down in winter. By the late 1970s otters had disappeared from most British rivers, surviving in numbers only in southwest England, Wales and the sea lochs of Scotland. In 1978 otter

hunting was banned, but by then the damage had been done. (A similar decline was occurring in northern Europe, notably Holland, Belgium, France and Germany.)

In Britain one organisation which spearheaded recovery has been the Otter Trust, a registered charity founded in 1971 by Philip and Jeanne Wayre, whose dedication has produced outstanding results. A skilful captive-breeding programme in their wildlife park at Earsham in Suffolk, has enabled them to put over 120 otters back into the wild: most of the releases have been made in the eastern half of England, but some have been in the south, and 17 animals were set free in the headwaters of the Thames.

The majority of the new colonists settled down and bred so well that the population of East Anglia is almost back to pre-war levels. Meanwhile West Country otters have been making a slow natural recovery, and there is every reason to hope that the two populations will meet somewhere in the middle of the country. On the debit side, many otters are killed on roads – at least 300 in the three years from July 1998, for example – in spite of specific measures taken to prevent accidents, among them the provision of under-passes and fences.

Much of the success in East Anglia has been due to the intensive campaign of habitat-enhancement carried out by the Otter Trust, in conjunction with the Environment Agency and the county Wildlife Trusts. As early as 1976 staff of the Trust began lobbying landowners to create havens on their land, and in only three years they set up 261 riparian sanctuaries in Norfolk alone, each safeguarded by a management agreement between the landowner and the Trust. Another major effort has been in education: parties of children visiting Earsham, or the Trust's outstations at Tamar in Cornwall and Bowes in County Durham, receive comprehensive information packs. The Trust also owns and manages three wetland nature reserves in East Anglia.

Also heavily involved in otter conservation in the 1970s was the Vincent Wildlife Trust whose Otter Haven Project improved and protected riversides in England and Wales, helping the comeback of fragile populations.

In 1998 the county Wildlife Trusts launched their Otters and Rivers project, aiming to promote natural recolonisa-tion of all the waterways and coastal areas which the animals used to frequent. More than 1200 volunteers sur-veyed 4000 km of river banks, improved habitat in many places and built 300 artificial holts – a programme which did much to speed recovery, not least in cities like Birming-ham, Glasgow and Newcastle. A survey in Wales revealed that the animals take advantage of the help they are getting: 60 per cent of artificial holts showed signs of occupation. In 2001 the Trusts started yet another major initiative, Water for Wildlife, with the object of restoring wetlands

and bogs for the benefit of all the species that live in them – not merely otters, but water voles, southern damselfly and reed-warblers among many others.

Pine Marten

Martes martes

Lithe, forest-dwelling carnivores, up to 80 cm long includ-ing the tail, pine martens look like highly coloured ferrets, with chocolate-brown bodies and yellow throats. They were once common in much of Britain; but in the eighteenth and nineteenth centuries they disappeared almost entirely from England, partly because they were trapped for their pelts, and partly because gamekeepers killed them to preserve pheasants and partridges.

Although in 1988 they received full protection under Schedule 5 of the Wildlife and Countryside Act, only tiny enclaves of maybe 50 and 100 animals respectively, remain in North Wales and northeastern England; a colony of about 30 has been re-established in Galloway, and the greatest surviving concentration is in northern Scotland, where the population is thought to number 3500. Martens are also found in Ireland – in small pockets in the east and bigger strongholds in the west, especially among the hazel woodlands of County Clare.

If a pine marten gains access to a hen-house, that is usually the end of the flock, for the raider has instincts similar to those of a fox: fluttering and screeching trigger its attack reflex, and it kills every bird in reach. But its normal diet consists largely of field voles, supplemented by mice, rabbits, songbirds, frogs and beetles, in autumn by berries, mushrooms and bumblebees' nests, and, in winter, carrion from dead sheep or deer.

A marten's preferred habitat is mature coniferous forest: it is an elusive creature, active mainly in the dusk or at night, and avoids open areas; yet, like a stoat, it is also very curious. It ranges over wide areas, often travelling 20 km in a night and marking trails with deposits of urine and scent from anal glands. Each animal makes several dens, in hollow trees, old squirrels' dreys or disused pigeons' nests, moving from one to another. Sometimes a female will chew her way into the attic of an empty holiday cottage to have her young.

The reintroduction of martens to Galloway, in south-west Scotland, carried out in the 1980s, showed that the species could be artificially augmented; but although the colony established itself successfully, it has never spread out beyond an area only 20 km across. Conservationists would like to make further reintroductions in other suitable sites, but they are cautious about going ahead until thorough studies have been carried out into the impact the predators

POLECAT, *MUSTELA PUTORIUS* (below)
BEING CLOSELY RELATED TO FERRETS,
POLECATS ALSO HAVE A POWERFUL
SMELL.

STOAT, *MUSTELA ERMINEA* (right) THE
STOAT'S SUMMER COAT IS CHESTNUT
BROWN ABOVE AND YELLOW-WHITE
ON THE CHEST.

would be likely to make on species such as red squirrels, dormice and black grouse, which themselves are already under pressure.

Another drawback is that the south of England, although increasingly well-wooded, does not have many large areas of forest free of motorways, and in some otherwise promising areas the risk of road casualties would be high. Nevertheless, the Weald of Kent, Dartmoor and the Forest of Dean have been proposed as possible sites, and a study by the Game Conservancy Council suggested that the British population may eventually climb back to 8000.

Polecat

Mustela putorius

Polecats are closely related to ferrets, and in fact many specialists consider that ferrets are merely domesticated polecats. Except that polecats are darker coloured, with light patches beside the nose and behind the eyes, the two animals are often closely similar. Certainly they both have the same powerful smell (*putor* is Latin for 'stench'), and cross-breeding between the two species has produced many hybrids.

Polecats were once common throughout Britain, but,

like pine martens, they were eradicated from most of the country by the excessive zeal of Victorian gamekeepers. By the beginning of the twentieth century they survived only in Wales, and their sole stronghold was a small area in the west of the Principality. Then, in the 1950s and 1960s, they gradually spread back into most of Wales, and on into the western Midlands of England.

The fact that some animals have apparently leap-frogged into areas like Hampshire and Wiltshire, separate from places properly colonised, suggests that people have been deliberately catching, moving and releasing them without the knowledge or permission of conservation agencies. A few are still being caught – often accidentally – by gamekeepers, but a greater threat to them is poison, picked up at second hand in rats which have eaten an anticoagulant such as warfarin.

Their return is by no means universally popular, for they are fearsome killers of poultry and young gamebirds: they live mainly on rodents, rabbits, birds, worms and carrion, but they also kill many frogs and toads, which they paralyse with a bite through the back. They breed in late spring, in underground dens or rock crevices lined with moss and grass, and a female has up to a dozen young, but usually half that. Being largely nocturnal, polecats may often take up residence in a new area without their presence being noticed for some time.

Stoat

Mustela erminea

Stoats have a rather sinister reputation, echoed by the Victorian writer Richard Jefferies, who recorded in his book *The Gamekeeper at Home* that 'labouring people – at least the elder folk – declare that they have been known to suck the blood of infants left asleep in the cradle upon the floor, biting the child behind the ear'. In fact stoats, weasels and ferrets all have a bad name – not least because of their activities in Kenneth Grahame's classic children's book, *The Wind in the Willows*, in which these denizens of the Wild Wood lay siege to Toad Hall and squat there while its owner, Mr Toad is in prison:

> A band of weasels, armed to the teeth, crept silently up the carriage-drive to the front entrance. Simultaneously, a band of desperate ferrets, advancing through the kitchen garden, possessed themselves of the back-yard and offices; while a company of skirmishing stoats who stuck at nothing occupied the conservatory and the billiard room.

The question of whether or not, in real life, stoats do hunt in packs has been much debated. Modern experts tend to dismiss the idea as rubbish; but in his spirited anecdotal

History of Mammals, published in 1854, the Victorian naturalist the Reverend J. G. Wood, of Merton College, Oxford, included this story:

> A gentleman was walking along a road near Cricklade when he saw two stoats sitting in the path. He idly picked up a stone and flung it at the animals, one of which was struck and was knocked over by the force of the blow. The other stoat immediately uttered a loud and peculiar cry which was answered by a number of its companions, who issued from a neighbouring hedge and sprang upon their assailant, running up his body with surprising rapidity and striving to reach his neck ...
>
> Most providentially a sharp wind happened to be blowing on that day, and he had wound a thick woollen comforter round his neck, so that he was partially protected. Finding that he had no chance of beating off the pertinacious animals, he flung his stick down, fixed his hat firmly over his temples and, pressing his hands to his neck so as to guard that perilous spot as much as possible from the sharp teeth of the stoats, set off homewards as fast as he could run.
>
> By degrees several of the animals dropped off, but others clung on so determinedly to their opponent that when he arrived at his stables, no less than five stoats were killed by his servants as they hung on his person. His hands, face and part of his neck were covered with wounds; but, owing to the presence of mind with which he had defended his neck, the large blood-vessels had escaped without injury. The distance from the spot where he had been attacked to his own house was nearly four miles.

The author of that passage was a seasoned observer, and similar stories have appeared elsewhere. But the notion of mass attack by stoats may simply derive from the way in which a mother sometimes leads her litter of young out when teaching them to hunt: a family on a training sortie does make an alarming sight as its members skim and ripple over a pile of cordwood or go surging through long grass, lithe as rust-red snakes.

Although small and light, weighing only 300 to 400 g, Stoats are highly effective predators, able to catch and kill rabbits three or four times as heavy as themselves. They are fast and agile, hunt by scent, and are extremely persistent: once on the trail of a rabbit, they will follow it for miles, across country or in and out of burrows. They sometimes stand upright on their hind legs and weave their bodies from side to side in a kind of sinuous dance – a ploy that seems to hypnotise a victim before they go in for the kill, which they achieve by means of a precision bite to the back of the neck. Being very inquisitive, they will respond to a

STOAT, *MUSTELA ERMINEA* (below) PEERING FROM A ROCK CREVICE, THIS STOAT WEARS ITS WHITE WINTER COAT.

WEASEL, *MUSTELA NIVALIS* (right) HALF THE SIZE OF A STOAT, THE WEASEL IS BRITAIN'S SMALLEST CARNIVORE.

whistle or a squeak by coming to the edge of cover and standing up to look for the source of the noise.

In summer their slender, lithe bodies are chestnut brown above and yellow-white on chest and stomach, but in winter, especially in the north, they turn white all over, except for the black tip of the tail, the change being triggered by a fall in temperature and designed to give them camouflage in snow. In earlier days the winter pelts (ermine) were valuable as furs, and noblemen and judges trimmed their ceremonial robes with ermine.

Stoats are active by day as well as at night, but because they are so low to the ground, and so elusive, they are rarely seen by humans. On grouse moors, for instance, they can run about under the heather, or along drainage ditches, without ever showing themselves. Since a single stoat will kill a whole brood of grouse or pheasant chicks if it gets a chance, they can be highly damaging to shooting estates, and gamekeepers are tireless in their efforts to trap them.

Besides rabbits and the eggs of ground-nesting birds such as curlews and partridges, they eat leverets, rats, mice and voles, hiding away any food that they do not need immediately. They are also agile enough to climb trees, and sometimes catch nesting woodpigeons. Whenever there is an abundance of prey, such as rabbits, in a particular area,

their numbers build up rapidly: one winter a gamekeeper in County Durham caught more than 200 stoats on his moor, and kept the whole lot in a deep-freeze to prove he was not exaggerating.

Such culling may well help grouse breed on a particular moor, but it seems to have little effect on overall predator numbers, and stoats' success as survivors is due largely to their strange sexual habits. Male and female mate in May and June, and the ova are fertilised in the usual way; but because the female has delayed implantation, the fertile cells go into a state of suspended animation, and do not start to develop until nine months later. Gestation begins the following March, and litters are very large: up to 13 kits are born after only about 25 days, in April or May, in a den in a rock cavity, rabbit burrow or hollow tree.

The most curious feature of the young is their sexual precocity. Soon after the mother has given birth, she comes into oestrus again, and attracts a male to her den, where he mates not only with her, but may possibly mate with her unweaned female kits. The male thus propagates his own genes through several females at the same time, for in spite of their youth the babies are sexually mature, and if they survive will bear his offspring the following year.

If the mother has to move her young to a safer refuge,

she carries them one at a time by the nape of the neck, and if threatened she defends them fearlessly. At about 11 weeks they start killing their own prey, but thereafter females mature more quickly than their brothers, becoming full-grown in six months, whereas males take nearly a year to reach full size.

When stoats' main prey species – the rabbit – was suddenly all but wiped out by the myxomatosis epidemic of the 1950s, the predators at first declined; but after an initial fall, numbers picked up strongly as rabbits started to make a comeback. The present population is thought to be some 460,000, and stable. Stoats occur all over Ireland, where they are commonly called 'weasels' (in fact, there are no weasels in Ireland). Conservationists' main worries are that stoats are being contaminated by secondary poisoning, contracted through eating rats or squirrels which have picked up rodenticides, and that good habitat is disappearing with the eradication of hedgerows and the loss of rough grassland.

Weasel

Mustela nivalis

Britain's smallest carnivore, the weasel is like a miniature version of the stoat, half its size, and with much the same colouring, except that it has a whiter belly, no white round its ears, and no black tip to its tail. It lives mainly on voles and mice, supplemented by occasional rabbits, birds and eggs, and its head – the widest part of its anatomy – is slender enough for it to pursue its prey down the narrowest of burrows and tunnels. Old drawings and paintings illustrate the legend that the head of a weasel can pass through a wedding ring. The animals are common all over England, Wales and Scotland, but there are none in Ireland.

Unlike stoats, which breed once a year, female weasels can produce two families, and have no system of delayed implantation. Adult females come into season in February, are quickly mated, and after 36 days' gestation produce up to eight kits. For the next few weeks all the mother's energy is taken up with suckling her young and bringing them food; but as soon as they are weaned, probably in May, she comes into oestrus again, and if feeding is good, can have a second litter that same year. The females from her first litter may also breed that same summer, since they become mature at only three or four months. The species is thus highly productive – and it has been calculated that if all her offspring survived and bred at the first opportunity, a single female could be responsible for the birth of 510 other weasels in two years.

In fact this will never happen, because mortality is high. Prey is not always abundant, and weasels are themselves

preyed on by cats, foxes, owls and kestrels. Disease is another limiting factor: like stoats, weasels suffer from canine distemper, and they are attacked by a parasite which penetrates through the nose and grows into a worm that eats away the bone of the skull

After the myxomatosis outbreak in the 1950s, the number of weasels actually increased. This was because, with the pressure of grazing lifted, grass grew longer and made better habitat for voles, which flourished in consequence, providing abundant prey. Today the population of some 450,000 weasels is thought to be declining, but the animals are notoriously difficult to count, and this figure is speculative.

In folklore weasels, like stoats, hunt in packs. Most experts doubt this – but the Rev J. G. Wood told a weasel story very like his account of the man who was attacked by stoats. In this case a walker had been passing an old wall and, seeing a weasel, had started to tease it. When the animal gave a scream, 'about 15 other weasels issued from the crannies of the wall and commenced an attack'. Another man, seeing the first in trouble, ran to his aid and laid about him with his whip, killing several of the marauders and putting the rest to flight.

Wild Cat

Felis sylvestris sylvestris

Few people in Britain have seen a wild cat in its natural surroundings, for the species exists here only in the Scottish Highlands, and is extremely wary and elusive. It was once widespread in Britain, but it had disappeared from lowland farming areas by the end of the eighteenth century, after which it gradually withdrew into the mountain fastnesses of the far north and northwest.

As its Latin specific name suggests, it is essentially a forest animal and needs extensive tracts of woodland, or at least of wild country, in order to flourish. The earliest fossils of wild cat bones in Europe date from about 250,000 BC: the creatures were then much larger than now, probably due to the abundance of prey. The European wild cat *Felis sylvestris sylvestris* belongs to the same species as the domestic cat (*Felis sylvestris catus*). The subspecies of wild cat found in Africa (*Felis sylvestris lybica*) is the progenitor of the domestic cat. Brought to Europe, probably by the Romans, it interbred with the European subspecies of wild cat *Felis sylvestris sylvestris* to produce the domestic *Felis sylvestris catus*.

Wild cats have much the same colouring as domestic tabbies, with dark stripes round their bodies, their main distinguishing features being their greater size, their broad, blunt heads and bushy tails, which are strongly marked with between three and five black rings, and end in a rounded black tip. So powerful looking is the tail that in some parts of the Highlands old people claimed it carried a hook on the end.

At up to 65 cm long and weighing as much as 7 kg, the cats are noticeably stockier and more powerful than most of their domestic cousins, and at the same time longer in the leg; but they readily mate with house cats to produce hybrids. Indeed, some naturalists believe that truly wild cats are now confined to the remotest glens, and that many sightings of animals believed to be wild are in fact of hybrids. These tend to retain wild-cat markings, but some are sandy coloured, and some melanistic, or black. In Scotland black hybrids are known as Kellas cats, after the village in Morayshire where the first one was seen. It has recently been suggested that in some areas such as Speyside there should be a drive to neuter feral and domestic cats, so as to give wild animals a better chance of retaining, or regaining, genetic purity.

If the spread of agriculture was the main cause of the original cats' retreat, another factor was persecution by Victorian and Edwardian gamekeepers, who saw them as a threat to their stocks of grouse and killed them at every opportunity. The animals got a reprieve during the First World War, when hundreds of keepers went off to join the armed forces, and from the 1920s they staged something of a a comeback, spreading into much of the Highlands, and southwards as far as the line between Glasgow and Edinburgh.

Wild cats were not fully protected until 1988, when they were added to Schedule Five of the Wildlife and Countryside Act. Estimates of the present population vary between 3500 and 6000, with the heaviest concentration in the relatively dry eastern Highlands.

In recent years young plantations have created much good new habitat for small rodents, and so have indirectly benefited wild cats, which tend to inhabit the borders between forests and open moorland. In summer they live mainly in the open, but in winter use dens in cairns of rock, piles of timber, disused badger setts and hollow trees, keeping away from areas frequented by humans. Their diet includes rabbits, squirrels, blue hares, rats, mice and voles, but they also eat birds, fish and frogs: they are strong enough to carry off a bird as big as a greylag goose. One tell-tale habit is that of eating a rabbit, turning the skin inside out and leaving it with feet attached.

A myth persists that they are untameable – and certainly no cat captured as an adult has ever turned into a relaxed domestic pussy; but if kittens are brought up on the bottle, and given plenty of attention, they tolerate the proximity of humans fairly well. If cornered in the wild, they spit, hiss and attack viciously: a stalker who caught one in a purse-net when ferreting rabbits never forgot what a job he had to release it, so violently did it fight.

In the wild, mating takes place in winter or early spring: one male often mates with several females, and kittens are born in summer. Only the mother feeds her young, which are sometimes taken by golden eagles, foxes and pine martens. At about three months kittens start to accompany their mother on hunting forays, learning to catch prey, and the survivors disperse at the age of about five months to find ranges of their own. Mature tom cats are solitary and often nomadic, moving around from the home territory of one female to that of another.

A study carried out by Ro Scott in the late 1980s for the Nature Conservancy Council (forerunner of Scottish Natural Heritage) showed that on the Ardnamurchan peninsula some males' territories extended to 1000 hectares. Live-trapping them – to fit radio collars – proved a lengthy exercise: they were so wary that one capture was made, on average, out of every 250 trap-nights. There, in the far west, the cats depend mostly on mice and voles, because rabbits are scarce; but radio tracking revealed that at night they travel as much as 5 km from the hills to hunt the few rabbits that live about the crofts on the shore.

WILD CAT, *FELIS SYLVESTRIS SYLVESTRIS*
ALTHOUGH THEY LOOK LIKE THEIR
DOMESTIC COUSINS, WILD CATS ARE
CONSIDERABLY LARGER.

Herbivores

Literally 'grass-eaters', herbivores live on green vegetation, twigs, bark and so on. Some, like domesticated cattle, are primarily grazers, and crop grass from the ground; others, like goats, are mainly browsers, picking leaves and small branches off trees and bushes. Some, like deer, have incisor teeth only on their lower jaw, and tear off vegetation by clamping it between their teeth and the horny pad on the upper gum. Many herbivores are ruminants — that is, they have four stomachs, in the first two of which, the *rumen* and the *reticulum*, cellulose fibres are fermented. Semi-digested food, known as the cud, then passes back to the mouth and is chewed again before going on to third and fourth chambers, the *omasum* and *abomasum*.

Deer

Considering that deer were for centuries the prime quarry of the chase, it seems strange that they are no longer officially classed as game animals. Most landowners regard them as a pest, and no game licence is needed to shoot them. Six species now live wild in Britain, but only two – red and roe – are indigenous. The others – fallow, sika, muntjac and Chinese water deer – were all originally imported. With the exception of the diminutive water deer, which are confined to East Anglia, all species are thriving to such a degree that in many areas they have become a menace to forestry and agriculture. Here is an apparent paradox: in spite of the developments which threaten much wildlife – intensive farming, land disappearing under concrete or asphalt, people taking to the countryside for recreation in ever-increasing numbers – deer are flourishing as never before.

There are two main reasons for this expansion. One is the spread of woodland, which began after the Second World War and continues to this day, providing deer with ideal habitat. The second is that deer are very adaptable, and, although shy, are quite willing to exist in close proximity to humans. Being largely nocturnal in their habits, lying up in cover during the day and coming out to feed at night, they often live near villages or the edges of towns without people noticing their presence.

Because they respect no boundaries, jump cattle fences with ease, and wander freely about the countryside, grazing and browsing as they go, they inflict serious damage on trees, farm crops, shrubs, ground flora and garden plants. In ancient times their numbers were kept in check by wolves, lynxes and bears; but today, with the major carnivores gone, their only predator is man. Since they are extremely prolific, increasing at a rate of 30 per cent a year unless checked, they have to be regularly culled. Unlike cattle or sheep, they cannot be rounded up and taken to a slaughterhouse, so that the job has to be done by marksmen using suitable rifles.

One of their main defences is the high state of alert which they habitually maintain: their eyesight and hearing are at least as good as those of human beings, but their sense of smell is infinitely keener – their noses can detect danger at distances of at least a kilometre. Unlike man, who has lost his ability to remain alert for long periods, deer do so naturally, and in any herd one or two animals are always keeping a lookout. Females are especially vigilant, and have a habit of trying to surprise anything that excites their suspicion. Whenever they spot something not to their liking, they glare at it for several minutes, then begin grazing again, having apparently satisfied themselves that all is well – only to whip up their heads suddenly and stare again at the same point, as if trying to catch the interloper in the open.

The early English kings set large areas aside purely for their deer hunting. Thus in 1079 William the Conqueror declared the New Forest in Hampshire a royal preserve in which he alone had the right to hunt, with draconian penalties for anyone who poached royal game. The Forest of Dean on the borders of Wales, owes its origins to a similar royal initiative. Exmoor, also, was for centuries a royal forest, and so on.

The term 'chase' is probably misleading, for the method of hunting was more of a drive than a pursuit. A line of beaters, working downwind with hounds on leashes, would advance through a wood in which animals were known to be harbouring, and try to push shootable ones out across open ground towards archers ensconced on the edge of the next patch of cover. 'Chase' meant either the whole hunting operation, or the unenclosed woodland in which it took place – Enfield Chase, for example.

At an early date owners of great country houses began to establish deer parks around their homes by enclosing extensive areas with walls or wooden palisades. Leaps were

left in the barriers so that wild animals could jump down into the enclosures from outside, but those inside could not escape. The Domesday Book of 1085–86 recorded 31 parks, and by the middle of the seventeenth century the number in England alone had risen to 700. Then, however, many were destroyed by the Roundheads, during the reign of Cromwell from 1653 to 1658, who smashed the fences and drove the deer out or killed them.

The role of the early parks was purely practical: to furnish the owner with animals to hunt, and with a ready supply of meat on the hoof. Later the captive deer came to be seen also as ornaments which enhanced the landscape and lent interest to the view. Some families went so far as to take their herd with them when they moved up to summer quarters. At Stonor Park in Oxfordshire, an 8-km temporary hedge of hessian was built every year beside drove-roads so that the deer could be run along it, up on to the Chilterns, when the household moved to its dower house, Watlington Park, for the summer months. Writing in 1892, Joseph Whitaker listed over 400 parks, describing Spetchley in Worcestershire, as having a 'grand old oak fence fastened with oaken pegs', and Thoresby in Nottinghamshire, as boasting 'a grand oak fence, many of whose posts have withstood the weather for fifty years'.

Today one of the finest deer parks in Britain is that at Woburn, where 1200 hectares of gently rolling grassland are bounded by a wall. The park contains no fewer than ten species – with the exception of roe, all those that are established in the wild – and an impressive collection of exotics: chital or axis deer (*Cervus axis*), Barasingha or swamp deer (*Cervus duvauceli*), hog deer (*Axis porcinus*), all from India; Rusa deer (*Cervus timorensis*) from Java, and the odd-looking Père David deer (*Elaphurus davidianus*), which

were bred back from the brink of extinction by the eleventh Duke of Bedford. The duke's enthusiasm – not to say mania – for collecting animals knew no bounds. Deer apart, he imported black squirrels, catfish and zander. At one point he had between 40 and 50 species of deer in his park, and although most of them died out, enough survived to establish a substantial and not altogether welcome presence in the United Kingdom. A century of selective breeding has made the Woburn red deer outstanding specimens. The duke collected their ancestors from all over Europe, and today the best stags carry over 40 points on their antlers, making Highland red deer look like goats. Embryos from the best stock are exported to the deer farm which Woburn runs in New Zealand.

A much later innovation was that of deer farms, the first of which were founded in the 1970s, many by the simple expedient of fencing enclosures on the lower slopes of Scottish hills and driving wild Red Deer down into them. It was found that deer quickly became so tame that they could be managed in much the same way as cattle or sheep, and supermarkets soon showed that they were prepared to pay higher prices for farmed venison from animals whose age could be guaranteed, than for meat from wild deer, which might be 10 or 12 years old.

In Scotland the practice of stalking deer became firmly established in the nineteenth century (see Red Deer, page 66); but in England no tradition of stalking existed until the second half of the twentieth century, and until the 1960s wild deer were treated as vermin, being culled in drives by men armed with shotguns – a crude and often cruel method, which failed to discriminate between good or bad, old or young, and left many animals wounded.

Then in 1959 came the Deer Act (Scotland) and in 1963 the Deer Act (England), which set close seasons, prohibited shooting at night, and laid down minimum calibres of rifle to be used. Later Acts refined the original provisions, and management has now become far more professional, with two organisations – the British Deer Society and the British Association for Shooting and Conservation – both running training courses for stalkers in England, and the Deer Commission (Scotland), a government body, in overall charge of culling north of the border. Every modern stalker's aim is – or should be – to assess his or her herd,

3

Wild Mammals
Herbivores

Deer

RED DEER, *CERVUS ELAPHUS* (right)
A HANDSOME STAG ON A SCOTTISH
MOUNTAINSIDE.

make a plan, and cull selectively, going first for animals that are old or sub-standard.

Poaching remains a hazard, and many deer are taken illegally with rifles, shotguns, bows-and-arrows, crossbows, snares or dogs. In the Scottish Highlands crofters often still regard it as their right to shoot the odd stag or hind that strays onto their ground, in defiance of the laird who owns the surrounding estate. In England, a far greater threat is motor traffic. It is thought that between 30,000 and 50,000 road accidents involving deer occur every year: in these some 400 people are injured and about ten killed. The total of deer destroyed is substantial but impossible to compute, as many disappear, mortally injured after a collision, never to be found, and newly killed animals often vanish in the boots of passing cars.

It is often supposed that deer belong to the owner of the land on which they happen to be at any one time, but this is not so. In law they are *ferae naturae*, creatures of nature, and while they are alive belong to nobody. Only when dead do they become the property of the landowner.

Throughout the centuries hunters, stalkers and others have retained traditional names for various classes of deer, which vary according to species:

	Male	Female	Young
RED	Stag	Hind	Calf
ROE	Buck	Doe	Kid
FALLOW	Buck	Doe	Fawn
SIKA	Stag	Hind	Calf
MUNTJAC	Buck	Doe	Fawn
CHINESE WATER DEER	Buck	Doe	Fawn

One obvious physical peculiarity of deer is that, unlike cattle, which keep a single set of horns for life, males cast their antlers and grow new ones every year. A young buck or stag grows a larger set in each successive year until he reaches maturity: then, after a year or two at maximum size, his antlers progressively diminish, and he is said to be 'going back'. When old antlers fall off each spring, coming away from the pedicles on top of the head, new ones begin to grow rapidly, covered in furry grey skin known as velvet. This is full of blood vessels, and so sensitive that the deer are careful not to damage it; but once growth is complete, the blood supplies to the antlers dry up, the velvet dries and peels off, accelerated by the deer rubbing their new antlers against trees, rocks or fence-posts. Velvet is highly prized by oriental manufacturers of aphrodisiacs, and for a few years the practice became established in Britain of sawing the still-growing antlers off park deer, so that their velvet

could be harvested. This, however, has now been banned. On the face of it, the annual renewal of headgear seems a great waste of energy, and scientists are by no means agreed on the biological reason behind it. Why should a stag or buck not keep his antlers for life? One theory is that it gives the animal a chance of replacing his main weapons if one of them should be broken off in a fight; another, that the rapid growth of new tissue is a means of dissipating the excess testosterone produced by sudden rich feeding in early summer. Either way, the process has one beneficial by-product, in that cast antlers form an important source of calcium for female deer, which chew them up and swallow them, sometimes in large lumps.

VENISON

All species yield excellent, healthy meat, rich in iron and exceptionally low in fat: compared with lamb (which has 12.3 g of fat per 100 g of meat), beef (12.9 g), whole chicken (13.8 g) and pork (15.2 g), venison is a clear winner, with only 1.6 g. It is also rich in fatty acids, which combat heart disease. Yet the British have never shown much interest in it, and producers have sometimes been forced to sell carcasses at rock-bottom prices, as low as 70 pence per kilogram.

The result is that in the past most venison has been exported to Europe, and in particular to Germany, where it is highly valued. Prices have fluctuated wildly, influenced by the ever-increasing volume of imports from New Zealand, and by events such as the fall of Communism in 1989, which, with the breaching of the Iron Curtain, released a flood of cheap venison from the former East Bloc countries into western Europe. During the 1990s the steady supply from deer farms encouraged British supermarkets to stock venison regularly; but the foot-and-mouth epidemic of 2001 had a disastrous effect on prices, for although the disease was not found in deer, all exports of meat were temporarily banned, and there was such a glut on the home market that some Scottish estates were obliged, when culling hinds, to leave the carcasses on the hill – a practice both wasteful and exceedingly distasteful to landowners and stalkers alike.

Red Deer

Cervus elaphus

Red deer are easily the largest wild land mammal in Britain. Deposits of bones in caves and peat bogs show that they were once plentiful all over Britain, and formed a staple item of early man's diet, besides providing him with skins for clothes. Now, however, England has only a few tracts of wild country extensive enough to accommodate such

3

Wild Mammals

Carnivores

Red Deer

66

wide-ranging animals: big herds survive on Exmoor, and smaller ones in the New Forest, Thetford Chase and the Lake District, besides several captive herds in parks. There are a few wild red deer in Ireland, but none in Wales, and it is in the Scottish Highlands that they have their last real stronghold.

Red deer are essentially woodland animals, and when they live primarily in the shelter of trees, they grow to an impressive size. A Thetford stag, comfortably ensconced in the pinewoods of Norfolk, can weigh 200 kg clean (without its intestines). In contrast, the Highland herds exist mainly on bare, open mountainsides: in that harsh environment so much of their energy is devoted to keeping warm that their physique has become much diminished, and a stag weighing 110 kg clean is considered a fine beast. Similar differences are apparent in their heads, or sets of antlers. Occasionally a Highland stag grows a head of 14 points and is known as an imperial; but normally the greatest number of points is 12 – a royal.

After the end of the last ice age, in about 8000 BC, trees grew all over the Scottish mountains, and the Caledonian forest of antiquity spread out until it covered the hills to a height of at least 600 metres with a mixture of Scots pine, birch, alder, oak and hazel. Gradually, however, most of the trees disappeared, killed by increasingly wet and cold weather or cut down by man, until by the end of the eighteenth century only a few stands were left. Then came an invasion of new and devastating intruders: sheep.

The 1780s saw the beginning of the notorious Clearances in Scotland in which landlords brutally evicted people from their homes in the glens and imported huge numbers of black-faced sheep, which (they were convinced) would make their fortunes. The cost in human suffering was immense – and so was the cost to the environment, for the sheep reinforced the native deer in their assault on the vegetation, and the combined grazing-power became such that the remaining patches of forest had no chance of regenerating.

In Scotland, as in the south, the pursuit of deer had long been a royal sport, and several immense hunts are recorded, among them a hunt in 1528, when the Earl of Atholl entertained King James V of Scotland, and another in 1563, also on Atholl ground, when the guest of honour was Mary, Queen of Scots, and 360 deer were killed in a single day. The method used on both occasions was the tinchel, in which several hundred men walked out for days to form a huge ring and then moved inwards, driving deer either to a narrow pass or into a man-made trap where long stone walls gradually converged into a funnel, so that the animals could be attacked at close quarters by hunters lying in wait with muskets, swords and axes.

It is impossible to tell how many deer the Highlands held during the Middle Ages; but with the eviction of the human population during the Clearances, poaching dwindled and numbers steadily rose – and probably it was reports of increasing herds that first attracted the attention of English shooting men. According to the second Earl of Malmesbury, himself a keen stalker, 1833 was the year in which the Highlands 'became all the rage' among the English gentry. Not only did well-to-do sportsmen begin travelling north in droves every autumn; more and more of them bought huge tracts of land in the mountains and declared them deer forests, building lodges, roads, bridges and pony-paths, to say nothing of the steam yachts which they had launched on lochs to provide smoother transport than was possible on bumpy tracks.

The craze continued until some three million hectares had become deer range. Paradoxically, the fact that the red deer had become highly valued as sporting targets meant that numbers steadily increased. Enthusiasm for Highland stalking continued unabated throughout the nineteenth and twentieth centuries. Today culling is coordinated by the Deer Commission, Scotland (formed as the Red Deer Commission in 1959), but most of the work is carried out by individual estates, many of which let stalking rights to outsiders.

Although thousands of animals are shot every year, the herd as a whole has kept increasing, and by the end of the millennium the total had risen to more than 300,000. One contributing factor was a run of relatively warm winters. In earlier years severe winter weather killed many thousands of deer, which starved or died of pneumonia; but with the onset of global warming, such mortality dwindled almost to nothing.

For 150 years at least Scottish landowners favoured deer at the expense of trees, and the result is that the herd had a powerfully damaging effect on the environment. Over millions of hectares, grazing pressure from deer and sheep created a barren, treeless desert, which offers poor feeding and little shelter. In the 1990s, however, the balance of opinion at last began to tilt in favour of trees, and on some estates – notably Mar Lodge, owned by the National Trust for Scotland – drastic culls were carried out in an attempt to begin restoration of the Caledonian forest, the hope being that if deer are reduced to a density of no more than one or two per square kilometre, Scots pine seedlings will have a chance to grow and reach maturity.

The annual cycle of red deer is much the same wherever they live. For most of the year stags and hinds stay apart in separate herds; but with the approach of the rut, which takes place in September and October, the stags break out from their gentlemen's clubs and go in search of mates. In

Scotland, 12 September is the traditional Day of the Roaring, when stags start to take up territories and challenge rivals with long-drawn-out bellows, also rolling in wallows of mud or waterlogged peat to blacken their hides and make themselves look more formidable.

For a stag, the effort of rounding up his harem – maybe 20 or 30 hinds – and keeping rivals at bay is such that in a month he can lose a third of his body weight – a process accelerated by the fact that he stops eating for the duration. In the frenzy of procreation two stags often warm up for a fight by walking parallel, side by side and only two or three metres apart, for a few steps before wheeling inwards and locking antlers in a ferocious wrestling match. Occasionally an animal is killed when an antler pierces its ribs, but generally a defeated competitor turns tail and runs.

The calves, born in June the following year, are strongly spotted with white for their first few weeks, but gradually lose their markings. Although now and then a hind produces twins, single births are more common. Mothers often leave their calves tucked down in grass or bracken while they go off to graze, knowing instinctively that their young are protected from predators by their lack of scent. People who find calves left on their own tend to assume, wrongly, that they are orphans, and either stroke them or (worse) pick them up. Either action is potentially dangerous, for when the mother returns she may well abandon the calf because it has been contaminated by human scent.

A few red deer may reach the age of 20, but 15 is a more normal lifespan. Stories like that of the legendary white hind of Loch Treig, which in the eighteenth century was thought to be 200 years old, are no more than folklore.

Fallow Deer

Dama dama

With their white-spotted coats and the wide, palmate antlers of the bucks, fallow are the quintessential deer of English parkland, presenting an even more picturesque spectacle than reds. Fossil remains show that fallow did once live in England, but they died out at an early date, and the ancestors of today's population originated in North Africa, whence they were brought to this country by invaders – according to different authorities, by the Phoenicians, the Romans or the Normans. They vary widely in colour, from creamy white to almost black, via the most strongly spotted variety, which are known as 'menil'. All varieties have a black stripe along the top of the tail and round the edges of the target, or tail end, so that when seen from behind they show a distinctive pattern of black and white.

For centuries precise nomenclature has been reserved for bucks of various ages: a second-year buck is a pricket, a third-year a sorel, a fourth a sore, a fifth a bare buck; and an animal attains the status of great buck only when he is seven. The points on the front of their antlers are known as tines, those on the back as spellers.

Fallow were confined mainly to parks for centuries, but during the Second World War, when falling trees breached walls or fences, many escaped into the surrounding countryside and established themselves in the wild. Feral fallow are now common in much of southern England, with lesser numbers in Wales, Scotland and Ireland.

Their habits are largely nocturnal: they feed out on farmland at night, and retire into woods at first light; this makes it difficult to count them accurately – an essential prerequisite of any culling plan. Conventional counts were done by moving the deer quietly through a wood, past observers stationed at strategic points; but this method often underestimates true numbers by up to 30 per cent. More recently, Forestry Commission rangers have successfully used thermal imagers, devices which pick up the

SIKA DEER, *CERVUS NIPPON* (below, right) DARK FACIAL MARKINGS ON THE STAG GIVES IT AN ANGRY EXPRESSION.

ROE DEER, *CAPREOLUS CAPREOLUS* (far right) ROE DEER BUCK DURING THE RUT IN HAMPSHIRE.

radiant heat given off by animals and are so sensitive that they can detect a creature as small as a rabbit a kilometre away. To someone looking through one of these chunky, whirring telescopes, living creatures show up pink against a black background, so clearly that deer and sheep (for instance) can easily be differentiated – and the potential value of thermal imagers was demonstrated one year in Mortimer Forest near Ludlow, where the experienced ranger, John Speed, reckoned he had about 200 Fallow, only to count 460 in a single night.

Fallow are the most mobile of British deer, in that they do not keep to any particular area, but move long distances across country, depending on the degree of disturbance and the availability of food. In summer they inflict severe damage on farm crops, and in winter they browse shrubs and the lower branches of trees: in heavily frequented woods there is often a clearly visible browse-line about 1.5 metres off the ground. This reveals the limit of their reach, and below it most twigs and leaves are eaten off.

Like red deer, fallow rut in September and October. Master bucks take up their positions on traditional rutting stands, to which (some people believe) they are drawn by ley lines. They seem to prefer areas of fairly open woodland, with overhead cover perhaps 3 metres off the ground: overgrown hazel groves are ideal. Instead of roaring as they parade up and down, males utter rattling grunts or groans, which sound as though they are emanating from enormous pigs. The noise attracts females and warns other bucks to keep their distance, and intense excitement grips all participants. Fights between competing bucks are common, but because of the shape of the antlers, serious injuries are less common than in red deer. Outside the rut fallow deer make very little noise, although does give out loud, gruff barks if they are alarmed. In winter females and young establish play-rings – places where they run round and round a fallen tree trunk or a hollow in the ground, apparently for the fun of it.

Sika

Cervus nippon

The presence of sika in Britain is due to the predilection, not to say mania, of Victorian landowners for importing exotic species. As their scientific specific name suggests, the deer come from Japan, and in 1857 the seventh Viscount Powerscourt secured three hinds and a stag from Charles Jamrach, the London dealer, for his park at Enniskerry in the Wicklow Mountains south of Dublin. Over the next three years he also brought in roe, Indian sambur, red deer, wapiti, eland and Sardinian wild sheep, but only the sika flourished – and in fact they bred so well

that soon he was able to export stock not only to other parts of Ireland, but also to England, Wales and Scotland – thereby sowing the seeds of an enormous long-term and widespread problem.

He himself obviously had no idea that he was creating trouble, for in his privately printed memoirs he cheerfully recorded that, quite apart from populating half a dozen parks in Ireland, he sold or gave sika to numerous landowners in England and Scotland: 'I also sold them to Lord Ilchester at Melbury, Dorset; Mr Myddleton of Chirk Castle, North Wales, and among many other places they were introduced at Tullyallan near Stirling, and by Mr Bignold at Auchnasheen, Ross-shire.'

Other landlords were also busy spreading trouble. In 1896 a few sika were released on Brownsea Island in Poole Harbour, and some swam ashore to the Isle of Purbeck – which, in spite of its name, is part of the mainland. These were joined by escapers from the park at Hyde House near Wareham, and today at least 1000 of their descendants are living wild in Dorset.

Sika have two main disadvantages. First, they do even more damage to trees than other species of deer, being

inveterate bark-strippers (in Japan they have destroyed large tracts of natural elm forest.) They also have superior digestive powers, and can thrive on poor vegetation, which enables them to live at high density and out-compete other species. The second problem is that they interbreed with red deer, producing hybrids. Although essentially wood-land animals, they readily take to the open hillsides; and now that the number of sika in Scotland has risen to nearly 20,000, experts fear that the genetic purity of the entire red deer herd may be compromised by this cross-breeding. At Luggala, a 2000-hectare estate in the Wicklow Mountains, sika have driven red deer clean off the range by the pressure of their competition.

Sika are slightly smaller than fallow deer, and drabber in colour, ranging from mid-brown in summer to grey in winter. The dark facial markings of stags tend to give them an angry appearance. During the autumn rut, stags issue their challenges with loud, long whistles that carry for hundreds of metres through the forest: the calls sound as if they come from the lips, but in fact they are made by a valve in the throat.

Roe

Capreolus capreolus

Many people find roe the most attractive of all deer. With their velvety black muzzles and delicate heads, they give an immediate impression of gracefulness – and they are instantly recognisable from behind by the fact that they have no visible tails: a cream-coloured caudal patch, bobbing off into the distance is sure to belong to a roe. The animal's ability to vanish into woodland has led the Spanish to give it a lovely name: *el fantasma del bosque*, the ghost of the forest. Roe are also – it must be said – excep-tionally good to eat, their venison being arguably the finest of any deer.

Fossil remains show that they have existed in Britain for many thousands of years. The surviving evidence suggests that at one period they almost died out in the south of England, but now they have come back with a vengeance, encouraged by the spread of forestry, and in particular by the thick cover available in new plantations. Nobody knows for certain how many there are in Britain, but estimates

ROE DEER, *CAPREOLUS CAPREOLUS*
(previous pages) THE DOE OFTEN GIVES
BIRTH TO TWINS AFTER DELAYED
IMPLANTATION.

REEVES'S MUNTJAC, *MUNTIACUS*
REEVESI (right) THE SMALLEST DEER IN
EUROPE, THE BUCK HAS PROMINENT
CANINE TEETH OR TUSKS.

vary between 500,000 and one million, which makes them easily our most numerous deer species. The total is still rising as roe colonise new areas like Kent and Cornwall, and if excessive damage to forestry is to be avoided, heavy culling must be maintained.

Unlike other deer, roe are generally not gregarious, and tend to live in small family groups, only coming together in herds if they are pushed out of the woods into open country. Their most remarkable biological characteristic is that of delayed implantation. The rut takes place in summer, but even if a doe is mated and fertilised in July, her embryos do not start to develop until late autumn, and this means that her kid or kids will be born the following June.

Partly because twins are common, concentrations of roe can build up at extraordinary speed. In 1970, before the forest of Eskdalemuir was created in Dumfriesshire, that area of rolling border hills was almost entirely grassland, and held only nine or ten roe in one small wood. Fewer than ten years later, when extensive areas had been planted with trees, the population had grown to 3000, and at the end of the century it was the same, kept down to that figure by an annual cull of 1000 beasts.

Small as they are, roe can inflict severe damage on young plantations, partly by browsing the leading shoots off saplings, but also by fraying: when bucks rub their antlers against springy stems to deposit scent and mark their rutting territory, they strip off the bark and kill or maim the young tree. Their destructive potential is such that they now have a strong influence on the design of new woodlands: foresters plant expendable species like hazel along the edges of rides, and leave wide open spaces so that when the trees grow up, the deer can be culled efficiently. By such means, damage to timber is minimised.

The general picture of roe stalking has changed considerably over the past 25 years. Until the 1970s, the main aficionados of British roe came from the Continent, where the tradition of woodland stalking is much older and stronger than ours. Belgians, Austrians and above all Germans were prepared to pay high prices for the best trophies – up to £1200 for a gold-medal head. Trophies are assessed on the internationally-recognised CIC (*Conseil International de la Chasse*) formula of points, awarded for length, thickness and conformation of antlers.

Later, however, the strength of the pound did much to suppress foreign demand, and at the same time native interest in stalking grew rapidly. The result is that more of the riflemen are now British, who on the whole do not care to pay heavily for trophies. Over the same period, the ever-growing population of roe has led to a ten-fold increase in the number of estates, firms or individuals that offer stalking on a commercial basis.

In summer the habits of the roe – which tend to feed at dawn and dusk – set stalkers a challenging but agreeable routine. Parties go out at 3.30 am and stay out until about 9 am, generally moving slowly around on foot from one likely spot to another. After breakfast, many clients go back to bed or at any rate take things easy. Dinner is at 5.30 or 6 pm, after which there is another outing, often spent up high seats, and this continues until dark, which in the north of England and Scotland does not fall until about 10.30.

The advantage of high seats, either free-standing or propped against trees, is that they give riflemen a clear view, and enable them to fire downwards towards the ground, which is far safer than shooting horizontally. Also, deer rarely look up above their own height, and the scent of man is generally carried away above their heads. The disadvantage of high seats is that they attract the attention of animal-rights activists, who smash or steal them, misguidedly thinking that they are somehow doing the deer a favour.

In his magisterial book *The Roe Deer*, the veteran specialist Richard Prior included a passage about a sixth sense that deer seem to possess. 'As a long-term deer-stalker,' he wrote, 'I have become convinced that fierce concentration on the object of a protracted stalk communicates to it some kind of awareness of approaching danger.' He believes, in effect, that there is 'some sort of primitive telepathy between predator and prey' – a theory which may explain why so many stalks go wrong.

Even at a distance deer seem able to distinguish between humans that mean them no harm and those that are after their blood. If hikers go pounding through a wood, wearing bright anoraks and chattering, deer often stand at no great distance and watch them without taking evasive action; but the moment they see someone moving stealthily and clad in camouflaged garments, they detect a sinister element in his gait, and make off.

Muntjac

Muntiacus reevesi

Like sika, muntjac, or barking deer, come from the Far East. The first animals to reach England, in about 1900, were introduced by the eleventh Duke of Bedford to Woburn Park, his home in Bedfordshire. These were Indian muntjac, and although they flourished for a while, it was decided in about 1920 to exterminate them in favour of the smaller and less aggressive Reeves's muntjac. Before long some escaped from the park and began to spread out from Woburn – but humans deliberately accelerated the distribution by secretly moving pairs long distances and letting them out on fresh territory, in Oxfordshire, Kent, Suffolk and Northamptonshire. The result was rapid expansion in

3

Wild Mammals
Herbivores

Roe Deer
Muntjac Deer

CHINESE WATER DEER, *HYDROPOTES*
INERMIS (below) THE BUCKS POSSESS
HINGED TUSKS THAT CAN BE USED
FOR FIGHTING.

PÈRE DAVID'S DEER, *CERVUS (ELAPHU-*
RUS) DAVIDIANUS (right) THIS SPECIES
HAS SURVIVED IN CAPTIVITY FOR OVER
2000 YEARS.

the 1970s, 1980s and 1990s. By the end of the century Reeves's muntjac had proliferated all over the south of England and made headway far towards the north.

Less graceful than other species of deer, muntjac tend to walk jerkily, with their heads lowered and their backs humped, in a rather pig-like attitude. The smallest deer in Europe, they stand a mere 45–52 cm at the shoulder. Their colloquial name comes from the loud, harsh, staccato, single barks which they give when alarmed, or in territorial disputes, especially at night. Once started, they often carry on barking for half an hour, letting fly once every 15 or 20 seconds. If surprised in the open, they either sink to the ground and lie frozen, or bound away with their tails raised high over their backs.

Bucks have two prominent canine teeth or tusks, one growing down from the upper jaw on either side, which are sometimes used for fighting. Another physical peculiarity of the species is that they have no set rutting time; rather, doe comes into season within a few days of giving birth, so that they are continually in production, and fawns are born all year round.

Muntjac are not gregarious, usually going about singly or in small family groups. They also appear to be strongly territorial, each group occupying its chosen area: when the population of a wood becomes too dense for comfort, some animals move out on to new ground, with the result that a form of creeping takeover progresses across the landscape. They inflict little damage on trees, but can have a disastrous effect on wild plants such as bluebells, primroses and orchids: in several ancient woodlands, especially in East Anglia, they have destroyed the ground flora by intensive grazing, allowing coarse grass to take over.

During the 1980s damage became particularly severe in Monks Wood, the National Nature Reserve in Essex managed by English Nature. Muntjac were so numerous that in some parts of the wood they killed 98 per cent of the bluebells, and their heavy browsing prevented coppiced areas from regenerating. For many years English Nature could not countenance culling the deer, for fear of upsetting members of the public, and enormous amounts of money were spent on unsightly electric fences in attempts to exclude muntjac from particular plots, so that plants and shrubs inside the barriers would have a chance to recover. Yet the deer, Houdini-like, kept penetrating the defences, and in the end planned culls had to be instituted to save the wood from total devastation.

Muntjac also wreak havoc in gardens, and seem to have a particular liking for rose bushes and runner beans.

Chinese Water Deer

Hydropotes inermis

These small deer, slightly bigger than muntjac but more delicate in appearance, are believed to be the most primitive surviving members of the family *Cervidae*. The adjective *inermis* – unarmed – refers to the fact that they have no antlers, but, like muntjac, the bucks carry weapons of a sort in the form of tusks on their upper jaw, which are so loose in their sockets that they are in effect hinged, and can be held backwards for grazing or brought forwards for fighting.

Woburn Park – once again – was the source of this exotic species. The eleventh Duke of Bedford imported foundation stock in the 1890s and again early in the twentieth century, and some of their descendants escaped into the surrounding countryside during the Second World War. By 2000 they had colonised several areas of East Anglia, particularly the Norfolk broads, but because their preferred habitat is reed beds and grassland near watercourses, they did not spread out anything like so widely as muntjac.

They rut annually, most often in November and December, and the does are the most prolific of all deer, frequently giving birth to four fawns at a time. Experts are puzzled as to why water deer have not expanded farther,

but one factor is high mortality among fawns, many of which die of hypothermia or are taken by foxes. In spite of such losses, the species is faring better in England than in its native China, where water deer are steadily declining.

Père David's Deer

Cervus (Elaphurus) davidianus

One day in September 1865 the French missionary Père Armand David, ever on the lookout for interesting natural phenomena in China, found a pile of sand against a wall of the old Imperial Hunting Park south of Peking. Scrambling up, he looked over the wall – the first Westerner to do so – and was amazed to see deer of a kind on which he had never set eyes before. Through a little bribery he obtained two skins and some bones, and sent them back to France, where the deer was recognised as a species new to Western science, and named *Elaphurus davidianus* in his honour.

Over the next few years he obtained permission from the Chinese government to send a few animals to Europe; most died, but the survivors were placed in various zoos, and maintained their numbers without ever increasing much. Père David returned to France in 1870. Then in the 1890s and early 1900s various disasters swept away the last of the animals remaining in China, and on their home territory they went extinct.

In England the Duke of Bedford realised that the only hope of saving the species was to bring all the survivors together, and he persuaded various European zoos to send him their animals, which then amounted to 18. These he released into his park at Woburn Abbey, where they did so well that by 1914 the herd had increased to 88. In spite of the privations caused by lack of winter feeding, which became impossible during the world wars, the deer came through both conflicts, and in 1945 a second herd was established by moving some calves to Whipsnade. In 1957

77

FERAL GOAT, *CAPRA AEGAGRUS HIRCUS* FERAL GOAT (bottom left) WITH KID.
(top left) MALE (BILLY) FERAL GOAT WITH BILLIES AND NANNIES LIVE APART UNTIL
MASSIVE HEAD-GEAR. FEMALE (NANNY) THE RUT IN SEPTEMBER AND OCTOBER.

there came a startling development, when, in spite of the Cold War and the hostility between East and West, a keeper from London Zoo took four sturdy calves to Peking, thereby reestablishing the species in its homeland.

By 2000 the herd at Woburn had increased to 460, with subsidiary herds established at several other places in England, and a total of more than 40 deer had been sent to China, where they appear to be breeding well, some in part of the old Imperial Hunting Park, and some in the Da Feng Milu reserve on the shore of the Yellow Sea 400 km north of Shanghai.

Père David's deer are large – stags weighing over 200 kg – and odd-looking: not for nothing are they known in China as *ssu-pu-hsiang*, 'the four unlike' – meaning that they have the antlers of a deer, the feet of a cow, the neck of a camel and the tail of a donkey. Physical peculiarites include very large feet, apparently evolved to enable them to walk over swampy ground, and long, irregular antlers, which throw enormous backward-pointing tines. It is thought that they became extinct in the wild soon after 200 BC: if that is so, it means they have survived in captivity for more than two millennia.

Reindeer

Rangifer tarandus (see page 400)

Goats

Feral Goat

Capra aegagrus hircus

The goats which live wild in the Scottish Highlands and elsewhere are almost certainly descended from escaped domestic stock – for animals of this kind quickly revert to the wild form. Perhaps in response to the harshness of the climate, they grow larger and hairier, with sweeping horns up to 110 cm long, and trailing, shaggy coats of many soft colours: grey, russet, brown, black-and-white or pure white. Some authorities believe that the white strain came originally from Scandinavia, and that Viking seafarers may have brought Norwegian animals to the west coast of Scotland. Wild white goats were once much in demand for making the aprons of regimental drummers in the British Army, and billies' beards or tassels were used on the sporrans of Highland regiments.

More browsers than grazers, goats eat twigs, leaves, shrubs and coarse weeds, rather than grass, and are lethal barkers of trees, especially in winter. Normally billies and nannies live apart, but they come together at the rut in September and October. Although they mate at the same time as the deer, their gestation period is shorter, and their young are born earlier, from the end of January to the end of March, rather than in June. The harsh weather of late winter ensures that only the strongest survive, weak kids being picked off by eagles and foxes.

Isolated herds of feral goats still live on several islands off the west coast of Scotland, and in parts of the Highlands, where the word *Gobhar* (goat) features in many place names. There are also groups in the north of England and in Ireland. One Scottish stronghold is the Letterewe estate, in Wester Ross: goats have been there for at least a hundred years, and there are more on the splendid mountain immediately to the north, An Tellach. Living for preference high up in such precipitous and rocky terrain, they have to be extremely agile: often they are seen on ledges to which there appears to be no access, but almost always they find a way up or down.

They can be a menace to deerstalkers, for they are exceedingly wild, and when disturbed make off with high-pitched snorts so loud that they scare any deer within a kilometre. Anyone who has passed downwind of them, even at a distance, will have no difficulty in appreciating the old belief, once prevalent in Wales, that the stink of a wild goat was enough to keep infection (or rats) at bay.

Numerous myths and superstitions cling to the animals. Among other accomplishments, they are supposed to be expert at killing adders, at forecasting the weather and at banishing evil spirits from mountain summits.

3

Wild Mammals

Herbivores

Feral Goat

Lagomorphs

Long ears, very long hind legs and short tails are the obvious characteristics of lagomorphs, a term derived from the Greek word meaning 'hare-shaped'. Herbivores of this order of mammals have several peculiarities. One is that, behind their front two upper incisors, they have another pair, called the peg-teeth; another, that they can open and close their slit-like nostrils by moving a fold of skin; and a third, that they eat their own droppings, thus passing food twice through their digestive systems.

Brown Hare

Lepus europaeus

THE HARE

*In the black furrow of a field
I saw an old witch-hare this night;
And she cocked a lissome ear,
And she eyed the moon so bright,
And she nibbled o' the green;
And I whispered, 'Whsst! Witch-hare,'
Away like a ghostie o'er the field
She fled, and left the moonlight there.*

From *Songs of Childhood*
By WALTER DE LA MARE

It seems odd that a creature as timid and graceful as a hare should be invested with connotations of devilry and witchcraft – but so it is. Perhaps because it is solitary and most active at night, the animal has long been credited with magic powers and the playing of sinister roles: men long thought a hare was dangerous to meet, because it might be a fairy that had snatched a dead child from its coffin, a changeling escaped from its home, a witch, the devil himself in disguise, or the agent which gave a hare-lip to the unborn child of any pregnant woman. A hare running down a village street always presaged a fire, and at sea nobody must mention the creature's name, but resort instead to some euphemism if need be.

The fact that in March hares went mad, leaping all over the place and sitting up on their hind legs to box, merely increased the sinister impression they made. On the other hand, fashionable ladies used a hare's foot as the best means of applying make-up, and the seventeenth-century diarist Samuel Pepys carried one as a cure for colic –

although he admitted that he was not sure whether his escape from the malady was due to the charm or to something else.

Brown hares are not indigenous to Britain. They are thought to have originated in the steppes of Central Asia, and they reached Europe by the Pleistocene era, but apparently spread northwards too slowly to cross the land bridge into England before the rising level of the sea created the Channel. It is known that the ancient Greeks, valuing hares highly, deliberately introduced them to new sites, such as Karpathos in the seventh century BC and Sicily in the fifth century; although some authorities maintain that the Romans brought the animals to Britain in the first century AD, fossil evidence suggests that brown hares have been in Britain since the Iron Age or perhaps the Bronze Age. Whenever they arrived, they gradually spread out to colonise all lowland areas of the country, displacing the smaller mountain hares already in residence and pushing them up on to areas 500 metres or more above sea level. Their introduction to Ireland for hunting purposes was relatively recent.

Because they were hunted by humans for food, and preyed on by wolves and foxes, brown hares probably did not become very numerous until the eighteenth century. Then the combination of land enclosure, improvements in farming and control of predators by gamekeepers allowed numbers to increase: Victorian keepers nursed their hare stocks so zealously that in the nineteenth century the population reached its zenith, estimated by latter-day specialists at four million animals. In his *Rural Rides*, published in 1830, the radical reformer William Cobbett left a vivid description of riding in company across Salisbury Plain. One of his companions:

> ...took a gallop round, cracking his whip at the same time; the hares (which were very thickly in sight before) started all over the field, ran into a flock like sheep, and we all agreed that the *flock did cover an acre of ground.*

For old-time poachers a hare was as great a temptation as a pheasant, and ever since the Roman occupation the animal has been prized for the table. In the Middle Ages the flesh of the hare was supposed to induce melancholy, but the eighteenth-century cookery writer Hannah Glasse was enthusiastic about it, and coined the celebrated phrase 'First case [skin] your hare', usually rendered wrongly as 'First catch your hare'.

Brown hares are twice the size of rabbits, and easily recognised by their yellower fur and long, black-tipped ears. Powered by their rangy back legs, they can run at 65 km/h, and their eyes, set on the sides of their heads, give them an almost 360-degree field of view. They live entirely

BROWN HARE, *LEPUS EUROPAEUS*
(below) LEVERETS ARE SUCKLED ONLY
ONCE EVERY 24 HOURS WHEN THE
DOE VISITS THEM BRIEFLY.

MOUNTAIN HARE, *LEPUS TIMIDUS* (far
right) SMALLER THAN THEIR COUSINS,
MOUNTAIN HARES TURN PURE WHITE
IN WINTER.

above ground, crouching by day in forms – hollows in grass or shallow scoops in the earth – and moving around the fields at night to feed on grass, young cereal crops, herbaceous plants and so on.

As already mentioned, a century ago hares were far more numerous than they are today: it is thought that the population in 1900 was about four million, compared with one million now. One main reason for the decline has been the reduction in the number of gamekeepers, and the consequent lack of predator-control; another, the intensification of farming. Strong and fast as they are, hares depend on finding suitable habitat, and the removal of hedges and the creation of enormous fields have worked against them, for huge expanses of wheat or barley become useless to them once the plants pass a height of 25–30 cm. Such crops provide food while they are in their early stages of growth, but once they have reached full height, with the tops out of the hares' reach, they become, in effect, deserts. Research at Loddington has shown that hares thrive best on a succession of crops planted in small patches, so that food and shelter are available all year round.

Another weakness in the hare's armoury is the doe's method of bringing up her young. Mating takes place in early spring, and the boxing in which mad March hares indulge – long thought to be between competing males – is often an unreceptive female fighting off the advance of a suitor. Since a doe gives birth in a form on top of ground, her three or four babies never have the same security as rabbits born in a burrow.

It is true that leverets are far more developed at birth, being fully furred and able to run; yet the doe leaves them on their own all day, and comes back to the area in which they were born, to feed them, only once every 24 hours, generally just after dark. For a few minutes the youngsters gather, suckling the mother as she moves along, but for the rest of the time they scatter. This leaves them vulnerable to attacks from foxes and stoats. A doe makes up some of the losses by producing up to four litters a year, but the survival rate is normally low.

In spite of the hazards, the overall hare population has stabilised during the past ten years, and appears to be sustainable at its present level. In particular areas the population can fluctuate widely from year to year depending partly on the weather in spring when the leverets are being born, and partly on the incidence of disease in the autumn. Conservationists would like to see the species more evenly distributed and the Biodiversity Action Plan calls for a doubling of spring numbers by the year 2010. As always, the species is flourishing best in the drier eastern half of the country. In Lincolnshire and Norfolk, and on the Berkshire downs hares are numerous enough to be an agricultural pest, and on shoots organised by farmers 200 or 300 are often killed in a day. The Game Conservancy estimates the present annual bag at 400,000.

Compared with that large total, the number of hares killed by hounds is very small – only 1500 a year. As a means of culling, hare-hunting is amazingly inefficient, but it remains a popular field sport, and its aficionados claim that it benefits the quarry, in that, because of their enthusiasm and advocacy, farmers tolerate more hares than they otherwise would.

Public fascination with hares was reflected in the immense success which the artist and writer Kit Williams achieved in the early 1980s by making a bejewelled, golden hare, burying it somewhere in England, and challenging readers of his book *Masquerade* to work out where it was, from clues embedded in 15 fantastical, intricately detailed paintings and various riddling rhymes. The response was phenomenal. As Lagomania spread round the world, *Masquerade* sold a million copies, and people searched every corner of the realm. Williams received some 30,000 letters, many from people seeking help with the puzzle or confident that they had solved it. When eventually the golden hare was run to earth two and a half years later, close to the cross that commemorates Catherine of Aragon in Ampthill Park, Bedfordshire, thousands of eager lagomanes were left sadly disappointed.

Mountain Hare

Lepus timidus

Heather moorland, high grassland and tundra are the home of mountain or blue hare, all round the northern regions of the Earth. The animals have been living in Britain for about 12,000 years, but when the brown hares arrived, most of them were driven up to high ground. Only in Ireland did mountain hares continue to inhabit the low ground.

During the nineteenth century shooting men made many attempts to introduce the species to new areas, but the only southern transplantation which had lasting success was the one in the Peak District of Derbyshire, which now has a population of about 500. The number in Scotland is estimated at 350,000, most of which are in the Highlands, while it appears to be extinct in Wales. The Irish population of mountain hare (*Lepus timidus hibernensis*) is a slightly larger and browner subspecies.

Mountain hares are visibly smaller than their lowland cousins, and in summer much greyer, with blue-grey under-fur which shows though on the flanks. In winter they turn pure white, which gives them camouflage in snow and to some extent protects them from airborne predators such as golden eagles.

Mountain hares generally live above ground, often making their forms in old, long heather, in which they hollow out a squatting-space by biting off stems; but they sometimes also dig holes, or take over rabbits' burrows, for protection in cold weather and as shelter for their leverets. A doe gives birth to four or five young in spring, and suckles them in the same way as a brown hare, returning to their place of birth to feed them once a day, sometimes more often. Mortality is high, but hares that survive to become adults disperse to extraordinary distances, the greatest recorded being 300 km.

Their distribution on the Scottish hills is patchy, and evidently some areas suit them better than others. In general they flourish on ground keepered for grouse-shooting, where predators are culled and the heather is regularly burnt so that different ages of plant are available for food and shelter. On some moors they are so prolific that regular culls have to be made to stop them damaging the heather and spreading disease through ticks.

Although in general solitary, they sometimes gather in quite large numbers to feed; if driven by a line of beaters on a shoot, they tend to run uphill. Owners of Scottish estates take advantage of this quirk and earn useful extra income by letting days to parties of foreigners, who prefer to be ferried to the top of a mountain in four-wheel-drive vehicles, rather than climb it themselves. Italians, especially, have a passion for hare meat: they come over in parties, eager to pay up to £10 for every hare they shoot, and make arrangements to freeze their bag immediately, so that they can fly it home with them.

Rabbit

Oryctolagus cuniculus

Rabbits are among our commonest and most familiar wild animals, yet they are not native to these islands. There is no Anglo-Saxon or Celtic word for 'rabbit', and no mention of the animal in the Domesday Book of 1086. The ancestors of the rabbits we know today were introduced to Britain by the Normans for their meat and fur, and although they have been present ever since, the population has fluctuated violently. In the Middle Ages huge numbers were kept in warrens, protected from predators by surrounding walls or fences and managed like other farm stock, for sale. Black rabbits were particularly favoured, their skins being popular not only in England, but also abroad.

Kent, especially, had numerous warrens, from which thousands of rabbits were sent every week to markets in London. Until the eighteenth century only the young of the species were called rabbits, or 'rabets'. Adult animals were known as 'coneys' and warrens as 'coneygarths' or 'conygers'. Today, any town or village bearing a name which includes 'Coney' is likely to be on or near the site of a former warren.

By the reign of Henry III (1216–72) rabbits were regarded as a delicacy, and every winter hundreds were sent from warrens for his royal Christmas feast. Nevertheless, it seems that the animals remained relatively scarce all through the Middle Ages. The fact that Gilbert White, describing the natural history of Selborne in minute detail, scarcely mentions rabbits suggests that there were very few in Hampshire during the second half of the eighteenth century. He did remark on a third product of the warrens

(after meat and skins): 'Rabbits make incomparably the finest turf, for they not only bite closer than other quadrupeds, but they allow no bents to rise; hence warrens produce much the most delicate turf for gardens.'

Only at the end of the eighteenth century did large numbers become established in the wild. Two factors are thought to have promoted the expansion: more active farming, especially in winter, and the ever-increasing activities of gamekeepers, who eliminated many of the rabbits' natural enemies, such as foxes and stoats. In due course rabbits became most plentiful in counties with sandy soil which allowed the creatures to excavate their burrows easily – Lincolnshire, Norfolk, Suffolk and Cambridgeshire – whence 'immense numbers are brought for the supply of the London market'.

Many country people kept tame stock of their own: William Cobbett – a tremendously practical man – gave instructions in his treatise *Cottage Economy*, published in 1821, and concluded: 'Rabbits are really profitable. Three does and a buck will give you a rabbit to eat for every three days in the year, which is a much larger quantity of food than a man will get by spending half his time in the pursuit of wild animals.'

Throughout these vicissitudes, many superstitions attached to rabbits. To see a black one was considered unlucky, since it might embody an ancestral spirit returned to Earth; a white one, equally, was potentially dangerous, as it could be a witch. Many people, to protect themselves, would chant 'Rabbits and hares!' early in the morning on the first day of every month, always making sure those were the first words they spoke – otherwise the charm would be ineffective.

By the end of the nineteenth century rabbits had become a major agricultural pest, and colossal numbers were trapped, snared and shot. The record bag for a single day's shoot was (and is likely to remain) 6943, killed by six guns at Blenheim Park in Oxfordshire, on 7 October 1898. Since rabbits were also the traditional quarry of poachers, thousands were taken illegally every year, and they formed the staple food in countless rural households. It used to be said that if a rabbit was shot or caught after it had run through wild garlic in spring, it came into the kitchen so highly flavoured that it needed no further seasoning.

In the wild the creatures spend most of the day underground, in burrows, and come out to graze on grass and arable crops in the evening, staying out all night unless disturbed; but poachers would operate at all hours of the clock, surreptitiously using ferrets to bolt rabbits from their burrows during the day, and at night setting snares on their runs across fields, or staking out long nets beside hedges and driving the animals, which had been out feeding in the open, back towards their burrows.

In spite of continual persecution, rabbits continued to flourish, kept going by their exceptional fecundity. Does start breeding in January or February and continue through most of the summer, producing up to 12 babies in a litter, and as many as seven litters a year. The young are naked, blind and deaf at birth, but their eyes open after ten days, and they are weaned at only one month. Young females become sexually mature at the age of 14 weeks, and so, if born early in the spring, are able to breed during their first year. The result of all this is a population explosion every summer, and hedges which seemed uninhabited in early spring are suddenly alive with rabbits of all ages, pouring out onto the fields early in the evening.

Scientists have pointed out that the rate of increase would be truly explosive, were it not for the fact that at least 60 per cent of litters conceived are never born, the embryos being absorbed back into the body of the mother. By the beginning of the 1950s some 40 million rabbits were being killed every year, but the survivors were doing between £40 and £50 million worth of damage annually to farm crops.

Then in 1954 there came a dramatic change: the introduction and spread of the highly infectious viral disease myxomatosis wiped out 99 per cent of the population, cutting it from perhaps 100 million to only one million. Myxomatosis is carried by fleas and breaks out in rabbits' burrows: it causes swelling of the mucous membranes and the growth on the skin of tumours composed of mucous tissue. A victim's eyelids become so puffed up, oozing with pus, that it gradually loses vision and blunders about, still grazing, but running into obstacles, unable to find its way or feed properly, until it dies of fever and starvation. The sight of stricken rabbits was so revolting that the RSPCA led a campaign to make intentional spreading of the disease illegal, and was rewarded by an amendment of the Pests Act.

After the first devastating impact, some rabbits reacted by living more above ground, away from fleas, and many developed resistance to the disease, so that although it now still recurs almost every summer, enough animals survive each new epidemic to keep overall numbers high. With the present population restored to some 38 million, rabbits are once again a menace to agriculture and forestry. Attempts have also been made to develop a contraceptive bait which would sterilise animals without harming them, but none is yet commercially available. Nobody wants to get rid of rabbits altogether, since they play an important role in the food chain, and are a vital source of food to species like the fox, stoat and buzzard; but farmers would certainly like to see their numbers reduced.

Rodents

The order Rodentia includes mice, rats, squirrels and voles. The name comes from the Latin *rodere*, 'to gnaw', and the animals' teeth, which keep growing through life, are self-sharpening, having an enamel strip along the outer rim which acts as a cutting edge. Most rodents eat seeds, but some also live on insects and some are omnivorous.

Mice

Mice are great fellow-travellers. Known to scientists as 'commensals' – creatures which live in partnership with humans – they appear to have come with man all the way from the steppes of Central Asia, where they originated. The association is thousands of years old: house mice were common in ancient Egypt, Greece and Rome, and, with the exception of man, they are now more widely distributed than any other mammal in the world.

Common *or* Hazel Dormouse

Muscardinus avellanarius

There was a table set out under a tree in front of the house, and the March Hare and the Hatter were having tea at it: a Dormouse was sitting between them, fast asleep, and the other two were using it as a cushion, resting their elbows on it, and talking over its head. 'Very uncomfortable for the Dormouse,' thought Alice; 'only, as it's asleep, I suppose it doesn't mind.'

The Mad Hatter's Tea Party, from *The Adventures of Alice in Wonderland* by LEWIS CARROLL.

With its pointed face, big black eyes, rounded ears and luxuriant whiskers, the dormouse is one of Britain's smallest and most appealing mammals, rendered all the more endearing by the fact that it spends over half its life asleep. Its sandy yellow fur and long, bushy tail make it impossible to confuse with an ordinary mouse; but because it is nocturnal, and hibernates for six months of the year, it is not easy to observe.

In recent years its range has contracted, and, except for a few outposts, it is now confined to the southern half of England, small outlying colonies in Cumbria and Northumberland and to parts of central Wales. Loss of good habitat has probably contributed to its decline, but the chief factor against it is our constantly changing maritime climate. Consistently hot summers and cold winters, like those of central Europe, are what suit it best.

Dormice live in woodland, and in summer spend almost all their time in trees and bushes, rarely descending to the ground. All four feet are prehensile, and they can turn their hind feet backwards, like squirrels: this enables them to climb and jump with great agility, to run head-first down tree trunks, and also to hang head-down while feeding on fruit and flowers. Radio tracking has revealed that they leave their nests of woven bark and grass about an hour after sunset, and spend the night foraging for food among the branches. In horizontal terms they do not travel very far, but they go up and down a great deal, climbing high into the canopy of tall trees. Just before dawn they return to base, or hole up for the day in an old birds' nest, a squirrel drey or a hollow tree.

Their food varies according to season. When they emerge from hibernation in late April or May, hawthorn flowers are generally in bloom. As these die off, they move on to the nectar of later flowers like those of honeysuckle; but in midsummer there comes a hungry gap, when there is not much available, and they turn to caterpillars and other insects. To help themselves through this difficult period, they may go into torpor – a kind of short-lived hibernation, during which their body temperature falls and they become immobile for the duration. If any predator discovers them in that state, they have no chance of escape, for they take about 20 minutes to come round.

Plenty returns in autumn with blackberries, elderberries and other fruit, but above all with hazel nuts, which they tackle while they are still green and relatively soft, taking up to 20 minutes to open up each shell and eat the kernel. Their presence in a wood is often given away by empty shells chewed into a distinctive pattern – a circular hole, with tiny tooth-marks round its outside rim.

The high protein content of nuts builds dormice up with the fat they need for hibernation, which begins with the arrival of cold weather in October or November. By then an adult's weight should have doubled, from about 17 g to 35–40 g. In contrast with their arboreal activities of summer, the animals sleep the winter away on the ground, rolled up tightly in nests made of woven bark and grass, and covered with leaves or moss. Because their temperature falls to that of their surroundings, and heartbeat and respiration slow down to a tenth of normal rates, they use almost no energy, and can go for weeks without emerging.

In comparison with other small rodents, they are slow breeders. Females have only one litter a year, of perhaps five young, and juveniles stay with their mother for up to

COMMON DORMOUSE, *MUSCARDINUS AVELLANARIUS* DORMICE ARE AMONG THE SMALLEST AND MOST APPEALING OF BRITISH MAMMALS.

two months. But this low rate of reproduction is offset by the fact that the animals live much longer than other rodents – four or five years, as against a vole's six months.

Conservation of dormice can be promoted by the provision of nesting boxes, to which they take readily, and by management of woodland to produce a favourable combination of shrubs and trees, varied in height and density. Recent reintroduction schemes have started to extend the creatures' range. In 2000, for instance, 33 were released into ancient woodland in Suffolk, and 200 nest boxes were put up. By October that year at least 87 dormice were known to be living in the wood, many of them babies.

Edible *or* Fat Dormouse
Glis glis

This little animal was a favourite food of the Romans, who kept the creatures in earthernware jars called *dolia* (normally used for storing wine) and fattened them up with nuts until they were fit for the table; and because one such jar was found at Verulamium (modern St Albans), there is a theory that the Romans introduced edible dormice to Britain. But there is no other evidence for their existence here before 1902, when a number were released into Tring Park, in Hertfordshire by Walter, Lord Rothschild.

Some sources say they were brought from Germany, others from Hungary. Either way, they bred extremely well, and soon became a nuisance, raiding farm crops and finding their way into houses, where they chewed through wood, ate electrical insulation and drowned themselves by falling into water tanks, thereby polluting the house's entire system. And yet, in spite of their early success, they have never spread much beyond their original territory in the Chilterns, where the combination of beech woods and conifer plantations suits them particularly well. For reasons not properly understood, they have never expanded into what seems ideal habitat to the north and south – but radio-tracking has shown that in general they move around very little.

A survey conducted in 1995 revealed that the animals were resorting more and more to human dwellings: many were being captured alive by householders and clandestinely released elsewhere – even though this is illegal – and some may have been taken to the New Forest, over 100 km to the southwest. Estimates of the population are largely guesswork – not least because the animals are mainly nocturnal, and hibernate during the winter – but they are thought to number at least 10,000.

Their food seems to be much the same as that of the common dormouse – tree flowers in spring, insects and caterpillars in summer, nuts and fruit in autumn. Since they feed mostly in trees, they are likely to eat birds' eggs also. As winter approaches and they build themselves up for hibernation, they become extremely fat.

Edible dormice bear a superficial resemblance to small

EDIBLE DORMOUSE, *GLIS GLIS* (top)
TWICE THE SIZE OF A COMMON DOR-
MOUSE, THIS CREATURE RESEMBLES
A GREY SQUIRREL.

HARVEST MOUSE, *MICROMYS MINUTUS*
(below): TINY BUT AGILE, THE HARVEST
MOUSE USES ITS PREHENSILE TAIL TO
CLING TO WHEAT STEMS.

HOUSE MOUSE, *MUS MUSCULUS*
(opposite page): IN BRITAIN, THE HOUSE
MOUSE HAS BEEN PRESENT SINCE AT
LEAST THE IRON AGE.

grey squirrels, but have shorter, chunkier bodies and much fluffier tails. Also, their foreheads are broader, and they have dark rings round the eyes. They are about twice the size of common dormice. Yet the appeal of their looks is not reflected in their habits. Inside houses, besides stripping electric wires, they raid larders and apple stores, deposit offensive amounts of droppings and urine in communal latrines, and bite viciously if cornered. Outdoors, like grey squirrels, they cause serious damage by gnawing the bark of trees, conifers especially. A survey made in Forestry Commission woods during 1990 estimated timber losses in some badly hit areas at £2000 per hectare.

Harvest Mouse

Micromys minutus

'Minutus' is the word: the harvest mouse is tiny, weighing 5–11 g (a third or less the size of a house mouse). Its blunt face and rounded ears give it the appearance of a vole, and its golden brown colour is quite different from the predominant grey of other mice; but its clearest distinguishing feature is its prehensile tail, which it uses like a fifth leg as a brake or anchor. This helps make it an exceptionally agile climber: with the tip of its tail curled round a twig or stalk, it can use its front feet for gripping food. Another of its vital assets is its exceptional sensitivity to vibration: through the soles of its feet, it can sense the movement of other animals in time to take evasive action.

Harvest mice move about with the changing seasons, seeking out areas of choice habitat, which consists of thick, tall vegetation like long, tussocky grass or reeds. They are great builders of nests, and carry on working all year round. Most constructions are quickly put together

from loosely woven grass and, not being designed for breeding, soon disintegrate. Breeding nests are another matter, and far more complex: the mice use living grass stalks as peripheral supports, and weave leaves tightly into a ball about 10 cm in diameter, sometimes as much as 1.5 metres off the ground. Once a shell is complete, the builder moves inside and draws in more leaves, shredded but still growing, through the walls, before making a lining of thistledown.

Young are born after about 18 days' gestation, and start exploring outside their aerial nursery when they are barely two weeks old: as adolescents, they are dull brown, and grow their distinctive golden coats only as adults. Harvest mice are by no means as sociable as their gentle appearance might suggest: they tend to be aggressive towards each other, and to fight, sitting up on their haunches to box and chatter. When the loser turns and runs, the victor snaps at its rear, and sometimes bits off the end of its tail or even a hind foot.

The world of harvest mice is prone to sudden, violent change. When hay or corn is harvested, their immediate environment is devastated in a day. When this happens, the survivors shift their ground – and they do so again in winter, when vegetation dies down, moving into barns, straw stacks or hollow trees. Not surprisingly, their life expectancy is short, and probably measured in months rather than years.

During 2001 the All England Tennis Club at Wimbledon gave the Wildlife Trusts in Avon, Glamorgan and Northumberland 350 used balls with which to make artificial mouse nests. With suitable access holes drilled in each side, and attached to stakes driven into the ground, the balls offered instant shelter and possibilities for development. Yet the best single innovation for harvest mice has been on the Game Conservancy Trust's experimental farm at Loddington in Leicestershire, where beetle-banks – long, low mounds of earth thrown up across fields – have given the mice a new and stable environment. The banks were orginally designed to harbour predatory insects, which eat pest species in cereal crops; but because the coarse grass on them is never cut, it provides ideal habitat for mice, with stems stiff enough to support their nests, and extraordinary numbers of nests have been counted – up to 400 along a single stretch of just a few hundred metres.

House Mouse

Mus musculus

As its name suggests, the house mouse is at home in human dwellings – and in almost any form of shelter, domestic, agricultural, industrial or commercial, but it is also common in hedgerows and open country. Anyone who lives in an old building is liable to share it with mice, for the creatures are extremely mobile, and constantly seek out comfortable new quarters

under floorboards, in ceilings or wall cavities. They are also extraordinarily active: agile jumpers and climbers (and good swimmers), they may visit 20 or 30 different feeding sites during a single night, and if they are using one site only, they may make 200 visits. Hence the scamper of tiny feet often heard in ceilings and behind wainscoting.

Mice eat a very wide range of substances, including soap, plaster, glue and plastic insulation, but their preference is for cereals, which they pick up in their forepaws, one grain at a time, and nibble, before dropping the remains and so leaving tell-tale deposits of small, chewed-up pieces. This, together with their habit of defecating 50 times a day, makes them a menace in corn mills, where they spoil or contaminate far more grain than they consume. Their activities are mainly nocturnal, but darkness is no problem to them, because they have good night vision and, like rats, use their whiskers for orientation, as well as

memorising specific routes about their territories. Their hearing, also, is exceptional. Their large ears move independently of each other, and can be swivelled round like radar dishes to pick up faint sounds.

Their ability to reproduce is legendary, exceeding that even of rabbits: one female can have up to ten litters a year, each of from four to ten young. In open country the population is kept down by cats, stoats, weasels, foxes, kestrels and owls, but in houses and (especially) farm grainstores numbers can reach amazing levels. In 1926 there was a celebrated plague of mice in California, where such colossal numbers built up in a crop of maize and barley that by the end there were estimated to be 200,000 in every hectare, or 20 to the square metre. Early in 2001 a householder in South London reported that he had been plagued by mice coming up from under the dining-room floor, and had caught 1359 of them in a live-capture trap set against a hole in the wainscoting.

A colony of mice set up an easily recognised, musty smell, and if one of them dies beneath floorboards, the stench of its decomposing body – small as it is – can render a room uninhabitable. Clearly, it is desirable to remove the corpse as soon as possible – but how to pin-point its position without ripping up half the floor? The traditional method is to capture some bluebottles, let them loose in the room and watch them flying around. When they start circling over a particular spot, begin investigations there.

Mice communicate by squeaks audible to the human ear, and also by ultrasonic signals. It is often the noise they make when feuding over territories, rather than movement, that betrays their presence to predators such as barn owls, which use their ears as well as their eyes to hunt.

WOOD MOUSE, *APODEMUS SYLVATICUS* (below) WOOD MICE DIG BURROWS – ONE FOR NESTING AND ANOTHER FOR FOOD STORAGE.

BLACK RAT, *RATTUS RATTUS* (right) ALSO KNOWN AS THE SHIP RAT, BLACK RATS SPREAD DISEASE AROUND THE WORLD VIA SHIPS.

Wood Mouse

Apodemus sylvaticus

Also known as the long-tailed field mouse, this has larger ears, eyes and hind feet than the house mouse: it is browner (and less grey) on the back, with yellowish-brown flanks and grey belly. It lives in woods, scrubland, arable fields and gardens, and is mainly vegetarian, eating grain, weed seeds, nuts, fungi and fruit (especially blackberries), but also insects, earthworms and snails. Wood mice dig themselves burrows, often with one chamber for nesting and another for the storage of food: they also store food in other cavities or old birds' nests. In spite of these provident habits, they suffer high mortality in early spring, and very few adults survive from one summer to the next, their normal lifespan being about 18 months. Pollution of the environment is an extra hazard.

Yellow-necked Mouse

Apodemus flavicollis

Large ears and eyes make the yellow-neck easy to confuse with the wood mouse, but it can be distinguished by its more vivid colours: bright brown fur on top, white underneath, and a larger yellow collar or bib on its throat. In Britain it lives only in the southern half of England, inhabiting mainly woods, hedges, gardens and orchards, and feeding on seeds, nuts and some insects. One of its more tiresome habits is to chew the heads off brightly coloured flowers like crocuses and tulips.

The mouse's own vivid colouring has the disadvantage of attracting predators – as witness an extraordinary incident which befell the naturalist Michael Clark one afternoon as he drove slowly along a road in Hertfordshire. On behalf of an elderly friend, he was deporting two yellow-necks which she had caught alive in her house but did not want

destroyed, and he was proposing to release them in a safe spot. He had the captives in a clear polythene bag, which he was holding in his right hand, outside the window of the car, when suddenly a kestrel stooped and made a grab at the passing target, which it clearly recognised, even though the mice were travelling at 30 or more km/h, in a manner which the hawk could never have seen before.

Rats

Black Rat

Rattus rattus

A rat's main asset is its teeth, and in particular its prominent incisors, which are so sharp that they can cut their way through wood, mortar and even concrete. Tradition holds that it was black rats and their parasitic fleas, travelling westwards with humans from eastern Asia to the Middle East, which brought plague to Europe between the eleventh and the fouteenth centuries. One version has it that they reached Europe in the baggage of the Crusaders, returning from the Holy Land in the twelfth century – and certainly in 1348 they let loose the Black Death in England, killing a third of the population and causing many of the survivors to abandon their villages in favour of unpolluted ground. Yet in recent years archaeological evidence has emerged to show that the creatures were here long before that, first reaching Britain by the third century AD.

Later, rats stowed away on ocean-going ships and spread disease all over the world. It was almost certainly an infestation of black rats that gave rise to the legend of the Pied Piper of Hamelin, the German town on the River Weser from which all the children were said to have vanished in 1268. For English readers, the story was immortalised by Robert Browning, whose narrative poem describes how a mysterious piper, dressed in fantastical clothes, got rid of the vermin, but then, because the Mayor and Corporation would not pay his fee of a thousand guilders, also lured away the town's children, who, all apart from one cripple unable to keep up with the rest, disappeared into the mountainside and were never seen again.

> Hamelin Town's in Brunswick,
> By famous Hanover city;
> The river Weser, deep and wide,
> Washes its walls on the southern side;
> A pleasanter spot you never spied;
> But, when begins my ditty,
> Almost five hundred years ago,
> To see the townsfolk suffer so

From vermin, was a pity.
Rats!
They fought the dogs, and killed the cats,
And bit the babies in the cradles,
And ate the cheeses out of the vats,
And licked the soup from the cooks' own ladles,
Split open the kegs of salted sprats,
Made nests inside men's Sunday hats,
And even spoiled the women's chats
By drowning their speaking
With shrieking and squeaking
In fifty different sharps and flats ...

From *The Pied Piper of Hamelin*
By ROBERT BROWNING

Contemporary accounts give a vivid idea of how rats harassed people in medieval England. 'Of all manner of vermin, Cornish houses are most pestered with rats,' wrote Richard Carew in his *Survey of Cornwall*, published in 1602. He described them as 'a brood very hurtful for devouring of meat, clothes and writings by day, and alike cumbersome through their crying and rattling, while they dance their gallop galliards in the roof at night.'

Today black rats are rare in Britain, driven out of most former habitat by brown rats: they are found only around some ports, on the cliffs of Lundy Island in the Bristol Channel and on three of the Shiant Islands in the Hebrides. They can be distinguished from brown rats by their longer ears, which are almost naked, larger eyes, and longer, thinner tails. In colour they may be black or brown, but the thick guard hairs on their backs and sides give them a slightly shaggy appearance.

They proliferate very fast. Gestation takes only 21 days; a single litter may contain 15 young, and one female can have up to five litters a year. Young are weaned in less than four weeks, and females become sexually mature in only four months. Population explosions are checked by the fact that mortality is high: life expectation is less than 18 months, most rats falling victim to poison or cats.

Brown Rat

Rattus norvegicus

The scientific name is misleading, for the brown or common rat did not originate in Norway, but in the Far East, and reached Europe only at the beginning of the eighteenth century. In Britain, the first certain record is from 1728, although they reputedly reached Ireland in 1722: the rodents are thought to have come ashore from Russian ships and their ability to run along mooring ropes makes such landings all too possible. The creatures are usually associated with human beings, and have always been a major agricultural, industrial and domestic pest.

For much of the year they live out in arable crops or in hedgerows, making dens in underground tunnel-systems: come autumn, however, they draw into the shelter of farm buildings and houses, where they cause phenomenal damage by gnawing through walls, floors and ceilings to make nests and runs in any cavity they can enlarge. So voracious are they, and so determined to reach sources of food that they undermine floors and cause whole buildings to collapse. Not only do they consume and spoil immense quantities of grain and animal feed: a high proportion of them also carry the bacteria which cause leptospirosis, or Weil's Disease, a form of infectious jaundice, excreting the organisms in their urine.

Like black rats, they multiply at alarming speed. A female can have up to 15 young in a litter, and five litters a year – but it is calculated that on farms, where active measures are taken against them, only five per cent survive their first 12 months. In the south of England many rats have developed resistance to anticoagulant poison, but thousands are trapped by gamekeepers or killed by predators such as cats, foxes, stoats, owls and buzzards.

They have highly developed territorial instincts, and often live in clans, driving off and even killing outsiders that try to intrude. Dominant rats feed mainly at night, but subordinate members of a community are sometimes forced to forage in daylight. Besides a repertoire of whistles, squeaks and chattering audible to humans, they communicate with each other by means of ultra-high frequency sounds, which do not alert predators. They have an acute sense of touch, and use their whiskers to orientate themselves in the dark. Tactile hairs all over the body enable them to memorise their surroundings and particular routes: if an object is removed from one of their trackways, they still make a detour round the spot.

Their habits are not pleasant. They eat almost anything, including the feet of live chickens brooding eggs. They are also cannibals: another rat, killed in a trap, is perfectly accceptable. By chewing away the plastic insulation on electric cables, they cause short-circuits and fires. Being very agile, with prehensile claws, they can climb vertical walls and run along narrow beams; where they squeeze through small holes, their coats leave a greasy deposit.

They are adept at stealing hens' eggs by rolling them along the ground, and there is a tradition that they also carry off eggs by turning themselves into sledges, one rat lying on its back and holding an egg on its chest while another pulls it along by the tail. Whether or not this tale has any real foundation, the creatures are extraordinarily versatile: on the Norfolk Broads they have alarmed conservationists by learning to dive almost a metre to forage for freshwater mussels.

3

Wild Mammals
Rodents

Black Rat
Brown Rat

Strong swimmers, they often reach shore from ship-wrecks and devastate local wildlife. One such instance was on Puffin Island, off the coast of Anglesey in north Wales. Rats from a late nineteenth-century shipwreck bred on the island, and did so well on a diet of eggs and chicks that by 1991 they had killed off all but about 20 pairs of the colony of puffins, which had been 2000 strong. They also severely depleted other seabirds that nest on the ground or on cliffs, among them razorbills, shags, guillemots, Manx shearwa-ters, fulmars and kittiwakes. In March 1998, under the direction of the Countryside Council for Wales and the Royal Society for the Protection of Birds, RAF helicopters lifted two and a half tons of wheat laced with warfarin onto the island: wardens deployed the poisoned grain, and managed to eliminate the invaders.

In poor African villages humans consider rats a delicacy, eating them with relish. Not many British people do the same – but, as the rural historian Roy Palmer recorded in his excellent book *The Folklore of Gloucestershire*, there have been occasions on which vermin have gone down the hatch. When farmers made cider, they often used to slip a joint of beef into the fermenting barrrel to improve the brew. One year a score of rats fell into a hogshead and drowned – and the cider that came out next summer was, by common consent, the finest of the season. When the cider barrel was drained, not a trace of rat remained.

'It had yut 'em, see?' explained the farmer.

'You'd drunk 'em', his companion replied.

'It had yut 'em', the farmer insisted, 'and we'd drunk 'em. Comes to the same thing.'

Squirrels

Grey Squirrel

Sciurus carolinensis

The name 'squirrel' derives from two Greek words mean-ing 'shadow tail' – an allusion to the way the creature sits up with its fluffy tail curved over its back. And yet, cuddly as it may look, the grey squirrel has proved one of the most unfortunate imports ever brought into Britain: an ecologi-cal disaster. The first pair, introduced from North America in 1876, was released at Henbury Park in Cheshire and never seen again. Five more animals set free in Bushey Park, North London in 1889, also disappeared. Not so – alas – the ten brought to the park at Woburn Abbey in 1890 by the Duke of Bedford: they flourished, and their descend-ants spread out, reinforced by at least 30 more releases to

GREY SQUIRREL, *SCIURUS CAROLINEN-SIS* (below) THE INTRODUCTION OF GREY SQUIRRELS HAS BEEN AN ECOLOGICAL DISASTER.

RED SQUIRREL, *SCIURIS VULGARIS* (right) THE RED HAS BEEN PUSHED OUT OF ITS TERRITORIES BY THE INVADING GREY IN MOST REGIONS.

Where woods are bordered by arable fields, the greys eat large quantities of cereals during late summer, and ruin more of the crops than they consume by knocking down ears and stalks; but their most destructive habit is that of stripping bark from deciduous trees, principally beech and sycamore. Young trees are particularly vulnerable, especially when a species such as beech is planted among conifers: the squirrels wait until the hardwoods are 10 or 12 years old, with trunks 8–9 cm in diameter and then chew away the bark just above the roots – a form of attack that leaves the trees maimed for life, or kills them entirely. In areas such as the Chiltern Hills numerous plantations have been entirely wiped out. Older trees are often ring-barked high up, so that the crown dies off.

There has been much debate about the reasons for such behaviour, which hardly occurs in North America, but in Britain starts during May and reaches a peak during June and July. Some experts believe that the damage is done by young male squirrels marking out their territories: observers have watched juveniles rush straight from fights with rivals and start bark-stripping, as if it were a way of working off aggression. Others think that they are feeding, and that they gnaw bark in early summer because it is sweet with rising sap. During the 1940s and 1950s damage to plantations became so widespread that the Ministry of Agriculture ran a scheme under which one shilling (5p) was paid for every tail sent in. Many thousands of squirrels were shot and trapped every year, but enough survived for the species to keep extending its range. Game-keepers and landowners found that even if they cleared a wood completely, it would soon be re-colonised by new-comers moving into the vacuum. In recent years a more effective control agent has proved to be warfarin poison, mixed with grain and set out in metal hoppers fitted with spring doors, so that only squirrels can gain access to the contents.

Grey squirrels are almost entirely vegetarian, feeding on acorns, beechmast, nuts, cereals, fruit, flowers and so on; but in spring they also eat the eggs and fledglings of song-

sites as far apart as Devon, Kent, Oxford, Yorkshire, Scotland and Wales between 1902 and 1929.

The earliest arrivals were considered amusing novelties, and they were expected to 'brighten up' the British wildlife scene; unfortunately, they turned out such good colonisers that within 50 years they had not only driven the native red squirrels from much of their range, but also established themselves as a major pest to foresters and farmers. As early as 1929 the naturalist Eric Parker was suggesting that county councils should launch local offensives to exterminate the newcomers, and the first national anti-grey-squirrel campaign was launched in 1931; but only in 1938 was it declared illegal to import the creatures or keep them in captivity – and by then the species was out of control.

birds. Like reds, they store surplus food in autumn, burying nuts in the ground or hiding them in holes in trees, and a bumper harvest of nuts and beechmast often produces a surge in breeding during the following spring. The squirrels sometimes live in hollow trees, but more often in spherical nests, called dreys, made of twigs and leaves, and lined with leaves and grass, placed high in the branches: a neat-looking, rounded drey is generally inhabited, whereas a dishevelled one has probably been abandoned or taken over by birds such as carrion crows.

In summer greys are out and about foraging for most of the day, and even on cold winter mornings they are abroad for several hours. When alarmed, they twitch their tails up over their backs and let off long bursts of scolding – *chuck, chuck, chuck, chuck* – which may go on for several minutes, and sound almost mechanical. In parks and gardens they become very tame, especially if people feed them; but in woods where they are hunted, if they spot a fox or a human

being, they tend to run up a vertical or steeply sloping branch and cling there, constantly scrabbling round so as to keep hidden from the intruder, or remaining still, belly to bark, until the threat has gone.

Grey squirrels are good to eat, their flesh tasting rather like chicken; but because they are relatively small and difficult to skin, and remind people of rats, they have never been high on British menus.

Red Squirrel

Sciuris vulgaris

It seems ironic that our most attractive squirrel should also be called *vulgaris*, or common, as it can no longer be found in most parts of Britain, having been driven out of its former haunts by the larger and heavier greys.

Red squirrels were once abundant all over the United Kingdom, but they have disappeared almost entirely from

95

RED SQUIRREL, *SCIURIS VULGARIS* (left)
RED SQUIRRELS PREFER THE SMALLER
SEEDS OF PINES AND NORWAY SPRUCE.

BANK VOLE, *CLETHRIONOMYS RUFO-
CANUS* (below): FEED ON GRASS, FRUIT,
SEEDS, INSECTS, SNAILS AND FUNGI.

the south, where the only places they survive in good numbers are the Isle of Wight and Brownsea Island, to which greys have never gained access. There are also a few in Thetford Chase in Norfolk; but otherwise they have been pushed back to the coniferous forests of northern England and Scotland.

It has often been said that greys attack or at any rate intimidate reds. Greys are certainly larger and heavier (up to 30 cm long in head and body, and weighing up to 700 g, as against 23 cm and 480 g), but there is no evidence of direct antagonism between the species. The truth seems to be simply that the greys are able to make better use of typical British woodland, in which broadleaved trees predominate over conifers. Whereas greys, with their more powerful jaws, eat green acorns, hazelnuts and beechmast, reds prefer the smaller seeds of trees like pines and Norway spruce.

Reds nest in spherical dreys (nests) made of twigs and lined with grass or moss, generally set in a fork against the trunk of a tree. In summer they are active for much of the day; in winter they do not hibernate, but may lie up for several days on end if the weather is cold. They are strongly territorial, with males and females occupying ranges of similar size – about four hectares.

Mating takes place early in the year, and litters of up to eight young are born between March and May, productivity depending largely on the food supply during the previous autumn. The squirrels are sometimes preyed on by rare pine martens, and also by buzzards and rare goshawks, against which their normal defence – of remaining motionless – offers little protection. However, more squirrels are probably killed by cats, dogs and cars than by any natural predator in Britain.

By the end of the twentieth century several conservation bodies were making strenuous efforts to halt the reds' decline. In 1993, for intance, no fewer than 120 individuals and organisations joined together in the north of England to form Red Alert North West, whose main aim is to give reds the best possible chance by adapting forests to suit them. The charity has identified several large blocks of woodland – ideally, separated from each other by farmland – which may become refuge sites for the reds, and in general the plan is to keep the two species apart by careful habitat management.

At Kielder in Northumberland, where the Forestry Commission owns 60,000

hectares, research has shown that although red squirrels can survive in plantations of pure sitka spruce, they do better if there is a percentage of Norway spruce. Felling and planting are therefore being tailored for the reds' benefit. In the south the National Trust spends more than £15,000 a year clearing rhododendron bushes from Scots pine woodland for the benefit of the 200 reds that live on Brownsea Island. Without this work, which has enabled regeneration to start again, the pines would all have died at about the same time, eliminating the squirrels' main source of food.

Voles

Bank Vole

Clethrionomys rufocanus

Although heavily preyed on by owls, foxes and weasels, bank voles are flourishing in mainland Britain, and spreading in the southwest of Ireland. Their coats are redder than those of field voles (*see page 98*). They live in scrub and deciduous woodland, and make spherical nests of grass, leaves, moss and feathers, often underground at the centre of several radiating tunnels. In addition to leaves, they eat grass, fruit, seeds, insects, snails and fungi. Should population densities become very high, evidence suggests that breeding will temporarily cease.

Common Vole

Microtus arvalis

In spite of their name, common voles live only on islands such as Orkney and Guernsey. They look very much like field voles, but their coats are shorter and smoother. Dry land is their favoured habitat, since they nest and store food in underground chambers and tunnels. Some of their habits are unusually tolerant: breeding pairs occupy nests within three or four metres of each other, nursing mothers allow other voles to inspect their litters, and on Orkney the males retrieve babies when they stray from the nest.

Field Vole

Microtus agrestis

Darker-coated and larger than the common vole, with a rather shaggy look, field voles are abundant throughout Britain, especially in rough grassland and young forestry plantations where the grass is high enough to give cover. Living mainly on grass and other plants, they are active at all hours of the day and night, but tend to be more nocturnal in summer. This makes them a good source of food for owls, which hunt by ear as well as by eye, and locate voles by the squeaks and chattering they give out during territorial disputes.

Field voles breed at a great rate, mainly in summer, but often all year round, even under snow. In spherical nests of shredded grass a female produces up to seven litters a year, each averaging from four to six young, which are weaned after only 14 days. The maximum recorded lifespan is two years, but only a tiny percentage of animals survive more than 15 months. Populations fluctuate violently between peaks and troughs every four or five years: in peak years voles become so numerous that their tunnels can destroy the surface of pastures. In 1934 they reached plague proportions in new plantations round Lake Vyrnwy in North Wales, devouring grass, weeds and young trees, so that the hillsides were left completely bare.

Water Vole

Arvicola terrestris

Millions of children have agonised along with Ratty, the water vole in Kenneth Grahame's *The Wind in the Willows*, as he and his friends struggle to win back Toad Hall from the squatting stoats. In the book the friends come out on top; but in real life Ratty is not doing so well.

In the last two decades of the twentieth century the water vole suffered a disastrous decline in Britain and became an endangered species, largely due to the depredations of American mink. The first national survey done by the Vincent Wildlife Trust in 1989–90 revealed that the species had disappeared from 68 per cent of sites occupied early in the century.

A second survey eight years later showed that the rate of decline had accelerated, and that water voles had vanished from almost 90 per cent of their former sites. The Trust predicted that if the downward trend continued, the animals would be extinct in Britain by the year 2003.

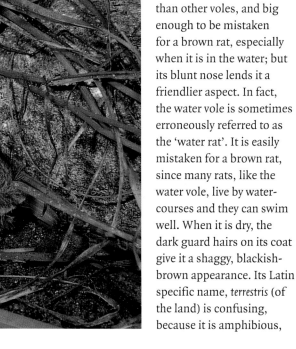

The creature is much larger than other voles, and big enough to be mistaken for a brown rat, especially when it is in the water; but its blunt nose lends it a friendlier aspect. In fact, the water vole is sometimes erroneously referred to as the 'water rat'. It is easily mistaken for a brown rat, since many rats, like the water vole, live by watercourses and they can swim well. When it is dry, the dark guard hairs on its coat give it a shaggy, blackish-brown appearance. Its Latin specific name, *terrestris* (of the land) is confusing, because it is amphibious, and spends much time swimming: the word refers to its habit of burrowing in the ground. Along with other aquatic rodents like the beaver and coypu, water voles have pelts of thick fur with air trapped in it, which gives them excellent insulation, and flaps of skin inside their ears keep water out while they are swimming.

Water voles, like their cousins the field voles are active both day and night, and live along the banks of streams, usually within a couple of metres of the water's edge, favouring areas with abundant vegetation. Grass is vital to them, both as food and as material for lining their nests which they make in burrows bored out of the banks. Their tunnels are on several levels, so that if the water rises, they can move up and remain dry. An occupied burrow can often be recognised by the small circle of grazed-down vegetation outside its entrance.

Their diet is almost entirely vegetarian, consisting of grass and other green plants in summer, and of fruit, roots and bulbs in autumn and winter. They particularly like apples, which are useful bait for anyone wanting to lure them into the open for observation; and the attitude in which they eat – sitting up, with food held between their forepaws – is very photogenic.

Like other small rodents, they are highly prolific, females producing up to five litters of five or six every year. Yet young leave the nest when only half-grown, and in some areas only about a third of the juveniles survive to become adults. Few live for more than two winters. One reason for such a high mortality rate is that they are hunted by many predators, including otters, pike, herons, stoats, weasels, brown rats, cats and owls – and to these there has now been added the extra menace of introduced American mink which has escped from mink farms (*see page 53*).

Voles can often escape their traditional enemies by diving into water and stirring up clouds of mud; but such

tactics are no defence against the American mink, which dive and swim at devastating speed. In some areas, especially North Yorkshire, these introduced predators have eliminated the entire population of water voles, and naturalists are concerned about the survival of the species as a whole.

It is a legal offence to disturb water vole burrows, but the animals themselves are not protected. Possible conservation measures include improvement and restoration of habitat along river banks, and a nationally coordinated programme of captive breeding.

Insectivores

Most insectivores are small — the hedgehog is easily the largest of those in Britain — yet they are phenomenal survivors, having existed since the mid-Cretaceous period, about 130 million years ago, longer than all other extant mammals. They are mainly nocturnal, and a very keen sense of smell, backed by some capability for echolocation, makes up for their poor sight.

Hedgehog

Erinaceus europaeus

To the Anglo-Saxons it was an il, a contraction of the German *igel*. By Shakespeare's day it was known as a hedgepig or a furzehog, from its habit of snuffling around in undergrowth. ('Thrice and once the hedgepig whined', chants the Second Witch in *Macbeth*). Today it is a hedgehog (or sometimes, still, an urchin), the object of more affection than many a less fortunate mammal, not least because of Beatrix Potter's portrayal of that 'very stout short person', Mrs Tiggywinkle.

Like pigs, the creatures were once thought able to see the wind and to know when storms were coming: the Elizabethan poet Chester wrote of a merchant in Constantinople who fed a hedgehog in his garden because it gave him 'just presagement' of the winds:

> The hedgehog hath a sharpe thicke thorned garment
> That on his backe doeth serve him for defence:
> He can presage the winds incontinent,
> And hath good knowledge in the difference
> Between the southerne and the northerne wind.
> These vertues are allotted him by kind.

In evolutionary terms, hedgehogs are essentially very primitive, and they have existed far longer than humans – at least ten million years. During the reign of Queen Elizabeth I the Act for the Preservation of Grain declared them vermin (along with rats, mice, sparrows and, illogically, all the small predators) and encouraged churchwardens to destroy them by offering a small bounty for every snout and tail handed in. For 300 years they remained an official pest, and in the nineteenth century gamekeepers persecuted them unjustly because they thought that hedgehogs ate the eggs of pheasants and partridges: records from one estate in East Anglia show that over a period of 50 years the keepers killed 20,000 hedgehogs. All sorts of crimes were laid at their door: they were said to suck milk from the teats of cows as they lay in pastures, and to steal apples by rolling on them, so as to impale them on their spines, and running off with a load on their backs.

Now things are different. The Wildlife and Countryside Act of 1981 gave the animals some legal protection, and their cause is championed by the British Hedgehog Preservation Society. Today they are common all over lowland Britain, also in Ireland and on several offshore islands – to which they must have been transported by humans. The only environments where they are scarce or absent are conifer forests, wetlands, moors and mountains. They are quite at home in urban gardens and parks. But their overall numbers are probably declining, due to intensive farming, the ripping-out of hedges, the removal of cover and the build-up of agricultural chemicals, from pesticides and herbicides in the invertebrates they eat.

Hedgehogs find particular favour with gardeners, since they eat many horticultural pests – slugs, caterpillars, beetles and insect larvae. (Before the advent of insecticides, people used to bring them into their houses to clean up the cockroaches.) Yet they are more aggressive and heartily carnivorous than their bumbling image suggests, gladly devouring the eggs and chicks of ground-nesting birds, as well as grass snakes, earthworms, mice and the occasional rabbit. Since hedgehogs were introduced to the Hebridean islands of North and South Uist in 1974, the population has built up to 5000, and they eat so many waders' eggs that they have had a seriously damaging effect on such species as dunlin, redshank and lapwing.

Folk stories suggest that they kill adders, and certainly they are well protected against snakebite: not only do their 5000 or more spines intercept strikes, but their blood has some immunity to adder venom. For many years naturalists doubted that hedgehogs had the ability to kill snakes, but the matter was settled once and for all during the 1830s, when Professor Buckland put a hedgehog and grass snake into a box to see what would happen. At the outset the hedgehog was rolled into a ball, but when it opened up and saw what was nearby, it gave the snake a hard bite and instantly rolled up again. Twice more it did the same thing. The third bite broke the snake's back, whereupon the hedgehog ran its jaws along the body, cracking it and breaking the bones at intervals. Having thus softened up its victim, it ate the whole thing, starting from the tail.

Hedgehogs' own defence against aggression is to roll up tightly into a ball and raise their spines, presenting a predator with a sphere of spikes. Foxes and badgers, nevertheless, do manage to kill and eat some, leaving cleaned out skins as evidence. A fox confronted by a ball of spines is said to roll it into a pool of water, and when the hedgehog puts its head out, seizes it in its jaws. But by far their

worst enemies are mechanical: thousands are squashed on roads every year, and thousands more chopped into pieces or severely injured by flail mowers cutting silage or trimming verges. If they escape a violent end, they may live for ten years, but three is probably the average.

The best-known fact about hedgehogs is that they hibernate. In autumn they build up stores of special brown fat around their necks and shoulders, and, when cold weather sets in, curl up in nests known as 'hibernacula'. They make these mainly from layers of fallen leaves, which provide good insulation, and they often position these nests beneath heaps of brushwood or garden clippings – a habit which leads to many an accidental roasting, when gardeners light bonfires without checking the bottom of the pile. During hibernation, temperature and pulse rate fall to very low levels, thus conserving energy; but hedgehogs rarely sleep through the whole winter. Rather, they arouse several times and prowl about before tucking up in a different nest.

Emerging in April, they set about mating – a tricky process for creatures so well armoured, but one which is facilitated by the sow's ability to lay her quills flat and to stick out her backside in the most accessible posture. After five weeks' gestation, she gives birth to four or five young,

which have smooth, pink skins: only after a few days do the first white spines start to appear, soon followed by brown ones. If the mother is disturbed during the first few days, she may eat her babies, but if an emergency arises when they are older, she will carry them one by one to a new nest. At about three weeks she starts to lead them out in little processions, teaching them to forage for themselves.

Many householders encourage hedgehogs by putting out bread and milk in their gardens; needless to say, this is not a good idea, since it gives the animals diarrhoea and sometimes serious enteritis. Nor are they ideal indoor pets, as, prevented from grooming themselves by their spines, hedgehogs carry large numbers of fleas and ticks, besides harbouring the virus that causes foot-and-mouth disease in cattle.

An old cure for fits was to feed the patient a cooked hedgehog, and gypsies used to bake the animals in bonfires. The Rev. J. G. Wood, writing in 1854, described how they singed off the bristles, wrapped the body in clay and put the whole bundle into the fire. 'After a time the clay cracks, and the hedgehog is pronounced to be properly cooked. The clay is then broken and the hedgehog extracted, having been baked in a manner not to be equalled in any oven.'

Mole

Talpa europaea

When William of Orange's horse tripped over a molehill and came down in a fall that led to the king's death in 1702, Jacobites raised their glasses in toasts to 'the little gentleman in black velvet'. But since then not many people have had a good word to say for moles, which madden farmers, gardeners and the keepers of golf-courses by wrecking lawns and greens and fouling mowers with the heaps of earth and stones that they throw up.

The animals are almost impossible to watch, and difficult even to see, for they spend practically all their time underground, emerging now and then in search of grass or other material for their nests. Normally the only mole that comes to light is a dead one, nipped by a fox but left uneaten, as if the carcass had an unpleasant taste. Nevertheless, the creatures have a fascinating and highly specialised way of life.

Constantly digging with their broad front feet and powerful shoulders, they create complex systems of tunnels in which they live and forage. When they move into a new area, they first make a kind of reconnaissance, opening tunnels just below the surface by forcing the turf or earth up into shallow ridges. With this preliminary network in place, they dig deeper to establish permanent

living quarters – and it is this phase of work that creates the all-too-familiar molehills.

Having scraped away at the work-face with claws and front feet, the mole drags loosened soil back past its body, then swivels round and pushes the debris along the new tunnel until it reaches an already dug vertical shaft. There it forces the soil to the surface, pushing with either front foot in turn and thus raising a typically pyramid-shaped heap. For an animal so small, its earth-moving power is phenomenal. It has been calculated that in 20 minutes one 100 g mole can shift 6 kg of soil – the equivalent of a medium-sized man moving four tons.

The result of all this excavation is a series of galleries on different levels, sometimes going down a metre below ground. By patrolling these burrows, moles get most of their food in the form of earthworms, which fall into the tunnels. When they catch one, they bite off the head and draw the body through clenched claws to squeeze out the earth that it has ingested. They also eat a variety of insects, and they hunt mainly by using their sense of smell, which is acute, storing surplus food in special larders. They are often supposed to be blind, but in fact they have rudimentary eyes which can recognise light and dark, and they also seem to have some power of orientation which enables them to retain a mental picture of their surroundings. They are certainly sensitive to vibration, and quickly cease digging if they detect an alien approach, lying doggo until the intruder has moved away.

Their programme of activity is a matter of some debate. They do not hibernate in winter, but remain active all year round, digging and hunting in bursts of several hours, with pauses to sleep in between. The fact that they get going early in the morning may or may not be connected with the arrival of daylight above; more likely, hunting is triggered by earthworms coming back to ground after their night in the open and falling into the tunnels.

For most of their time moles are solitary and aggressive, each defending its own territory. The Victorian naturalist the Rev. J. G. Wood was highly censorious of their behaviour. 'Dull and harmless as it may appear to be,' he wrote, 'it [the mole] is in reality one of the most ferocious animals in existence.' Only in the spring mating season do males and females come together, and young are born underground in nests of woven grass. Suckled by the mother, and taught by her to explore the tunnel system, they are cast into the world at the age of nine weeks, to establish tunnels and territories of their own.

In the old days many professional trappers caught moles for a living, and their pelts were much in demand: moleskin waistcoats and breeches were all the rage among farmers. Today a few trappers survive; but most mole control is carried out by rodent operatives using poison or pellets that release gas. For anyone who wants to get rid of moles but does not want to kill them, there are various traditional remedies. One is to place mothballs in the runs, and another – not so handy in front gardens – is to station horses above them, the theory being that the vibration of stamping hoofs will persuade the tunnellers to decamp and go elsewhere. Luckily for gardeners across the water, there are no moles in Ireland, north or south.

Shrews

Shrews belong to the order *Sorex* and are among the oldest surviving mammals, their ancestors having evolved in the Tertiary period about 50 million years ago. They are mainly nocturnal, and their prominent snouts – long, pointed and adorned with bristling whiskers called *vibrissae* – give a clue to the fact that, although their eyesight is poor, they have a keen sense of smell, which enables them to hunt and feed at night. Some species have glands in their flanks which give off a strong smell, with the result that although predators such as foxes and domestic cats often kill them, they generally leave the bodies uneaten (birds, which mostly have a relatively poor sense of smell, do eat them). Even if the scent glands do act as a defence, their primary purpose is probably to provide a means of marking runs and territories. Shrews also have toxins in their saliva for stupefying or killing prey. Experiments with saliva taken from the submaxillary glands at the back of a shrew's mouth showed the substance contained poison potent enough to kill a rabbit in five minutes, acting rather as snake's venom does, by slowing the heart until breathing stops.

Perhaps it was these unusual natural attributes that gave shrews their ancient reputation as creatures of evil. They were once supposed to possess the power of bewitching people, and to create an antidote one had to make a hole in an ash tree, push a shrew into it, immure it with a plug and leave it to die – after which any branch or twig plucked from the tree would cure whatever mischief the creature had managed to perpetrate. The eighteenth-century naturalist Gilbert White recorded that near the church at Selborne, his village in Hampshire, there stood a very old, hollow, pollarded ash which for generations was regarded as a shrew-ash, until the vicar had it cut down. Dictionaries still define the shrew as 'a small, mouse-like

animal formerly thought venomous...an evil being...a brawling, troublesome person...a scold'. To Shakespeare 'shrewd' meant 'ill-natured' or 'mischievous', rather than 'acute', and in *The Taming of the Shrew* he gave Katharine torrents of wonderfully sharp, spiteful invective.

Common Shrew

Sorex araneus

Well distributed all over Britain, but absent from Ireland; the upper half of the common shrew's body is dark brown, sometimes almost black, and and its belly much paler. Shrews live in deciduous woodland, but also in tussocky grass, especially along road verges, and their food consists mainly of invertebrates such as slugs, snails, earthworms, spiders, beetles and woodlice.

Shrews often dig for prey, which they locate with their snouts, and they use a combination of smell and echo-location to find their way around. They hunt mainly at night, and at dawn and dusk, and normally consume about 90 per cent of their body weight in a day; but a lactating female packs away twice that amount. Having a high metabolic rate, like moles, the creatures must eat every few hours,

and if they cannot find normal prey, they often turn cannibal. Aggressive territorial encounters are frequent, and marked by high-pitched screams. Common shrews remain active all year round, but in winter spend most of the time underground in burrows. Mortality is very high among the young, and the maximum lifespan is less than two years.

Pygmy Shrew

Sorex minutus

As tiny as its name suggests, the pygmy shrew has a head and body length of about 5 cm and weighs at most 7.5 g, but it has a relatively long and hairy tail. It is widespread in Britain and Ireland. It is more active in daylight than the common shrew, climbs and swims better, and spends less time underground.

Water Shrew

Neomys fodiens

Largest of European shrews, very dark on the back and almost white on the belly, the water shrew is a good swimmer and diver; but the air trapped in its coat makes it

so buoyant that, in order to initiate a plunge, it has to break the surface by leaping off the bank. Fringes of silver bristles on the outer edges of its feet increase its paddling power, and similar bristles on the tail help it steer.

It usually lives close to water, on the banks of streams, and particularly favours watercress beds, feeding on aquatic crustaceans, molluscs and small fish, which it can locate with its whiskers. But it also forages on land for beetles and worms, and stores spare, half-eaten food in little caches. Venom in its saliva helps overcome small mammals. Water shrews make a good deal of noise, churring and squeaking, but appear to be less aggressive than other species of shrews and live in close groups.

Bats Order *Chiroptera*

By no means everyone likes bats. Children are often fascinated by them, but some people fear that if one flies into the house, it will land in their hair and infest them with fleas. These fears are unfounded, because bat fleas cannot survive on humans – but revulsion is probably compounded by the creatures' peculiar shape, by the fact that they are nocturnal, and by the associations with Count Dracula that inevitably hang about the only flying mammals. Popular sayings enshrine many misconceptions. Bats do not live in belfries, which are too noisy for their liking. Nor are they blind or batty in the sense of being irrational.

Bats belong to the order *Chiroptera* (literally 'hand-wings'), and in spite of their strange appearance, are not much different in structure from other mammals, except that the bones in their fingers are greatly extended to carry membranes of skin, and their knees bend backwards, making it difficult for them to walk on the ground. The German name *fledermaus* (flying mouse), is misleading, for they are more nearly related to humans than to mice.

Bats are divided into two major groups, namely insect-eating microbats and fruit-eating megabats. The earliest known microbat was *Icaronycteris*, whose fossil remains were discovered in early Eocene sediments 54 million years old. Megabats came later: the first, *Archaeopteropus*, dates from 37 million years ago.

Because they are nocturnal, microbats have developed echolocation of prey to a high degree, and for this many species have evolved large ears and (in some cases) growths of skin on their faces. The fact that their food is abundant only in summer has made them refine techniques of hibernation in winter; and their habit of going into a torpor during the day is another device for energy-saving, needed by small creatures that put out a lot of effort when flying.

In all there are over 950 species of bat (about 20 per cent of all mammals). More than 30 (all microbats) survive in Europe, but only 16 still live and breed in England; some of them have become extremely rare, and all are suffering from a decline of good habitat, as feeding grounds and roost sites are lost to development and changes in land use. Although all are fully protected under Schedule 5 of the Wildlife and Countryside Act of 1981, so that it is an offence to kill, injure or even disturb them, the removal of hedgerows, felling of ancient woods, drainage of wet areas, use of pesticides and conversion of old buildings all remain damaging influences. One activity particularly dangerous to bats is the spraying of roof timbers with insecticides. The creatures are made vulnerable by the fact that they tend to live in large communities, which can be suddenly wiped out if a tree falls down or a building catches fire.

In summer they spend the day roosting in colonies, in roof spaces, attics, barns and hollow trees, where they hang upside-down, holding on with their sharp claws. This posture guarantees them a fast take-off, and is probably a form of defence against predators. It also obviates any need for standing or walking, with the result that the creatures have extremely light pelvises, and knees that bend in the opposite way from ours. They rarely land on the ground, because they have difficulty taking off again.

Towards dusk they start to fly around inside their roosts, and then emerge into the open as dark is falling. All British bats feed on insects caught at night, detecting prey by echolocation – a system of ultrasonic signalling. Sounds emitted through mouth or nose are reflected back so rapidly that the sender can detect if an object is soft or hard, whether it is stationary or moving, and, if it is travelling, at what speed and in which direction. Because flying burns a lot of energy, numbers of insects consumed are phenomenal: one pipistrelle, tiny though it is, can put away 3000 victims in a night.

In the autumn bats build up their weight by piling on fat. When the weather turns cold and prey becomes scarce, they hibernate. Some bats migrate hundreds of kilometres, others only a few hundred metres, seeking out cool places like caves and old mine shafts, where the temperature will remain stable through the winter. They conserve energy by dropping their body temperature and slowing their metabolism so that they can survive for weeks or months without food, living on their accumulated fat. If the temperature rises, they may wake occasionally, for a short period, but they do not become fully active again until the spring, by which time they have used up all their reserves. A lesser horseshoe which in autumn turned the scales at 9 g may well have lost half its weight when it comes out of hibernation in April.

Female bats have a unique system of delayed fertilisation.

After mating in autumn, they retain the male's sperm separate from their eggs, so that if they are in poor condition in spring, they can avoid ovulating, and thus prevent pregnancies which they might not be able to sustain. When a female does give birth, she produces a baby with about a quarter of her own body weight – the equivalent of a woman of 60 kg producing a 15 kg infant. She is a slow breeder, not starting to produce until several years old. In comparison with other small mammals, bats are extremely long-lived, often surviving for 30 years or more. One species, the mouse-eared bat, has recently gone extinct in Britain, and those that survive in Britain are listed below.

Barbastelle

Barbastella barbastellus

Endangered in much of Europe, and with only one breeding colony known in Britain, the barbastelle is considered rare. Medium-sized, with long, silky fur, its head and body measure 45–58 mm and its wingspan is 260–290 mm. Although preferring woodland, it has a wide range of habitat, from mountains and wooded river valleys to municipal parks, and spends the summer in caves, tree-holes, nest boxes or roof spaces. It hunts low along woodland edges, keeping close to the trees, or over water, and snatches insects, mainly moths, out of the air or off leaves – but, having a small mouth and weak teeth, it cannot crunch prey with hard shells.

Bechstein's Bat

Myotis bechsteinii.

With only one known breeding colony, this bat is now considered rare. Skeletons in deposits from 1000 BC show it was once much more common. The main reason for its decline has been loss of deciduous woodland. Bechstein's bat has exceptionally long ears which reach beyond its nose when folded forward, and are held straight even when hibernating. Its head and body measure 45–55 mm and its wingspan is 250–300 mm. It lives mainly in damp woodland, also in parks and gardens, and roosts in holes in trees, but hibernates in caves, mines and buildings. On windy nights it does not venture out, but is prepared to hunt in wet, cold weather; it flies quite low (about 10 metres from the ground) and slowly, with fluttering, highly agile flight.

Brandt's Bat

Myotis brandtii.

Principally a woodland species, Brandt's bat can occasionally be seen in daylight as it emerges from its daytime roost earlier than others. In terms of numbers, its status is considered to be vulnerable. Its head and body measure 39–51 mm and its wingspan is 190–240 mm. It has long fur, dark grey-brown at the base, but its back is sometimes lighter than that of the whiskered bat, which it resembles very closely. Other differences between the species, which are not discernible in the course of normal observation, are in the relative shape of teeth and penises.

Brown Long-eared Bat

Plecotus auritus.

This species of bat is numerous enough to be considered not under threat. Its ears are nearly as long as the body but this is not always apparent, as it tends to curl its ears back or tuck them under its wings. The brown long-eared bat's body and head measure 37–52 mm while its wingspan is 230–285 mm. It usually roosts in the attics of old houses. Broad wings and tail allow it to hover and manoeuvre sharply at low speeds, and to fly among foliage to pick insects off leaves and bark. This bat's particular habit of landing on the ground to catch insects leaves the creature vulnerable to attack by predators, especially domestic cats.

Daubenton's Bat

Myotis daubentonii

Living mainly in open woodland with water nearby, this bat hawks for insects over water, skimming along with slow, flickering wing-beats. It is said to use its large feet as gaffes and tail membrane as a scoop, to snatch prey off the water surface. It measures 40–50 mm with a wingspan of 230–270 mm. In winter it hibernates in cellars, old wells and mines, often clustering together in packs of 100 or more. It is not considered to be under threat.

Greater Horseshoe Bat

Rhinolophus ferrumequinum

Its range was much reduced during the twentieth century, and it is now restricted to southwest England and southwest Wales, with less than ten per cent of the former population surviving. The Wildlife Trusts estimate that there are only 4000–6000 greater horseshoes left in Britain, leaving them endangered. One reason for their decline has been the loss of feeding grounds, principally old pasture, which has been ploughed up.

The greater horseshoe is the largest horseshoe bat in Europe, measuring 58–70 mm with a wingspan of 350–400 mm. When coming to roost, it approaches the point chosen, then turns a forward somersault, folds its wings

GREATER HORSESHOE BAT, *RHINOLO-PHUS FERRUMEQUINUM*: WHEN HIBER-NATING, IT HANGS FROM THE ROOF OF CAVE, CELLAR OR TUNNEL.

and grips on with its hind feet. It sometimes hangs by one leg, echolocating at the same time. When hibernating, it hangs from the roof of cave, cellar or tunnel, rather than tucked into a crevice, and so is relatively easy to count.

Grey Long-eared Bat

Plecotus austriacus

Now restricted to a few areas of southern England, the rare grey long-eared bat has a very dark face and blackish ears, which are more prominent and rounded than those of the brown long-eared. It frequents low-lying farmland, roosting in buildings during summer, and migrates only short distances in winter – generally less than 20 km – to hibernate in caves or old mine tunnels during winter.

Leisler's Bat

Nyctalus leisleri

This vulnerable bat is rarely seen in England but is relatively common in Ireland. It lives in woodland, roosting in holes or crevices, buildings and bat boxes. The fur is light-coloured, red-brown on its back, yellow-brown underneath. Its body measures 48–68 mm, with a wingspan of 260–320 mm. It flies high and fast, making shallow dives. In autumn males establish mating roosts where each is visited by up to nine females. It migrates seasonally over longer distances than any other British bat, generally north to south.

Lesser Horseshoe Bat

Rhinolophus hipposideros

Restricted to southwest England, west Wales and the west of Ireland, this vulnerable bat is one of our smallest species: when hanging with its wings wrapped round its body, it is about the size of a plum (it measures 35–44 mm with a wingspan of 200–250 mm). It flies close to the ground – generally within five metres of it – circling over promising areas and sometimes snatching prey off branches or stones. Up to 500 bats may assemble in one winter roost in a cave, mine or cellar.

Natterer's Bat

Myotis nattereri

Widespread throughout Britain and Ireland, this vulnerable bat is very light coloured, almost white round the neck and back of the head. Its face and limbs are rather bare and pink – it is sometimes called the 'Red-armed Bat'. About 40–50 mm long with a wingspan of 250–300 mm, it inhabits open woodland and farmland, roosting in tree holes or roof spaces. In summer, females roost in large maternity and nursery colonies, with up to 200 bats in each. The creature's broad wings and tail enable it to hover while hunting, catching insects in flight or flicking them off leaves with its tail to catch them in its mouth.

Noctule Bat

Nyctalus noctula

One of our largest bats, up to 80 mm long in head and body, with tail another 4–6 cm, and a wingspan of

Wild Mammals
Bats

Grey Long-eared
Bat
Natterer's Bat

320–450 mm, the vulnerable noctule bat can be identified in flight by its size and sharply angled wings. It has glossy brown fur and roosts in holes or splits in trees, occasionally in buildings and rock crevices, often in urban surroundings. When hunting, it flies fast, straight and high – sometimes at 50 km/h and 70 metres above the ground, making sudden turns and dives, catching large insects in flight and eating them on the wing. It also gives off loud, clicking calls when airborne. In winter the sexes hibernate together in mass roosts 1000 strong, packing on top of each other like roof tiles. They can withstand very low temperatures – down to −4° C – but sometimes large numbers freeze to death.

Common Pipistrelle Bat

Pipistrellus pipistrellus

The smallest bat in Britain: with wings closed, one would fit into a matchbox. Pipistrelles are also our commonest bats, but in decline due to loss of insect-rich wetlands and hedgerows, and the use of organochlorine pesticides.

They look very dark on the head, with blackish brown nose and ears; their wing membranes are also black, but they have orange-brown backs and yellow-brown stomachs. The most urban of bats, they live happily in the roofs of housing estates on the outskirts of towns. In summer females congregate in nursery colonies, often 100 strong.

When hunting at or just above head height, twisting and diving sharply in pursuit of insects, they utter high-pitched calls which are audible to humans with good hearing, and quite different from their echolocation transmissions.

If disturbed during hibernation or their daily torpor, they sometimes feign death by lying flat on their backs with their wings folded alongside their bodies; but they tend to hibernate less than other species, and often emerge in winter if the ambient temperature rises.

The **Soprano Pipistrelle** (*Pipistrellus pygmaeus*) has only recently been identified as a separate species. **Nathusius' Pipistrelle** (*Pipistrellus nathusii*) was thought to be only a vagrant, but is now considered a rare resident breeder.

Serotine Bat

Eptesicus serotinus

One of the largest British species – 58–80 mm long and 320–380 mm wingspan – this vulnerable bat lives mostly in the roofs of houses, going in and out under the eaves or through gable ends. Its preference for lofts and roof spaces makes it vulnerable to chemical treatment of woodwork for worm, dry rot and so on. Its flight is slow and erratic, punctuated by steep dives. Serotines are often seen flying circuits round street lights or above rubbish tips. Their tails look rounded rather than wedge-shaped, their broad wings nearly straight. In winter, they hibernate singly rather than in clusters, usually in buildings, and sometimes come out to hunt if the weather turns warm.

Whiskered Bat

Myotis mystacinus

This and Brandt's bat are so similar that until 1970 they were classed as the same species. Considered vulnerable in terms of numbers, the whiskered bat has long, rough-looking fur, dark brown or grey on the back and lighter underneath. It measures 35–48 mm with a wingspan of 210–240 mm. It frequents woodland edges, gardens and parks, but is more likely to live in the roof space of a building than in a tree hole. When hunting at night with its rapid, jinking flight, it often works regular beats along hedges or the sides of woods, or low over fields and flowing water, picking insects from the air or off foliage. If disturbed, it sets up a long, shrill twittering.

Cetaceans

Cetaceans — whales, dolphins and porpoises — are mammals specially adapted to life in the sea. Like their counterparts on land, they are warm-blooded, breathe air and give birth to live young, which are suckled on their mothers' milk. Eleven species are regularly seen in British and Irish waters; some remain here throughout the year, but others migrate south in winter. In British waters all species are protected by law, and may not be killed, captured, injured or harassed. The best places for watching are the west coast of Scotland and around the Scottish islands: binoculars are essential, and a telescope still better.

Strange as it seems, whales are descended from the mesonychids (*see page 16*), the small, hoofed predators which flourished in the Palaeocene and Eocene periods, from 65 to 38 million years ago. It appears that otter-like mesonychids gradually adapted to living in the sea, and that one of them, *Pakicetus*, was among the first of the now-extinct sub-orders of early whales, the Archaeoceti.

Cetaceans' adaptations include a streamlined body which slips easily through water, and a thick layer of blubber which insulates them against cold. Their hindlegs have disappeared, and their forelegs have evolved into flippers which help them balance and steer. The fluke – a powerful tail – moves up and down horizontally (unlike a fish's tail, which swings from side to side) for propulsion, and they have hyper-efficient lungs which absorb 10 per cent of the oxygen they breathe in, as against the 4 per cent that land mammals can use. While on the surface they breathe through nostrils or blow holes set on top of their heads; underwater, they can hold their breath and compress their lungs for several minutes. Back on the surface, they force out used air through their blow holes, creating clouds of spray. To communicate, they use a complex system of moans, grunts, snores, chirps, whistles and clicks, including echolocation.

Different species feed in different ways. Baleen whales, such as the blue, minke and humpback whales, have rows of baleen or whalebone plates in their mouths, through which they strain water to catch plankton and small fish. Those with teeth – the sperm, and killer whales, dolphins and porpoises – eat fish, squid and other marine animals.

Every cetacean has a unique pattern of markings and fin-shape which allows it to be identified as an individual, much as fingerprints identify humans. Other clues to identity are the number, height and direction of the blows which different species make.

Humans have hunted whales for over a thousand years, with the Norwegians always leaders in the industry. It was they who, in 1870, invented the harpoon fired from a gun, and with the development in 1949 of an electric harpoon, which stunned or killed the target, hunting became even more efficient. In 1955–6 nearly 60,000 whales were killed, some 80 per cent of them in Antarctic waters. Products from carcasses included oil, (used as a lubricant or in soap, candles and margarine), whalebone (used by corset manufacturers and in the brush trade), meat and ambergris, a valuable ingredient of perfume.

The industry, admired for its romance and danger, but hated for its cruelty, produced one literary classic – *Moby Dick*, the novel by the American writer Herman Melville published in 1851. The eponymous hero is a huge and crafty whale who has caused so many disasters among men bent on his capture that he has become an object of superstitious terror. The book tells how the obsessive, one-legged Captain Ahab pursues Moby Dick and how, after an epic battle, the whale comes out the victor.

The International Whaling Commission was set up in 1946 to conserve stocks and regulate the whaling industry. In 1982, with stocks severely depleted, the Commission decided to set the catch-limits for all commercial whaling at zero – in other words, to suspend commercial whaling for the time being. The ban came into force for the 1985–6 season and has been upheld ever since, in spite of appeals from various countries. Norway lodged objections to the ban and exercised its right to set national limits for catching minke whales round the coast, killing several hundred each year. At its fiftieth annual meeting in 1998, the Commission called on Norway to halt all whaling operations, but its appeal was ignored. The main consumers of whale meat are still the Japanese, and the best hope of establishing effective control of whaling seems to be through CITES, the Convention for International Trade in Endangered Species.

All inshore cetaceans face the threat of pollution. Those with teeth are at the top of the food chain, and so tend to accumulate high concentrations of heavy metals such as mercury and organochlorines, some of which may be passed on from mother to calf through the wall of the placenta or in milk, and so may cause abnormalities of development, reproduction or immunity. The tissues of dolphins in British waters have been found to contain large concentrations of potentially harmful pollutants.

Whales

The eleven species of whale most often sighted around the coasts of Britain are listed below.

Blue Whale

Balaenoptera musculus

The biggest creature the world has ever known is only an occasional visitor to British waters. The longest individual reliably recorded was landed at South Georgia in 1909 and measured 33.58 metres. That monster was not weighed; but a 25-metre female, cut up and weighed piecemeal in 1948, with due allowance for blood and stomach contents, turned the scales at 134 tons; and it has been calculated that a whale of 33 metres would weigh about 160 tons – the equivalent of two *Brachiosaurus* dinosaurs.

Whales have been hunted for their meat and oil since time immemorial, and in the first half of the twentieth century blue whales were the main target of the world's whaling fleets. In 1934 alone 30,000 were caught – a third of the entire estimated population – and by 1967, when the animals received full protection, it was thought that only 600 or 700 survived. This must have been a serious under-estimate, for after that date Soviet whalers killed another 8000. Numbers in the North Atlantic are believed to have increased slightly to between 500 and 1000, but the global population is probably no more than 3500.

In summer, blue whales migrate northward to feed in cold waters, and in winter they return to subtropical ocean areas to breed. After mating in November, a female gestates for nearly a year, then gives birth to a single calf, which she suckles for six or seven months. Mature whales can swim at 50 km/h; they can live up to 80 years.

Wild Mammals
Cetaceans

Blue Whale

Fin Whale

Balaenoptera physalus

Slate-grey all over its back and sides, and white on the belly, the fin whale has the peculiarity of asymmetrical colouring on the head, its right lower 'lip' being white, in contrast with the left, which is dark grey. Males are about 21 metres long and weigh 50 tons, and females are slightly bigger: besides being very large, they are also long-lived, sometimes surviving for 90 years. The world population is estimated at 78,000. They are occasionally sighted off northern Scotland, the Outer Hebrides, Shetland and the west coast of Ireland.

The function of the irregular head colours is not clear, unless it is to break up the whale's outline and fool prey species like fish which have good vision. One theory is that as a whale advances on fish, it rolls on to its right side, so that the dark half of its face is upwards and the pale half downwards, improving its camouflage.

Humpback Whale

Megaptera novaeangliae

Two features make this whale easy to identify: first, the line of its back, which looks almost as though it is broken, dropping sharply behind the small dorsal fin; and second, its exceptionally long usually white pectoral fins (4 metres or more), which protrude downwards and backwards from the sides of its chest, and have a knobbly look, as does its head. (*Megaptera means* 'big wing' or 'big fin'.)

Considering its weight – females can reach over 30 tons and are slightly larger than males – the humpback is a great performer: every now and then it hurls most of its body out of the water, then crashes down; pokes its head up above the surface (known as 'spy hopping'), smacks the water with its tail ('lobtailing') and waves its fins. Yet these antics are not laid on to amuse human onlookers. Rather, they have the practical purpose of stunning prey species of small fish or driving them into concentrations, so that the whale can swallow hundreds in one gulp. Several whales sometimes combine forces to attack a school of fish, forcing them together by releasing streams of bubbles from beneath them.

Humpbacks migrate northwards in summer and return to tropical waters in autumn, with young whales following their mothers to learn the routes. Adult males have a complex system of communication, and some of their songs can go on for 24 hours.

Killer Whale (Orca)

Orcinus orca

Easily recognisable from its bold black-and-white colouring – black body, oval white patch behind each eye, white chin, throat and undersides of flukes, with a black dorsal fin nearly 2 metres tall – the killer whale is in fact a very big member of the dolphin family, reaching a length of about 10 metres and a weight of 5 tons. The male is twice as long as the female. The greatest concentration is in Antarctica, but killer whales are also found in the North Atlantic. Their total world population is estimated to be at least 100,000 individuals.

They live in family groups known as pods until they are fully adult. They normally dive for up to five minutes, then surface with as many as five noisy blows. Very fast swimmers – up to 55 km/h – they hunt and eat large fish, seals, other species of whale and penguins – and follow prey species for hundreds of kilometres. Their vision is good, and they have highly developed hearing and echolocation.

Minke Whale

Balaenoptera acutorostrata

The Latin specific name, meaning 'sharp-snouted', is a good clue to the appearance of the minke, which has a flattened, elongated head and a pointed nose. Another good indicator is the broad band of white angled across the pectoral fins found in northern hemisphere animals. Smallest of the baleen whales, in the North Atlantic minke males reach about 8 metres and weigh 10 tons. They got their name from an eighteenth-century Norwegian whaler called Minke, who was notorious for persistently breaking rules about size and species of the prey he hunted that all small whales came to be known as 'Minke's whales', and the name was formally adapted for this species.

They seem to migrate north and south less than other whale species, but tend to move out away from the shore into the deep ocean in the autumn. Minke is the species most likely to be seen off British coasts, especially in northwest Scotland and Ireland, either singly or in pairs.

Northern Bottle-nosed Whale

Hyperoodon ampullatus

A high, bulbous forehead and short beak protruding nearly at right angles from its base give this, the largest British member of the beaked whale family, a distinctive appearance. But even if it resembles a dolphin in profile, it is far larger, reaching a length of 9 metres and a weight of perhaps 7 tons. In colour, it is very dark on the back, ranging from chocolate to greeny brown, with lighter flanks. Its single, crescent-shaped blowhole is set in a hollow just behind its head: when it blows – once at a time – the column of water goes only 1–2 metres up, and slightly forward.

In spring and summer bottle-nosed whales migrate to the Arctic, passing west of Britain and Ireland, and return to warmer seas in autumn. If any member of a group is injured, other whales are said to take care of it.

Sperm Whale

Physeter macrocephalus

Known also as the 'Cachalot', this, the largest species of toothed whale, has a huge, blunt, barrel-shaped head which typically takes up a third of its entire length. As a male can be 20 metres long and weigh 70 tons, its head is a major feature. Its single blowhole is near the front and on the left, so that blows are angled forward at about 45 degrees and slightly to the left. Corrugations in the greybrown skin give the whole body a wrinkly, shrivelled look, and mature males often carry deep scars, probably inflicted by other males during mating fights.

Within the head is the spermaceti organ, composed of highly vascular tissue filled with a mixture of fatty oils. The function of the organ is not precisely known, but because the oils liquefy at 32°C and solidify below that temperature, it is thought that it may help provide neutral buoyancy, and contribute to the animal's system of echolocation.

Sperm whales live mainly on squid and various kinds of fish in deep water. When feeding, they typically dive for 45 minutes, then surface for 5–15 minutes, giving noisy blows every ten seconds or so. Females and young males form 'pods' about 10 strong, and these in turn form part of larger schools. Senior males live in bachelor groups, which gradually diminish as the whales grow older: the oldest of all become solitary and live alone.

During the whaling era sperm whales were caught all round the North Atlantic and the population was greatly reduced. Apart from blubber, meat and ambergris, the most valuable product was spermaceti wax, from the organ of that name in the head.

3

Wild Mammals
Cetaceans

Killer Whale
Sperm Whale

Dolphins

Short-beaked Common Dolphin

Delphinus delphis

Dolphins seem to delight in keeping boats company: for stretches of 15 or 20 minutes they gambol just ahead of the bows, turning their heads on one side and apparently grinning up at anyone watching. Doubtless it was this behaviour that gave rise to the ancient Greek legend of the dolphin which saved the life of poet Arion. It is said that when he found the crew of his ship were plotting to murder him, he struck up on his lute and jumped into the sea – whereupon a dolphin, attracted by the music, bore him safely home to Corinth. (The crew, arriving later, claimed that he had gone of his own accord; but their plot was detected and they were put to death.) People who swim with dolphins notice that although the creatures take little notice of divers cruising a few metres down, they love to frolic with humans on the surface.

Only recently have common dolphins been split into two species: the short-beaked and the very similar long-beaked common dolphin of the eastern north Pacific.

Most common dolphins are about 2 metres long and some weigh up to 110 kg. Bold colouring makes them easy to identify: they have black backs and upper flanks, with broad yellow-and-white lower sides, fading to grey towards the tail. They live on fish and can dive to great depths (almost 300 metres), staying under for as long as 8 minutes, but dives are usually much shorter, averaging 10 seconds to 2 minutes. They move about in schools, sometimes of only a dozen, sometimes of hundreds or even thousands. A female gives birth to one calf at a time, and members of her school will help to protect youngsters.

Bottlenose Dolphin

Tursiops truncatus

This is the species most often exhibited in aquaria – although all the dolphinaria in the United Kingdom and many other countries have been closed, as a result of concern at the behavioural and physiological disorders that captives develop. The bottlenose is nearly twice the length of a common dolphin, and therefore more spectacular, reaching a maximum length of 3.9 metres and weighs far more – a large individual can reach up to 650 kg. Its colour

3

Wild Mammals
Cetaceans

Short-beaked
Common Dolphin
Bottlenose Dolphin

114

is more subdued – brownish grey above, and paler below – but its short beak and protruberant jaw make it look as though the creature is grinning. Its high dorsal fin is in the middle of the back.

Behaviour appears to vary widely, but in general the animals are highly social. They usually go around in small groups of ten or fewer, although sometimes solitary individuals are seen, and they are known to hunt as a pack, herding fish into concentrations near the surface of the water. They are clearly intelligent, and enjoy associating with humans; people have taken to swimming with dolphins for a variety of therapeautic reasons, but their alleged healing powers cannot be scientifically validated.

As with all species of whales and dolphins, calves are born tail-first, so that they can swim to the surface and breathe the moment they are clear of the mother. Among bottlenose dolphins, a second female often assists at the birth; mothers are very protective of their young, which they suckle for 18 months, although they sometimes leave a calf with another adult as a babysitter while they make a long dive.

Risso's Dolphin

Grampus griseus

A blunt, rounded, beakless head coming up out of the water, is likely to be the first clue to this dolphin's identity. Its body is mainly dark brownish-grey, often heavily marked with scars, and it has a tall, sickle-shaped fin half way along its back. Its chest and belly are light grey or white. Males grow to a length of 3.8 metres and weigh up to 500 kg, females being slightly smaller.

White-beaked Dolphin

Lagenorhynchus albirostris

Over twice the weight of a common dolphin, this species is common in the North Atlantic. It may grow 2.5–2.8 metres long and weigh 180–275 kg. It has not only a short, white beak, but a white throat and belly, a white streak curving over its flank, and the black of the upper body lightens into grey behind the dorsal fin.

Atlantic White-sided Dolphin

Lagenorhynchus acutus

Similar to the white-beaked dolphin in length (1.9–2.5 metres), but slimmer (165–200 kg) and more vividly marked, with grey, white and yellow bands running back along the flanks. The eyes stand out more because they are set in dark patches against pale grey and white back-

grounds. A narrow, dark stripe runs down from each corner of the mouth to the flippers, which are black and sickle shaped, curving backwards. The tail end of the body looks rather bulbous, as it remains thick until suddenly narrowing just in front of the flukes (the two horizontal parts of which the tail consists).

Porpoises

Harbour or Common Porpoise

Phocoena phocoena

This species frequents coastal waters, especially bays and estuaries, and comes into large rivers. Harbour porpoises are quite small – less than 2 metres long, and weighing only about 60 kg. Black or dark grey on the back, and white on the belly, they have smaller fins than dolphins, and their bodies tend to look more chunky. They can sometimes be seen floating on the surface as they rest.

They are solitary creatures, or live in small bands of two, three or four, except during migration in spring and autumn, when they assemble into large groups. Their main prey is herring, which they hunt mostly at dawn and dusk, when the fish come to the surface to feed, but they also take whiting, mackerel, capelin and cod. There is thus an echo of reality behind the nonsense in Lewis Carroll's *Alice in Wonderland*:

> 'Will you walk a little faster?' said a whiting to a snail,
> 'There's a porpoise close behind us, and he's treading on
> my tail.'

Unlike dolphins, which can live for 40 years or more, porpoises have a lifespan of only 20 years or less, and a female probably produces only three or four calves in her lifetime.

Since 1960 the population in the English Channel and North Sea has fallen sharply. One reason is that many young porpoises drown when they become entangled in fishing nets, attracted by the thrashing of fish already caught, and apparently unable to detect monofilament mesh, either visually or acoustically. Another cause may have been the decline in stocks of herrings brought on by over-fishing.

Tradition held that porpoises had some power over the winds, and foretold storms by gambolling about.

Other ccasional visitors to Britain include the **Beluga Whale**, **Cuvier's Beaked Whale**, **Sei Whale**, **Sowerby's Beaked Whale** and **True's Beaked Whale** and the **Striped Dolphin**.

Seals

COMMON OR HARBOUR SEAL, *PHOCA VITULINA* (below and page 118) CONSIDERABLY SMALLER THAN THE GREY, ITS FUR IS GREY OR BROWN.

GREY SEAL, *HALICHOERUS GRYPUS* (right) GREY SEAL PUPS ARE WHITE AT BIRTH AND MAY GAIN UP TO 2 KG EACH DAY.

The Latin name '*pinnipedia*', means 'feather- or fin-footed' and applies to three families of animals: true seals, eared seals and walruses. The two true seals in Britain have webbed feet that are usually longer than the short limbs to which they are attached: on land they drag themselves forward with their front flippers, using their back flippers for propulsion in the water. Although they live primarily in the sea, and feed there, they have to give birth on land; as this exposes the young to danger, they have evolved the ability to produce rich milk, on which babies grow rapidly. Inquisitive creatures, they have a habit of suddenly bobbing up round boats in inshore waters or sea lochs and watching the occupants closely: with their bulging dark eyes and bristling whiskers, they look like maritime Labradors.

Common or Harbour Seal

Phoca vitulina

A pattern of fine, dark spots on grey or brown fur differentiates the common or harbour seal from the grey seal, which is marked with bigger blotches, and has a longer muzzle. The common is also a good deal smaller, weighing at most 130 kg – not much more than half the weight of a big grey. Pups used to be hunted for their skins, and excessive culls led to the Conservation of Seals Act (1970), which gave the species protection during their breeding season. The latest survey produced in 1995 gave them population figures of around 35,000, mostly around the coasts of Scotland.

Common seals feed in the sea, mainly on fish such as herring, sand eels and whiting, but also on crustaceans. In the water they are solitary, but they gather in huge groups when they haul out to rest on rocky shores or beaches. Their hearing and vision are both better under water than in the air.

They mate at sea during July and August, and after delayed implantation females give birth the following summer. Pups are usually born with adult colouring (not white, like grey seals): they can swim from birth, and grow very quickly on their mothers' rich milk. If danger threatens, a mother may dive into the water holding a pup in her mouth or between her front flippers. Males, in contrast, show no interest whatsoever in pups, but spend much time fighting rivals in the water.

In 1988 a severe outbreak of distemper killed 3000 common seals around England alone. The disease was known to have been caused by a virus, but its origin was uncertain. After that plague, seals were given year-round legal protection.

Grey Seal

Halichoerus grypus

Grey seals are hefty creatures, males reaching a length of up to 250 cm and a weight of 250 kg or more. With their bulbous eyes and wrinkled but scarcely indented necks – heads running straight into bodies – they are no beauties, but hardly as hideous as their scientific name ('hook-nosed little sea pig') suggests. They live mostly round rocky northern and western coasts, spending about two-thirds of their time hunting and feeding in the sea; between tides they haul out onto rocks or secluded beaches, usually on islands.

They are greatly detested by game fishermen, as one of their favourite foods is salmon, and they congregate off estuaries when salmon are running into the rivers from the sea. Not only does each seal eat 5–6 kg of food every day: it is also a wasteful feeder, often taking one large bite out of a fish and letting the rest go to waste.

Seals damage the cages in which salmon are artificially

reared on farms, releasing valuable stock, and they are especially destructive when wild salmon are already caught in nets – but it may be that they do the worst damage of all when smolts – young salmon – are about to go to sea for the first time. For several weeks the smolts gather in the estuary, as if waiting to make sure that all their number are present, before they push out into the deep, and the predators cut through the shoals, eating huge numbers. Recent research has shown that they also eat sand eels in large quantities.

Seals are protected to some extent by a close season from 1 September to 31 December; but they may be shot with suitably high-powered rifles in the open season, and if they are causing an excessive nuisance, fishery owners and managers can obtain licences to cull them in the close season as well. Some operators pay bounties of up to £25 per tail to professional hunters.

In spite of disease and sporadic culling, between 1960 and 2000 the number of grey seals in British waters doubled to nearly 100,000 – a figure which amounts to half the world population of grey seals. This species somehow escaped the worst effects of the distemper plague that killed many common seals in 1988: of the 3000 animals found dead, only 300 were greys. Their colonies are often very large, running into thousands of individuals. For instance, on the Farne Islands off the Northumberland coast, the gathering numbers between 3000 and 4000, and sheer weight of use has led to much erosion of the soil. In breeding sites, known as rookeries, mortality is high, partly because both bulls and cows are extremely aggressive.

Pups are born above the high-tide mark, generally between September (in West Wales) and December (in the Farne Islands). They weigh about 14 kg at birth, and for the first two weeks of life their fur is white; they grow fast on their mothers' rich milk, which contains up to 60 per cent fat, putting on about 2 kg a day, building up a thick layer of blubber beneath their skins – essential insulation when they take to the sea. But many of them are lost during their first three weeks, either because they are abandoned and starve, or because they are trampled to death or washed off the rocks into the sea. Infant mortality of 20 per cent is common, but it may be as much as 80 per cent in some localities. Rookeries are noisy places, since females howl at each other, pups cry like human babies, and bulls give out low-frequency grunts like the noise of steam trains. Male grey seals live for 25 years and females up to 45 years, although 35 is more typical.

3

Wild Mammals
Seals

Grey Seal

4 HORSES

The horse's most distant ancestor, *Hyracotherium*, was so unequine in most respects that when its fossil bones were found in London clay in 1839, they were mistaken for those of a hyrax, a rabbit-like animal the size of a dog. Its brain, teeth, limbs and feet were quite unlike those of a horse; with four toes on its front feet and three on the back, it walked on the pads of its feet, using its little hooves only for pushing off when it started to run. Yet later, when its true place in evolution was discerned, it was renamed *Eohippus* or Dawn Horse. Fifty million more years of evolution were needed to turn it into modern *Equus*, via several intermediary stages.

Modern horses are undoubtedly descended from wild horses, but experts differ as to whether their direct ancestors were Przewalski-type animals, like those depicted in the cave-paintings at Lascaux and elsewhere in Europe, or Tarpans, which originated in southern Russia, were once widely distributed in Europe, and survived in the Ukraine until the middle of the nineteenth century. Przewalski's horses (*see page 144*) were, and are, between 12 and 14 hands high, a yellow-dun colour on the back, with lighter sides and belly, and have stiff, upright manes (a hand is 10 cm or 4 inches). Tarpans (*see page 27*) were smaller, and mouse-grey, also with upright manes, but with a dark stripe along the back from neck to tail.

Whatever the precise relationship of the two, wild horses were hunted for their meat thousands of years before man domesticated them. Fossil remains found in caves consist mainly of limb bones split to extract the marrow, and skulls similarly opened to get at the brain, but very few backbones or ribs – which shows that the hunters hacked the legs and heads off their victims and carried them back to base, rather than try to drag the whole carcass.

Domestication of the horse is thought to have begun

121

MARES AND FOALS IN A RIVER LAND-
SCAPE (previous pages) OIL PAINTING
BY GEORGE STUBBS 1724–1806.

JARDINE'S TARPAN HORSE (below)
ENGRAVING PUBLISHED IN THE
NATURALISTS LIBRARY SERIES, 1841.

NORMAN CAVALRY AT HASTINGS
(bottom) DETAIL FROM THE BAYEAUX
TAPESTRY c.ELEVENTH CENTURY.

ORNAMENT IN THE FORM OF A
HORSE'S HEAD (right) CELTIC FIRST-
CENTURY AD BRONZE (11 CM).

THE TARPAN. WILD HORSE. Native of Russia.
primeval bay stock.

about 3000 BC in the Far East; but it seems unlikely that tame horses reached Britain until the second century BC, when the Belgae crossed the Channel, bringing animals which they rode bareback, and chariots. It was these aggressive people who attacked Julius Caesar's troops during his two invasions of Britain in 55 and 54 BC: the Roman commander was impressed by the tribesmen's horsemanship, and by the degree of control which they had instilled into their mounts:

> In cavalry battles they often dismount and fight on foot, training the horses to stand perfectly still so that they can quickly get back to them in case of need. In their eyes it is the height of effeminacy and shame to use a saddle, and they do not hesitate to engage the largest force of cavalry riding saddled horses, however small their own numbers.

Caesar described how the British would begin a battle by driving their chariots all over the field, hurling javelins: 'Generally the terror inspired by their horses and the noise of the wheels is sufficient to throw their opponents' ranks into disorder.' They achieved their expertise by daily practice, attaining such proficiency that, having jumped down to fight on foot, while their drivers waited to pick them up, they could 'run along the chariot pole, stand on the yoke and get back into the chariot as quick as lightning'.

When the Romans occupied Britain a hundred years later, it was often the home cavalry and charioteers who caused them most trouble – and no individual harassed them more effectively than Boadicea, the hard-driving queen of the Iceni tribe, who led a major revolt in 61 AD. Having massacred the Roman garrisons at St Albans and Colchester, her forces devastated London before being almost annihilated in a battle with the army of Suetonius Paulinus – whereupon the warrior queen ended her own life by taking poison.

Boadicea's horses seem to have been very small – and so, to judge from the Bayeux Tapestry (below), were the animals on which William the Conqueror's cavalry rode to victory in the conquest of 1066: in the long string of horses depicted, some of the knights' feet almost touch the ground. These warriors are lightly armoured in chain mail helmets and body-suits; but their mounts have no protection, and over the next century, as the technology of bows and arrows improved, giving archers greater range, it became expedient to armour the horses as well.

This meant that bigger, stronger animals were needed, and led to the importation of *destriers* – heavy horses with thick legs and shaggy fetlocks – from the Low Countries (*see illustration on page 124*). By the time a big horse, like its rider, was fully armoured, it was carrying a load of at least 200 kg and could only lumber along, in danger of becoming bogged whenever it crossed soft ground. It was these same heavy horses that Crusader knights rode to the Middle East during the eleventh and twelfth centuries.

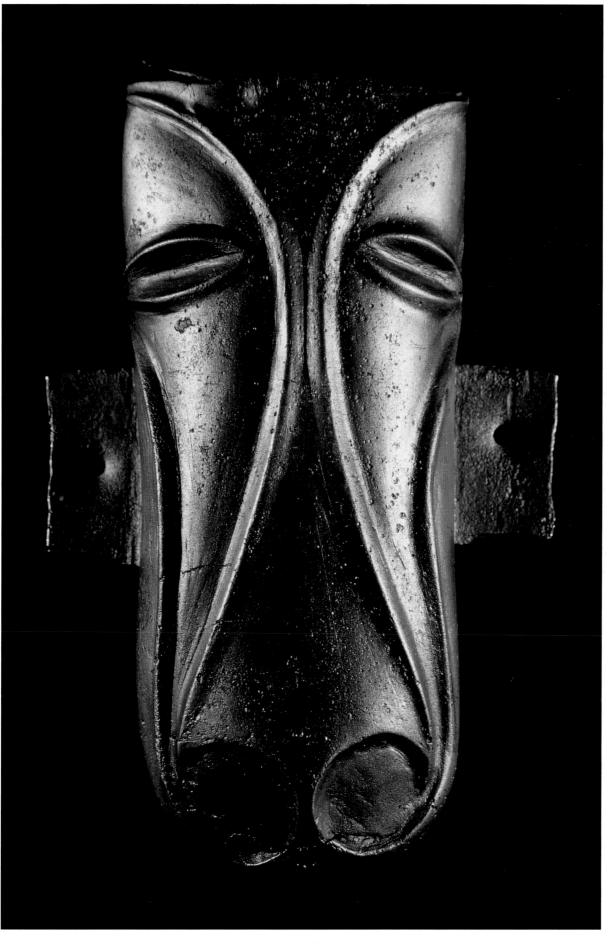

4

Horses

Equus

poiloit eſtoit la aie le roy nagauement, et il avoit nom teſtu enfant avnoulz ſauz faull tout ce eſtoit bon. Et quant il ot la thoſe ap pauſee il retouona a ſa femme. Et ſinent les fais du roy lors le biaul fik charles le chauf.

Soldiers needed powerful, young horses, and when their mounts became too old for active service, they sold them off to farmers for ploughing and transport. In those days breeders did not castrate their stallions – partly because they hoped to sell them for war-horses – and the result was a great deal of indiscriminate mating.

This tended to produce mediocre animals, and in efforts to raise standards the medieval kings from time to time brought over heavy stallions from Europe. In about 1200 King John imported 100 black Flemish stallions, and a few years after the Battle of Bannockburn in 1314, when huge numbers of horses were killed, falling into the camouflaged pits dug by the army of Robert the Bruce, Edward III arranged for another large consignment to be sent from Europe. As a result of that military disaster, horses became so scarce in England that their export was banned, and the prohibition was extended by a series of Acts until the reign of Henry VIII.

At the Battle of Bosworth Field near Leicester, on 22 August 1485, the final encounter in the Wars of the Roses, the loss of his mount proved fatal for Richard III. 'A horse! A horse! My kingdom for a horse!' he roars in Shakespeare's play, as he is about to be struck down by the Lancastrian Earl of Richmond, later Henry VII.

Around that time it was widely believed that the phases of the moon had a strong influence on mating, and could determine the sex of a foal. Many owners were convinced that only by having their mares mated when the moon was waxing or waning could they get a colt. This superstition was roundly debunked by Anthony Fitzherbert, a Derbyshire farmer who dismissed it as nonsense in his *Boke of Husbandry* published in 1523, but it persisted nevertheless. For centuries before that, horses had been fertility symbols, of great importance to the harvest, and the hobby-horses that still take part in May Day ceremonies echo the tradition.

In Britain the mounted knights, drawn from the ranks of the nobility and leading landed families, became for a while the most potent force on any battlefield. Yet their supremacy was ended by the invention of gunpowder early in the fourteenth century, and even though some later cavalry regiments considered it more dashing to charge bearing only drawn swords or lances, most took to carrying loaded firearms which they could discharge as soon as they came in range.

Firearms notwithstanding, during the seventeenth century numerous cavalry regiments were created – dragoons, hussars and lancers. (The word 'dragoon' came from the French *dragon*, first applied to a cavalryman trained to fight on foot. 'Hussar' derived from the Hungarian *husz*, meaning 20, since every twentieth household was once required to furnish a man for the cavalry; and lancer regiments were armed with lances.) Several of the units were created by wealthy private individuals – for instance the Seventh Dragoon Guards, raised in 1689 by the Duke of Devonshire; and many distinguished themselves overseas – in the Peninsula War, at Waterloo, in the Crimea, India, the Sudan and South Africa. But the first few battles of First World War showed that riders charging on horses were no match for modern weapons such as machine guns, and over the next few years the cavalry regiments converted to armoured-car or tank units, many merging with each other.

Appalling numbers of horses were lost in cavalry campaigns: 30,000 during the French retreat from Moscow in 1812, 256,000 by the British alone on the Western Front in 1914–18. It was largely the plight of horses in the Boer War of 1899–1902, and in the First World War, that led to the establishment of the organisation now known as the Blue Cross. Formed in 1897 as Our Dumb Friends' League, the charity became famous for its work treating horses wounded on the battlefields – the Blue Cross for animals being the equivalent of the Red Cross for humans.

Today, the only British survivors of the glorious but doomed company of mounted warriors are the King's Troop of the Royal Horse Artillery, whose animals pull gun carriages on ceremonial occasions, and the Household Cavalry Mounted Regiment, drawn from the two units of the Household Cavalry, the Life Guards and the Blues & Royals. In campaigns like the Falklands, the Gulf, Bosnia and Kosovo, the Household Cavalry has been at the forefront in its armoured fighting vehicles; but more familiar to the public is its special role in providing a personal bodyguard for the Queen on State occasions like the opening of Parliament, when members of the Mounted Regiment escort the Sovereign through London on their black horses, splendidly arrayed in plumed helmets and gleaming breastplates. Police forces around the country also maintain a considerable number of horses, mainly for purposes of crowd control.

Just as, for hundreds of years horses formed an indispensable element of any military force, so in civilian life they remained the principal means of travel and transport. In the countryside they were the only method (except walking) of moving from one isolated community to another. When the admirable roads left by the Romans eventually fell into decay, there were no easy routes: in wet weather such roads as existed became quagmires, and the only way for a rider or packhorse to make progress was to deviate more and more widely from the central track, cutting across cultivated fields if necessary, so that the road became 50 or more metres wide.

By the middle of the seventeenth century, in spite of the difficulties, post-horses and chaises were travelling swiftly the length and breadth of the country. Every town had at least one posting house, an inn at which horses were stabled and vehicles kept, and there was a constant passage, day and night, of travellers moving through, all needing transport for the next stage of their journey. A big inn would have stabling for 50 or 60 post-horses, which pulled the light post-chaises in pairs, and the same number for coaches.

Noblemen, also, kept huge stables. When the Duke of Devonshire drove to Doncaster races in 1827, he travelled in his coach-and-six accompanied by 12 outriders. To employ 18 horses on such a journey, at that date, was pure show. Earlier, outriders had furnished useful protection against highwaymen, and they had also acted as couriers, hurrying on ahead to book accommodation at hostelries or pay tolls in advance, so that their masters could pass through the gates without delay. A large family, making its seasonal move from one country home to another, might easily take half a dozen vehicles and 50 horses with it.

In the heyday of stagecoaches – the early nineteenth century – leading operators needed huge numbers of

4

Horses
Equus

animals to maintain fast services. William Chaplin, who worked out of five yards in London, owned 1300 horses, and so swiftly were they worn out that a third of them had to be replaced every year. At the main coaching centres on the outskirts of London, where teams were changed, extensive equine accommodation was needed. The depot at Hounslow, on the junction of the Gloucester, Bath and Exeter roads, had stabling for 2500.

RACING

It is impossible to say when the first horserace was held in Britain; but many historians date organised racing back to the reign of James I, who was addicted to field sports of all kinds, and supervised the drafting of a code of rules. By 1612 private matches between gentlemen riding their own horses had become common, and important races were known as 'bell courses', because the winner was presented with a bell.

The sport was well established by the time of the Civil War in 1648, when, according to the Earl of Clarendon, a group of Royalists met on the Downs at Epsom 'under pretence of a horse-race, intending to cause a diversion on the King's behalf'. Clearly, racing was common by then – and after the Restoration in 1660 Charles II's personal enthusiasm did much to foster competition.

No doubt some Arab blood had already found its way into British blood-lines by that date; but all present British thoroughbreds trace their descent from three foundation sires, which were imported during the late seventeenth and early eighteenth centuries.

The Byerley Turk was acquired after the defeat of the Turks outside the walls of Vienna in 1683 by Captain Byerley, who used him as a charger at the Battle of the Boyne in Ireland in 1690, and later retired him to stud in Yorkshire. The Darley Arabian was a good-looking bay colt of excellent pedigree, about 15 hands, bought in the Syrian desert in 1701 by Thomas Darley, a merchant living in Aleppo. Darley was clearly aware of the horse's unusual looks, with three white socks and a large white blaze down its face, for he wrote to his brother, who had a stud in Yorkshire, saying that he hoped the horse would not be 'too much disliked' in England.

The sale had barely been completed when the treacherous sheikh who owned the horse gave orders that his prize stallion was not to be removed from the royal stables, on pain of death. However, the Consul persuaded some sailors from a British man o'war to row ashore at night, overpower the stable guard and return to their ship with the prize. In vain the sheikh wrote to Queen Anne complaining that 'my incomparable Arabian is worth more than a King's ransom, and he was foully stolen from me by your subjects.'

From the stud in Yorkshire, which he reached in 1704, the Darley Arabian sired numerous winners, among them the outstanding Whistlejacket and Flying Childers. His great-great-grandson Eclipse was one of the most successful horses ever seen on the English turf – not only never beaten, but never even extended, and himself the sire of 335 winners.

The Godolphin Barb or Arabian, described as 'an ugly little horse with lop ears and a vile temper', was one of eight presented to Louis XV of France by the Bey of Tunis (Barbs came from Barbary, the northwest corner of Africa). The stallion was so miserable-looking and vicious that he passed from one owner to another, and finished up hauling a cart for a wood merchant in Paris. In 1729 he was rescued by an English visitor, Edward Coke, who took him

back to his stud in Derbyshire, where he became known as the Paris Barb and founded a line that has included many celebrated horses, not least the American champion Man O'War.

The first Derby was held at Epsom on 4 May 1780. There were nine starters, and the winner, a chestnut colt called Diomed, carried off a prize of 1075 guineas. The race has been run every year since, and today is the most valuable event of the season, worth £1 million to the winner. One of its most spectacular moments occurred in 1913 when the suffragette Emily Davison threw herself out from the railings at Tattenham Corner and brought down King George V's Anmer: the horse and its jockey escaped serious injury, and luckily they were near the tail of the field, so that they did not fell anybody else; but Miss Davison's skull was fractured, and she died in hospital the following Sunday.

The winner of the 1981 race – Shergar – became still more famous when, after two years at stud, he was kidnapped in 1983, allegedly by the IRA. A ransom of £3.9 million was demanded from the stallion's owner, the Aga Khan, but word came out that the horse had been killed within hours of being stolen. Persistent rumour claims that Shergar mated with a female donkey that was put in his field to keep him company, and sired a hinny.

Steeplechasing – originally riding hell-for-leather across country from one church steeple to another – gradually developed into racing over fences. Easily the best-known of today's steeplechases is the Grand National, still held at Aintree in Lancashire, where 17 horses and riders first lined up for a race of 'four miles across country' in 1839. The rules on that occasion specified that no jockey might open a gate or ride for more than 100 yards along any road, path or driftway; and one of the obstacles, Becher's Brook, received the name it bears to this day, when Captain Martin Becher was catapulted off his mount into a stream and came out saying that he had never known how dreadful water tasted without the benefit of whisky.

Today the Grand National attracts worldwide interest, and in 2001 nearly ten million people watched the race live on television in Britain alone. Of all the horses that have triumphed at Aintree, none is more famous than the diminutive Red Rum, whose unique achievement was to win the gruelling contest three times, in 1973, 1974 and 1977, besides coming second in 1975 and 1976. This legend is buried beside the winning-post at Aintree.

Racing has become very big business in Britain. Under the auspices of the British Horseracing Board, which in 1993 took over from the Jockey Club as the governing authority, some 78,000 runners competed at 1142 meetings in the year 2000. The country's 59 racecourses range from Perth in the far north to Newton Abbot in the south, from Great Yarmouth in the east to Ayr in the West; and racing, together with breeding, supports some 60,000 jobs around the country.

More than 9000 active owners have 14,000 horses in training, each one costing an average of £16,000 a year in training fees, feed, stable wages, veterinary and shoeing expenses, transport to and from meetings, entry fees and jockeys' remuneration. Of course everyone hopes to produce winners, and there is plenty to be won: prize-money totals £80 million a year. During the past 20 years Arab owners have increasingly dominated the British racing scene – a fitting state of affairs, considering that every thoroughbred on the course derives ultimately from Arabian stock.

Sales are still conducted in guineas (one guinea was £1 1s, or £1.05 in modern terms), and a promising young thoroughbred can cost anything from a few thousand guineas to a few hundred thousand. Many people spread the expense by forming syndicates and each owning a share of the same animal. On its cheerful website, which encourages everyone to have a go, the British Horseracing Board illustrates the success of some 'notable purchases' – from Papillon, who was bought at Doncaster sales for 5300 guineas, went on to win the Grand National, and by 2001 had earned £393,378 in prize money, to the famous Irish hurdler Istabraq, who was much more expensive as a colt (£38,000 guineas at Tattersalls) but became the Champion Hurdler and by 2001 had won £1,027,175 in prizes.

The highest-earning stallion of all time is Sadler's Wells, who was foaled in 1981 and 21 years later is still standing in rude health at Coolmore Stud, in County Tipperary. Although he won only six of his eleven races, his breeding success proved second to none. By the time his son Galileo had won the 2001 Derby, Sadler's Wells' stud fee had risen to £200,000 – and in 2000 he covered 196 mares, so that his stud fees for that year alone amounted to more than £30 million.

The number of people who go racing each year (about 5 million in 2000) is far out-numbered by those who watch horseracing on television. From the Queen down, women show keen interest: some 40 per cent of racegoers and 38 per cent of terrestrial television viewers are female. A huge amount of money is spent on betting every year – some £7 billion off-course, and £94 million with the Tote on-course.

HORSE TRIALS

Also known as 'eventing' or 'combined training,' horse trials evolved from the military exercises practised in the cavalry schools of Europe. The sport has three phases – dressage, cross-country and show-jumping. All three are held on the same day in one-day events, but more demanding competitions extend over three days, with dressage on the first, a test of speed and endurance on the second, and show-jumping on the third.

In dressage, the rider teaches the horse to perform extremely precise movements, giving the animal aids with hands, seat and legs to make it go forwards, backwards, sideways and at various other angles, at the same time changing its gait – for instance to an extended trot – in response to signals. The movements, which derived ultimately from the need for bodies of cavalry to manoeuvre in tight formation during battle, demand a high degree of concentration from rider and horse alike.

Speed and endurance tests consist of a ride along roads and tracks – about 13 km – and a cross-country course of 6.8 km, with 30 or more varied obstacles – fences, walls and ditches – to be jumped along the way. Three-day events also include a steeplechase – a 3.5-km race over regulation steeplechase fences, round a figure-of-eight course, which is held between two sections of roads and tracks. Show-jumping takes place in an arena, over fences which fall down easily if touched. There are generally two rounds: in the first, the riders' aim is to complete the circuit without making a mistake, and speed is unimportant; but in the second, speed is crucial, as time may be the factor which decides between riders who have had clear rounds.

The three-day event first appeared at the Olympic Games of 1912 in Stockholm, and the first British event took place at Badminton, the Duke of Beaufort's estate in Gloucester-shire in 1949, when the organisers boldly described it as the greatest event in the equine world. That year there were only 22 entrants; but today Badminton attracts over 80 top-class riders and horses from 20 or more countries, who compete for a first prize of £30,000. Purists pine for the informality of the old days, when the Queen and other members of the royal family used to sit among the spectators on straw-bales; but the event has now become so large that such informality is no longer possible, for Badminton draws a crowd of 250,000, one of the biggest such gatherings in the world. Other leading three-day events are held at Burghley, Bramham, Blenheim and Windsor.

POLO

The first recorded game took place in 600 BC, when a team of Turkomans beat a team of Persians. In the fourth century AD King Sapoor II of Persia learned to play at the age of seven, and the game evidently flourished in his country during the sixteenth century. By then the Mughuls had adopted polo farther east, and the Emperor Babur established it in India.

In the 1850s British tea-planters discovered the game, and formed the first polo club in the world, at Silchar, west of Manipur. The oldest surviving club, the Calcutta, was founded in 1862. Six years later the game took root in Malta, where British army and naval officers called on their way home from India; then Edward 'Chicken' Hartopp of the Tenth Hussars read an account of polo in the Field, and was so enthused that together with some brother-officers he organised the first match in England, known as 'hockey on horseback', and played on a hastily rolled area of Hounslow Heath.

The new sport quickly spread to other countries – to Argentina in 1875, to America and Australia in 1876. Handicaps were introduced by United States players in 1910, a practice soon followed in England and India. Today polo is played in nearly 80 countries. From 1900 to 1939 it was an Olympic sport, and it has now been recognised as such again. In Britain the governing body is the Hurlingham Polo Association, which was founded in 1874.

The game – the fastest ball-sport in the world – is played on a field 300 yards long and 160 wide (more than double the dimensions of a football pitch) between two teams of four. A game consists of between four and six chukkas,

each seven minutes long. The riders' aim
is to hit the ball between the goalposts at
either end, and every time a goal is scored,
the teams change ends. There are usually
two mounted umpires on the field, and a
referee on the sideline. The pace is so fast
that in a normal game each rider needs at
least two horses.

RIDING TODAY

A survey conducted by the British
Equestrian Trade Association in 1998
suggested that the number of horses in
Britain had risen rapidly over the past few
years to a total of nearly one million. Casual
observation certainly backed up the idea
that there had been a sharp increase: as
farmers felt less pressure to grow food,
more acres were given over to horsiculture.
Especially in the Home Counties, there was
a proliferation of paddocks beaten down
to seas of mud and dotted with brightly
striped obstacles for ponies to jump.

According to the British Horse Society
(BHS), about 65,000 animals are owned
professionally for racing, eventing, polo,
use in riding schools and so on; but the vast
majority are in private hands. More and more people are
keeping horses of their own, and there is also an unprece-
dented demand for livery stables, which board animals as
paying guests. In spite of the high charges levied – up to
£90 per week – the BHS and its website are besieged by
callers seeking equine accommodation. It is thought that
some three million people ride for pleasure, and a work-
force of 125,000 (75 per cent female) supports the industry.

One particularly vigorous body is the Pony Club, the
international youth organisation founded in England in
1929 and now represented in 15 countries, with a total
membership of over 100,000 – the largest association of
riders in the world. The club's 360 UK branches organise
full programmes of rallies and competitions, culminating
in annual summer camps, the aim being to encourage
young people to learn all kinds of equine sports, including
show-jumping, dressage and polo, and to look after their
animals properly.

Most Pony Clubbers grow up into responsible owners.
Yet there is another side to this coin. Owners frequently
ring the BHS to say that a horse is no longer rideable, and
ask if the society will take it over. The answer is always
'No': callers are told that if they cannot afford to keep the
animal, the best course is to have it put down.

Many people, however, take the cowardly, cheaper
option of dumping the unwanted animal in some stranger's
field, along with a horse already in residence – and this
abdication of responsibility throws a heavy burden on the
country's numerous horse sanctuaries, all of which are
running at capacity. One of the largest, Redwings, looks
after more than 1000 superannuated horses, donkeys and
ponies on its farms in Norfolk. The sanctuary has the use
of 400 hectares of land, most of which it owns, a paid staff
of 180 and an annual budget of £5 million, all of which
comes from volunteer supporters and legacies. Well-
organised though it is, the place cannot possibly take all
the animals offered it: the organisation receives 2000
requests a year, and, painful as it is, has to turn people
away all the time.

Many of the horses that do come to the sanctuary are
identified by its 108 equine welfare officers – all unpaid
volunteers – spread across Britain. Almost every day a
call comes from a member of the public who has seen an
animal that looks in bad shape, and although two thirds of
the alarms turn out to be false, the remaining third often
bring to light cases of neglect or cruelty. Some owners,
when confronted by a welfare officer, are grateful for help
and glad to hand the horse over, because they realise they

cannot look after it adequately themselves. Most, however, are initially hostile and resent the intrusion. If there seems to be a case for prosecution, the welfare officer calls in the RSPCA.

Horse-lovers though they may be, British people in general are not impressive in the way they look after their charges. Only 57,000 belong to the BHS – a tiny proportion of owners – and if double that number joined up, the Society would be able to mount far more effective campaigns on such key matters as the prevention of accidents on roads.

Riding for the Disabled

Early in the 1960s independent groups began to offer riding as a form of therapy for disabled people, and in 1969 the Riding for the Disabled Association was formed as a registered charity. Five years later the organisation recognised the benefits of carriage driving, and made that another of its activities. Today, with HRH the Princess Royal as its enthusiastic president, the RDA is a federation of almost 650 member groups spread through Britain and Northern Ireland, run by more than 14,000 committed volunteers, who give up their time and energy to provide half a million rides and drives a year. Group members own some 4000 ponies and donkeys.

Instructors work closely with physiotherapists and other health professionals to encourage every individual to aim for realistic goals, and ensure that all riders and drivers receive a high standard of tuition tailored to their personal capabilities. For most of those who take part, the activity is enormously rewarding, in psychological as well as physical terms. The mere fact of sitting on the back of a horse means that someone normally confined to a wheelchair is raised to a new height above the ground, and so gains a fresh outlook on life, besides a feeling of independence.

It is also beneficial for riders or drivers to spend time with different people, in rural surroundings, away from institutional life. Especially during the holidays which the RDA organises, they feel a new freedom, and derive great satisfaction from being more or less in control of large animals. Physical contact is also important: to groom or feed a horse or donkey makes a child feel that, for once, it is not being helped, but rather is helping another creature.

Logging

In recent years there has been a return to the practice of using horses to extract timber from forests on steep or fragile terrain. The advantage of animals is that they can manoeuvre in confined spaces, and their hooves cut up the ground much less than heavy machines. Equipped with a Norwegian device known as an arch, which has steel shafts and a hooped arch with four small winches ranged along

it, so that the front ends of logs can be lifted clear of the ground, even a medium-sized animal can drag out ten tons of wood in a day and pull it to a roadside site for loading onto lorries.

The British Horse Loggers' Group now has over 100 members. Most are keen amateurs, who keep their own animals and work in the woods during their spare time; but grants from various sources have enabled them to restart management of woods that have lain derelict for generations. It is estimated that 70 per cent of traditional hardwoods in Wales have been abandoned as uneconomic for as long as anyone can remember; but now, with ecological awareness growing fast, and horses back on the scene, activity has resumed in many places.

Horseshoes

Since time immemorial a horseshoe has been regarded as a symbol of luck. Nailed over the doorway of a house, it kept evil at bay and brought good fortune to the occupants – although opinion differed as to which way up the shoe should be (some said that if the points were downward, luck would run out). It was also good fortune to find a horseshoe lying in the road, and the correct procedure, in this happy event, was well-known: the finder should pick the shoe up, spit on it, make a wish and throw it away over his left shoulder without looking back. The antiquarian John Aubrey confirmed that a shoe found in the highway was effective 'against the mischiefe or power of Witches'.

Veterinary Practice

It is scarcely an exaggeration to say that the entire veterinary profession was founded by a horse – the great Eclipse, who was never beaten on the racecourse. When he died in 1789, at the age of 25, his record seemed so remarkable that a decision was taken to hold a post-mortem examination, not only to ascertain the cause of death, but also, if possible, to determine the physical origins of his exceptional performance. At that date there was no veterinary school in Britain, and the only qualified vet in England was a Frenchman, Charles Benoit Vial de St Bel, who was invited to examine the body.

He duly did so – rather as Soviet surgeons dissected the brain of Lenin in the 1920s, trying to discover the source of his revolutionary genius –and published his findings. Yet St Bel's purpose in crossing the Channel had not been to carry out post-mortems: rather, he came in order to establish a veterinary school in England – and he found allies in the enlightened gentlemen of the Odiham Agricultural Society, who for some time had been seeking ways to improve animal husbandry. In May 1790 they formed a committee in London, and there St Bel met one of their

ARABIAN STALLION (below) LIGHTLY
BUILT AND OF MEDIUM SIZE, ARABS
ARE AMONG THE OLDEST BREED OF
HORSE IN THE WORLD.

CLYDESDALE MARE LUCINDA, 1939
(right) THE BREED'S AGILITY AND
STRENGTH MAKES IT IDEAL FOR
WORK 0N STEEP TERRAIN.

members, Granville Penn, grandson of William Penn, founder of Pennsylvania. In 1791, as a result of their deliberations, the Veterinary College, London, was set up in Camden Town, and on 4 January 1792 four students began a three-year course.

LEADING BREEDS

Appalloosa

The name Appalloosa is a corruption of the term used to describe the spotted horses bred by the Palouse Indians in North America; but because similar animals are depicted in cave drawings in Southern France that date from 20,000 BC, it is believed that the their origins were in Europe, and that some were taken across the Atlantic by the Conquistadores in the sixteenth century. Others may have swum ashore in Britain and Ireland from wrecked ships of the Spanish Armada: spotted horses appear in early manuscripts, and Charles II had a strangely marked grey with red on its rump, which caused it to be named 'Bloody Buttocks'. At the beginning of the twentieth century horses in American travelling circuses brought fresh blood to English and Irish strains.

The aim of the British Appalloosa Society is to create a pure breed from what it calls the 'cocktail' of spotted horses deriving from various sources. Stallions are now licenced, and only animals of a high standard are allowed to go forward for breeding purposes. In the Society's words, 'inconstancies in type and quality of the foundation stock are gradually being smoothed away to produce a superior riding horse'.'

Arab

The Arabian horse is claimed to be the oldest breed in the world – and it is certainly one of the most attractive. Its most obvious characteristic is its dished face: in profile, it has a bend or hollow at the base of the forehead and above the nose. Large eyes, a fine muzzle, an arched neck and a habit of carrying the tail high all contribute to its elegant appearance. Arabs are lightly built and of medium size, averaging 15 hands.

They originated in the Middle East,

where tribesmen, using them for warfare, depended on animals which would carry them fast across open desert with little food or water. Tribal families kept the breeding of their horses secret, but all sought much the same qualities of excellence and purity. Apart from the three foundation sires (*see page 126*), the vogue for bringing pure-bred Arabians to England started in 1881, when Wilfred and Lady Anne Blunt travelled through Arabia, befriended tribesmen and chose the best bloodlines, to import 29 mares and stallions.

The Arab Horse Society was founded in 1918 to promote breeding and importation. A registered charity, the Society now arranges its own programme of racing, and holds some 15 meetings a year.

Hackney

The name 'hackney' comes from the old French word *haquenée*, which described a type of horse with a comfortable trot or amble, and over the years the term has become synonymous with an animal whose special pace is the trot. The breed was highly esteemed by Henry VIII, who penalised anyone exporting an animal without authority, and during his reign hackneys were much used as light cavalry horses.

In the north of the country, Yorkshire particularly, the horses were known as 'nags'. Crossing with Arab blood during the eighteenth century refined the breed, and hackneys, which showed exceptional stamina and soundness, were widely used as coaching animals. Road races also became popular, with heavy bets being placed. As horse-drawn vehicles became more elaborate during the Regency period, more and more well-to-do owners wanted flashy

carriage-horses – and so evolved the modern hackney, with its high-stepping knee action. The celebrated mare Nonpareil is said to have trotted 160 km in just under ten hours, and on 10 June 1895 another mare, called Lady Combermere, established a record by trotting 31 km in an hour.

The Hackney Horse Society was founded in 1883, and today the animals are much in demand for show-jumping and carriage-driving.

Irish Draught

This breed, developed over the centuries by farmers in Ireland, is not, as its name suggests, a ponderous draught horse in the sense generally understood in Britain. Rather, it is usually crossed with thoroughbreds to produce a multi-purpose animal, good for riding, driving and light farm work. A great many top-class competition horses have Irish draught in their pedigrees, and Ireland has long been recognised as an excellent source of high-class hunters.

HEAVY HORSES

Cleveland Bay

Now much prized for dressage, the Cleveland bay was selectively bred for harness work by crossing pack-ponies with heavy horses and then introducing thoroughbred blood into the mix. Since publication of the breed stud book in 1884, no extraneous blood has been admitted: all

animals must be bay with black points, the only white permitted being a small star on the forehead.

Clydesdale

These heavy draught horses were developed in Scotland by crossing imported Flemish stallions with the old, pack-horse type of mare used in the Clyde Valley. The breed was established in Lanarkshire during the eighteenth century. Stallions grow to a height of 17.2 hands, but the Clydesdale is not as massive as the Shire, and its combination of agility and strength makes it ideal for work on steep terrain, particularly in forests. Clydesdales are bay, brown or black – but hardly ever grey – with much white on legs and face. Their lower legs grow long hair known as 'feather', which looks good in the show ring, and gives good protection on wet or muddy ground.

In 2001 the only British farmer still relying exclusively on horse-power was John Dodd of Sillywrae Farm in Northumberland, who was still working his 80 hectares with a team of five Clydesdales.

Shire

The biggest and most powerful English heavy horse, standing up to 19 hands high, the shire was selectively bred from the sluggish black horse of the Midlands and smaller, more active types of horse. Long association with humans has made these gentle giants exceptionally amenable and easy to handle; but the rapid advance of mechanisation on farms after the Second World War put most of them out of a job, and the breed fell to a low ebb. Shires are now used

mainly by breweries for promotional purposes and to pull their drays on short delivery rounds; in cities, on routes of 15–20 km they are reckoned more cost-effective than mechanised vehicles, due to heavy traffic congestion. A few still work on farms, and some take part in organised ploughing competitions.

Suffolk

Traditionally always chesnut coloured – spelt with no 't' in the middle – the Suffolk is the oldest breed of heavy horse in Britain. Seven shades of chesnut are recognised as authentic: bright, red, golden, yellow, light, dark and dull-dark. The animal's legs sometimes appear too short for its massive body, giving it the nickname Suffolk Punch, but this low-slung structure produces enormous pulling power. The standard for the breed has never included a specific height, but mares are generally from 16.1 to 16.2 hands, and stallions from 17 to 17.1 hands.

Suffolks derive from the county of their name, but experts believe that the genes which give the horses their large size came originally from Belgium. In their heyday, huge numbers worked on the land in East Anglia, and well-known local firms produced the latest forms of plough, seed drill and wagon specially for them to draw.

134

PLOUGHING TEAM, (left) RETURNING HOME, EARLY TWENTIETH-CENTURY PLOUGHING TEAMS IN BURNHAM, BUCKINGHAMSHIRE.

SHIRE HORSES (bottom left) PRESERVING A DYING SKILL, A PLOUGHING COMPETITION BETWEEN TEAMS OF SHIRE HORSES.

EXMOOR PONIES (below) THE EXMOOR PONY HAS CHANGED LITTLE SINCE IT EVOLVED DURING THE ICE AGE AROUND 130,000 YEARS AGO.

And yet, for all their renown, Suffolks did not start to spread westwards until the 1930s, and by then it was too late for them to make much progress, for the tide of mechanisation was sweeping the era of farm horses away. Numbers fell drastically: there are records of farms getting rid of 40 horses in a day, all to slaughterhouses.

Extinction seemed imminent, and the breed sank so low that in 1966 only six foals were born. Today careful restoration work by members of the Suffolk Horse Society (founded in 1877) has restored the number of breeding mares to about 75, and a fine historical exhibition has been established in the museum at Woodbridge.

PONIES

Britain has more breeds of pony than any other country in the world. Some have recently disappeared, and others are threatened with extinction. Lincolnshire Fen ponies vanished when the Fens were drained; Cornish Goonhillies, Irish Hobbies and Scottish Galloways are no longer distinct breeds.

Connemara Pony

Andalucian blood imported in the seventeenth century has made Connemaras larger than most other breeds. They grow to between 13 and 15 hands, and, being agile, athletic and well suited to equestrian sports, make excellent ponies for teenagers.

Dartmoor Pony

Fifty years ago there were 20,000 ponies wild on Dartmoor. Small, strong and sure-footed, they would carry shepherds all day over the roughest terrain. Now that traditional role has largely disappeared, with the animals supplanted by quad bikes, and numbers are nearer 2000.

Eriskay Pony

The origins of the Eriskay pony are ancient, and certainly have Celtic and Norse connections. Carvings of animals with proportions similar to those of today have been found on Pictish stones in the north and west of Scotland. DNA tests have shown that they are genetically different from all other horses and ponies. They are between 12 and 13.2 hands tall, and predominantly grey, with an occasional black or bay. Foals are often born brown or black, but turn grey with maturity.

In earlier times the ponies were widely used for traditional tasks such as carrying peat and seaweed in creels (or baskets) slung in pairs across their backs, but in the nineteenth century they quickly declined, until only a small number of pure-bred animals remained on the island of Eriskay, betweeen South Uist and Barra in the Outer Hebrides.

With the formation of the Eriskay Pony Society in 1970, intensive efforts began to restore the breed. Numbers have now risen to about 100 registered mares, and 300 animals in all, but the Rare Breeds' Survival Trust still lists Eriskays as 'Category 1: Critical'.

Exmoor Pony

The chunky little Exmoor pony, about 12 hands tall, is an astonishing survival. Not so much a breed as a race, it has hardly changed from animals that evolved in the Ice Age 130,000 years ago. Almost every other type of horse has been altered by humans deliberately breeding to influence size, shape, colour and markings; but, first because of the isolation in which it lived, and later through owners' efforts to keep the strain intact, the Exmoor has come through as a natural blueprint – nature's design for a wild pony – almost exactly the same as the animals that Celtic farmers tamed and used to pull their chariots.

All Exmoors are similar in colour and markings, and their 'mealy mouths', or pale muzzles, resemble those of other primitive species like Przewalski's horse. Their skulls have deep jaws and large teeth, well adapted for grazing coarse plants, as do the fossil remains of prehistoric horses found at various sites in Britain; and their legbones have similarly common characteristics.

DARTMOOR PONY (below left) SADLY THE POPULATION HAS DECLINED FROM 20,000 IN THE 1900s TO A MERE 2000 INDIVIDUALS TODAY.

ERISKAY PONY (below right) WITH ONLY 300 INDIVIDUALS LEFT, ERISKAYS ARE LISTED AS CATEGORY 1 CRITICAL BY THE RARE BREEDS TRUST.

CONNEMARA PONIES (bottom) STALLION (IN FRONT) AND SMALLER MARE. THEY ARE GENERALLY LARGER THAN OTHER BREEDS OF PONY.

The first written record of the breed dates from 1818, when Sir Thomas Acland, the last Warden of the Exmoor Royal Forest, drove 20 of the ponies on to his own land on Winsford Hill. Descendants of those animals still run on the same ground and now form the main foundation of the breed.

Exmoors are listed as 'endangered', because the total population amounts to fewer than 1200 individuals. Of these, some 180 still live free on Exmoor, in separate groups, remaining out all year round, except for the brief period late in October when they are rounded up in the traditional gathering, for the inspection, branding and registration of foals. Natural selection continues to ensure that the breed remains true to type.

Exmoors make excellent children's ponies, and have the merit of being weatherproof. Their thick winter coats give such good insulation that falling snow does not melt on them, but piles up until they shake it off, and short hairs at the root of the tail form an unique rain- or snow-chute which sheds water. Fleshy rims round their eyes – 'toad eyes' – give extra protection, and their short ears minimise heat loss. In the year 2000 some 30 ponies were released on to the South Downs above Lewes in the hope that they would eat down the invasive tor grass and promote the growth of herbs, orchids and other wild flowers found on chalk grassland.

Fell Pony

Them that asks no questions isn't told a lie.
Watch the wall, my darling, while the Gentlemen go by!
 Five and twenty ponies
 Trotting through the dark –
 Brandy for the Parson,
 'Baccy for the Clerk;
 Laces for a lady, letters for a spy,
Watch the wall, my darling, while the Gentlemen go by!
 RUDYARD KIPLING: A Smuggler's Song

It is thought that Fell ponies have existed as a recognisable breed since Roman times, when imported Friesian stallions were mated with indigenous mares in the north of England to produce strong, dark-coloured animals about 13 hands high, bigger and more powerful than the pure native strain. They have a chunky, deep-bodied appearance: their legs are sturdy, and made to look even more so by the fine feather of hair on their fetlocks. The only admissible colours for the breed are black, brown, bay and grey. The ponies' small heads, short ears, large eyes and nostrils give them an alert look.

In earlier times they made excellent packhorses and draught animals, especially in the building of defensive structures like Hadrian's Wall. The Vikings used them for ploughing and pulling sledges, and later they became the main means of transport for the cattle rustlers known as the Border Reivers. Along northern coastlines smugglers found them ideal for shifting contraband inland, particularly when they had sacking wound under their hoofs to deaden the sounds of their passing. Some ponies were owned by Cistercian monks, who may have developed the grey strain, since light colour was a sign of monastic ownership.

In the early days of the Industrial Revolution during the eighteenth century they found a new role transporting iron ore across country; but the coming of the railways made them redundant, and many were sold for slaughter. After the Second World War they declined even further when mechanisation rendered horse-power obsolete on farms and in villages.

Today a few herds still breed on the hills in a semi-wild state, but it has been the active interest of the Fell Pony Society that has brought the breed back into demand for riding, carriage-driving, trekking, shepherding and hunting. Carriage-driving, in particular, has enjoyed a strong renaissance, not least because of the close interest taken in it by HRH the Duke of Edinburgh, the Society's Patron.

The **Dales Pony** is very similar to the Fell in size and appearance. It comes from the eastern slopes of the Pennines, rather than the west, but its past career as packhorse and draft animal has been much the same, and today it, too, is used for driving.

Highland Pony (*also known as* Garron)

Ideal pack animals, strong, sure-footed and long-lived, Highland ponies have been moulded by their harsh environment into hardy survivors. The earliest records refer to horses of this kind being ridden in southern Scotland during the fourteenth century, not least by King Robert the Bruce.

Although not very tall – the maximum is 14.2 hands – they are exceptionally powerful, the sturdiest of all British ponies, and they range in colour from white to black, via a variety of mouse, yellow, grey and cream. For centuries they were used for all kinds of farm work. When the Scottish Highlands were opened up for deer-stalking and grouse-shooting in the nineteenth century, they quickly established themselves as the favourite means of transport for parties going to the hills: they carried cartridges and lunches up in panniers, and returned with the shot grouse. Later in the season they brought down carcasses of stags and hinds, lashed onto special saddles.

When Queen Victoria began to keep Garrons at Balmoral,

NEW FOREST PONIES (below)
ALL SHAPES AND COLOURS, THE
WILD PONIES ARE AMONG THE CHIEF
ATTRACTIONS OF THE NEW FOREST.

HIGHLAND PONY (right) THESE STURDY
LOAD CARRIERS ARE USED FOR PONY-
TREKKING AND EXTRACTING TIMBER.

their fame spread. Other landowners set up formal studs, and in the 1880s the Department of Agriculture established a stud of the best sires at Inverness, for the use of crofters. Pedigree records have been kept since 1896, and the Highland Pony Society was founded in 1923.

Today, even with all-terrain vehicles widely available, Garrons are still much used for bringing shot deer off the hill. Not only can they go where machines cannot, especially on rocky ground, numerous owners prefer to retain traditional methods. The loading up of a stag is often a curious sight, for if a horse is nervous about having a dead beast heaved onto its back, the ghillie blindfolds it by draping his jacket over its head and tying the arms loosely beneath its chin, until the burden is secure.

Many Garrons double as trekking or driving ponies in summer, and they are also still used for extracting light timber from forests on difficult slopes.

Miniature Horses

Not a breed so much as a category, diminutive equines qualify for the description Miniature Horse if they are 8.5 hands (85 cm) or less at the shoulder. The British Miniature Horse Society, formed in 1994, has some 300 members, and claims that its charges 'make ideal pets, relating well to human beings, and enjoy pulling tiny traps and being ridden, if large enough'. Certainly the tiddlers are often used as companions for racehorses, and as mascots, and they win many hearts (and much money) fund-raising for charities.

New Forest Pony

Wild ponies are one of the chief attractions of the New Forest in Hampshire. All shapes and all colours, they can be seen everywhere, grazing on road verges, out on open heaths, lurking under ancient trees. They live free in small herds, being brought in only once a year in the traditional drifts, or round-ups, when a posse of riders goes out into the Forest and drives them into pounds to be wormed and branded.

They belong to the 400-odd Commoners, whose age-old right it is to run horses and cattle in the Forest, and the wild ponies play a vital part in the maintenance of the environment, for without their constant browsing and grazing (helped by the deer and cattle) undergrowth would choke the woodland, and scrub would invade the glades and open spaces beloved of the 8 million tourists who visit the place every year.

A few ponies generally die in the autumn, poisoned by excessive consumption of newly fallen green acorns, but most come through the winter in reasonable shape, not least because they eat holly, happily scrunching up the sharp-spined leaves which the foresters cut down for them. A much more lethal agent is the motor car. Even though many of the animals wear fluorescent collars, and strict speed limits apply throughout the Forest, more than 100 ponies (along with a few cattle and donkeys) are killed in road accidents every year.

The sad fact is that although the ponies were once much favoured as children's mounts, there is now so little demand for them that foals have been sold for only £1 apiece. The result was that many owners stopped even taking their foals to sales, and by 2000 the pony population had grown to almost 4000 – a figure which everyone concerned agreed was much too high. Habitat was being ruined by excessive grazing, and the animals themselves were losing condition.

The Commoners knew that they should bring themselves to organise a cull, especially of old mares. The trouble was (and is) that many families have run horses on the Forest for generations, and the tradition is so deeply rooted that people now keep ponies for sentimental rather than practical reasons – which makes it very hard to get rid of any. But then nature took a hand. The fouly wet winter of 2000 caused high mortality, and, together with a limited cull, reduced the numbers to 3200, a more manageable total.

SHETLAND PONY (previous pages)
ON SOUTH UIST, OUTER HEBRIDES,
HAS A THICK COAT TO PROTECT IT
FROM THE HARSH CLIMATE.

WELSH MOUNTAIN PONIES (below)
BEING ROUNDED UP AT CWM OWEN
IN THE BRECON BEACONS IN 1958.

DONKEY *EQUUS ASINUS* (right)
THERE IS ONLY ONE BREED OF
DONKEY IN BRITAIN, ALTHOUGH
OTHERS EXIST ELSEWHERE.

Shetland Pony

These tiny ponies – the smallest native breed – were originally developed for farm work on the Shetland Islands; but during the Industrial Revolution in the nineteenth century many were taken south and used as pit ponies, pulling trolleys in the mines and living their entire lives underground. Large heads, short necks and broad backs make them better for carrying packs than for riding. Thick coats insulate against harsh weather, and large nasal cavities warm freezing air before it enters their lungs.

Welsh Pony

Arguably the prettiest of our native breeds, the Welsh pony is like a miniature Arabian, with a dished face and plumed tail. A nineteenth-century writer described it as 'one of the most beautiful little animals that can be imagined...He will live on any fare and never tire.' The Arabian look is thought to date back to the Roman occupation, when the invaders may have brought with them Arab horses acquired during their African campaigns.

Owners are confident that their breed has existed since

prehistoric times, and that it is mentioned in the laws of Hywel Dda, written in 930 , when the good king specified three types of horses or ponies then extant in Wales: the palfrey, or riding pony; the rowney or sumpter (a packhorse), and the *Equus operarius*, a lightweight but wiry working animal that pulled a sledge or small cart. For centuries the ponies ran wild, to the considerable annoyance of shepherds and farmers; and when Henry VIII ordered the destruction of all stallions under 15 hands and mares under 13 hands, on the grounds that such small animals were useless for warfare, a good number managed to escape into the hills, where the harsh conditions sharpened their survival instincts.

By the fifteenth century farmers had bred a larger version of the pony, the **Welsh Cob** – probably a descendant of the *Equus operarius* – 15 or more hands high, and strong enough to carry an adult or to pull a cart. The sixteenth-century poet Tudur Aled left a glowing description of a stallion called the Abbot of Aberconwy:

> He has the outlook and gait of a stag, eyes like two ripe pears, bulging and dancing in his head, a dished face, a wide forehead, his coat like new silk.

In about 1700 farmers realised that the cobs and ponies had some value and began bringing them to markets and fairs. As more people took an interest in their breeding, selectivity increased. In 1901 a number of enthusiasts formed the Welsh Pony and Cob Society and opened the first stud book. At first there were only 200 members, but the fame of the horses spread across the world, and by 1920 between 100 and 200 were being exported every year to countries as distant as Australia and the United States. Today the Society has 6800 members, and ponies are much in demand for carriage-driving as well as for riding.

OTHER MEMBERS OF THE HORSE FAMILY

Donkey

Equus asinus

To many people it is a moke; to Americans it is a burro, and to some Scots it is a cuddy. But in fact there is only one breed of donkey in Britain. Others exist elsewhere, such as the French Poitou and the American Mammorth; and there are several types still living wild, including the Kiang in India and Nepal, the Somali wild ass (with zebra-striped legs), the Nubian ass, and the Onager in Mongolia, Turkestan, Iran and Syria.

Cave paintings in Europe and Africa show that donkeys were among the first animals to be domesticated by early man, who no doubt found them easier to control than horses, which can move much faster. As everyone knows, they are renowned for their stubborness and stupidity; but their supporters claim that in fact they are just intelligent and naturally cautious, 'and will not be commanded into a situation of danger like a horse'.

They are certainly patient, sure-footed and persistent; they also eat less than a horse, and live longer (40 years is common). It was these qualities that made them much valued for carrying burdens or pulling carts. Their huge ears and shatteringly loud voices are supposed to have developed from the fact that they are less sociable than horses, and in the wild live with more space between them: hence the need to communicate and pick up messages, over long distances. A good bray is said to carry for 3 km – a claim not likely to be disputed by anyone who has had the misfortune to intercept one at close range.

British domestic donkeys are traditionally grey or brown (although they can also be white, black or even pink), and between 10 and 14 hands. All have a black cross on their shoulders – the mark which their forebears are supposed to have carried ever since the first Palm Sunday, when an ass bore Jesus into Jerusalem. The dark hairs from the cross were long believed to have strong curative powers, excellent for whooping cough or toothache.

The ancestors of today's stock were brought here by the Romans, who used them as pack-asses and harnessed them four-abreast to draw wagons – and they have been part of the British landscape ever since. Anglo-Saxon paintings show donkeys harnessed and pulling a plough, and they feature in many medieval paintings. At the peak of their popularity there were 100,000 working donkeys in London alone, and on a Saturday morning late in the nineteenth century there would be 2000 donkey barrows jostling on the streets round Covent Garden, ready to distribute fruit and vegetables through the city. Within the capital there was also one milking herd, since asses' milk – in which the Egyptian Queen Cleopatra is supposed to have bathed – was thought to be very good for premature babies and delicate children.

It is said that there were no donkeys in Ireland until the seventeenth century, when some were introduced by tinkers, sword-sharpeners and ladies of easy virtue, who used them for transport when they followed Cromwell's army. Today about 800 donkeys still give rides on British beaches in the summer, over 200 at Blackpool alone. Some are used for trekking, and some still help on farms, although more to attract visitors than to provide horsepower. At Carisbrooke Castle on the Isle of Wight an ass still treads the big drum that turns a windlass to raise water from the well, but other such donkey wheels have long since rolled to a halt. Most of today's animals are pets, but in recent years there has been a strong upsurge of interest in donkey-driving, particularly among disabled people, who find the animals' calm temperament reassuring.

The Donkey Breed Society was founded in 1967, and a stud book was opened in 1969, recording the parentage of over 3000 animals. More recently a general register has been added to keep track of as many donkeys as possible, whether or not they are eligible to be entered in the stud book. Even so, there is no reliable estimate of the overall population in Britain.

The Donkey Sanctuary, started in 1969 by Dr Elizabeth Svendsen, is now the biggest such establishment in the world. The sanctuary is the fifth-largest animal charity in the United Kingdom: it is based in Devon, and has 11 farms, with a total of 700 hectares. No animal is ever refused admittance, and nearly 8500 have been taken in during the past 30 years.

Mule

A mule is the hybrid offspring of a donkey and a horse. The most frequent cross is between a male donkey, or jack, and a mare; the less common, between a stallion and a female donkey, produces a hinny, which is smaller than a mule. Both forms are sterile and cannot breed. A mule is often nearly as tall as a horse, but it has the long ears, clumsy head, thin legs and small feet of a donkey.

The phrase 'stubborn as a mule' accurately reflects one aspect of the animal's nature; but the creatures have many merits, not least that they are intelligent, agile, sure-footed, able to live on the roughest of food, and tough enough to withstand hardships that would overcome either of their parents.

In the past they have served nobly with the armed forces in many theatres, most notably in the two world wars, when they acted as pack-animals, carrying ammunition and other vital supplies, and performed prodigious feats in hauling artillery pieces over terrain with which horses could not cope. Especially in Flanders during the First World War, and in Burma during the Second, mules proved themselves indispensable, and it is entirely fitting that two mules should have pride of place in the fine memorial to Animals in War, conceived by the sculptor David Backhouse for a site on an island near the top of Park Lane. They are depicted struggling, heavily laden, towards a gap in a curved wall on which are depicted in relief all man's fellow combatants, from an elephant to a glow-worm.

Today there are more mules in Britain than one might think. The British Mule Society puts the number at between 3000 and 4000, almost all of them the result of animals mating accidentally, but a few deliberately bred. Some owners use them for driving, some for riding; a few haul timber in forests, and at least one family of London totters still has mules to pull its cart.

Przewalski's Horse

Equus caballus przewalskii

This wild horse was discovered in Mongolia during the 1870s by the Russian explorer Colonel Nikolai Przewalski; and when he presented the skull and skin of a three-year-old animal to the Zoological Museum in St Petersburg, the remains caused no little excitement, for they seemed to belong to a form of wild horse thought long extinct. Some experts considered that the animal had been a mule, a cross between a horse and a wild ass; but later breeding experiments showed that such hybrids were sterile, and that Przewalski-type horses were, and are, capable of breeding normally. The creature was therefore deemed to be a genuine wild horse, dun-coloured, with a heavy head and short, stiff mane, standing about 13 hands.

In 1901 the Duke of Bedford, anxious to have a herd at Woburn, commissioned the leading German animal collector Carl Hagenbeck to procure six foals, and after an arduous expedition through Mongolia, Hagenbeck's emissary Wilhelm Grieger returned to Germany with no fewer than 28 mares and foals. Six of them went to Woburn, as agreed, and the rest were sent to various European zoos;

but none of them did very well, and in 1954, with the English colony failing, the Zoological Society of London founded a separate herd by importing a pair of animals from Prague.

In the wild, Przewalski's horse is thought to have gone extinct during the late 1960s: the last wild stallion was seen in 1969. But since then several European zoos have run successful breeding programmmes, and a number of animals have been returned to the wild in Mongolia. Marwell Zoo in Hampshire, has alone produced more than 150 foals, and in the year 2000 it deployed a group of four colts to graze a 70-hectare site on Eelmoor Marsh, next door to the airfield at Farnborough, the aim being that the animals should grow to maturity in semi-natural conditions, and also improve the environment by their selective grazing. European zoos hoped to send a further consignment of some 18 horses to Mongolia during the summer of 2002, their destination being Takhin Tal, close to the border with China, in the area where Przewalski's horse used to roam wild.

Some people possess the power to heal horses within their own bodies, a gift handed down from one generation of a family to the next

Horse healers

VAV SIMON IS IN SUCH DEMAND as a healer of horses that she often treats 10 or 12 animals in a day. As she runs her hands over one, it often goes to sleep, so soothing is her touch – and yet strong forces are involved. On one occasion, as she finished working on a horse with a swollen foot, the stable girl holding the animal was hit by such a charge of negative energy that she went into a trance and began to sway about.

As Vav moved to help her, she too was hit. 'I felt as if I'd been kicked in the solar plexus,' she remembers. 'I called, "Get her out of the box!" As I brought her out, I was gasping for breath, and had tears streaming down my face. My husband, who didn't know what had happened, said, "Oh, my God – is the horse dead?" The horse was fine, but I had to rebalance the girl, ground the energy and settle her down. She didn't come back to work for a week, but when she did, she felt terrific, and had no memory of what had happened.'

A direct and friendly person, not in the least fey, Vav came from a farming family on the Isle of Lewis, and only by degrees did she realise that she had inherited what were known as 'the old ways' – ancient methods of healing. One day when she was six she was sitting at her grandmother's dressing table, admiring the mirrors, the silver-backed hairbrushes, the powder bowls – 'all the things that fascinate young girls.' In one of the mirrors she saw her granny approaching with a blue velvet cloth in her hands. From the cloth the old woman brought out a crystal ball, which she handed over with the words, 'One day you'll know what to do with this.'

At that moment Vav's mother entered the room, and a terrible argument broke out, the mother screaming from a mixture of fear and anger that the child was being initiated into dangerous mysteries. The scene has haunted Vav ever since, and it took her many years to understand the cause of the tension. The truth was that ever since Christianity had become established in the Outer Isles, 'the old ways' had come to be seen as something sinister and unpleasant, and women like her grandmother who practised them 'were put into the witch class'. So for much of her life she hardly dared trust or speak about the gift which she knew had passed to her.

For a long time her career lacked direction. After dropping out from a physical education college in Dunfermline, she went to live with her boyfriend, whom she later married, and with whom she had two children. She worked as an accountant in a bank until she found the job too boring, then became a personal assistant to a potter. She also trained as a dancer with the Scottish Ballet, and taught dance to children.

All this time people were bringing horses, cats and dogs to her, because healing was in her blood. She was also treating dancers, but she thought it important to get proper qualifications, and so she trained in massage and physiotherapy, took a degree in chiropractics at the McTimoney School in Oxford, then an MSc in animal chiropractics. After the break-up of her first marriage she spent some time on her own, then met her present husband, David, a psychologist: with her own two children, two of his, and two more jointly, they have amassed a brood of six.

She still often uses Gaelic phrases to soothe animals, but in fact her grasp of the language is fragmentary – and once, when provoked by an insistent journalist to explain an aside she had just made to a horse, she instantly invented a bogus translation: 'I told him I'd said, "Stand up, you silly bugger. The knackerman's coming!"'

She has such a rapport with animals that her mere presence soothes them, but her work sometimes involves the expenditure of considerable force. To straighten a horse's pelvis, for instance, she may have to hoist one of its rear legs high off the ground – no easy task for a person of modest size.

She sees herself as a channel for the powers she possesses, and feels honoured to

act as such. Yet she is by no means as ordinary as she looks. She now knows that the energies to which she tunes in work through the prehistoric stone circle at Callanish, on the island of Lewis – but she found this out only through a chance meeting with a North American Mohawk elder at a healing conference in Cirencester. Her ambition is to take part in scientific research which may establish exactly what happens when she heals.

She is not surprised to find that her daughter seems to have inherited her gift. At a Welsh pony stud the little girl, then aged three, saw her inspecting an old horse in a field, and immediately said, 'Mummy, that horse has got a sore foot'. When Vav asked, 'How d'you know that?' the reply was, 'I can hear it'. She did not challenge this curious answer, because she realised that the old powers were surfacing again, in another generation.

5 FARM ANIMALS

When the Romans

came to Britain in 43 AD, they brought with them donkeys and longwool sheep, and probably reintroduced fallow deer; but otherwise they had little influence on the fauna during the four centuries of their occupation. On the other hand, they certainly took advantage of fertile land, especially in the south, and many large country villas were built from the profits of agriculture.

The most important farm animal was, and remained, the Celtic Shorthorn, *Bos longifrons*, which itself was apparently descended from the aurochs, and from which the small, dark breeds of Welsh and Scottish cattle derived. Huge numbers of bones found in Neolithic deposits show that the beasts had been an important item in the diet of Stone Age people; and from the abundant remains of calves, it has been inferred that the primitive farmers killed off young stock in infancy so that their mothers' milk would be available to humans, who depended heavily on it.

During the Roman period, even though farming expanded, only a small proportion of the land was occupied by humans. The Anglo-Saxons, who began migrating into Britain from northern Europe in the fifth century AD, were also energetic farmers, and brought more ground into cultivation with their oxen and heavy ploughs; yet for centuries huge areas of Britain remained virgin forest or marsh, inhabited by wolves, bears, lynxes, deer and Wild White cattle. The historian Matthew Paris recorded that in the time of Edward the Confessor (1004–66), Leofstan, Abbot of St Albans, cut through the thick woods which extended from the Chilterns almost to the fringes of London, building bridges and levelling roads to make travelling safe, because the forest was 'the habitation of numerous and various beasts, wolves, boars, woodland bulls and stags'.

The life of an Anglo-Saxon farmer was exceedingly

simple. He built his own frail house from rough-hewn wood and thatch, and shared it with the pair of oxen that pulled his plough, the cow that supplied him with milk, butter, cheese and replacements for his ploughing team, and sheep that produced mutton, more cheese and wool for clothes. He might also own a sow and piglets, and some poultry. As for the nature of his cattle – many of the red breeds that survive today are thought to derive from animals which the Anglo-Saxons imported with them from what is now Germany.

By the time of the Domesday survey of 1086, the coastal marshes in the southeast were heavily stocked with sheep. The flats around the shores of Essex alone carried 18,000 head, and East Anglia as a whole produced large quantities of sheeps' cheese. Sheep were valued not only for their meat, wool and milk, but also for their manure, and in consequence were carefully looked after. Not so pigs, which were allowed to wander freely, finding what food they could in woods and fields. In late winter they were fattened with a little grain, but the meat they produced must have been lean and tough as old boots.

When it came to ploughing, the rival merits of horses and oxen were a subject for debate as early as the thirteenth century. Walter of Henley, who wrote a treatise on agriculture, thought a mixed team the best, partly because the different animals, naturally moving at their own speeds, kept each other in check, and partly because in heavy ground oxen would battle on when horses would give up and stop. Another advantage, he reckoned, was that oxen were four times cheaper to feed, and in the end were themselves edible: 'When the horse is worn out, there is nothing left but the skin, but ten pennyworth of grass will make an ox fit for the larder.' (Five hundred years later the Duke of Bedford presented Thomas Coke of Norfolk with 30 oxen, which walked the whole way from Woburn Abbey in Bedfordshire to Holkham Hall in Norfolk, where the great agricultural innovator used them for ploughing.)

There is little evidence that any of the Norman kings had much enthusiasm for farming. Their interest lay rather in hunting, and they frequently afforested (or set aside) good agricultural land in order to give their deer herds more grazing: thus Henry II extended Windsor Forest to take in most of Surrey. Management of livestock remained primitive, and was often governed more by superstition than by common sense. One cure for contagious abortion, for instance, was to nail an aborted foetus on to the wall of the barn, where all the cows could see it, and where it would act as a warning to the rest of the herd. Many farmers believed that if they laid a hand on the back of a calf, the animal would fall ill or meet with an accident.

The fourteenth century brought a great increase in the numbers of sheep, as wool became England's principal export. Agricultural historians believe that, even then, two main types of sheep existed: the shortwools of the western marches and northern uplands, and the longwools of the south, which included an early version of today's Cotswold breed. It was the longwool fleeces that were most highly valued and formed the bulk of the export trade. 'White gold', people called them. The wool was processed and made into fine cloth at hundreds of water-powered mills.

Fortunes were made, churches and great country houses built, schools and universities founded, all on the backs of the grazing flocks, and much former arable land was put down to grass to provide pasture for an ever-increasing army of mouths. By the early fifteenth century the sheep industry had become so overpowering that numerous commentators complained about it. 'Sheep have eaten up our meadows and our downs, our corn, our wood, whole villages and towns,' wrote Thomas Bastard; and Thomas Latimer, preaching before Edward IV, proclaimed, 'Where have been a great many householders and inhabitants, there is now but a shepherd and his dog.'

DROVING

The practice of droving – of moving animals around the country on foot – goes back into the mists of antiquity. In Kent the sunken trackways that cross the downland from northeast to southwest show that, long before the Norman conquest, farming was based on the practice of *trans-humance*: in summer, herds migrated from settlements north of the Downs to pastureland in the Weald and on Romney Marsh.

In the Middle Ages the passage of animals steadily increased as the ever-growing populations of cities and towns concentrated the demand for meat into particular areas. The greatest magnet and market for meat was always London, whose citizens ate their way through phenomenal quanties of beef, mutton and pork – and this meant that, before the advent of railways or mechanised transport, cattle, sheep, pigs and even geese were constantly moving from every corner of the land, on the march towards the capital (see page 154 for an account of the Scottish Drovers). Geese had their feet dipped in tar and coated with gravel to prepare them for the trek.

Huge numbers of cattle paused in Norfolk, to be fattened on the marshes between Norwich and Yarmouth, and thousands were sold at St Faiths, a village north of Norwich, where a fair opened on 17 October every year. Meanwhile other droves, which had set out from southwest Scotland, went down through Carlisle and crossed the Pennines on their way to fairs along the Great North Road, in Huntingdonshire and Hertfordshire.

Cattle

TWO PRIZE BORDER LEICESTER RAMS IN A LANDSCAPE (previous pages) BY THOMAS WEAVER (1774–1843).

WILD WHITE CATTLE (below) THE MODERN REMNANTS OF AN ANCIENT HERD AT CHILLINGHAM PARK.

For thousands of years cattle have been mankind's most valuable animal. Living mainly on grass, whether fresh or dried, and often without much shelter, they provided successive generations not only with meat and milk, but also with hides that yielded leather for clothes, shoes, ropes, boats and roof-coverings, and with the power to pull ploughs and wagons.

Wild White Cattle

Closest to the aurochs in appearance and temperament are the Wild White cattle which survive in a few English parks. The best-known, those of Chillingham Park, in Northumberland, are thought to be living relics of animals that roamed the forests of prehistoric England and were sacrificed by the Druids. The Chillingham herd is known to have existed for at least 700 years: the Tankerville family, which owned them for generations, believed that their ancestors enclosed a herd during the thirteenth century, the aim being to have a ready supply of meat on the hoof, and to stop rustlers from the north driving cattle off across the Scottish border.

From the towers of Chillingham Castle, which stands within the park, the cattle are generally in sight, and in the past their behaviour gave the inhabitants valuable early warning if raiders were in the offing. The animals were – and are – wild enough to attack strangers, and from the way they were reacting, watchers could tell if a large body of men was approaching with hostile intent.

The shape of the animals' skulls, and the way in which their wide, upswept horns grow out of them, are similar to those of the aurochs; but analysis of blood samples has revealed that the Chillingham strain is unique among the cattle of Western Europe. Its origins therefore remain mysterious, as does the source of its pure white colour: the herd always breeds true to type, and has never produced a coloured or even partly coloured calf.

Numbers have fluctuated over the years, from a high of 80 in 1838 to a low of 13 after the dire winter of 1946–7, when snow drifted to a depth of twelve metres in the park,

and, in spite of intensive efforts to feed them, 20 animals died of starvation. Today the herd is almost 50 strong, and geneticists are astonished by the way it has survived centuries of inbreeding without enfeeblement. Old skulls recovered from the park suggest that the cattle have diminished in size, but apart from that they have remained remarkably true to type, retaining not only their physical characteristics, but also their wildness and ferocity.

Refusing grain and concentrates, they eat only grass, meadow hay and occasionally straw: even when starving in 1947, they would not accept the oats and cattle-cake offered them. They can never be treated by vets, because any animal that has contact with humans is ostracised by the rest – in any case their natural resistance to disease is remarkable.

Their vitality seems to be due to the fact that the strongest and fittest bull always establishes himself as king, and, for as long as he can, sees off challengers in ritual combats, thus ensuring that he sires all the calves. When a cow is about to give birth, she detaches herself from the herd and secretes her calf in deep grass or bracken, like a deer. If a human approaches, she attacks – and when she is ready to show the new arrival to the herd, she goes through a formal process of introduction. As she approaches, the king bull comes out to meet her and escort her in; the other cows then inspect the calf and sniff it, and once they have given it their approval, they accept it as a new recruit.

In 1939, with costs of maintenance rising, the eighth Lord Tankerville formed the Chillingham Wild Cattle Association as a charity, which took over care of the herd, and when he died in 1971 ownership passed to the new body. Fresh problems arose on the death of the ninth earl, in 1980, when the family decided to sell the Chillingham estate; but after a personal intervention by the Duke of Northumberland the park and its surrounding woodland were bought by the Sir James Knott Charitable Trust, which granted the association a 999-year grazing lease. The herd is now looked after by a warden.

Foot-and-mouth has been a recurrent threat: during the outbreak of 1967 it came within 5 km of the park but fortunately did not affect the herd. After that narrow escape, a party of animals was despatched to a secret location in Scotland, to establish a reserve which could keep the breed going in case of future disaster, and there are now 15 tucked away on that site. In the more recent epidemic of 2001 the herd again survived unscathed, and because the animals have already shown that they are immune to tuberculosis, brucellosis and other ailments from which domestic beasts suffer, many people believe that their natural way of life may have given them immunity to foot-and-mouth as well. Even at the risk of killing one of them, it has been suggested that there may be a case for immobilising a cow and taking a blood sample, to discover if it contains antibodies which could be developed and used on a wide scale.

Aurochs

Aurochs redivivus

So far as anyone knows, all domestic cattle derive from one common ancestor, the splendid aurochs, which disappeared from Britain in about 1000 BC but survived until the seventeenth century in Poland, where one herd lived on in the Jaktorowka Forest near Warsaw. Then in 1627 the last of the line died and the species went extinct, leaving us with one painting, as well as with skulls and bones, to show what the breed was like.

Early in the twentieth century two distinguished German zoologists, Heinz Heck and his brother Lutz, conceived the idea of trying to re-create the animal; and in the 1920s they began a series of experiments to see if they could reconstitute an aurochs by crossing breeds of cattle that embodied various characteristics of their original ancestor. Dr Heinz Heck was Director of the Munich Zoo, and into his melting pot went Hungarian and Podolian steppe cattle, Scottish Highland cattle, grey and brown Alpine breeds, piebald Friesians and half-wild Corsicans. After a few years his trials produced a male and a female which had the physical characteristics he was looking for, and the calves of these reborn *Urochsen* bred true to type.

A similar experiment, by Professor Lutz Heck, was started in 1951 at the Zoological Gardens in Berlin, this time using cattle of southwest European origin (including Spanish fighting bulls), but also park cattle from England. This produced even better results, and in a shorter time – and one of the most fascinating features of the hybrids was that they seemed to possess not only the physical attributes of the prehistoric wild animals, but also their mentality: they were fast-moving, evasive, temperamental and fierce.

NEW BREEDS

Before the Enclosures – the bounding of fields by hedges or walls, authorised by Acts of Parliament, which began in the seventeenth century and carried on until the nineteenth – owners grazed their cattle on common land, where they were mated haphazardly, by any bull that happened to be around, probably one belonging to the lord of the manor. Peasant farmers had to put up with what the lord provided, and had no chance of doing any selective breeding to improve their stock. The development of pedigree lines was out of the question. The result was that most medieval cattle were narrow-bodied, long in the leg, and well suited to pulling the plough, but not to producing milk or beef.

153

Before the days of
mechanised transport,
the only way for farmers
and dealers to move
their beasts to market
in the cities and towns
was on foot

....

The
Scottish
drovers

THE PRACTICE OF WALKING cattle from the far corners of Britain to the hungry cities and towns in the south had already been established, in embryo, in 1359, when two Scottish drovers were granted a letter of safe conduct for travelling through England with horses, oxen, cows and other merchandise. In spite of intermittent export bans imposed by the Scots Parliament, and the passion for reiving, or rustling, cattle that was rife in the north, especially in the Borders, spasmodic traffic continued over the next 300 years; yet it was only in the second half of the seventeenth century that droving came to be officially recognised as an honourable occupation, and the despatch of meat on the hoof was actively encouraged. By 1663 the annual total of beasts passing through the town of Carlisle had reached 18,574, and in 1680 a Commission was appointed in Scotland to encourage the further export of cattle and other goods south of the border.

Highlanders were not easily parted from their traditional pastimes, and cattle raiding continued for another century at least. But gradually more and more men who had a liking for dangerous journeys through wild country and rough weather harnessed their energies to peaceful rather than warlike ends.

Especially in the early stages, their journeys were extremely demanding: no maps existed, and although they sometimes travelled on tracks or green roads, they often had to cross unmarked mountains, so that they needed close knowledge of the country, particularly when mist came down on the hills. A few of them owned ponies, which they rode or used to carry supplies, but most went on foot. If they could, they stopped for the night at an inn or outlying farm, but they spent many a night out on the hill, wrapped in their plaids. Their food was exceedingly plain, consisting mainly of oatmeal, which they boiled and made into porridge if they had access to a fire, or ate cold, mixed with water, if they were in the open, and washed down with whisky. Their dogs lived on the same rations. They also sometimes drew blood from the cattle, and mixed that with oatmeal and perhaps onions to form black pudding.

Even in times of unrest – as after the rising of 1745 – drovers were licenced to carry weapons in order to protect themselves and their cattle. As a precaution against rustlers, most armed themselves with gun, pistol and sword, and in their thick, homespun tweed plaids they were clearly a memorable and intimidating sight: one observer described them as 'great stalwart hirsute men, shaggy and uncultured and wild, who look like bears as they lounge heavily along'.

The assembling of cattle began early in May, when dealers or drovers went out into the Highland glens to negotiate, often with tenant farmers so poor that they might have only one animal for sale. The beasts were then walked down to some convenient collection point and formed into droves, which might consist of anything from 100 to several thousand head. The planning of each journey demanded a high degree of skill and knowledge, for success depended on finding every huge herd enough food and water to sustain it throughout its marathon trek to the south.

In hill country a normal day's march was 16 or 20 km. The drovers would set off from their resting place at about eight in the morning, and move the cattle slowly on, allowing them to graze a little as they went. Surviving stretches of drove road show that the animals usually moved in parallel strings, side by side, spread out over a front 30 or 40 metres wide. At midday the cavalcade halted so that the men could eat and rest, and the cattle graze more extensively. Towards evening the drove stopped at a 'stance', or resting place, where there was enough pasture and water for the night. During the night the animals were not corralled: generally they were too tired to stray far, but in the early stages of a journey some often had a tendency to try to head for

home, and at least one man was awake throughout the hours of darkness to make sure that none wandered off. At the outset of the journey the cattle were unshod; but when they were about to come on to gravelled roads, the animals were fitted with thin, crescent-shaped metal plates nailed to their hooves – no easy business with half-wild creatures, as each beast had to be thrown down and held on the ground with its feet tied while the blacksmith was at work.

Of the numerous hazards along the way, among the worst were rivers, most of which, being still unbridged, had to be forded or swum. Even relatively small burns could become impassable when rainstorms produced sudden spates and such bridges as did exist often proved even more dangerous than crossings in the water, for if they were made of wood, they thundered under the feet of the cattle, causing them to panic and then stampede.

The travellers' destination lay hundreds of kilometres to the south; and even if many of the Scottish cattle paused for fattening in East Anglia, most finished their journey at one of the London markets. In 1794 the number of cattle sold at Smithfield alone reached 109,000, and it seems that at least 80 per cent of these were Scottish.

Only in the age of steam did these great annual migrations start to falter. With the advent of fast ships during the 1830s, Scottish farmers changed their tactics: instead of sending beasts off on droves, to be fattened in the south, they began to finish cattle at home and despatch them to market by sea. The railways took longer to make an impact, but by the 1880s large numbers of fattened cattle were travelling from Aberdeen to London by train, and in 1889 the Highland Railway company carried 250,000 sheep to the south.

Once fields were enclosed, and farmers could control their herds, everything changed. The idea of a planned breeding programme became fashionable, especially among the upper classes, who controlled more and more of the land; but no systematic attempt to breed specially for milk or beef was made until the mid-eighteenth century. Then there emerged the outsized figure of Robert Bakewell (1725–95), a big, fat farmer from Dishley Grange in Leicestershire who was so far advanced in his ideas that he toured the Continent in search of new agricultural methods, carefully filled in hollows to level his fields, and irrigated 80 hectares of land with a network of small waterways so effective that he was able to cut his grass four times a year. He also built a canal so that he could float his heavy turnip crop down to the yard, rather than have to transport it in carts.

'The Wonder of Dishley' was described as 'tall, broad-shouldered, stout, of brown-red complexion, clad in a loose brown coat and scarlet waistcoat, leather breeches and top boots' – and a contemporary painting (see below), now owned by the Royal Agricultural Society, confirms his

solidity: there he sits on a horse as cobby as himself, with his ample belly pushing out the front of his three-quarter-length frock coat. An engraving of 1842 also emphasises his hefty build, but the most striking feature of that portrait is the alert, penetrating look of his eyes, which surely missed nothing. One Bakewell relic in the Society's possession is a high-backed, broad-bottomed chair made at his own direction out of a willow tree that grew on his farm. An inscription records that it was his favourite seat, and that the back 'served as a screen while seated by his fireside calculating on the profits, or devising some improvements on his farm. Thousands of pounds have been known to exchange hands in the same.'

Bakewell kept large sheepflocks of his own, and hired out his best rams to neighbouring farmers. His celebrated ram Two Pounder earned 1200 guineas in stud fees during 1789 alone. He himelf became notorious for the secrecy with which he guarded his methods, but he availed himself freely of outside information when he rode round the countryside checking the quality of the lambs, so that he could recover the best sires for his own use.

For a while he enjoyed no mean success: in developing the longwool Leicester sheep by careful inbreeding, and by introducing some Ryeland and Merino blood, he produced an animal that fattened quickly. Towards the end of the eighteenth century large numbers of Dishley Leicesters were exported to Ireland: Bakewell himself was enthusiastic about the trade, and sent his son-in-law across the water to promote his breed. At first there was resistance to the newcomers, some of which were deliberately killed by locals, but they soon took on.

And yet, although his refinement of Longhorn cattle and Leicester sheep had lasting effects on British and Irish farming, Bakewell himself died in poverty – some said because he was so profligate with his hospitality, others because his Irish customers failed to pay him. Apart from entertaining in the normal sense, in his farmhouse kitchen, where he himself dined on his own at a small, round table in a corner by the window, he received many young men who came to stay and work with him purely for the experience. In the words of one American, Dishley 'rapidly became an institution of higher learning'. For the better instruction of his pupils, in the hall he kept joints of meat pickled in brine and skeletons of animals to illustrate the effects of heredity.

Among Bakewell's numerous friends was Thomas Coke, first Earl of Leicester ('Coke of Norfolk'), another agricultural pioneer, whom he advised on sheep and cattle, and whom he described as 'like a Prince of the best kind' among his tenants, 'being loved by many and feared by few'. Coke was widely known for advocating the benefits of muck, or manure, and for 43 years he held an annual sheep-shearing festival at his home, Holkham Hall. Eighty guests from as far afield as Russia and America stayed in the house, and every day the park filled with visitors as tenants, independent farmers and neighbours poured in to watch the shearing, see the prize cattle, inspect the farms and walk the pastures.

Inspired by Bakewell's example, other farmers like the Collings brothers, Charles and Robert, from near Darlington, carried selective breeding forward, and so laid the foundations of a pedigree stock industry that produced the world-beating cattle and sheep which Britain has today. In 1780 the Collings collected four cows and one bull, all carefully chosen animals with short horns and heavy bodies, and by judicious selection – rejecting any calves which did not conform to the high standards they were seeking – created one of the world's most famous breeds.

The original Collings Shorthorn was a dual-purpose animal, good for the production of both milk and beef, but later the breed was split by further selection into specialist milk and beef strains. No slouch when it came to creating publicity, Charles fattened up one calf until it reached the amazing weight of 1.3 tons and became known as 'the Durham ox', whereupon he commissioned a special carriage to transport it for exhibition around the country.

Over the generations many local types of cattle, sheep and pigs faded into extinction, but many were fostered and kept going by individual breed societies. In 1969 a Gloucestershire farmer, Joe Henson, began to collect rare breeds at Bemborough Farm, his home high on the Cotswolds, and a year later he took over most of the animals which had formed the rare breeds' gene bank at Whipsnade Zoo. In 1971, to finance his conservation projects, he opened his farm to the public, calling the new enterprise the Cotswold Farm Park, and in 1973 he founded the Rare Breeds Survival Trust, a national charity, to ensure the continued existence of all endangered British farm livestock.

The trust is now a national institution, based at the National Agricultural Centre at Stoneleigh, in Warwickshire, and it has had widespread success in helping bring breeds back from the brink of extinction; today it has over 10,000 members, with the Prince of Wales as its patron. Because rare cattle are often kept in small herds by enthusiasts who cannot afford to own a bull, the Trust ensures that artificial insemination is available to any owner wanting to produce pure-bred calves.

Mr Henson gives three reasons for wanting to preserve strains of animal no longer needed in mainstream agriculture. First, he says, his rare breeds form a living museum in which people can see the kinds of animals our ancestors farmed. Second, he feels it is important to study the characteristics of these old-fashioned breeds in detail; and third, it is vital that breeders of the future should have a pool of genetic material to fall back on. Who is to say, he asks, that we may not need some of the ancient characteristics again? In his view, we are 'highly fortunate to have 64 breeds of sheep in these tiny islands, and all that genetic material to choose from.'

The success of the Cotswold Farm Park has demonstrated the interest that ordinary people have in unusual animals. For many years the park attracted 100,000 visitors during its six-month opening season. Until 2000 the trust's long-term policy for the preservation of rare breeds was to have small groups of animals dotted all over the country, thus ensuring that some would survive any major epidemic. Yet the outbreak of foot-and-mouth disease which began in February 2001 was so disastrous that it brought major change. Simply to keep living populations no longer seemed enough: it was decided that resort should be had to cryogenics – that semen, embryos and ova should be kept deep-frozen, preferably on several different sites, to spread risks even further, and an appeal for £2.5 million was launched to finalise that operation.

ABERDEEN-ANGUS CATTLE (below) BRED FROM BLACK CATTLE OF NORTH-EAST SCOTLAND IN THE NINETEENTH CENTURY.

AYRSHIRE COW (bottom) A NATIVE SCOTTISH BREED FROM THE SOUTH-WEST OF THE COUNTRY, PRODUCING EXCELLENT MILK AND BEEF.

BELTED GALLOWAY (right) A WHITE BELT ROUND THE MIDDLE AND LACK OF HORNS DISTINGUISH THE GALLOWAY.

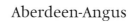

PRESENT BREEDS OF CATTLE

British livestock farmers have recently suffered two serious outbreaks of disease – bovine spongiform encephalopathy (BSE, or mad cow disease) and foot-and-mouth. BSE first appeared in November 1985: over the next 15 years it killed 180,000 cattle and led to the precautionary slaughter of millions more. When foot-and-mouth broke out in February 2001, government action was so confused and dilatory that over the next eight months over 6 million animals were destroyed. Cynics claimed that even if the epidemic was not deliberately started, it was allowed to spread, as a means of reducing the size of the national herd (11 million cattle) and sheep flock (42 million sheep), in response to demands from Brussels.

Aberdeen-Angus

Coal-black Aberdeen-Angus, billed as producers of the world's finest beef, were developed by selective breeding early in the nineteenth century from the polled (that is, hornless) and predominantly black cattle of northeast Scotland, known locally as 'doddies' and 'hummlies'. The pioneers were three outstanding farmers: Hugh Watson of Keillor in Angus, William McCombie of Tillyfour in Aberdeenshire, and Sir George Macpherson-Grant of Ballindalloch on the River Spey. A herd book was established in 1862, the first show of bulls was held at Perth in 1863, and the Aberdeen-Angus Cattle Society was founded in 1879. By then Aberdeen-Angus were taking root in the United States, and in 1901 the Americans registered more pedigree cattle than the British. The breed spread rapidly to other parts of the world – Canada, Australia, New Zealand, South Africa and South America – but for the first half of the twentieth century Britain continued to be regarded as the fount of pure stock, and exports flourished. In the 1920s and 1930s, however, British breeders deliberately reduced the size of their animals, partly because they felt that housewives wanted smaller joints, and partly because of the demand from overseas, particularly from Argentina and North America, where smaller beasts suited the different system of management – rearing cattle on the range, and having them on grass throughout their lives.

This policy of diminution proved a serious mistake, for the 1960s saw the arrival in Britain of large-muscled, draught-bred Continental cattle such as Charolais and Limousin, which the emerging supermarkets preferred because of their larger carcasses and higher proportion of prime cuts. British Aberdeen-Angus farmers, finding themselves in trouble, started to breed bigger animals again. For veterinary reasons they could not import live cattle from the United States, but, from 1972, they did begin to bring in Canadian stock, besides semen and embryos from America. By these means they have bred back to a larger, heavier animal, but one which retains the original characteristics.

The Society now has nearly 2000 members, and its patron from 1938 to 2002 was Her Majesty Queen Elizabeth the late Queen Mother, who herself had a notable herd of Aberdeen-Angus at the Castle of Mey.

Ayrshire

The body patterns of Ayrshire cattle often look like maps of strange countries surrounded by off-shore islands: multiple red-brown splodges scattered on a white background. This native breed originated in southwest Scotland and was first recorded officially in 1877, when the Ayrshire Cattle Society herd book was inaugurated.

Such has been its predominance as a leading dairy animal that it is now established in many countries, and the Society's commercial arm, Cattle Services (Ayr) Ltd, formed in the 1960s, markets genetic material all over the world: in 1999 alone the company exported over 10,000 straws of semen. In 1968 a world federation of Ayrshire breed societies was formed, and 13 countries are now members, all aiming to promote the cattle and improve them still further. Milking apart, Ayrshires produce excellent beef, especially when crossed with Limousins or Belgian Blues.

Beef Shorthorn

Once the Collings brothers had perfected their Shorthorns in the eighteenth century, the breed was split into distinct types, one designed for milk production, the other for meat. The Beef Shorthorn established itself firmly in Scotland, whence it was exported to many other countries, mainly to cross with, and improve, local breeds. Changes in fashion and world markets sent it into decline, but since the formation of the British Shorthorn Cattle Society in 1959 it has made a strong comeback, epitomised by the Society's bullish slogan: 'Join the revival. Breed from the breed with the oldest history and the brightest future.'

Belgian Blue

First imported into Britain in 1982, Belgian Blues are specialist producers of lean meat, and have become famous for their 'double muscles' – the bulges of flesh which stand out from their hindquarters.

Belted Galloway

Black, dun or red at both ends, the small, hardy Galloway is distinguished by the belt of white round its middle. Black animals look very like Belted Welsh (*see page 160*) except that they have shorter legs and no horns, and tend to have a wilder temperament.

Their origins are obscure: there are references to belted cattle in twelfth-century Bohemia and to 'sheeted cattle' in Britain during the time of Charles II; but the first clear mention comes from Scotland in about 1790, from the area south of Glasgow – and that is where most of the larger herds are found today. Some authorities believe the animals inherited their striking colour scheme from a belted Dutch breed, the Lakenvelder, which was imported in the seventeenth century.

Belties are hardy upland animals, with an efficient double coat of long outer hair and mossy inner growth, which means that they can happily spend the winter out of doors. A few animals were recently deployed to graze the steep slopes of Colley Hill near Reigate in Surrey, so as to stop trees and shrubs invading the wild-flower meadows. It is also hoped that the cattle's feet will encourage desirable plants to grow by breaking up the turf.

Belted Welsh

Devotees of the Belted Welsh are confident that their cattle are a separate breed which evolved centuries ago, but that their present black colour is of relatively recent origin. Earlier, all colours were present – black, red, smoky, line-backed, blue. Old market tolls, on which farmers described the beasts they brought in for sale, show that belted cattle were common in the Welsh hills by the eighteenth century, and when the drovers moved herds across country on their treks to markets in England, they always liked to have a few Belts because the white girdles showed up in the dark. Then in 1902 farmers around Caernarfon formed a breed society and chose black as their trademark, deliberately suppressing other colours by selective breeding.

When the Rare Breeds Survival Trust was formed in 1973, it did not recognise Welsh Belts as a separate breed, and it was left to owners to start their own society, *Gwartheg Hynafol Cymru* (the Ancient Cattle of Wales), in 1981. This now represents all the surviving strains, but some of them

have fallen to perilously low levels. The society's first herd book, produced in 1991, listed only one line-backed female, and no blue bull. The Belts are now relatively strong: fortunately they cross well with Welsh Blacks: a belted bull on a Welsh Black cow almost always yields belted offspring, which, with their fresh blood, can be mated back to a pure strain

Blonde d'Aquitaine

Long in the body, heavily muscled and attractively cream coloured, Blondes originated in southwest France, where for centuries they were used primarily as draught animals. The first stock was imported to Britain in 1972, and the animals have been so successful here as producers of beef that there are now about 8000 registered breeding cows in this country. Farmers claim that carcasses yield an exceptionally high ratio of lean meat to bone, and the British Blonde Society has 600 members.

British Friesian

During the nineteenth century black-and-white Friesians were frequently shipped into the east-coast ports of England and Scotland from the lush grassland of Holland; but in 1892 live imports were stopped because foot-and-mouth disease was endemic on the Continent. Some of the animals landed here were evidently better than others, for the *Livestock Journal* of 1900 referred to both 'exceptionally good' and 'remarkably inferior' Dutch cattle, recording that some were 'handsome in form and good milkers', but that others were 'so ugly and so poor in appearance that they almost shamed the owners.' Another drawback of the breed was that the cows were considered to be 'great eaters', needing more sustenance in winter than British breeds.

In any case, when a census was taken in 1908, there were so few of the animals in the country that they were not included in the return; but members of a breed society, formed in 1909, inspected nominated cattle and gradually compiled a pedigree herd book. Further major importations took place in

1914 and 1936, and the breed expanded rapidly in Britain right through until the end of the 1980s.

Then in the 1990s owners began bringing in stock, embryos and semen from the United States in attempts to increase milk production still further; but this Americanisation did not prove by any means a complete success, as the new strains of cow proved unable to fulfil their potential in British conditions, especially since dairy farmers were driven by ever-increasing economic pressures to feed their herds as much as possible on grass, rather than relying on concentrates.

British White

Not to be confused with the Wild White cattle, British Whites are one of the oldest native breeds. They may well be ultimately descended from wild stock, but the fact that they are naturally polled – they grow no horns – suggests some ancient Scandinavian influence. It is known that a herd of white polled cattle was running at Whalley Abbey in Lancashire, at the time of the Dissolution of the monasteries in 1537; this was later dispersed, and its members

were used to establish several herds in Norfolk, which remains the breed's stronghold.

The cattle were originally used for dairy purposes, but during the 1970s many farmers gave up milk production, and the number of pure-bred females sunk to between 100 and 150. Then came a strong revival, as owners switched to raising them for beef: by 1994 there were 111 registered herds, scattered over Britain and Northern Ireland, and the total of pedigree females had risen to 1200.

The cattle are creamy white, with black ears, muzzles, socks, hooves and eye-sockets. Apart from being decorative, the black points have a valuable role, in that they reduce the risk of sunburn and eye cancer, especially in hot climates like that of Australia and South America.

Charolais

First brought over from their native France in 1962, the big, cream-coloured Charolais have established a major presence in British farming. The cattle have existed in France for centuries, but they were not registered there as a distinct breed until about 100 years ago. In the early days of imports to this country, the sheer size of the breed alarmed owners of rival beef cattle – a cow can weigh up to 1200 kg – and the Charolais' good conformation and rapid growth rate did indeed erode the market share of others; but now the British Charolais Cattle Society has 2200 members, and there are some 40,000 registered cattle in Britain.

Dexter

These miniature black cattle were developed in Ireland during the nineteenth century by crossing small examples of the Irish Kerry to produce an ideal cow for smallholders. Most Dexters are less than a metre tall at the shoulder, and cows weigh only 300 kg – about half the weight of commercial types. In 1975 the breed was classed as 'endangered', with fewer than 250 cows, but today is has reached the status of a minor breed, with over 1500.

Galloway

These remained one of the leading British beef breeds all through the eighteenth century. Bred on the hills of southwest Scotland, the calves were taken down to the lowland pastures of the coast and there reared to the age of four or five, before setting out on foot to market in London. On the way some cows mated with Longhorn bulls in Westmorland or Cumberland, thus producing crossbreeds, but the majority were fattened on turnips in East Anglia before being driven on to Smithfield market in London, where they were slaughtered during the winter.

Gloucester

An ancient breed, Gloucester cattle were numerous in the Severn Vale by the thirteenth century. They were much valued for their milk, for their beef, and for working as strong, docile draught oxen. Their milk was ideal for making Double Gloucester cheese because of its small fat globules – an important consideration in days before mechanical or refrigerated transport was available for transporting it to towns and cities. Later, however, they went out of fashion, unable to compete with specialist milk producers such as the black-and-white Friesians.

By 1972 only one herd remained, belonging to the Dowdeswell sisters at Wick Court near Gloucester, and the breed was listed as 'critically rare' with only 12 bulls and 60 females surviving; but luckily, at the sale when it was due to be dispersed, a group of buyers came together to ensure that the herd remained intact. The Gloucester Cattle Society was revived and today it has 700 cows on its register.

Their distinctive feature is the white stripe that runs along their spine, down over (and including) the tail, known as 'finching'. Their faces and lower legs are black, and their bodies are otherwise blackish brown, with a lovely tinge of dark red, like mahogany, set off by their white underparts. They are renowned for their longevity, often breeding for 12 or 15 years.

Guernsey

Owners of Guernsey cattle trace the breed back to 960 , when Robert, Duke of Normandy sent a group of militant monks to the island a few kilometres off the coast of France. One duty of the holy men was to teach the islanders how to cultivate the soil, and they took with them some of the best French cattle of the day – Norman Brindles (also known as Alderneys) from Isigny, and Froment de Leons from Brittany. From these developed the Guernsey, which today is renowned for the high quality of its milk.

Guernsey milk appears to be almost entirely free of the protein beta casein A1, which is present in other milk, and is thought to cause heart disease in people whose immune systems have been compromised. Instead, Guernseys produce beta casein A2, which is apparently benign. Public health statistics show that the islanders, who use no other milk, have a 27 per cent lower incidence of heart disease than people on the mainland – a record echoed by that of the Maasai tribe in Kenya, whose cattle are also A2 producers, and to whom heart disease is almost unknown.

The cattle are established in many countries; but in 1999 a Guernsey Global Breeding Plan was launched, with the aim of keeping standards high and securing the breed's future on a worldwide basis.

Hereford

This native British animal is such an efficient converter of herbage into meat, and so easy to manage, that it has become the cornerstone of beef-producing industries in more parts of the world than any other breed of cattle. With its solid, chunky outline, its rich red body, white face, crest, chest and underparts, the animal is a familiar sight all over the British Isles.

It was developed 250 years ago by farmers in Herefordshire and on the Welsh borders, but even in the United Kingdom the breed has been much diluted by the introduction of other blood, and there are now only 15 true, traditional Hereford herds in Great Britain: only 350 cows can be identified as deriving entirely from stock bred in this country. Yet its future is secure, for in 1996, when the Rare Breeds Survival Trust created a new category of livestock called 'Native Breeds', the Hereford was the first entry.

Highland

Highland cattle are great bluffers. With their wide, curving, pointed horns, they look formidable customers – and indeed the confirmation of their horns and skulls suggests descent from the wild and aggressive aurochs; but in fact the breed has long been favoured as much for its docility as for its hardiness. Highlanders thrive in harsh conditions and on rough herbage. Not only do they live and breed happily in the open, without artificial shelter: their grazing habits complement those of sheep, and so actively improve upland environments. Their shaggy coats, as thick as duvets, are impervious to even the heaviest rain. Calves look like woolly toys.

Most Highland cattle today are a rich, gingery red, but in the seventeenth century their ancestors were black. The change of colour began early in the nineteenth century, when reddish animals from Glenlyon were exported to the Hebrides and elsewhere, and their genes proved dominant. To this day a herd is known as a fold, from the days when the cattle were brought into stone-walled enclosures at night to protect them from wolves.

The Highland Cattle Society, founded in 1884, has nearly 38,000 animals registered in its herd book, and every year new folds are founded in Britain and overseas. Some owners keep the cattle purely for their picturesque appearance, but in fact they yield excellent beef, especially when crossed with Hereford, Aberdeen-Angus or Charolais bulls.

Irish Moiled

The name comes from the Irish *maol*, meaning 'a little mound', and refers to the pointed crown on the animal's polled head. The cattle vary in colour, some being almost white, with reddish ears; but many resemble Gloucesters, in that they are mainly red, with white underparts and a white stripe down the back.

The breed comes from Northern Ireland, but in the 1980s the population of Irish Moiled sadly fell to only about 20 cows.

HIGHLAND CATTLE (left) THEIR SHAGGY COATS, AS THICK AS DUVETS, ARE IMPERVIOUS TO EVEN THE HEAVIEST RAIN OR SNOW.

JERSEY COW (below) TAN, WITH BLACK FEET, MUZZLES AND TAIL-BRUSHES, JERSEYS ARE THE MOST ATTRACTIVE OF COWS.

CAVE PAINTINGS AT LASCAUX (bottom) LIMOUSINS BEAR A STRIKING RESEMBLANCE TO THE CATTLE DEPICTED AT LASCAUX.

Jersey

The eponymous Jersey is the only type of cattle present on the largest of the Channel Islands, and the purity of the breed is maintained by a strict ban on imports of any other kinds of cattle, which has been in place for over 150 years. There are fewer than 6000 Jersey cows on the island itself, but such is the animals' excellence as milkers that they have become the second most popular dairy breed in the world, surpassed in popularity only by Holsteins.

Like Guernseys, they derive from a mixture of French breeds. They were originally known as Alderneys (after the Channel Island) and have been kept on mainland Britain for at least 250 years. Their characteristic colours – tan, with black feet, muzzles and tail-brushes – make them the most attractive of cows – and they are relatively small, weighing only between 400 and 450 kg.

Their milk is exceptionally rich in protein, minerals and trace elements: its golden colour derives from carotene, which the cows naturally extract from grass. The Jersey Cattle Society was founded in 1878, and today has about 1000 members.

Kerry

Claimed by its fanciers to be one of the oldest breeds in Europe, the Kerry is a medium-sized, black animal with a skull very similar in formation to that of the aurochs (*see page 153*). Its closer ancestors were probably the little black cows known as Celtic Shorthorns, brought northwards by Neolithic man as he migrated across what is now Europe from the Mediterranean basin. The Kerry was the world's first real dairy cow: it was bred mainly for milk production by the Celts in Ireland, who depended heavily on its produce, and stored milk treated with herbs, possibly in the form of cheeses, and possibly yoghurt in earthenware jars underground.

The Kerry Herd Book has been kept by the Royal Dublin Society since 1887. Today the breed is classified as Category 3 (Vulnerable) on the Rare Breeds' Survival Trust list, and there are only about 120 Kerries in Great Britain.

Limousin

With their big, golden red bodies, Limousins bear a striking resemblance to the cattle depicted on the walls of the Lascaux Caves near Montignac in France. It seems, therefore, that the history of this breed may well reach back 20,000 years.

The animals originated in the Massif Central of France, a region of harsh climate and poor granite soil, which forced them to develop exceptional sturdiness and adaptability. Moreover, because the area was isolated, local farmers were able to develop their cattle with little genetic influence from outside.

Since those early days, selective breeding has transformed Limousins into highly specialised producers of

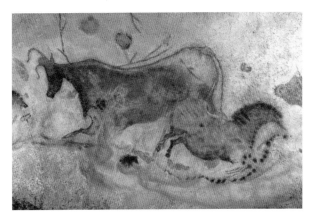

5

Farm Animals
Cattle

Jersey
Limousin

beef, with well-muscled carcasses and not too much fat.
The first pure-bred bulls and heifers to reach Britain
arrived at Leith Docks outside Edinburgh, in February 1971,
and farmers formed such a high opinion of them that the
animals rapidly challenged the traditional Herefords as the
country's leading beef animal. By 1998 they had become
the most numerous beef breed in the United Kingdom.

Longhorn

Hardy cattle with long, downward-curving white horns
have been bred in the midland counties of England since
time immemorial. They may have varied in colour from
black, through various stages of roan to white, but they
were all much of a type, long in the back and valued more
for their staunchness in pulling the plough than for their
meat or milk.

Robert Bakewell, in the latter half of the eighteenth
century, set out to create an outstanding producer of beef –
and so successful was he that his Leicestershire Longhorns
were exported to many parts of the world. Not only did his
animals mature in half the time taken by others: they were
also capable of providing a carcass which was 'two-fifths
boil to three-fifths roast'. After his death in 1795, the fame
of the breed spread to all corners of Britain and Ireland –
witness a notice in the Belfast *Newsletter* of April 1810:

SULTON A beautiful young bull of the Longhorned
Leicestershire breed will be let to cows this season at 5s 5d
per leap. He is a full-bred son of LEICESTER TOM. His
dam a thorough bred cow of equal beauty ... He stands at
Glenville, four miles from Belfast on the Falls Road.

Yet nobody had quite Bakewell's intuitive feeling for the
work, and the breed went into decline until new champions
took it up and formed the Longhorn Cattle Society in 1878.
Latter-day farmers found the cattle difficult to manage,
because of their lengthy horns, especially in the 1950s and
1960s, when the trend was to keep animals indoors and feed
them cereals. By 1975 the breed had become endangered,
with fewer than 250 cows remaining, but 20 years' careful
restoration work lifted it back to the status of a minor
breed, with about 2500 breeding cows.

Owners and keepers of Longhorn cattle claim that the
breed produces beef that leaves all others standing in
terms of flavour and texture.

Lincoln Reds

The big, rugged Lincoln Reds are almost certainly
descended from animals brought to eastern England by
successive waves of Viking invaders. Their hardiness is
legendary – as it needs to be, with icy winds whistling in
off the North Sea – and they are excellent at converting

Farm Animals
Cattle

Longhorn
Lincoln Reds

rough herbage into meat. In the eighteenth and nineteenth centuries Lincoln Reds were developed as a dual-purpose breed, for milk and meat, but later the emphasis swung onto beef, the aim being to produce bigger and bigger animals. Then in the 1950s fashions changed: butchers decided that the Reds were *too* large, and went for smaller beasts like Aberdeen-Angus and Herefords. With demand for their animals declining, Lincolnshire farmers worked out a new strategy: taking advantage of the fact that the Reds mature very fast, they began to market steers at 15 or even 12 months, when they were still relatively small. This proved successful, and the breed gradually built up again. As a result of a selective breeding programme begun in the 1940s, all Lincoln Reds are now polled.

Red Poll

No great antiquity is claimed for the chunky, medium-sized Red Poll. The breed was created in East Anglia at the beginning of the nineteenth century by the fusion of the Norfolk Red with the Suffolk Dun, and classes for it were first held at the Royal Show in 1862. The Breed Society was formed in 1888, since when the cattle have spread all over the world, highly valued as dual-purpose animals, the heifers giving good yields of milk over exceptionally long spans, and steers producing excellent beef. The Red Poll's pigmentation protects it against skin diseases associated with strong sunlight and this has made it popular in countries such as Jamaica and Brazil, where it has been successfully crossed with local breeds.

Vaynol

In 1872 a single herd of cattle was moved from Scotland to Vaynol Park in North Wales. The animals seem to have derived largely from White Park cattle (see right), perhaps with some Highland blood thrown in, and possibly with some Indian influence as well. For years the herd ran more or less wild, but recently it was taken into more active management, and the animals, though still primitive, are easier to handle.

Whitebred Shorthorn

The origin of Whitebred Shorthorns is not clear, but it seems that they derived from the Shorthorn cattle of northern England. They are bred mainly on the borders of Scotland and England, where, in the mid-nineteenth century, farmers found that the white strain of Shorthorn, when crossed with a Galloway, produced an attractive blue-grey animal which quickly became popular, not least because it was exceptionally good at making the most of rough hill grazing.

The selected White Shorthorns became known as Whitebreds, and although crossing was always directed towards blue-grey production, breeding was somewhat arbitrary until the Whitebred Shorthorn Association was formed in 1962. Today the cattle are recognised as a breed by the Rare Breeds Society, and there are about 200 registered females.

White Park

One of the most ancient breeds of British cattle, the White Park are mentioned in the old Irish sagas and in the tenth-century code of the Welsh King Hywel Dda. In about the thirteenth century several herds were enclosed in parks, and three of the original collections survive to this day – at Dynevor, Cadzow and Chartley. With their wide, elegant horns and fine colouring – white, with black noses, ears and feet – the animals are extremely decorative, and are now kept in many rural parks, as well as in some commercial herds. During the Second World War the government considered the breed such an important part of the British heritage that a small herd was shipped to the United States for safe-keeping.

The Chartley Herd of White Park cattle can be traced back to 1248, when wild animals were driven out of the Forest of Needwood in Staffordshire and confined to the park at Chartley, home of the Shirley family. Tradition held that the number must never exceed 21, and that if a black calf were born, it must be slaughtered at once: otherwise, it would presage the death of a member of the owner's family within a year.

In spite of these restraints, the total number of White Park at Chartley rose at one stage to 50, only to fall sharply, until in 1904 only eight cattle survived, These were sold to the Duke of Bedford, to add to his collection at Woburn Abbey; but their journey to the south proved disastrous: the straw provided for their bedding in the railway wagons caught fire, and several beasts were so badly burned that they died.

The Duke decided to cross the survivors with Longhorn cattle, to infuse new blood into the breed; but the wild White strain was so dominant that the hybrids reverted to type, and when the thirteenth Earl Ferrers bought back the herd – by then 24 strong – in 1970, they were indistinguishable from the original stock. A separate herd of 17 more cattle had been established at Whipsnade Zoo, from animals presented by the Duke of Bedford, and in 1973 Earl Ferrers bought these individuals as well, thus reuniting the whole herd.

Sheep

All domestic sheep (*Ovis aries*) are thought to have originated from the wild Asiatic mouflon (*Ovis orientalis*) which, living in social groups in the mountains, were easier for early man to round up and catch than fleet-footed deer. The origins of British animals are lost in the mists of time, but our indigenous breeds must have been developed from wild strains by selective breeding. They are fundamentally different, in that they are covered with wool, whereas wild species are coated only in kemp,or coarse hair. Thousands of years of improvement have developed the soft underfur of primitive types, and it has superseded the stiff guard-bristles that formed their original covering. Inextricably mixed with native stock are the various strains brought in by successive invaders such as the Romans, Vikings and Normans.

For centuries sheep have been an important element in British farming, and in hill country – which consitutes much of our landscape – harsh weather and sparse grazing have helped create breeds that can survive tough conditions. Yet it was only at the start of the eighteenth century that sheep were recognised primarily as a source of meat. Until then they had been bred mainly for their wool, which was already famous far beyond our shores in Roman times, and by the Middle Ages was in demand even in Turkey. In his huge survey *Britannia*, published in 1601, the historian William Camden wrote of the Cotswolds:

> There feed there great numbers of sheep, long-necked and square of bulk and bone, by reason (as it is commonly thought) of the weally and hilly situation of their pasturage; whose wool being most soft and fine is had in passing great account among all nations.

The task of putting meat on the bone was begun by Robert Bakewell, who had little interest in fleeces but in 1755 began breeding to produce compact animals which grew more quickly than his traditional stock. Innumerable other farmers have followed his example, with the result that British sheep are now bred all over the world.

Sheep are far less stupid than non-farmers suppose. In St John's Gospel, Jesus tells the Pharisees that the animals will always follow their shepherd, 'for they know his voice. And a stranger they will not follow, but will flee from him: for they know not the voice of strangers'. That truth, evident 2000 years ago, was recently confirmed by research and observation conducted in Cambridge, which confirmed that sheep not only recognise different human beings, but have quite efficient memories.

PRIMITIVE BREEDS

Castlemilk Moorit

One of the rarest breeds in existence, this was developed by the Buchanan Jardine family at Castlemilk Estate Park, in Dumfriesshire, early in the twentieth century. An amalgam of several rare breeds, it was designed to produce moorit-coloured (tan) wool; but by 1973 there were only ten survivors, and the flock was dispersed. Six of them went to the Farm Park, and four to a neighbour. By means of a careful breeding programme, numbers have been built up again: there are still fewer than 300 ewes, but it is hoped that the breed has been saved from extinction.

Hebridean

Black as the night and bristling with horns, a Hebridean ram is an amazing sight. Legend has it that the ancestors of these strange-looking sheep, which grow two, four or sometimes even six horns, were brought to Britain by the Vikings during their wave of expansion in the second century AD. Archaeological evidence of multi-horned breeds survives in many places associated with the Scandinavian invaders, among them the Isle of Man, Shetland, Iceland and even North Africa and the Canary Islands.

Although no longer found in the Scottish islands, the Hebrideans survive as ornamental animals in many small flocks. Most are black, but on the Isle of Man only the moorit or tan colour survives. By 1975 the breed had fallen to critical level, with fewer than 300 ewes remaining, but since then the active support of a breed association has trebled numbers.

Manx Loghtan

A remarkable survivor from prehistoric times, the Manx Loghtan is a small mountain sheep which often has four horns, two spread upwards in a wide V shape, and two curling down round its neck. The word 'loghtan' or 'loaghtan' is Manx for the dark chocolate colour of its fleece, and

CASTLEMILK MOORIT (below) THIS RARE SHEEP WAS BROUGHT DOWN TO ONLY 10 INDIVUDUALS; NOW THERE ARE JUST UNDER 300 EWES.

MANX LOGHTAN (bottom) BRED SELECTIVELY FOR ITS DISTINCTIVE LOGHTAN-COLOURED FLEECE, THIS BREED HAS TWO SETS OF HORNS.

seems to be derived from *lugh* (mouse) and *dhoan* (brown) or from *lhosht dhoan* (burnt brown). Until the eighteenth century the animals were generally white; some were grey and some black, with only a few brown, but the Loghtan wool was highly prized, and farmers bred selectively until it was the only colour left. Today, if white markings appear on any part of the body, they disqualify the animal from registration.

During the last century the breed steadily declined, and by the 1950s only a handful of Loghtans remained. Then interest revived, and by the time a breeders' group was established in 1988, a total of 69 flocks were registered. Some retain their primitive ability to shed their fleeces in early summer, but some have to be sheared, and the wool is usually woven or knitted without being dyed.

North Ronaldsay

This breed, now rare, was originally brought to Britain by the Vikings, and it still shares a number of characteristics with primitive breeds of Norwegian sheep. 'Ronnies' can be almost any colour, from white to grey, brown and black. During the Highland Clearances in the eighteenth and nineteenth centuries they were ousted from mainland Scotland by the more prolific Blackface, and eventually retreated to the most northerly Orkney island of Ronaldsay.

Living outside the high seawall, originally built to keep them off the crofts inland, they adapted to a diet entirely of kelp, or seaweed, which over the decades produced unique physiological changes. The ewes' milk, for example, contains a high level of iodine, which it is thought may help combat diseases like foot-rot and mastitis. On the other hand, the seaweed is high in molybdenum, which inhibits copper absorption – and this may lead to problems if the animals are moved to a different environment and grazing diet, where they are liable to take up too much copper and be poisoned.

Even though, in 1973, there were 2000 animals on Ronaldsay, Joe Henson, founder of the Rare Breeds Survival Trust, considered that the breed was at risk, because it was all in one place and could be wiped out by an epidemic or an oilspill. As a result he flew to Orkney, bought Linga Holm, a 40-hectare island surrounded by big kelp beds, and moved 150 North Ronaldsays to it as an insurance. He

Manx Loghtan
North Ronaldsay

PORTLAND (below) BOTH SEXES OF
THIS ENDANGERED BREED HAVE
HORNS; THOSE OF THE RAM SPIRAL
FINELY AND HAVE FINE BLACK LINES.

SOAY FLOCK (right) THIS PRIMITIVE
BREED IS SMALL, LIGHT-BONED WITH
SHORT TAILS. THEY WERE TAKEN TO
SOAY BY BRONZE AGE FARMERS.

BALWEN WELSH MOUNTAIN (bottom
right) ITS DARK BODY IS RELIEVED
BY WHITE ON ITS FOREHEAD, FACE,
NOSE, FEET AND TAIL.

was fascinated to see that although the sheep had access to grass in the middle of the island, they made straight for the seaweed and ate that first, coming on to dry land only at high tide. After seaweed they went for the stinging nettles and docks, not really taking to grass at all. Mr Henson also moved 100 individuals south, to establish mainland flocks and expand and enhance his own group of Ronaldsays in the Cotswolds.

The North Ronaldsay Sheep Fellowship was formed in 1997, and has over 60 members. There are still between two and three thousand sheep on the island, and about 800 breeding ewes on the mainland.

Portland

Legend has it that the ancestors of Portland sheep swam ashore from a wrecked Spanish ship as the survivors of the Armada fled anti-clockwise round the coast of Britain in the autumn of 1588. Whether or not that is true, the breed certainly contains Spanish blood, and was the first in Britain that could have lambs at any time of year (native sheep come into season only in the autumn, and lamb in the spring). Two other breeds derived from the Portland – Dorset Horn and Polled Dorset – share this ability.

It seems more likely that Portlands were introduced by the Romans, for in Saxon times large numbers of sheep were kept on Portland Island, where people traded wool and paid their tithes in cheese made from ewes' milk. King George III (known as 'Farmer George'), on his frequent visits to Weymouth, is said to have insisted on eating Portland mutton, which he considered a delicacy.

In the twentieth century quarrying for stone brought about a decline in farming on the island, and the last sheep left for the mainland in 1920. A survey by the Rare Breeds Survival Trust in 1974 revealed that only 86 breeding ewes

remained, and Portlands were listed as Category Three (endangered). Now the Breeders' Group, formed in 1993, represents some 90 flocks, and the total of Portlands is back over 500.

Both sexes have horns: those of the ram spiral finely, and are often marked with longitudinal black lines. Lambs are born with foxy-red coats, but these soon turn creamy white.

Soay

Ancestors of all modern sheep, these have remained unchanged since prehistoric times, isolated on islands off the west coast of the Scottish Highlands. Like all primitive breeds, they are small and light-boned with short tails, and shed their dark brown wool in spring. Each flock has a king ram, groups of breeding females with a clear hierarchy and parties of young bachelor males.

They were taken to Soay, one of the islands in the St Kilda group, by Bronze Age farmers, and they have remained unchanged ever since.

Confusion arose from the fact that some people called Hebridean sheep (a separate breed) St Kildas, whereas in fact the island of St Kilda is stocked with Soays. The sheep once called St Kilda are now known as Hebridean. Because of their small size and thrifty nature, Soays are useful in conservation areas, where light grazing is needed to keep vegetation at a moderate level.

Another breed of small, horned primitive sheep from the St Kilda group is the Boreray, which inhabits the island of the same name.

HILL BREEDS

Balwen Welsh Mountain

The savage winter of 1946–7 reduced this Welsh mountain breed to one small flock in the Upper Towy valley, its homeland in South Wales. Balwens have down-curling horns and unusual, attractive colouring, their dark bodies relieved by a white blaze down the forehead, face and nose, white feet, and white end to the tail. The combination is thought to derive from some foreign strain, introduced by Irish seamen or Dutch settlers.

5

Farm Animals
Sheep

Portland
Balwen Welsh
Mountain

170

Clun

A hill breed originally from Shropshire, which took its name from the market town of Clun, these odd-looking sheep are mainly off-white, but with dark-brown legs, faces and ears. Each has a curious pom-pom or powder-puff of wool on the top of its forehead. Their fleece is short, but dense and fine, and comparatively free from coarse fibres. A Clun ewe crossed with a Border Leicester ram produces the English Halfbred.

Cheviot

Chunky-looking Cheviots have faces and heads covered with short, white hair, but their fleeces are so thick that a ruff of wool piles up behind their ears and makes them look as though they were wearing fur coats and collars. From their original home in the Cheviot Hills on the Scottish borders they have spread to many parts of the world. A reference to a 'small but very hardy race' of sheep in 1372 suggests that they already existed in the fourteenth century. Their wool once formed the basis of the Border tweed industry, and earned farmers' substantial income; but it has now declined to be of marginal importance, and the main purpose of Cheviots is to produce high quality lamb, often from crosses with other breeds such as the Suffolk or Texel. Kindred strains, the Brecknock Hill Cheviot and the North Country Cheviot, are found in mid-Wales and the north of Scotland respectively.

Dartmoor or Greyface Dartmoor

A medium-sized sheep, with short legs and a deep chest, the Dartmoor looks like a mobile powder-puff, so luxuriant is its curly wool, which covers its head and legs as well as

JACOB SHEEP (below) ALTHOUGH LISTED AS A MINOR BREED, JACOB SHEEP HAVE BECOME RELATIVELY COMMON IN RECENT YEARS.

SHETLAND (right) THE FINE WOOL FROM SHETLANDS IS LEFT UNDYED AND USED TO MAKE THE PATTERNS IN FAIRISLE SWEATERS.

the rest of its body. The animals' attractive appearance makes them (as a breed leaflet puts it) 'a natural focal point whenever they appear'.

Because they are descended from local breeds which grazed the low ground round the fringes of Dartmoor, they have developed constitutions strong enough to withstand the severe winters that characterise the moor. Their long lustre wool was traditionally used for blankets, serge, carpets and cloth.

The Dartmoor Sheep Breeders' Association was formed in 1909 to standardise and improve the breed, and today flocks are established on many farms in England, Wales and southern Scotland.

Jacob

Joseph's coat of many colours is supposed to have been made from the wool of Jacob sheep, which carry large, chocolate blotches on a creamy background. In Chapter 30 of the Book of Genesis there is much talk of spotted cattle and sheep, and a description of how Joseph's father Jacob took rods of green poplar, hazel and chestnut, put white stakes among them, and set the whole assembly in his drinking troughs, so that his animals might conceive off-spring 'ringstraked and, speckled and spotted' when they came to drink.

Alas, modern Jacobs rather spoil the story by having long tails and not shedding their wool naturally – two traits which suggest they are not primitive sheep at all. It seems that they were introduced to Britain from Spain in the

sixteenth century, perhaps bringing elements of Viking ancestry with them (like the Hebridean, they grow multiple horns). In 1973 they were classified as a minor breed, but research showed that in fact there were over 3000 ewes scattered about in small flocks in Britain, and now so many enthusiasts have taken them up that they have become relatively common.

Herdwick

The rugged hills of the Lake District are the home of the Herdwick, hardiest of British sheep, which were kept by rich abbeys in Norman times. Their long, coarse wool, which makes hard-wearing carpets, is dark blue-grey when they are born, but tends to grow lighter with age, and their faces are white.

Hill Radnor

A hardy mountain sheep, described by its aficionados as 'gay in appearance and active', with a tan face, the Hill Radnor is a heavy breed indigenous to the Welsh border counties of Brecon, Radnor, Hereford and Monmouth. Its origins are lost in the mists of time, as the Flock Book was established only in 1948; but registration as a rare breed in 1993 stimulated much local interest and today the society has over 40 members. Of these, probably fewer than ten run commercial flocks, and the rest keep a few animals as a hobby.

Kerry Hill

A breed from the Welsh borders, Kerry Hills are some of the prettiest sheep in Britain. They have creamy fleeces and black feet and knees; and with white faces offset by black ears and nose, and black patches round the eyes, they bear a super-ficial resemblance to pandas. They were once common in the Border counties, but now have gone out of fashion and are much reduced, on a watching brief.

Llanwenog

A medium-sized hill sheep, with a black face and no horns, the Llanwenog was traditionally bred on family farms in West Wales,

particularly in the Teifi valley. It was developed in the latter part of the nineteenth century by crossing clean-faced Shropshire rams with a local breed (now extinct) of horned, black-faced ewes. The result is an animal with a placid temperament, easily managed, and prolific.

Wider interest in the breed was first aroused by a succession of wins in national lambing competitions during the 1960s, when Llanwenogs six times won the coveted Thomas Memorial Trophy with a lambing average of 215 per cent – an annual production of well over two lambs per ewe. A further advantage is durability: the sheep's teeth tend to wear out rather than drop out. The Llanwenog Sheep Society now has 120 members, with 3120 breeding ewes and 140-odd rams, in flocks spread all over Britain.

Lleyn

This hill breed is exceptionally productive, as ewes can bear up to five lambs in one litter. It originated in the Lleyn peninsula, in North Wales, but now is found throughout Wales and the Welsh Borders. Lleyns are medium-sized, compact-looking, and white all over, except for a black nose and sometimes a black spot on the ear. Until the start of the twentieth century the ewes were often milked for cheese-making, but today the breed is valued for its long, fine wool, which is ideal for hand-knitting.

Norfolk Horn

These handsome sheep, horned and black-faced, missed extinction by a whisker. Strictly speaking, they are not hill sheep, having been traditionally bred in the flat, bare, sandy Brecklands of Norfolk, where they are known to have existed for at least 400 years. But their sparse environment resembled that of the hills, in that the sheep had to walk many kilometres every day to find enough sustenance. Lean, agile, long-legged and often bare-bellied, they were described as 'restless', and had a reputation for jumping hedges and walls like goats; but their mutton, said to taste like venison, was renowned for its leanness and succulence, and because they were so fit from constant ranging, they could walk the 160-odd kilometres to market in

London without losing much of their condition.

In the eighteenth century the breed declined, and although it was crossed with Southdowns to produce the highly successful Suffolk, the pure Norfolk strain steadily ebbed away until in 1965 only six ewes and seven rams were left. By then the sheep were so inbred that expansion of the flock was extremely difficult, and in 1968 a programme of back-crossing was started, using Suffolk ewes as a foundation, and the remaining pure-bred Norfolk rams, to reconstruct the breed. Numbers of nearly pure animals gradually built up, and in 1985 the breeders felt confident enough of having achieved 80 per cent purity to apply to the Rare Breeds Trust for recognition.

Norfolk Horn went on the Priority List, Category One (Critical) that same year. The recovery continued so well that by 1994 there were 40 flocks (some very small), and owners met to form a breeders' group. In 1998 this had 60 members, and the Combined Flock Book showed 54 rams and 377 ewes. The new-style Norfolks tend to be chunkier than their rangy forebears, but they still taste delicious, and they can still jump.

Shetland

In spite of the fact that its fine wool is highly prized, the Shetland became rare in the 1970s, when fewer than 900 ewes survived. Now it has seen a renaissance, not least because many owners of small flocks are interested in spinning. The wool is exceptionally soft and fine, and comes in many natural colours, from black through various shades of grey, moorit, and brown to white. The wool is used undyed to make the patterns in Fairisle sweaters.

BLUE-FACED LEICESTER (below) BIG,
AND LONG-LEGGED, THESE SHEEP
INHERITED THEIR FRAMES FROM
LEICESTER LONGWOOLS.

WELSH MOUNTAIN RAM (right)
THIS HANDSOME FELLOW'S FINE
SPIRALLING HORNS ARE TYPICAL
OF THE BREED.

Swaledale

This mountain breed still flourishes in the North Yorkshire dale from which it takes its name. Both sexes have horns and exceptionally long white wool (up to 25cm), which hangs down over their black-and-white speckled faces. Similar types are the **Dalesbred** in the Pennines, the **Rough Fell** in the Cumbrian hills, and the **Lonk**, renowned for its hardiness. The **Derbyshire Gritstone** is claimed to grow the finest fleece of any blackface mountain breed.

Welsh Mountain

The second most common breed in Britain, Welsh Mountain are small sheep with white faces and legs. The rams have fine, spiralling horns, but the ewes are polled. Like all mountain sheep, they have a strong sense of survival: they know when bad weather is on the way, and take care to find shelter for themselves and their lambs. Living in family groups, they get to know every corner of their range, and become hefted to it – that is, they regard it as home, and try to return to it if moved elsewhere.

The South Wales Mountain is bigger than its northern cousin, and grows a heavy fleece with a brown collar. The Black Welsh Mountain is larger still and is known as

Torddu, meaning 'black belly', while Badger-faced Welsh are called *Torwen* – 'white belly'.

Whiteface Dartmoor

One of Britain's most ancient breeds, the Whiteface was once spread over much of west Somerset and Devon; but as more land was enclosed, it was pushed back onto Dartmoor, where it became firmly rooted and now continues to flourish. Most of the flocks still live and thrive on the moor, grazing at altitudes between 150 and 600 metres above sea level, protected against wet and cold by their long, thick wool. A flock book was opened in the 1950s, and over 3000 breeding ewes are now registered.

White-faced Woodlands

These short wool sheep have existed on the borders of Yorkshire, Lancashire and Derbyshire since time immemorial. Once known as Penistones, after the market town in which they were sold, they were renamed after the Woodland Dale which links Derwent and Ladybower to the Snake Pass and Glossop. Both sexes have horns, those of the rams being large and spiralling. Due to the importation of Merino blood by George III in the eighteenth century, the sheep have some of the finest fleeces of all British mountain breeds.

During the First World War, enthusiasm for Whitefaced Woodlands declined, and they remained on only a few farms in the Pennines. But then, after the formation of the Rare Breeds' Survival Trust in 1973, interest revived, and over the past few years the breed has expanded and spread to new areas.

LONGWOOL BREEDS

Blue-faced Leicester

These are big, long-legged animals, which have inherited their large frames from Bakewell's improved Leicester Longwools. In spite of their name, their heads and faces are white, only the skin beneath the short hair being dark blue. High Roman noses lend them an imperious look, rather undermined by the fact that they have no wool on their legs, which gives them a spindly appearance. The breed was evolved

during the nineteenth century to produce high-quality cross-bred ewes, and today a Blue-faced Leicester ram crossed on to a mountain ewe produces the Mule, one of the most popular commercial half-breds.

Border Leicester

Easily recognised by their Roman noses, clean faces and long, upstanding white ears, Border Leicesters are one of the most famous British breeds, and are established in many other countries of the world interested in commercial sheep-farming, including Australia, New Zealand, South Africa and the Americas. Their wool is of high quality, and its natural elasticity makes it ideal for hand knitting; but the sheep were originally developed in the Scottish Borders specifically for meat production and for crossing with other breeds.

Cotswold

These are the sheep that so impressed William Camden. Cotswolds are descended from the large, long woolled animals imported by the Romans, and a pair of shears found in the ruins of the Roman villa at Chedworth, in Gloucestershire, is identical with the hand-shears used to this day, showing that the care of them was not much different two millennia ago. They grow thick, curly fleeces (which hang down even over their faces), and during the Middle Ages their wool produced great wealth in the Gloucestershire hills, enabling local merchants to build fine houses and churches.

During the nineteenth century the Cotswold entered a second golden age, this time as meat-producer. Rams were eagerly sought for crossing with other breeds, and were exported to many countries. Yet between the two world

LINCOLN LONGWOOL (left) THIS
LINCOLN LONGWOOL LAMB WILL
GROW TO PRODUCE A FLEECE THAT
ALMOST REACHES THE GROUND.

MERINO (below) ORIGINALLY FROM
SPAIN, MERINOS PRODUCE HEAVY
FLEECES OF VERY FINE WOOL, AND
GOOD MEAT.

wars the demand for smaller joints of meat, and the take-over of the woollen industry by Merinos, sent the breed into such a decline that by the 1970s it was on the brink of extinction, with only 300 ewes left, and only now is it recovering.

The Cotswold Sheep Society, established in 1892, is an exceptionally active charity, which works to promote and conserve the breed. Training forms an important part of its work, and the society holds its own annual show. Cotswold wool has come back into fashion among home weavers and spinners because it is ideal for home work.

Galway

Galway sheep are often regarded as a joint Anglo-Irish product. Their development began late in the seventeenth century, when English Longwools were exported to Ireland and crossed with local animals, and it was continued apace by Robert Bakewell a century later. The improvement brought about by English blood was evidently marked, for a visitor to Ballinasloe Fair described the original Irish animals as 'ugly sheep with nothing to recommend them except their size' – whereas by 1824 these thuggish aboriginals had been replaced by much finer specimens.

By 1870 the improved type had become known as the Roscommon, after Lord Roscommon, later the Earl of Sheffield, who had given Bakewell much help, and it bore a close resemblance to those of Bakewell's sheep that appear in prints and paintings. By the 1920s, however, the Roscommon was losing ground, and in 1923 it was superseded by the Galway. The Galway Sheep Breeders' Society, formed that year, admitted 600 ewes and 20 rams to its stock book, and the breed did so well that in 1965 a third of all the sheep in Ireland were of Galway stock.

Thereafter a decline set in, as imported animals like Texels and Suffolks became fashionable, and by March 1994 Galways had fallen back so much that only 300 pedigree ewes remained. Vigorous action by the society reversed the downward trend, and the breed now looks secure – especially as, in 1990, Galways were introduced to England by the importation of a selection from seven of the leading flocks in Ireland.

Leicester Longwool

A thick, heavy fleece hanging down in ringlets, cloaks the Leicester Longwool from head to toe, dangling even over its face and half-covering its ears. Yet the animal is now valued more for its meat than for its wool, and it has fallen far from the pre-eminence which Dishley Leicesters enjoyed in the late eighteenth century.

Lincoln Longwool

A neighbour and close relation of the Leicester Longwool, Lincolns also grow tremendous coats. This breed is thought to have been the origin of all the longwool types in England, and excelled as a wool-producer well before Bakewell began his experiments late in the eighteenth century.

Its home territory is on the rolling slopes of the Lincolnshire Wolds, where there is little shelter from persistent cold winds – and no doubt these conditions contributed to the evolution of its exceptional fleece, which reaches almost to the ground all round it. One ram is on record as having produced a fleece weighing 21 kg, and the record length of staple, clipped from a yearling ewe at first shearing, is 80 cm.

Lincolns have been exported to countries all over the world, and demand is so strong that in many years it cannot be met in full. The sheep have been crossed with others to create new breeds – for instance the Corriedale, a mixture of Lincoln and Merino, which is now popular throughout the southern hemisphere.

Merino

Deriving from Spain, where the king once had the sole right to own them, Merinos have spread all over the world. Some 3000 were sent to England in 1480 and the same number in 1560. The breed first reached South Africa in 1789, when a small flock sent from Spain as a gift to the House of Orange could not adjust to the wet weather in the Netherlands and were passed on to the Dutch military commander at the Cape of Good Hope. Since then their ability to produce heavy fleeces of fine wool, as well as good carcasses, has made them favourites in many countries.

TEESWATER (below) MASSES OF HANGING RINGLETS, SOME OF WHICH COME OVER THE FACE PRODUCE FINE LUSTRE FLEECES.

WENSLEYDALE LONGWOOLS (below right) LIKE TEESWATERS, THESE SHEEP HAVE EXTRAORDINARILY LONG RINGLETS OF FLEECE.

Teeswater

A large, hornless breed with black noses and feet, Teeswaters grow fine lustre fleeces made up of a mass of hanging ringlets, some of which come down over their faces. They are indigenous to Teesdale in County Durham, and have been bred by farmers in that area for at least two centuries: in 1804 a consignment was sent from the Duke of Northumberland's estate to Tasmania.

Along with all other longwool sheep in the north of England, they were influenced by Bakewell's experiments in the eighteenth century. But the breed retained its integrity, and until 1920 remained comparatively rare, never found far from its native habitat. Then its excellent crossing qualities began to be appreciated, and today Teeswaters, as well as Teeswater half breds known as Mashams, are found all over Britain. In the north of England young ewes are known as gimmers. The fine, long wool of Mashams is used for making carpets and tweeds.

Wensleydale Longwool

The founding sire of this breed was a ram called Bluecap, born in 1839 in the hamlet of East Appleton, in North Yorkshire. His father was a Dishley Leicester ram, his mother a Teeswater Mugg, a local longwool breed now extinct. His dark skin, enormous size and superb wool were so outstanding that they determined the breed type without any further infusion of Leicester blood.

Wensleydales are probably the heaviest indigenous

British breed, and they are visually striking, partly because of their alert, bold carriage, and partly because of their exceptionally fine wool, often known as 'poor man's mohair', which hangs down in ringlets, even over their blue faces in a forelock known as the 'topping'. The fleece yields the most valuable lustre longwool in the world, similar to mohair, with which it is often blended. Its special qualities are genetically transmitted to cross-bred lambs – which makes a Wensleydale ram the leading wool-improver. The sheep are also excellent milkers, and it was from ewes' milk that white, crumbly Wensleydale cheese was originally made.

In 1890 two rival breed societies were formed, and the pair feuded for the next 30 years, each claiming superiority. Not until 1920 did they amalgamate, with 197 members and over 3000 ewes put to the ram; but from that moment the breed lost popularity, and only 226 ewes went to the ram in 1973. That same year the newly formed Rare Breeds Survival Trust listed Wensleydales as Category 1 – Critical. Interest revived, and by 1995, when a Wensleydale was selected as Reserve Supreme Champion at the Royal Show, the number of breeding ewes had leapt to 1246.

Although several flocks were culled during the foot-and-mouth outbreak of 2001, the breed is now widespread throughout the United Kingdom, and there are small flocks in Holland, France and Denmark. Wensleydale cheese is still produced in the dairy at Hawes in the dale, but it is now made from the milk of cows, rather than of sheep.

Scottish Blackface

This breed has caused more human misery than any other animal in Britain, for it was the mass introduction of Blackfaced sheep to the Scottish Highlands that led to the evictions known as the Clearances, in which villages were cleared of their inhabitants, the houses burned, and the people cast penniless upon the world. The process, begun in the 1780s and lasting for 75 years, devastated the Highlands, not only destroying hundreds of little communities, but also wrecking the habitat. The constant grazing of the sheep, reinforced by the grazing and browsing of the ever-expanding red deer population, prevented regeneration of trees and shrubs, and so reduced several million hectares to a mountain desert of rough grass, heather and rock.

The Clearances caused immense anger when they were happening, and they still stir resentment today, particularly in areas like Sutherland, where some of the most brutal evictions took place. The crowning irony of the whole, lamentable saga was that the sheep, far from yielding the huge profits which landowners had been led to expect,

soon began to fail; but by the time their fallibility became evident, the damage had already been done. Today, in countless glens, one can look down from above and make out the pathetic traces of a settlement that flourished there long ago: the stumpy remains of house-walls are outlined under turf, and parallel ridges in the bracken mark the lazy beds where the crofters once grew potatoes.

Execrated though it is in much of Scotland, the Black-face remains the most numerous breed of sheep in Britain, making up 30 per cent of the total pure-bred population.

SCOTTISH BLACKFACE RAM (right)
THIS HANDSOME SPECIMEN WAS
PHOTOGRAPHED IN THE LAMMERMUIR
HILLS, SCOTLAND.

It is a hardy creature, with a heavy, coarse fleece, which grows to a prodigious length if an animal escapes the annual gathering and shearing: a two- or three-fleecer looks like a ragged, walking duvet. The fact that its wool is much used for European mattress-making is of little interest to deer-stalkers, because the animal becomes exceedingly wild, and if disturbed makes off with explosive, far-carrying snorts, which bolt any deer within earshot.

MEAT BREEDS

Beltex

Not a British breed at all, but now established here as a meat-producer *par excellence*, the Beltex was developed in Belgium. It is distinguished by the immense size of its backside, which is all meat and no fat – the ultimate in modern sheep production.

Dorset Down

In its official 'Standards of Excellence' prescribed for Dorset Downs, the breed association declares that the sheep should have 'a leg at each corner'. That is exactly how it looks: a chunky, thick-set animal, clad in a fleece of short, tight wool, with bare brown ears sticking out horizontally from a rounded, hornless head.

It is almost 200 years since Mr Homer Saunders of Watercombe near Dorchester, began to refine the Down sheep of Bovington by selecting thelargest ewes and rams. His work, carried on by numerous other farmers, has produced spectacular improvements: in the past 100 years the weight of a typical ewe has increased from 40 kg to 90 or 100 kg, and that of lambs has similarly doubled. Dorset Downs have been exported to countries all over the world and have consistently done well. At home, particularly good lambs are obtained when a Dorset ram is crossed with commercial breeds of ewe. The breed association was formed in 1906 and now includes 50 flocks, with about 2500 pedigree Dorset Downs registered in Britain and Northern Ireland.

Oxford Down

Largest of the Down group of sheep, Oxfords grow to impressive dimensions: ewes often weigh nearly 100 kg. They have black noses, muzzles, eye-patches and ears, and their dense fleeces grow right down to their feet, adding

still more to the impression of solidity created by their heavy bodies and prominent breast bones. They originated with the crossing of Cotswold rams on to Hampshire Down ewes in the 1830s, and over the next decade the breed was streamlined by (among others) Samuel Druce, who had a small farm at Eynsham and won prizes at the Oxfordshire county show. At first the new sheep were called Down-Cotswold, but in 1857 the name was changed to Oxford Down. By the time the breeders' association was formed in 1889, and the first flock book published in the same year, Oxfords were winning many prizes and attracting attention not only in England, but in France, Germany, Denmark, America and elsewhere.

After the Second World War, a swing towards smaller carcasses hit many large breeds, and Oxford Downs particularly. From the 97 flocks registered in 1960, the total fell to 34 in 1975. In the initial survey carried out by the Rare Breeds Survival Trust, Oxford Downs entered in Category 2, the tenth rarest British sheep.

Ryeland

Like a child's toy, the Ryeland is small, chunky and cuddly looking, with tight wool covering most of its body, including face and legs. It derives from the native sheep of Herefordshire, once famous for the fine quality of their wool, which was known as 'Leominster ore'. At the end of the eighteenth century they were crossed with Down rams, which improved the shape of carcasses, but spoilt the quality of their fleece.

Shropshire

Several old breeds from the Welsh borders and West Midlands – among them the Morfe Common and the Longmynd – went into the creation of the Shropshire breed, which has black faces and ears. Heavy Southdown rams helped evolve an animal with good meat-producing qualities. The breeders' society, formed in 1882, was the first such body in Britain, and its first flock book was published in 1883. Today Shropshire rams are renowned for their ability to sire excellent lambs for meat-production when crossed with other breeds.

Southdown

Like the Dorset Down, the Southdown is small and very compact, and 'should have a leg at each corner, well fleshed down to its hocks'. Sheep of this kind have grazed the Sussex Downs since time immemorial, and there is a record of some being exported to America in 1640; but it was John Ellman of Glynde near Lewes, who began to improve them radically at the end of the eighteenth century, by selective crossing within the breed.

They continued to be popular all through the nineteenth century, and many large estates had flocks of 1000 or more. One enthusiastic owner was Thomas Coke of Holkham Hall ('Coke of Norfolk'), who switched from Merinos to Southdowns, kept a flock of 2500, and persuaded neighbours to take up the breed. Southdowns were exported all over the world, but their greatest impact was in New Zealand, where rams were used to produce 'Canterbury Lamb'.

The breed society was formed in 1891. During the 1960s membership was only about 60, but since Southdowns were declared a rare breed in 1985, interest has revived sharply, and today there are over 300 members. Controversy still smoulders about the size of the sheep: some owners want the bigger animals produced by the importation of French and Australian blood, while others champion the compact stature that has always been the breed's hallmark.

Wiltshire Horn

Both sexes of this old-fashioned meat sheep have curving horns, and those of the rams grow to an impressive length in more than one full circle. The sheep have very short wool, which they shed in early summer as they grow a new coat, so that they never need shearing. The breed was once known as the Horned Crock.

Skeletons and bones excavated on the Wiltshire downs show that the sheep of 2000 years ago were only 4–5 cm shorter at the shoulder than their successors today. The origins of those ancient animals are impossible to determine: they may have been imported by the Romans, or by the Phoenicians, who came in search of copper and tin. Some experts believe the short fleece indicates a Welsh mountain influence.

Whatever the truth, by the Middle Ages, and even more by the eighteenth century, enormous numbers of Wiltshire Horn sheep swarmed over Salisbury Plain, astonishing visitors such as John Aubrey and Daniel Defoe. Later, various factors sent the breed into decline. The formation of a breeders' association in 1923 revived it for a while, but by the early 1970s it was again in trouble, handicapped (in some people's view) by the fact that it produced no saleable wool. The Rare Breeds' Survival Trust classed the Wiltshire as 'in need of monitoring'. In the past 25 years it has made something of a comeback. The lack of a fleece is now seen as a positive asset, since it means that the sheep are easier to look after, and in any case the price of wool has fallen to an uneconomic level. The Wiltshire Horn Society now has 150 members.

MILKING BREEDS

Sheep's milk, which is pure white, contains 50 per cent more solids than cows' or goats' milk, and twice as many minerals such as calcium, phosphate and zinc. All breeds of ewe should give milk after lambing, but some yield more than others, and only placid animals are suitable for dairy use: a nervous ewe will not let down her milk satisfactorily, and is liable to upset others. But most ewes learn a new routine quickly, and soon settle down to regular milking, feeding and handling. Sheep's milk is often used in cheesemaking, a craft that goes back thousands of years: it was common in regions with harsh, inhospitable landscapes where sheep were more successful than cows.

Friesland

The only specialist milk sheep in the United Kingdom at this point, Frieslands are kept by farmers who supply dairies or make their own cheese. The Friesland comes from Holland, where the breed traditionally lived on the Dutch polders. It is a large, white, long-legged animal, slimmer than those designed for meat production, with a long head and no horns. Two rams and eight ewes were imported into Britain in 1957, and a further draft of five rams and 15 ewes arrived in 1964. Since then there has been a ban on further imports, and in order to avoid the problems of inbreeding, owners have mated Frieslands with other types of sheep such as the Scottish Blackface

5

Farm Animals
Sheep

Friesland

183

BAGOT (below) THIS GOAT IS THOUGHT TO BE DESCENDED FROM ANIMALS BROUGHT BACK FROM THE CRUSADES BY RICHARD THE LIONHEART.

GOLDEN GUERNSEY (right) WITH UNUSUALLY SHAPED HORNS AND A SOFT GOLDEN COAT, GUERNSEYS ARE EXTREMELY RARE.

and the Dorset Horn – which produces excellent crosses.

Among the specialised new breeds created in this way are the British Milksheep (a combination of Friesland, Blue-faced Leicester, Dorset and Lleyn) and the Cambridge, which has no Friesland in its make-up, but includes elements of 12 other breeds. The pure-bred Dorset Horn is also suitable for milking.

Texel

Originally from the Island of Texel, off the Dutch Coast, Texels were much improved during the twentieth century by an infusion of Leicester and Lincoln blood. They are good dual-purpose sheep, being good milkers and yielding excellent lambs for the butcher. In contrast with their chubby, round bodies, their bare white faces make their heads seem rather small.

Goats

Goats, which belong to the genus *Capra*, are notorious for the destructive power of their browsing. At ground level no vegetation escapes them and they are agile enough to climb sloping trees. Who can forget the *cri de coeur* of Captain Joshua Slocum, who, during his solo voyage round the world in 1898, misguidedly picked up a goat on the island of St Helena and took it to Ascension, some 1100 km to the northwest. On the way to Ascension the animal ate his Panama hat, his chart of the West Indies and much of the rigging. 'Alas,' he lamented, 'There was not a rope in the sloop proof against that goat's awful teeth.' On the other hand goats have been kept by humans for their fleeces and their milk since time immemorial.

Angora

Prized for their fine, silky mohair fleece, which is shorn twice a year, Angoras originated in the Middle East and were first brought to Britain from New Zealand, Australia and the United States in the 1970s. Both sexes have horns and their long lop ears droop downwards. The mohair which they produce is not to be confused with the wool of Angora rabbits.

Bagot

This large, handsome, parkland breed, with black neck and shoulders, and the rest of the body white, is thought to be descended from animals brought back from the Crusades by Richard II. In the 1390s some goats were given to Sir Richard Bagot by Richard in return for a good day's hunting, and their descendants remained in Bagot Park near Blithfield in Staffordshire, for more than 500 years. In 1953, when the park was flooded to form an extra reservoir for the city of Birmingham's water supply, a small herd of the goats was saved by Nancy, Lady Bagot and the naturalist Phil Drabble, who lived near the park. Lady Bagot gave three Bagot goats to the Cotswold Farm Park, founding the herd there; and although the breed has built up from its low point of 50 nannies in 1973, it still has only about 100 individuals and remains critically rare.

Golden Guernsey

These beautifully soft-coloured goats, with honey-gold hair, are thought to derive from a mixture of French, Syrian and Maltese ancestors. The first reference to them in the Channel Islands dates from a book published in 1826. They were almost eliminated during the Second World War, when the islands were occupied by German forces, and many animals were slaughtered for food.

The Golden Guernseys were saved by one enthusiast, Miriam Milbourne, who first saw some grazing in 1924, and herself began to breed them on the island in the 1950s. The first successful imports to the mainland were made in 1967, but the animals are still extremely rare: they are now classed as vulnerable, with fewer than 300 nannies. Their long ears turn upwards and outwards, and this characteristic has contributed to the belief that they may be descended at least in part from Syrian goats, described by the Greek historian Herodotus in the fifth century BC as having wonderful ears that 'turn upwards and outwards at the tips in tribute to Apollo, who gave them their golden coats'.

Other breeds of goat found in Britain included the **Saanen**, a Swiss animal with a calm temperament from the valley of that name, where goats have been selectively bred for centuries. Also of Swiss origin are **Toggenburgs**, which are mid-brown to grey, with white markings on the face, and were first imported in 1882. The **Anglo Nubian** is easily recognised by its Roman nose and lop ears, and the **British Alpine** is black, with white face markings and feet. Largest of all is the **Lop-eared Boer**, which is white,

with a brown head and neck, and can weigh up to 150 kg. The **Lop-eared Angora** yields mohair – not to be confused with the angora wool produced from rabbits; and cashmere wool comes from the soft undercoat of any species.

The Harness Goat Society was formed in 1987 by enthusiasts keen to resume the Victorian custom of having animals pull small carts. British Goats are animals registered with the British Goat Society but not eligible for any specific breed; they can be any colour, and are noted for their hybrid vigour.

Golden Guernsey

Pigs

The intelligence of pigs has long been recognised and appreciated. Country people used to believe that the animals could see the wind, and reckoned that if they ran about with straw in their mouths, it was a sign of gales approaching. Travelling circuses kept pigs that would tell the time or people's fortunes by stopping opposite huge playing cards laid out in the ring. Of course, the animals could not read or count, but they were trained to react to very small signals, like the clicking of two fingernails that was imperceptible to the audience, and naïve rural spectators fully believed that they had superior mental powers.

Strict rules once governed the times at which a pig might be killed. The deed must not be done on a Monday, or when the moon was waning – otherwise the meat would shrink when cooked, or not take up salt when being cured. Ghost pigs have been reported from many areas, not least the Isle of Man, where one, wearing a red hat, is said to be harmless, but another, a big white boar, is supposed to snatch humans and carry them off upriver and through a cave to the underworld.

In the Middle Ages, when the inhabitants of the New Forest were forbidden to keep dogs large enough to hunt, they had recourse, instead, to pigs, which they trained to find and retrieve game. One creature of exceptional abilities, although at a later date, was Slut, the eighteenth-century sow who grew up half-wild in the New Forest until suddenly, at the age of 18 months, she showed unexpected prowess at pointing and retrieving game.

Her owners, the brothers Edward and Richard Toomer, were well known dog-breeders and trainers; but as soon as they spotted their new recruit's potential, they brought her into service, using her to point partridges, pheasants, black grouse and rabbits, all of which she would retrieve. In the words of Daniel's *Rural Sports*, 'When called to go out Shooting, she would come home off the Forest at full Stretch, and be as elevated as a Dog upon being shown the Gun.' Her one *bête noire* was a hare, which she disdained to recognise as quarry. She continued to live wild, but dashed in if she heard a whistle, the summons to go shooting.

For centuries pigs were kept in towns as well as in the country. In Jacobean London one starchmaker had 200 in his backyard, and straying pigs were a common hazard of urban life, often biting and sometimes even killing young children. Out in the country there was a wide variety in the methods and standards of husbandry. Some farmers simply put their animals in fields of clover and left them to graze on green fodder for the summer. Those with access to woods turned pigs out in autumn to grow fat on acorns and beech mast, or nuts.

Dairy farmers specialising in cheese and butter kept pigs to make the most of their by-products – skimmed milk, buttermilk and whey. Brewers and distillers did the same, feeding the spent barley used in the manufacture of beer or spirits. In the production of bacon, pork and ham, fatness was everything: the aim was to grow colossally solid animals, which no butcher would look at today. Hence the portraits of immense, rectangular bruisers, supported on a tiny, stick-like trotter at each corner.

Compared with the rate at which breeds of cattle and sheep were refined and improved during the eighteenth century, the husbandry of pigs was slow to develop, mainly because the majority of animals were kept by individual country folk to provide essential supplies for the home. Only late in the eighteenth century did rangy British pigs begin to assume new shapes as a result of the importation and crossing of small, fat animals from China. In the same period, ideas about feeding changed, as farmers began trying out new methods of fattening, using potatoes either boiled or raw, carrots, cabbage, peas and barley meal to bolster the household scraps and traditional wild food like grass, acorns and beech mast which pigs picked up at different seasons.

With Chinese influence, the Berkshire breed, for instance, evolved from a long, shallow-bodied animal into something much more thick-set. Yet some breeds like the Yorkshire Large Whites remained intact and scarcely known outside their own territory until, in 1851, the Yorkshire weaver Joseph Tuley caused a sensation at the Royal Show with his huge boar Sampson.

The nineteenth-century radical William Cobbett reckoned himself an authority on the subject: he assumed that every cottager should keep a pig, and gave detailed instructions for its care. No doubt his advice was excellent at the time, but not all his recommendations would find favour today. He remarked, for instance, that if the animals were turned loose on ground alongside public highways they would find their own food for much of the summer; and it is clear that he had never heard of cholesterol. Feed the pig peas or barley meal to make him as fat as possible before slaughter, he insisted: 'The last bushel, even if he sit as he eat, is the most profitable. If he can walk two hundred yards at a time, he is not well fatted.'

Today pigs are seen as valuable aids to conservation and the management of woodland. In the New Forest the Commoners' traditional right of pannage allows them to turn pigs out into the forest on a certain date in the autumn, the aim being that the animals should clean up the annual harvest of acorns, which otherwise might poison the cattle and wild ponies. The pigs – which were once a significant part of our natural ecosystem – also do good by digging up the forest floor, thereby making the soil more permeable, improving aeration, accelerating the decay of leaf-litter and reducing insect pests by eating grubs like those of cockchafers and click beetles. Wherever they rootle and trample vegetation, loosening the earth, they encourage the growth of seedling trees. The Nottinghamshire Wildlife Trust, also, has found pigs an asset. In Treswell Woods the canopy of ash had become so dense that the hazel beneath it was dying; but when three-quarters of the ash was thinned, brambles grew so vigorously that they

BRITISH LOP (below) A USEFUL PIG
SINCE IT CAN SUBSIST LARGELY ON
GRAZING. THIS PARTICULAR PIG IS
SUFFERING FROM SUNBURN.

BRITISH SADDLEBACK (bottom)
WEARS ALL BLACK EXCEPT FOR
A DISTINCTIVE BAND OF WHITE
AT THE SHOULDERS.

GLOUCESTER OLD SPOT SOW (right)
ANOTHER PIG WHICH LENDS ITSELF TO
AN OUTDOOR LIFE, IT USED TO GRAZE
IN ORCHARDS.

swamped the forest floor. A local farmer then offered the services of his pigs, a cross between Gloucester Old Spots and Large Whites: in they went, and they cleared the brambles in short order. They also trampled and rootled the ground into mud, but the result was an unparalleled blossoming of bluebells the following spring. With light let in and the hazel rejuvenated, the Trust hopes that dormice may return to the wood. In the meantime, people who eat pork from the woodland pigs declare it the finest they have tasted.

PRESENT BREEDS

Pigs are members of the Snidae family. Today the British pig industry is dominated by a few breeds such as the Large White and Landrace, and most others are rare.

Berkshire

This breed originated in the Thames Valley, possibly round Wantage, at the end of the eighteenth century, and was a devlopment of the Old English Pig. It began as a large, tawny-red animal spotted with black, and had a long, thick body, short legs and drooping ears. Early in the 1800s the introduction of Chinese or East Asian blood, which came via Italy, made it shorter and more compact, besides lightening its head and ears. The British Berkshire Society, founded in 1883, was the first pig society in England.

In the middle of the twentieth century Berkshires fell out of favour so severely that they almost went extinct; but the importation of new blood from Australia, New Zealand and the USA led to a strong revival, both in terms of numbers and in carcass quality. Today's Berkshires are almost entirely black, with white feet, tail and snout, but carcasses dress out white. The flavour of the meat is much appreciated in the Far East, where exported Berkshire pork is marketed as a rare delicacy.

British Lop

A hardy breed that thrives outdoors all year round, and can subsist largely on grazing, the British Lop is a large, multi-purpose pig, good for the production of both pork and bacon. It originated in Cornwall and the Tavistock area of Devon, and is thought to have shared ancestors with breeds now extinct in Glamorgan, Ulster and Cumberland.

A breed society was established in 1920 with the title 'National Long White Lop-Eared Pig Society,' but the name seemed too cumbersome, and in the 1960s it was abbreviated to the British Lop Pig Society. With the move towards outdoor pig production, interest in the breed has increased in recent years, and British Lops have spread all over the United Kingdom.

British Saddleback

You can hardly mistake a Saddleback, for its colour scheme is extremely distinctive, like that of a Belted Galloway cow: black all over, except for a band of white wrapped round the shoulders and

extending down to include front legs and feet. The back feet and the tip of the tail are also white.

The modern breed is a mix of the Essex and Wessex Saddlebacks from East Anglia and the southwest respectively, which are believed to be almost pure representatives of the Old English Pig. From that distant source it derives its ability to live outdoors and its readiness to eat grass – both very useful assets. The Saddleback was still common on commercial farms 25 years ago, but today the breed is listed as endangered, with fewer than 200 sows.

Duroc

Now one of the most numerous breeds in the world, Durocs were developed in the mid-nineteenth century from the Old Duroc of New York and the Red Jersey of New Jersey, and were first imported to Britain from Canada in 1968. The British genetic base was expanded by further imports from Canada and the USA in the mid-1970s and 1980s, and more recently from Denmark. Carcasses are lean, which makes the pigs a favourite choice for crossing with other breeds such as Landrace and Large Whites. Durocs are already an important element in the national herd, and the demand for pedigree stock is increasing.

Gloucestershire Old Spots

An Old Spot – the 's' is normally dropped in everyday usage – is a heavy, lop-eared creature, with big, black splodges on a whitish background. The breed was not formally registered until 1913, but in pubs, on postcards and on trays there are representations of spotted pigs taken from paintings at least 150 years old, and it is clear that the animals, or something very like them, existed early in the nineteenth century.

Thirty years ago the breed declined to a low ebb, but now it is strongly in the ascendant, due partly to the enthusiasm of a few dedicated farmers, and partly to the reaction of consumers against the pallid pork which is all that supermarkets are prepared to handle. Old Spots are

recognised as endangered by the Rare Breeds Survival Trust, but after the resurgence of interest the Gloucester Old Spots Pig Breeders' Club has over 600 pedigree sows on its register.

Among modern owners, few are keener than Eric Freeman, who keeps the pigs on his farm at Taynton near Gloucester. As he puts it, 'They're much the happiest living in the open, so they lend themselves to the new movement for eating animals that have been looked after kindly and naturally fed.' Also, he says, 'they're quite characters, some of them. What they get up to – sometimes you can't help falling on the gate and laughing.'

In earlier times Old Spots were known as orchard pigs, because they lived in the cider orchards of the Severn Vale, grazing the grass in summer, rooting among the trees, and guzzling on windfall apples in the autumn until (it was said) their meat acquired a magically sweet flavour. Legend has it that the black spots were originally bruises, caused by the impact of falling fruit. The pigs shown in old paintings have barely credible dimensions: bloated rectangles teetering on tiny pins, they could hardly have survived if they really had been that shape. One longs to know how

they would square up against Foston Sambo the 21st, an Old Spot who holds the record for the highest price paid for any pig in Britain, having fetched 4000 guineas (£4200) when sold at auction in 1994.

Hampshire

Although black-haired, Hampshire pigs dress out completely white, and they are now firmly established as a British commercial breed, having been introduced from the USA. They are particularly robust animals, and thrive in many other countries with a wide range of climates.

Kune Kune

The name of these medium-sized pigs means 'fat and round' in Maori, but during the 1970s the New Zealand aboriginals stopped using the breed for meat, and it nearly went extinct. One peculiarity is that each animal has a pair of skin tassels called piri piri dangling from its throat. The first Kune Kunes reached Britain in 1992, but there are now over 600 pure-breds registered here.

5

Farm Animals
Pigs

Gloucester Old
Spots
Kune Kune

192

Landrace

Known a 'the breed for every need,' the British Landrace, introduced from Sweden in 1949, has rapidly increased in numbers to become one of the Britain's most popular pigs. It can live indoors or out, and its long, lean carcass is idea for the production of bacon; but perhaps its greatest asset is its ability to improve other breeds when crossed with them to produce hybrids.

Large Black

'EARS – Long, thin and well inclined over face ... NECK – Long and clean ... SHOULDERS (IMPORTANT) – Fine and in line with ribs ... BACK – Very long and strong ... HAMS – Very broad and full ...' The Standards of Excellence laid down by the British Pig Association for the Large Black breed are exacting in many particulars, and any defect such as 'thick, coarse, cabbage-leafed or slopping ears' rules an animal out of serious contention.

The lop-eared Large Black is one of the country's oldest breeds, having originated in the Old English Hog of the sixteenth and seventeenth centuries. By the late 1800s it had two main strongholds, far apart, in East Anglia and Devon and Cornwall, but the formation of the Large Black Pig Society in 1889 encouraged exchanges of stock between the two areas. Early in the twentieth century the breed became very fashionable, and a Large Black sow was Supreme Champion at the Smithfield Show in 1919.

Then in the 1960s, demand for leaner meat, and a growing prejudice against coloured pigs, sent the breed plummeting, and in the 1970s the Rare Breeds Survival Trust placed Large Blacks on its critical list. Today small herds are established throughout the British Isles: the pigs are renowned for their docility, their ability to do well out of doors, and their succulent meat. But at the latest survey in 1998, there were still only 58 registered boars and 244 sows.

Middle White

The short faces and turned-up snub noses of Middle Whites point to the introductions of Chinese stock which took place in the late eighteenth century. Known as 'the beautifully ugly pigs,' they were developed as special pork-producers in Yorkshire in the 1850s by Joseph Tulley, a weaver from Keighley. The breed was recognised almost by accident, for when Tulley exhibited his pigs at the Keighley agricultural show, the judge deemed them too small to compete with the Large Whites, and too large to take on the Small Whites – but he reckoned them so good that, after a special meeting, a new section was introduced.

Small Whites went extinct in 1912, but by the 1920s Middle Whites were one of the most popular breeds in the country. After the Second World War government policy decreed that all pig production should be directed towards the bacon market, with the result that specialist pork types became less popular. Middle Whites fell away rapidly until they were the rarest British breed, with fewer than 100 sows left. Since the formation of the Middle White Pig Breeders' club in 1991, numbers have picked up again: there are now about 240 pedigree sows and 70 stock boars kept by some 100 breeders.

In Japan the animals are revered for their flavour, and a monument has been erected to the Middle White's 'outstanding eating qualities'. 'Middle York' pork sells at a premium in high-class food shops in Tokyo.

Tamworth

Of all British pigs, the bright brown Tamworths are the least influenced by Far-Eastern or Neapolitan importations, and remain the oldest pure English breed. They were here in Roman times, and take their name from the region in Staffordshire, but they are very much the type of animal

that was kept throughout central Britain since the early Middle Ages. Their long snouts and pricked ears give them a very alert appearance.

Being hardy, they do well out of doors; but because they could not compete with more prolific, faster-growing strains, producing litters of only 7 or 8 piglets, they went out of fashion in the 1960s, and by 1975 the remaining population was so small that it had become seriously inbred. Fortunately numerous Tamworths had been taken to Australia, and in 1975 Joe Henson, founder of the Rare Breeds Survival Trust, brought back three unrelated boars. These helped revitalise the breed, but Tamworths remain endangered, with fewer than 200 sows.

> Touching animals, and
> even more having to look
> after them, can have a
> powerfully therapeutic
> effect on children,
> especially those who live
> in concrete jungles

Contact with animals

It is sad but true that children who live in cities often have no idea where food comes from. Boxed into urban environments, they have practically no contact with animals or the countryside, and no first-hand knowledge of either. Milk, to them, starts life in a carton on a supermarket shelf, meat in a plastic wrapper. Many do not realise that potatoes grow in the earth or that frozen peas have been shelled out of pods.

In 1974, in an attempt to combat such ignorance and deprivation, the prize-winning children's author Michael Morpurgo and his wife Clare – both teachers – set up a charity, Farms for City Children. Soon a chain of coincidences led them to buy

Nethercott, a Victorian mansion with land above the River Torridge in North Devon. By the beginning of 1976 they had managed to furnish the house and opened for business, taking in children for a week at a time. After a slow start, schools in London and Birmingham began to send parties, and by 1979 Nethercott was fully booked. Yet the enterprise lost money consistently, and Clare was obliged to become a fund-raiser – a role at which she proved extremely proficient.

Then along came representatives of the National Trust with the news that several farmhouses in Wales were surplus to requirements. The result was that the Morpurgos took a lease of Lower Treginnis Farm, on a peninsula close to St Davids. To put the listed buildings in order cost £1 million, and stretched their finances to the limit. Nevertheless, by 1990 they had the place up and running, and within a few years it was flourishing, thanks not least to the energy of Paul Raggett, a former Trust warden, who set up Friends of Treginnis, to support children who could not afford to pay. The fact that the community backed the enterprise so strongly gives some idea of how local people value it.

Before Treginnis was finished, the Morpurgos' architect saw what he described as a 'fantastic property' close to the River Severn near Gloucester. Clare said, 'I can't cope with any more – it's too frightening.' To which he replied, 'If you see it, you'll do it' – and they did.

Wick Court, at that stage, was a wreck. Basically a moated Elizabethan manor, the house incorporated elements dating from the thirteenth century. From 1919 it had belonged to the Dowdeswell family, but the clan gradually dwindled until one old spinster was living there on her own. After her death in 1985 the house stood empty: when the Morpurgos first saw it in 1991, the floors had all gone, and bits of the stairs were missing. The architect demonstrated the state of the 10-metre-high south wall by leaning against it: when he put his shoulder to it, the entire structure swayed.

Undeterred, the Morpurgos again swung into action, and took a lease from the Dowdeswell family trust. By then Princess Anne was showing strong interest in their work, and in October 1991 she came to the launch of their appeal for funds. Because the house was so dangerous, the ceremony had to take place in the cowshed, but it went off triumphantly. Altogether they raised £1.2 million towards refurbishment of house and outbuildings, and the purchase of 60 hectares of surrounding farmland. This last was financed by Sainsbury family trusts, after passionate advocacy from the late Poet Laureate Ted Hughes, who was a neighbour of the Morpurgos in Devon.

Primary school children from inner cities come to Wick Court in batches of about 35 with their teachers, for a week at a time, and are immediately plunged into the life of the farmyard, not only feeding the animals, but mucking them out as well. In spring they help with lambing, and in autumn they make cider and perry, crushing the fruit in an old stone mill.

When they arrive on a Friday afternoon, they become very excited, but many are also frightened – of the open spaces, the animals, the chickens. Oddly enough, it is the chickens that scare them most: the idea of touching feathers seems to have a special horror for boys and girls brought up in the tower blocks and estates of Birmingham or Greater London.

Even if, in winter, dark has already fallen, the newcomers are sent straight out to feed the cattle, pigs and sheep. The pigs, especially, are a shock. Storybook pigs are small, round, pink and clean. Here the Tamworth sow is two metres long, nearly a metre tall, bristly, plastered with muck and squealing like a banshee. Yet the children have no alternative but to work: they are told that if they don't feed the pigs, the animals will go hungry.

The farm, all organic, is run by Jonathan Crump, who owns the livestock. An enthusiast for ancient breeds, he has Gloucester cattle, Old Spots and Tamworth pigs, Cotswold and Jacob sheep. His chickens, ducks, geese, turkeys and guinea fowl are at large in the yard and the surrounding orchards. He enjoys seeing the children respond to challenges, but is sometimes surprised by their reactions. 'Strangely enough, the sight of a dead lamb doesn't bother them,' he says. 'In fact, if anything dies, they quite like it.'

Within two or three days negative attitudes vanish, and they learn to work with each other in little teams. At the end of a week they go home different people, often having absorbed more in seven days than they normally do in a year, not just about the countryside, but about living in general.

Being a teacher himself, Michael Morpurgo can see how profoundly they benefit. 'It isn't just that they learn where food comes from, and easy things like that,' he says. 'It goes far deeper. Before they come to one of the farms, most of them have never been extended, physically or mentally. Here they simply have to work, and after three days they're knackered. But the gain in confidence is phenomenal: they go back able to tackle tasks which were beyond them before. With luck, they get some inkling of the fact that work is the thing from which you gain most satisfaction and fun in life.'

The enterprise also has the broader effect of bridging the ever-widening gap between town and country. Many parents of today's primary school children never go into the countryside, and have no interest in what happens there. Teachers tend to be just as urban. At least the farms show a few children that life on the land goes on, and can be richly rewarding.

Today Wick Court is solid, warm and cheerfully decorated, yet still full of fascinating old beams, cubby holes and secret passages. According to the farm director, Heather Tarplee, various ghosts, inside and out, do not worry the young visitors. After one girl had woken up to find a woman in white standing by the window, and Heather asked her how she knew the figure was a ghost, the lass replied robustly, 'Cos it had no head!'

Poultry

Feelings sometimes run just as high among poultry keepers as they do among owners of any other livestock. When the Poultry Club was founded at the Crystal Palace in November 1877, the inaugural meeting was described as a 'mission of reformation', made necessary by the widespread improprieties prevailing at the time, and the first code of rules included one for the 'suppression of fraud and dishonourable conduct'. The club got off to an erratic start; shows that it promoted in 1882 and 1889 incurred heavy financial losses but by 1902 it had attracted 1100 members. It survived the difficulties and food shortages caused by two world wars, to reach the millennium — in the words of an official account — 'more lively, more secure than at any other point in its history'.

Its membership may have slipped back from a high point of 2500 to 1200, but according to its secretary, Michael Clark, interest in high-class fowl is again rising fast — not just because people are keen to eat free-range eggs, but also because keeping chickens has a therapeutic effect and helps relieve stress. As Mr Clark says, 'You can talk to them, and although they answer, they never argue.'

Chickens

The domestic chicken, *Gallus domesticus*, is descended from *Gallus gallus*, the red jungle fowl. Selective breeding of poultry has been practised for at least 150 years. Ever since Queen Victoria – a keen fancier – exhibited her Cochins at the Dublin Show in 1846, many members of the royal family have kept poultry, among them the club's long-serving patron, Queen Elizabeth the late Queen Mother, whose own involvement went back to her childhood. The main interest of many club members now lies in exhibiting their birds at agricultural shows all over Britain. More than 130 breeds are recognised, and there are over 50 separate breed clubs, each championing the cause of some rare strain, from Appenzellers to Scots Dumpies and Wyandottes. Prize-winning fowl can command enormous sums – up to £300 for an outstanding bird – but a normal price is around £15.

Thousands of other keepers are more interested in poultry's practical uses – the production of meat which they know contains no artificial ingredients, and eggs which are infinitely superior to any that can be bought in shops. Today's fanciers do not at all mind being described as 'cloth-cap people', for they tend to be more friendly and cooperative than the breeders and showers of dogs.

Fashions change rapidly as one breed or another moves up or down in public esteem, but some remain perennial favourites – and none more so than the hefty **Buff Orpington**, named after the place in Kent where lived its main developer, William Cook. Officially described as a bird 'that is majestic in appearance, docile and friendly', the Buff is also hailed as the layer 'of a good quality tinted egg'. In 1977 the presentation of some birds to Queen Elizabeth the late Queen Mother by Will Burdett, long-serving chairman of the Buff Orpington Club, further confirmed the breed's status.

Another breed with royal connections is the **Cochin**, for the first birds to reach Britain from China were presented to Queen Victoria. The magnificent amount of body-feathers which they carried led people to believe that the Chinese had been breeding them to stuff duvets. Today the Cochin is admired for its dignity and its rotund, maternal look, which reflects its excellence as a broody. Unfortunately, says one admirer, 'the rotundity extends to its metabolism, as the birds are prone to fat and heart problems, compounded by their desire to be idle and decorative.'

Also from China is the **Croad Langshan**, an ancient breed that originates from the north of the country, and was first imported into Britain in 1872 by a Major F. T. Croad. Both here and in the United States disputes broke out as to whether or not the Langshans were the same as Cochins, but in time the two were recognised as distinct, and the name Croad was added to Langshan as a tribute to the importer's niece, who had worked hard to establish the breed's independence. The earliest birds were black; the majority still are, although with a few whites thrown in, and their eggs are a pinkish plum-colour.

Brahmas, with feathers extending right down their legs and over their feet, come from India. The first pair to reach America, in 1846, were bought in New York harbour off a ship alleged to have come from Lakipur, near the mouth

BUFF ORPINGTON: A HEFTY AND PERENNIALLY POPULAR CHICKEN, IT IS NAMED AFTER THE PLACE IN KENT WHERE IT WAS DEVELOPED.

of the Brahmaputra river; but there was some scepticism about their provenance, and it was only in the 1860s that importations to Britain confirmed that the birds' origins were Indian. In spite of their size and clumsiness – they are so hefty that they can scarcely fly – they became popular here, only to fall out of favour so severely that in 1969 they were officially classed as a rare breed. Oddly enough, rescue came from Germany, where, in spite of the Second World War and the devastation of the country after it, Brahmas were somehow raised in good numbers during the 1950s and 1960s. The revival in Britain was so strong that no fewer than 108 birds were entered for the National Poultry Show in 1999.

No indigenous cockerel is more handsome than the **Dorking**, with its rich red comb, gleaming white cape, black-and-white body and finely-arched black tail. Aficionados claim that when, in 30 BC, the Roman writer Columella praised a table bird as being 'square in shape, with sturdy short legs and five toes,' he must have been describing a Dorking, since the characteristics he mentioned are those of the bird today. Thus it is claimed that the breed dates back at least 2000 years. Although slow to grow, Dorkings are still much fancied as table birds, and reach noble proportions if properly fed: an adult cock may weigh 5 kg – but his sheer size can be a hazard, and he may suffer from 'bumble foot', an infection of the pad of the foot usually caused by too hasty a descent from high places.

The antiquity of **Silkies** is undisputed. The birds may look like fluffy teapot cosies, with powder-puffs for heads, but in their native China they have commanded immense respect for at least 500 years. A book about medicine, written during the Ming dynasty, contained a long section on the fowl, and to this day the Chinese value them highly for their health-giving and curative properties. Huge numbers are farmed there for pharmaceutical products and for meat. Here, the Silkie Club was formed in 1898, and for a century enthusiasts have battled to retain the purity of the breed: membership has grown from 22 in 1977 to more than 230, and the birds have become serious contenders on the show circuit.

For beautiful brown eggs, there is no bird to beat a **Marans**, whose ancestors made a surreptitious entry into this country some 70 years ago. Lord Greenway, visiting the Paris exhibition of 1929, was impressed by a table fowl that came from a remote and marshy area of France; but since a ban on livestock imports was in force at the time, all that could be brought to Britain were eggs, smuggled in a luncheon-basket under the guise of being hard-boiled. From them came today's Marans, which are renowned for their rapid growth and exceptional laying-power. The Marans Club was formed in 1950, and to mark its fiftieth anniversary in 2000 every member was presented with a ceramic keepsake.

For many years in the nineteenth century the **Sussex** was the mainstay of the poultry industry in its own county and in Surrey. Dealers, known locally as 'higglers', would collect the fowl from breeders and fatten them for market. Then, in 1903, owners decided to form a club, and within 20 years, to quote one enthusiast, 'the club and breed soared to world-wide fame'. The Sussex maintained its popularity until the 1950s; but then the advent of hybrid birds put it into a long decline, from which an enthusiastic breeders' club has only recently retrieved it.

At one time or another most, if not all, of the fowl mentioned here have been deliberately diminished by selective breeding, to produce bantam-sized versions of the original; but in many cases owners decided that bigger was better, and reverted to birds of full dimensions.

In 1969 the Rare Poultry Society was formed, to represent breeds which had no club of their own. Lack of space prevents detailed description here, but a few mentions will show how diverse are their origins. The **Brabanter** is an

Farm Animals
Poultry

Marans
Sussex

BANTAM COCKEREL (left) BANTAM-
SIZED VERSIONS OF MANY BREEDS
HAVE EMERGED, BUT THE FULL-SIZED
VERSIONS SEEM TO BE FAVOURED.

MARANS (below) ILLICITLY INTRO-
DUCED TO BRITAIN BY LORD GREENWAY
IN THE LATE 1920s, MARANS PRODUCE
BEAUTIFUL BROWN EGGS.

old Dutch breed; **Transylvanian Naked Necks** come from Hungary; the **Sultan** hails from Turkey, the **Yokohama** from Japan, while the **Sicilian Buttercup** derives not from where its name suggests, but from North Africa; and no explanation is needed for the **Russian Orloff**, a very old breed in which a 'gloomy, vindictive expression' is *de rigeur*.

IT IS A SAFE BET that all the breeds mentioned above live healthy outdoor lives; but the sad fact is that the vast majority of British chickens are reared intensively, either for eggs or for meat, in conditions which meet official requirements but confer no sort of freedom on the birds.

A genuinely free-range chicken is amazingly active. In the course of foraging it walks several miles a day, and delivers many thousand stabbing pecks at blades of grass, insects, earthworms and other delicacies, not excluding dead mice. This makes it fairly destructive of any tidy environment such as a garden – hence most people's habit of keeping their birds confined, even if in large pens. A hen in a barn, in contrast, gets very little exercise, and a bird in a cage none at all.

Anyone who eats chicken regularly should reflect on the fact that the bird almost certainly never went out of doors.

It was reared in a barn or shed, packed in among thousands of others, with just enough space to move about on litter of wood shavings or chopped straw. Far from seeing the light of day, it lived in almost-permanent artificial light, with only one hour of darkness in every 24, to make it eat more and grow faster. Even if, in accordance with present regulations, its beak was never trimmed, and it was not given any antibiotic growth-promoters, it never had a chance to exercise any of its natural instincts, except to eat and drink, and its existence was so artificial that its life ended at the age of six or eight weeks, only half the time its predecessors of a few years ago took to reach market weight. Over 15 million British chickens are killed and eaten every week – a rate of 2.5 million a day, 1500 every minute – and the RSPCA claims that 100,000 birds die prematurely every day, crippled by deformities.

Turkeys

All domestic turkeys derive from the wild turkeys of North America, where hunters regard the birds as a prime game quarry. Etiquette, however, is entirely different from in England: turkeys may be shot only on the ground, not while

BRONZE TURKEY (below) THE MOST POPULAR BREED IN BOTH BRITAIN AND AMERICA, MALE AND FEMALE ARE SHOWN HERE.

NORFOLK BLACK MALE (opposite) A PURE BREED, BELIEVED TO BE DERIVED FROM THE FIRST TURKEYS TO ARRIVE IN ENGLAND.

they are flying – a practice that would induce apoplexy in the Home Counties.

The first birds to reach Europe were brought to Spain via Mexico in about 1519, and some reached England a few years later. The **Common Turkey** (*Meleagrus gallopavo*) is the species most familiar in Britain. Millions of birds are produced by commercial growers like Bernard Matthews of Norfolk, principally for the Christmas trade; but when individual enthusiasts founded the Turkey Club UK in 2000, they quickly attracted 70 members, all keen to promote the rearing and maintenance of pure breeds. The formation of the club aroused interest from large commercial firms, which may need pure stock for future breeding, and from America.

To its fanciers, a turkey is extremely handsome, but its looks do not entrance everybody. The top of its head is bumpy and red. A long, red, fleshy appendage called a snood hangs down from its forehead over its bill; a fleshy wattle grows from its throat, and a tuft of hairy black feathers sprouts from its breast.

Commercial birds are double-breasted and chest-heavy, but pure breeds are high-breasted and very active: they fly like pheasants and mate naturally. The pure breeds include **Norfolk Black**, believed to derive from the first turkeys to arrive in England, and developed in Norfolk; **Bourbon Red**, with chestnut mahogany plumage, which originated from Bourbon County, Kentucky; **Bronze**, the most popular of all, in both America and Britain; **Narragansett**, the oldest variety, now close to extinction, and the strikingly coloured **Crollwitzer** (black and white) and **Blue**, which is ash-blue or lavender all over.

Guinea Fowl

Numida meleagris

With their small heads, long necks and mottled grey and white plumage, guinea fowl have a rather outlandish appearance – which is hardly surprising, as they come from Africa. Not only are they delicious to eat, with a flavour half way between a pheasant and a chicken: they also make excellent watch dogs, for they are alert and nervous, and raise a loud, gabbling cackle at the first sign of a threat, be it from fox, dog or human. Many poultry farmers and gamekeepers use them as voluble sentries.

AYLESBURY DUCK (below) BRED FOR THE TABLE, THIS DUCK IS THE LARGEST AT ABOUT 5 KG.

KHAKI CAMPBELL (bottom) A LIGHT BREED OF DUCK, THEY ARE EXCEPTIONALLY PROLIFIC LAYERS.

MUSCOVY DUCK *CAIRINA MOSCHATA* (opposite) ORIGINATES FROM SOUTH AMERICA.

5

Farm Animals
Poultry

Aylesbury Duck
Khaki Campbell
Duck

204

They are naturally gregarious, and in the wild live in small flocks. Although well able to fly in order to escape from predators such as leopards or (in Britain) foxes, they prefer to stay on the ground and run for it, if they can.

Ducks

Ducks are basically aquatic birds with feet webbed for swimming, and broad bills designed for dabbling in water; but domestic varieties are fully amphibious, and, if they get the chance, happily waddle about on land around the fringes of muddy ponds. Almost all domestic ducks were developed from the wild mallard (*see page 295*). Until the Second World War most farms had small flocks of ducks and geese, kept for their eggs or for the table; but in the 1960s commercial companies began turning out hybrids by the thousand, and many old breeds declined almost to the point of extinction. More recently, enthusiastic members of the British Waterfowl Association (BWA) have brought about something of a revival.

Of the breeds known as 'heavy' ducks, reared specially for the table, the largest are the traditional, pink-billed English **Aylesbury**, which can weigh up to 5 kg, and the French **Rouen**. When the Chinese **Pekin** was introduced to North America and Britain late in the nineteenth century, it made such an impact that it immediately began to replace the Aylesbury. In 2001 the BWA, alarmed by the decline of the exhibition-standard Aylesbury, launched a campaign to save the breed from extinction. Other heavy breeds include the **Blue Swedish**, the **Rouen Clair** and the **Silver Appleyard**, developed by a breeder of that name in the 1930s. **Drake Silver Appleyards** are particularly handsome, the bottle-green head of a mallard being enhanced by silver eyebrows and throat. The **Muscovy duck** (*Cairina moschata*) is a different species from the rest, originating from South America.

Prominent among light breeds are **Khaki Campbells**, which are exceptionally prolific layers, and **Indian Runners**, which are slim, upright and fast-waddling: a small flock is sometimes marshalled by sheepdogs during demonstrations at agricultural shows.

Geese

Legend has it that St Martin, the fourth-century Bishop of Tours, was once annoyed by a goose, which he ordered to be killed and served up for his dinner. Since he died from a surfeit of the rich meat, Martinmas, 11 November, became the day of a great goose-feast in France.

Even if the birds have less significance in Britain, they are valued for the table, not least at Christmas, when many people prefer their strong, dark meat to the blander flesh of the traditional turkey. Some owners keep them for egg production, and as guardians of the farmyard, since they are highly vigilant, and, like guinea fowl, cackle noisily if they spot an intruder. Many people keep them purely as pets – although ganders can be ferocious, especially when

DOMESTIC GEESE (previous page)
VALUABLE FOR THE TABLE, FOR EGG
PRODUCTION AND AS GUARDIANS
OF THE FARMYARD.

CHINESE GOOSE (below) DOMESTIC
WHITE FORM OF CHINESE GOOSE,
WHICH WAS DEVELOPED FROM THE
WILD SWAN-GOOSE.

harassing small children. One advantage of geese is that they need little looking after and largely feed themselves. Being voracious grazers, they are useful as self-propelled grass-mowers – but with the inevitable result that their copious grey-green droppings foul the sward they create. For an owner, the main requirement is that they are penned or shut up at night – otherwise a fox will get them.

Fourteen breeds are recognised in the United Kingdom, but only three – the **Brecon Buff**, the **Pilgrim** and the **West of England** – are considered indigenous. Others range from the heavy white **Emden** (up to 15 kg) to the small **Roman** (also white and weighing around 5 kg). All these are descended from the wild European goose, the greylag; but also present are the white and grey **Chinese**, developed in the Far East from the wild swan-goose, and the tall, ashy-brown **African**, which in fact also emanates from China. Russian breeds include the **Tula**, **Asamas** and **Kholmogory**, and the fine-looking blue **Steinbacher** was recently introduced from Germany.

Ostrich

Struthio camelus

Ostriches have been farmed for nearly 150 years in South Africa, for their excellent red meat, their hide, which makes fine leather, and their feathers, once all the rage as fashion accessories. But it was only in the 1990s that the birds began to be reared commercially in England. The demand for breeding stock increased so fast that prices rocketed: a mature female became worth £10,000, and eggs changed hands at £100 apiece.

The first few companies in the business invited investors to buy birds which the firms themselves would manage, and they put out seductive brochures showing what enormous returns a client could expect. Unfortunately, it turned out that the most prominent firm, the Ostrich Farming Corporation, was being run by con-men, who in 1996 decamped to Belgium, taking many of their clients' birds with them. Police inquiries revealed that numerous ostriches had been sold several times over, and after a lengthy investigation the directors of the company were gaoled for fraud, leaving more than £70 million worth of claims from former investors outstanding.

After that setback, the industry took some time to settle down, but by the end of 2000 it was making steady progress. There are now thought to be over a hundred ostrich farms in Britain, holding perhaps 50,000 birds. Prices dropped to a realistic level: £200 for a yearling female, £400 for a mature breeder.

Neverthelss, everything about ostriches is on a large scale. They are among the oldest living species, having existed for 120 million years, and the largest birds on Earth. They grow to 2.5 metres tall and weigh up to 150 kg. They are the second-fastest animals in the world (giving best only to cheetahs), and can maintain 65 km/h for at least half an hour. They can deliver a vicious kick, striking forwards with their three-toed feet. Each egg weighs over 3 kg, and a hen can lay 50 eggs a year.

For mating, one cock bird is paired off with two hens, and the trio are put into a large, fenced enclosure of their own. Hatching the eggs in incubators is no easy business: temperature and humidity have to be carefully controlled, and the eggs must be turned regularly. When chicks hatch, after 42 days, they are already 25 cm tall, and grow as much again in their first month.

In the year 2000 nearly 6000 birds went for slaughter, at prices between £150 and £200. As an ostrich is flightless, and has practically no pectoral muscles, the meat comes from its thighs: it sells at about £15 per kilo, tastes much like beef, and is exceptionally low in cholesterol, with a high iron content.

Other Species

Alpaca

Lama oacos

Alpacas are camelids – of the same family as llamas – and are bred for their fibre or wool, which, being fine, light and warm, is worth up to £50 a kg. They are smaller than llamas and more amenable: they do not spit or kick when handled, and are easy to keep since they eat only grass and hay, and prefer to live in the open, disdaining shelter even when it is available.

They graze energetically, with quick, thrusting movements of the lower jaw, and canter with a springy, loping action. Some of their antics are agreeably ridiculous: they indulge in communal rolling and sudden, sideways jumps, and from time to time utter extraordinary creaking, grinding noises, like barn doors shutting on rusty hinges, which seem to express irritation.

In their native South America alpacas were originally lowland grazers, but the herds were slaughtered by the invading Spaniards in the sixteenth century to make way for sheep and cattle, and the survivors were taken on by peasant farmers living high in the Andes. There they had to adapt to thin air, poor grazing and extremes of heat and cold.

They were first bred on British farms early in the 1980s. but it was only in 1996 that Arunvale, an Australian-backed firm with a base in Sussex, really got things going by flying in large contingents from their native South America.

Most early imports came from Chile, where the animals are all colours from dark, chocolatey brown to grey and off-white. Later, pale Peruvian alpacas became more fashionable. As the demand for breeding stock increased, prices rose to astronomical levels: by the end of the century a good female was worth £9000 or £10,000, and a female *cria*, or baby, the same; but as numbers built up, prices fell to a third of those amounts. The total number of alpacas in Britain is thought to be about 2500, but those in the business reckon that the national herd will have to grow to 25,000 before the annual production of fibre is great enough to sustain a cost-effective manufacturing industry.

Bison

Bison bison

Various types of bison lived in prehistoric Britain, but all went extinct many thousands of years ago, and it was only in 1891 that a small herd again set foot on British soil. In that year the celebrated American animal catcher and dealer Charles Jesse 'Buffalo' Jones shipped ten animals to Liverpool and drove them on the hoof to Lord Derby's park at Knowsley, where their descendants are still living.

The first man to farm American bison commercially in this country was Colin Ellis, who during the 1980s established a group on his farm in Dorset. The original patriarch of his herd, Harvey, made history when he literally joined the great herd in the sky, and parts of him were served up as bison steak to passengers on Concorde's transatlantic flights.

Since then Mr Ellis – now Lord Seaford – has expanded his herd to 80 animals, and the demand for bison meat, which contains significantly less cholesterol than beef, has become so strong that he has had to make good the shortfall with Canadian bison, which are very similar. The British Bison Association has 30 members, of whom 11 actually keep the animals, and there are thought to be altogether some 300 in the country. Although formidably large and powerful, standing 1.8 metres at the shoulder, with massive heads and weighing up to a ton, bison are placid giants and easy to manage, as they live entirely on grass. Nevertheless, they are wild animals, and need to be treated with respect. Because they do not like to be touched, it is hard to help them if, for example, a cow gets into difficulty while calving and has to be separated from the herd.

Water Buffalo

Bubalus bubalis

British farmers seeking new lines began to import water buffalo early in the 1990s. The first consignment was Italian, but most of the imports have come from Romania, where the animals are used for draught, as well as for producing milk and meat. There are now thought to be some 1500 in the United Kingdom. Their milk is rich and creamy, lower in cholesterol than cows' milk, and makes excellent hard cheese, besides the more famliar mozzarella. Their meat tastes like old-fashioned beef, and is claimed to contain 70 per cent less fat.

Although armed with formidable-looking horns, water buffalo are gentle and easy to manage, not least because they do well on poor fodder, such as maize stalks, straw, low-grade hay and potatoes. They can also be useful as agents of conservation: when the West Wales Wildlife Trust wanted to improve its wetland reserve on the River Teifi, a herd of five buffalo grazed out invasive plants, and their wallowing created pools suitable for dragonflies and wading birds.

Water buffalo live longer than other cattle – up to 20 years – and have more individuality, often recognising their individual names; but they do not like the combination of wet and cold in which English winters specialise, and owners find it best to bring them in at night.

Sympathetic farming and attention to detail have yielded numerous benefits for wildlife on 280 hectares of Leicestershire countryside

....

Loddington

NOWHERE IN BRITAIN are the results of careful habitat management more clearly demonstrated than on the experimental farm at Loddington in Leicestershire, run by the Game Conservancy Trust. Friendly farming, combined with the culling of predators in spring, has produced enormous benefits not only for gamebirds, but for many other species as well, and at the same time has created a much better-looking environment.

When the Trust bought the 283-hectare property in 1992, it had been farmed in typical modern fashion, with large fields of wheat and barley and some grassland. The new policy was, in general, to reduce the size of the fields, to grow a wider variety of crops, and to provide more cover for birds. The small areas of woodland were thinned, restocked and augmented by the planting of new spinneys, and several silted-up ponds were dug out.

One vital innovation was that of the conservation headlands already pioneered by the Trust on other sites. These are strips of ground, 6 metres wide, round the edges of arable fields, which are sprayed with as few chemicals as possible, so that beneficial weeds and insects can flourish. Strips of set-aside land, and cover crops such as kale and quinoa, provide food and shelter for song- and gamebirds alike.

Another important introduction was that of beetle-banks – long, low mounds of earth which run across the middle of fields, planted with tussocky grass. The idea is that these should harbour useful beetles which, in summer, march out into the surrounding cereal crops to devour harmful aphids, thus reducing the need for pesticides. The policy has worked well, but the banks have had the further advantage of creating excellent nesting habitat, not only for birds but also for harvest mice, which have bred in amazing numbers: one year researchers found 47 nests in every kilometre stretch, compared with 5 in normal field boundaries.

From the start these innovatory practices were backed up by vigorous suppression of predators in spring. The resident gamekeeper never hoped or tried to exterminate all the predators in the region: rather, his aim was to keep his ground clear in the birds' breeding season, between March and July. This he did by shooting foxes at night with high-velocity rifle and spotlight, catching magpies and crows in Larsen live-capture traps, and maintaining strings of tunnel-traps for stoats, weasels, rats and grey squirrels.

One result of the new regime was a spectacular increase in the numbers of wild pheasants, which went from 126 in 1992 to 616 in 2001, and enabled a small surplus to be shot annually. Even more striking was the resurgence of the brown hare – a species nationally in the doldrums. When the Trust took over, a count revealed a total of 15 hares on the entire property. Six years later the population had rocketed to 211: hares had become so plentiful that two batches were caught and exported to Pembrokeshire, to restock the gunnery ranges at Castlemartin, and now shoots are needed in most winters to keep the numbers to a tolerable level. Meanwhile, on other farms roundabout, still run on traditional lines, the hare population remained at rock-bottom.

The experiment at Loddington was launched primarily as a study in game management; but the new regime has also given enormous encouragement to songbirds. By the autumn of 2000 there were 430 songbird territories on each of the farm's 3.3 square kilometres, and all the species named in the national Biodiversity Action Plan were flourishing. In the six years between 1992 and 1998, song thrushes – on a national scale the most severely depleted species of all – increased by 243 per cent, linnets by 111 per cent, bullfinches by 83 per cent. Altogether, species in national

decline went up by 129 per cent, while those remaining stable elsewhere, or increasing slightly, grew by 42 per cent.

Because of national concern over the decline of thrushes, a special study was started in the summer of 2000, when a few birds were fitted with miniature radio back-packs in an attempt to plot their movements while foraging for young. It is known that thrushes are a very productive species, and if freed from predation (chiefly by magpies and crows) may rear three broods of chicks a year. The study was designed to reveal more about the birds' summer behaviour; but much remains to be learnt about what happens to thrushes in winter. Do surplus birds die from starvation, or do they migrate out into new territories?

For any visitor to Loddington, the most obvious change is in the landscape, which has become far more attractive under the new regime. Smaller fields, more breaks between crops, more copses – everything combines to give the land a varied and interesting look. Perhaps the most surprising feature of the whole enterprise is that the farm still makes a profit – and the moral is that, in agriculture, attention to detail pays rich rewards in conservation. Conventional farmers blunder about with heavy machinery and poisonous chemicals, obliterating the insects which sustain chicks and the seeds that keep birds going through the winter. At Loddington, the importance of such humble links in the food chain has been identified, and practices adapted to make better use of what nature provides.

6 DOMESTIC ANIMALS

Dictionaries define pets as 'cherished tame animals' or 'indulged favourites', and over the centuries both phrases have applied to an enormous variety of living creatures. Apes, tortoises, foxes, owls, squirrels and bears have, at one time or another, held pride of place in some humans' affections. During the 1920s, the white settlers in the Happy Valley in Kenya kept even more outlandish animals: Diana Broughton, a mongoose; Juanita Carberry, cheetahs; Alice de Janzé, a lion cub called Samson.

Britain now harbours amazing numbers of pets: almost exactly half the country's 24 million households keep an animal, bird, fish of some description. In 2000, there were 6.5 million dogs, 8 million cats, 26.6 million fish, 1 million budgerigars, 4.5 million rabbits, 850,000 guinea pigs and 800,000 hamsters.

The number of dogs is slowly falling, as people tend to live in smaller houses and flats, but the total of rabbits is increasing at an extraordinary rate. A survey conducted by the University of Warwick, completed in 2002, concluded that rabbits are well-suited to modern lifestyles, and revealed that of the 3000 members of the Rabbit Welfare Association almost 90 per cent are adults, a high percentage of them professional women in the 20–40 age group.

The majority of pets are doubtless loved and wanted; as the social historian Keith Thomas remarked, 'the fact that so many people feel it necessary to maintain a dependent animal for the sake of emotional completeness tells us something about the atomistic society in which we live.' Nevertheless, the pre-eminent sharers of human households (mice and fleas apart) have always been dogs and cats – partly because the animals readily return love, and partly because they perform the useful functions of guarding the household and vermin control.

213

Dogs

One of the most moving passages in Homer — all the more powerful for its brevity — describes Odysseus' return to Ithaca. After the ten-year siege of Troy, and ten more years' wandering, he eventually comes home to his palace disguised as a beggar. So gaunt and ragged is he that the humans do not know him, but he is immediately recognised by his dog Argus, whom he reared as a puppy.

The old hound is at death's door, lying outside the gate amid the dung of mules and cattle; but as his master approaches, he raises his head and pricks up his ears, then wags his tail and drops his ears again. That is all he can do: he is too weak to move. Odysseus, that much-travelled man of many wiles, is momentarily overcome. A tear rolls down his cheek and he has to look away. To avoid revealing his identity, he asks a question of his companion Eumaeus, who tells him that the hound belonged to a great hero who has perished far from home. Then the two men go on into the palace. 'But as for Argus – the black fate of death seized him, the moment he had seen Odysseus, in the twentieth year.'

Homer ensured that Argus's fame would be immortal. But humans had kept dogs (*Canis familiaris*) for thousands of years before the siege of Troy. One of the earliest known was found at Star Carr, the Mesolithic site in Yorkshire: a skeleton dated to 7600 BC, when Britain was still part of Europe. The animal was of medium stature, about the size of a modern collie; but what makes it of intense interest is the fact that it had jaws like a wolf, with teeth that overlapped each other. It was, in fact, a form of domesticated wolf, and confirms that all dogs derived ultimately from that source: genetic analysis has shown that the two have interbred for 100,000 years. Even today many of a dog's habits – circling before lying down, rolling in filth if given a chance – are identical with those of its ancestor.

The dogs of the Mesolithic period were presumably kept for hunting, as guards and maybe for eating. Few specimens survive from the Neolithic or Bronze Ages, but those that remain were all of much the same size, and cut-marks on the bones show that some creatures – either humans or other dogs – had eaten them. From the Iron Age there is more variety, and the Celts, who arrived in Britain about 400 BC, were great lovers and users of dogs: they brought with them mastiffs of immense size and ferocity, which were trained to fight in war. Julius Caesar, invading in 55 and again in 54 BC, came partly in search of such hounds – and it is in Shakespeare's tragedy that Antony, mourning his murdered leader, prophesies that

> And Caesar's spirit, ranging for revenge,
> With Ate by his side come hot from hell,
> Shall in these confines with a monarch's voice
> Cry 'Havoc!' and let slip the dogs of war.

By the time of the Roman occupation, a hundred years later, there is clear evidence also of toy dogs, little more than half a collie's height at the shoulder, and too small to have had any function beyond that of pets: but it was the big mastiffs which became famous in Europe, and were much sought after. Later a special official was posted to Winchester to arrange the collection and export of British dogs to Rome, probably for wild-beast shows in the arena.

Another breed much admired by the Romans was the great Irish hound – now extinct – which could out-run and pull down wolves, deer, wild boar and hares. One skull recovered from an Irish bog gives an idea of the animal's dimensions: at 42.5 cm from front to back, the skull is a quarter as long again as that of a modern wolf-hound – so the original must have stood some 120 cm at the shoulder (as opposed to 95 cm), and its speed must have been devastating. Yet the best known type of all at that date was the greyhound, known to the Romans as *vertragus*, and described by the poet Martial as able to catch hares and bring them back in its mouth unharmed.

War dogs feature strongly in early Irish sagas, which describe hounds going into battle wearing bronze armour and broad collars to protect their throats, trained not only to attack the enemy, but also to defend their masters, should they be wounded or killed, by standing over their bodies and driving off other dogs, wolves or humans. This usage persisted well into the Middle Ages. When Sir Piers Legh fell wounded at the battle of Agincourt in 1415, his mastiff bitch stood guard over him until he could be carried off the field; and although he died of wounds in England, the bitch, besides attending his funeral, founded the Lyme Hall line of mastiffs which continued unbroken for 400 years. Size and strength made mastiffs formidable guard dogs:

SLEEPING BLOODHOUND

(previous pages) BY SIR EDWIN HENRY
LANDSEER, OIL ON CANVAS, 1835.

TWELVE FAVOURITE DOGS

(below) BY EDWIN FREDERICK
HOLT, 1883.

chained at the gates or door of a house, and let loose in
the grounds after dark, they effectively deterred thieves or
would-be murderers, especially as many of them seemed
to have a sixth sense which enabled them to detect when
a human harboured sinister intentions.

Another form of war dog was the talbot, forerunner of
the modern bloodhound. Even in the Middle Ages it was
called a bloodhound (or 'limer' or 'limehound') from its
uncanny ability to follow a trail, and on countless occasions
it was used to track an enemy, a cattle rustler or a sheep-
stealer, worked by its handler on a liam or long leash made
of horsehide. King Philip II of Spain, who despatched
the Armada against England in 1588, bought some British
bloodhounds and sent them to the Spanish Indies, where
they became famous for tracking down runaway slaves and
other absconders.

Holy men and women were great keepers of dogs, which
sometimes gave offence by howling during divine service
and eating food destined for the poor. The tender-hearted
prioress in Chaucer's *Canterbury Tales*, who wept if she saw
a mouse caught in a trap, and wore on her sleeve a broach
bearing the slogan *Amor vincit omnia*, brought with her on
pilgrimage several

> smale houndes that she fedde
> With rosted flesh, or milk and wastel-bred.

Also on the pilgrimage was a monk 'that lovede venerye'
and brought along his greyhounds, 'as swifte as fowels in
flight'. In the Middle Ages dogs were welcome at church,
and special pews or benches were provided at the back for
them to sit on – although one main purpose of commu-
nion rails was to keep them away from the altar.

Scholars have pointed out that Shakespeare appears to
have hated dogs, and that no favourable reference to one
occurs anywhere in his work. In his *Recollections of Past Life*
Sir Henry Holland pointed out that Lord Nugent, the

6

Domestic Animals

Dogs

215

greatest Shakespearean expert of his day, declared that no passage could be found in Shakespeare 'commending, directly or indirectly, the moral qualities of the dog'. Sir Henry bet Nugent a guinea that he was wrong, but after a year's vain search had to pay up.

Among royalty and noble landowners, hunting was an immensely important activity, not to say an obsession, and the dogs used for it were principally greyhounds, of various breeds. Great Irish hounds and deerhounds from the Scottish Highlands, both with rough coats, were used to hunt stags, wolves and wild boar; smaller, smooth-coated dogs – perhaps showing the influence of imported Italian greyhounds – went after hares. In the fourteenth century a newcomer appeared on the scene: the spaniel, so-called because it came originally from Spain, was used to hunt birds, often by a falconer. Like setters, the dogs were trained to point birds, and then to flush them when the falcon was waiting on overhead; but contemporary remarks, not least by Edward, second Duke of York, show that then, as now, spaniels tended to be as wild as the hawks they were supposed to be helping, and often caused chaos.

The first full account of British dogs was compiled by the sixteenth-century savant Dr Johannes Caius, founder of Caius College, Cambridge, who became court physician to Edward VI, Mary and Elizabeth. Replying to an inquiry from his friend the Swiss naturalist Konrad Gesner, Caius wrote a long letter in Latin which, although often obscure, contained much interesting information. In 1576 *De Canibus Britannicis* was translated into English by Abraham Fleming, who himself had a delightful turn of phrase, under the title *Of Englishe Dogges*.

Caius described several breeds recognisable today. He particularly admired the sagacity of bloodhounds, and their ability to stick to the right scent, especially when tracking thieves – or, as he called them, 'desperate purloiners':

> The nature of these dogs is such, and so effectual is their foresight, that they can bewray, separate and pick them out from an infinite multitude and an innumerable company, creep they never so far into the thickest throng, they will find him out notwithstanding he lie hidden in wild woods, in close and overgrown groves, and lurk in hollow holes apt to harbour such ungracious guests.

Such dogs, he wrote, were much in demand about the Scottish Borders, where they were first taught to hunt cattle, and then trained to pursue rustlers. Mastiffs (or 'bandogs') also impressed him with their power and ferocity, and their willingness to take on bears or lions ('three of them against a bear, four against a lion are sufficient'). He reported that harriers of different sizes were used to hunt a variety of prey, from deer, foxes and hares to lobsters [sic]; the job of terriers was to flush

badgers and foxes from underground ('to hayle and pull them perforce out of their lurking angles, dark dungeons and close caves'). Greyhounds also hunted deer and foxes; gazehounds ran down foxes and hares, and limmers – lightly built hounds – took game with what Caius called 'a jolly quickness'.

There were also 'tumblers', which sound like small greyhounds and were used for rabbiting; poachers' dogs, which appear to have been lurchers; spaniels and setters for pointing gamebirds, and water spaniels for retrieving birds from lakes or rivers. Shepherds' dogs (collies?) were so highly trained that they would marshal and move flocks at the slightest whistle or hand-signal from their masters. The author was anxious that his learned Swiss friend should understand the English method of shepherding:

> It is not in England, as it is in *France*, as it is in *Flanders*, as it is in *Syria*, as it is in *Tartary*, where the sheep follow the shepherd, for here in our country the shepherd followeth the sheep.

Caius evidently felt much sympathy for the 'currish' pack-dogs (presumably mongrels) which carried panniers loaded with the wares of lazy tinkers – 'metal meet to mend kettles, porridge pots, skillets and chafers, and other such-like trumpery requisites for their occupation and loitering trade, easing him of a great burden which otherwise he himself should carry on his shoulders'.

About all these types and their skills, the author was enthusiastic; but he had less time for dancing dogs – mongrels dressed up in fancy clothes and taught to cavort to the beat of a drum or a set of bagpipes – and he considered ladies who kept lapdogs ridiculously affected – even though acknowledging that when somebody was sick, an animal could draw off the affliction if carried against the bosom.

Early owners were evidently careless, many letting their dogs breed at random, for by the middle of the seventeenth century the canine population of London and other centres had reached intolerable proportions, and thousands of animals were running wild. Without knowing that disease was carried by fleas, people were beginning to suspect that the swarms of dogs, cats and rats were somehow connected with the upsurges of plague that occurred every summer, and purges were instituted in what came to be called the dog-days of August. In 1666, at the height of the plague, 40,000 dogs and 200,000 cats were killed in London alone. What people *did* know was that hydrophobia or rabies, was highly dangerous to humans as well as to animals, and it remained a threat for centuries.

Through all these changes one breed carried on as before: the turnspit, whose job was to work a treadmill connected to a spit on which a joint of meat rotated over the fire in the kitchen. Sometimes the treadmill was built round an extension of the spit itself, using the same axle, sometimes linked to it by a gear-chain. Turning it was such hot and relentless work that many households kept two long, low-backed dogs which worked on alternate days: contemporary descriptions make them sound miserable creatures, living in fear of loud-mouthed cooks. Only in the middle of the nineteenth century did the invention of a mechanical turnspit relieve them of their drudgery.

Bull- and bear-baiting, after being temporarily suppressed by Cromwell, started up again under Charles II, but by then bulldogs and bull terriers were replacing mastiffs; and the king himself was the first man to embrace lapdogs, having lost his heart to a small black-and-white spaniel brought over from France.

The eighteenth century saw the specialised breeding of greyhounds for coursing, in which two dogs were slipped simultaneously in pursuit of the same hare, and points were awarded for the way they performed, either turning the quarry or killing it. One of the new sport's leading advocates was George Walpole, Lord Orford, an eccentric Norfolk squire who founded the Swaffham Coursing Society and, by judicious crossing-in of bulldogs and lurchers, made prodigious efforts to improve the dogs' speed and stamina.

He once had a narrow escape while driving four red deer stags which he had trained to pull a phaeton: he was on his way to Newmarket when suddenly he found himself and his team being hunted by a pack of hounds. Defying every effort to restrain them, the stags went away like the wind; but fortunately they had already been to the Ram Inn in Newmarket, knew their way there, and hurtled into the yard, where the ostlers and stableboys slammed gates and doors, shutting them and his lordship into a barn, just at the hounds, in full cry, appeared at the gate.

In the end Orford's mania did finish him. In old age he had been certified insane, but escaped from house-arrest by jumping out of a window and rode to a coursing match nearby to watch his own greyhound Czarina perform. The excitement proved too much: charging after her, he fell off his horse and was killed instantly.

His work with greyhounds was taken up by another eccentric and even more flamboyant sportsman, Colonel Thomas Thornton, but he too over-reached himself, and in the end was obliged to decamp to France, to escape his creditors. The National Coursing Club, which flourishes to this day, was founded in 1858, and the Greyhound Stud Book was opened in 1882. The principal event of the coursing year was, and remains, the Waterloo Cup, held at Altcar, near Liverpool.

Another eighteenth-century fashion was for the importation of foreign breeds. From Denmark came the Great Dane, which in England became a carriage dog, running beside its owner's vehicle to keep ordinary people clear. A similar function was performed by Dalmatians, which many people thought the height of glamour but others considered impossibly brainless. From across the Atlantic the Newfoundland quickly established itself as a wonderful water dog, always ready to leap in and help anyone in difficulties, and so was a welcome member of the crew on naval vessels. The Labrador, originally a fishing dog, trained to bring fish out of the water, took to British soil no less readily: it first came here in about 1800, probably on the cod boats which docked at Poole and other ports, and became the most popular dog in the country, able to hunt as well as to retrieve (see pages 220–24).

No doubt many owners looked after their animals well; but cruelty was still ubiquitous. Writing in 1802, the Reverend William Daniel felt it necessary to defend the way in the British treated their dogs by comparing it favourably with the habits of some foreigners. In the Society Islands, he recorded, dogs were specially fattened for human consumption, like turkeys; and to emphasise the degree of barbarity involved, he added the charming detail, 'They are killed by strangling, and the extravasated blood is preserved in cocoa-nut shells and baked for the table.'

Even after dog-fighting had been officially banned in Britain by an Act of Parliament in 1835, it continued surreptitiously, as did the practice of cutting off puppies' ears, so that opponents would have less to get hold of. There was more justification in the kindred sport of ratting, and outstanding practitioners became famous for their prowess. One such was Tiny, a bull terrier which once killed 50 rats in just over 28 minutes. In his *Illustrated Natural History* the Reverend J. G. Wood reckoned that the dog put paid to 5000 rats during his lifetime, or half a ton of vermin:

> He used to go about his work in the most systematic and business-like style, picking out all the largest and most powerful rats first, so as to take the most difficult part of the task when he was fresh. When he was fatigued by his exertions, he would lie down and permit his master to wash his mouth, and refresh him by fanning him, and then would set to work with renewed vigour.

Another age-old task of dogs was to carry goods in panniers or pull small carts and wagons. In city streets with cellars beneath they had an obvious advantage over horses, whose weight might send them crashing through: in London, butchers' carts were often drawn by dogs, and perishable goods like fish, which had to travel fast, went by the same means from the south coast to London.

Everybody knew that transport dogs were often half starved, beaten to keep them going, and frequently died of exhaustion; but a campaign by the newly founded Society for the Prevention of Cruelty to Animals, which came into being in 1824, gained little public sympathy until someone made the entirely fictitious claim that excessive work in transport was a cause of rabies. In 1840 the Metropolitan Police banned the use of dogs for draft within 15 miles of Charing Cross, and after further vigorous lobbying by the SPCA, canine transport was finally abolished by Act of Parliament at the start of 1855.

The ban, followed by the imposition of a dog tax nine years later, precipitated a huge fall in the canine population. Owners who could not afford to pay the tax, and could not bring themselves to shoot or hang their pets, simply turned them out, and towns were overrun with strays: thousands were rounded up and killed – but by then two ladies in Islington had founded the first dogs' home, and the modern idea of taking in rejects was born.

In the second half of the nineteenth century the British at last evolved from being a nation of dog users and abusers to one of dog lovers. The first show open to all breeeds was held at the Town Hall in Newcastle on 28–29 June 1859, and there were 60 entries. A year later the first 'Exhibition of Sporting and Other Dogs' drew 267 entries to Birmingham. The first annual 'Grand Exhibition of Sporting and Other Dogs', held in Chelsea over six days in March 1863, attracted 1214 entries, and even that huge total was eclipsed a few weeks later, when 1678 dogs were entered for the first 'Great International Dog Show', held at the Agricultural Hall in Islington in May, and one commentator reckoned that over 2000 animals were present.

So the idea of shows developed rapidly. But in 1860 Mary Tealby, a divorced woman seriously ill with cancer, had been so distressed by the number of strays roaming London streets that she opened 'The Temporary Home for Lost and Starving Dogs' in a stable yard in Holloway. Her initiative was not well received, because conventional wisdom held that it was immoral to spend money on dumb animals when human familes were starving and children were living on the streets. Nevertheless, her courageous lead attracted many followers, not least Charles Dickens, who published an article comparing what she was doing favourably with early dog shows; and even though she died in 1865, her canine refuge survived as the Battersea Dogs' Home, having moved to its present headquarters in 1871.

The Kennel Club, founded in 1873 with Edward, Prince of Wales as its patron, quickly began raising standards by publishing pedigrees of all breeds in its stud books. The year before, a go-ahead young man called Charles Cruft, fresh out of college, had taken a job with James Spratt in London, selling dog 'cakes' all over the country. (Spratt, of Cincinnati, Ohio, had travelled to London to sell lightning conductors, but after watching dogs scrounging discarded ship's biscuits on the quayside, he had turned his attention to producing biscuits especially for canines.)

Soon Cruft was travelling on the Continent, and he so impressed French breeders that in 1878 they asked him to organise the promotion of the canine section of the Paris Exhibition. Back in London in 1886 he held a terrier show which attracted 600 entries, and the experiment was such a success that he made it an annual event: in 1891 he put his own name to the show, opened entries to other breeds, and awarded prizes to the winners in various classes.

His show went from strength to strength, and when he began to issue detailed, illustrated descriptions of each breed, written by experts, he created an entirely new market, for owners became ready to pay high prices for animals of good pedigree. When Crufts celebrated its fiftieth anniversary in 1936, its creator achieved his lifetime's ambition of attracting 10,000 entries – a world record that he thought would never be broken.

Meanwhile, another formidable canine organisation had been growing swiftly. In 1873 the ever-increasing popularity of shows led to the formation of the Kennel Club, whose committee formulated a code of rules governing dog shows and announced that only animals from societies which adopted the rules would be eligible for inclusion in the stud book which it was compiling. That autocratic stance has persisted ever since, and although owners have sometimes resented the dictatorial control which the club exercises, nobody can deny that it has been immensely successful. It now registers some 250,000 pedigree animals every year and, among many other activities, runs a Good Citizen Dog Scheme, the largest training programme in the United Kingdom.

After the death of Charles Cruft in 1938, his widow ran the show for one more year, but then handed it over to the Kennel Club, which, after a break necessitated by the Second World War, resuscitated it in 1948 at Olympia in west London. There it remained until 1979, when numbers of entries and visitors forced a move to Earls Court. By 1991 even that arena had become too small, and the show shifted again, to the National Exhibition Centre in Birmingham. Little could its instigator have imagined that in four days of May 2001, with quarantine laws relaxed for the first time, so that overseas entries had become possible, Crufts would attract 20,500 dogs and 118,000 humans – more than double his own world record. In one section of the show alone, the Discover Dogs area, more than 180 pedigree breeds were exhibited.

To an outsider, there is something faintly appalling

about Crufts. Whether from the overpowering press of the crowds, the ill-concealed ambition of human competitors, or the steely and aloof professionalism of the judges, the whole event produces a feeling of over-kill. Luckily the dogs themselves seem to enjoy what to them is a tremendous social gathering, and cheerfully ignore the tension fizzing in the air around them.

TOO MANY PETS?

Consider the story of the boy in ancient Sparta who stole a tame fox, hid it under his cloak, and rather than betray its presence to his interrogators, stood motionless and silent as it gnawed away at his vitals, until he fell down from loss of blood. How many dog owners would show such devotion and courage today?

As the number of pets in Britain climbs ever higher, it is clear that there is an enormous variation in the level of care which the creatures receive. The majority are greatly loved, and some are ridiculously spoilt; yet all too many owners are as heartless and irresponsible as the people who, in days gone by, took surplus pets to the Tower for the delectation of the lions. Why else should rescue organisations always see a surge in the numbers of unwanted animals around holiday times, when people decide simply to get rid of their dog or cat, rather than find alternative accommodation for it while they are away?

Why else should the RSPCA have to find homes for 25,000 dogs and 35,000 cats every year, and have to put down more than 10,000 dogs and nearly 20,000 cats, which are either ill or for which no homes can be found? Why else should the society annually have to mount 800 prosecutions for cruelty and secure court orders banning about the same number of people from keeping animals? Countless owners, too craven even to hand an animal in to some rescue organisation, simply turn it out on to the road or into a field. In a town, if it does not starve, its most likely fate is to be run over, and in the country it will almost certainly be shot by a gamekeeper or caught in one of his traps as it gradually wastes away,

unable to fend for itself because it has never learnt to hunt.

In London the Battersea Dogs' Home plays an indispensable role in controlling the capital's errant or surplus pets. Every year the home receives more than 8000 calls from people who have lost a dog or cat within the ring of the M25, and at any one time there are usually about 500 dogs and 90 cats on the premises. Every effort is made through a computer system to match descriptions with animals brought in either by the police or by dog-wardens. Many, however, are not lost, but are handed in, or have been dumped by owners who cannot cope with them any more.

In 2000 the Home took in an average of almost 30 dogs a day – nearly 11,000 during the year. New owners were found for more than half these rejects, and every animal passed on was given full treatment: microchipped, vaccinated, neutered and furnished with a personality assessment. Yet many thousands dogs and cats had to be put down either because they were unfit or because nobody wanted them.

Much of this waste derives from impulse-buying and lack of forethought. Overcome by the charm of a puppy or kitten, people buy one without realising how large it will grow or how much attention it will need. Many pets are bought at Christmas as presents for children, with little thought for the amount of work, money and time that pet care requires. People fail to anticipate the expense – not merely of food, but of essential visits to the vet, who may easily charge £100 for taking an x-ray and a blood-sample.

BLACK LABRADOR RETRIEVER (below)
LABRADORS VARY IN COLOUR FROM
JET BLACK, THROUGH TO YELLOW
AND CREAM.

ENGLISH COCKER SPANIEL (far right)
ORIGINALLY HUNTING DOGS, NOW
MOST TEND TO BE HOUSE OR
FAMILY DOGS.

GOLDEN RETRIEVER (right, bottom)
DESCENDED FROM CAUCASIAN
SHEEPDOGS, THEY WERE PIONEERED
BY LORD TWEEDMOUTH.

Numerous other excuses are always to hand: a new boy-friend is allergic to animals, mother-in-law has put her foot down, and so on.

The rate at which stray dogs can multiply is graphically illustrated by the example of Rumania, where during the 1980s, the crazed dictator Nicolai Ceaucescu became paranoid with suspicion that his subjects were hatching plots against him. In order to improve state surveillance, he ordered the demolition of whole villages, and moved the inhabitants into huge, featureless blocks of flats on the outskirts of towns. The result was that people had to leave their dogs behind, and after Ceausescu's assassination in 1990, the country was alive with stray animals. By 2000 it was reckoned that there were over two million stray dogs in Rumania, and 120,000 of these were in the capital of Bucharest.

Top Dogs

Britain's favourite dogs are highly pampered. Every year the Kennel Club produces a list of the Top Twenty breeds, based on the number of pedigree animals registered during each 12-month period. The placings change little from one year to the next, but reveal some surprising preferences.

Who would have guessed that Labradors out-gun all other types by such a margin, or that German Shepherds – so large and expensive to maintain – are miles ahead of all smaller breeds? Many popular types – lurchers, for instance – are not recognised by the Kennel Club, but it seems strange that collies and fox terriers (to name only two which *are* recognised) have no place in this ark of favourites. Neither do Corgis – those jewels of the Crown – nor Pekingese; but Pekes must be mentioned here, if only to include that brilliant summary of their character in the breed's National Anthem, by E. V. Lucas:

> The Pekingese
> Disdain to please
> On any set design,
> But make a thrall
> Of one and all
> By simple Right Divine.

The Lion Dog of China first reached Britain in 1860, when army officers brought back five animals after the sack of the Summer Palace at Peking. One, called Looty, was given to Queen Victoria, and survived for a dozen years. The breed quickly established itself as a popular toy, and was officially recognised by the Kennel Club in 1898. E. V. Lucas's verse points accurately at the Peke's supreme independence: although tiny, it cares for no other dog, and enslaves owners by its fearless individuality.

Sporting dogs designed primarily for showing tend to be more heavily built than those destined for field-trial work or purely for shooting. The Top Twenty list for 2000 was as follows, with numbers of registrations alongside.

Labrador Retriever 34,888

For year after year the Labrador retains its place as easily the most popular pedigree dog in Britain. To people who own one, its charms need no extolling – but perhaps its greatest merit is its versatility: at one minute it can be the soppiest of house pets, licking babies' faces or curled up on the living room sofa, and the next it can be a tenacious hunter, able to track and if necessary pull down a wounded deer. Add to this a strong sense of humour.

Although in the shooting field Labradors are used principally as retrievers, they also hunt well. Their keen noses make them ideal sniffer-dogs, used by Customs, police and army to search out drugs, hidden firearms and illegal immigrants, and their intelligence and gentleness ensure that they are first choice as guide dogs for the blind (see page 225).

In colour, most Labradors range from jet black via various shades of yellow to cream. The same litter often includes black and yellow puppies, even if both parents are the same colour. Chocolate Labradors have recently gained in popularity, even though many people consider them thick-witted – a charge vigorously refuted by their owners.

German Shepherd (Alsatian) 17,852

When this breed arrived in Britain at the start of the twentieth century, it was known as the German Sheep-dog – a direct translation of its original name, *Deutscher Schäferhund*, and a reflection of its original role. The First World War, however, ruined its chances for the time being, and because the next importations came from Alsace, in 1919, its name was changed to the Alsatian Wolf-dog – an almost *less* felicitous title, which carried hints of savagery.

In the 1920s the breed was not merely unpopular: it was positively hated by a great many people, mainly because at that time the dogs tended to be highly strung and inclined to bite strangers. Whenever an Alsatian did bite someone and was reported in the press, it was invariably described as a dangerous wolf hybrid.

Since then selective breeding has eliminated most of the tendency to nervousness, and German Shepherds are now widely used by the police, the rescue services, the army and, above all, by the Guide Dogs for the Blind Association.

Cocker Spaniel 13,445

Spaniels of a kind certainly existed in the sixteenth century, for they were described by Dr Caius in *De Canibus Britannicis*, which mentions white hunting dogs spotted with black, red or 'marble blue'. At that date no distinction was made between different kinds of spaniel: only later were they divided into larger animals called Springers or Starters, and smaller ones which became known as Cockers. A pair of red-and-white spaniels sent from China to John Churchill, later Duke of Marlborough, were first known as 'Blenheim spaniels,' but later, because they proved good at flushing woodcock from thick cover, they were called 'cocker spaniels'.

The breed was officially recognised by the Kennel Club in 1902, and its popularity increased so rapidly that in 1938 nearly 8000 Cocker Spaniels were registered. Today they are more often house or family dogs than active workers in the shooting field, where their long ears tend to get caught up in brambles.

West Highland White Terrier 13,051

Except for their black noses, eyes, paws and toenails, Westies are all white, with a coarse top coat and softer fur underneath. They were bred from a variety of other terriers in Scotland at the beginning of the twentieth century, primarily for hunting foxes and otters; now they are mainly pets, but their primeval instincts still surface fast enough if they pick up the scent of a squirrel or rabbit.

Golden Retriever 12,722

Unlike the Labrador, which came from the west, the Golden Retriever derives from the east, being a direct descendant of the Caucasian sheepdog. The pioneer of the breed in Britain was Lord Tweedmouth who, in about 1850, saw a troupe of Caucasians performing in a circus at Brighton, bought the whole lot, and took them to his estate in Inverness-shire to be trained as retrievers. They responded so well that he bred from them extensively.

At the beginning of the twentieth century various attempts were made to improve the original, crossing it with bloodhounds to give it better powers of scenting, and with Irish Setters to refine its shape. For a while the heavy bloodhound type persisted, but in time selective breeding produced the finer-looking animals favoured today.

6

Domestic Animals
Dogs

German Shepherd
Golden Retriever

221

KING CHARLES SPANIEL (below) ALTHOUGH SMALL, KING CHARLES SPANIELS ARE SURPRISINGLY TOUGH DOGS.

ENGLISH SPRINGER SPANIEL (opposite) IMMENSELY ENERGETIC, THEY ARE GOOD RETRIEVERS AND WONDERFUL HUNTERS.

English Springer Spaniel 12,599

Springers, developed via an intermediate version of the breed known as the Norfolk, are longer in the leg than other spaniels, and immensely energetic: they are good retrievers, wonderful hunters, leap into water at the first opportunity, and will keep going all day. But they also have an entrenched reputation for wildness and are difficult to control. Usually they are white with heavy black or liver markings.

Cavalier King Charles Spaniel 11,415

In the seventeenth century King Charles II had so many little spaniels about his palaces that a courtier was once heard to remark, 'God save Your Majesty, but God damn your dogs!' The diarist Samuel Pepys was also irritated by the monarch's obsession, and wrote in September 1666: 'All I observed was the silliness of the King, playing with his dogs all the while, and not minding his business.'

Although very small (about 25 cm tall), and often known as Toy Spaniels, Cavalier King Charleses are in fact quite tough dogs.

Staffordshire Bull Terrier 11,026

With the emergence of white bull terriers in the 1860s (see below), the coloured Staffordshire version lost favour, and the breed was not recognised by the Kennel Club until 1935. An authority on dogs writing in 1948, expected that the word 'Bull' would soon be discarded from its name, to distance it from its close rival – but no such change has come about, and the Staffordshire has made its own way up in owners' estimation.

Boxer 10,573

Boxers stem from the German *Bullenbeisser* or Bulldog, literally 'bull-biter', which was used for baiting large animals like bulls and bears. They are taller and less deformed-looking than British bulldogs, but still power-fully built, and on the Continent they are in demand as guard dogs, used extensively by police and army.

Yorkshire Terrier 6787

Only about 20 cm tall at the shoulder, and weighing perhaps 4 kg, the Yorkshire Terrier is one of the smallest dogs in the world. It was created in about 1850 from a mixture of other terriers – Old English, Black and Tan, Clydesdale, Scottish – and bred by coal miners in the West Riding of Yorkshire, who liked to take good rat-killers in their pockets when they went down the pits.

In those days it can hardly have had the long, silky coat which today reaches down to the ground on all sides. Nor can it have been so pampered as today's toy specimens, which are constantly shampooed and have socks put on their feet to stop them scratching.

Rottweiler 5226

A reputation for ferocity and bad temper tends to mask the Rottweiler's better qualities of strength, obedience and loyalty. In the past, in central Europe, it had many roles, being used originally for hunting wild boar, later as a cattle dog and for police work. Rottweilers were first brought to England in 1936, and exhibited at Cruft's a year later; but the Second World War

blocked further importa-
tions, and for a while the
breed seemed to have no
future in this country.

Border Terrier
4312

The tough Border Terrier,
long legged and rough
coated, is descended from
a Lake District strain which
was recognised as a good
working dog nearly 300
years ago. By the middle of
the nineteenth century hill
shepherds in Cumberland,
Westmorland and Northum-
berland were using Border
Terriers to hunt foxes,
badgers and otters. The
breed was recognised by the
Kennel Club in 1920, and by
the American Kennel Club in
1932. Its neat, alert head is
balanced by its short tail,
which it carries upright and
curled forward.

Shih Tzu
3782

The Shih Tzu – a form of oriental terrier – is a close relative
of the Tibetan Apso (see below). For centuries the Dalai
Lama of Lhasa used to send Apsos as special presents to
the Emperors of China and Japan, as well as to a few high-
ranking officials, and at some relatively recent date Chinese
owners crossed the dogs with Pekingese, producing the
Shih Tzu. The dogs can be all colours, from black to white,
and they are covered with long, wavy hair down to the
ground, which makes their feet look enormous, and hangs
down in a thick curtain over their eyes.

Lhasa Apso
3450

The name Apso is a corruption of the Tibetan *rapso*, which
means 'like a goat', and the adjective is apt, for the dogs are
coated from head to toe and tail with long, shaggy hair. This
can be sandy or honey-coloured, but more often is blue-grey
or slatey. Many people believe that Apsos and Shih Tzus are
the same, but in fact they are quite different, the first being
a purely Tibetan breed, and the second partly Chinese.

Just as the Dalai Lama used to present Shih Tzus to
Chinese Royalty and dignitaries, so, from the sixteenth to
the early twentieth century, he would also give Apsos, in
the belief that the dogs brought luck to the recipient.

Dobermann
3198

This black-and-tan breed, of German origin, took its name
from one Herr Dobermann, who produced it in Thuringia
late in the nineteenth century by mixing Pinscher, Weimaraner and Vorstehhund blood lines. If not immediately
attractive – its head looking rather small for its body – the
Dobermann compensates for a lack of beauty with speed,
agility and toughness, all of which, combined with a tendency towards aggression, make it an excellent guard dog.
In Germany it is much used by the army and the police.

Bull Terrier
2925

In the eyes of owners the bull terrier is handsome, but
to others it has a thuggish appearance, which accurately
points to the bulldog in its ancestry. Originally bred by

crossing bulldogs and terriers, it was produced purely for fighting other dogs, bears, bulls, lions or badgers. When bear-baiting died out, fights between dogs became highly popular, and the bull terrier's ferocity earned it an enormous reputation.

The breed's image was improved largely by the efforts of James Hinks of Birmingham, who bred out some of the bulldog's less desirable characteristics such as bowed legs, and created a more streamlined shape. In the second half of the nineteenth century pure-white dogs were all the rage, but later other colours became acceptable. In India, in the closing days of the Raj, the bulldog became very fashionable, being one of the few British breeds which could stand the climate.

Dalmatian   2752

Also known as carriage or coach dogs, Dalmatians once performed the useful function of running alongside or behind horse-drawn conveyances, first to deter highwaymen and thieves, later as fashionable ornaments to set off their owners' equipages. They also had a curious connection with fire engines, which they used to accompany, especially in New England.

Their provenance is by no means clear, but they are believed to have originated from Istrian pointers (Istria being a peninsula in the north of Yugoslavia), with the possible addition of some Great Dane blood. Legend has it that they were brought to Dalmatia by Indian gypsies – but how they acquired their multiple black spots remains uncertain. Their present popularity owes much to the author and playwright Dodie Smith, whose children's novel *A Hundred and One Dalmatians* became a bestseller immediately it was published in 1956, and the fame of the breed was secured by the film of the book made by Walt Disney.

Latter-day owners agree that Dalmatians are perhaps not all that bright, but they love them for their genial nature, high spirits and boundless energy.

Weimaraner   2694

Sometimes known as 'the grey ghost', from the lovely silver colour of its coat, which has an almost metallic sheen, the Weimaraner is a large pointer, similar to but bigger than a Hungarian Vizsla, and stands about 65 cm at the shoulder. The antiquity of the breed is shown by the fact that the Flemish artist Hubert van Eyck painted a dog of this exact description early in the fifteenth century. Weimaraners are thought to have been bred by crossing bloodhounds with pointers or other hunting dogs.

Miniature Schnauzer   2399

If any dog looks like a toy, it is the Miniature Schnauzer, with the rectangular shape of its face in profile, its turned-over ears and the stiff, forward tilt of its stance. Seen from the front, its facial hair curves down on either side of its muzzle in the form of an immense moustache.

The breed was established in the United States by 1923, but did not arrive in Britain until 1928. Its larger relative, the ordinary Schnauzer, is a German breed which was once used by drovers for moving cattle, sheep and pigs, and probably has poodle and wire-haired pinscher in its ancestry. Schnauzers also make excellent ratters, and did good service in granaries and warehouses.

6
Domestic Animals
Dogs

Dalmatian
Miniature
Schnauzer

224

Bichon Frisé

A lapdog *par excellence*, the Bichon looks like a fuzzy toy poodle, covered in curly white fur, with an appealing, rounded head, black nose and black button eyes. Of Continental origin – possibly Italian – the breed was recognised by the Kennel Club only in the 1970s.

DOGS AT WORK

DOGS AT WAR

Many times in the twentieth century dogs reverted to their old role of fighting alongside humans in war, although now they relied on speed and powers of scent, rather than merely on their teeth, to render assistance on the battlefield. The earliest British military school for dogs was set up during the First World War in Essex, where Airedales, collies, lurchers and whippets, sent on indefinite loan by their owners, were trained to carry messages back from the front line. Although casualties were heavy, many dogs performed admirably during the trench warfare in France, and crossed ground that no human could have survived. Besides acting as runners, they laid out telephone lines by carrying drums of cable which unreeled as they ran, and killed thousands of the rats which swarmed over the corpses at the front.

In the Second World War an Army War Dog School was set up at Potters Bar. Again, private owners were invited to lend their pets: many proved unacceptable, but 3500 were taken for training, especially as guard dogs, to be deployed on airfields, ammunition dumps and prisoner-of-war camps. In the first war, Airedales had been pre-eminent, but for this role the big, strong Alsatian came into its own.

Many dogs learnt to parachute and dropped into action with their units: they were trained, when they came to earth, to lie still until their handler came up and released their harnesses. Sheepdogs and Labradors proved excellent mine-detectors, sitting down when they scented an alien object buried ahead of them, and being able to pinpoint not only metal, but plastic and wood as well.

These abilities were again invaluable during anti-terrorist operations in Northern Ireland, where dogs repeatedly sniffed out caches of arms and explosives. So highly skilled did many become that, even when shown into a strange room for the first time, they would quickly tell to a place where a floorboard had been taken up and replaced, or bricks prized out of a wall and built back: they seemed to carry in their heads a complete scent picture of what a normal room should be like, and they could instantly detect any anomaly, where dust patterns had been rearranged, whether or not there was anything in the cache.

GUIDE DOGS FOR THE BLIND

A far more worthwhile occupation than fighting is guiding blind humans, and the success of the Guide Dogs for the Blind Association is the most heartening canine story of the century. The idea of using dogs as human eyes originated in Germany in 1916–17, when animals were trained to lead soldiers blinded in the First World War; but it was a rich American, Mrs Dorothy Harrison Eustis, who brought the international guide dog movement into being. In the 1920s she herself trained Alsatians in Switzerland for the customs, police and army, and in 1927 an article about German guide-dog training which she wrote for the *Saturday Evening Post* sparked such excitement in the United States that she set up schools of her own, first in Switzerland and later in America.

In 1931 Mrs Eustis sent a trainer to England, and the idea took root here. The first four British dogs completed their training that same year, and in 1934 their success led to the formation of the association, which began training from a lock-up garage in Wallasey, in Cheshire. The first dogs were almost all Alsatians, but later Labradors and Golden Retrievers were found to be just as good, if not better, and today all three breeds are used, as well as crosses between them.

The characteristics most needed are willingness to work, acceptance of other animals and people, and immunity to noise and crowds. A vivid illustration of how human attitudes change is provided by the fact that, in the early days of the scheme, passersby often criticised, abused or even physically obstructed trainers when they were out on the streets, goaded by the belief that it was cruel to make an animal work. Little did such critics realise how much the dogs enjoyed what they were doing, or what an immense difference they made to the lives of their partners.

From that modest start the charity has grown so enormously that it now costs £45 million a year to run. Its success, in both physical and psychological terms, would be hard to exaggerate. It has some 5000 guide dogs out working in Britain, and has become the world's largest breeder and trainer of working dogs, producing 1200 puppies a year from sires and bitches chosen for their intelligence and temperament.

The brood bitches live out in family homes scattered round the country, and their offspring get their first taste of training at only six weeks, when volunteer walkers introduce the puppies to the sights, smells and sounds of the world in which they will work, taking them on buses and trains, along busy streets and into shops. Walkers start

GREYHOUND RACING (below) THERE
ARE 33 GREYHOUND TRACKS IN BRITAIN
AND BETTING IS BIG BUSINESS.

BORDER COLLIE (right) JOCK, A
BORDER COLLIE AT REST DURING
SHEARING IN THE HIGHLANDS.

BEAGLES (right, below) KEPT AS
HARE-HUNTING DOGS AND AS
FAMILY PETS.

giving their charges simple commands like 'Sit,' 'Down,'
'Stay' and 'Come', and teach them to go ahead on the
leash, rather than to walk at heel.

At the age of a year the puppies return to the Guide
Dogs' Centre for specialised training, learning to walk in
a straight line along the centre of a pavement, not to turn
corners unless told to do so, to stop at kerbs and wait for
the command to cross the road, to judge height and width
of gaps so that the owner does not bump head or shoulder,
and generally to deal with traffic.

One difficulty in training a guide dog is that the handler
cannot work to develop any natural instinct. Hounds and
gun dogs react to scent, as does an animal being trained
for police or customs work, and so need little encouragement to follow a trail; guide dogs, on the other hand, work
only to please their handlers. Willingness to work and
eagerness to please are thus essential elements in their
characters, and trainers often use small rewards like pieces
of baked liver to back up praise when it is due. Outsiders
tend to think that guide dogs are particularly chivalrous
and altruistic characters, but this is not so. They simply do
what they are trained to do, without understanding the true
purpose of their lives.

By no means all the pupils pass their final exams; but
those that do – the majority – are carefully matched with
potential owners. Factors taken into account include the
owner's height, length of stride and general habits. The
pair go through up to four weeks of intensive training
together: when they pass out, the owner hands over a
token fee of 50 p and the dog exchanges its brown training
harness for a white one.

So begins a partnership which, with luck, will last for
the dog's working life of seven years. For the human, a four-
footed leader means new freedom, often almost a new life.
For the dog, work demands great concentration, but has
the reward of close companionship that all canines love.
The association pays for the dog's food and veterinary care
throughout its working life: the cost of breeding, training
and supporting each one is £35,000.

When the time comes for a dog to retire, it often stays
on as a pet with the owner's family, and the association
guarantees to replace it with another fully trained animal,
so that there is no gap. Nevertheless, the moment of trans-
ition is often painfully emotional, so fond has the owner
grown of his or her constant companion. The fact one
person may go through six or seven guide dogs means that
the distressing business of handing over has to be repeated
several times.

GREYHOUND RACING

The idea of setting greyhounds to chase an artificial hare
was first put into practice at the Welsh Harp in Hendon in
1876, when dogs were set to pursue a target drawn along
by a wire wound in on a windlass. Today there are 33
registered tracks, and the hare is generally a wooden or
metal cut-out, travelling on the outside track. The length
of races varies from 237 to 916 metres, but the majority
are run over about 450 metres, for which a good time is
28 seconds. Betting is an all-important ingredient of the
sport: more than 20 per cent of all bets in the United
Kingdom, including those on horse-racing and football
go on the dogs.

6
Domestic Animals
Dogs

Dogs at Work

WORKING DOGS

Basset

Bassets are claimed to be the oldest breed of hound, with records going back to 1304, and their name derives from the French *bas à terre* – low to the ground. They stand only about 35 cm at the shoulder, and with their stumpy legs, huge heads and drooping ears, they have an endearingly ridiculous appearance; but it was because of their low-slung frame, which enabled them to wriggle under dense undergrowth, that French huntsmen used them to flush out boar, deer and other game. To this day the scent of deer is so deeply engrained in their subconscious that if they cross the track of a deer, they are liable to abandon the line of the hare they are supposed to be hunting, and take off in pursuit.

Compared with the ubiquitous beagle, they have become relatively rare. At the end of the century there were only ten packs of bassets in Britain and one in Pennsylvania, USA. Aficionados love hunting with them, partly because they are slower than beagles, and partly because what they lack in speed, they make up in skill and tenacity: their scenting powers are second only to those of a bloodhound, and it is said that if they lose a hare at the end of one day, all the huntsman need do is stick a marker in the ground and come back next morning, whereupon his hounds will pick up the line.

Many bassets are kept for showing, or simply as pets. As in other breeds, show dogs tend to be more heavily built, with creases of skin folding over their ankles and jowls sweeping the ground.

Beagle

Beagles are about the same height as bassets – 35 cm at the shoulder – but much more lightly built, and they are generally coloured in a mixture of black, tan and white, like miniature fox-hounds. Many are kept as pets, but the animals' forte is hunting hares as a pack.

Because they do not generally move very fast, huntsmen and followers are always on foot. But for most of the people involved, speed is not the point. The fascination of beagling lies in the exercise of an age-old art, the skill with which a huntsman manages his hounds, laying them on or lifting them at the right moment, controlling them with the horn, and knowing when they have switched from one hare to another.

Border Collie

Thousands of farmers keep black-and-white, long-coated collies to help them marshal and move grazing animals, particularly sheep. In such dogs herding sheep is a natural instinct, and it can be honed by training to a fine art. The pleasure that a sheepdog gets from working is evident in the attitude it adopts when awaiting the order to go – quivering in every muscle, crouching belly to the ground, head right down, eyes focused intently on the quarry – and in the speed with which it dashes off when it gets the command.

Fox Hound

As the craze for fox-hunting spread during the eighteenth century, each hunt established its own stud book, and soon packs of hounds bred specifically for the sport outnumbered those of harriers, which chased hares. Two basic strains of fox hound evolved – the smaller Northern hound, and its heavier, slower Southern counterpart, which made up for other deficiencies by its excellence at following a scent. Another important influence was the traditional, long-coated Welsh hound, famous for its keen nose and perseverance.

By studying pedigrees and watching individual hounds at work, masters and huntsmen constantly refined their packs to produce speed and stamina. Today's hounds stand from 58 to 70 cm at the shoulder, and range in colour from all white to various combinations of white, tan and black. At the end of 2001 there were some 16,000 fox hounds in Britain. Hounds are never bought or sold: rather, puppies are given or swapped from one kennel to another.

Along with their hounds, practitioners developed terriers small and fierce enough to go down an earth and drive a fox out. Rough-coated terriers were preferred, because their long hair gave them some protection against bites, and colour did not matter: black, tan, white – anything was acceptable. **Harriers** between fox hounds and beagles in size, have been bred to hunt hares. There are 20 packs in England and Wales.

In size and shape, **Stag Hounds** are almost identical to fox hounds, but there are far fewer of them – only three packs in England. In earlier days the breed had its own bloodlines, but now new blood is frequently imported by crossbreeding with fox hounds. The proponents of stag-hunting claim that their traditional method of culling is best for the red deer herds in the West Country, first because it is selective, and weak or old animals are taken out before healthy ones, and second because the sport encourages local farmers to tolerate a much higher deer population than they would otherwise accept.

In 1998 a bitter controversy arose when the National Trust banned stag-hunting on its land in Somerset and Devon, even though the donors who had given the properties to the Trust had specified that the sport should continue.

The sixteen packs of **Drag Hounds** in England and Wales are essentially fox hounds trained to follow an artificial scent, which is laid by a human runner or some-times by a rider – the scent being made up of chemicals, or from the excreta of wolves and foxes. Packs are much smaller than those of fox hounds, with only eight or ten couples out at once.

Bloodhound

Larger, heavier and slower than fox hounds, blood hounds are a quite different breed, but also trained to hunt the line of an artificial drag, In 2001 there were 14 packs, most of

A COUPLE OF FOX HOUNDS (left)
BY GEORGE STUBBS, OIL ON
CANVAS 1792.

SIBERIAN HUSKY (below) WITH A
WOLF-LIKE APPEARANCE, HUSKIES
RETAIN MANY WILD CHARACTERISTICS.

them privately owned. Their deep cry can make the hair on your neck crawl, but when they catch up with their quarry, they are sloppiness itself, showing no desire to eat or even molest the runner, but slobbering all over him.

Husky

In spite of their wolf-like appearance – often with one eye white or pale blue and the other amber – individual huskies are usually gentle with humans. It is only when they get going as a pack that their wild tendencies assert themselves. At night they indulge in bouts of communal howling, and the prospect of going out on a run rouses them to a state of frenzied excitement, so that getting them harnessed and hitched up to a sledge or bogey is no job for anyone nervous.

They have a limited understanding of international commands. *Jee* (left), *hoar* (right), *mush* (go) and *whoa* (stop) are about the limit of their comprehension, and it is hard to train them to do anything except what they enjoy most – running in a team. Why, then, do people find them so fascinating and spend considerable sums on keeping racing teams? The answer seems to be that huskies retain many wild characteristics, and to secure cooperation from such creatures of nature is exceptionally rewarding.

Pointers and Setters

When pointers and setters scent game, they instinctively come to a point: that is, they stop and stand rigid, with their noses directed straight at the quarry, sometimes with one paw raised. A steady dog will hold the point until its handler comes up and either flushes the game himself or urges the dog forward; but a less well-trained animal is liable to rush in on its own without waiting for any further command.

English Pointers are slender and rangy, about 65 cm tall, and usually multicoloured in liver, tan, black and white. **German Short-haired Pointers** – the same height, but more heavily built and often solid liver, or liver and white – are also much used for shooting, and for tracking wounded deer. Hungarian **Vizslas** are generally deep honey-coloured and smooth-coated.

Field trials for gun dogs have become extremely popular, and because only a limited number of entrants can be accommodated, many owners are frustrated at not being able to take part. On a typical day, a small team of four or five guns is invited to shoot partridges or pheasants, and every time a bird falls, one of the competitors is given the chance to retrieve it, while judges keep close and award points for skill and perseverance.

Retrievers

As their name suggests, the main task of retrievers is to find shot game and bring it back to their handlers; but many will also hunt for birds and ground game. Easily the most popular breed is the **Labrador** (*see page 220*), which can be black or yellow. The **Golden Retriever** looks like an outsized yellow Labrador with a long coat, but the **Flat-Coated Retriever** is always black or liver.

Alsatians

Recent tests have shown that the scenting powers of Alsatians exceed those of all other dogs by a wide margin, and German Shepherds (*see page 221*) have proved so effective at sniffing out drugs and explosives that more and more of them are being used by the army, police and security agencies, both in Britain and in the United States. After the terrorist attacks of 11 September 2001, the demand for Alsatian puppies rocketed in America, and the value of a trained dog rose to as high as $20,000.

The most flamboyant
and dangerous of
England's traditional rural
pastimes, fox-hunting
has attracted followers
from every walk of
life for more than
250 years

The history of fox-hunting

THE CIVIL WAR of 1649 brought profound changes in hunting with hounds, for, in their vendetta against the King and Cavaliers, the Roundheads vindictively destroyed hundreds of deer parks, smashing the walls and fences, driving the deer away or killing them. The massacres put an abrupt end to the fashionable sport of buck-hunting, and country gentlemen started, with initial reluctance, to hunt foxes instead. It was not long, however, before the speed, guile and subtlety of this new quarry began to command respect; and during the next 150 years the breeding of faster, more enterprising hounds required to catch 'Charlie', (as the quarry came to be nicknamed after the eighteenth-century gambler and politician Charles James Fox) changed the whole character of English hunting.

It has often been claimed that fox-hunting exercised a profound influence on English history because it promoted harmony in the countryside. Whereas shooting had always been divisive, being an occupation of the rich which was denied to the poor, hunting embraced all classes of country people, from squires to farm hands, who, even if they had no horse, could always follow on foot – a point wilfully misunderstood by the sport's detractors. The historian Carson I. A. Ritchie said, 'It was fox-hunting men, much more than Methodist preachers, who saved England from a French Revolution, by keeping the different classes in constant and amicable contact.'

As packs of fox hounds proliferated and the sport became more fashionable, the land was divided into 'hunting countries', within each of which a particular pack held sway. By degrees the practice of meeting at dawn in order to trace a fox by his 'drag' from the previous night's foraging gave way to overnight earth-stopping, followed by a mid-morning meet. Nearby coverts would then be drawn and hunted until nightfall.

In the early days a great landowner such as the Earl of Berkeley could hunt a country stretching from Berkeley Castle in Gloucestershire to Berkeley Square in London – a distance of more than 160 km; but gradually private packs became the exception, replaced by subscription packs run by committees, to which invited members, subscribers and local farmers contributed in cash or in kind – a system which continues to this day. So, too, does the wearing of eighteenth-century hunting dress – boots and breeches, swallow-tailed coat with brass buttons bearing the hunt's insignia, and starched white hunting tie, though modern protective headgear of velvet-covered skull-cap has largely replaced the silk top hat of yesteryear.

The spread of the railways in the nineteenth century gave fox-hunting a powerful boost, making it possible to transport horses to distant meets; and hedges planted as a result of the Enclosures Acts sharply increased the thrill of the chase, for jumping obstacles became an essential part of riding to hounds. Nor was it only men who exulted in what Adam Lindsay Gordon described as:

> The leap, the rise from the springy turf,
> The rush through the buoyant air,
> The light shock landing ...

That 'light shock landing' often turned into a crashing fall, yet soon dashing women such as Catherine Walters, the famous *demi-mondaine* of the 1860s known as 'Skittles', were showing their mettle over fences and hedges. Despite his wife's disapproval, Lord Stamford, Master of the Quorn, was so impressed by her riding that he said she was always welcome to follow his hounds, adding firmly, 'And damn all jealous women!' The sport attracted many outrageous characters, and none wilder or more arrogant that John Mytton, the squire of Halston in Shropshire, who was born in 1796 and drank himself to death (in prison) at the age of 38.

Today, famous Shires packs – Quorn, Pytchley, Fernie and Belvoir – hunt five or even six days a week and attract fields of 300 mounted followers. The huntsman and kennelman are generally paid professionals, and the Master or Masters may be professionals or amateurs, paid or unpaid. At the other end of the scale are the small packs of the Lakeland Fells and the Welsh Borders, many of whom go out on foot, because the terrain is too steep for horses. In such wild, inaccessible areas of the country, the hunts offer not merely entertainment, but – more important – an essential means of pest control.

The number of hounds in a pack varies from 75 couple in a big, busy kennels to perhaps 17 couple in a humbler hunt. Hounds are entered at about 18 months, reach their career peak at three, and seldom go on hunting beyond the age of six, after which they are put down.

Few sports have attracted so eclectic a following or given rise to so much tradition, lore and literature. Among today's keenest fox-hunters can still be found princes, philosophers, poets, politicians, authors, doctors, journalists and men of the cloth, as well as the farmers, shopkeepers, and countrymen and women who have always provided bedrock support. Among legion authors, R. S. Surtees and Anthony Trollope remain pre-eminent, while Siegfried Sassoon's *Memoirs of a Foxhunting Man*, first published in the 1920s, comes closest to explaining the sport's enduring fascination for intellectuals as well as men and women of action.

Hunting people claim, with some justification, that their activities maintain a healthy population of foxes, because hounds kill off old, weak, and maimed animals which would otherwise die a lingering death from starvation. Equally important are the benefits to landscape conservation and biodiversity, for the creation and maintenance of suitable fox habitat provides a vital refuge for many other species threatened by modern methods of farming.

For experts, the fascination of the sport lies in watching a huntsman work his hounds, and seeing the pack follow scent. Most followers do not take part in order to see a fox killed. Rather, they go hunting for the sheer excitement of riding hell-for-leather across country, often being swept along (as in skiing) rather faster than they would wish, and always keenly aware that a mistake over the next fence or hedge could land them with a broken leg, collar-bone, arm or even neck.

Cats

It is thought that cats were first domesticated some 5000 years ago in the Middle East, and that today's typical domestic moggy with tabby markings, is descended from the African wild cat (the word 'tabby' derives from *Al Attabiya*, a district of Baghdad, where a type of black and white watered silk was produced). The ancient Egyptians were fascinated by the animals because of the way the pupils of their eyes dilated and contracted. This, people thought, in some mysterious way represented lunar changes: cats were under the influence of the moon, and should be propitiated. The creatures were therefore treated as sacred, and thousands were buried, mummified, in specially consecrated graveyards. The goddess Bastet was represented as a woman with a cat's head, attended by sundry felines, and her temple at Bubastic was the centre of cat worship.

Pet cats were spread throughout Europe by the Romans, who brought them to England in the first century AD, and they have been here ever since, usually but not always welcome as household companions and killers of vermin. They were highly regarded in medieval Wales, where, in the ninth century AD, the legendary ruler Hywel Dda (Hywel the Good) enacted that the price of a kitten before its eyes opened should be one penny; if later it caught a mouse, its value was raised to two pence, then to four pence. If anyone stole or killed the cat that guarded the prince's granary, the owner was compelled to forefeit either a ewe or as much wheat as would cover the cat when suspended by its tail.

In the Middle Ages, on the other hand, many people supposed that cats were dangerous for purely physical reasons, and should be avoided as much as possible. Edward Topsell, writing in 1601, concluded that the flesh of cats could 'seldom be free from poison' because the animals habitually ate rats and mice. 'Above all,' he thought,

> the brain of the cat is most venomous, for it being above all measure dry, stoppeth the animal spirits [so] that they cannot pass into the ventricle, by reason thereof memory faileth and the person falleth into a phrenzie ... The hair

also of a cat, being eaten unawares, stoppeth the artery and causeth suffocation.

Cats were often regarded with deep suspicion, as being the familiars of witches. Black cats were the worst, because they were reckoned to be agents or symbols of Satan, and the treatment meted out to them was diabolical, as in the practice known as *taghairm*, or 'giving the devil his supper', described by Lewis Spence in his book *The Magic Arts of Celtic Britain*:

> Lachlan Oer and a companion, Allan ... shut themselves up in a barn near the Sound of Mull, and, impaling black cats on spits, roasted them alive by a blazing fire. Other cats entered the building, setting up an infernal cater-wauling, which well-nigh daunted the men, but they remained inexorable until a greater cat of ferocious appearance entered and remonstrated with them, threatening them that if they did not desist from their horrid employment they would never see the face of the Trinity. Lachlan struck the hideous animal on the head with the hilt of his sword, whereupon the Devil, for it was he, assumed his appropriate shape and asked the pair what it was they wanted of him. They replied that they craved prosperity, and a long life to enjoy it. This was granted, and it is said that Lachlan, for his part, never repented of the dreadful act, even upon his deathbed.

Conversely, some people reckoned that black cats had their uses: an Irish superstition held that the liver of a jet-black animal, cooked, dried and ground into powder, acted as a powerful aphrodisiac and would cause the person who took it to fall in love with the one who administered the dose. In his eighteenth-century *Diary of a Country Parson* the Reverend James Woodforde described how, when once much troubled by a stye on his right eyelid, he rubbed it with the tail of a black cat, and 'very soon after dinner I found my eyelid much abated of the swelling and almost free from pain'.

Optimists have always regarded black cats as lucky, and many households used to keep one purely to ensure prosperity. On the coast of Yorkshire the wives of fishermen believed that if they kept a black cat in the house, their husbands would return safe from sea; and in Scarborough this conviction was so strong that cats were constantly being stolen. Further south, that matchlessly graceful Indian cricketer Prince Ranjitsinji also believed in the creatures' efficacy: twice in succession, he reckoned, the appearance of a black cat at a critical moment was instrumental in winning a county match for Sussex.

Countless celebrated people have become besotted with cats of any colour. Florence Nightingale kept 60 cats, and refused to travel without them. The author Ernest

LILAC-POINT BIRMAN CAT WITH

KITTENS BIRMANS ARE AMONG THE
TOP TEN BREEDS KEPT IN BRITAIN.

Hemingway had so many at his farm in Cuba that he was obliged to build a separate house for them. In his *Life of Johnson* James Boswell recorded how the great savant himself used to go out and buy oysters for his cat Hodge, 'lest the servants having the trouble should take a dislike to the poor creature'. Wretched Boswell hated cats, and 'frequently suffered a good deal from the presence of the same Hodge'.

Like pigs, cats can be trained to astonish visitors by their apparent precocity. There is one record of an animal which, when presented with a large-scale map of London, would place its paw smartly over any principal building that the guest cared to name. The secret was that it had been taught to swat flies on the walls when carried round a room, and struck out at any dark spot. Since each of the capital's main edifices was marked with a bold black dot, the owner could make the cat appear to read the map by holding it close to the right place.

One curious historical feature has been the number of cats found, bricked up in the walls of buildings and mummified by air rather than by any chemical preservatives. Some obviously got stuck while hunting and died miserably of starvation, but others were set up after death and placed in position, probably in the hope of scaring off vermin. One gruesome, dried-out specimen from the seventeenth or eighteenth century, was found in a house in Southwark, holding one rat in its jaws and trampling another under foot.

During the nineteenth century the families of soldiers and administrators posted to far corners of the British Empire began bringing back exotic breeds of cat with them when they returned home from service overseas, among them the Seal Point Siamese. Long-haired animals also became popular, and in the latter part of Queen Victoria's reign, people started to breed cats selectively, for show purposes. The first major show took place at Crystal Palace in London in 1871, organised by the redoubtable Harrison Weir, first president of the National Cat Club.

By the end of the century, when a few other cat clubs had opened, confusion was growing from the fact that different organisations had different systems of registration, and not all recognised their rivals' standards. In due course everyone concerned agreed to set up a new body which would hold all the registers and oversee the running of shows. So it was that in 1910 the Governing Council of the Cat Fancy was formed with the aims of keeping the registers, licencing and controlling shows, ensuring the welfare of pedigree cats and seeing that rules were not broken. Today the GCCF is the feline equivalent of the Kennel Club: it has 139 affiliated clubs, oversees about 125 shows and licences an average of 32,000 pedigree cats every

233

year. The major event of its year, the Supreme Cat Show held over two days in Birmingham, attracts more than 12,000 visitors.

In the Fancy's own words, 'the whole purpose of the pedigree breeding is to attain cats of a specific shape and colour' and a Standard of Points is laid down for each colour and breed. Judges at shows have to be on their mettle, for continuous refinement leads to progressive change, even within a breed. The difference in head shape between Persian and Siamese, for instance, was once relatively small, but now there is little resemblance between the two. The Fancy produces annual popularity charts which clearly show which breeds are favourites. The top ten registered in 2000 were:

Persian Long Hair	5157
British Short Hair	4704
Siamese	3786
Burmese	2737
Birman	2099
Bengal	1698
Ragdoll	1463
Maine Coon	1251
Oriental Short Hair	1224
Exotic Short Hair	652

The Fancy strongly advises members of affiliated clubs not to buy cats from pet shops. Nevertheless, it is from pet shops or private sales that the vast majority of British felines emanate, for common-or-garden animals outnumber pedigrees by at least ten to one. If you want a top-notch Persian kitten, you may well have to pay £300, but you can pick up a perfectly adequate mouser for £25 or so.

In 1983 the Cat Association of Britain was formed 'as an alternative to other existing bodies', and to represent Britain on the *Fédération Internationale Féline*, a non-profit body composed of worldwide cat-fancy organisations. The Association's aim is to encourage responsible breeding and to promote the welfare of domestic cats, one specific purpose being to reduce the amount of blindness, which is especially prevalent in white animals. The association runs its own Rescue Express service, designed to help cats in need.

Occasionally a new breed comes into being by chance. In 1951 a kitten with folded ears was born in a farm cat's litter near Coupar Angus in Scotland. When the same cat gave birth to another white kitten with folded ears, a local shepherd, William Ross, decided to see if he could establish a new breed with this engaging characteristic – and in due course he succeeded in producing what is now called the Scottish Fold, a chunky-looking cat, either black and white or tortoiseshell and white, with a round head and ears pointing downwards in the direction of the nose.

Some idea of the problems that cats pose is given by the work of the country's largest feline charity, Cats' Protection, whose role since its foundation in 1927 has always been to

rescue and rehome strays and unwanted animals. Founder-members were shocked by people's ignorance of how to treat their pets, and the aim at the outset was 'to promote the interests of cats'. To this end, attempts were made in the 1930s to produce a cat-door or flap, and in 1940 during the Blitz the Tailwavers' Scheme was introduced to relieve distress among bombed-out cats and kittens. The name came straight from the Greek for cat – *ailouros*, which means tail-waver – and after the war surplus funds from the scheme were used to set up a clinic and shelters.

Today, through its nationwide network of 29 permanent shelters and 245 voluntary branches, the organisation helps some 170,000 cats and kittens every year, rehoming about 200 animals a day. Pointing out that a single female could, in theory, be responsible for producing 20,000 descendants in five years, it spends £2.5 million a year on neutering and strongly advises all owners to spay or neuter any animal from which they do not want to breed. Ninety per cent of the work is carried out by 5000 volunteers, and the organisation's helpline answers over 650 calls a day.

The choice of a cat is an intensely personal matter, for the variety available is enormous. The vast majority of the nation's cats are non-pedigree, and among this plebeian horde tabbies probably predominate. Yet even here there is room for careful selection, since experts list Red Classic, Blue Mackerel, Brown Mackerel, Brown Classic, White and Brown and Brown Mackerel among the colours in which tabbies may come.

Manx cats have no tails, and to some eyes look rather deformed, but are said to be particularly intelligent.

Siamese, with their long, slim bodies and sleek, short hair, are undoubtedly elegant, and they are rated as 'affectionate', but not everyone can stand their raucous voices. Besides, there are nearly twenty recognised varieties – Cream Point, Lilac Point, Seal Tortie Point and so on.

Maine Coons enslave their owners – and very handsome they are, with their wide-set eyes and luxuriant, silky fur. But it is easy to see why **Persian Long Hairs** top the pure-bred popularity chart: the 40-odd varieties are all colours from white to black, via blue, chocolate, tortoiseshell and marmalade, and all are characterised by an irresistible fluffiness.

Almost all cat-owners are faced with a dilemma: they know that their darling pets are born killers, and that even if fed to the eyeballs, they will go out and kill some harmless victim the moment they get a chance. A survey carried out by the Mammal Society in 1997, and entitled 'Look What the Cat Brought In', suggested that Britain's 9 million cats kill 200 million mammals, 55 million birds and 10 million reptiles and amphibians every year, their prey including such rare and declining species as water voles, dormice and house sparrows.

The survey estimated that even a properly domesticated cat may have a home range of 28 hectares, and may hunt up to 1 km from home – which means that it is not just suppressing rodents around the house, but foraging on a much wider scale. The society urges all owners to keep their cats indoors at night and to put bells on their collars. It also recommended that garden birds should be fed, to cut the time and effort birds need to put into looking for food, and so makes them less vulnerable.

6

Domestic Animals
Cats

Other domestic animals

The less trouble a pet is to look after, the more popular it is likely to be. In contrast with dogs, which are extremely demanding, as they need to be fed, let out and exercised at frequent intervals, the animals described here can all look after themselves for quite long periods.

Rabbit

Oryctologus cuniculus

Every year the British Rabbit Council, which deals only with exhibition animals, issues about 60,000 identification rings (for slipping on to the back leg of each baby), but these rabbits are no more than the tip of a huge iceberg of less distinguished pets, which are estimated to number about 4.5 million.

Exhibitors of pedigree strains are highly active: about a thousand shows take place every year, with competitors divided into three categories – Fancy, shown for their breeding and conformation; Fur, shown for their coats, and Rex, shown for their particular velvety texture. The 50-odd recognised breeds range from the **Alaska** to the **Vienna**, via such favourites as the **British Giant** (which must weigh at least 5.7 kg), the **Lop English** (whose ears sweep the ground) and the **Chinchilla**.

Gerbil

Meriones unguiculatus

Also known as sand rats, gerbils are small burrowing rodents about 12 cm long, which are native to Africa and Asia. Those now widely domesticated as pets are the Mongolian variety: their large eyes and ears, along with very soft grey or brown fur and calm temperaments, make them engaging pets. Nobody knows for sure how many there are in Britain, but the total is probably several hundred thousand. When they escape, gerbils apparently survive for quite some time in the wild, for their remains are found in the pellets of waste material regurgitated by owls. The British Gerbil Society holds eight or ten shows a year, generally as one element of some larger exhibition.

MINI REX RABBIT SIAMESE SABLE
(below left); GUINEA PIG, SILVER
AGOUTI REX (below right).

Guinea Pig

Cavia porcellus

A domesticated species of a South American rodent, guinea pigs were first brought to Europe in the sixteenth century, and later became not only much fancied as pets, but also widely employed for medical research, especially in bacterial diseases – hence the application of the term 'guinea pig' applied to any person, thing or process used for experimental purposes. Being stout, short-legged and about 25 cm long, with small ears and no external tail, the animals appeal strongly to children; but, as many parents have found to their cost, their fecundity is phenomenal. A female may breed three times a year, producing up to eight young per litter after a gestation period of only eight or ten weeks.

Hamster

Cricetus

Large cheek pouches, used for carrying food, are the most obvious features that distinguish hamsters from other small rodents. Common hamsters live in the steppes and farmland of Europe and western Asia, where they dig elaborate burrows, with separate chambers for nesting and storing grain, fruit, insects and other food, which they collect industriously.

The ubiquitous pets are **Syrian** or **Golden hamsters** (*Mesocricetus auratus*), every one of which is supposed to derive from a single family caught in Syria in 1930. Apart from the fact that it is clean, easily tamed and cared for, a hamster's chief virtue is that it is a solitary animal, content to live on its own. For owners, this is just as well, since a female hamster can produce up to 18 young every year, in several litters, after a gestation period of only about 20 days.

A form of population control is sometimes exercised by the animals themselves: if a captive female is stressed or disturbed, she may turn cannibal and eat her offspring. Escapees have been eliminated by pest-control measures, although some have survived for quite a time by going into hibernation for the winter and thus creating the impression that they are already dead.

Mouse

Mus

Keepers of fancy mice are relatively few, but immensely enthusiastic. The National Mouse Club, founded in 1895, has only 120 members, yet each may own 100 animals, and competition at shows is keen. The club recognises about 15 varieties and a number of colours. A trio of good-looking mice – a buck and two does – may fetch a price of £10; and as life expectation is only about two years, turnover is fast.

Rat

Rattus

The National Fancy Rat Society has about 1000 members, each of whom owns an average of four rats. Rat clubs have existed since the beginning of the twentieth century, but the NFRS was founded only in 1976. It promotes the welfare of pet rats in general, and recognises many varieties: 'dark-eyed self-coloured' rats may be white, black, mink, chocolate, blue or buff, while 'pink-eyed self- coloured' are either white or champagne. More exotic types include the **Himalayan** (white), the **Cinnamon** (warm russet) and the blue **Agouti** (blue ticking over fawn background). Disqualifying faults include 'lack of whiskers' and 'intractability'. Baby rats are known as 'kittens'. The society holds numerous shows; it discourages breeders from selling rats to 'people who do not take their responsibilities seriously,' and its journal, *Pro-rat-a*, is published every two months.

Rats are fully weaned from their mother after 4–5 weeks, and females become fertile when 5 to 12 weeks old. They will normally live for around two years, although some individuals may live for three years or more .

7 BIRDS

Birds are easily our most visible form of wildlife.

They live in every part of Britain – in cities, in towns and villages, on the coast, in mountains and plains, in bogs, in woods and on farmland – and they arouse strong emotions in human beings. Most of us are bird-lovers; a few people hate killer species like sparrowhawks and magpies, but most enjoy the sight and sound of birds, envying the creatures their grace, freedom and mobility. Requests for money to bolster species in decline elicit enormous responses – witness the £450,000 raised for lapwings by the RSPB with a single appeal – and colossal amounts are spent on bird food every year. Twitchers – tireless seekers of rarities – travel thousands of kilometres with their binoculars, telescopes, cameras and tripods, in their attempts to clock up sightings, and rivalry between them sometimes becomes acrimonious.

The earliest known ancestor of birds was *Archaeopteryx*, a small, winged dinosaur about 30 cm long whose remains were discovered in the middle of the nineteenth century, in limestone quarries between Munich and Nuremberg, in southern Germany, where it lived 150 million years ago. The creature had many reptilian features, among them solid (rather than hollow) bones, teeth, a long, bony tail, and three clawed fingers at the ends of its forelimbs, or wings. Yet it also had feathers, much like those of modern birds, and a small wishbone, to which some of its pectoral muscles may have been attached.

There has been intense debate about how well *Archaeopteryx* could fly. Its pelvis and long legs show that it was a good runner, but other anatomical details suggest that it was a poor performer in the air. Some experts have thought that it could only flutter and scrabble its way up trees or rocks, gripping with its claws, and then glide down, or that it used its wings to levitate as it was running, and so increase its speed; others, judging from the shape of its feathers, think it was capable of powered take-offs.

Whatever its performance, its successors have taken an amazing variety of forms. They evolved hollow bones containing air sacs, and strong pectoral muscles that gave them the power of sustained flight. Some of them became enormous: witness the teratorn, a carniovorous bird that lived in Argentina between eight and five million years ago. This monster, which may have been an early ancestor of the stork, had a wingspan of 7.5 metres and must have weighed over 120 kg. There is no absolute proof that it could fly, but ornithologists believe it did.

How many hundreds or thousands of other species have evolved and gone extinct? The one that everybody remembers is the flightless dodo, which died out on the islands around Mauritius in the seventeenth century, hunted out of existence by Dutch sailors.

For centuries men looked on wild birds mainly as food: a few species such as owls and ravens were considered obnoxious and a potential threat; but for the rest, if they could be caught or shot, they were eaten. The catholic nature of taste at the end of the sixteenth century is shown by an account of the presents sent by sheriffs of various towns for the delectation of the judges of assize on the Western and Oxford circuits. At Salisbury their honours received a dressed bustard; at Dorchester and other places, a heron; in Cornwall, gulls, curlew and puffins; at Exeter, a kite; at Taunton, plovers, golden and green; at Chard, a peacock; at Winchester, a swan.

In those days blackbirds, thrushes and larks were all eaten with relish; but no small bird was more highly prized than the wheatear – even though, in northern counties, there was a superstition that its song gave warning of approaching death. The Mecca for wheatear-eaters was Sussex, where the birds were reported to be of surpassing succulence – as recorded in the seventeenth century by the 'Water Poet', John Taylor:

> There were rare birds I never saw before,
> The like of them I think to see no more:
> Th' are called wheat-ears, less than lark or sparrow.
> Well roasted, in the mouth they taste like marrow.
> When once 'tis in the teeth, it is involved,
> Bones, flesh and all is lusciously dissolved.

When men began to study bird behaviour, they were much puzzled by the phenomenon of migration. The anonymous author of a paper in the *Harleian Miscellany*, published in 1744, discussing the migration of storks, argued that if they flew horizontally on their seasonal journeys, they would be seen by many travellers. But because he had read no reports of such sightings, he concluded that the birds' route must be perpendicular, and that their destination could only be the moon. Leading intellectuals thought that swallows spent the winter under water, and even that great savant Dr Johnson believed that when the birds disappear in autumn, 'a number of them conglobulate together by flying round and round and then, all in a heap, throw themselves under water and lie in the bed of a river'.

Before the days of efficient cameras and binoculars, the only way that anyone could examine a bird closely was to obtain a specimen by shooting or catching one. The Victorian hunter-naturalist Charles St John, though greatly admiring owls and hawks in general, thought nothing of downing a short-eared owl simply because it appeared to be rather different from others that he had seen, and he wanted to get a better look at it. In his book *Wild Sports of the Scottish Highlands* he wrote a glowing account of how, early one morning, he massacred two golden eagles which had been seen eating one of his companion's sheep; and in 1848, on behalf of some unnamed gentleman collector, he made a special expedition into the wilds of Sutherland to shoot ospreys and bring back their eggs.

Such behaviour would seem outrageous today – yet St John was deeply interested in birds and animals, an acute observer, and ahead of his time in many of his attitudes. For generations, it was shooting men like him who took the closest interest in wild life, and only in the twentieth century did the idea of conservation start to grow among townspeople.

Today the Royal Society for the Protection of Birds is the largest and richest privately funded wildlife conservation body in Europe. With an annual income of over £50 million, it is able to buy large areas of land for bird reserves – for instance, at Abernethy on Speyside (14,000 hectares acquired in 1988 for £1.8 million) and Forsinard in the Flow Country of Caithness (17,127 hectares acquired in 1995) – and so to have an active influence on habitat.

More than 550 species of birds have been recorded in Britain, and even specialist books struggle to describe them all in single volumes. Here, a small selection is given of the more common species, and of those birds which, in recent years, have given rise to most anxiety or controversy. The population estimates are those given by Chris Mead, of the British Trust for Ornithology, in his excellent survey *The State of the Nation's Birds*, published in 2000.

Anyone wishing to improve his or her identification would do well to acquire one or more of the excellent compact discs available from the British Trust for Ornithology, and from the Royal Society for the Protection of Birds, which contain not only text and pictures, but also recordings of many species' song: calls are notoriously difficult, if not impossible, to render in words, but the recordings are admirably clear.

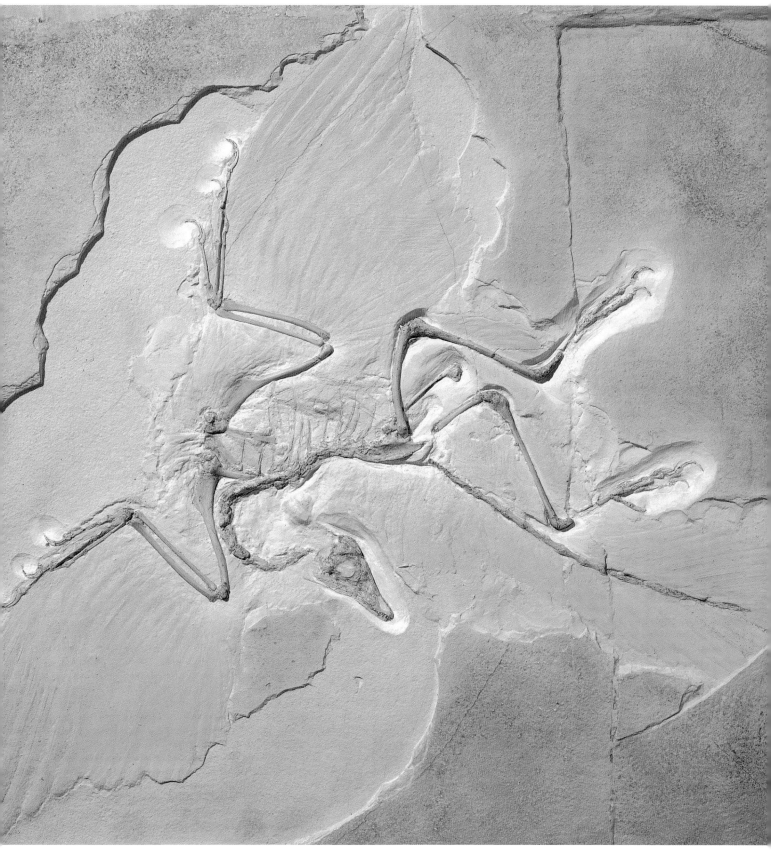

Farm, garden & songbirds

The decline of farmland and songbirds has been a constant lament of the RSPB for the past 30 years. Falls in population have been disastrous, and there is no doubt about the main causes: excessive use of pesticides and consequent lack of insects; absence of winter feeding grounds, caused by immediate ploughing of stubble after harvest and planting of winter corn; removal of hedges which give nesting cover. All these problems have been well identified — yet it was only at the millennium that the government started to take effective remedial action by making financial incentives available to farmers who were prepared to manage their land in a manner more sympathetic to wildlife.

Corn Bunting

Miliaria calandra

The decline of this rather dull-looking, streaky brown bird, half-way in size between a sparrow and thrush, led to a special study by the Game Conservancy Trust and the University of Sussex. The buntings nest in or near the edge of cereal crops, and a pilot survey conducted in 1994 revealed that the density of the birds was four times greater on traditionally farmed land than on areas under intensive agricultural regimes. The main research, carried out on the Sussex Downs between 1995 and 1997, showed – not surprisingly – that the abundance of invertebrates in the crop margins fell in proportion to the amounts of insecticide and herbicide that were used.

When feeding chicks, the birds foraged wherever invertebrates were most numerous – that is, in areas on which less chemicals had been used. If the supply of invertebrates near the nest was poor, the parents had to fly farther to find food, the chicks were underweight, and survival rates were low. When invertebrates were more plentiful, the reverse was true. In spite of the knowledge gained, prospects for corn buntings are gloomy: already they have disappeared from most former haunts, and, with only about 20,000 remaining in Britain, experts fear they may vanish altogether. There is still, however, a large population in southern Europe and North Africa.

Finches

Small, lively finches were greatly prized by the Victorians as cage-birds. Thousands were trapped, especially the gaudier species and the best singers, and most went into decline. Some have now recovered well, but others are still in trouble.

By far the commonest is the **chaffinch** (*Fringilla coelebs*), which is sometimes as bold as a robin, and prepared to take food from a human hand. A male chaffinch is a very fine fellow, resplendent in blue cap, deep pink cheeks and breast, green back and black and white wings; the female is duller, with the same white bars on her wings, but otherwise mainly olive green. Apparently not much affected by changes in farming – perhaps because they frequent woods and gardens so much – chaffinches are on the increase.

Next most common, but only a tenth as numerous, is the **greenfinch** (*Carduelis chloris*), with a stable population of 530,000 breeding pairs. Females are mostly olive green, males brightened by yellow on tail and belly. Greenfinches are principally seed-eaters. Equally numerous, but holding its ground far less well, is the **linnet** (*Carduelis cannabina*), which depends largely on weed seeds, and so has lost out to modern methods of agriculture, the use of herbicides in particular.

The stout and splendidly coloured **bullfinch** (*Pyrrhula*

CHAFFINCH MALE *FRINGILLA COELEBS*
(bottom, left) THE MOST COMMON
OF FINCHES, CHAFFINCHES ARE ON
THE INCREASE.

BULLFINCH *PYRRHULA PYRRHULA*
(below) NUMBERS HAVE DROPPED
AND THERE ARE FEWER THAN 200,000
BREEDING PAIRS IN BRITAIN.

pyrrhula) was a target for nineteenth-century bird-catchers. With its bright pink breast and cheeks, its black cap and tail, grey back and white rump, a male would decorate any cage. Owners of orchards were not sorry to see it decline, for it is a great nipper-off of buds. Legal protection enabled it to revive, but now, with fewer than 200,000 breeding pairs in Britain, it is struggling again, discouraged by the loss of overgrown hedges, the general intensification of agriculture and predation by sparrowhawks.

Even gaudier is the **goldfinch** (*Carduelis carduelis*), with its extraordinary combination of red, white, black, yellow and buff. Another species much reduced by Victorian trappers, it was again hit by the advent of chemical herbicides, but now, although relatively scarce (22,000 breeding pairs), seems to be recovering, perhaps because it has learnt to frequent gardens and eat from hanging feeders.

Larger and heavier-looking is the **hawfinch** (*Coccothraustes coccothraustes*), whose thick, powerful bill enables it to break open large seeds and nut kernels, including cherry stones. Like the bullfinch, it also eats buds with relish, as well as caterpillars and other grubs; but, being essentially an elusive and very shy woodland bird that prefers to stay in the tops of trees, it has not taken to gardens and so is in decline with only 5000 pairs breeding in Britain.

7
Birds
Farm, Garden &
Songbirds

Finches

ROBIN *ERITHACUS RUBECULA* (below)
BRITAIN'S BEST-LOVED BIRD, IT NUM-
BERS 4 MILLION BREEDING PAIRS.

SKYLARK *ALAUDA ARVENSIS* (opposite
top) NUMBERS HAVE FALLEN BY
60 PER CENT SINCE THE 1970s.

HOUSE SPARROW *PASSER DOMESTICUS*
(opposite bottom) THE POPULATION
HAS COLLAPSED TO ONLY 50,000 PAIRS.

Nightingale

Luscinia megarhynchos

Summer is the time for nightingales. In spring they migrate from Africa to breed in southern England, and as the weather warms up, their glorious, slow, piping song floats out of the dense thickets in which they lurk, usually after dark, but also in the dusk. For all the beauty of their voices, they are rather dull-looking: brown-bodied, with a dark eye, faint speckling on the back and a red-brown tail, they are seldom easy to see.

Latest estimates are that about 5000 pairs breed in Britain. A recent fall in numbers has been caused largely by loss of good habitat, due not least to the spread of deer, which devour the thick underbrush in which nightingales prefer to nest.

Robin

Erithacus rubecula

Best loved of British birds, the robin redbreast has featured on countless million Christmas cards as a midwinter symbol of cheerfulness and goodwill. Yet its very familiarity with man – its habit of keeping people close company as they work in the garden, of perching on the handle of a fork or spade, even feeding out of their hands – has given rise to much superstition.

One legend held that its breast was first stained red by the blood of Christ as it ministered to him on his way to Calvary; another, that the ruddy feathers were scorched by the flames of hell as it carried water to sinners there. To kill or even detain a robin was long thought unlucky; a robin entering the house boded ill fortune, and one pecking three times at a windowpane would herald impending death.

Essentially loners, robins have their own territories, which they defend with remarkable pugnacity against all comers, especially of their own kind, lurking in dense undergrowth. They are excellent gardeners, in that they eat large numbers of insects, as well as seeds and fruit, and they have a beautiful, melodious but rather melancholy song. The species as a whole is doing well, with a population estimated at 4 million breeding pairs, perhaps helped – paradoxically – by the building of new houses, most of which have sheltered gardens.

Skylark

Alauda arvensis

'Hail to thee, blythe spirit,' wrote Shelley. 'Bird thou never wert' – and the skylark's song remains one of the most

7

Birds
*Farm. Garden &
Songbirds*

Nightingale
Skylark

244

magical evocations of British summer mornings. As the continuous, bubbling warble floats out of the sky, it is often difficult to spot the singer, so high is he fluttering – hovering, briefly – above the Earth. But then he puts in one of his sudden, sliding descents before climbing again, and so reveals himself to the listening watcher. Usually he is too far for his fine, streaky brown colours to be apparent, but at close quarters he is a handsome little fellow.

Yet the skylark is in trouble. Since 1970 numbers have fallen by nearly 60 per cent, to not much over a million breeding pairs. The worst decline has been on farmland, and, once again, the main cause seems to be inimical agriculture, not least the forage-harvesting of silage crops, which, even if it does not mince sitting birds to pieces, ruins their nests in early summer.

Like many other small birds, skylarks can rear two or three broods in a summer if there is plenty of food available; but all their efforts are in vain if the fields in which they nest are swamped with chemicals.

House Sparrow

Passer domesticus

Scientists are at a loss to explain the collapse of the house sparrow population. Once omnipresent in cities, towns, villages and farms, these cheerful, bustling, energetic, noisy little birds, which enjoy living close to humans, have dwindled to a shadow of their former selves. In earlier times they bred to excess and ate – besides insects – such huge quantities of cereal crops, and made such a mess, that many villages had sparrow clubs whose sole purpose was to rid the parish of the pests. The British population is still some 3 million breeding pairs, but losses appear to have occurred mainly in towns. Although gregarious, and usually seen in flocks, house sparrows mate for life, and a pair returns to the same nest year after year, often under the eaves of buildings.

The **Tree Sparrow** (*Passer montanus*) is on an even sharper downward trend, in both Britain and Ireland. A smaller and more retiring relative of the house sparrow, but closely similar in appearance, it lives in overgrown hedgerows and trees, rather than around habitations, and in recent years this preference has proved disastrous, for by removing hundreds of kilometres of hedgerows farmers destroyed much of the bird's habitat, and pesticides killed

off many of the insects on which it lives. The result was that in the last quarter of the twentieth century the population collapsed from a million pairs to 50,000, and in the autumn of 2001, in an attempt to arrest the decline, the RSPB appointed a tree sparrow recovery officer.

There is an amazing disparity between the present scarcity of tree sparrows in Britain and the immense population that built up in China during the 1950s. Then Chairman Mao became exasperated by the flocks infesting cities, and incited residents to kill as many as possible.

245

STARLINGS *STURNUS VULGARIS* (below) A KNACK FOR MIMICRY IS ONE OF THEIR MOST STRIKING CHARACTERISTICS.

STONE CURLEW *BURHINUS OEDICNEMUS* (opposite top) NEST ON DOWNLAND, HEATH AND ARABLE FARMLAND.

WREN *TROGLODYTES TROGLODYTES* (opposite bottom): MORE THAN SEVEN MILLION BREEDING PAIRS IN BRITAIN.

The **Hedge Sparrow** or **Dunnock** (*Prunella modularis*) is not in the same family as other sparrows, but may be closer to nightingales and thrushes. Its colouring is drab, streaky dark brown and grey, and it is more retiring, keeping in dense cover when disturbed. Whereas the eggs of house and tree sparrows are similar – white speckled with grey – those of the hedge sparrow are plain, bright turquoise.

Starling

Sturnus vulgaris

The Red Arrows have nothing on starlings: the jet pilots may thrill crowds at airshows, but they will never fly with anything like the agility and precision shown by starlings when they mass for their evening manoeuvres. Flocks of birds, coming from all quarters and from miles away, unite into immense clouds, and hundreds or even thousands of them, in the closest possible formation, climb, dive, wheel and turn in unison, all making incredibly abrupt, synchronised changes of direction.

It seems impossible that, in a split second, the whole mass can react in exactly the same way – and yet they manage it, and when they decide it is time to go to roost,

they pour down into laurels or other thick bushes (or even on to the ledges of tall buildings), their wings roaring like a cataract. While thus engaged, they keep up a terrific barrage of screeching and chattering – and woe betide the area on which they settle, for the uric acid in their droppings can rot stonework and kill trees and bushes.

On the ground, they bustle about at a quick, jerky walk, and although from a distance they look black, from closer-to their iridescent plumage gives them an attractively spangled appearance. Yet their most striking characteristic is their ability to adapt their own strident whistles so that they imitate whatever sounds take their fancy.

This knack of mimicry has amused humans for thousands of years – and one person who appreciated it was Mozart, who bought a starling in May 1784, and was fascinated by the way in which it learned to whistle the tune from the beginning of the final movement of his piano concerto in G Major, K. 453, which he completed that spring. Such was his admiration for the bird that when it died three years later, he gave it a solemn funeral, and then wrote 'A Musical Joke', which seems to contain some elements of a starling's song.

When birds appear in large flocks, it is hard to believe

7

Birds
Farm, Garden & Songbirds

Starling

that their numbers are falling overall; yet this is the picture, and although there are still over a million breeding pairs of starlings in Britain (with about a third as many in Ireland), their severe decline is causing concern.

Stone Curlew

Burhinus oedicnemus

Another nationally threatened farmland species, the stone curlew sank to its lowest ebb in 1985, when the entire population amounted to 160 pairs. Now, thanks largely to the fact that farmers have taken up special schemes designed to create suitable habitat, the birds have recovered strongly: a Biodiversity Action Plan target of 200 pairs was set for the year 2000, but the curlews passed it two years in advance, and now have built back to 250 pairs – another conservation success. Even simple measures like putting in sticks to mark nests, so that tractor drivers do not obliterate them, have proved beneficial.

There is something agreeably mysterious about stone curlews, which look like out-sized plovers with long yellow legs. They are semi-nocturnal, and even in daylight their protective colouring of brown, grey and white makes them hard to see on rocky ground. Only their huge yellow eyes show up strongly. They walk with a measured, stately tread, and when alarmed, bob up and down, tipping forward and back.

They breed on dry, stony soil on down-land, heathland and arable farm land, mainly in Wessex – Dorset, Wiltshire and Hampshire – and in the Breckland of East Anglia. They are demanding in their choice of site, in that they like to have a large clear area open round the nest – and on some of the military training areas of Salisbury plain army engineers have bulldozed spaces the size of football fields clear of vegetation, in the hope of making them feel at home.

Wren

Troglodytes troglodytes

Tiny as it is, the wren was known to the Druids at the king of birds, and for centuries it had symbolic associations. On the Isle of Man and elsewhere, especially in Ireland, there was a traditional pastime called Hunting the Wren, which took place on Christmas Day or the day after, St Stephen's Day, and which persisted into the 1960s. Boys armed with sticks would sally out at dawn to beat the bushes, flush out a wren and kill it. They then suspended the body in a garland of flowers, ribbons and evergreens, and carried in a procession from house to house, plucking its feathers and handing them out as a defence against witchcraft. In the evening the boys would bury the wren's body – by then naked – in a corner of the churchyard.

In spite of such persecution, wrens have survived in immense numbers: with 7 million breeding pairs in Britain, and nearly 3 million in Ireland, they are easily the most common British birds. In the past, cold winters caused heavy mortality, but the apparent onset of global warming has given them a better chance of survival.

Plump-looking, stumpy little brown creatures with turned-up tails and smartly barred wing feathers, wrens are

YELLOWHAMMER MALE, *EMBERIZA CITRINELLA* (bottom) ALTHOUGH THERE ARE STILL 1.2 MILLION PAIRS, THEY ARE IN DECLINE.

SONG THRUSH, *TURDUS PHILOMELUS* (right) MODERN FARMING METHODS ARE LARGELY TO BLAME FOR THIS BIRD'S DECLINE.

miracles of miniaturisation. Often in a wood their agitated alarm call – *tick – tick – tick* – betrays the presence of a predator such as a cat or stoat, and they make short, sudden flights from one perch to another, with their wings whirring furiously.

Their scientific name, derived from the Greek for 'cave-dweller', or 'one who goes into a hole', refers to the shape of their nests, which are beautifully made spheres of moss and grass, the size of small grapefruit, with an entrance hole on one side: the cock bird builds several preliminary structures called cock's nests, and his mate brings soft material to line the one in which she intends to lay.

Yellowhammer

Emberiza citrinella

Strange as it seems, this brilliantly coloured songbird has often been associated in folklore with the devil. In Scotland and the north of England it is said to drink a drop of the devil's blood every May day morning – and for this reason it was once persecuted by boys, who wrecked nests, smashed eggs and killed nestlings. One possible reason is that the markings on its eggs look like scribbled writing, and may once have been thought to contain hidden meanings.

An adult male can hardly be mistaken for any other bird, since he is bright yellow all over his head and body; females are duller, with fine dark streaks on head, face and chest. Numbers are still fairly high – 1.2 million pairs – but in recent years these birds of heath and farmland have gone into such a steep decline that Chris Mead of the BTO speaks

of the species being in 'dire straits and still falling: out of control'. One place in which they have done well, however, is on the Game Conservancy's experimental farm at Loddington (*see page 210*), where the benevolent farming regime has increased their numbers.

THRUSHES

Blackbird

Turdus merula

A species of thrush, this has fared better than the ailing song thrush, even though its diet is much the same. Females can be mistaken for song thrushes, as their colouring is similar, though duller; but the male is unmistakable, with his glossy black plumage, orange bill and eye rims. As blackbirds alight and balance, they have a distinctive habit of raising their tails with an easy motion. One idiosyncracy is that they have two distinct alarm calls. A low *tuk, tuk, tuk*, steadily repeated as the caller dodges about the undergrowth, invariably signals danger on the ground – a cat, fox, stoat or weasel; but an airborne predator such an owl sets off a loud, agitated screeching, generally delivered when the bird is in flight.

Mistle Thrush

Turdus viscivorus

Larger than the song thrush, the mistle (or missel) thrush has stronger brown spots on its chest and underparts, bright white underwing flashes (visible only when it is flying), a greyer back and a more upright stance when on the ground. Its voice is quite different – a harsh chatter, like a scaled-down version of a magpie's call – and it lives more in the open. During the breeding season the birds are fiercely independent, and will try to see off anyone who goes too close to a nest; but in autumn they form quite large flocks and feed together, flying from tree to tree

Song Thrush

Turdus philomelus

The steep decline of this garden bird has caused conservationists great

concern. In the last three decades of the twentieth century the population fell by half, and comparative research carried out by the RSPB in West Sussex and Essex strongly suggested that modern farming techniques were to blame. In Sussex, where farming is still mixed, with a combination of arable crops and livestock, pairs of thrushes were found to be rearing two or three broods of young every summer; but in Essex, which has fallen victim to agribusiness and the creation of endless empty hedgeless prairies, each pair was struggling to bring up one brood.

Song thrushes are solitary birds, and rarely congregate in flocks. They like environments with plenty of cover – woods, thickets, gardens, shrubberies. Although they eat spiders, insects, berries and so on, their main food consists of earthworms and snails, which they crack open by hitting the shells on stones. The sound of a thrush preparing its dinner – repeated tapping and cracking – can be heard from a good way off.

The RSPB survey found that the main cause of thrushes' decline has been the loss of good feeding habitat, such as wet ditches, woodland and damp, grazed farmland, where snails are abundant. Excessive drainage and drier summers are at least partly to blame. Unable to find enough food, the birds were abandoning their efforts to raise young half way through the summer, stopping after only one brood, instead of going on to two or three. In spite of the losses, the population of Britain is still estimated at a million breeding pairs.

The **fieldfare** (*Turdus pilaris*), a handsome member of the thrush family, migrates southwards from Iceland, Scandinavia and Russia to overwinter in Britain. It is distinguished by its slate-grey head, nape and rump, which contrast with its bright chestnut back and black tail. A golden-brown chest and white underparts, both boldly spotted, complete its cheerful colour scheme. Fieldfares head southwards and westwards in autumn, moving in large flocks of 100 or more as they shift from one field to the next, and chattering as they fly about, but they rarely nest in Britain.

Yet another species of thrush, the **redwing** (*Turdus iliacus*) is also a winter visitor and passage-migrant, arriving in southern Britain in September and leaving in April. Redwings resemble song thrushes quite closely, except that they have curved whitish stripes above and below the eye, and red flanks and leading wing feathers. During winter months they are gregarious, and feed in flocks on open fields. Their thin, lisping flight-calls can sometimes be heard at night as they migrate.

Cuckoo

Cuculus canorus

The composer Delius may have written a lyrical piece about the bird – *On Hearing the First Cuckoo in Spring* – but the truth is that the habits of a hen cuckoo are as deceitful as they are inexplicable. Not only does she, a parasite, impose herself on birds many times smaller than herself, and by deception force them to raise her offspring: she also lays an exceptional number of eggs – up to 25 in a season – and so extends her destructive influence to many victims.

Cuckoos migrate northwards from Africa in spring, reaching the south of England in the middle of April. (Semi-serious discussion of the subject, often between clergymen, usually breaks out in the correspondence columns of *The Times* around this period.) It is the male who sends out the familiar, two-note call, either from a tree or on the wing, while the female hunts the hedges for host-nests, and occasionally gives her own, completely different call, a kind of bubbling chuckle. Both sexes can be mistaken for sparrowhawks, as they are blue-grey above, with barred underparts, and when they fly give the impression of having all their weight up-front, in their flat heads and necks.

Having selected a nest, the female lays one egg – and somehow she has the uncanny ability to adapt its colour so that it more or less matches that of her chosen fosterer, and the resident bird accepts it as one of its own. This is usually a meadow pipit, dunnock (or hedge sparrow), robin, reed warbler, sedge warbler or pied wagtail; but whatever the species, the cuckoo's egg has such a short incubation period that it often hatches before the clutch of the host, and the young cuckoo pushes the other eggs or fledglings over the side of the nest, one by one. Left alone, it grows to such a size that it soon overflows the nest, and its tiny foster-parents, having lost their own brood, struggle to feed the monstrous invader, until it flies at the age of about three weeks.

As the season goes on, the male bird's call changes from *cuck-koo* to *cuck-cuck-koo*, and then, quite soon, the birds disappear, their purpose fulfilled. Their short season is reflected in the nursery rhyme

> In April come he will,
> In May he sings all day.
> In June he changes his tune,
> And in July he flies away.

The cuckoos' disappearance was once accounted for by the belief that in winter the birds turned into hawks. Another theory was that they hibernated in hollow trees or holes in the ground, and in the Scottish Highlands they were supposed to join the wee folk, or fairies, for the duration, going to ground in their hidden dwellings. About 20,000 pairs now breed in Britain every year, but numbers are falling slightly, perhaps because their favourite host species, dunnock and meadow-pipit, are in decline.

Golden Plover

Charadrius apricarius

Unlike lapwings, which are essentially lowland birds, golden plovers mostly inhabit upland moors and bogs. They move around in flocks, and fly fast, all changing direction at the same instant with astonishing precision. Lacking the lapwing's head crest, the golden plover looks a much more compact bird, strongly mottled on the back in gold and dark brown. Unfortunately the species is in decline, not just in Britain, but all over Europe, perhaps due to the intensification of agriculture.

Lapwing (Peewit or Green Plover)

Vanellus vanellus

Another species in trouble, the lapwing went sharply down-hill once before, during the nineteenth century, when its eggs were systematically collected for the table. Now, after a recovery, numbers have fallen again. A survey carried out by the RSPB and the BTO in 1998 revealed that the total of breeding birds in England and Wales had dropped by almost half during the ten years since the previous count, and that the declines were worst in Wales and the southwest of England, where the population had fallen by three-quarters.

The cause seemed to be changes in farming, for lapwings, which nest on the ground, prefer rough grassland and arable fields sown in the spring. The acreage of rough grass has been steadily diminishing, and winter-sown corn is already too high for the birds by the time they start to breed in late March or early April. The lapwing used to be known as the farmer's best friend, since it eats many insects that damage crops: now that chemical sprays have super-seded natural pest control, ornithologists are trying to persuade farmers to modify some of their regimes for the birds' benefit.

The lapwing has a very distinctive appearance and call: a long crest of black feathers sweeps upwards and back-wards from its black-and-white head, and its alarm cry – *pee-wit-wit-wit, pee-wit* (or, as some have it, *be-witched, witched, witched, be-witched*) is unmistakable. The bird has a fascinating method of decoying intruders away from its nest, which is nothing but a scrape in the earth or grass, in the middle of a field. If a lapwing brooding eggs or chicks sees danger approaching, it runs some distance from the nest before taking off, and then flies a whole repertoire of diversionary manoeuvres over some other part of the field, screeching out its alarm call and swooping about in such tight loops that its pinions make a loud rushing noise as they cut through the air. The closer the intruder goes to the nest, the more frantic the display becomes – a facet of behaviour beautifully described by the Elizabethan poet Chester, in *Love's Martyr*:

> *The lapwing hath a piteous mournful cry,*
> *And sings a sorrowful and heavy song,*
> *But yet she's full of craft and subtlety,*
> *And weepeth most being farthest from her young.*

People in Lancashire once thought that every plover harboured the soul of a wandering Jew, and that if seven were seen together, they foretold misfortune. Today the affection that people have for these brave birds was revealed when an appeal launched by the RSPB for lapwing work raised the amazing total of £450,000.

Nightjar

Caprimulgus europaeus

As the light dies, late on a summer evening, a strange, almost mechanical whirring sound comes faintly over the heathland. Its origin is strangely hard to pinpoint, for the source of the noise seems to move around, rising and falling slightly as it carries on for minutes at a time. Somewhere a male nightjar is sitting on a dead tree-branch, sending out his territorial call. Then another answers him, and another, so that the churring emanates from three directions at once.

Nightjars are agreeably mysterious birds, for their activities are largely crepuscular. They are slim and falcon-like, with flat-topped heads and hunched, powerful-looking necks, and they are never easy to see. As they sit on the ground during the day, their protective colouring of mottled, streaked brown, buff, grey and black renders them almost invisible, and only as night is coming on do the males take to the air, to send out territorial challenges and hawk for moths in the twilight. In transit from one vantage point to another, they fly straight, giving an occasional loud clap of their wings to warn rivals off their areas; but when hunting they wheel and dive abruptly, faltering and flickering through the dusk like angular bats. Females, meanwhile, are already nesting on bare earth.

Myths have hung about the nightjar for thousands of years. It was known to the Romans as *Caprimulgus*, the goat-milker, and was supposed to snuggle up to goats as they lay on the ground, fastening on to one of their teats, and, apart from draining the animal, rendering it blind.

The scientific name of the species that migrates from Africa to nest in England is *Caprimulgus europaeus*: to this day country people refer to it as 'the goat-sucker', partly because of its enormous mouth, which gapes open in flight to capture insects. In the Middle Ages it was regarded as sinister, and in parts of northern England it was thought to embody the soul of a child who had died unbaptised. In the eighteenth century Gilbert White, although ridiculing the popular belief about goats, recorded the various other names by which the bird was known: churn-owl, eve-jarr, fern owl and puckridge.

Like many other species, nightjars declined in the middle of the twentieth century, perhaps due to a succession of cool, wet summers, perhaps through loss of their favourite heathland habitat, much of which had been planted with trees or taken into agriculture. A survey by the BTO in 1981 discovered only 2100 nesting pairs – but another count eleven years later showed the total up by 50 percent, and they are still recovering well, helped by the felling of ill-sited conifer forests and the reinstatement of heathland.

Nuthatch

Sitta europaea

Among the sleekest and smartest of all small birds, the nuthatch has enormous charm. It is blue-grey above and pinkish buff below, with a black stripe running back from its eye to separate the two colours, and the plumpness of its body is accentuated by its rather flat head and sharply pointed bill. It sometimes feeds on the ground, but its most characteristic action is to scud up, down and round tree-trunks in jerky little jumps, clinging on with its claws and never needing to brace itself with its tail. It moves with amazing facility, often head-downwards, as it searches for insects or hacks open acorns, hazelnuts, beechmast or seeds which it has wedged in the crevices of the bark. Its

energetic battering often produces a tapping noise, like that of a thrush smashing a snail.

Nuthatches nest in holes in trees or banks. Both sexes help to reduce the size of the entrance-hole by packing it with mud, and they also fill in any other openings before lining the cavity with dried leaves or chips of bark.

Like the nuthatch, the **Treecreeper** (*Certhia familiaris*) goes up trunks in a series of jerks as it searches for insects, climbing with its feet wide apart and tail braced against the bark. Having spiralled round and round until it reaches the top, it flies down to the base of another tree and starts up again. Its colouring is relatively dull – streaky brown above, and pale below.

Meadow Pipit

Anthus pratensis

In spite of a decline in recent years, these hyperactive little birds are still numerous. Insect eaters, they spend the summer in the uplands, living especially on rough grass-land and in young forestry plantations, and surviving predation by merlins and (to a lesser extent) hen harriers. In winter they tend to return to the lowlands, but they remain in Britain all year round. The population numbers some 2 million pairs, with another 900,000 in Ireland.

Tree Pipit

Anthus trivialis

Of much the same size, and with the same streaky plumage – pale on the breast and grey-brown above – the tree pipit can easily be confused with its meadow cousin; but it is more a bird of forestry edges and clearings than of open country. Also, it is much more scarce, with only 120,000 breeding pairs, and on the decline. The **rock pipit** (*Anthus petrosus*) is rarer still, with 34,000 pairs in Britain and 12,500 in Ireland, and lives on rocky coasts, feeding on debris along the tide line and insects in grass farther from the shore.

Swallow

Hirundo rustica

Traditional harbingers of summer, barn swallows arrive suddenly in April after their migration from Africa: one day there are none to be seen, and the next the air is full of them, hawking swiftly after insects, easily identified by their slender bodies and long, forked tails. Wonderfully agile fliers, they cover enormous distances while hunting the same area, constantly changing direction and varying their altitude.

LONG-TAILED TIT *AEGITHALOS CAUDA-TUS* (below) EASILY RECOGNISABLE WITH A TAIL AT LEAST AS LONG AS ITS BODY.

BLUE TIT *PARUS CAERULEUS* (bottom) THE MOST BRIGHTLY COLOURED OF THE TITS, IT LIVES MAINLY ON INSECTS.

GREY WAGTAIL *MOTACILLA CINEREA* (right) HAS EXTENDED ITS RANGE OVER MOST OF BRITAIN IN THE LAST CENTURY.

Country lore holds that if they fly high in the evening, fine weather is imminent, but that when they skim low over the fields, they presage rain – and often the truth of this old saying is borne out. On the other hand, no one has ever seen them performing a more curious feat once attributed to them, of bringing a stone from the seashore to give their fledglings sight. Nevertheless, like house martins, they are seen as friendly birds, whose presence is beneficial – hence the rhyme:

> Martin and swallow,
> God's mate and marrow.

Swallows nest on beams or rafters in barns, sheds and outhouses, building up sturdy cups of mud and straw, and returning to the same sites year after year. Unlike swifts, which rarely touch down, they often settle on telegraph wires or roof-ridges (though hardly ever in trees), and in autumn, when they are preparing to migrate, they assemble in large gatherings. In spite of the loss of farmyard animals, and therefore of insects, swallows seem to be holding their own, with more than half a million pairs breeding in Britain.

The **House Martin** (*Delichon urbica*) is superficially similar, but has much shorter, blunter tail-feathers and a white rump, and is generally plainer coloured, lacking the swallow's chestnut-red patches on throat and forehead and the male bird's buff underparts. The **Sand Martin** (*Riparia riparia*) – plain brown above and white below, but for a distinctive brown breast band – is smaller than either house martin or swallow. Also a summer visitor, it nests in horizontal burrows which it bores in sand and gravel pits, river banks and sea cliffs. The **Swift** (*Apus apus*) is dark, sooty brown all over, except for a white patch on the throat, and has conspicuously slim, curved wings. Another phenomenal flier, it remains airborne for days, even weeks, on end, ceaselessly wheeling, dashing and gliding in its pursuit of insects.

Tits

Small and plump, with short bills and generally some black on the crown, tits live in small flocks and give an impression of busyness, hopping about on the ground and making their short, direct flights from bush to bush. All the species mentioned here behave in much the same way. When feeding on insects in trees, they hang from twigs in acrobatic postures, and in winter several different species often collect together.

The most brightly coloured of the family is the **Blue Tit** (*Parus caeruleus*), with its cobalt-blue crown and tail, white face and lemon-yellow underparts. Living in gardens, close to houses, it is often caught in the act of pecking through the tops of milk bottles or tearing up the post. In spite of these predilections, it exerts a beneficial influence, as it lives mainly on insects.

The **Great Tit** (*Parus major*) is noticeably larger (about 14 cm long, including the tail) and much darker: its glossy, blue-black crown and nape surround its white cheeks, and the black continues down over its breast in a broad band. The **Coal Tit** (*Parus ater*) is smaller and less flamboyant, with a white patch on the back of the black crown, underparts buff, and no black band down its chest. The **Marsh Tit** (*Parus palustris*) and the **Willow Tit** (*Parus montanus*) are much the same size as the coal tit, and, with their black caps, grey-brown wings and pale bodies resemble each other so closely that the easiest way to distinguish between

them is often by their calls. In spite of its name, the marsh tit does not particularly frequent wet areas, but the willow tit does prefer damp woods and stands of alder containing plenty of rotten timber, just as the **Bearded Tit** (*Panurus biarmicus*) frequents reed beds and the **Crested Tit** (*Parus cristatus*) pine woods.

Nobody can fail to recognise a **Long-tailed Tit** (*Aegithalos caudatus*), for its tail is at least the same length as its body, and its plumage a combination of pink, black and white. It is probably no more busy than other tits, but the constant flicking of its tail – a matter of balance – makes it seem more frenetic. The nest built by a pair of long-tailed tits is a small miracle: shaped like a large goose egg standing on end, it is a soft, domed structure made of moss, hair, feathers and lichen, woven into the twigs of a thorn bush, with a circular entrance hole just big enough for the parents to fit through on one side near the top. In this tiny, snug enclosure the female lays up to a dozen miniature eggs, and somehow raises a family, which grow so fast that they fly when only 15 days old. It seems extraordinary that they can all fit in such a confined space.

Wagtails

Slim, graceful and quick-moving, wagtails bustle about on the ground, walking fast or running, jerking their heads back and forth and constantly flicking their long tails, with the occasional flutter-jump into the air after a passing insect. Their flight is undulating, with long glides between bursts of wing beats. The **Grey Wagtail** (*Motacilla cinerea*) is blue-grey on the back and dull yellow below: it frequents fast-running water, along streams or by sluice gates and weirs. It used to breed only in Scotland, Wales and Ireland, but during the last century it extended its range to most parts of Britain, and in recent years has probably been helped by global warming. The **Yellow Wagtail** (*Motacilla flava*) is a similar shape, but green on the back and brighter yellow on the breast, and in summer adult males have a black bib. The **Pied** or **White Wagtail** (*Motacilla alba*) looks quite different, being boldly marked in black and white. It too, often feeds near water, but also in open farmland. Some birds live in Britain throughout the year, but others migrate to southern Europe in the autumn.

WILLOW WARBLER *PHYLLOSCOPUS TROCHILUS* (below) BUILDS ITS DOMED NEST ON THE GROUND.

GREATER SPOTTED WOODPECKER *DENDROCOPOS MAJOR* (right) SECOND LARGEST OF BRITAIN'S WOODPECKERS.

Warblers

These small, slim insect-eaters are mostly rather non-descript in colouring – from olive green to grey-brown – and it not always easy to differentiate between the various species, except by their song. All spend the winter in Africa, arriving in Britain to breed in early spring, and returning southwards in autumn. Their success or failure depends partly on conditions in the United Kingdom, but also on the winters in the far south: droughts in Africa can cause high mortality.

Easily the most plentiful species in Britain is the **Willow warbler** (*Phylloscopus trochilus*), whose population of 2. 3 million pairs appears to be stable. The birds like thickets of birch, hawthorn and young willow in which insects abound, and build their domed nests on the ground. Although far less numerous, with 660,000 pairs in Britain and 120,000 in Ireland, the **Whitethroat** (*Sylvia communis*) is on the increase, at home in rough, overgrown hedges and gravelpits gone to seed. So, too, is the **Chiffchaff** (*Phylloscopus collybita*), now at its highest ever recorded level – 640,000 breeding pairs in Britain, 290,000 in Ireland. Also on the up is the **Blackcap** (*Sylvia atricapilla*) – 580,000 pairs, which has spread widely across Britain during the last century, with some birds remaining here all year round, or migrating from mainland Europe for the winter. The male's small black cap, topping a grey head, makes him distinctive.

The **Sedge warbler** (*Acrocephalus schoenobaenus*) winters in tropical Africa and migrates to Britain in April, feeding on insects taken from low down in reeds, sedges and other plants. At 250,000 breeding pairs it is stable (with 110,000 in Ireland), having recovered after a severe decline in the 1970s, caused by drought in its wintering grounds. The

Reed warbler (*Acrocephalus scirpaceus*) arrives a week or two later, and although relatively scarce, with 60,000 pairs, has shown good recent increases, due perhaps to the proliferation of flooded gravel pits and small nature reserves. In contrast, the **Wood warbler** (*Phylloscopus sibilatrix*) has gone into a sharp decline, especially in the east of Britain, from which it has almost disappeared. Of 17,000 breeding pairs, a third are now in Wales.

Woodpeckers

There are three species of woodpecker in Britain, all gaudily coloured. The largest is the **Green Woodpecker** (*Picus viridis*), which is nearly as big as a woodpigeon, and green-backed, with a vivid red cap on its head. It is also known as the yaffle, from its high, laughing call, and although it spends much time pecking at the bark of tree trunks, its main food is ants. Next in size is the **Greater Spotted Woodpecker** (*Dendrocopos major*), boldly pied black and white, with red on its tail coverts and on the head of the male. Smallest is the **Lesser Spotted Woodpecker** (*Dendrocopos minor*), also pied, but less vividly, and without any red under the tail. All three have a looping, undulating flight, putting in fast wingbeats to gain height, then gliding for a few seconds before turning on the power again.

The most astonishing features of woodpeckers are the speed and force with which they drum their beaks on branches and tree trunks, to send out territorial messages or to bore holes. High-speed film shot at 2000 frames per second has revealed that an acorn woodpecker delivers each hit in one-thousandth of a second, and that the deceleration of its beak on impact is about 1000 G, or 1000 times the pull of gravity (a fighter pilot, in comparison, can pull only seven or eight G in a tight turn without starting to lose consciousness). It seems incredible that a bird can do this without severely damaging its head – but the secret is that its small brain is encased in a cranium lined with spongy bone, and that its muscles absorb the shock.

Territorial drumming echoes through spring woods like the fire of toy machine-guns – brrrrrrp, brrrrrrrp, coming from various directions. Although individuals of the same species sound the same to human ears, minute variations in timing and intensity are all-important to the drummers, each of which has a call sign that others can recognise. The great spotted woodpecker's drum roll accelerates as it goes on, whereas that of the lesser spotted

retains the same pace throughout – although the overall speed depends on the season: in winter it drums at only 10 or 12 hits per second, but in spring it goes much faster.

Drumming apart, woodpeckers bore into dead trees in search of insects, or to hollow out nest chambers. A few wood chips at the base of the hole suffice as lining for their nests. The entrance to a green woodpecker's nest is circular, and sometimes only a metre or so above the ground; but both the spotted species aim higher – from 3–4 metres up to 20 – and their entrances are elliptical, being higher than they are wide.

PIGEONS

Wood Pigeon

Columba palumbus

Although more of an agricultural pest than a gamebird, the wood pigeon is the number one target species for thousands of shooting men. Large numbers are killed all year round, most of them in direct response to farmers' appeals for crop protection, for if a big flock feeds undisturbed even for a few days, it can wreak havoc on crops like new-sown peas.

Partly because of our moderate climate, and partly because of the crops which our farmers grow, Britain is the only European country in which pigeons remain throughout the year. Elsewhere they migrate, heading south in late autumn and north in spring. On one typical autumn day observers in France counted 1.3 million of them streaming southwards over the foothills of the Pyrenees into Spain and Portugal.

Here, even though they move up and down the country according to season, they stay on or over British soil, and after starlings and rooks are our commonest birds. Nobody knows for sure how many there are in Britain, but most people accept as a working base the figures produced by Dr Ron Murton, an expert from the Ministry of Agriculture who studied the birds intensively during the 1950s and 1960s, and in 1965 estimated the population at between three and five million pairs.

Counts made by the British Trust for Ornithology suggest that since then numbers have doubled and are still rising. Thus it seems that Britain and Ireland are home to over 10 million wood pigeons, and the annual cull, far from depressing the population, is failing to contain it. Two main causes lie behind the continual increase: first,

the proliferation of oilseed rape, which
provides pigeons with abundant food all
winter, and second, the lack of severe
weather, which used to kill off the weaker
birds in large numbers.

The fact that they cause severe damage
has not stopped them becoming the subject
of heated argument. The European Union
Bird Directive of 1979, designed to protect
migrating species, required member states
to introduce legislation complying with its
terms; but Britain's response was the
Wildlife and Countryside Act of 1981, which
gave pigeons no protection, and British
gunners continued to shoot them throughout the year. This led to a protest from the
German Green Party, who lodged a com-
plaint in Brussels; but British shooting men
succeeded in getting pigeons moved from
Article 7 of the Directive to Article 9, so that
they could still be shot for purposes of crop
protection. Since 1 January 1993 year-round
shooting has continued under a general
licence issued annually by the government.

Stock Dove

Columba oenas

Smaller and more compact than the wood
pigeon, the stock dove is darker coloured,
and lacks white on wings and neck. It also
flies faster, with very quick wingbeats, and
is also less inclined to form large flocks. Its
habits are similar to those of wood pigeons,
except that it nests in holes, rather than in
trees, often in old rabbit burrows. Country
people sometimes refer to stock doves as
'blue rocks', but this is misleading, as the birds are of a
different species from the **Rock Dove** (*Colomba livia*), which
lives only on the coast, nesting in sea caves and gliding
along cliff faces, and is distinguished by the two strong
black bars on each wing, also by a white patch on the rump.

now over 200,000 breeding pairs in Britain, and 30,000 in
Ireland, and the totals are still increasing.

The doves are elegantly coloured, with narrow black
collars standing out from their pale, pinkish-grey heads,
soft brownish-grey backs and bright pink legs Their main
call is distinct – coo-COO-coo – always three syllables.

Collared Dove

Streptopelia decaocto

The rapid northward spread of this species since 1900 has
been hailed as one of the great conservation events of the
twentieth century. The first birds reached Norfolk in 1955,
and after a slow start in the east, their successors colonised
the rest of the country with extraordinary speed. There are

Turtle Dove

Streptopelia turtur

The gentle, purring, crooning song of the turtle dove is
always thought of as one of the quintessential sounds of
the British summer. Yet in fact it is migrant from West
Africa which comes north only to nest. It superficially

7

Birds
*Farm, Garden &
Songbirds*

Stock Dove
Turtle Dove

258

resembles a wood pigeon, but is much smaller, and distinguished by its reddish-brown wing coverts, flecked with black, and by its long tail.

During the past 30 years the breeding population has fallen by nearly three-quarters, and as a result, turtle doves are now recognised as a priority species in the government's UK Biodiversity Action Plan. One reason has been that the doves are heavily culled by Mediterranean hunters, but an intensive study by the Game Conservancy Trust concluded that the main cause of their decline here has been changes in farming.

An earlier survey, made in the 1960s, found that the doves were living almost exclusively on weed-seeds; now there are so few weeds that the birds are forced to eat predominantly cultivated seeds, such as those of wheat and oilseed rape, and this has reduced their reproductive capacity so severely that each pair produces only half as many chicks as their predecessors. A contributory factor has been the removal of hedgerows, which has cut down good nesting sites.

Racing Pigeon (Rock Pigeon)

Columba livia

Developed from rock doves, which have the same Latin name, racing pigeons are immensely valuable. The record price paid for a British bird is £106,000, and even a good-looking, run-of-the-mill pigeon fetches £500 or £600. The Royal Racing Pigeon Association – the largest body of owners – has 60,000 members, and licences 1.5 million birds every year. The Association's Patron is the Queen, who is said to be a keen fancier and a canny flier.

Pigeons have been used as message-carriers at least since Roman times, and during the First World War many performed such heroic feats that they were awarded the Dickin Medal, an avian Victoria Cross. Like human athletes, the pigeons have various builds, some suitable for sprinting, some for long-distance races, and 15 distinct colours are recognised. They are now taken to start-points in air-conditioned lorries, some carrying as many as 6000 birds, and they are accompanied by minders known as conveyors, who make sure they are properly fed and watered. On release they head for home at speeds averaging 60 km/h. In spite of intensive study, their homing mechanism is not yet properly understood; but scientists believe that they follow the invisible contour-lines of the Earth's magnetic field.

A town pigeon is generally a mixture of several breeds, but almost certainly is descended from the rock dove (Columba livia) – a handsome, grey-blue bird with two black bars on its wings and a white patch on the rump. True rock doves nest around the coast on cliff ledges and in caves but the domesticated varieties are at home in urban surroundings, and when they collect in large numbers, as in Trafalgar Square, they become a nuisance, fouling pavements and buildings with their droppings.

OWLS

Since time immemorial humans have been uneasily fascinated by owls. With their nocturnal habits, their silent flight, their mournful cries and their apparent wisdom, the birds have a prominent place in mythology, superstition and folklore. An owl was the emblem of Athene, patron goddess of ancient Athens, who is frequently described in Homer as 'glaukopis' – 'with gleaming eyes' or 'owl-eyed'. An image of the bird appeared on countless Greek coins, and it was also closely identified with Minerva, the Roman goddess of wisdom. Roman soothsayers found it a bad omen if an owl hooted during the daytime.

In Shakespeare's Hamlet Ophelia's enigmatic remark – 'They say the owl was a baker's daughter' – reflects the strange story of how Jesus went into a baker's shop in search of something to eat. The mistress at once put some dough into the oven, but her daughter, claiming the piece was unnecessarily large, cut it in half. In the baking, however, the dough swelled to a gigantic size, and the daughter, seeing it, cried 'Heugh! Heugh! Heugh!' – whereupon she turned into an owl.

Barn Owl

Tyto alba

The barn owl's face is beautifully white and round, but it is also highly functional, in that the bowl-like depressions on either side, separated by a ruff of tightly packed feathers, act as parabolic reflectors, focusing light into its eyes and high-frequency sounds into its ears. Not only that: the right ear points slightly upward, so that it is more sensitive to sounds coming from above, and the left ear is trained in the opposite direction. The result is that the bird receives three-dimensional stereophonic signals, which make it able to detect and place the faintest of sounds, and to hunt in the dark with deadly precision.

During the day barn owls roost in church towers, buildings or dark trees, standing upright and looking very long-legged. Come dusk, they take to the air in lovely, faltering flights, flitting like ghosts across open spaces. They do not hoot, but utter eerie shrieks while flying, and loud snoring noises when at rest.

During the twentieth century they suffered a severe

decline, the number of breeding pairs in England and Wales falling from 12,000 in 1930 to 4000 in the mid-1980s. The main reasons appeared to be the reduction of good feeding habitat (mainly rough grassland), the loss of nesting sites in trees, old barns and other farm buildings which have been converted into houses, and high mortality on roads, over which owls hunt at night. Narrow country lanes cause many deaths, but so do motorways – and it is a curious but sad fact that owls hit on motorways almost always have their right wings broken. This is because, as they launch out across a carriageway from a fencepost, they dip low to pick up speed over the first few metres of their flight, and are struck by vehicles coming from their right.

During the 1980s many individual conservationists made well-meaning but misguided attempts to increase the population by breeding owls in captivity. It was easy enough and perfectly legal to buy a pair of barn owls for about £40, and the hen birds proved extremely prolific, able to lay more than 30 eggs every spring. The young could be hatched in incubators, and reared on surplus day-old chicks from commercial chicken farms. Trouble set in when birds were released, for they had no idea how to hunt or look after themselves, and inevitably starved. The practice came to an end when the law was changed to make release illegal except with special licence.

In recent years, determined joint efforts by the British Trust for Ornithology and the Hawk and Owl Trust have begun to reverse the downward trend in wild owls, particularly in East Anglia. For Project Barn Owl, a major survey begun in 1996, 1200 specially trained volunteer field-workers spent three winters and summers searching for signs of breeding owls in all parts of the United Kingdom and the Republic of Ireland.

More than a third of the barn owls seen during the survey were found breeding in nest-boxes put up by BTO volunteers or individual property owners. One useful by-product of this great effort was that the volunteers were able to make an estimate, also, of the little owl population, which they put at between 5000 and 9000.

Farmers like barn owls, because the birds keep down rodents, and the information provided by the BTO survey encouraged them to take steps to help them, for instance by extending patches of rough grass, which are anyway promoted by schemes like those for Environmentally Sensitive Areas.

Little Owl

Athene noctua

Named after the goddess of Athens, the little or French owl was introduced to Britain during the nineteenth century, and has a very distinctive shape and flight. Sitting on a roof or fencepost, it looks like a small block of wood, compact and plump, with a square top to its head, its grey-brown feathers smartly mottled, barred and spotted with white. Its facial discs are flattened above the eyes, making it look as though it is frowning. When suspicious or worried, it goes into a comical routine of bobbing up and down, bowing and straightening again in rapid succession.

In flight it keeps low to the ground and progresses in a series of loops, like a heavy woodpecker, as a burst of wingbeats allows it to climb a few metres before it glides to the next stretch. Frequenting hedges, especially ones with old pollarded trees in them, it lives in open country rather than thick woods, and is by no means purely nocturnal, often on the move during the day, as it hunts insects and invertebrates. Its usual call is a plaintive, monotonous *kiew kiew*.

Long-eared Owl

Asio olus

Being almost entirely nocturnal, the long-eared owl rarely appears in daytime, which it spends roosting (for preference) in thick conifers. It is smaller than a tawny owl, and easily recognised by its prominent, upstanding ear-tufts. Its main call is a low, long drawn-out *oo-oo-oo* – a moan rather than a hoot. In Ireland it is the commonest of all the owls.

Short-eared Owl

Asio flammeus

In contrast with its long-eared cousin, the short-eared owl is largely diurnal, and can often be seen hunting over moors, fells and young plantations in full daylight, wheeling, wavering and feinting on its long wings, low over the ground. Although it can capture birds on the wing, its principal prey is voles, snatched from the ground.

Foresters value its presence highly because it can control the rodents, which sometimes multiply so fast that they destroy whole stands of young trees. Whenever a plague sets in, word seems to go out through the owl community, and raptors congregate to share the feast. Since one short-eared owl can eat 2000 small rodents a year, the impact made by a whole gathering can be decisive in saving a tree plantation.

Tawny Owl

Strix aluco

It is the tawny or brown species that gives out the mellow hoots which most people associate with owls. Both sexes go *hoohoo, hoohoo*, but when a wood resounds with calls coming from different directions, the chances are that two males are letting each other know their territorial ambitions. The birds also have a quite different contact call – usually rendered *kee-wick* – and at close quarters use a variety of grunts, mews and hisses for communication.

Sound is also important to them in hunting, as they are almost entirely nocturnal. Their excellent night vision is augmented by an extraordinarily accurate system of sound location and analysis, which enables them to pinpoint the rustles and squeaks given off by mice with devastating accuracy, and instantly to interpret the signals they receive so as to create a complete sonic map of their surroundings.

A tawny owl's eyes have more than twice the nocturnal sensitivity of human eyes. This enables it to fly safely in the dark, even through thick woodland, and also to spot prey already located by sound. Yet to hunt successfully at night, every bird still needs to build up complete knowledge of its territory. Rather than cruise about in search of targets, it visits a series of vantage points, and at each one sits in wait over a fruitful area of open ground.

Although tawny owls do not normally attack other birds, their presence in a wood causes acute alarm among smaller species such as blackbirds, chaffinches and tits, which set up a hysterical chorus whenever they spot one. If the mobsters succeed in dislodging an owl from its perch, they follow it, keeping up the racket and making mock-attacks as they try to chivvy it off their territories.

It is easy to see where an owl has sat or roosted, for the ground beneath its perch is splashed with bright white droppings, the colour coming from the calcium in the bones of its prey. Owls tend to swallow their victims whole, and regurgitate indigestible parts like skin and sinews in the form of pellets. The present population of tawnies is about 20,000 pairs, but the species is potentially at risk from new rodent poisons.

Other owls, known as vagrants because normally they only pass through Britain on migration, include the small **Scops Owl** (*Otus scops*), which resembles the little owl, but has ear-tufts and a longer face; **Tengmalm's Owl** (*Aegolius funereus*), about the same size, but with no ear-tufts, and a larger, more rounded head; the **Eagle Owl** (*Bubo bubo*), an enormous bird about 70 cm long with prominent ear-tufts and a fierce expression; the **Snowy Owl** (*Nyctea scandiaca*), also very large, the male predominantly white, the female white with strong brown barring.

LITTLE OWL *ATHENE NOCTUA* (below)
A NINETEENTH-CENTURY INTRODUCTION
TO BRITAIN, IT LIVES IN OPEN COUNTRY.

7
Birds
Farm, Garden &
Songbirds

Little Owl

Gamebirds

For centuries deer were eagerly hunted with hounds; but as the area of forest was gradually reduced and the numbers of large animals diminished, interest turned more and more to the pursuit of birds, and the age-old art of falconry flourished. Under the Normans the privilege of keeping hawks was strictly structured, and reserved for people of the highest rank. Later monarchs continued to give hunting birds strict protection: in the time of Henry VII anyone caught stealing or destroying the eggs of a falcon (a female hawk) could be imprisoned for a year and a day.

Hawks were obtained in two ways. Birds taken from the nest, known as 'eyasses', were reared in confinement and then trained to fly from the owner's wrist. 'Passage' hawks were those captured after they had left the nest but before they had grown into their mature plumage. Then, as now, the only way a handler could control a bird was by feeding it. Romantic notions of some sort of special relationship between a falconer and his hawk were, and remain, nonsense: only because the bird knows it will get a reward in the form of some meat does it sacrifice freedom and return to the handler's wrist. Trained falcons were flown at partridges, pheasants, duck and (in the north) grouse, and although the sport largely gave way to shooting towards the end of the eighteenth century, when flintlock weapons became relatively small and reliable, it is still practised today by dedicated enthusiasts.

The British Falconers' Club – successor of the Victorian Old Hawking Club – now has 1000 members, and seeks to maintain the highest standards of professional conduct, warning beginners (for instance) that to keep a hawk requires a lot of time and effort, and that nobody should own a bird unless he or she has the space in which to fly it. Since all wild hawks are now protected by law, there is no longer any supply of birds from wild sources; but in recent years major advances have been made in techniques of captive breeding, so that the most sought-after species – peregrines, lanners, goshawks, sparrowhawks and American Harris hawks – can be legitimately acquired.

Better weapons, and the practice of driving, meant that more birds could be shot in a day, and the improvements led to a general gearing-up of game production. More and more landowners employed gamekeepers, not only to protect their preserves, but to rear pheasants and partridges artificially by catching hens when the shooting season finished, keeping them in laying-pens, and hatching their eggs under broody chickens.

The census of 1871 showed 17,000 keepers working in England, Scotland and Wales, but by 1911 the number had risen to 23,000, and this ever-growing army of guardians unleashed a fearful war on any creature they considered detrimental to their cause – not only in the lush farmland of southern England, but far north in Scotland as well. There in the mountains and moors well-to-do gentlemen had embraced the new sport of grouse-shooting with enthusiasm, and they urged their keepers on as keenly as did their counterparts in the south. The ensuing slaughter was prodigious – as is shown by a list of predators exterminated on the Glengarry estate between 1837 and 1840:

11	foxes	198	wild cats
246	marten cats	106	polecats
27	white-tailed eagles	15	golden eagles
301	stoats & weasels	67	badgers
48	otters	78	house cats (gone wild)
3	honey buzzards	462	kestrels
18	ospreys	98	blue hawks
7	orange-legged falcons	6	gyr falcons
83	hen harriers	11	hobby hawks
5	marsh harriers	275	kites
1431	hooded crows	475	ravens
35	horned owls	63	goshawks
71	fern owls	285	common buzzards
3	golden owls	8	magpies
371	rough-legged buzzards		

It is easy to condemn the Victorian gamekeeper, in his top hat, his luxuriant beard and side-whiskers, his velveteen waistcoat, his frock coat and leather gaiters; and certainly some of his habits today seem deplorable – not least that of exhibiting his victims by stringing their bodies up on gibbets in the woods, where they hung until they decomposed and fell apart. By today's standards the man had limited understanding of ecology; yet he was only doing the job for which he was paid, and practising what he took to be conservation. Whatever the morality of such extermination policies, the results were far-reaching. In Scotland the osprey and white-tailed (or sea) eagle went extinct; wild cats survived only in the remotest glens, and all other predators were greatly reduced. Yet the keepers' harsh regime did wonders for grouse. Even on a forest as high and wild as Glenfeshie in the Cairngorms, the English tenants were able to shoot 3632 birds in 1839 – a total never since approached on that estate.

Down south, the red kite disappeared except in Central Wales, and buzzards were wiped out in the eastern half

England. Another casualty was the great bustard –itself once a prized quarry – although its demise was due more to increased enthusiasm for farming than to the mania for preserving game. According to the Victorian ornithologist William Yarrell, 'Down to the time of Henry VIII it occupied all the undulating plains and wolds from the British Channel to the Firth of Forth'. Yet with the enclosure of land, this large bird – a kind of slender turkey of the open plains – gradually dwindled, until in the 1830s it remained only in Yorkshire, Suffolk and Norfolk. Most landowners of that time seem to have had regrettably little idea of conservation. In East Anglia, according to Yarrell, the decline of the species was hastened by the fact that it was treated as an enemy of agriculture. By the middle of the nineteenth century the great bustard was extinct in Britain, and attempts to reintroduce it have so far met with no success.

On the other hand, pheasants and partridges flourished as never before, and the craze for shooting driven game, led by members of the royal family, principally Edward VII and George V, became the main winter obsession of the aristocracy. Every weekend great country houses were flooded by parties of shooting men and their ladies. In the field, each guest was equipped with two guns and a loader, sometimes with three guns and two loaders, and if the Monarch was invited, the numbers of birds could never be too high.

The First World War wrought havoc in the countryside. Landowners, their sons, their gamekeepers and farm workers were swept up into the armed forces, and many died on the battlefields in France, breaking the continuity of management at home. After the war estates were split up and sold to new owners who had neither the inclination nor the money to shoot on the scale of their predecessors.

The Second World War brought most game-shooting to a halt, and afterwards the growing emphasis on efficient agriculture, with its ever-increasing use of chemical weed-killers and insecticides, gave wild gamebirds little chance to flourish. Only a few enthusiasts like Sir Joseph Nickerson (*see page 266*) successfully went back to the old ways. More and more shoots turned to rearing tame birds as a means of supplementing wild stocks.

Those involved point out in self-defence that the management of land for shooting does much to enhance the environment: woods are thinned to encourage the growth of shrubs, coppices are planted, hedgerows are maintained and allowed to spread, so as to offer better nesting cover. A survey of 712 landowners, carried out by the Game Conservancy Trust in 1996, showed that on estates on which pheasants were being reared, 61 per cent of owners had created new woods, compared with only 21 per cent on non-shooting properties. In short, estate owners who shoot are prepared to spend large amounts on enhancing the landscape. Research has also shown that an understorey of shrubs which is good for pheasants also benefits many songbirds, including willow warblers, spotted flycatchers, chiffchaffs, song thrushes, blackcaps, garden warblers and nightingales.

Pheasant

Phasianus colchicus

Today the pheasant is by far the most numerous gamebird in the British Isles, for artificial production and rearing have reached astronomical proportions. More than 20 million pheasants are reared and released every year, and about 12 million are shot: the demand for renting days of 250–350 birds, at up to £30 per bird, seems unlimited, and the sport has become so popular that even if bags on individual days do not approach the massacres of yesteryear, the annual total of birds shot is five or six times higher than in the Edwardian heyday.

Pheasants are now so common in Britain that many people suppose them to be indigenous. In fact they originated in the Far East, and were probably imported by the Romans. The adjective *colchicus*, meaning 'of Colchis', reflects the legend of Jason and the Argonauts, who went to seek the magical golden fleece in Colchis – now part of Georgia – and returned to Greece bringing pheasants with them. Reality was almost certainly more prosaic: it was probably ordinary Greek traders, plying across the Black Sea, who brought the birds home with them.

Pheasants are essentially ground-living creatures, which fly only to escape danger during the day and to go up to roost in the evening. Strong runners, they can cover miles on their feet. When they do take off, they put in a succession of short, powerful bursts with their wings to gain height, and then tend to glide.

Persecuted though they are during the winter, large numbers of pheasants survive until the end of the season on 1 February, and cocks especially seem to have an uncanny grasp of the calendar: having disappeared from view for weeks, they emerge from their hiding places and saunter about in the open, becoming ever gaudier as the red wattles above their eyes grow larger and the ear-like tufts on their crowns extend.

After a period of territorial disputes, which includes much beak-to-beak posturing with other males, and occasional fly-up, tumble-down fights, each cock assembles a harem of five or six hens. In April, after mating, each hen goes off and nests in a shallow scrape among undergrowth, laying up to 15 olive-brown eggs which she incubates for 21 days, coming off her clutch only for short periods to eat and drink. Being on the ground, she is vulnerable to

predators, foxes especially, but she is protected to some extent by the fact that while she is sitting her metabolism slows down, so that her scent is much reduced.

In the old days gamekeepers used to catch hen pheasants at the end of the shooting season, keep them in laying pens, and hatch their eggs under broody chickens. Now the initial process is the same, but almost all hatching is done in incubators. In recent years many estates have imported Japanese (or green) pheasants in attempts to make the birds fly better. Other strains including Scandinavian and Michigan Blue have gone into the melting pot, so that the present pheasant population of the United Kingdom is truly multiracial.

Grey Partridge

Perdix perdix

Scientists have come to see the grey or English partridge as an indicator species, which gives a clue to the state of the environment as a whole. If partridges flourish, many other species do the same; but if the gamebirds go into decline – as they did in the last 40 years of the twentieth century – things are seriously wrong.

The partridge's ability to multiply, given the right conditions, was well recognised by the Victorians and Edwardians; but it was never more impressively demonstrated than in the 1950s at Rothwell, the estate in the Lincolnshire Wolds belonging to Sir Joseph Nickerson, where on 3 October 1952, his team of six guns shot 2119 wild partridges – an all-time record. If anyone deplored slaughter on such a scale, Nickerson would point out that, far from exterminating the birds, he kept them going at a very high level year after year.

Few other landowners had the will, or could afford, to do the same; and as the number of gamekeepers continued to fall, the grey partridge went into such a steep decline that in 1968 the Game Conservancy inaugurated the Partridge Survival Project, a detailed ecological study on the South Downs in Sussex. The project officer, Dick Potts, soon discovered that one of the main problems was a shortage of food for young chicks, which depend on protein from insects in the first few days of life. The introduction of chemical herbicides during the late 1950s had drastically reduced the amount of arable weeds in cereal crops, and this in turn had cut the density of invertebrate insects which live on such weeds. This meant that newly hatched partridge chicks could not find enough food, and that few were surviving, in spite of the fact that both sexes of adults are assiduous parents, the male helping his mate to incubate her eggs.

Every year from 1970 the Game Conservancy has

RED-LEGGED PARTRIDGE *ALECTORIS
RUFA* (bottom) AT LEAST 2 MILLION
ARE REARED AND RELEASED EACH
YEAR FOR SHOOTING.

CAPERCAILLE *TETRAO UROGALLUS*
(right) THE LARGEST GROUSE IN
THE WORLD, IT WEIGHS IN AT A
HEFTY 4 KG.

monitored details of weeds and cereal invertebrates in the third week of June (the peak hatching time for partridge chicks), and has also counted the birds themselves in autumn, after harvest. Data from this, the longest-running such project in the world, show that in the past 30 years the density of invertebrates in cereal crops has fallen by half, contributing to the decline not only of partridges, but also of small birds such as skylarks and corn buntings. From this knowledge has evolved the Game Conservancy's practice of leaving conservation headlands – six-metre strips round the edges of arable fields – which are treated with as few chemicals as possible so that insect life can flourish. This system has now been taken up on numerous estates, with very little damage to crops or loss of yield.

In spite of the knowledge gained, grey partridges remain at a low ebb, except on a few farms and estates where special efforts are made to sustain them. Elsewhere the aggressive use of chemicals, exacerbated by the removal of hedges, has reduced them to critically low levels, and they are now one of the species in the Biodiversity Action Plan. Already these charming birds are almost extinct in Ireland, and it would be a thousand pities if they disappeared from England also. The creaking territorial calls that coveys utter as they settle down for the night in the middle of fields are one of the archetypal sounds of the British countryside.

In 2001 the Game Conservancy launched a major new scheme in Hertfordshire, giving partridges every possible assistance in a core area of 800 hectares, to see if the species can be boosted by meticulous husbandry.

Red-legged Partridge

Alectoris rufa

The red-leg (also known as the French partridge or Frenchman) was introduced into mainland Britain in 1673, when Charles II sent his gamekeeper, Favennes de Mouchant, to the Château de Chambord, to fetch birds with which to stock the royal parks at Windsor and Richmond. Frenchmen are slightly bigger and a good deal gaudier than their English counterparts, with white encircled by a black band on throat and cheeks, and flanks strongly barred with black, white and chestnut stripes. Great runners, they will scuttle long distances unless obliged to fly, and when they do get up, they tend to scatter rather than remain in coveys. When it comes to breeding, they should in theory out perform grey partridges, for the hens are able to lay two clutches of eggs every summer, and their chicks need fewer insects in the first days of life, eating more seeds and vegetable matter; yet, being of Mediterranean origin and used to a hot climate, they have never done as well here in Britain as in their home territory of Portugal, Spain and France.

Today the wild population is impossible to estimate, because immense numbers of red-legs – at least two million a year – are reared and released for shooting. In country where they can be induced to fly across deep valleys, they make fast, challenging targets, and in the eyes of shoot-managers one of their great merits is that they mature at least a month earlier than pheasants, so that operations can begin in September rather than late October or early November.

During the late 1960s game farmers realised that the chukar partridge (*Alectoris chukar*) and chukar-red-leg hybrids were almost twice as prolific as ordinary red-legs. The first ones, released in 1970, quickly became popular on shoots, but it soon became apparent not only that chukars and hybrids would scarcely breed in the wild, but that hybridisation was threatening the genetic purity of the wild stock. The release of chukars and hybrids was therefore prohibited in 1992, since when the breeding success of wild red-legs has improved. Nevertheless, it remains disappointing: on many estates large numbers of Frenchmen are left at the end of the season, but during the winter they dwindle and vanish. Some simply go down off high ground onto lower territory, in search of warmer weather; others provide a bonanza for foxes – and, either way, few if any remain by the following spring.

7

Birds
Gamebirds

Grey Partridge
Red-legged
Partridge

Capercaillie

Tetrao urogallus

If you think of a red grouse as single-bottle size, and of a blackcock as a magnum, the cock capercaillie is a jeroboam or even a methuselah, the equivalent of four or eight bottles and the largest grouse on Earth. His name in Gaelic is *Cabhar coille*, the Old Man of the Woods. Standing more than 50 cm tall, he weighs 4 kg and is as big as a slim turkey, with a big, hooked beak, plumage of black and bottle-green, and a scarlet flash above the eye. Females are smaller and more soberly coloured.

These magnificent birds were formerly common in Ireland, England, Wales and Scotland, but they now appear to be heading for extinction in Britain. Already they have died out once, and the signs are that they may soon do so again.

In the eighteenth century caper flourished in Scotland, but about 1785, for reasons no longer clear, they went into a decline and disappeared. Then in 1837 a Norfolk squire, Sir Thomas Buxton, arranged for his Irish gamekeeper, Larry Banville, to visit Sweden and bring back as many birds as he could collect, for release on the Earl of Breadalbane's estate at Taymouth Castle in Scotland.

So well did the immigrants do, after this and later reintroductions, that within a few generations capercaillie had become a menace to forestry, because in feeding they nipped so many buds and leading shoots from young trees, mainly pines. By the 1920s, to keep numbers down, gamekeepers had taken to stamping on their eggs in spring and trampling chicks to death, and in winter landowners organised drives that often yielded bags of 100 birds in a day.

Today the idea of such deliberate murder seems inconceivable, for although caper survived quite well until the 1960s, they have gone downhill ever since. The decline has been blamed on various factors, among them overgrazing by sheep and deer, which degrades the habitat and in particular suppresses bilberry plants, on which caper depend for food and shelter. Like blackcock, they need old established forest, and in particular a combination of mature pine trees and open glades: serried ranks of conifers, planted for commercial reasons, are no use to them.

Another damaging influence was the weather: a series of cold, late springs meant that there was little food for newly hatched chicks, which must be able to find protein from insects during their first few weeks of life.

Yet another threat was, and is, the deer fence. For years keepers had been finding the remains of birds which had flown into the 2-metre high wire barriers erected to keep deer out of new plantations, and radio-tracking confirmed that the fences were major killers not only of caper, but of black grouse as well. The risks appear to be worse in spring, when the birds are homing in on their traditional leks or mating grounds. Once a dominant cock has established himself, he sends out low-frequency calls, which a human ear cannot detect, but which hens can apparently pick up a kilometre or more away. Drawn by these siren sounds, they come gliding low along the glens with their minds on other things, and in the half-light of dawn do not see the lethal obstructions in their flight-path.

Removal of deer fences – or at least the siting of fences in gullies – is one measure that may help capercaillie recover. Another is control of predators, hooded crows and foxes especially. Because the birds nest on the ground,

BLACK GROUSE MALE *TETRAO TETRIX*
(below) CONSERVATIONISTS WORRY
AT THE DECLINE IN THE BLACKCOCK
POPULATION.

RED GROUSE *LAGOPUS LAGOPUS* (right)
HARDY CREATURES, LIVING HIGH IN
THE HILLS, THEY CAN ENDURE HARSH
WINTER WEATHER.

eggs are at risk from predators from the instant they are laid, and chicks from the moment they are hatched.

Considering their size, caper are suprisingly agile flyers. They make a loud clatter as they leave a perch, but thereafter fly fast and silently, dodging through the trees. Although in normal circumstances extremely wary, a cock caper sometimes becomes so crazed by lust during the rut that in defending his territory he will attack sheep, horses, humans or even vehicles, jabbing at them with his beak, uttering loud clucking noises, and delivering violent strikes with both wings at once.

In spite of all the efforts being made on their behalf, capercaillie ended the millennium in a precarious position. In the last ten years of the century their numbers collapsed from perhaps 20,000 to barely 1000, and their future looked bleak. In 1999 RSPB Scotland appointed a Capercaillie Project Officer to coordinate work on the species, and in October 2001 the Caledonian Partnership – a group of participating organisations – submitted a bid for £4.5 million to the European Union to fund management of special protection areas.

Black Grouse

Tetrao tetrix

There is no mistaking a blackcock. Double the size of a red grouse, glossy black, with a red wattle above the eye and a long tail swept out at the end into two curved branches like a lyre, he is altogether a splendid bird. His females, known as greyhens, are smaller and less vivid, more the colour of red grouse, with their brownish mottling above and grey and white stripes below.

Black game are essentially birds of the forest edge, and prefer to live where scattered birch, alder and pine give out on to open moorland. Dense plantations do not suit them. Their flight is direct and deceptively swift: their wingbeats are relatively slow, but they usually travel faster than a red grouse. In summer they eat leaves and shoots of ground vegetation such as bilberries, as well as seeds, berries and fruit, and in winter they switch their attention to the buds of birch and other trees.

The high point of the blackcock year is the lek – a term that covers both the gathering which the birds form when they are about to mate, and the area in which the congregation is held. Usually this is a stretch of open ground covered in tussocky grass, either in a forest clearing or just outside the trees, and it is used year after year. If you creep silently into a hide at one edge of it, just as dawn is breaking on a morning early in May, you will witness a spectacle never to be forgotten.

As the light strengthens, black shapes come gliding in from all points of the compass, to plump down in the grass, until a dozen or more are dotted about the arena. For a while they remain still; then each cock bird begins his antics, fluffing up his tail, holding his head low and sweeping it from side to side, puffing out the air-sacs in his chest, then abruptly springing into the air to perform a series of tumbling flutter-jumps.

To a human eye he has thrown dignity to the winds and is making an utter fool of himself as he up-ends himself and falls about – yet to admiring females, he is clearly one hell of a fellow. Lured by his bubbling song, they too come gliding in to the lek, but once they have landed in the rough grass or heather, they are hard to spot because their colours blend into the background. They seem to pay no attention to the posturing males – and yet they must, for every now and then one of them succumbs to the charms of a particular blackcock and allows herself to be mated.

In recent years conservationists have been much worried by the progressive decline in the blackcock population. The species has disappeared from the West Country, where it was once common, and there are perilously few birds left in North Wales. In northern England a five-year project run launched in 1996 by the Game Conservancy Trust, the RSPB, Northumbrian Water and the Ministry of Defence, suggested that the birds had managed an encouraging

increase, with the total of displaying males rising from 650 to 800. But on a national scale they are a threatened species. Only in Scotland are they still relatively numerous, and even there they are dwindling.

The most successful attempt to bolster their numbers has been made by the RSPB, on its 15,000-hectare reserve at Abernethy, a stretch of gloriously wild country that rises from the valley of the river Spey to some of the highest Cairngorm peaks. The Society bought the estate in 1988 because it encompassed a substantial remnant of the ancient Caledonian pine forest which once covered much of Scotland, and it was one of the last refuges of black grouse and capercaillie.

One of the RSPB's first decisions – a brave one, as it might have upset many members – was to reduce the resident herd of red deer from 900 to 300 with a series of heavy culls. These, and the removal of sheep, combined with careful thinning of the trees, led to better natural regeneration of Scots pine, and allowed the bilberry and heather to become more luxuriant, providing deeper cover for ground-nesting birds. Another major initiative was to take down 40 km of deer fences, and a third arm of the policy was to cull hooded crows and foxes.

Within five years these measures had a beneficial effect. A count on the black-cock leks in May 1997 revealed 197 males – more than the total on 17 other Strathspey estates combined. Capercaillie, though less numerous, seemed to be holding their own. Then in 1999 the RSPB amazed and disconcerted outside observers by suspending predator control, claiming that it must make a full scientific assessment of all the factors involved.

Many people felt that, with woodland grouse in such a precarious state, it was madness to deny them all possible help, and that the RSPB had given in to political pressure. In any case, with crows and foxes once again unchecked, the number of blackcock counted on the same leks dropped to 130 in 1999. In 2000 the RSPB reinstituted predator control, agreeing that it must be an essential part of their conservation programme on Speyside, but in 2001 only 77 lekking cocks were counted.

Red Grouse

Lagopus lagopus

In purely financial terms, the red grouse, found only in Britain and Ireland, is easily our most valuable gamebird. Solid and chunky, like outsize partridges with furry legs, red grouse are among the fastest flyers in creation. Whistling down over mountain contours at 100 km/h, changing direction with one dip or lift of a wing, they make such exciting and challenging targets that well-to-do shooting men cheerfully pay £100 per brace to take on driven birds. The revenue that red grouse produce enables landowners to pay for the upkeep of heather moorland which otherwise they would not be able to afford, and at the same time finances the control of gamebird predators, to the benefit of many other upland bird species.

Grouse live on the high-lying moors of northern England and Scotland. There are still a few in north Wales – where there were once large numbers – and some in Ireland. The birds' major attraction to sportsmen is that they are genuinely wild. Because they live mainly on heather shoots, supplemented by cotton-grass flowers in spring and bilberries in autumn, they cannot be reared artificially in large numbers, like pheasants or partridges, and this means that the only way of maintaining good stocks of red grouse is to manage their environment sympathetically.

Moorland gamekeepers spend every dry day of the winter burning strips of heather in rotation, so as to ensure continual renewal: their aim is to create a mosaic of patches, some of young heather to provide food, some of older plants to give shelter. Regular burning also helps prevent invasion of the moor by bracken, which harbours disease-carrying ticks. A joint study by the RSPB and the Game Conservancy, completed in 2001, showed that golden plovers, curlews and lapwings – in general decline elsewhere – are five times more abundant on managed grouse moors than on other ground.

Grouse are hardy creatures. Living high in the hills, they can endure harsh winter weather. Weak birds may die during spells of snow and frost, but gamekeepers welcome this natural mortality because it leaves the stock strong. Yet grouse are also susceptible to outbreaks of disease, which cause disastrous cyclical population crashes, usually about every five years.

One cause of such collapses is the sickness known as louping ill, which is carried by sheep ticks, and kills chicks in early summer; another, which strikes in winter, is the parasitic strongyle threadworm, which kills many birds and reduces the productivity of others. Some gamekeeepers try to minimise disease by putting out small piles of medicated grit (which grouse eat to help digest their food), and other keepers go to the extreme of creeping up on birds as they roost in the heather at night, netting them, and dosing the birds individually with worm-killer. Many landowners, however, feel that such interference with nature is liable to weaken the stock and make matters worse in the end.

The cocks are highly territorial, and in March the moors resound with their rattling calls – which end with *Go-back! Go-back! Go-back!* – as they fly about to claim their own stamping grounds and fight off rivals. Once a cock and hen have formed a pair, they settle down in a relatively small area, and there in April the hen lays a clutch of between six and nine eggs, their buff-coloured background mottled with darker brown, in a depression in the heather. She

alone incubates, but her mate keeps watch nearby, and stands guard whenever she briefly leaves the nest in search of food or water. Chicks hatch in late May or early June, and when they are two or three days old the mother takes them off to some nearby boggy area in which insects such as crane flies are abundant – for the chicks need a rich protein diet until they are big enough to digest heather.

If all goes well, they grow rapidly, and are fully mature by 12 August, the traditional start of the grouse-shooting season. Families stay together in coveys of up to a dozen until mid- or late September; then, as wilder weather sets in, they begin to consolidate into enormous packs, often several hundred strong.

The sport of grouse shooting first became fashionable early in the nineteenth century. At first most birds were shot walking-up – that is, with guns and beaters advancing across the moor in line abreast – or else over dogs, with pointers or setters working ahead and freezing whenever they scented grouse. Later, as stocks increased, driving became the order of the day: a long chain of 15 or 20 beaters would sweep huge areas of moor towards lines of butts made of stone, turf or wood and often sunk into the ground to give the waiting guns concealment.

On big days, to maintain a maximum rate of fire during the drives, each shooting man would have two guns and a loader, or sometimes three guns and two loaders. The biggest bag ever recorded was 2929 birds, shot at Littledale in Lancashire on 12 August, 1915 (the First World War notwithstanding); but the most selfish massacre of all time was that perpetrated at Blubberhouses in Yorkshire, on 30 August 1888 by the sixth Lord Walsingham, who killed 1070 birds to his own guns, with two lines of beaters repeatedly driving coveys over him.

In the last quarter of the twentieth century ever-rising costs inevitably meant that grouse-driving became increasingly commercial. Earlier, moor owners simply invited friends to come and shoot in autumn, but now if a party is coming from the United States, prepared to spend £20,000 on a 200-brace day, the most professional organisation is called for.

Without grouse-shooting, the United Kingdom would have far less heather moorland. Aerial photographs show that since 1940 active Scottish grouse moors have lost only 17 per cent of their heather, whereas there has been a loss of up to 50 per cent on moors not used for shooting.

It should not go unremarked that grouse – particularly young ones – are delicious to eat. For many years a few leading hotels and restaurants in major cities have made special arrangements to secure a supply on the first day of the season, and to serve roast grouse for dinner on the evening of the Glorious Twelfth.

Ptarmigan

Lagopus mutus

The ptarmigan is a high-altitude grouse, which in Britain lives only in the Scottish Highlands, almost entirely on or above the 600-metre contour. In summer it is a mixture of stony grey, brown and white, which gives it excellent camouflage among rocks and screes; but in winter its plumage becomes entirely white, except for some black around each eye and on the tail, so that it blends into drifts of snow and, by crouching low, can often escape the eye of a peregrine falcon or golden eagle sweeping past overhead.

Its behaviour varies widely with the weather. On calm, sunny days, a whole covey of ptarmigan will toddle along in front of a human hiker, only a few metres away, apparently quite fearless and relaxed; but in a high wind they will spring up 20 or 30 metres off, and swing out over the glen in a whirl of white wings. Sometimes they cross right over to the next mountain, but more often they sweep round in a big circuit and come back to another point on their own hill. The Latin name *mutus* is misleading: the bird is not mute at all; but on the contrary has a most curious cry – a kind of creaking whirr which continues for several seconds at a time, rising and falling as the caller turns its head.

In the high, harsh environment which ptarmigan inhabit, there often seems to be nothing to eat – and indeed a Highland gamekeeper, asked what the birds live on, once replied, ' Stones, mostly'. In fact they come down to the edge of the rocky ground to eat heather shoots and, in autumn, bilberries and crowberries. Nevertheless, their survival in winter always seems something of a miracle, especially as eagles and peregrines are constantly on the lookout for them; but they burrow into snow to find shoots, and, if they can evade predators, generally come through until the spring.

Woodcock

Scolopax rusticola

Most elusive and mysterious of gamebirds, woodcock have a peculiar fascination for the shooting fraternity. Because they feed on worms and and grubs by pushing their long beaks into soft ground, they cannot be reared artificially, and so, like grouse, are truly wild. Not only are they difficult to find: they are also hard to hit. Their jinking flight through trees, broken by sharp changes of direction and sudden climbs and dives, makes them testing targets, and their mystique is increased by the way in which they come and go unpredictably, present in a wood one day, gone the next.

WOODCOCK *SCOLOPAX RUSTICOLA*
(below) WITH HER MOTTLED COLOUR-
ING, THE HEN IS ALMOST INVISIBLE
ON THE NEST.

SNIPE *GALLINAGO GALLINAGO* (right)
ESSENTIALLY BIRDS OF BOG AND
MARSH, THEY THRIVE WHERE FIELDS
ARE ALLOWED TO FLOOD.

Some birds spend the whole year in Britain, and nest here: the breeding population is thought to be about 20,000. But maybe ten times that number migrate north and south according to the season. During the winter, hard weather in Scandinavia and Russia often brings what is known as a 'fall' of woodcock, especially at times of full moon, as the birds come in to rest on British soil after their passage across the North Sea.

In the bitter winters of 1946–47 and 1962–63, prodigious numbers arrived. Since they are not great long-distance fliers, it is assumed that, if they hit headwinds on the way, thousands must go down in the water; but the survivors land on the northeast and east coasts and pause there before heading on southwestwards towards the warmer climate of Devon, Cornwall, South Wales and Ireland. If the weather in the far north remains open, they do not come at all.

Because they fly at night, people rarely see them migrating, but when they suddenly arrive in November or December, word flashes round shooting communities. Who can forget the story of the Norfolk squire who went off to London, leaving instructions with his keeper, George, to send him a message if or when the woodcock came in. In due course the gentleman received a letter which said, in its entirety:

> Horned Sir
> The kaks becum
> Jarge

In winter the birds sit around in woodland, often under holly bushes, preferably in areas with wide rides and open glades, which give them easy flight paths. When flushed, they get up with a loud clap of wings. In the evenings they flight out to feed in grass fields.

The woodcock that stay here to breed invest warm summer evenings with particular magic, for males perform a ritual known as roding, in which they fly back and forth above their chosen territory, sometimes in enormous elliptical loops, sometimes in figures of eight perhaps almost a kilometre long. In contrast to their flickering passage through trees, their roding flight is steady, with slow, heavy wingbeats. They travel with beaks pointing downward and heads turning from side to side, as if scanning the ground, and as they go they utter an unique combination of calls – deep, guttural croaks, almost like those of frogs, interspersed by high-frequency squeaks. Often a watcher can hear the sounds approaching in the dusk long before the bird appears.

As the male manoeuvres overhead, the female waits on the ground, close to the site which she has already chosen for her nest, and when she is ready, flutters up as a signal. Down comes the male, plummeting like a stone, to join her briefly; but once the mating is over, he leaves her to carry on and raise his offspring alone while himself continues with his demonstration flights in the hope of making another conquest. Each male may mate with up to four females in a season.

The female nests on the ground, often in a drift of old leaves, among which her marbling of buff, brown and black renders her almost invisible: often her bright and protruberant dark eyes, set high on the sides of her head, are the only feature that attract a searcher's attention. Yet she seems to be aware of this risk, for as the sun goes round during the day, she slowly rotates on her nest to keep her face away from it. During her incubation period of 21 days she sometimes leaves the nest briefly in order to feed, but her eggs – generally four in a clutch – are protected by their own mottled camouflage.

When chicks hatch, they are naturally vulnerable to predators such as stoats and foxes, but the mother has a method – extraordinary for a bird – of keeping them safe. If danger threatens any particular spot, she will shift her brood to somewhere safer, carrying one chick at a time between her thighs. People who have not

witnessed this feat claim it to be an old wives' tale, but plenty of reliable observers have seen it done.

Snipe

Gallinago gallinago

Snipe look much like miniature woodcock, with similar mottled colouring and long, probing bills; but they are essentially birds of open bogs and marshes, and rarely if ever frequent woods. Because they are wild and unpredictable, and their flight is highly erratic, they are greatly prized as sporting targets: they spring from the bog with a curious, creaking call and twist violently away, climbing into the distance as if the devil was after them.

As with woodcock, some stay in Britain all year round, but millions more pour through on migration. The breeding population in Britain may be 55,000 pairs plus perhaps 15,000 pairs in Ireland, but it is thought that in winter between 20 and 30 million come down from Finland, Scandinavia and Russia, passing through Britain and Ireland on their way to mainland Europe.

The resident population in Britain fluctuates according to the degree of agricultural activity: when farming is depressed, as it was in the 1930s, and drains are not maintained so that pastures become waterlogged, snipe benefit and increase. But when fields are regularly drained, ploughed, fertilised and treated with herbicides, the resulting sward is much less suitable for this bird. Besides, many broods are lost to the trampling of cattle. The best way to conserve snipe is to improve their habitat by deliberate blocking of drains and reflooding of low-lying fields.

POACHERS (right) BY JAMES LAWTON
(1846–1924), OIL ON CANVAS.

In the 1890s, there was still real poverty in the country and many families were so short of food that a rabbit, a hare or a pheasant was a priceless commodity

....

Poaching

FOR EIGHT CENTURIES after the Norman invasion a series of repressive measures denied ordinary country people, who formed the great bulk of the population, the right to take game. That privilege was reserved for royalty and for landowners with substantial holdings, and Act after Act enforced the law with appalling severity: at various dates penalties for poaching included blinding, hanging, public whipping, transportation for seven years, imprisonment and fines. Quite apart from having recourse to the law, gamekeepers exacted fearful penalties with their spring-guns and mantraps, whose savage, serrated jaws were driven by springs powerful enough not merely to penetrate flesh, but to splinter the bones in a man's leg.

All through the eighteenth and early nineteenth centuries newspapers were full of the 'desperate affrays' and 'fatal conflicts' that erupted in the countryside at night. Not until 1831 did the Game Reform Bill sweep away the landowning qualification and allow anyone who bought a Game Certificate to shoot – and even then guerrilla warfare continued unabated between poachers on one side and the landed gentry, backed by their armies of gamekeepers, on the other.

In spite of the penalties, the urge to poach – to score off the rich landlord – never died down. Gilbert White, the eighteenth-century sage of Selborne, believed that the mere existence of wild animals and birds was bad for the morals of country people – for, as he put it, 'Most men are sportsmen by constitution, and there is such an inherent spirit for hunting in human nature, as scarce any inhibitions can restrain.' The essayist and wit, the Reverend Sydney Smith (1771–1845) echoed this truth when he wrote: 'The same man who would respect an orchard, a garden or a hen-roost scarcely thinks he is committing any fault at all in invading the game coverts of his richer neighbour.'

Because poachers were almost invariably working-class people, public sympathy generally lay with them rather than with the landlords, especially as the courts were thoroughly partisan, tending to favour the rich at the expense of the poor. In 1821 feeling ran dangerously high when, after being tried at the Winchester assizes, two young men were hanged, the first for having assisted in the murder of a gamekeeper, the other for simply having fired a shot at one.

Another writer who sympathised with poachers was Richard Jefferies – although he took a gentler, more romantic view of their activities. When he was writing *The Amateur Poacher*, in the 1870s, there was still real poverty in the country, and many families were so short of food that a rabbit, a hare or a pheasant was a priceless commodity. Yet many rough customers went poaching out of sheer devilment, to score off a hated landlord or gamekeeper, and for the excitement of the chase.

Jefferies himself was no stranger to nocturnal operations, and *The Amateur Poacher* memorably evokes the strangeness and excitement of being abroad on winter nights:

> When the moon is full and at its zenith, it seems to move so slowly that the shadows
> scarcely change their position ... Leaning against the oak and looking upwards, every twig
> is visible against the moon.

One of Jefferies' favourite characters is Oby (short for Obadiah), an inveterate poacher who goes 'a-navigating' (navvying), doing piecework on farms so that he always has an excuse for loitering about the fields and lanes. To this day his rustic vernacular survives almost unchanged: 'If they sees I with a gun, I puts un in the ditch till they be gone by.' From his work on farms Oby 'knows every hare in the parish, and every copse to which pheasants resort in the autumn'. He also knows the habits of the farmers: 'them as bides out late at night at their friends, and they as goes to bed

early'. Equipped with such knowledge, he remarks, 'You may do just as you be a-mind'. Yet he also knows that 'hitting is transporting', so he avoids getting into fights with gamekeepers, and does not mind if he occasionally comes up before the magistrate and has to pay a token fine.

Victorian and Edwardian poachers often used a small-bore shot-gun, maybe with a sawn-off barrel, hinged at the breech so that the carrier could fold it in two and secrete it under his jacket. On windy nights the pop of such a weapon would not carry far. Yet many a prowler preferred methods entirely silent: a net draped across a gateway to intercept a bolting hare, or raisins soaked in brandy and scattered along a pheasant feed ride, which would leave birds so stupefied that they could be picked up and slipped into a sack as easily as acorns. A crueller trick was to thread individual raisins with hairs from a horse's tail: a pheasant that swallowed such a bait would exhaust itself trying to rake the hair out of its beak, and lacked the will or strength to escape when the poacher came to collect it.

Even today, it does not seem to matter that the quarry may be worth very little: the mere sight of it, or even the knowledge that it exists, can overcome reason and incite age-old hunting instincts to prevail.

from THE SONG OF THE LINCOLNSHIRE POACHER
When I was bound apprentice in famous Lincolnshire,
I served my master faithfully for more than seven year.
Then I took up a-poaching, as you shall swiftly hear –
Oh, 'tis my delight on a shining night in the season of the year!

Raptors

Many human beings hold raptors in the highest esteem – and for good reason: birds of prey are fierce, handsome and wonderful fliers. The fact that they are carnivorous and must therefore kill other creatures for food does not worry their admirers. On the other hand, if anyone suggests that a particular species of hawk should be culled or managed to take the pressure off other species, the idea is greeted with furious resentment. In recent years there has been bitter disagreement on this subject between the RSPB, which has steadfastly championed birds of prey, and the Game Conservancy Trust, which has proposed responsible control of some raptor populations (*see page 314*).

(*see page 314*)

At present all British raptors are protected by the Wildlife and Countryside Act of 1981, which makes it an offence to interfere with them in any way; but recent experience has repeatedly shown that penalties are too light to deter criminals such as egg thieves, and bird crime continues to cause much anxiety. In 1999 the RSPB recorded 691 incidents of crime against wild birds in Britain, which included 153 shootings or destruction of raptors, 70 poisonings, 245 nest robbberies and 63 reports of illegal taking, possession or sale of wild birds. Figures for the first nine months of 2000 showed an alarming increase in these crimes, particularly in the number of poisoned raptors, which included 14 red kites, 11 peregrine falcons and 3 golden eagles.

Prospects for wildlife improved significantly in 2000 with the passing of the Countryside and Rights of Way Act, which introduced custodial sentences for serious offences, raised fines to a maximum of £5000 and generally increased penalties. The Act also gave police officers the power to arrest wildlife offenders in order to prevent them destroying evidence like poletraps or egg collections. In the past police were able to arrest suspected egg thieves (for instance) only for some peripheral offence such as being in suspected possession of a stolen car.

Egg stealers seem to be driven by peculiar, dark compulsions: although repeatedly caught, identified, fined and vilified in the press, they return again and again to rob nests, especially those of raptors. Personal ambition – to amass the eggs of more and rarer species than anyone else – is apparently one of the forces that goads them; another may be resentment of authority, and a desire to score off anyone guarding an important site.

The first person to be jailed in the United Kingdom for illegally collecting wild bird eggs was Barry Sheavils of Blyth, Northumberland, who in September 2001 was sentenced to four months' imprisonment at Bedlington Magistrates' Court. He had four previous convictions for collecting, and only in May that year he had been fined £1000 for possessing over 1200 wild birds' eggs, including those of goshawk, osprey and golden eagle.

The RSPB reckon that there are probably 300 serious collectors in Britain, all targeting the nests of rare birds especially, and constituting a significant threat to species like osprey and cirl bunting. As far as the Society knows, there is no trade in eggs within Britain; but there is certainly a trade in young peregrine falcons, which may fetch between £500 and £1000 apiece from falconers in the United Kingdom, more than that if smuggled across the Channel in the boot of a car, and a great deal more if they reach the Middle East. Oddly enough, the tip-offs that lead to surveillance and arrest often come from wives or girlfriends disgruntled with their partners' illegal expeditions.

Buzzard

Buteo buteo

This large raptor, about 50 cm long from beak to tail, has made a strong comeback, after being eliminated from much of England. By the early twentieth century buzzards survived only in the west of the country, but now they have spread back to many of their former haunts.

They are easily distinguished by their broad, blunt-ended wings and the sweeping circles in which they ride air currents. When it comes to soaring, they are amazingly efficient: many a glider pilot has been startled to see a buzzard climb rapidly past him in the centre of a thermal, effortlessly rising on set wings. Lower down, though, they are clumsy fliers, and take off with laboured wingbeats.

The reputation for villainy which they had with gamekeepers was largely unjustified, since they rarely take gamebirds, but live mainly on small mammals such as rats, mice and young rabbits. Especially in spring, when they are establishing territories, they give off long, wild-sounding whistles.

The **Honey Buzzard** (*Pernis apivorus*) resembles a buzzard but has long wings that are more pinched in at the base and a longer tail. It has an extraordinary penchant for raiding the nests of wasps and bees: it eats the young of both species, and the thick feathers on its face apparently

make it immune to stings. The bird is relatively rare in Britain; most pass through after migrating from Africa through Europe to breed in northern and eastern Europe, but a small number breed here. In 1999 some 55 pairs nested in England, and numbers have increased slightly since then, perhaps because of global warming and a consequent increase in the population of wasps and bees.

Golden Eagle

Aquila chrysaetos

One of the largest and most spectacular of British birds of prey, golden eagles inhabit wild regions of the Scottish Highlands, where the population is thought to be about 420 pairs, and stable. With a wingspan of 2 metres, the birds look enormous when seen from close quarters: more often, though, they appear wheeling majestically in the distance against the sky, and when they glide out across a glen, they travel for long stretches with no perceptible movement of the wings. In spring they climb, tumble and dive in spectacular mating displays.

Each pair holds a huge territory of up to 60 square km, and they return year after year to one or other of several traditional eyries in inaccessible rockfaces or isolated trees. Their nests are big, untidy masses of sticks and heather lined with dead grass; the hen lays two or sometimes three eggs, one of which is usually white and the rest heavily mottled. Incubation lasts for six weeks, and both parents bring food to the nest for the young, which fly at the age of about three months. Because the rarity of golden eagles makes their eggs prime targets for egg thieves, many eyries are now guarded day and night during the nesting season.

7

Birds

Raptors

Golden Eagle

279

HEN HARRIER FEMALE *CIRCUS CYANEUS*
(below) IN DECLINE DUE TO HABITAT
LOSS AND ILLEGAL PERSECUTION.

KESTREL *FALCO TINNUNCULUS* (right)
LIVES MAINLY ON SMALL RODENTS,
INSECTS AND EARTHWORMS.

When hunting, eagles sweep low along hillsides in search of hares, rabbits, grouse or ptarmigan, snatching prey off the ground or out of the air. They also eat carrion from dead sheep or deer. If they stoop on a potential victim from a height with claws extended below them, their passage through the air sets up a loud roar, and they sometimes put in a feint attack on a herd of deer in the hope of scaring a calf and driving it to its death over a cliff.

Their powers of consumption are astonishing. In the nineteenth century Charles St John recorded that in Sutherland he twice heard of eagles 'unable to rise from over-eating', and since then their appetites have not diminished. One day in the 1990s a Highland gamekeeper, driving up the glen, looked across at his crow trap and saw that he had seven captives fluttering around inside the wire-netting cage. Returning an hour later to knock them on the head, he was astonished to find that the only live occupant of the cage was a golden eagle, which, having dropped down the central funnel, had killed and eaten all seven crows in short order. Nothing remained but a few feathers and 7 pairs of feet – and when the keeper opened the door to let the eagle out, the great bird was so gorged that it scarcely managed to take off.

Goshawk

Accipiter gentilis

Like a very large sparrowhawk, with similar colouring, the goshawk has curved wings and a long tail. Males are noticeably smaller than females, which reach a length of up to 62 cm (compared with a female sparrowhawk's maximum 38). Goshawks live mainly in open woodland, with a preference for the conifer forests of wild hill country such as that of Shropshire and the Welsh borders. They are breeding well there and in Scotland, but they are one of the worst-persecuted birds of prey, their nests being robbed by egg collectors and illegal falconers.

Although so large, the birds can thread their way between tree-trunks and branches with amazing facility, but for nesting they prefer trees with soft foliage, such as larch, which does not damage their feathers. They make scarcely any noise, but if alarmed they utter a sharp, high, staccato kik-kik-kik-kik. The present population is between 400–500 pairs.

Hen Harrier

Circus cyaneus

In recent years no raptor has caused greater controversy than the hen harrier: the effects of its predation on grouse-moors are discussed elsewhere (*see page 314*). It is a spectacular bird – long-winged, long-legged and long-tailed – and it frequents open country, hunting low over the ground. It is unusual among raptors in that adult males and females are quite different colours – the female having mottled brown and cream plumage, but the male being slatey-grey on the back and the upper side of the wings, and white beneath, with conspicuously black wingtips.

It is the relative scarcity of hen harriers that concerns organisations like the RSPB. Although occasionally seen in the south of England, the birds are mainly confined to the uplands of the north. Because they nest on the ground, sitting females and their chicks sometimes fall victim to foxes. While females are brooding chicks, males bring in prey and yield it up in the course of high-speed food-passes, during which the female springs into the air and snatches the dead bird or rodent in her talons as her mate flashes past. Closed-circuit television, set up at nest sites such as those at Forsinard in the Flow Country in Caithness, now gives visitors a thrilling view of harrier life at close quarters.

Montagu's Harrier (*Circus pygargus*), though smaller and even more elegant, closely resembles the hen harrier, males being light grey above and cream-coloured below, females predominantly brown with streaked underparts. The species disappeared from Britain in the 1970s, but has now made a limited comeback, mainly in East Anglia. The **Marsh Harrier** (*Circus aeruginosus*) also went extinct in

Britain, but much earlier – in 1900 – and is now recovering fast. As many as 200 pairs breed here, mainly in the reedbeds of East Anglia, the Wash and the Fens, but also in Lanashire, Yorkshire, Somerset and Scotland (for the first time) and in Ireland after an absence of 150 years. The marsh harrier is the largest of the British harrier species, noticeably bigger than the rest, with broader wings, a heavier flight, and both sexes predominantly dark brown. It hunts low over marshes and reedbeds, preying on water-birds, frogs and small mammals.

Hobby

Falco subbuteo

Among the most beautiful and agile of all falcons, the hobby lives mostly south of a line drawn from the Humber to the Severn, and it is doing well, with its numbers expanding; up to 624 breeding pairs were counted in 1997. With its long, slender, pointed wings, and a rather short tail, its slatey upper-parts and streaked breast, buff and cream, it resembles the merlin; but the male has vivid orange thighs and a broad, white collar reaching almost round to the back of his neck.

Hobbies are magnificent flyers: when cruising, they alternate bursts of fast wingbeats with short glides, but in an attack they are fast enough to catch even such speedy victims as swallows and swifts. In hunting they use various tactics, including peregrine-type stoops from above, but often they flash straight through a flock of smaller birds and grab one as they pass. Insects, especially dragonflies, seized in their talons feature in their diet. Hobbies do not build nests of their own, but take over the derelict dwellings of crows or squirrels. Males bring prey to the site and hand items over in food-passes.

Kestrel

Falco tinnunculus

Hovering is the kestrel's main characteristic: this slender little falcon, bright chestnutty red above, with streaked underparts, can often be seen poised in the air above motorway verges, its wings vibrating furiously, as it scans the long grass for mice or voles. Unlike the sparrowhawk, it poses little danger to other birds, for it lives mainly on small rodents, insects, earthworms and so on. It is also less furtive than the sparrowhawk, and, rather than skulk about woods and hedges, has a habit of perching in the open on telephone wires. When a farmer is cutting grass, a kestrel will often sit watching, as if it knows that the operation is likely to expose prey animals to its gaze.

For breeding, kestrels take over old nests built by crows or magpies, or make new ones in hollow trees, and often during the nesting season they can be heard even if not seen, since parent birds communicate with each other and their young with thin, very high-pitched screeching cries. Kestrels have declined recently, probably because of a shortage of prey caused by intensive agriculture, but they are still the most common bird of prey in Britain: in 1991 the population was estimated at 50,000 pairs with another 10,000 pairs in Ireland.

Merlin

Falco columbarius

Slender and fast, with grey (male) or brown (female) backs and underparts streaked with brown and cream, merlins can be mistaken for sparrowhawks; but both sexes, and especially the male, are a good deal smaller, 25–30 cm

OSPREY *PANDION HALIAETUS* (below)
THEIR RETURN HAS BEEN A MAJOR
CONSERVATION SUCCESS.

GOSHAWK *ACCIPITER GENTILIS* (right)
A PERSECUTED RAPTOR, ITS NESTS ARE
ROBBED BY EGG COLLECTORS.

long, as against the sparrowhawk's 28–40 cm. They generally frequent hilly areas, such as those in central Wales, the Pennines, Scotland and Ireland; their main prey consists of small birds, on which they stoop in mid-air, but they also occasionally snatch mice and voles from the ground. When a female is brooding chicks, the male hunts continuously for prey, and whenever he is heading for the nest with a victim, he announces his approach from several hundred metres off with a shrill, squeaking call.

For much of the last century their numbers were low – first because they were persecuted by gamekeepers, then because they fell victim to chemical pollution. Now they have recovered strongly, not least because they seem to have realised that it is safer to nest in trees than on the ground, and they are increasingly inclined to take over old structures made by crows

Osprey

Pandion haliaetus

The return of the osprey to Scotland has been a major conservation success. Harassment by egg collectors, specimen hunters and gamekeepers exterminated the birds from Britain by 1916; but in 1954, after an absence of almost 40 years, one pair on migration from Europe to Scandinavia broke their journey at Loch Garten on Speyside and nested there, opening a new era.

In that first year and the three that followed, the birds did not succeed in raising any young; but interest was so strong that in 1959 the RSPB built a viewing-point from which visitors could observe the hawks at close quarters. That year alone 14,000 people went to the site, and by 2001 the total of visitors had risen to two million.

In 1995 the RSPB opened a new and much-improved Osprey Centre, built of native Scots pine extracted from the nearby Abernethy Forest Reserve. The centre is equipped with closed-circuit television, so that watchers have the feeling of being taken almost into the nest, and get memorable close-up shots of parents feeding their chicks.

Ospreys are much smaller than golden eagles, but with a wingspan of some 150 cm they are impressive birds, easily recognised by the strong contrast between their dark brown upper parts, white under parts and whitish head. They live almost entirely on fish, and hunt by gliding over water and plunging to snatch a target in their talons, often hovering briefly before launching an attack.

Over 130 pairs are now breeding in Scotland, and in 2001, to the delight of

ornithologists, one pair, reintroduced from a Scottish nest, hatched a single chick in their nest on Rutland Water in England. It remains to be seen whether or not they will ever again become as numerous as they evidently were in the sixteenth century, when the chronicler Holinshed recorded how country people often took advantage of the birds' skill in fishing:

> We have ospraies which breed with us in parks and woods, whereby the keepers of the same doo reape in breeding time no small commoditie; for so soone almost as the young are hatched, they tie them to the butt ends or ground ends of sundrie trees, where the old ones, finding them, doo never cease to bring fish unto them, which the keepers take and eat from them.

Holinshed had admitted that he had never seen an osprey – and perhaps if he had, he would not have written that the bird 'hath one foot like a hawke to catch hold withall, and another resembling a goose with which to swim'.

Peregrine Falcon

Falco peregrinus

One of the most spectacular birds in existence, the peregrine is a creature of superlatives. It has binocular vision eight times as efficient as a man's, and it can travel at 180 km/h or more when diving on prey. Its stoop from a height, ending in an explosion of feathers as it knocks a grouse or pigeon out of the air, breaking its neck or back with the impact of its extended talons, is a thrilling sight. Even in level flight it exudes power, giving a few quick beats with its long, sharply pointed wings, then gliding on with wings extended. With its slatey-blue upper parts and strongly barred breast and legs, it looks not unlike a large version of a sparrowhawk.

It was the steep decline of peregrines during the 1950s

PEREGRINE FALCON *FALCO PEREGRINUS* (below) CAN TRAVEL AT 180 KM/H OR MORE WHEN DIVING ON PREY.

SEA EAGLE *HALIAEETUS ALBICILLA* (right) THIS SPENDID RAPTOR HAS STRUGGLED BACK FROM THE BRINK.

RED KITES *MILVUS MILVUS* (next pages) MAKE A MAGNIFICENT SPECTACLE AS THEY SOAR ON ANGLED WINGS.

and 1960s that helped raise the alarm about organochlorine pesticides. Research revealed that the shells of the birds' eggs were being drastically thinned by their uptake of poisonous chemicals which had already been ingested by prey species such as pigeons, with the result that few of the raptors' chicks were hatching. The number of breeding pairs in the UK fell to 360.

By the end of the millennium, however, full legal protection and withdrawal of dangerous chemicals had enabled the UK population to recover to its pre-Second World War level of 1300 pairs, along with perhaps twice that number of single birds, even though in some places they were still being killed illegally by unscrupulous gamekeepers or owners of racing pigeons. Because peregrines normally inhabit wild mountain country, they are difficult to watch; but one place where excellent views of them can be had in

the breeding season is Symonds Yat in Monmouthshire, where a public viewpoint looks out across a spectacular gorge, with the River Wye flowing far below.

Unlikely as it sounds, there is now quite a good chance of seeing peregrines in towns and cities, for in recent years the birds have taken to urban nest sites – no doubt because there is so much easy prey around. A national survey carried out by the BTO in 1991 found seven successful nests on man-made structures in urban areas; two years later, a dozen pairs were nesting on buildings, bridges, railway viaducts, pylons, industrial towers and chimney stacks, undeterred by the commotion going on below them.

Red Kite

Milvus milvus

The return of the red kite is another great conservation success story. Fossilised bones show that this fine scavenging raptor existed in Wales 120,000 years ago, and even if it was driven out of Britain by the cold of the final ice age, it returned when Neolithic farmers began to open up the forests in about 2500 BC. From then on it flourished, and in

the Middle Ages it was common throughout England, not least in London, where it played a useful role, along with ravens and pigs, in clearing human refuse from the streets.

Later, however, kites came to be regarded as vermin, and persecution by Victorian gamekeepers reached such a pitch that the birds were exterminated from most of England by about 1870. Only in remote parts of Wales did a tiny population hang on into the twentieth century.

Full legal protection and hard work by dedicated ornithologists, and by enlightened farmers and other local people nursed this remnant back to health and strength: by 1991 the number of breeding pairs had increased to 101. By then, however, a separate bold initiative had been launched by English Nature and the RSPB, which in 1989 had begun importing kites from Sweden and Spain. The first release, made in great secrecy, was at Wormsley, a heavily wooded estate in the Chilterns. Others followed in Scotland and Yorkshire and the hawks took to their new surroundings so well that numbers built up rapidly: one evening in the winter of 1997 the gamekeeper at Wormsley counted 76 kites which had collected in a single spiral before going to roost, and by 2000 the total British population had increased to 431 breeding pairs.

Sad to say, this triumph has been marred by numerous cases of poisoning, some accidental, some intentional. Kites are liable to pick up rats killed by highly toxic poison, and others take baits deliberately put out for them by people whose ideas are rooted in the past. In the last decade of the twentieth century 70 kites fell victim to illegal measures of this kind.

In spite of such setbacks, red kites are securely re-established in Britain. Most gamekeepers realise that, because they are essentially scavengers and feed mostly off carrion, they do little harm to live gamebirds. In the Chilterns they have become a familiar sight, especially to motorists driving on the M40, and they make a magnificent spectacle as they soar effortlessly on angled wings, using their forked tails to help them steer.

Sparrowhawk

Accipiter nisus

Towards the end of the twentieth century a groundswell of hostility built up against sparrowhawks, which had grown so numerous in some areas that they were perceived by many people to be wiping out songbirds and racing pigeons at an intolerable rate. Pigeon fanciers, in particular, became outraged by the losses they were suffering, and demanded an amendment of the law so that special licences could be issued for culling excessive predators.

At the end of 2000 amateur ornithologists in Bristol

formed Songbird Survival, an action group which called for control of 'selected predatory species', including sparrowhawks, to reduce the pressure on small birds. Working from the British Trust for Ornithology's estimate of the sparrowhawk population – 34,000 breeding pairs, and the same number of unattached single birds – the group concluded that the hawks must be eating about 107 million sparrow-sized birds every year, and that such predation was having a significant effect on numbers, besides putting the birds that survived under continual stress.

Such popular perceptions, however, do not tally with scientific investigations by the BTO and the Institute for Terrestrial Ecology. Surveys conducted during the 1990s showed that sparrowhawks had declined by a third in large study areas of Northamptonshire and Dumfriesshire, probably from a lack of the small birds on which they mostly live.

Although relatively small – only about 25 cm long, with females dramatically larger than males – sparrowhawks are deadly hunters, and a female can bring down a wood pigeon twice its weight. They are wonderfully agile fliers, and when one streaks low through a wood at dusk, twisting between trees and bushes like a slate-grey arrowhead, it strikes terror into every small bird along its route, so that a wave of agitated twittering and screeching sweeps ahead of it, heralding its passage. Often a patch of feathers on the ground – white and blue from a pigeon, dark brown from a blackbird – marks the spot where a sparrowhawk has brought a victim down.

White-Tailed or Sea Eagle

Haliaeetus albicilla

This splendid predator was wiped out in 1917 when the last pair were shot from their nest on the Isle of Skye. Attempts at reintroduction were made in 1959 and 1968, but it was not until the Nature Conservancy Council (forerunner of Scottish Natural Heritage) had imported more than 80 chicks from Norway and released them on the Island of Rhum in the 1970s and 1980s, that the foundations of success were laid.

In 1985 came the successful fledging of the first wild-bred chick to survive in Scotland for 70 years. During the 1990s, in a second-phase release, this time on the mainland, SNH and the RSPB imported 59 more chicks from Norway, and in 1996 the first pair of wild-bred Scottish sea eagles reared one young. By 2000, 19 pairs had established territories, and the total of chicks fledged since 1985 reached 100. Visitors can now watch the eagles nesting on closed-circuit television at the Aros Centre on Skye, and from a hide on Mull.

The restoration has been hailed as another major conservation success. Sea eagles are the biggest native eagles in Europe, with a wingspan of up to 2.4 metres. They are larger and heavier than golden eagles, from which adults can be distinguished by their relatively long necks and very short white tails. Their diet includes fish, deer, rabbits, hares and coastal birds, besides offal and scraps from fishing boats. Unfortunately they also take lambs, and SNH offers farmers on Mull compensation for losses; farmers are also paid to keep their sheep away from nest sites, and to scare eagles away from their flocks.

Man's long association with the raptors was revealed by the presence of remains in the 5000-year-old Tomb of the Eagles in Orkney, which suggest that Neolithic people regarded the birds with superstitious respect. The Anglo-Saxons believed that the eagles' bone marrow had healing properties, and the Faroese thought their talons could cure jaundice. Fishermen in the Shetlands, convinced of the birds' supernatural qualities, used to smear their bait with sea eagle fat to increase their catch.

Corvids

Noisy and very conspicuous, this family of large, perching birds have black or boldly patterned plumage. Other characteristic features are their powerful, longish bills and strong legs and feet. Corvids thrive on a wide range of food and some species are known to hoard surplus in the autumn. There are seven regular British species within this family, which include crows, jays, magpies, choughs, jackdaws, crows and ravens.

Carrion Crow

Corvus corone corone

No bird should be criticised for its habits, but those of the carrion crow are not very attractive. Its tough, black beak makes short work of lesser birds, eggs, frogs, toads and small mammals, and it has often been seen to gouge out the eye of a still-living sheep or lamb that has gone down with hunger or disease. It is clever enough to smash the shells of crabs, molluscs and walnuts by dropping them from a height; and crows are such efficient hunters and scavengers that in areas where they are not culled by gamekeepers, they wipe out the nests of partridges and pheasants, along with those of many songbirds.

They can be distinguished from rooks by the fact that they are slightly larger, and intensely black all over, with no white on the face. Also, their flight is heavier, with laboured wingbeats. They are generally less gregarious than rooks, and mostly live in pairs or family groups. Each pair also nests on its own, high in a tree, the male having proclaimed his territory with a harsh call of *kaaarrk, kaarrk* for days on end in early spring.

Superstitious beliefs cling to crows as they do to ravens: to meet a single bird in the morning is unlucky, and if one perches on the roof of a house, it presages death for somebody inside. The reputation of the bird has not changed in 500 years, since the Elizabethan poet (and Member of Parliament) George Gascoigne wrote:

> *The carrion crow, that loathsome beast,*
> *Which cries against the rain,*
> *Both for her hue and for the rest*
> *The devil resembleth plain.*

7

Birds

Corvids

Carrion Crow

CARRION CROW *CORVUS CORONE CORONE* (bottom left) INTENSELY BLACK, CARRION CROWS LIVE IN PAIRS.

JAY *GARRULUS GLANDARIUS* (below) DISTINGUISHED BY ITS GAUDY AND INTRICATE COLOUR-SCHEME.

Chough

Pyrrhocorax pyrrhocorax

Red beaks and legs distinguish choughs, which are otherwise black all over, from jackdaws. When airborne, their wings look very broad and conspicuously deep-fingered – that is, with long, separate feathers on the tips – as they glide and dive and perform acrobatics. Mainly birds of the coast, they frequent sea cliffs and crags, nesting in crevices or holes in the roofs of caves. Cornish people still sometimes say that King Arthur lives on in the form of a chough (or raven), so that to kill the bird is highly inadvisable.

Hooded Crow

Corvus corone cornix

A grey mantle and underparts give 'hoodies' a quite different appearance from that of the carrion crow. Their main haunts are the uplands, in the north of England, Ireland and Scotland. Their diet is much the same as that of the carrion crow, and includes carrion, especially in the Highlands, where, like ravens, they appear overhead within minutes of a stag or hind being shot.

Hoodies, also, are cunning hunters, as scientists investigating the habits of grouse found to their cost. When researchers stuck sticks into the heather to mark grouse nests, the crows, realising what they signified, promptly moved in and ate the eggs. Only when the scientists started putting their markers a certain distance away, on a pre-arranged bearing, did they foil the raiders. Hoodies are much blamed for the decline of woodland grouse – the blackcock and capercaillie.

Jackdaw

Corvus monedula

Smaller than rooks, and smoky grey about the back of the head and neck, jackdaws move jerkily both on the ground and in the air, walking with a quick, jaunty action and flying with fast wingbeats. They are intensely sociable birds, almost always going about in small flocks, and maintaining a chatter of conversation. They must have started more house fires than any other species, since they have an ungovernable penchant for nesting in chimneys – and not building simple nests, either: sometimes they make huge structures of sticks, a metre deep, which create a merry blaze when a fire is lit in the hearth below. (Perhaps this is the origin of the superstition that if one flies down a chimney, it heralds a death in the house.) Jackdaws also breed communally in hollow trees, setting up a strong, musky smell around the area.

As to diet – they are less objectionable than magpies, for although they do eat eggs and fledgling songbirds, they concentrate more on insects, slugs, worms and other invertebrates. But their reputation as thieves is well founded, for they pick up any shiny object that catches their eye and carry it off to a cache.

Jay

Garrulus glandarius

The presence of a jay is usually signalled by its alarm call, a harsh screech, echoing through the wood, which it gives at the sight of a fox, an owl or a human intruder. As it slips through the trees with its characteristic, looping flight, like that of woodpeckers, its gaudy and intricate colour scheme is revealed: body mainly pinkish-brown, crown of head striped black and white, moustache black, throat and rump white, wing- and tail-tips black. Yet its most striking features are the feathers on its wing-coverts, which are barred in brilliant blue and black.

Acorns are its staple food, and in autum a jay will return repeatedly to the same oak for supplies, which it stores in a cache. But in spring it is more carnivorous, and eats young birds, eggs, mice, worms, insects and spiders. Although jays sometimes congregate in groups, they are more often solitary or in pairs.

Magpie

Pica pica

In the last 20 years of the twentieth centtury, owners of gardens became more and more annoyed by the rise in the number of magpies, which, every spring, robbed the nests of songbirds, eating eggs and chicks alike. Since, at the same time, the songbird population was sinking fast, it seemed obvious to ordinary citizens that the magpie was one of the villains causing the decline.

MAGPIE *PICA PICA* (below) CONTRO-
VERSY SURROUNDS MAGPIES AND
THEIR EFFECTS ON SONGBIRDS.

RAVEN IN THE TOWER *CORVUS CORAX*
(right) IF THE RAVENS DEPART, LEGEND
HOLDS THAT DISASTER WILL FOLLOW.

hedgehogs and pheasants are run over every year; but if the totals for badger and fox casualties (50,000 and 100,000) are anything to go by, the number must be prodigious.

It seems hard luck that birds as good-looking as magpies should be so destructive, with a reputation not only as killers but also as thieves. They are said to have acquired their bold black-and-white colouring because they refused to go into full mourning, along with all the other birds, after the Crucifixion; and another echo of the same legend is the belief that the birds can be forced to abandon their nest if someone carves a cross into the bark of the tree in which they have built. To this day many people remain superstitious enough to bow or spit and salute whenever they see a magpie, to ward off any bad luck it may bring, and everyone knows the nursery rhyme:

> One for sorrow, two for joy,
> Three for a girl and four for a boy.

Many people find their voices exceptionally aggravating: their harsh chatter, interspersed with thick, fruity clucks, grates on human nerves. But their nests are marvels of engineering, and heavily defended, with a cup of baked mud fashioned inside a mass of sticks, and roofed over with a dome of twigs – as if they were expecting other species of birds to take up their own form of guerrilla warfare, and attack them at home.

And yet, according to the experts of the RSPB and the BTO, this popular correlation was wrong. A report issued in October 1998 announced that 'extensive data collected since 1962 in the BTO's annual Common Bird Census were subjected to rigorous statistical analysis,' and this showed that neither magpies nor those other commonly accused predators, sparrowhawks, were responsible for the song-birds' plight.

The report acknowledged that the number of magpies had trebled during the past 20 years, partly because persecution of them by gamekeepers had relaxed, but pointed out that the birds are 'only seasonal killers,' and rob nests only in spring. 'Exactly!' replied the man in the street. 'That's when they do the damage.'

In the far north, on its huge Speyside reserve, Abernethy, the RSPB gave ground to the extent of culling crows and magpies in a last-ditch attempt to save capercaillie and black grouse from extinction (*see page 271*). Meanwhile, all over Britain, people took matters into their own hands and acquired Larsen traps, which use live decoys to lure birds of the same species into a cage: thus equipped, many a householder caught 15 or 20 magpies each year, and so cleared his immediate area for the breeding season.

The major reason for the magpie explosion has probably been the carnage of wildlife on the roads. Every dawn presents them with an extensive menu of freshly run-over carrion: never before has so much high-protein food been served up to them. Nobody knows how many rabbits,

Raven

Corvus corax

Largest and most powerful of the corvids, ravens long had a sinister reputation as harbingers of pestilence, famine and death, doubtless derived from their jet-black plumage, and from their inevitable attendance on battlefields, where they gathered to feast on the corpses of the slain. Never mind that in the Old Testament the birds brought Elijah bread and flesh, morning and evening, as he hid by the brook Cherith: in the ancient world a skirmish between ravens and kites, or ravens and crows, prognosticated a mighty battle.

The Romans looked on the birds with dread, and if one

passed from left to right at a critical moment, saw it as a sinister omen. In 43 BC Cicero was forewarned of his death by the fluttering of ravens, and it was said that on the day of the orator's murder one bird entered his chamber, pulling off the bedclothes.

During the Middle Ages people took a more positive view. Ravens were actively protected in Scottish towns and villages because of the service they rendered in cleaning up offal and rubbish. With slops being tipped out of windows,

and pigs foraging among heaps of garbage, the birds performed a useful task, just as kites did in London. In 1584 the German traveller Baron von Wedell, riding through Northumberland, recorded that Berwick-on-Tweed was full of ravens, 'which it is forbidden to shoot ... for they are considered to drive away bad air'.

And yet – has anyone ever read Edgar Allan Poe's haunted poem *The Raven* without a shudder? There is something infinitely disturbing about his picture of the 'ghastly grim and ancient raven' which comes tapping at his door as the fire is dying on a December night. When he lets the creature in, it perches on a bust above the door, and will neither leave nor speak, except to utter the one word, 'Nevermore'.

Ravens normally inhabit wild mountain country such as the Scottish Highlands, where they appear from nowhere, giving their abrupt, dry, barking cries – *ark, ark* – within a minute or two of a stag or hind being shot, knowing that the beast's *gralloch*, or intestines, will furnish them with a week-long banquet. Yet the most famous ravens in the world are those at the Tower of London. Almost always, ever since Charles II issued a decree in the seventeenth century, there have been six ravens in residence, backed up by one or two auxiliaries in case a bird should be lost: legend has it that if ever the ravens depart, the White Tower will crumble and disaster will overtake the kingdom. (In fact there were no ravens in residence in 1946 – a moment in history at which the kingdom had narrowly escaped destruction.)

At the end of 2001 the Tower's unkindness – the collective name for a gathering of ravens – included four males and three females, all with names and identified by coloured leg-rings. The oldest, Hardy (named after the writer), came from Dorset in 1981, and the youngest, Thor, was born in Hampshire in 1995. Two of the females are Hugin and Munin ('Mind' and 'Memory'), their names taken from the pair that traditionally sat on the shoulders of Odin, the Norse war god, flew information-gathering sorties over the world every day, and returned in the evening to tell him what they had seen.

The birds at the Tower are free to come and go, but they have the feathers of one wing trimmed so that they cannot fly very far, and although one occasionally escapes, they generally stay within the walls. Because they cannot indulge in the high-level mating manoeuvres to which wild ravens resort, they do not breed much: the last time a pair produced chicks was in 1991, and the young birds were given away on condition that they would be returned if ever a shortage threatened.

The man in charge of the ravens in the Tower is Derrick Coyle, the Raven Master, one of the Yeoman Warders, resplendent in his Tudor uniform, and the birds look up to him as the senior member of their flock. He feeds them twice a day, in the morning with scraps left over from the cafeteria, including fried eggs and sausages, and in the evening with raw meat. Occasionally he comes back from the country with a rabbit, which they rip up, fur and all. In the evening he whistles them down to their cages and shuts them in safely for the night. In short, they live a pampered life – and one can only hope that instinct does not make them pine for the wild places where their fellows fly free.

Rook

Corvus frugilegus

If rooks are among the most sociable of all birds, they are also among the noisiest. When feeding on the ground, they are quiet, but whenever they are airborne, especially coming off roost early in the morning, they raise a tremendous clamour, wheeling about in huge flocks, as if arguing about where to go next. They nest together in traditional rookeries, returning year after year to the same trees, to refurbish the big, untidy bundles of sticks left from the previous spring, and even when busy breeding they maintain ceaseless cawing, squawking and squabbling.

As adults, they can be distinguished from carrion crows by the fact that they are always in flocks, rather than single or in pairs, and by their bare, grey-white faces, quite different from the all-black head of the crow. Since they live mainly on insects, they are welcomed by farmers, for they gobble up many pests such as wireworms. Nevertheless, in earlier times, farmers used to shoot young birds as they came off their nests on 12 May, to make traditional rook pie – a dish still occasionally eaten in rural districts.

One of the birds' characteristics is that they continue to forage on fields far into the twilight, staying on the ground dangerously late, when foxes are already abroad. Shakespeare knew this – and even if he muddled up his corvids, he caught the atmosphere of approaching dusk perfectly in *Macbeth*:

> *Light thickens, and the crow*
> *Makes wing to th' rooky wood;*
> *Good things of day begin to droop and drowse*
> *Whiles night's black agents to their preys do rouse.*

Waterbirds

Britain is of outstanding international importance for waterbirds, because it lies on some of the major migratory routes used by species that nest in the Arctic. Our relatively warm winter climate and extensive areas of wetland, notably estuaries, attract aquatic species in large numbers – and the United Kingdom thus has moral as well as legal obligations to conserve both the birds and their habitat.

Each winter since 1947 extensive surveys have been made to monitor developments. The Wetland Bird Survey, known as WeBS, is conducted by a partnership formed from the British Trust for Ornithology, the Wildfowl and Wetlands Trust, the Royal Society for the Protection of Birds and the Joint Nature Conservation Committee. The counts, taken at a wide variety of sites, and synchronised so that birds are not counted twice, reflect the enthusiasm and dedication of some 3000 volunteer ornithologists. The results are collated in a substantial book, published every year.

The two principal groups of waterbirds are *waders*, which live mainly on or about the shore, and *wildfowl*, which move inland to feed on fields and waterways, usually at night. The best habitats for both categories are the east coast estuaries like that of the Humber, with their extensive mud flats.

The total of waders counted in January 2000 was 1,589,141 with the breakdown of the most numerous species as follows rounded up to the nearest thousand:

DUNLIN	371,000
LAPWING	322,000
OYSTERCATCHER	242,500
COOT	106,000
CURLEW	89,000
REDSHANK	75,000
BAR-TAILED GODWIT	49,000
GREY PLOVER	18,000
MOORHEN	14,000
BLACK-TAILED GODWIT	11,000
TURNSTONE	11,000
GREAT CRESTED GREBE	9000
RINGED PLOVER	8000
SNIPE	7000
SANDERLING	6000
LITTLE GREBE	4000
AVOCET	4000
GREY HERON	3000
PURPLE SANDPIPER	1000

In the same month, wildfowl totalled 1,282,508 and the most numerous species were:

WIGEON	326,700
MALLARD	134,000
TEAL	122,000
DARK-BELLIED BRENT GOOSE	86,000
PINK-FOOTED GOOSE	73,000
SHELDUCK	57,000
TUFTED DUCK	55,000
CANADA GOOSE	49,000
POCHARD	36,000
BARNACLE GOOSE	24,000
GREYLAG GOOSE	21,000
GREYLAG GOOSE (ICELAND)	19,000
MUTE SWAN	19,000
PINTAIL	17,000
EIDER	16,000
GADWALL	16,000
GOLDENEYE	14,000
SHOVELER	8000
WHOOPER SWAN	7000
RUDDY DUCK	5000
EUROPEAN WHITEFRONT	4000
GOOSANDER	3000
COMMON SCOTER	3000
RED-BREASTED MERGANSER	3000
SCAUP	3000
BEWICK'S SWAN	2000

The most numerous gulls were:

BLACK-HEADED GULL	268,000
COMMON GULL	74,000
HERRING GULL	71,000
LESSER BLACK BACKED GULL	8000
GREAT BLACK BACKED GULL	6000

DUCKS

Mallard

Anas platyrhynchos

Probably the most familiar British duck since it lives happily on lakes, ponds and rivers in urban as well as rural suroundings, the mallard is also the number one quarry species of wildfowlers. It has been estimated that at least one million birds are shot every year, but since most of these are artificially reared, the annual cull appears to have no effect on wild stocks. The number of wild pairs that breed in Britain is smaller than that of the birds that winter on our coast.

Drake mallard are resplendent with bottle-green heads, white collars, purple-brown breasts and brown-and-grey bodies; and ducks, though plainer brown, are also distinguished by the white, black and turquoise flashes on their wings. It is the females who give the distinctive *quark, quark, quark* call: the male's voice is higher and less emphatic.

Mallard sit on the water during the day, then as dusk comes on, flight out to feed on corn, acorns and seeds in fields and marshes, their departure preceded by minutes of loud warm-up chatter. They also feed on insects, shellfish and other aquatic animals. In the breeding season, females generally nest on the ground, but sometimes up trees, so that the ducklings have to flutter down to the ground as soon as they are hatched. If danger threatens a brood, the mother decoys the intruder away by feigning injury in a convincing manner, fluttering along the ground, always just out of reach, tumbling over as though she had a broken wing – only to get up suddenly and fly back in a circle, unharmed, when she considers it safe.

7

Birds
Waterbirds

Mallard

PINTAILS *ANAS ACUTA* (below) FEMALE
IN BUFF, BROWN AND GOLD; (bottom)
DRAKE WITH HIS MORE DRAMATIC
COLOURING.

WIGEON MALE *ANAS PENELOPE* (bottom
right) THE MOST COMMON DUCK ON
BRITISH COASTS IN WINTER, IT GRAZES
HAPPILY ON LAND.

Pochard

Aythya ferina

A bright chestnut-red head and neck above a black, white and light grey body make the drake pochard stand out among all other ducks. His mate is much plainer, mainly brown. Pochard stay mainly inland on open fresh water, and if disturbed, tend to swim into the distance, rather than fly. If obliged to take off, they do so only after a heavy, clattering run across the surface.

Shelduck

Tadorna tadorna

Sheldrake also have a bold colour scheme: bill red, head dark green, body mainly white, but with a broad band of chestnut round the breast, and black on wings and tail. A large bird – half way between a mallard and a farmyard goose – it flies heavily and stays largely about the coast. Females nest in rabbit holes or under gorse and bramble bushes, and lay exceptional numbers of eggs – usually 8 to 10 but up to 15 or even 20. After her brood has hatched, the female leads them to a food-rich site, where they often form a creche with chicks from other broods.

Pintail

Anas acuta

A pintail drake looks like a painted duck, so complex and sharply defined is its colour scheme. The chocolate of its head is set off by the white of its breast, which continues up each side of its neck in a curving, narrowing band. The sides of a drake's body are a fine grey, with a creamy patch in front of its black tail coverts, and the trailing edge of the inner wings in both sexes are dark, glossy, bronze and green, orange, black and white. The drake's long, pointed central tailfeathers, from which the species takes its name, are most obvious while the bird is in flight, while on the water or on land they can be surprisingly inconspicuous when lowered.

Teal

Anas crecca

Only half as big as mallard, and extremely fast on the wing, teal are easily identified by their small size, by the way they rocket up off water, and by their abrupt changes of direction in the air: small flocks swerve and wheel violently in unison. From a distance drakes look grey, but at close quarters they are stylish little birds, with grey wings and bodies, and chestnut heads with yellowish-cream lines encircling green bands round the eyes. Females resemble miniature, more boldly mottled versions of female mallard.

Teal feed on seeds, shoots, roots and aquatic insects, flighting in to ponds and marshes at night. They breed mostly in northern areas, nesting in vegetation near water.

Tufted Duck

Aythya fuligula

Conspicuous for the pure white on his flanks and belly, the drake is otherwise jet black, and his tuft of feathers hangs off the back of his head. The female is brown rather than black, but gives an almost black-and-white impression in flight. Only about 7500 pairs of tufteds breed wild in Britain, but they are one of our most familiar ducks, because they live happily on lakes and ponds in urban parks, where they can be seen diving for molluscs, crustaceans and insects, popping back onto the surface like corks between explorations.

Wigeon

Anas penelope

As the table on page 294 shows, by far the most common duck on the coast in winter is the wigeon; and yet very few – only about 400 pairs – breed in Britain, coming inland to breed on isolated moorland ponds and peat bogs. Drakes are predominantly grey and white, with chestnut heads, yellow foreheads and pink breasts; females are a dull grey-brown, but both sexes have white bellies and dove-grey underwings. In winter huge flocks frequent coasts and muddy estuaries, where they feed on grass, sedges and rushes. They are strongly gregarious, and often form enormous rafts when resting offshore. When disturbed, they take off almost vertically and fly fast, often in V-formation, with drakes giving out loud, wonderfully musical whistles.

GEESE

There is something infinitely romantic about wild geese, a quality born of the huge distances over which they range. Anyone who has been out in the Scottish Highlands and heard geese coming south in the autumn will know how their far music can set the scalp crawling. Often, at first, you cannot identify the origin of those strident cries: then, looking up, you realise that geese are right above you, high in the sky, spread out in big, V-shaped skeins as they ride the winds towards their wintering grounds. Their voices sound as though they are bringing news from the ends of the Earth.

Yet geese thrill different kinds of people for different reasons. They appeal to straightforward bird lovers on an aesthetic and emotional plane. Wildfowlers, in contrast, consider them the ultimate quarry, difficult to outwit and

approach, but worth any amount of discomfort from cold and filthy weather encountered in the pursuit. To farmers, geese are often a menace, not just because seven of the birds may eat as much grass or winter corn as a sheep, but also because their droppings foul acres of pasture.

Nowhere has the conflict of interests been better illustrated than on the island of Islay in the Hebrides, which is the winter haunt of many thousands of barnacle and whitefronted geese. There in the old days (good or bad, according to viewpoint) the principal landowners used to have the geese counted every year, and met to decide how many should be shot. This annually adjusted cull kept the population in check, with minimal expense, and the island's dairy farmers were happy.

Then professional conservation bodies took over. The European Birds' Directive of 1979 led to the Wildlife and Countryside Act of 1981, which gave protection to barnacle and whitefronted geese in Scotland. With shooting banned, the number of barnacles on Islay rose to intolerable heights: the birds destroyed farmers' crops by grazing them down and plastering the fields with excrement. In 1996 the ensuing controversy led to the establishment of a Goose Forum, later replaced by the Goose Review Body, which advises the Scottish Executive on management schemes.

When two Islay farmers applied for culling licences, and were granted them, the move was strongly opposed by the RSPB and the Wildfowl and Wetlands Trust, on the grounds that the application was to shoot on parts of the island that had been designated specially protected areas. After complex legal arguments, the Scottish Executive lost, and the licences were withdrawn. Instead of a cull being carried out by locals at no charge, a whole team from Scottish Natural Heritage was deployed on Islay at enormous expense: a Goose Management Officer, five counters, one scarer, two part-time marksmen and five office staff.

The aim, moreover, was not so much to reduce numbers as to keep the geese on the move. The field workers not only count the birds, but also shift around a complex battery of alarming devices, including kites, gas-guns, squawkers, rotating flashers and orange 'scarymen' which inflate intermittently. To show the flocks that explosions are not always innocuous, the marksmen shoot a few hundred birds every winter. Farmers are paid compensation for playing host to the geese, according to the density of the flocks and the kind of land they are on.

On the best land – arable fields or improved grassland – and at maximum density of 15 geese per hectare, a farmer, in 2000–01, got £269 per hectare per year. The cost in straight compensation paid out over that winter was £595,000, and with some of the SNH team's costs thrown in, total expenditure was £637,000. It was some relief to all concerned to find that the number of barnacles had remained static, at about 35,000, for three winters running.

In Britain as a whole, barnacle, bean and brent geese are

BARNACLE GEESE *BRANTA LEUCOPSIS* (left) BOLD BLACK AND WHITE COLOURING MAKES THEM EASY TO SPOT.

PINK-FOOTED GEESE *ANSER BRACHYRHYNCHUS* (below) IN FORMATION OVER THE WASH, NORFOLK IN NOVEMBER.

fully protected, and never shot except with a special licence. The principal quarry species – Canada, pinkfoot and greylag – can be shot in the open season, which runs from 1 September until 31 January above the high-water mark and 20 February below it, although the government has powers to suspend shooting of all wildfowl and waders during periods of severe weather. There is no official limit on the number of geese that any gunner may shoot in an outing, but shooting organisations like BASC do suggest voluntary limits.

Barnacle Goose

Branta leucopsis

A bold black-and-white colour-scheme makes barnacle geese easy to spot even at a distance: black caps, white faces, black necks and breasts, white underparts, black legs – the colours alternate all over. It was once widely believed in Britain and Northern Ireland that barnacles hatched from timbers rotting in the sea – a curious theory of their origin believed by many authors, including Giraldus Cambrensis, whose *Topographia Hiberniae* published in the twelfth century, recorded that the birds grew hanging by their beaks from the sides of wrecks, like festoons of seaweed. The erroneous belief that the geese were thus more fish than fowl meant that they could be eaten during Lent or other periods of fasting.

Brent Goose

Branta bernicla

There are two races of brent goose around British coasts, the dark-bellied and the light-bellied. The first is by far the more common, and from a distance looks like a big, black duck, dark all over except for its white tail coverts. Brents are intensely gregarious, and form large flocks, but instead of flying in skeins, like other geese, they move in loosely knit packs. They over-winter mainly in eastern and southern Britain, and in April or May migrate to the far north, where they breed on open tundra.

Pink-footed Goose

Anser brachyrhynchus

Even if the pink legs are not visible, this species' dark head and neck, contrasting with a rather pale body, make it fairly easy to spot. Pinkfeet breed in Iceland, Spitsbergen and Greenland, and migrate south in September and October, thousands coming to spend the winter in Britain. The geese congregate in enormous flocks, roosting on coastal sandbanks and estuaries, but coming inland to feed on grass and cornfields at night. In spite of considerable annual culls, the winter population has risen to 240,000 and is steadily increasing.

Canada Goose

Branta canadensis

Originally imported from North America in the late seventeenth century for Charles II's collection of waterfowl in St James's Park, in London, Canada geese gradually spread through England, Wales and Scotland, either by free migration, or through other landowners obtaining eggs or goslings to stock lakes on their own estates. They are easily identified by their large size and black heads and necks, set off by a white chinstrap. A few wild Canadas, of much smaller, darker subspecies, migrate across the Atlantic, flying from the eastern Canadian Arctic to winter on the west coast of Ireland and Scotland.

A census taken in the late 1960s estimated the feral population in Britain at over 10,000, but the 1996 figure showed that in 30 years the number had quadrupled, and it was rising so fast that it was expected to reach six figures by the year 2000. Somehow this never happened, and the population appears to have stabilised at about 61,000.

Canada geese are now so numerous as to be a menace,

CANADA GOOSE, *BRANTA CANADENSIS*
(left) THE LARGEST GOOSE IN BRITAIN,
IT IS NOW NUMEROUS.

BEWICK'S SWAN *CYGNUS COLUMBIANUS*
BEWICKII (bottom left) MIGRATE UP TO
8000 KM EVERY YEAR.

MUTE SWANS *CYGNUS OLOR* (below) AN
ADULT AND TWO CYGNETS; MUTE SWANS
LIVE IN BRITAIN ALL YEAR ROUND.

particularly in public parks, where the birds – the largest geese in Britain at 90–100 cm long – carpet the grass with their droppings. Three birds are reckoned to eat the same amount of herbage as one sheep, and their defecations have been timed at one every four minutes. Another problem is that they are more sedentary than other geese, and do not migrate in spring and autumn: they seem to have lost the instinct to move north and south, and remain in the same areas all year round.

In spite of the obvious nuisance they cause, people fly to their defence if plans for a cull are mooted. In 1993 a proposal by Wandsworth Borough Council to shoot some of the 250 birds that were wrecking Battersea Park aroused strong protests, with people camping out all night in attempts to prevent a cull. Yet action of some kind was essential, for the birds had taken to roosting on the wooded islands in the 8-hectare lake in such numbers that they were destroying the environment. They had killed the vegetation on the islands' banks, were filling the water with unacceptable amounts of nutrient from their droppings, and were fouling the public areas of the park.

In spite of the protests, 200 geese were shot at night, and thereafter the authorities resorted to less violent methods of control, obtaining licences to prick eggs so that they do not hatch. They also fenced off the islands, so that the geese could not gain access to them, and replanted the banks. The result was that the resident population fell to only twenty birds, and local people now accept that some form of control is essential.

Greylag Goose

Anser anser

The largest species of native wild goose, up to 90 cm long, greylags are almost exactly the same as farmyard birds, which are

descended from them. They have orange bills, grey-brown backs barred with white, and pink legs. Birds that breed in Iceland come south to Britain for the winter, grazing on grass and young corn, and sometimes causing severe damage to farm crops. Like other species of geese and swans and ducks, they lose the ability to fly for a few weeks during their summer moult.

White-fronted Goose

Anser albifrons

Superficially like greylags, and about the same size, white-fronts are slightly darker, and distinguishable by the bold white patch on their face, extending from the back of the bill up to the forehead. They breed in the far north, in Greenland and northern Russia, and migrate south in the autumn, arriving in Scotland, Ireland and England during October, or later if the weather remains open.

SWANS

Bewick's Swan

Cygnus columbianus bewickii

Named after the celebrated wood engraver Thomas Bewick, these swans overwinter in Britain after their marathon migration from the Russian Arctic, where they breed. When Sir Peter Scott founded the Wildfowl and Wetlands Trust at Slimbridge on the River Severn in 1948, he soon realised that every Bewick's has a different arrangement of black and yellow markings on its beak, and from these patterns, as precise as fingerprints, he was able to identify thousands of individual birds and keep records of their

7
Birds
Waterbirds

Canada Goose
Bewick's Swan

movements over the years. Thus he knew that the most famous Bewick's of all, Lancelot, made the heroic migration to Nova Zemlaya, where the swans nest on the tundra, 23 times, flying 4000 kilometres to the northeast every spring, and the same back in time for Christmas. Bewick's mate for life, and it was when Lancelot's wife, Elaine, arrived at Slimbridge on her own at Christmas 1986, that staff realised her old consort must at last have gone down.

Bewick's catch the imagination, partly by overcoming the hazards of their great annual migration, partly by the regularity with which they return to base, partly because of their marital fidelity. But why do they (like other swans) make such tremendous journeys?

One theory is that at the end of the last ice age, with the climate warming up, breeding grounds in Europe became congested, and some birds set off in search of more room farther north. They found it on the Russian tundra, where space is unlimited, the summer is short but fierce, food abounds in the form of leaves, grass, rhizomes and tubers, and chicks grow fast because they can feed round the clock in the continuous daylight. Yet those pioneers that explored the Arctic also somehow knew that they must set out for the south before savage winter weather closed in on

them – and so they came back to Europe. The number of Bewick's wintering in Britain and Ireland varies according to the severity of the weather, but often there are 9000 birds on various reserves.

Mute Swan

Cygnus olor

Most of the swans that live in Britain all year round are of this species: snow white, gliding majestically on rivers, lakes and village ponds, with their necks arched in S-shaped curves, they add timeless elegance to any scene, rural or urban. Generally they make no sound, and the fabulous song they are supposed to sing before they die exists only in human imagination. Nor is it true, as superstition relates, that their eggs cannot hatch without a crack of thunder. But they are not as mute as their name suggests; for if annoyed or threatened when nesting, they let go explosive hisses, snorts and trumpetings.

When they want to fly, being big and heavy, they need a long takeoff run: as they gather speed, their wings smack the water and churn up a line of froth until at last they are airborne. In the air, the heavy beat of their wings sets up a

melodious, throbbing hum, which may help to keep individuals in an airborne flock in touch with one another.

All swans were once deemed royal birds, and in Elizabethan times the penalty for stealing an egg was a year and a day's imprisonment, with a fine at the king's discretion. Every year the birds on the Thames were rounded up to be checked and marked, and to this day the ancient practice of swan-upping still takes place in summer, when Her Majesty's Keeper of the Swans, in full nautical regalia, directs operations in which flotillas of punts gradually close in to corral and apprehend indignant victims. A male is still called a cob, a female a pen.

Until recently, many swans were poisoned by eating the lead weights used by anglers to sink their lines. After a government ban on the supply or import of these weights was introduced in 1987, the species began to recover, and the British population is about 7000 breeding pairs.

Whooper Swan

Cygnus cygnus

Like the Bewick's, this is a winter visitor, but more likely to be seen in Scotland and the north of England than in the south. Whoopers are bigger than Bewick's, and differ in that their bills are longer and deeper, and have a larger area of yellow, which extends in a wedge at least to the end of the nostrils.

They, too, are tremendous fliers, and cover vast distances on migration. On 9 December 1967 a party of about 30 whoopers was seen by the pilot of an aircraft over the Inner Hebrides, heading south from Iceland on the way to western Scotland at a altitude of 8230 metres and a speed of nearly 140 km/h. Still more extraordinary than their altitude and velocity was the fact that the temperature of the air in which they had chosen to fly was −48°C.

GREBES

Great Crested Grebe

Podiceps cristatus

Long-necked and elegant, with sharply pointed bills, grey on the back and wings and white on the breast, great crested grebes grow black ear tufts and extraordinary ruffs of chestnut-coloured feathers round their necks and cheeks in summer. They live almost entirely on water, and although they are expert divers, they rarely fly except when migrating. If disturbed, they tend to dive or swim away, rather than take off.

In the nineteenth century they were severely reduced, as they were killed for their skins, but since then they have recovered, encouraged by the proliferation of flooded

7
Birds
Waterbirds

Whooper Swan
Great Crested Grebe

gravel pits, and the number breeding in Britain is thought to be about 8000. The birds are also doing well in Ireland, with 750 pairs breeding on Lough Neagh alone. Although mainly freshwater birds, some winter along sheltered bays and estuaries.

The **Little Grebe** (*Podiceps ruficollis*), also known as the dabchick, is almost as common, but smaller and less spectacular: having a rather dumpy body and lacking ornamentation about the head, it looks like a duck without a tail. Much rarer are the **Black-necked Grebe** (*Podiceps. nigricollis*), with seldom more than 50 pairs breeding, though not all successfully, and the **Slavonian Grebe** (*Podiceps auritus*), with about 40 pairs in recent years. Still more elusive is the **Red-necked Grebe** (*Podiceps grisegena*), of which a single pair is reported to have bred in Scotland. All grebes live on small fish, molluscs and other aquatic creatures, and all are threatened by the spread of feral mink.

Birds of Inland Waters

The term 'inland water' covers a multitude of habitats including rivers and streams, lake and ponds, reservoirs and flooded gravel pits, freshwater marshes and reedbeds, bogs, fens and wet grasslands. Sadly, due to agricultural practices and other development, many wetland areas have been lost: not only the birds that inhabit those areas but all manner of animals have been displaced. The following are simpy a few species that can be found around inland water habitats.

Bittern

Botaurus stellaris

Skulking and secretive, bitterns are hard to see, partly because they lurk in reeds and swampy vegetation, partly because they only emerge at dusk to feed, but also because they have become exceedingly scarce. Once they were common in many parts of Britain, a favourite quarry for falconers, and esteemed as choice birds for the table; but now their only remaining stronghold is in East Anglia, with a few birds in Lancashire and elsewhere.

These members of the heron family are mottled and barred in brown, buff and black: their overall colour is reminiscent of female pheasants, but they are much larger – about 75 cm from head to tail – and they stand very upright, made to look even taller by their long, dagger-like bills, slim heads and elongated bodies. They are celebrated for the loud, booming call – audible from more than 5 km away – that males give out when they display in spring. The sound has been likened to that of someone blowing across the neck of a large bottle, and it has such carrying-power that early ornithologists believed the birds made it with their bills pushed down into the mud – but later observation has shown that they deliver it with the bill held straight upwards.

Because individual birds can now be identified by their voice-prints, the calls can be used to produce accurate counts of the population. In the 1950s there were about 80 males in seven different counties, but numbers fell to their lowest ebb in 1998, when only 11 were left in the entire country, their decline having been caused by a number of factors including reduction of good habitat, lack of food and pollution of the water.

Living mainly on fish and amphibians, bitterns stand still in the water or move slowly forward before stabbing down with their beaks. They are liable to starve in cold winters if the temperature falls low enough for their wetland environment to freeze over. A few birds migrate to England from Europe to escape harsh weather there. Now, though, there are welcome signs of recovery among the resident population. A grant of £1.5 million from the European Union's LIFE programme enabled the RSPB, the Wildlife Trusts and English Nature to launch extensive schemes for the restoration of habitat, including the creation of new reedbeds; and these, backed up by a series of mild winters, brought the number of booming males back to 27 in 2001, causing conservationists to hope that the birds had turned the corner.

Huge excitement greeted the appearance of three bitterns in the the reedbeds of the new Wetland Centre at Barnes in West London, during January 2002: the birds were thought to have been driven from their normal haunts by exceptionally cold weather in France and the Netherlands.

Dipper

Cinclus cinclus

There is something endearing about dippers, which always live near water, typically fast-flowing upland rivers and streams, and have the tubby shape of a wren, although in fact they are the size of small thrushes – about 18 cm long. At rest on a branch or rock, they bob up and down as if on springs, and then whizz across the stream like grey and white bullets, skimming low over the surface with their dark wings going furiously. They are the only songbirds that habitually feed underwater: they wade, swim and dive in search of insects and crustaceans, spreading their wings and lowering their heads underwater so that the flow over their backs pushes them down.

GREY HERON *ARDEA CINEREA* (left)
WHEN NOT FEEDING, HERONS REST
TOGETHER IN FAVOURITE SITES,
OFTEN HUNCHED ON ONE LEG

KINGFISHER *ALCEDO ATTHIS* (below)
RARELY SEEN, BUT MEMORABLE FOR
THOSE WHO CATCH A GLIMPSE OF
DAZZLING COBALT BLUE.

Grey Heron

Ardea cinerea

The grey heron is one of Britain's biggest birds, standing almost 1 metre tall, with a wingspan nearly double that; but so peculiar is its shape – all beak, neck and legs, with a pendant of feathers hanging off the back of its head – that it looks like the result of some cruel practical joke on nature's part. In order to fly it has to double its neck back on itself, and in the air its feet trail far behind its body. Yet it functions perfectly well, and in fact is an efficient predator. Slowly pacing along the bank of a pond, or standing motionless in the shallows, it stabs down on prey with its powerful beak – and woe betide any fish, frog, vole or duckling within range.

For much of the time herons are solitary, going about singly or in pairs. Often in the early morning or late evening they commute between resting and feeding grounds: a single harsh krarnk signals the passage of a lone bird, high overhead, flying with slow, heavy wingbeats. To breed, however, they congregate in large heronries, returning to traditional sites year after year, and refurbishing the enormous nests of sticks and branches left over from previous seasons. The noise of a heronry is prodigious – a continual cacophony of raucous squawks and honks – and the smell never to be forgotten.

The heron was once the falconer's ultimate quarry, and was hunted with peregrines. In Tudor times the bird was carefully preserved and a law was passed forbidding its capture by any means except falconry or long bow. Today it is again protected, and numbers are at the highest level ever.

Kingfisher

Alcedo atthis

Few people are lucky enough to see a kingfisher flash across a pool in a streak of brilliant cobalt blue, with its wings whirring so fast that they are nothing but a blur. In fact the little bird, only 16–17 cm long, is highly coloured – chestnut underparts, white patches on throat and ears, bright red feet – but it is the dazzling blue that takes the eye. Legend has it that the creature was once grey, but that when Noah released it from the ark during or after the Flood, it flew so high that it assumed the colour of the sky, and got its reddish parts by soaring too close to the sun.

Later, observers were struck by the fact that kingfishers never seem to moult (in fact they do, but little by little, so that practically no change in their plumage is visible). This led to the belief that their skins not only did not decay, but had the power of preserving anything with which they were in contact: hence the custom of housewives keeping a skin in linen cupboard or clothes chest. Nor was that the only reason why kingfishers were once persecuted: in the nineteenth century it became all the rage for a lady to sport a stuffed specimen on her hat, and many were killed so that their brilliant feathers could be used for tying fishing flies.

Kingfishers haunt freshwater ponds, lakes, rivers and canals. They perch on any useful eminence, watching for movement in the water below, and then dive suddenly to grab a fish, insect or crustacean in their beaks. If the victim is not dead, they beat it on some hard surface before swallowing it. They nest in chambers hollowed out of sandpits or earth banks, some distance from water.

Moorhen

Gallinula chloropus

From a distance this common freshwater bird looks black, but in fact it has a slatey-grey body with a white stripe along the side, dark olive-brown wings and green legs. On ponds, lakes and rivers it swims about near reedbeds, and takes off after a long, noisy run across the surface, wings thrashing and legs paddling furiously until it is airborne. On land it may scuttle for cover, rather than take off. Often the first indication of its presence is an abrupt, strident and very loud single *kurruk*, which seems to bounce across the water.

Although mostly vegetarian, moorhens also eat small fish, tadpoles, worms, slugs and so on. They build large nests of dead reeds and twigs, lined with grasses and finer vegetation, often attached to clumps growing in the water. If two females lay in the same nest, they may produce 20 mottled eggs between them. Survival rates tend to be low, because young moorhens are preyed on by pike, herons and mink.

The **Coot** (*Fulica atra*) is a larger and more solid version of the moorhen, black all over except for its white bill and frontal shield. It tends to inhabit more extensive stretches of water and to be more gregarious, congregating in large numbers, especially outside the breeding season. It is also a more accomplished diver than the moorhen and a habitual one, diving very often to obtain water plants from up to 7 metres or more below the surface. This is how the coot obtains most of its food, in marked contrast to the moorhen, which feeds mainly on waterside vegetation and on the banks and adjacent land, generally diving only to escape danger.

Coastal and Seabirds

Huge numbers of birds seek food, shelter and breeding grounds around the British coastline, which provides a variety of habitat, including rocky beaches, estuaries and saltmarshes, sandy, muddy and shingly shores and sea cliffs as well as offshore islands and the open sea itself.

Cormorant

Phalacrocorax carbo

With the possible exception of herons, no birds are more disliked by fishermen than cormorants, for these predators have increased enormously since gaining legal protection in Britain in 1967 and Ireland in 1976, and they make serious inroads into fish stocks. The RSPB estimates the summer breeding population in Britain at 7600 pairs, and in winter the British and Irish population reaches over 20,000 individuals, as some birds migrate back and forth between here and the Continent, Denmark and Holland particularly.

Cormorants are not among nature's most elegant creations. With their long, serpentine necks and hefty black bodies, they have a rather sinister appearance; their scientific name comes from two Greek words meaning 'bald-headed raven', and although their heads are not in fact bare, they do tend to have an unkempt look. When one stands on a rock holding out its wings to dry, its angular outline becomes almost prehistoric, like that of a pterodactyl.

In the past, cormorants were often regarded as pests, and were kept down by culling: indeed, during the 1950s the Ministry of Agriculture ran a control scheme, paying a shilling (5p) a beak sent in. Protection has undoubtedly helped the birds increase; but another cause of the inland build-up is that over the past thirty-odd years many coastal waters have become polluted or fished out, so that the cormorants have been forced to seek food elsewhere.

In the same period, the clean-up of sewage and industrial effluent has dramatically improved the quality of lakes and waterways, and this in turn has encouraged freshwater fish to extend their range into the lower reaches of rivers that were once polluted. Estuarine species of fish have moved farther upstream – the

MOORHEN *GALLINULA CHLOROPUS*
(bottom left) MOORHEN FEEDING
HER CHICK IN APRIL.

CORMORANT *PHALACROCORAX CARBO*
(below) THERE ARE ONLY ABOUT 7600
BREEDING PAIRS IN BRITAIN.

salmon now found regularly in the river Thames are an indication of the trend.

British cormorants were traditionally coast-dwellers, nesting on cliffs and offshore islands, and used to come inland only during the winter. In recent years, however, the pattern has shifted, and increasing numbers of birds tend to stay inland all through the year.

These changes have imposed severe pressures on fisheries, not least those in the Lea Valley, which runs south from Hertford to join the Thames in the East End of London. A report published in 1994 called for urgent remedial action, since the number of cormorants recorded in the London area had shot up from 150 in 1954 to 2600 in 1985, and it was estimated that the birds in the Lea Valley alone were eating some 100,000 kg of fish a year. With coarse fish costing £6.50 a kilo, the annual loss suffered by local angling clubs was reckoned to be approaching £750,000.

Aggrieved parties can, in theory, obtain special licences to shoot some of the marauders; between 100 and 200 licences are taken out every year, but each permit allows the holder to cull only five or ten birds, so that the effect of shooting is more to move flocks on than to achieve any significant reduction in numbers. Official policy is that all possible 'non-lethal deterrent measures', such as scaring the birds away with gas-guns, should be tried first, and that refuges for fish, in the form of submerged cages, should be introduced.

There is much dispute about how much fish each bird consumes, the figures given by anglers naturally being far higher than those produced by scientists or ornithologists. A cormorant in captivity gets through about 500 g a day, but fishermen argue that a wild bird burns up far more energy, and eats at least double that amount. What makes matters worse is that hundreds of fish die uneaten from stab-wounds inflicted in botched attacks. Coarse fishermen feel particularly aggrieved, because the evidence suggests that cormorants prefer fish about 20 cm long –

and since most artificially reared trout are bigger than this by the time they are put into lakes and reservoirs, the weight of attack falls on species like bream and roach.

In 1999 and 2000 Martin Read, an angler from South Yorkshire, suffered such damaging attacks at Ravensfield Park, the fishery which he had spent 20 years developing at Rotherham, that in 2001 he drew up a petition calling for a change in the law, to allow the free culling of cormorants, and quickly collected more than 26,000 signatures.

Notwithstanding the nonsense-poem ('The common cormorant or shag/ Lays eggs inside a paper bag'), the **Shag** (*Phalacrocorax aristotelis*) is a separate species, similar to the cormorant, but slightly smaller, and a coastal breeder that is rare inland.

7
Birds
Waterbirds

Cormorant

GANNET *MORUS BASSANA* (left) NESTING IN COLONIES ON CLIFFTOPS, MOSTLY AROUND WESTERN AND NORTHWESTERN COASTS.

GREAT BLACK-BACKED GULLS *LARUS MARINUS* (below) A LARGE PREDATOR OF SEABIRDS, FISH, MICE, RATS AND RABBITS.

BLACK-HEADED GULL *LARUS RIDIBUNDUS* (bottom) ON THE NEST; IT IS OFTEN CONFUSED WITH THE LITTLE GULL.

Gannet

Morus bassanus

Flying over the sea, gannets look exactly what they are: powerful marine predators. Up to 100 cm long, white and streamlined, they have narrow, black-tipped wings, pointed tails and long beaks like daggers. They live almost entirely on fish, and when hunting make spectacular headlong dives into the water, either vertically from as high as 30 metres, or from low level at a shallow angle, slicing deep into the water to reach relatively large prey such as herring or mackerel. They remain at sea the whole year, except during the breeding season which lasts for several months.

They nest in colonies, often thousands strong, generally on cliff ledges. If they overflow on to cliff tops, they are often so closely packed together that the nests may touch each other. Each female lays one egg, and incubation is very slow, taking from 43–45 days. Having being fed by both parents for almost three months, the chick leaves the nest and jumps off the cliff into the sea. At this stage it is so well fed – having been stuffed with oily fish by its parents – that it has no need to eat for the next three weeks.

In the British Isles, most gannet colonies are round the western and northwestern coasts.

Gulls

Several species of gulls live on or about British coasts, and many come inland, especially during rough weather, to settle on fields and lakes, and to scavenge on rubbish tips. A farmer ploughing a field on a tractor is often followed by a cloud of birds wheeling and screaming as they compete for the earthworms and insects turned up.

The largest species is the **Great Black-backed Gull** (*Larus marinus*), which can be identified by its size, its flesh-coloured legs and black back. A ferocious predator, it kills and eats seabirds smaller than itself, fish, mice, rats, rabbits and

even weak lambs. The **Lesser Black-backed Gull** (*Larus fuscus*) is similar in appearance, but noticeably slimmer and smaller, with its back dark slate grey rather than black. Its range of food is almost equally wide, and includes fish, crustaceans, worms, mice, voles, carrion and garbage.

From a distance the **Herring Gull** (*Larus argentatus*) and the **Common Gull** (*Larus canus*) look very much alike, both having white bodies and silvery-grey wings tipped with black and white; but the common gull is a good deal the smaller, with a more slender bill and in general a more delicate appearance. Both species come far inland to feed, pulling up earthworms on arable and grass fields, and raiding refuse tips for scraps.

The **Black-headed Gull** (*Larus ridibundus*) is smaller and

PUFFINS *FRATERCULA ARCTICA* (below) NORMALLY LIVE AT SEA AND BREED MOSTLY ON WESTERN COASTS AND ISLANDS.

ARCTIC TERN *STERNA PARADISAEA* (bottom right) MIGRATION TAKES IT DOWN THE WEST COAST OF AFRICA TO ANTARCTICA.

slighter than the common gull, and can be recognised in its breeding plumage by its dark chocolate hood and dark-red bill and legs. An inveterate food-thief, it often snatches succulent morsels from waterbirds on lakes and lapwings on land, and also grabs insects in flight. The aptly named **Little Gull** (*Larus minutus*), at 26 cm long the world's smallest gull, has a larger, jet-black hood covering the whole head in breeding plumage, which it loses in autumn. It has a more erratic, buoyant, tern-like flight than larger gulls, and often picks insects from the water surface.

The black legs and solid black wingtips of the **Kittiwake** (*Rissa tridactyla*) distinguish it from the common gull, which it otherwise closely resembles. It is less likely to be seen inland than other gulls, generally staying out to sea except during the breeding season, when it nests in colonies on cliff ledges, raising a continuous clamour. Kittiwakes are great followers of ships.

Petrels

Small, very dark birds no bigger than starlings, but with longer wings, petrels look scarcely robust enough for a life spent almost entirely at sea. Yet they come to land only to breed, and then only under cover of darkness. They feed by flying low over the surface, hovering and dipping to snatch tiny fish, other marine creatures and offal from trawlers but never diving.

The **Storm Petrel** (*Hydrobates pelagicus*) looks like a heavily built house martin, with more rounded, swept-back wings and a blunt tail, and with its erratic, twisting flight, interspersed by glides, it often follows ships, fluttering back and forth across the wake. **Leach's Petrel** (*Oceanodroma leucorrhoa*) has more angular and sharply pointed wings, and a forked tail. Both species nest in colonies, often digging burrows out of peaty soil, storm petrels on islands off the west coasts of England, Wales and Scotland, Leach's petrels only on islands in the far northwest. In autumn they move out to sea and spend the winter over the Atlantic.

Puffin

Fratercula arctica

With their portly black and white bodies, orange feet and huge, red-tipped beaks, puffins have an endearingly clownish appearance. They normally live at sea, feeding on fish, but for breeding they come in to turf-topped islands and nest in large colonies, laying their eggs underground in burrows excavated by themselves or appropriated from rabbits or shearwaters. Incubation of the eggs is very slow, lasting for six weeks, and the young are fed by both parents until about 40 days old, when the parents leave them to fast in the nest for several more days, until they flutter out and down to the water.

Most puffin colonies are on western coasts, and Lundy Island, in the Bristol Channel, was once a major stronhold. Before the Second World War 3500 pairs bred there, but now the number of pairs is a dozen or less. The prime suspects blamed for the decline are black rats, which still abound on the island – and since the birds nest in holes, their eggs and chicks are easy meat for the predators.

Terns

Slender, graceful, fork-tailed and predominantly white, with black caps on their heads in breeding plumage, red legs and grey backs and wings, several species of sea-going tern closely resemble one another. Except for the Arctic tern, which reaches Antarctica, the birds winter in Africa but migrate north to breed around British coasts in spring and early summer. When fishing, they fly slowly or hover over the water, then dive at a target, and surface to eat the catch.

The **Common Tern** (*Sterna hirundo*) is primarily sea-going, feeding on fish, crustaceans and molluscs, but in recent years it has shown an increasing tendency to nest inland in colonies around lakes and along rivers, or on the islands in gravel pits. The **Arctic Tern** (*Sterna paradisaea*) is hard to distinguish from the common tern, except when at rest on land: if it stands on a rock, its exceptionally short legs give it away. In flight it looks particularly slim and elegant. The **Roseate Tern** (*Sterna dougallii*) is whiter, has longer tail-feathers, and breeds only at a few sites on the coast. Its name derives from the rosy flush that comes out on its breast during the breeding season. The **Little Tern** (*Sterna albifrons*), apart from being obviously smaller, has yellow legs and a yellow bill tipped with black. Its Latin

specific name – literally 'white front' – refers to the white forehead. Its habit of nesting in shingle beaches right at the edge of the water means its eggs are often washed away by high tides, or covered by wind-blown sand. The **Sandwich Tern** (*Sterna sandvicensis*) can be distinguished by its hefty appearance, black legs and long black bill with yellow tip. In fishing, it dives from a greater height, and so makes a bigger splash when it hits the water. It nests in large colonies, often several hundred pairs strong, mainly on sand dunes, shingle or sandy islands.

The **Black Tern** (*Chlidonias niger*) is a different customer altogether. First, in spring and summer it is sooty-black and slate-grey all over, except for under its tail-coverts, which are white; second, it is much smaller than sea-going terns (about 23 cm long, compared with the common tern's 33 cm); and third, it breeds around marshes, fens and reedy lakes, rather than on the coast. In summer it lives mainly on insects and small aquatic creatures, but at other times relies on fish.

OYSTERCATCHERS *HAEMATOPUS OSTRALEGUS* (top left) HABITUALLY NEST ON THE COAST, BUT HAVE STARTED TO MOVE INLAND.

REDSHANK, *TRINGA TOTANUS* (bottom left) BREEDS IN WET MEADOWS AND ON COASTAL SALTMARSHES.

DUNLIN *CALIDRIS ALPINA* (below) MOST ABUNDANT OF ALL COASTAL WADERS IN WINTER, ESPECIALLY IN WINTER.

CURLEW *NUMENIUS ARQUATA* (bottom) LARGEST OF ALL EUROPEAN WADERS, WITH A VERY LONG, DOWN-CURVED BILL THAT PROBES MUD FOR FOOD.

WADERS

Curlew

Numenius arquata

The long, bubbling trill of the curlew is one of the most magical sounds of the uplands, the spirit of wide open spaces. Although a wader, and found in great numbers outside the breeding season on the shore, this long-legged bird, with its long curved bill and streaky brown plumage, is also at home on high moors and rough farmland, probing the ground for worms and insects. Along the coast it congregates in large flocks, but inland it is more likely to be single or in nesting pairs. In earlier years it nested only on high ground, but it has recently shown a tendency to move on to farmland.

Dunlin

Calidris alpina

Elegant dunlin are easily the most common waders on our estuaries in winter: at low tide they scurry about the mudflats on their rather short legs, probing with their beaks for worms and molluscs. Yet relatively few – fewer than 10,000 pairs – breed in Britain, and those that do nest here are harassed by predators, including feral American mink which recently appeared on the Hebridean islands of North and South Uist. In winter dunlin are mostly grey-backed and white-breasted, but in spring, during the breeding season, adults develop brighter colours – dark streaks on the chest, a black patch on the belly, and mottled brown and black on the upper side of the wings.

Oystercatcher

Haematopus ostralegus

This large, sturdy-legged wader is unmis-takable, because its colour scheme is so bold: black head, black neck and back, white underparts, and bright orange-red bill and eye-ring and reddish-pink legs. The oystercatchers' insistent, piping calls are one of the features of the foreshore, where they feed on ragworms and other invertebrates as well as their staple diet of mussels and cockles which they prise off the rocks and open by inserting their beaks between the two halves of the shell. The breeding population is about 38,000 pairs, and the birds, which once nested only on the coast, increasingly breed inland.

Redshank

Tringa totanus

A medium-sized long-legged wader, the redshank looks quite dark when standing or walking, but when displaying or landing it reveals the bright, white underside of its wings. A restless and noisy bird, it bobs up and down when suspicious, in typical sandpiper fashion. Redshank feed on beaches, saltmarshes and estuaries, reservoirs and on sewage farms and flooded fields, probing in mud or water for worms and crustaceans.

7

Birds
Waterbirds

Curlew
Redshank

An acrimonious debate
has arisen between those
who shoot grouse and
those who wish to
preserve the dwindling
numbers of raptors that
prey on gamebirds

The Langholm Debate

LANGHOLM is a 12,000-acre grouse moor in Dumfriesshire, belonging to the Duke of Buccleuch, and in the last years of the twentieth century it became the focus of acrimonious debate between shooting men on the one hand and the Royal Society for the Protection of Birds on the other.

In 1992 the Duke offered the moor as the site for a study designed to settle one key question: can birds of prey such as hen harriers and peregrine falcons make serious inroads into grouse stocks? Under the auspices of the government's advisory body, Scottish Natural Heritage, a team of researchers from the Game Conservancy Trust and the Institute of Terrestrial Ecology closely monitored the estate as its five gamekeepers went about their normal business, burning heather in patches to bring on fresh growth, and culling foxes and crows, but leaving protected raptors strictly alone. One of the bodies funding the research was the RSPB, which naturally took a close interest.

The study proved what the keepers had been saying all along: that raptors were having a lethal effect on Langholm's grouse. In five years the number of resident breeding female hen harriers rose from 2 to 14, and that of peregrine falcons doubled from 3 to 6. In the same period the seasonal bag of grouse declined from 4000 to 100, and instead of earning enough income to pay for its management, the moor became unviable. On other moors nearby bags remained much the same.

The findings of the study were extremely unpalatable to the RSPB, which champions the total protection of birds of prey. Publication of the Langholm report was repeatedly delayed as conservationists haggled over details of the text, but when it finally appeared in November 1997, it pinned the blame firmly on hen harriers at Langholm, which had killed 30 per cent of the breeding grouse every spring, 37 per cent of the chicks every summer and 30 per cent of the surviving birds every autumn.

What was to be done? Everyone concerned agreed that, in the prevailing climate of opinion, licensed culling of raptors was not an option; but, faced with unassailable evidence, the Game Conservancy produced an ingenious plan whereby hen harrier eggs would be taken from some nests under licence, the chicks reared artificially, and grown birds released on other moors where (in theory) they could live on their other staple foods, principally meadow pipits and voles. According to Dr Dick Potts, the Conservancy's Director, the aim was threefold: to increase the overall number of hen harriers overall, to relieve the pressure on Langholm and make it a viable shooting moor again, and on a wider front to reassure gamekeepers that harriers and grouse can coexist. The RSPB, however, declined to endorse any such scheme

Another suggested innovation, which was put into practice, was that of experimental 'buffer feeding'. For two summers the hen harriers at Langholm were pampered with supplies of white rats and day-old chicks, delivered to their nest sites daily. In 1998 alone nearly 250 kg of food was put out for them, and the birds soon learnt to snatch the offerings off fenceposts. The cost of the food itself was minimal, but the expense of distributing it ran into thousands of pounds: even on a quad bike, it took a man up to 7 hours to get round 10 nest sites. The experiment convinced Simon Thirgood, head of raptor research at the Game Conservancy, and leader of the Langholm study, that although such artificial feeding may help save some grouse, it could never be viable in the long term.

The shooting fraternity felt that the whole of the Langholm inquiry had been wasted. But in the words of the late Gareth Lewis, who was then factor (or agent) for the estate, 'The point about the study was that it brought together people who won't normally speak to each other, and provided a forum for informed debate.'

Ornithologists pointed out, unofficially, that the population of harriers at Langholm had built up rapidly during the period in which the gamekeepers were under constant observation, and therefore unable to take action against them – for instance by destroying their nests.

Meanwhile the moor itself was dying. Some fox control was still carried out for the benefit of surrounding farmers, and some heather burning was still being done in the hope that one day things might return to normal. But the golden plover and wheatears soon disappeared, grouse sank to a low ebb, and the number of passerines such as meadow pipits and skylarks fell drastically. Brian Mitchell, the former head keeper, calculated that in 1997 harriers must have killed 20,000 of them. Of the five gamekeepers who used to work on the estate, one died, one took early retirement, two were redeployed onto control of deer and rabbits, and one went to another estate.

Even the RSPB agrees that management of the habitat for shooting, provided gamekeepers do not cull raptors illegally, is the best regime for the uplands: regular burning promotes good heather, keeps bracken and coarse grasses at bay, prevents invasion by trees and provides a perfect habitat for many birds besides grouse. Also, shooting brings much-needed money into remote areas. It is not just that rich marksmen pay up to £100 a brace to shoot driven grouse, thereby providing the wages of keepers and beaters. They also stay in local hotels and their wives spend freely in nearby shops, contributing substantially to the local economy.

Langholm lost all these advantages and the Duke's magnanimous gesture in lending his moor for the experiment was disastrously rewarded.

8 FISH

For people living on the sea-
shore or close to inland rivers and lakes,
fish have been an important source of food
since time immemorial. The Mesolithic
wanderers who came up out of Europe at the
end of the final ice age ate molluscs by the
thousand, as well as any more mobile fish they
could catch by setting out primitive traps made of
wickerwork, by casting spears into the water, draining pools or building dams and stockades.

Apart from being nutritious, fish and shellfish were
thought to have medicinal properties. In the Middle
Ages people believed that anyone bitten by a rabid dog
could be saved by pickled fish, 'applied topically'. The
brains of a dogfish boiled in oil were a sure remedy for
toothache, and burning lint greased with dolphin's fat
was supposed to end any woman's fit of hysterics.

It is impossible to tell at what date fishing evolved from
a necessity into a sport. The earliest book on the subject –
The Treatise of Fishing with an Angle – was written in about
1420 and published in 1496, but the content makes it clear
that angling for amusement was already well established,
and had been practised for centuries. One of the fascina-
tions of that early text is the fact that it seems to have
been the work of a nun and a noblewoman, Dame Juliana
Berners, who gently and humorously extolled fishing as
the finest field sport, free from the vexations suffered by
huntsmen, fowlers and falconers.

Two centuries passed before the appearance of another
major work on the subject, and then came easily the best-
known English work on fishing, Izaak Walton's *The Compleat
Angler, or The Contemplative Man's Recreation*, which was
published in 1653 and has been reprinted several hundred
times since. The author, born in 1593, was apprenticed to
an ironmonger, and by the time he was 21 had a business
of his own; but at heart he was a poet and writer, and he

Freshwater Fish

produced several biographies, including a life of his fishing companion, the cleric and poet John Donne. *The Compleat Angler* still enchants, with its enthusiasm not just for the river, but for all outdoor recreation; and the leisurely conversations between the three main characters – Piscator (the fisherman), Venator (the hunter) and Auceps (the birdcatcher) – have a timeless charm.

Today fishing is easily the most popular field sport in Britain, although it is hard to determine exactly how many people take part. Angling organisations claim that more than 3 million people regularly go down to the water, but nowhere near that number buy licences. In 2001 the Environment Agency issued 1,120,000 annual licences for coarse fish and non-migratory trout at £21 each and a further 112,000 junior licences at £5. Licences for salmon and sea trout (at £60) numbered only 24,350. (No licences are needed in Scotland.) Many anglers took out permits for shorter periods, but coarse fishing in general is thought to be in decline, with youngsters glued to computer monitors rather than drawn by the lure of river, canal or lake.

Most anglers think of salmon, brown trout and sea trout as game fish, and regard other species as coarse. But many practitioners would count charr and grayling as game fish – so classification is imprecise. Yet there is no doubt that the salmon is still king of the river. As Dame Juliana remarked 550 years ago, 'the salmon is the most stately fish that any man can angle for in fresh water' – and that remains so to this day. Purists lament the artificial stocking of rivers and lakes with species like rainbow trout, but the income generated by fishing enables owners to keep their water in good order.

Coarse fishermen have little interest in eating their catch. Clubs compete keenly with each other in matches; captives are put into keep-nets and carefully weighed at the end of the day, before being returned to the water.

During the last decades of the twentieth century immense amounts of work and investment went into the cleaning up of inland waterways, and in many rivers the habitat for fish was greatly improved. Salmon once again began to run up the Thames, and in November 2001 three were caught in the Mersey, in which no such fish had been recorded for years. Yet sometimes the reduction of low-level pollution had the effect of reducing fish populations. From the 1950s to the mid-1980s the Ribble and the Trent Rivers regularly yielded large bags of coarse fish: 50 kg catches of roach and chub were by no means rare. But over-purification of the water reduced the amount of food in the rivers (mainly invertebrates), and made such large hauls impossible. Acid rain, pesticides running off farm land and the excessive abstraction of water all pose further threats to fish stocks.

Britain and Ireland have a wide variety of freshwater environments. In the north and west of Scotland small spate rivers rise rapidly after rainstorms, and then fall as quickly. In the south, bigger rivers such as the Thames and the Severn maintain a steadier flow. Many of the canals that thread the landscape are being restored, as are village ponds, and the area of water is expanding as worked out gravel pits are flooded, creating new habitats for fish and other aquatic life.

Atlantic Salmon

Salmo salar

King of British game fish, the salmon is immensely valuable, not simply for its succulent pink flesh, but because anglers are prepared to pay fortunes for a chance to catch it. On great rivers like the Spey, Tweed and Findhorn in Scotland, and the Test and Wye in England and Wales, demand for beats is intense: every fish caught is worth between £6000 and £8000 in fees alone, and the total market value of the sport in Scotland is over £400 million a year.

If salmon were easy to catch, their mystique would no doubt diminish; but their magic is increased by the fact that they are capricious and unpredictable, and that much about their lifecycle remains mysterious. During the autumn the fish migrate upstream to the headwaters of the river in which they were born, leaping up falls and churning through shallow runs to reach the gravel beds known as redds high up in the streams or burns. There a mature hen salmon wriggles to create a groove or trench, in which she lays her spawn – maybe 2000 eggs for every kilo of her weight, or 10,000 for a 5-kg fish. A male salmon fertilises the spawn by depositing his milt on it; the spent fish, known as kelts, drift back downriver, but few survive long enough to breed again.

When the eggs hatch in the following March, in their first stage of life they are known as alevins – tiny, translucent creatures, each with its own supply of food in a sac attached to its throat. In a month or so the alevins emerge from the gravel as fry, and these in turn grow into parr, camouflaged by vertical stripes or fingermarks on their sides (parr was an old English word for 'finger'). Depending on the habitat, this phase lasts from one to

TROUT AT WINCHESTER (previous pages) BY VALENTINE THOMAS GARLAND (fl. 1867–1914).

ATLANTIC SALMON *SALMO SALAR* (below) WILD SALMON MAKES A DIFFICULT JOURNEY TO ITSPAWNING STREAM.

three years, and during that time the tiny fish – only about 10 cm long, and decorated with bright-red spots – take up individual territories, each hiding under a stone on the river bed. They prey on insect larvae and other very small living organisms, but in turn they are heavily preyed-on – by other fish (not least brown trout), by otters, mink and birds such as herons, cormorants and mergansers.

At the next stage, the parr smolt – that is, they change into smolts, turning silver, whereupon they become gregarious and start to migrate downstream in shoals. Having congregated in the estuary, they are attacked by many new enemies (gulls, seals, other fish, including conger eels); but the survivors leave the river and disappear out to sea, where they feed on smaller fish and crustaceans, and grow rapidly to 20 or 30 times their original weight before returning to their own river to breed. A fish that comes back after only one winter at sea is known as a grilse, and may already weigh 6 kg; but many salmon do not return until they have spent four or five winters in the ocean. They apparently find their own river from the taste of the water coming down it; but how do they navigate in the open sea and round the coast? Why, since they stop eating when they re-enter fresh water, do they sometimes take the flies and other lures that fishermen cast over them? Why have many of the biggest fish taken on rod-and-line been caught by women? And why, above all, did catches of wild salmon decline catastrophically in the last quarter of the twentieth century?

One main agent of destruction has undoubtedly been salmon farming, which began in the 1970s and has since

8
Fish
Freshwater Fish

Atlantic Salmon

grown into a major industry. Most of it takes place on the northwest coast of Scotland, where salmon are reared from the smolt stage in cages, in the sea lochs into which many Highland rivers flow; and nobody now disputes that the artificial cultivation of fish has had a disastrous effect on native stocks. The figures speak for themselves. In 1983 Scottish waters produced 1220 tons of wild salmon and 4000 tons of farmed. By 1999 the wild catch had fallen to 200 tons – about 55,000 fish – but industrial production had soared to 127,000 tons, or 70 million salmon.

Damage is inflicted in several ways. Farmed fish, living in unhealthy concentrations, attract immense numbers of sea-lice, crustaceans which bore through the skin and into the flesh, eating the host alive. To control the parasites, operators use toxic pesticides: these pollute the sea lochs but do not kill all the lice, which infest young salmon and (particularly) sea trout on their way to the ocean.

Almost worse is the threat posed by escapees. Cages are often broken open by storms, and it is reckoned that in in the year 2000 alone nearly 500,000 salmon escaped. These farmed fish, not being tied to any particular river, lack the homing instincts of their wild cousins, and by milling around in estuaries upset the natural pattern of migration, and by mating with wild fish progressively weaken age-old genetic instincts. A further hazard of farming is that high stocking densities increase the incidence of diseases such as infectious salmon anaemia, which was apparently imported from Norway during 1998 and forced Scottish operators to destroy 4 million fish.

Enormous efforts are being made to revitalise stocks of wild salmon. On many rivers groups of riparian owners have bought out the firms which once had the right to net the estuaries. The movements of salmon up- and down-stream are being studied by tagging and radio-telemetry. On more and more rivers anglers are required to put back the fish they catch, or to keep only one at most. In the headwaters of catchment areas much work is being done to improve habitat, by stabilising the banks of tributaries, increasing the flow of streams and clearing fallen timber and other rubbish from gravel beds, to provide good conditions for spawning.

And yet, whatever man can achieve on land or in fresh water, he cannot control the salmon's marine environment. The greatest worry, now, is that so few fish are returning from the sea, and that the reason may be long-term climate change. It is thought that warm water, drifting up into the Atlantic, is pushing the salmon's cold-water feeding grounds further north, with the result that many fish either do not reach the rich feeding areas at all, or never gain the size and strength they need to complete the long journey home.

Charr

Salvelinus alpinus

Members of the salmon family, charr are found in the deep lakes of Scotland, Ireland, North Wales and the Lake District. Unlike Arctic charr, (a subspecies of *Salvelinus alpinus*) which migrate to the sea to feed and enter rivers to spawn, lake charr remain in fresh water all their lives. They are thought to be descended from migratory stock which was cut off from the sea towards the end of the last ice age, when moraines from melting glaciers dammed outlets and formed land-locked stretches of water.

They usually live deep down, and have been found in Loch Ness 130 metres beneath the surface. They feed on tiny crustaceans, insect larvae and small fish, including baby perch; they reach a length of about 35 cm and a weight of 0.75 kg, and are themselves eaten by salmon and trout. The British lake most celebrated for its charr is Windermere: in earlier days potted charr was a speciality of the Lake District.

Trout

Salmo trutta

Many anglers suppose that brown trout and sea trout are different species; yet although the two behave quite differently, there is no genetic variation between them. The first remain in fresh rivers or lakes all their lives, whereas the second, like salmon, migrate to sea to feed and grow into adults, returning later to breed.

Both are highly prized by fishermen as sporting quarry, and dry-fly fishing – casting an imitation fly, so that it lands as softly on the water as a real insect, and in the right place – is reckoned the highest piscatorial art. A few people still practise the old poachers' trick of tickling trout – of lying on the river bank above a resting fish, lowering an arm stealthily into the water, and stroking the trout's belly until, with a sudden grab, it can be seized round the body in front of the tail and flipped up on to the bank.

Trout spawn in much the same way as salmon. In November and December they move upstream to deposit and fertilise their eggs in gravel beds. The eggs hatch into alevins, which then become fry and, in due course, parr. After a period that varies from one year to four, fish destined to become sea trout grow silver skins, and, as smolts, go downriver to the sea; but those that remain in fresh water take on adult trout colouring without going through a smolt stage.

For most of the year river trout are solitary, each fish keeping to its own lie, which may extend to only about 1 by 3 metres, and chasing away lesser fish that intrude.

BROWN TROUT *SALMO TRUTTA* (below)
BROWN TROUT LIVE THEIR ENTIRE
LIFESPAN IN FRESH WATER, WITHOUT
GOING THROUGH A SMOLT STAGE.

SEA TROUT *SALMO TRUTTA* (bottom)
GENETICALLY IDENTICAL TO BROWN
TROUT, SEA TROUT MIGRATE TO SEA
TO FEED AND MATURE.

reservoirs are artificially restocked with reared fish, both brown and rainbow, which are easier to catch.

On the west coasts of Scotland and Ireland sea trout have been severely reduced by the damaging effects of salmon farming (*see page 320*). When smolts migrate to the sea, they tend to stay in inshore waters, rather than head for the deep ocean, and this makes them more susceptible than salmon to the ravages of sea-lice. Numerous fish have returned to rivers eaten to the backbone, little more than living skeletons.

Rainbow Trout

Oncorhynchus mykiss

The west coast of North America is the natural home of the rainbow trout, and the first consignment of eggs to reach England, which arrived at the National Fish Culture Association in Buckinghamshire in February 1884, was sent by the Blair Trout Hatchery on the McCloud River in northern California. Over the next 40 years large numbers of rainbows

Food is brought to it by the current – insect nymphs and larvae, drowned flies and freshwater shrimps.

The chalk streams of southern England, steadily fed from subterranean aquifers, are far richer in food than the spate rivers of the north, and so produce much larger fish. In 1822 the Wiltshire Avon yielded a trout of 11.4 kg; but this was an exceptional monster, and today a fish of 2 kg is considered excellent. Trout in spate rivers grow much more slowly, and rarely attain the same size as less active fish. For many fishermen, wild brown trout remain the ultimate quarry, because they are so difficult to outwit; but today most commercially managed rivers, lakes and

were liberated in lakes and rivers all over England and Wales, and a survey conducted in 1940 found that they were present in more than 50 waters (only one of which was in Ireland.) Follow-up research carried out in 1971 showed that rainbows had spread to nearly 500 waters, of which 21 were in Northern Ireland and eight in the Republic. By the end of the century, rainbow trout had been introduced to over 800 waters throughout Britain; even so there are fewer than 50 naturalised breeding populations in Britain; the other populations being augmented by restocking to keep up the numbers.

In the wild, rainbows breed in chalk streams, and some

RAINBOW TROUT *ONCORHYNCHUS MYKISS* (previous pages) AN INTRO-DUCED TROUT FROM THE WEST COAST OF NORTH AMERICA.

CARP *CYPRINUS CARPIO* (below) ALSO AN INTRODUCED SPECIES FROM ASIA, PROBABLY BROUGHT TO EUROPE BY THE ROMANS.

are *anadromous* (literally, running up), migrating to sea to feed before returning to fresh water to spawn. These are known as 'steel-heads'; but other varieties spend their entire lives in lakes and rivers.

Feral rainbow trout grow faster than brown trout – which makes them an attractive proposition for the owners of commercial fisheries – reaching a maximum length of 35 cm and a weight of 3–4 kg. They can be distinguished from native trout and salmon by the colour of their tail-fins, which are covered with strong black spots on a pale background, and also by the bright, rose-pink bands along the sides of their silvery bodies.

Barbel

Barbus barbus

The Thames in London used to be alive with barbel, and the Victorian writer William Yarrell recorded that 150 lbs weight (68 kg) of them were once caught in five hours at Shepperton and Walton. These powerful, bronze-backed fish – members of the carp family – are still a prime target for anglers. Their name derives from the four barbels (or barbules), slim, finger-like projections which hang from their mouths, a short pair from near the tip of the nose, and a longer pair from the angle of the jaw. These are sensors that register touch and taste to guide the fish when they are feeding on the bottom in deep, fast-flowing rivers. Barbel's size alone make them an attractive proposition for fishermen: they run up to 7 or 8 kg – but their fitness for the table is a matter of debate, and most people consider their flesh too muddy to bother with. Various sources have stated that the eggs or ovaries of barbel are poisonous and that they are not considered edible.

Bream

Abramis brama

Like barbel, bream are bottom-feeders, and suck in such delicacies as worms, snails, midge larvae and water hog-lice as they forage with their mouths extended into feeding-tubes. Clouds of mud rising to the surface in lakes or slow-moving rivers often betray the fact that a shoal of them is at work below. Bream are handsome, but have a faintly ridiculous shape, being (when seen from the side) too deep for their length. A small head leads into a body that is exceptionally deep from top to bottom, but also flat-sided. They grow up to 80 cm long and can weight 5 kg.

Carp

Cyprinus carpio

There is much dispute about who introduced carp to Britain: some fishermen believe they were indigenous in eastern-flowing rivers, which were once connected with the Rhine. Carp are native to Asia from Manchuria west to Black Sea rivers. For centuries the fish were a staple food in monasteries, convents and other religious institutions which observed days of abstinence from meat. They were kept in stew ponds (large artificial ponds or tanks for keeping fish for eating purposes). Today carp are rarely eaten in Britain, and have a reputation for tasting muddy; but evidence discovered in the 1960s by Jack Hatt, a farmer and hydraulic engineer, showed that early monks had elaborate systems for raising the fish, and that careful husbandry almost certainly improved their flavour.

During the 1960s Mr Hatt was asked to investigate some old stew ponds at Weston Park near Telford, by the owner, Lord Bradford. Research on the site and in Poland revealed that in the tenth or eleventh centuries Polish monks came across to demonstrate their methods. Seven lakes on the estate were drained in rotation, one every year, the fish being graded and moved to other waters. When a lake had dried out, barley was planted in its bed, and harvested that autumn. Dung was then spread on the stubble, and the lake was refilled. Carp wanted for eating were placed in special tanks, set in a wall between two stew ponds, and for three weeks they were purged by living in a flow of fresh spring water and feeding on barley meal.

Feral carp favour lakes with slow-moving or still water and a muddy bottom, surrounded by dense vegetation. Feeding on worms, snails, algae, seeds, midge larvae, crustaceans and water fleas, they live for 40 years or more and grow to a substantial size, reaching a length of 90 cm and a weight of over 25 kg. Anglers testify to their apparent intelligence: seasoned carp have often been seen herding innocent younger fish away from anglers' baits.

In southern England the hen fish spawns in May or June, depositing up to a million eggs on aquatic plants – and these, if the water is warm enough (between 18°C and 20°C) hatch out a few days later. In winter, as the water temperature falls, the fish's metabolism slows down to a point at which it almost goes into hibernation. That, at least, is what used to happen. With the onset of global warming and milder winter weather, carp now keep eating all year round, with the result that the record weight for Britain is constantly rising. In 1980, when the leading expert Chris Yates caught a monster weighing 23.4 kg, the fraternity was amazed, because he had beaten the previous record by no less than 4.5 kg. Yet now the record has crept up to 26.8 kg, and everyone is agog to see who pushes it over 27 kg.

The presence of a leviathan in a particular lake acts as an irresistible magnet. Rumours of a big carp being spotted flash round the angling community, and within hours people are seeking permission to fish the water. Even if the big fellow has been caught many times before, the mere chance of getting him on the line is enough to attract anglers from far and wide. As for the idea of eating such a captive – it is unthinkable. 'It would be like eating my own brother,' says Chris Yates. 'I just shake him by the fin, apologise for inconveniencing him, wish him good luck, and send him on his way.'

European Catfish *or* Wels

Silurus glanis

The biggest freshwater fish in Europe, these catfish were introduced to a few English lakes towards the end of the nineteenth century, and they have bred here for more than 100 years, especially in the lakes at Claydon in Buckinghamshire. In eastern Europe and Russia they grow to a colossal size – up to 300 kg – but here a 20-kg fish is considered a good one. No beauty, the 'cat' has a wide, gaping mouth, with a slightly protruding lower jaw. Two long barbels, or feelers, grow from its upper jaw, and four shorter ones trail from behind its lower lip. The name 'Wels' is a corruption of the German *wälzen*, to wallow, and refers to its habit of wallowing in mud as it feeds on the bottom. Being a night-

WHITE-CLAWED CRAYFISH *AUSTRO-POTAMOBIUS PALLIPES* (below) A RELATIVE OF THE MARINE LOBSTER.

COMMON EEL, *ANGUILLA ANGUILLA* (opposite) MATURE EELS GROW TO A LENGTH OF ABOUT 50 CM.

feeder, the catfish has small eyes: it also has a voracious appetite, eating fish, water voles, moorhens and ducks.

Chub

Leuciscus cephalus

Gluttonous habits make the boldly biting chub easy to catch: they have been taken with an amazing variety of baits, including frogs, flies, cheese, dough, sultanas, bacon rind, snails and water voles. They are sizeable fish – about 40 cm long and weighing 2–3 kg, and so make tempting targets for anglers, especially as they tend to live in shoals. Unfortunately – as experts from Izaak Walton onward have reported – they are all but inedible: to Walton their flesh was 'not firm, but short and tasteless'.

Crayfish

Austropotamobius pallipes

Not a fish but a freshwater crustacean, this crayfish is a small relative of the marine lobster. The white-clawed or native crayfish live mainly in clear, fast, shallow rivers, tucking themselves into holes in the banks, under stones or between submerged tree roots. They are a dull greeny-brown, usually less than 10 cm long and equipped with five pairs of legs: these enable them to walk about the bottom, but they can also swim backwards by flicking their tails. They are scavengers and predators, able to grab snails, insect larvae and dead or dying fish with their claws and tear them apart. They are also cannibals: young crayfish

often devour others, especially when the victims are moulting their shells.

Much damage has been done to home stocks by the importation of the American **Signal Crayfish** (*Pacifastacus leniusculus*) which is larger and more aggressive than our own. At one stage these aliens were advertised as a fine commercial proposition: owners of ponds were incited to farm them, and assured that they would quickly make enormous profits. What nobody realised was that the crayfish are amphibious: on wet nights they clamber out, crawl overland into streams, and so spread out of control, eradicating the natives by killing them, eating them or merely driving them off their own territory, and devastating the environment with their habit of clipping off weed near the bed of the waterway. Besides, the immigrants brought with them a fungal disease so deadly that it has quickly wiped out several populations of native crayfish.

Eel

Anguilla anguilla

It is well known that baby eels, known in Britain as elvers, hatch in the Sargasso Sea, thousands of kilometres out in the Atlantic. But nobody knows how these tiny, translucent, flattened worm-like creatures navigate across the ocean. It is thought that they can change their buoyancy, and so to some extend control their depth, but they do not appear to have any means of steering, except by rising or falling into different currents, rather as hot-air balloon pilots can change direction by seeking higher or lower airstreams. They come into British rivers like the Severn as 'glass eels' and drift upstream on incoming tides, to grow to maturity in fresh water. However they manage it, they arrive here in March, and keep coming until May, and every night men are out along the banks of rivers, trying to scoop up the elvers in fine mesh nets, for they are now almost worth their weight in gold. In earlier times, when no wider market was available, country families would practically live on them during the season, either fried and scrambled with egg, or made up into a kind of fishy bread. Boys would go round the cottages selling their surplus stocks for sixpence (2½ p) a pound. In the Gloucestershire village of Frampton-on-Severn

elver-eating contests were staged every year, and in 1972 the winner, Les Coole, established a record by devouring a pound in 32 seconds.

Then, early in the 1980s, the whole nature of elvering was undermined by the appearance of middlemen, who began to buy up catches live and export them all over the world for breeding and restocking rivers. The price rocketed past that of smoked salmon until it almost rivalled that of caviar: at £60 per kg, no local could afford to eat a single elver, let alone a plateful, and the annual competitions were abandoned.

During the 1980s catches fell disastrously; and although some people blamed overfishing, experts pointed out that the decline had set in too early for that to be a major cause – for a male eel takes seven years to reach maturity in a river, and a female 15. Fishermen and conservationists alike hoped that eel numbers would pick up again, and that elvers would continue to make their mysterious way across the ocean.

Mature eels grow to a length of about 50 cm. They live in rivers, lakes and canals, and can reach isolated ponds by crawling overland; but they cannot ascend waterfalls or dams. They feed mainly at night, eating invertebrates, small fish and decaying animal remains. In summer they are olive-brown on the back and yellow on the belly, but in autumn these colours change to black and silver as they head back to salt water and begin their long journey to their spawning grounds.

Their oily flesh is excellent to eat, especially when smoked. In earlier times generations of countrymen believed that the best way of avoiding cramp was to wear an eel-skin garter round the calf, next to the skin – and it was reckoned that anyone addicted to alcohol could be cured by slipping a live eel into his drink.

Goldfish (Asiatic)

Carassius auratus

It is thought that the first goldfish to reach Britain came on board a ship of the East India Company which sailed from Macao in September 1691 and berthed in London next spring. Importations of these exotic creatures increased steadily during the early eighteenth century, and among the first English fanciers was Horace Walpole (later the fourth Earl of Orford), the Member of Parliament, collector, publisher and author who lived at Strawberry Hill in Twickenham, and kept goldfish in his garden pond. 'They breed with me excessively, and are grown to the size of small perch,' he wrote to a friend in June 1752. 'There are some Mandarin cats fishing for goldfish, which will delight you.'

Goldfish are long-lived: there are records of them surviving for 30 years in captivity, and, like most pets, they sometimes weary their owners, who dump them in the nearest pond or stream. As a result, many rivers (including the Thames at London and the Kennet in Berkshire) now have populations of feral goldfish, as do innumerable ponds and lakes all over Britain.

Grayling

Thymallus thymallus

Sometimes known as 'the lady of the stream', the grayling is an elegant cousin of the salmon and trout, distinguished by its high, swept-back dorsal fin, like a sail horizontally banded with delicate stripes of orange, green and black. The fish reach a length of 30–40 cm and a top weight (in Britain) of 2 kg. They live mainly in the middle reaches of rivers which have deep pools between shallow runs, but they also inhabit clean lakes. Unlike salmon and trout, they spawn in spring, and males compete vigorously, raising clouds of spray, for the privilege of fertilising a female's eggs as she deposits them on gravel.

Although grayling feed mainly on invertebrates on the the beds of lakes and rivers, when flies are hatching on the surface of the water, they go shooting up to snatch one, before returning to station near the bottom. They are one of the most sought-after quarry fish, not least because they are excellent to eat, and they are now widespread in Britain, after many introductions to rivers in the west and north.

Lamprey

One of the few useless bits of knowledge retained by many schoolboys is that in 1135 AD King Henry I supposedly died of a surfeit of lampreys. Certainly, lampreys were considered a delicacy for thousands of years: witness the enormous numbers of their teeth found in Viking latrines. In England they were caught in eel nets or basket traps, and were still a valuable commodity in Victorian times.

In 1894 the dignitaries of Gloucester City Council revived an ancient custom and sent a lamprey pie to Queen Victoria at Balmoral; in return they received a hand-written note saying that the dish had been served for lunch and dinner in the castle, and that the queen had enjoyed it. In 1953 and 1977 Gloucester repeated the gesture, sending pies to the present Queen to mark her coronation and Silver Jubilee; but there is no record to show that anyone at Buckingham Palace dared tackle the offerings, let alone that anybody enjoyed them.

Fossil remains show that these primitive, eel-like creatures have existed for 450 million years or more, and that in all those aeons they have scarcely evolved at all. They are fish-like vertebrates, without jaws, scales or paired fins, but with funnel-shaped, sucking mouths and protrusible tongues equipped with horny teeth. They also have seven gill openings, or breathing holes, on either side of the head. Medieval Germans supposed these openings to be eyes, and so, counting in the real eyes, they called lampreys *Neunaugen* – 'Nine-eyes', the name which the creatures retain to this day in Germany. (The arithmetic is faulty: with seven breathing-holes and one eye on each side of the body, the total should be 16.)

Three species exist in Britain: the **Sea lamprey** (*Petromyzon marinus*), the **River lamprey** or **Lampern** (*Lampetra fluviatilis*), and the **Brook lamprey** (*Lampetra planeri*). All spawn in fresh water, spending their first five to eight years there; during this larval period they are known as *prides*, and they live in mud or sand at the bottom of pools, feeding on organic matter and bacteria, which they strain from their immediate surroundings.

Sea lampreys (*Petromyzon marinus*) grow to be heavily mottled with grey or brown on their backs; they reach a length of 90 cm and weighing up to 2 kg. As adults they migrate to the sea, and there fasten on to a variety of host fish, including haddock, cod and salmon. Parasites, the lampreys clamp their large mouths on to victims and use their muscular, toothed tongues to rasp off patches of flesh, reducing it to pulp, and at the same time sucking out the host's blood and vital juices until the fish dies or turns inside out.

After two or three years, when sea lampreys reach sexual maturity, they return to freshwater rivers and canals to spawn in beds of gravel, gripping individual stones with their sucker-mouths and rearranging them so to make trenches in which to deposit their eggs.

River lampreys (*Lampetra fluviatilis*) also migrate to sea, but stay there for only about a year, feeding parasitically on other fish in the same way as sea lampreys, before returning to fresh water in order to spawn.

Brook lampreys (*Lampetra planeri*), which are only about 20 cm long, do not migrate to the sea, spending their entire life cycle in fresh water; they are non-parasitical. As adults they do not feed at all, and use their mouths only for holding on to stones. Both river lampreys and brook lampreys are a uniform olive-grey on the back and white on the belly, with brown dorsal fins.

In earlier days the creatures were reckoned a powerful aphrodisiac – witness these lines from the eighteenth-century poem by John Gay, *To a Young Lady with some Lampreys*:

Why then send lampreys? Fie, for shame!
'Twill set a virgin's blood on flame.
This to fifteen a proper gift!
It might lend sixty-five a lift.
I know your maiden aunt will scold.
And think my present somewhat bold.
I see her lift her hands and eyes.
'What, eat it, niece? Eat Spanish flies!
Lamprey's a most immodest diet:
You'll neither wake nor sleep in quiet.

Today lampreys are still eaten in Europe, and especially in Scandinavia, but normally in Britain their bloody, pulpy flesh is used only for fishing bait.

Minnow

Phoxinus phoxinus

Tiny and quick and uncarp-like as they look, minnows are nevertheless members of the cyprinid or carp family. Following a policy of safety in numbers, they swim about in tightly packed shoals; even so, thousands fall victim to carnivorous fish and birds such as kingfishers.

Humans no longer bother to catch them, except for use as bait. But they were once a staple food of country people, who fried them like whitebait or cooked them with eggs; and Izaak Walton recommended a minnow tansy – a kind of pudding – as 'a dainty dish of meat'.

Perch

Perca fluviatilis

A high and sharply spined dorsal fin makes perch easy to recognise but uncomfortable to handle: the best way to grip one is to slide a hand over it from the front, thus laying the spines down. Bright orange or red pelvic, anal and tail fins confirm the identity of this chunky, medium-sized fish, which in Britain grows to a length of 35 cm and a maximum weight of 2 kg.

Perch live in lakes, canals and slow-moving rivers, usually in shoals made up of the same age group. They normally feed on small fish such as bleak (freshwater sprats), but if they run short of other prey, they eat their own young. Almost all the perch caught nowadays are returned to the water; but anglers who have cooked one over a wood fire on the bank, and peeled away the blackened skin, before sprinkling the white flesh with salt and pepper, swear that no fish tastes finer.

Pike

Esox lucius

Rows of viciously pointed, backward-facing teeth give an accurate idea of the pike's character: it is a formidable predator, a beautiful killing machine which lurks in solitary ambush, camouflaged in a mixture of olive flecked and

PIKE *ESOX LUCIUS* (below) A FORMID-
ABLE PREDATOR, PIKE ARE EQUIPPED
WITH VICIOUSLY POINTED TEETH.

ROACH *RUTILUS RUTILUS* (opposite)
FOUND IN A VARIETY OF HABITATS, IN-
CLUDING LAKES, RIVERS AND CANALS.

banded with green, gold and white, before making a
sudden rush to snatch a lesser fish (even one of its own
kind), a frog, a rat, a mouse, a vole or a duckling, and
swallow it whole.

Pike live for many years – certainly 20, if not the 200
with which myth sometimes credits them – and females
grow to a fine size, especially in the limestone loughs of
Ireland, where fish of 18 or even 20 kg are not uncommon.
The celebrated Dowdeswell pike, found dead in a reservoir
near Cheltenham in 1896, weighed 27.3 kg. For reasons
not fully understood, males are far smaller and rarely
exceed 5 kg. The fecundity of females is astonishing: in
the ovaries of a 14-kg fish, the Victorian naturalist Frank
Buckland counted 595,000 eggs.

Both sexes are opportunist feeders, detecting prey by
scent or from vibrations. In winter, when rivers are high,
they move into backwaters to keep out of the current, and
if the water becomes very cold, they feed less frequently.
Then, if the water suddenly warms up, they go into what
fishermen call a feeding frenzy – and these are the times
that give anglers the best chance of catching them.

Large dorsal, anal and tail fins enable them to accelerate
rapidly in launching attacks – but sometimes they over-
reach themselves and tackle a target too big to swallow.
Pairs of pike have occasionally been found dead, locked
together, one having tried to swallow the other by grabbing
its head, and then having been unable to release it.

In earlier days pike's white flesh was highly valued.
King Edward I (1274–1307), set its price as double that of
salmon, and more than ten times that of turbot or cod; and
at ceremonial banquets pike often formed the chief dish.
Germans now consider pike (*Hecht*) their finest game fish,
and in France *quenelles de brochet* are frequently on the menu.
But in Britain there is little demand for it, since it is full of
fine, Y-shaped bones, which make its preparation for the
table a laborious task.

Roach

Rutilus rutilus

British anglers catch more roach than any other coarse fish
– mainly because the species is highly adaptable and lives
in a variety of habitats, including lakes, rivers and canals.
With its deep body, silver scales and orange fins, a roach

food consists of minute crustaceans and the larvae of midges and mosquitoes. In spring a male builds a nest in vegetation near the bottom of the water; after the female has laid her eggs in it, the male fertilises them and guards the nest until the young leave.

can be confused with a **Rudd** (*Scardinius erythrophthalmus*); but the rudd is olive green on the back and bronze-yellow on the flanks, has duller, less red eyes and a dorsal fin nearer to the tail. Both are easy to catch, because they take bait greedily, but neither is now considered worth eating. Both reach a maximum weight of about 1.5 kg.

Sturgeon (Atlantic Sturgeon)

Acipenser sturio

This huge and primitive fish – producer of caviar – is rarely seen in British waters, but occasionally one appears in the Severn, Wye or even the Thames. The Atlantic or green sturgeon grows to a length of about 3.5 metres, and the heaviest recorded in England weighed 209 kg. Captures were, and remain, rare enough to cause excitement. The Victorian naturalist Frank Buckland recorded that one fish, caught in a salmon net at Llandogo, above Chepstow, measured 2.4 metres, weighed 178 kg and yielded 12.3 kg of caviar. Traditionally, all sturgeon were reserved for the table of the monarch, and in his *Dictionary of the Thames*, published in 1880, the novelist Charles Dickens recorded that any such fish caught in the Thames 'is always, when taken, sent direct to grace the table of majesty'.

Nine-spined Stickleback

Pungitius pungitius

Smallest of British freshwater fish, sticklebacks – known to every budding angler as 'tiddlers' – are often less than 5 cm long. Their eyes look far too big for their slender, grey-green bodies, giving them a worried appearance. The nine-spined species inhabits the backwaters of rivers and weed-choked ponds, and is able to live in water with such low oxygen-levels that no other species can survive. Its

Three-spined Stickleback

Gasterosteus aculeatus

This is slightly thicker and longer – up to 10 cm – than the nine-spined stickleback. In spring males develop bright blue eyes and red colouring along their throat and belly, and attract females by going into zig-zag courtship dances. Some populations migrate to sea, then return to the river to spawn, but others live in seashore pools the whole time. Both types swim in spurts, resting and fanning with their fins between bouts of activity.

Tench

Tinca tinca

A chunky-looking member of the carp family, with a body both thick and deep, the tench has a smooth and slimy olive-brown skin, large grey fins and a startlingly red eye. It is found mainly in the southeast of England, and grows to a length of 60 or 70 cm, with a weight up to 2 kg. It used to be known as the 'doctor fish' because (it was believed) other fish that had been injured rubbed against it to heal themselves, and many human ailments, including headache and toothache, were treated with an application of tench slime.

Zander or Pike-Perch

Stizostedion lucioperca

With good feeding this large, grey-green fish can reach 1.3 metres long and weigh 12 kg. A powerful, solitary predator, it is a member of the perch family, and carries the same kind of high, spined first dorsal fin, streaked with dark marks. It feeds in much the same manner as pike, lurking in ambush and making sudden rushes to attack other fish such as bream, roach and perch; but, unlike pike, which prefers clear water, it does well in cloudy rivers and shallow lakes. Zander come from eastern Europe and were first introduced to Britain in 1878. Today they breed in lakes and the lower reaches of rivers such as the Great Ouse.

8

Fish

Freshwater Fish

Sturgeon
Zander

331

Sea Fish

Sea-fishing is still big business, in spite of overfishing and the depletion of stocks. In the year 2000 the British fleet landed some 748,000 tons of fish, worth millions, in home and foreign ports. About 22,000 people were employed in the fish-processing industry, and 1400 fishmongers were still in business.

Basking Shark

Cetorhinus maximus

In spite of its formidable appearance – powerful black body, gaping mouth and red gill-slits – the basking shark is harmless to man, as it feeds entirely on plankton, which it filters out of the water with the horny gill rakers in its mouth. An immense volume of water – some 7000 litres per hour – passes through its mouth and out of its gills as it feeds. It is the world's second largest fish, reaching a length of 11 metres or more and a weight of 3000 kg. It was once keenly hunted by harpoon fishers from Norway, Ireland and Scotland, mainly for its enormous liver, which can amount to almost a quarter of its body weight and yield over 2000 litres of oil. It is believed that basking sharks hibernate in winter, but they can sometimes be seen in summer off the west coasts of Britain.

Bass

Dicentrarchus labrax

To the French the sea bass is the *loup de mer* or sea wolf – a good name for this silvery, voracious predator, which hunts in shoals and lives on lesser fish, crustaceans and squid. It grows to a length of over 40 cm, and a weight (sometimes) of 5 kg, and although primarily a saltwater fish, it comes into freshwater estuaries during summer. The delicious flavour of its white flesh has made it a favourite item on restaurant menus.

Blue Shark

Prionace glauca

In theory blue sharks are a threat to bathers, as they have been known to attack humans, and appear from time to time off the southwest of Britain, where anglers used to catch considerable numbers; but in reality they do not often come close inshore. Powerful predators, they are deep blue on the back, lighter blue on the flanks, and white

Basking Shark
Blue Shark

BASKING SHARK *CETORHINUS MAXIMUS*
(opposite) COMPLETELY HARMLESS TO
HUMANS, BASKING SHARKS FEED
ONLY ON PLANKTON.

BASS *DICENTRARCHUS LABRAX* (below)
A VORACIOUS, SILVERY PREDATOR
THAT LIVES ON LESSER FISH, CRUS-
TACEANS AND SQUID.

COD *GADUS MORHUA* (bottom) COD
NORMALLY LIVE IN DEEP WATERS, BUT
MOVE TO SHALLOWER AREAS IN EARLY
SPRING IN ORDER TO SPAWN.

on the belly, with long, swept-back pectoral fins, and grow to a length of about 3.5 m, living principally on fish such as mackerel (their favourite) and pilchards, and often raiding fishermen's nets to burgle some of the haul.

Like most other sharks, female blue sharks give birth to live young, up to 50 at a time, each about 40 cm long.

Cod

Gadus morhua

For at least 500 years cod fishing has been an important industry, not only in Europe, but also off the northeast coast of America. Now, however, excessive exploitation has reduced stocks to a critically low level, and the annual survey for 2001 conducted by the International Council for Exploration of the Seas showed that cod had become dangerously scarce in the North Sea, partly due to overfishing, partly to a rise in temperature of two degrees over the past decade. There was a clear need for a ban, to give the species time to recover.

Cod have a distinctive, hefty shape, with three blunt dorsal fins rising from their mottled backs, two ventral fins, and a single barbel descending from the point of the lower jaw. Essentially coldwater fish, they live in all the northern seas, with separate populations based in the North Sea, Iceland, Greenland and Newfoundland. In the seventeenth century fish weighing 200 kg were not uncommon, and even 50 years ago a 40 kg cod was normal. Today, however, a fish of 15 kg is considered a good one.

Cod normally live in deep water – up to 600 metres down – but in order to spawn (from February to March) they move into shallower areas, where females lay amazing numbers of eggs – a single fish can contain eight or nine million. The fry, which hatch at a depth of about 100 metres, gradually go down into deeper water to feed on crustaceans and then, as they grow larger, on other fish. In autumn adult cod migrate, and it is then that they can be caught with rod-and-line from beaches.

Conger Eel

Conger conger

One of the most voracious predators in the sea, the conger eel will eat any other creature it can catch – fish, crusta-ceans, squid – and it is very much larger than the common eel, growing to a length of more than 2.5 metres and a weight of 65 kg. Around Britain, large eels are found mostly in deep water off rocky western coasts, where they hide in crevices and underwater caves during the day and use sunken wrecks as lairs. Mature eels live up to 15 years, and then repair to the Atlantic between the Azores and Gibralter, where they spawn at depths of up to 4000 metres: a female can lay up to 12 million or more eggs, and after spawning both she and the male die. Commercial fishermen detest them, because they raid lobster pots and fish nets.

Haddock

Melanogrammus aeglefinus

Living close to the seabed at depths up to 300 metres, feeding on worms, molluscs and other small creatures, haddock are dark on the back and silver-sided, with three dorsal fins, a black lateral line running along each flank from head to tail, and one obvious, round black spot on each shoulder. Tradition asserts that these two blotches are the marks left by the finger and thumb of Simon Peter when, sent out by Jesus to collect money for the tribute collectors, he went down to the Sea of Galilee and found a coin in the mouth of the first fish that he hooked.

Haddock are members of the cod family and grow to a length of about 75 cm, and weigh about 2.5 kg. They are caught in large numbers by bottom-trawlers, and in commercial importance are second only to cod. In recent years they, too, have become scarce, partly from overfishing and possibly because of changes in currents in the northern North Sea, where the fish spawn in spring, and where their eggs drift for 15 days before hatching.

In winter, when haddock migrate, immense shoals used to gather off the Yorkshire coast, the fish collecting in masses that could be 120 km long and 5 km wide. Such vast assemblies are a thing of the past, but very large shoals still sometimes appear.

The celebrated finnan haddie is a smoked haddock, so-called because the fish were once smoked over open cottage fires in the Kincardineshire village of Findon.

Herring (Atlantic Herring)

Clupea harengus

Once ubiquitous around Britain, herrings have been an important source of food since time immemorial. Immense shoals were frequently to be seen offshore, but now the species has been greatly reduced by overfishing. Although mainly silver, up to 40 cm long and weighing about 250–300 g, the fish are delicately tinted with pink and greeny-blue. In the past, Norwegian herrings have been the most important for British trawlers.

A female or hen fish takes between three and seven years to become mature: then in early spring she spawns off the coast, producing up to 40,000 sticky eggs, which sink to the bottom and attach themselves to rocks or seaweed. Thereafter the fish disperse and migrate through the North Sea towards Iceland, moving a hundred metres or more up and down in the water as they hunt for plankton. In Europe most of the catch is pickled and salted, or smoked to make kippers.

Smaller than the herring, but related to it, is the sardine or pilchard (*Sardina pilcharus*), which is commerically important in much of Europe, being canned or smoked for human consumption, and made into meal for animal feed. Sardine oil is used in the manufacture of paint and linoleum.

Mackerel

Scomber scombrus

Slender and streamlined members of the tunny, (or tuna) family, with fins that can be flattened against their bodies, mackerel are built for the speedy pursuit of lesser prey. Weighing up to 700 g, the mackerel have blue-green and black stripes on their backs to camouflage them from predators swimming above, and on a freshly caught fish the colours shimmer brilliantly; but the speed with which they go dull once a mackerel is dead indicates how quickly the fish turn bad because of the action of chemicals in their muscle tissue. Mackerel are delicious if cooked within an hour or two of capture, and their oily flesh is excellent when smoked.

When spawning in May and June, mackerel migrate into relatively shallow waters, particularly off Britain's western coasts, and inshore fishermen catch large numbers, often on hooks baited with artificial feathers. Out to sea, however, trawlers now compete with boats from Russia and eastern Europe, which take off much of the catch.

Monkfish

Squatina squatina

A relation of the shark family, and an extraordinary looking creature, the monkfish takes its name from the shape of its blunt, bulbous head, which is thought to resemble a monk's cowl. It is also known as the angel fish, from the broad fins that spread out on either side like wings. Grey-brown above and white below, it lives on the seabed and often half-buries itself in sand, waiting for prey, such as molluscs, worms, crustaceans and flat fish to swim or drift past. Its eyes are very small, and set just above its wide mouth: higher up its forehead are two breathing holes, or spiracles, which look like half-closed eyes, and give the fish the appearance of dozing.

In summer females give birth to as many as 20 young. Monkfish grow to a length of nearly 2 metres: their flesh, which is exceptionally meaty, white and well-flavoured, is often cooked as a substitute for scampi, but some chefs are now refusing to serve it because the fish have become so scarce. A popular fish in much of Europe, monkfish is referred to as *lotte* or *baudroie* on menus in France, as *rape* in Spain, and as *coda di rospo* in Italy.

Pollack

Pollachius pollachius

A hefty member of the cod family, weighing up to 9 kg, pollack is found inshore all around Britain's coasts, especially during summer, and it is a favourite with anglers, as it feeds near the surface and comes readily to a bait or lure. Pollack tend to feed around wrecks and rocky outcrops. Some pollack are also taken by trawlers, but they are not generally considered an important part of the commercial catch.

In appearance, they have several cod-like characteristics: big eyes, a dark lateral line along each side of the upper back, and three prominent dark dorsal fins, contrasting with their yellow flanks and white bellies. They feed on smaller fish, cod included, and small crustaceans.

Whiting

Merlangius merlangus

This slender and relatively small member of the cod family is grey-bronze on the back, white on the flanks and belly, with a prominent black spot beside the base of each pectoral fin. Usually about 30–40 cm long and weighing 375–500 g, it is are a commercially important fish, since it forms a large proportion of the European catch.

For much of the year whiting live in shallow water, and they are often caught by coastal anglers. They feed on other fish, shrimps and crustaceans. Juveniles, hatched from their mother's spawn, often take refuge among the trailing tentacles of jellyfish, presumably as a form of protection from predators. Young fish have a barbel, or fleshy feeler, protruding from the lower jaw, which disappears later on.

Ballan Wrasse

Labrus bergylta

There are 300 species of wrasse, but most are tropical or subtropical, and only seven exist in north Euopean waters. Around Britain, and particularly off rocky western coasts, the ballan wrasse is the most common – and its lifecycle is exceedingly odd. All ballan wrasse are born female, and after taking six to nine years to reach sexual maturity, some change sex internally to become males. Having done that, they may live for another 25 years and may reach a length of 60 cm although 30–50 cm is more common.

Females spawn in mid-summer, building nests of seaweed in rocky crevices; juveniles are bright green, and some remain that colour as adults, but others turn red-brown. Their scales have pale centres and dark edges, giving them a mottled appearance. One identifying characteristic is the high dorsal fin running right along the back, armed with spines for most of its length. In its throat the wrasse has two batteries of teeth, upper and lower, used for crushing molluscs and crustaceans; sailors used to carry the lower set – known from its shape as a ballan cross – as a charm against drowning. Although ballan wrasse is edible, its flesh is considered to be rather coarse.

Lesser Sand Eel

Ammodytes tobianus

In spite of its name this is not a true eel, but a slim, silver fish up to 15 cm long that has evolved an eel-like body shaped so that it can both swim and burrow in the sand. Of the five species of sand eels found on North Atlantic coasts, the lesser sand eel is the most common around the United Kingdom. It feeds on smaller fish, worms and plankton, and is eaten by a wide variety of other fish such as herring and mackerel, as well as by seabirds.

Nearly a million tons of sand eels are caught every year in the North Sea by trawlers using fine-mesh nets, and because these are liable to scoop up a great many immature fish of other species, they are widely blamed for the general decline in stocks. Some of the eels are fried, salted or dried for human consumption, but most are converted into agricultural fish meal.

Thick-lipped Grey Mullet

Chelon labrosus

It is surprising that grey mullet taste so good, for their method of feeding is curious, to say the least: they swallow mud, which their powerful stomachs grind up so that they can digest the plant and animal life caught in it. They are solid-looking, silvery fish resembling sea bass, up to 75 cm long, with six or seven lines of dark spots running along each side of the body, and large coarse scales. They reach a weight of 4 or 5 kg. In summer, trawlers often catch them in the Channel and off southern Ireland; the fish sometimes move up the estuaries of southern rivers and spend time in fresh water. Grey mullet is widely eaten in Europe and its roe was the original ingredient in *taramasalata*, the Greek dip now made from cod's roe.

The **Striped Red Mullet** (*Mullus surmuletus*), attractively coloured in longitudinal stripes of pink and yellow, is only about half the size of the grey, and is less common around Britain, but it is highly prized as a table fish. There is a similar but unstriped species, the **Plain Red Mullet,** but it is found only off the south coast of England

Lesser Spotted Dogfish

Scyliorhinus canicula

Known also as the Rough Hound, or simply as the dogfish, this is the commonest shark in European waters. It is very slim in proportion to its length, being only 10 or 12 cm in diameter and up to 100 cm long, and its back and upper flanks are light brown dappled with hundreds of darker spots. Dogfish generally live on the seabed, where they hunt molluscs, crustaceans and other fish by scent. Capsules of their eggs, laid in shallow water during autumn and winter, are sometimes washed ashore, and are known as 'mermaids' purses'.

Thousands of tons of dogfish are caught annually by trawlers, and much of the catch appears in fish-and-chip shops as 'rock salmon', 'huss' or 'flake'.

Porbeagle

Lamna nasus

This chunky-looking shark – pointed at both ends, but thick in the middle – hunts shoals of fish such as mackerel and herring on or near the surface of the sea, and can in theory attack humans. But there is no record of any such assault round British coasts, partly because porbeagles rarely come within 15 km of shore.

They grow to a length of 3 metres, and are regarded as a pest by trawlers because they damage nets when raiding them for fish. However, in recent years they have been classified as Vulnerable in the northeast Atlantic, because their numbers have fallen to a dangerous level. Their flesh is often eaten in continental Europe, but is rarely eaten here in Britain.

FLATFISH

Fish that live on the bottom have evolved flattened bodies, camouflaged on the upper side so that they merge with colours of the seabed, wherever they happen to live. The species described here are compressed laterally, from side to side, rather than vertically, from top to bottom, so that they lie on one side or the other, and have both eyes on the upper side of their heads. Young flatfish hatch out the same shape as ordinary fish, but as they grow, the head develops asymmetrically, until both eyes are on the same side. At the same time, the body becomes deeper and more compressed, and the fish starts swimming on its side, blind side down, until it becomes a bottom-dweller.

Dover Sole (Common Sole)

Solea solea

Although relatively small – no more than 50 cm long – Dover sole are perhaps the most relished of all British sea fish, their white flesh having a delicious texture and taste. It is a luxury fish and as a result it is expensive and not as plentiful as it once was. Dover soles may weigh up to 1 kg and have an almost perfect oval shape, with circular dark-brown blotches on a lighter brown skin, but the marks disappear when the fish is dead.

The **Lemon sole** (*Microstomus kitt*) is a similar shape, but a quite different fish from the Dover sole; bigger (up to 65 cm) and more reddish brown on its upper side: its smooth skin feels very slimy to the touch. It is considered to have a perfectly fine flavour in its own right but not anything like that of the Dover or common sole. Its name is misleading, since it is more closely related to a plaice (*see page 338*) than to a true sole.

Halibut

Hippoglossus hippoglossus

Biggest of British flatfish, the halibut lives in deep water, often on the bed of the sea, and off the coasts of North America reaches a length of 2.5 metres and a weight of over 300 kg. British fish are generally a good deal smaller – but also better-tasting. A voracious predator, with a large mouth and pointed teeth, it is brown or blackish on its eyed side, and white below. It feeds on other fish and large crustaceans. Its name, a corruption of 'holibut', probably derives from the fact that it was once eaten on holy days, and its firm, white flesh is still highly esteemed. Because it lives so deep in the cold North Atlantic, halibut is not affected by seasonal changes and is available most of the year round.

PLAICE *PLEURONECTES PLATESSA*
(below) COMMON IN THE NINETEENTH
CENTURY, NOW THEIR NUMBERS ARE
GREATLY REDUCED

TURBOT *PSETTA MAXIMA* (opposite)
CLEVERLY CAMOUFLAGED. ITS SANDY-
BROWN SKIN IS COVERED WITH SMALL
BUMPS INSTEAD OF SCALES.

Plaice

Pleuronectes platessa

As it lies flat on the seabed, white belly downwards, a plaice is well camouflaged by the grey-brown of its upper surface, broken by orange spots; but although its colouring may save it from predators, it does not confuse the nets of bottom-sweeping trawlers. At one point early in the nineteenth century plaice were so common that the Lord Mayor of London, wishing to get rid of a glut, distributed them free among the city's poor. Today they still have a regular place on fishmongers' shelves, but overfishing and poor spawning have reduced their numbers greatly. One problem is that they are slow growers: males need between 3 and 6 years to reach maturity, females up to 7. Given a chance, they can live for 20 years and reach a length of up to 90 cm although this is exceptional and 50 cm is more likely, and a weight of 3.5 kg.

Turbot

Psetta maxima

Another large flatfish, up to 90 cm long, the turbot is almost as round as a dinner-plate, and on its upper side the sandy-brown skin is covered with small bumps, instead of scales. It has long been considered a delicacy – but not by everyone. The fish did not please the Edwardian author Thomas Welby, who wrote in *The Dinner Knell*: '"Turbot, Sir," said the waiter, placing before me two fishbones, two eyeballs and a bit of black mackintosh.'

CRUSTACEANS

Such a wide variety of crustaceans exists that it is hard to give any general description. But they generally have a shell or outer skin known as an exoskeleton, which encases and supports the body. They also have two pairs of antennae, and a variable number of paired legs or appendages, some used for feeding and a range of other functions, and others for walking or swimming. Although creatures of the water, they are not fish. Crustaceans include lobsters, crabs, prawns and shrimps.

Edible Crab

Cancer pagurus

The biggest of common crabs in Britain, edible crabs have a potential lifespan of 20 years though only a few individuals live that long, and they can reach a weight of several kilos. The phrase 'moving crabwise' comes from the way crabs crawl sideways on their eight crooked, hairy legs. They are omnivorous scavengers, but also predators, and pugnacious with it, relying on their heavy armament of hard shells and powerful pincer-claws to keep them out of trouble in combat. Fights between males are common: when backed into a crevice or under a rock ledge, a big crab can defend itself against all comers, and it has the ability to regrow any limb that it loses. A female does not mate until she is five or six years old: she may then lay 2–3 million eggs, which float in mid-water. Most are lost, but some go through a series of moults to become minute juveniles, sinking to the sea floor after about four weeks.

Lobster

Homarus gammarus

People who have seen only cooked lobsters, which are orangey-red and white, are often surprised to find that, when alive, the creatures have greeny-blue-black shells. Common lobsters reach a length of about 50 cm and a maximum weight of 5 kg, scavenging dead fish and crustaceans, but catching some live prey also. They live for up to 30 years, mainly on rocky coasts, walking about on four pairs of legs known as swimmerets, or propelling themselves backwards

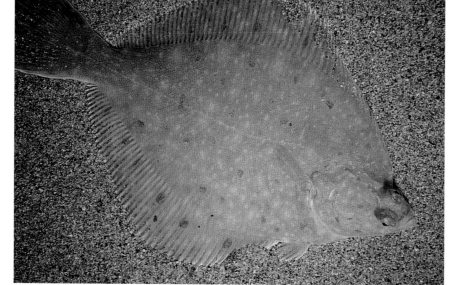

COMMON LOBSTER, *HOMARUS GAMMARUS* (below) MAY LIVE UP TO 30 YEARS OFF ROCKY COASTS.

COMMON PRAWN *PALAEMON SERRATUS* (opposite top) EQUIPPED WITH 5 PAIRS OF LEGS, 2 WITH PINCERS.

COMMON SHRIMP *CRANGON CRANGON* (opposite bottom) OFTEN HARD TO SPOT DUE TO SANDY COLOURING.

8

Fish

Crustaceans

Lobster

Prawn

through the water by flipping their abdomen and tail. Their front pair of legs, modified into two large claws, are of uneven size, the larger being used for crushing and the smaller for cutting. Their eyes are on short, moveable stalks, and they have two pairs of antennae.

Females do not spawn until they are 5–7 years old. Then each lays a mass of orange eggs – up to 150,000 – which remain attached to her legs for 9 months before hatching into shrimp-like larvae. Fishermen trap lobsters in 'pots' or cages made of netting, wood or plastic and baited with fish or offal, lowered to the ocean floor and anchored by a rope to a buoy on the surface.

Common Prawn

Palaemon serratus

Resembling lobsters in miniature, except that they have a long rostrum or beak protruding between their eyes, prawns grow up to 10 cm long. They have almost transparent bodies, and five pairs of legs, the first two of which are equipped with pincers, for picking up pieces of food. Their antennae and eyes on moveable stalks enable them to maintain all-round vigilance, and if attacked, they can move sharply by bending and flexing their abdomen. Nevertheless, they fall victim to numerous marine predators.

Common Shrimp

Crangon crangon

Shrimps, 5–9 cm long, are often hard to spot, partly because they are much the same colour as sand, and partly because their habits are mainly nocturnal. During the day they bury themselves in sand by digging with their legs and swimmerets – the short, flattened limbs under the abdomen. At night they come out to feed, walking on two pairs of legs and using the third to check any objects that they encounter. Strong claws enable them to tear apart worms, young fish and organic remains.

MOLLUSCS

Humans have eaten molluscs from the dawn of history, for the creatures' relative immobility makes them easy to collect; early man could prize mussels off the rocks and dig cockles out of the sand. Many shellfish are hermaphrodites, shedding both eggs and sperm into the water, and others change sex during their lifetime. Molluscs also include the octopuses, cuttlefish and squids (all cephalopods).

Common Cuttlefish

Sepia officinalis

Among the strangest-looking of all sea creatures, the cuttlefish is a relative of the octopus and squid. Up to 30 cm long, it is normally striped in a zebra pattern of brown and white, but able to change colour at will, to hide itself by ejecting a cloud of ink into the water, and to propel itself rapidly backwards by squirting a jet of water from a valve under its head. Big eyes are set wide apart in a broad forehead, and ten tentacles protrude forwards in a bunch from around its mouth. Its internal shell is made up of small chambers which act as buoyancy tanks: by filling or emptying them, it can sink or float. By day it burrows into sand for protection, and when hunting, mainly at night, it cruises slowly forward, camouflaged by constantly changing waves of colour that fluctuate through tentacles and body. When it comes within range of a target, two of its tentacles, much longer than the rest, dart out to snatch the victim, gripping it with the suckers on the spoon-like ends.

Common Octopus

Octopus vulgaris

Eight tentacles, each armed with a double row of suckers, give the octopus not only its name but also formidable gripping power. Having no hard shell, but a soft, rounded body, this predator favours evasive tactics, and has many tricks up its sleeves: it can quickly change colour to merge into any background, and if necessary can propel itself rapidly backwards by forcing a jet of water out of a nozzle at the base of its body. Lurking among rocks, it grabs prey such as crab with a swift strike, envelopes the victim in the skin stretched between its arms, and then bites it, injecting poisonous saliva which quickly brings on paralysis.

There is a huge disparity in size between the sexes: whereas females rarely exceed 1 kg in weight, males grow to 25 kg and 90 cm long. Mating rituals are unique: after

CUTTLEFISH *SEPIA OFFICINALIS* (below)
NORMALLY STRIPED BROWN AND
WHITE, CUTTLEFISH CAN CHANGE
COLOUR AT WILL.

COMMON MUSSELS *MYTILUS EDULIS*
(right) MUSSELS CLUSTER ON ROCKS
AT LOCH SUNART, ARGYLL IN SOUTH-
WESTERN SCOTLAND.

entertaining the female with a display of tentacle-waving, the male fertilises her at arms' length, transferring batches of sperm to her in one specially adapted tentacle. Having laid 50,000 or more eggs like translucent grains of rice, the female guards and fans them until they hatch, 40–50 days later, and soon afterwards she herself dies.

Common or Edible Cockle

Cerastoderma edule

With their pale, ribbed, oval shells, up to 5 cm across, cockles are a familiar sight on most sandy beaches – but those visible on the surface are probably only a fraction of a huge army deeply buried: some beds contain 10,000 cockles per square metre. These bivalve molluscs feed by drawing in water through one tube or siphon, straining out plankton in their gills, and expelling the waste water through another tube. They can move slowly by flexing their single, muscular foot, but not fast enough to escape birds such as oystercatchers, which prey heavily on them.

Common Mussel

Mytilus edulis

With their shiny, pointed, blue-black shells packed in tight clusters, mussels grow on rocks all round British coasts, and are one of our commonest shellfish. Caution is needed when harvesting these bivalve molluscs, because they ingest any toxins present in the water, and these become concentrated in their flesh. Mussels anchor themselves by secreting a thick fluid which hardens on contact with water and forms tough threads known as byssus; the creatures

can reabsorb the material and move around, but as they grow older, they tend to stay put.

Edible Oyster

Ostrea edulis

Oysters generally live in the shallow tidal waters of estuaries and sea lochs, attached by a hard-setting paste to rocks. Thick shells, corrugated on the outside and hinged together by an elastic ligament, protect them from most natural enemies, but some predators such as starfish, are able to prize these bivalve molluscs open. Having started life as a male, an oyster changes sex each time it spawns: sperm discharged into the sea is taken in by females, which retain the fertilised eggs as they develop into larvae. Since one oyster is naturally drawn to another, juveniles often fasten on to old shells, thus increasing the size of a bed, and they take 5–6 years to grow large enough for the table.

Great Scallop

Pecten maximus

Scallops are among the most delicious of sea foods, and their ribbed, fan-shaped shells have featured as a motif in art for centuries. These bivalve molluscs live on beds of sand, gravel or mud, digging out small hollows for themselves by forcing water out through valves; they feed by opening their shells to draw in water, and straining out edible particles. At any hint of danger, the shells snap shut, propelling the creature smartly backwards if need be.

Common Limpet

Patella vulgata

Everyone knows the expression 'clinging on like a limpet', which accurately reflects the grip exerted by this gastropod mollusc's suction pad of a foot when it fastens onto a rock. With its ribbed shell shaped like a blunt cone and a diameter of 6 cm, it occupies a base position on a rock, where it either grinds away the surface or wears down its own perimeter so that it fits the surface perfectly. At night it moves off perhaps a metre to graze on seaweed, but then returns, following its own trail.

Common Whelk

Buccinum undatum

Known also as the buckie, the whelk has a heavy yellowish-white shell that is flecked with black: this whorled and ribbed shell grows to about 11 cm at its greatest diameter. From its broad end protrudes a siphon, or antenna, which detects the smell of prey or carrion and so guides the whelk, which is a gastropod mollusc, to its food – and sometimes to its doom, for, moving on a large foot which extends from the main shell opening, it easily falls victim to bait set out in a wicker or mesh pot. Females which have been mated spawn communally, each producing up to 2000 fibrous egg capsules, containing perhaps 1000 eggs apiece. Several females stick their capsules together in a spongy ball, but only a small proportion of the eggs develop, and the growing young use the remainder of the unhatched eggs as a source of food.

Common Winkle (Periwinkle)

Littorina littorea

Winkle-picking has been both a hobby and a commercial activity for centuries in Britain. Thousands of tons of these gastropod molluscs are eaten every year in Britain, yet they survive in immense numbers. They live among rocks, in crevices or on seeweed, feeding on seaweed and dead vegetation, and their whorled, conical shells, only about 3 cm high, protect them when they are flung about by waves in rough weather. Part of their success is due to the fact that they can manage well in estuaries, where the water has low salinity.

9 REPTILES AND AMPH

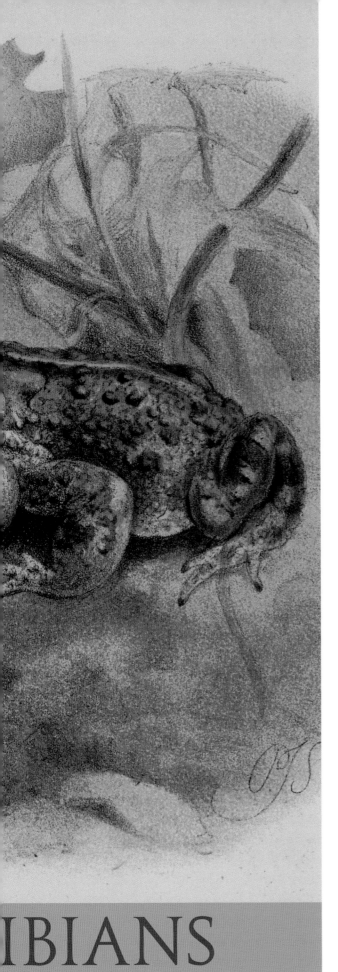

IBIANS

Both reptiles and amphibians are vertebrates – that is, they have backbones; but unlike birds and mammals, they are 'cold-blooded'. Rather than creating their own heat by chemical reaction in their bodies, they rely on heat from outside, and their temperature goes up and down according to the temperature of their surroundings: hence their habit of basking in the sun in cool weather, or seeking the shade when it is hot. In fact 'cold-blooded' is not a particularly apt term: in summer the body temperature of a common toad is normally about 27°C, and that of a natterjack toad about 30°C. The advantage of drawing heat from radiation in the environment is that the body needs relatively little food to keep it going. Small mammals such as shrews have to eat practically all the time to stay alive. Almost all reptiles and amphibians, in contrast, need to eat comparatively small amounts, and in winter when hibernating, their consumption falls to zero.

One peculiarity of amphibians is their method of breathing. Like other animals, they need oxygen, and they have lungs which transmit oxygen into the bloodstream. But they also breathe through the skin, and through the lining of the mouth, taking in oxygen and passing out carbon dioxide: even under water their soft, damp skin acts in the same way as the lining of their lungs. It is this ability that enables frogs to hibernate for months in mud at the bottom of ponds, breathing gently through the skin.

Reptiles and amphibians are poorly represented in Britain. We have only three species of snakes, one of frogs, two of toads, and three of lizards. Yet Ireland is even poorer. It was allegedly St Patrick who kept such creatures out of the Emerald Isle: he had total success with snakes and common toads, but let natterjack toads slip through his net.

Reptiles

Mostly land animals, reptiles are an exceedingly old group, having first appeared on Earth some 340 million years ago, and early forms included the dinosaurs. They have skins covered in horny, overlapping scales which are waterproof and help retain body moisture. In most cases, as a reptile grows, and its skin becomes too small, it grows a new covering and sheds the old one. A snake sheds its old skin all in one piece, starting from the head, whereas lizards slough theirs off in flakes or pieces.

Most reptiles have good vision and hearing, but they also have a third method of checking out their surroundings: through the Jacobson's organ, which is a pit in the roof of the mouth. A lizard or snake flicks out its tongue to pick up chemicals in the air, and then retracts it into the pit, to analyse the traces it has collected.

Reptiles have evolved various defence strategies. A grass snake, if cornered, will play dead, keeping absolutely still, with its head hanging down. The tails of lizards have special breaking points, so that if a predator grabs the end, it will come off. The broken-off section usually goes on twitching for a while, keeping the attacker interested while its potential victim makes good its getaway — and then the lizard grows a new end to its tail.

Snakes

Even in a largely irreligious age, the snake cannot shed its reputation as the bringer of original sin to the Garden of Eden. Partly because of that, partly because of their slithery nature, partly because some snakes are venomous and therefore potentially dangerous, people fear the creatures and associate them with evil. In Britain such an attitude is not very realistic, for of our three native species of snakes, only the adder poses any threat.

Snakes (Ophidia) are probably descended from lizards that gradually lost their legs, and they have evolved several physical peculiarities. In their long, thin bodies stomach, liver, kidneys and ovaries are greatly elongated, as is the right lung. The left lung, in contrast, is very small or absent in some snakes. The flexible backbone is made up of 160–400 vertebrae.

The loosely anchored bones of the jaws enable a snake to swallow a victim whole, even if the diameter of the prey is greater than that of the predator. Ingestion is helped by the backward slope of the teeth, which force prey down the gullet, and by the fact that the ribs at the front of the body are not attached to the backbone, allowing wide expansion. Even with these advantages, ingestion may take half an hour, and a single meal may last the snake several days. Sight and hearing are limited, but useful information is picked up from vibrations transmitted through the ground.

Adder (Northern Viper)

Vipera berus

Known also as vipers, adders are the only poisonous snakes in Britain, and are easily distinguished by the bold, black zig-zag pattern along their backs. Females are generally about 55 cm long, while males average 50 cm. Their colour varies greatly: males are mostly grey, yellowish or whitish, females reddish or brownish. All-black individuals are quite common in some localities. Their armament consists of a pair of teeth, set at the front of the upper jaw and pierced by fine tubes, through which they squirt venom as they bite victims. Humans rarely die from adder-bites, but dogs quite often succumb, especially if they are punctured in the nose and do not receive prompt attention. In other words, adders are potentially dangerous: they exist in most of Britain, and care should always be exercised when walking in summer over the kind of heath or moorland on which they tend to live.

Like other reptiles, adders depend on ambient heat to raise their body temperature to a level at which they can become active. In spring and autumn they bask in the sun whenever they can, but in summer the air temperature is often high enough for them to move around and search for prey all day. They hunt by scent, testing the air with their flickering tongues: having crept up to within range of a mouse or vole, they let loose a lightning strike with their heads and inject venom into their target. The wounded animal bolts for cover, but within a couple of minutes it is

NATTERJACK TOAD *BUFO CALAMITA*
(previous pages) PLATE TAKEN FROM
'THE TAILLESS BATRACHIANS OF
EUROPE' BY G. A. BOULANGER, 1897.

ADDER *VIPERA BERUS* (below)
DISTINGUISHED BY ITS BLACK ZIG-
ZAG PATTERN, IT IS BRITAIN'S
ONLY VENOMOUS SNAKE.

disabled or killed by the poison, and the snake follows it at its leisure. The venom also starts to break down tissues, making digestion easier.

As winter approaches, and the weather grows colder, vipers become increasingly lethargic, before going into hibernation at the beginning of October: tucked down under roots or in an old rabbit burrow, they survive on stores of accumulated fat. There are records of up to 40 adders, lizards, slow worms and toads all hibernating in the same hole. Come spring, the snakes emerge again and set about the vital business of mating. Females lay scent trails from glands at the base of the tail, and males follow them by smelling with their tongues.

When male and female come together, they indulge in protracted courtship, with the male flicking his tongue over the body of his prospective mate, before copulation takes place. If a rival appears, the first male gives chase, and a pursuit often ends in the ritual known as 'the dance of the adders', in which both combatants rear up, trying to force each other to the ground, without any resort to biting. In the end one gives way and makes off.

Adders are viviparous – that is, they give birth to live young, which may be encased in a membrane that breaks when the 15 cm-long babies push against it from inside. From day one the young can fend for themselves and give poisonous bites, but they generally stay with the mother for a while, and sometimes seek refuge under her if danger threatens – a habit which gave rise to the old wives' tale that adders eat their babies. Other physical peculiarities include the absence of ears and eardrums, the possession

9

**Reptiles &
Amphibians**

Snakes

Adder

of heat-sensitive pits on the sides of the face, which enable snakes to pinpoint warm-blooded prey, and the ability to slough off a complete old skin.

In earlier days fear of adders led country people to credit the snakes with supernatural powers. In Lincolnshire, for instance, it was believed that a hungry adder would take up station beneath a skylark fluttering high in the air, and spit poison at it, paralysing the bird so that it would drop into the mouth waiting below.

In the event of a snakebite, traditional first aid was to make incisions across the wound and try to suck out the poison, but this procedure is to be avoided at all costs. Rather, the bitten limb or area should be immobilised with splint or bandage, and physical effort reduced as much as possible to restrict absorption of the venom until professional treatment can be obtained.

Grass Snake

Natrix natrix

Lemon yellow patches on the neck, with bold black marks behind them, make the grass snake easy to identify. Twice the size of an adder, and up to a metre or more long, its body is olive-coloured, with short, slanting black bars spaced out along its flanks. It is a good swimmer, but also much given to basking in the sun. It feeds mainly on frogs and fish. Although non-venomous, it sometimes hisses when threatened, but rarely strikes at an aggressor; its normal means of defence is to disappear rapidly if danger threatens; but if it is cornered, it may feign death, and if picked up, release a foul-smelling secretion.

This is the only native British snake that lays eggs: in June and July females lay clutches in compost heaps and other rotting vegetation, where the natural heat incubates them, until miniature snakes hatch out in the autumn.

Smooth Snake

Coronella austriaca

Found only on dry heathland at low altitudes, especially in Dorset, Surrey, Hampshire and West Sussex, the smooth snake is Britain's rarest native reptile. It needs a warm habitat with an open, sunny aspect, and over the past two centuries most of Britain's lowland heath has been lost – to forestry, farming, roads, building and mineral extraction.

A smooth snake gets its name from the fact that its scales are flat and smooth, unlike those of the adder and grass snake, which have ridges down the middle. It grows to 50–60 cm long, grey or dull brown, with two rows of black dots along the back, a heart-shaped mark on top of its head, and an eye-stripe running back from the head and neck into the front of the body. It lives mainly on lizards

GRASS SNAKE *NATRIX NATRIX* (left top) FEIGNING DEATH AS A METHOD OF DEFENCE.

SMOOTH SNAKE, *CORONELLA AUSTRIACA* (left bottom) HAS FLAT, SMOOTH SCALES.

COMMON LIZARD, *LACERTA VIVIPARA* (below) FEEDS ON INSECTS, SPIDERS AND OTHER INVERTEBRATES.

and small mammals, which it catches by a sudden strike followed by tightly coiling its body round them to subdue them before swallowing the prey alive. A female produces up to 15 young, which are born alive, emerging from membranes as they come into the open. In winter smooth snakes hibernate in holes or under heaps of brushwood and dead vegetation.

Lizards

Britain's three lizard species are fast-moving little creatures that live mainly on insects. Lizards (Lacertilia) have long been seen as benign creatures – witness the old belief that if a person was sleeping outdoors, and a lizard saw a snake approaching, it would wake the human and so avert danger.

Common Lizard

Lacerta vivipara

Small, brown and fast-moving, this lizard usually grows up to 13–15 cm long, including the tail, and lives in a variety of environments – sea cliffs, dry-stone walls, moors, heaths and common land. It likes open, sunny surroundings, but also bogs, and it feeds on insects, spiders, centipedes and other invertebrates which it catches by flicking out its tongue. It is known as *vivipara* because it gives birth to live young, which at first are jet black, but later turn coppery before acquiring their adult colour.

Both sexes are mainly brownish on the upper parts; but they can be distinguished by their undersides, which in a male are bright yellow or orange spotted with black, and on a female pale grey-green, bluish, yellowish or orange, with few or no spots.

Sand Lizard

Lacerta agilis

At up to 19 cm or more in length, the sand lizard is noticeably larger and heavier than its common cousin – nearly twice its size – and, as its name suggests, lives on sandy heaths or dunes. It depends absolutely on such environments, for females lay their eggs in sand and rely on the heat of the sun to incubate them. After widespread loss of good habitat, the sand lizard is now extremely rare, occurring naturally only in a few southern counties and on the coast of Merseyside; but it has recently been reintroduced to sites in the West Country, West Sussex, Wales, Scotland and sites in its existing range.

Male sand lizards have bright green sides, which become still more vivid during the breeding season (April–May), when males sometimes fight. Both sexes sport lines of bold dark spots along their backs. The species is fully protected by British and European law.

Slow Worm

Anguis fragilis

Although it looks like a long, slim snake, the slow worm is in fact a legless lizard, about 40 cm long, whose eyelids and flat, shallowly notched tongue betray its true identity. Its very smooth scales give its body a shiny, polished look, and both sexes often have a dark stripe along the back; females tend to be coloured brown or bronze, with dark sides, and males are generally greyer, though they can be brown or reddish.

Slow worms feed on slow-moving creatures such as slugs, give birth to live young in autumn, and tend to lie up under roots, stones, old planks, tussocks of grass or compost heaps. They are common throughout Britain, but there are only a few in Ireland on the Burren, and these were introduced.

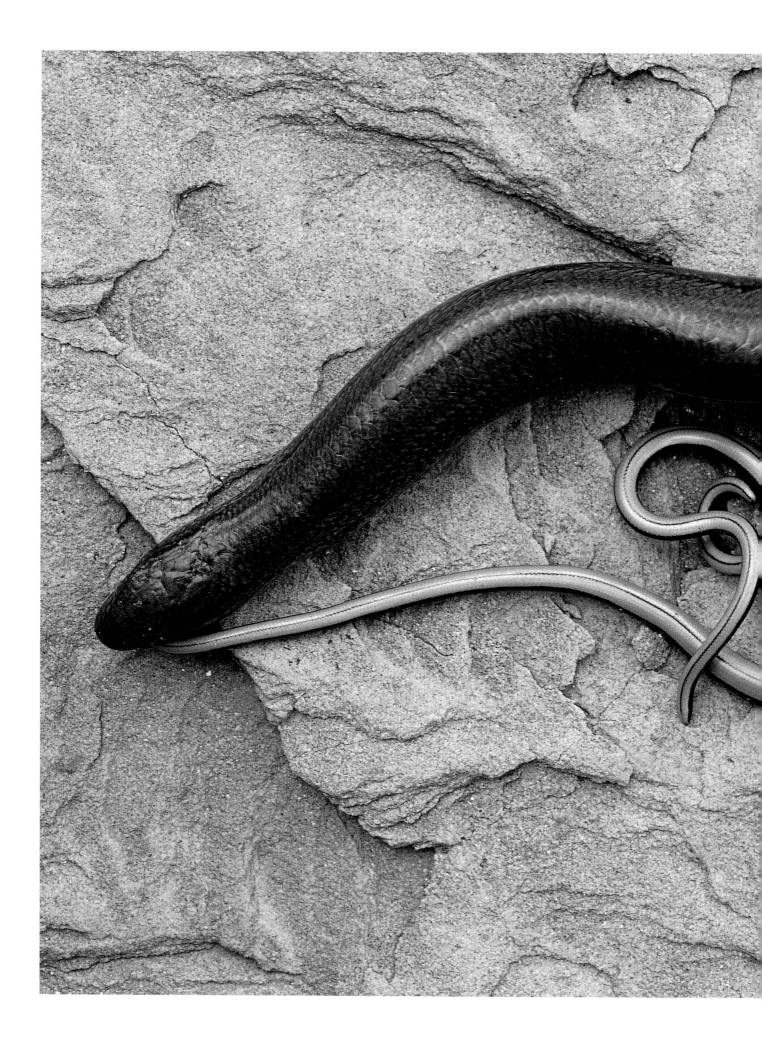

Amphibians

Derived from Greek, 'amphibian' means 'living a double life', and describes vertebrates that are equally at home on land or in water. The species found in Britain spend most of their time ashore and take to the water only to breed. All are four-footed: frogs and toads are tailless and have powerful back legs, whereas newts have tails and legs the same length.

Common Frog

Rana temporaria

Frogs are amazingly successful creatures. Harassed though they are by many enemies and habitat destruction, they live all over Britain and Ireland in a great variety of damp habitats, from suburban gardens to the Scottish Highlands, where they can often be found on mountain-sides 600 metres or more above sea level.

Their main requirements are a moist atmosphere and water – ponds or lakes – in which to breed. Having sat out the winter in mud at the bottom of ponds and ditches, absorbing oxygen through their skins, and often packed together in crowds, they generally spawn in March, finding their way to breeding ponds by following the distinctive smell of glycolic acid produced by algae in the water. A female lays up to 3000 eggs, each protected by a globule of jelly, and the spawn of several frogs, coming together, floats in large masses on the surface of the water. In two or three weeks the eggs hatch into tadpoles, which are like tiny, fast-wriggling fish, brown speckled with gold, and equipped with external gills. Gradually, the tadpoles develop into frogs: the gills are absorbed at four weeks, and hind legs appear at seven weeks, front legs at 12 – at which time the tail is absorbed into the body. Only a minute fraction of juveniles reach maturity, since they fall victim to numerous predators, diving beetles, fish, newts, shrews and birds among them. Adult frogs grow to a length of about 8 cm and are olive-brown, with black markings on the back, and two lighter stripes along each side.

Common frogs of all ages are eaten by predators such as herons, buzzards and foxes, but not – fortunately for them – by humans. The hind legs, which taste like chicken and are eaten in millions by the French, are more likely to come from the **edible frog** (*Rana esculenta*), which exists only in a few places in Britain, even though numerous attempts have been made to introduce it. Other species which have established toeholds in this country are the **pool frog** (*Rana lessonae*), a close relative of the edible species, and the **marsh frog** (*Rana ridibunda*), largest of European frogs and up to 13 cm long, which was brought from Hungary and released into a garden pond on the edge of Romney Marsh in Kent in 1935.

Common Toad

Bufo bufo

Ancient prejudice labelled the toad, or paddock, a creature of the devil, probably because it goes on the move at dusk and is abroad through the hours of darkness. Who can forget the incantation chanted by Shakespeare's witches in *Macbeth*?

Round about the cauldron go;
In the poisoned entrails throw,
Toad, that under coldest stone
Days and nights hast thirty-one
Sweltered venom sleeping got –
Boil thou first i' the charmed pot!

Even in the eighteenth century, Thomas Pennant, who published the first serous zoological work in Britain, described toads as 'the most deformed and hideous of all animals – objects of detestation'. Legend claimed that every toad carried in its head a jewel, the only antidote to the poison in the warts on its skin. Nobody now believes

SLOW WORM *ANGUIS FRAGILIS* (previous pages) WITH YOUNG BORN LIVE. THE SLOW WORM IS, IN FACT, A LIZARD.

COMMON FROGS *RANA TEMPORARIA* (below, left) A MASS OF COMMON FROGS SPAWNING IN MARCH.

COMMON FROG *RANA TEMPORARIA* (below) A FEMALE LAYS UP 3000 EGGS IN GLOBULES OF JELLY.

such a slander – yet still many people fear toads and would run a mile rather than pick one up.

The amphibian's dry-looking, warty skin does contain powerful toxins, that include hallucinogens and cardiac glycosides strong enough to stop heartbeat; these poisons are excreted by the parotid glands – the long, raised lumps behind the toad's ears. Women claiming to be witches certainly used to render these toxins down for their potions – as did wives who wanted to poison husbands – by throwing the creatures live into pots of boiling water. The natural chemicals are a defence mechanism which is activated only in moments of danger, and they protect the owner from potential predators such as foxes, which readily eat frogs, but know that toads taste disgusting and are potentially

dangerous unless they are skinned before consumption.

Although it does not exist in Ireland, the common toad is widespread in Britain, and is very long-lived: some in captivity have reached the age of 50. But in the wild there is heavy mortality, especially in spring, when toads cross main roads as they move down out of drier areas towards the ponds and lakes in which they breed, travelling mainly at night.

In the 1980s, on the road between Henley-on-Thames and Marlow, so many were being run over on their migration towards the Thames that the surface of the road became carpeted with squashed bodies: not just a waste of wildlife, but a positive danger to humans. Devoted local volunteers did what they could to mitigate the slaughter by

9

Reptiles & Amphibians

Frogs & Toads

Common Toad

COMMON TOAD *BUFO BUFO* (below)
LONG-LIVED, SOME TOADS KEPT
IN CAPTIVITY HAVE LIVED FOR AS
LONG AS 50 YEARS.

NATTERJACK TOAD *BUFO CALAMITA*
(bottom right) THE MALES' MATING CALL
CAN BE HEARD OVER QUITE LONG
DISTANCES.

and speckled with gold, emerge in August, often after heavy rain. In winter toads often congregate in comfortable refuges, and spend the cold months there in the company of newts, lizards and snakes.

The Hampshire naturalist Gilbert White told a sad story about a group of ladies who took a fancy to a garden toad and fed it, year after year with maggots, until it grew to a monstrous size:

> The reptile used to come forth every evening from a hole under the garden steps; and was taken up, after supper, on the table to be fed. But at last a tame raven, kenning him as he put forth his head, gave him such a severe stroke with his horny beak as put out one eye. After this accident the creature languished some time and died.

collecting the migrants in buckets and carrying them to safety, but the massacre continued.

Then in stepped the Flora and Fauna Preservation Society, who with the help of a firm called ACO Polymer, installed a 20-metre tunnel with walls of 30-cm-high polythene funnelling into its entrances. The toads took to their new underpass at once: on one evening alone nearly 600 went through, with another thousand moving in along the approach walls. There may well have been even more, as the travellers were being counted by a photo-electric eye, and many were joined together, copulating on the move. In any case, mortality was cut by 90 per cent, and the layout was later copied at many more of the 250 major migration sites recorded in Britain. Elsewhere in the country members of the Wildlife Trusts organise hundreds of toad patrols to minimise slaughter during March and April.

Toads feed on any live prey small enough for them to swallow. At night, if they are hungry, they wander around in search of food, and their bulging eyes give them good vision in the dark – although only at short ranges. But if they find a well-stocked area, they become quite sedentary. They can also live for a long time in cellars, into which they sometimes fall down old coal-chutes. Their life cycle is much the same as that of frogs, except that their spawn is laid in strings, rather than clumps – double rows of black eggs being held in a continuous strand of clear jelly up to 3 metres long, wound round stalks and leaves. The tadpoles are also black, and protected from carnivorous fish by the unpleasant taste of the toxins in their skin; but most of them are eaten by predators such as great diving beetles, water boatmen and great crested newts. Toadlets, which are tiny,

In the eighteenth century country fairs were frequented by toadies, or toad-eaters, who went from place to place in the company of quack doctors, swallowing the amphibians for a living. Having downed one, the toady would drop writhing to the ground, apparently at death's door, only to be revived by a dose of the quack's patent remedy forced between his lips – whereupon the doctor would go round the crowd, selling little bottles of his elixir. Whether or not the trickster actually swallowed the animal, or slipped it up his sleeve by sleight of hand, remains a matter of doubt; but it was through his antics that the word 'toady' acquired its secondary meaning of 'sycophant' or 'creep'.

Natterjack Toad

Bufo calamita

The natterjack's Latin specific name makes it sound as if the species were heading for disaster; in fact the word derives from *calamus*, a reed or rush, because males often hide among these plants. Natterjacks tend to run rather than hop. The toad gets its common name from the raucous calls that males give out at night during the summer mating season, far noisier than those of a common toad, and so loud that they can be heard a kilometre or more away, as they try to lure females to them.

The natterjack is smaller than the common toad, and

can be distinguished by the yellow stripe running down its back. Once common on heaths in southern England, it is now scattered in pockets over 60 different sites, with its main strongholds on the coasts of Merseyside and Cumbria, and outposts on the Solway Firth, in East Anglia and south-west Ireland. Sand dunes and salt marshes are its prime habitat, for it generally lives in a burrow which it has dug for itself, and breeds in the warm, shallow pools between ridges, where each female lays up to 7500 eggs at one time, deposited in single file (as distinct from the common toad's double) along a strand of jelly.

Like other amphibians, it is carnivorous, and catches insects, snails or worms by flicking out its sticky-ended tongue. Usually it hunts by keeping still, in ambush, but occasionally it hurries after a scurrying beetle. Although able to go for days without food, it will eat an enormous amount at one sitting if it gets the chance. Natterjacks spend the winter deep in soft sand, either digging holes themselves, or using those made by other creatures such as sand martins. At one stage the natterjack was extinct in Wales, but it has now been reintroduced to 13 sites, and in many places dunes are being managed to prevent invasion

by scrub. Even though there are no common toads in Ireland, natterjacks are found in a few isolated places in County Kerry in the southwest. The question of how they got there puzzles herpetologists: were they there before Ireland was separated from England and Wales, or did somebody introduce them?

Newts

Minute though they may be in comparison with reptiles of prehistory, newts, belonging to the family Salamandridae, are faintly reminiscent of dinosaurs. Their primitive looks – tubular bodies, heavy tails and jagged crests along the back – evoke images of vast antiquity.

Only three species exist in Britain, and all are under pressure from loss of good habitat as ponds and ditches are filled in to create bigger fields or more space for roads and houses. Yet efforts to conserve them are increasing, and the Internet carries numerous sites offering advice on how to encourage them. Some people keep them as pets, and the creatures have any number of articulate fanciers, not least the left-wing politician Ken Livingstone, who became mayor of London in 1999.

Britain is a stronghold of the great crested newt: one population of over 30,000 adults near Peterborough is said to be the largest in the world. However, it is also true that the great crested newt, like the other two species in Britain, has suffered a massive decline over the past 50 years, and may be decreasing even faster than any other British species of amphibian or reptile.

Great Crested Newt (Warty Newt)

Triturus cristatus

The largest newt in Britain – up to 16 cm long – but also the most threatened, the great crested is dark brown or black on the back, with a rough, warty, dark-brown skin. Females, which are slightly the larger, have no crest, but in spring a male grows a jagged, dragon-like crest along the whole length of his back, and a separate, straight-edged crest on top of his tail, which has a silver stripe along each side. The male also develops a bright orange belly spotted with black. Like toads, these newts secrete poison in the warts on their skin, and an experiment by a dauntless Victorian researcher, Miss Ormerod, showed that the venom can have distressing effects even on creatures as large as human beings.

> The first effect was a bitter astringent feel in the mouth, with irritation of the upper part of the throat, numbing of the teeth...and in about a minute a strong flow of clear saliva. This was accompanied by much foam and spasmodic action, approaching convulsions...The experiment was followed by headaches lasting for some hours, general discomfort and slight shivering fits.

In winter the newts hibernate under cover on land, but they are difficult to see, because when they do move about, they are mainly nocturnal. Then, in the breeding season, they move into ponds. In elaborate courtship rituals, males dash about in the water, demonstrating in front of females, before depositing a capsule of sperm on the bottom of the pond – whereupon the female moves in to pick it up on her cloaca, the opening of her intestinal and urinary duct, as she passes over it. She then lays up to 300 eggs on water plants.

Newts are entirely carnivorous; in the water they eat whatever they can catch – frog tadpoles, worms, shrimps and insects. In midsummer they leave the ponds and live in long grass or under stones, emerging on damp nights to hunt worms and slugs. If prey is abundant, numbers quickly build up; but newts need a lot of food, and they have suffered a major decline, chiefly through the loss of breeding ponds,

PALMATE NEWT *TRITURUS HELVETICUS*
(below left) MOST COMMONLY FOUND
ON HEATHLANDS AND MOORS.

GREAT CRESTED NEWT *TRITURUS CRISTATUS* (below) THE MALE GROWS A
CREST ON HIS BACK IN SPRING.

filled in for farming or development. They are now strictly protected by British and European law, which makes it an offence to kill, injure, capture or disturb them in any way.

form of toxins in their skin, huge numbers are eaten by fish. With breeding over, they take to the land and frequent damp places, tucked under logs or stones.

Smooth *or* Common Newt

Trituris vulgaris

This most common of British newts grows to a length of about 10 cm, and during the breeding season, from February to June, lives in ponds. Females are plain brown, but males are spotty, and grow wavy crests along their backs during the mating season. Both sexes have yellow or orange bellies with black spots, and these extend up the throat, enabling one to distinguish them from palmate newts, which have plain throats. Newt tadpoles, known as efts, breathe through feathery gills behind their heads, and develop their front legs before their back – the opposite of frogs and toads; and as they have no natural defence in the

Palmate Newt

Triturus helveticus

A plain throat, yellow or pink, is the feature to look for in trying to decide if a newt is a palmate. The creature is smaller than a smooth newt – often not much more than half the size – and has darker markings on the sides of its head. A male palmate newt in breeding condition is relatively easy to spot, as it has a low crest in the middle of its back, black webs on its back feet, and a filament at the tip of its tail. Because they prefer shallow ponds formed in acid soils, palmate newts are most numerous on heathland in the south and west of Britain, and in the high tarns on moors and bogs in the north.

357

Humans dislike insects because

they sting, bite, spread disease and cause general annoyance. Everyone knows that fleas carry bubonic plague, lice typhus and mosquitoes malaria. Nobody wants cockroaches in their kitchen, and anyone who has suffered a violent physical reaction to a bee- or wasp-sting goes in genuine fear of becoming a victim. Yet insects are amazingly versatile creatures. As the naturalist Eric Parker remarked, they are miners and masons, weavers, woodworkers, tailors, papermakers, unholsterers, gardeners and musicians.

They display mysterious instinctive behaviour, and undergo magical transformations in the course of their lives. Moreover, insects perform numerous services such as pollinating flowers and making honey, and many, like ladybirds, eat harmful species of insects by the thousand. They provide an indispensable source of food for birds, fish, frogs and other creatures. They exist in inconceivable numbers. In the world as a whole a million different kinds have been identified, and in Europe alone there are more than 100,000 species, of which there is room to mention only a handful here.

Annelids, molluscs and arachnids, all of which we glimpse briefly in this chapter, are, like insects, of immense antiquity. Annelids – among them earthworms and leeches – live in the sea, in fresh water and on land. Land-based molluscs are soft-bodied invertebrate animals, either encased in shells of calcium carbonate (snails), or bearing only vestigial traces of shells (slugs). Arachnids – among them ticks, spiders, scorpions and mites – are a group of arthropods well represented in Britain.

Insects

Most insects begin life as eggs, secure inside tough, waterproof shells, which enable them to withstand a wide range of temperatures, even if they are exposed to the air on branches or twigs. In due course the eggs hatch into larvae, which moult several times in the course of their growth, each time shedding their old, outer skins. The larvae of many insects – butterflies, moths, bees, wasps, ants and flies among them – are totally unlike adults, having no wings and taking the form of caterpillars or grubs. When it reaches full size, each larva splits its skin again and emerges as a pupa or chrysalis. To an onlooker this appears to be inactive, but inside its tough outer covering the finished body of the insect is developing, and when it is fully formed, it emerges, the adult insect being known as the imago. The whole development cycle is known as metamorphosis.

Butterflies & Moths
Lepidoptera

It is easy to see why butterflies have long been associated with human souls: flitting lightly about in the air, these most beautiful of insects could easily be the spirits of either the living or the dead – and in the past people's treatment of them depended on what view they took. If you thought, as they did in Northern Ireland, that a butterfly might be the soul of an ancestor, you accorded it respect; but if you considered (as folk did in Lincolnshire) that the first butterfly of the year meant bad luck, you did your best to kill it.

Nobody in Britain now kills butterflies in the hope of securing good fortune; on the contrary, many specialists are working to help the insects, which have suffered from the changes in climate, agriculture and other uses of land that have occurred during the past half-century. Entomologists have studied butterflies intensively for at least 200 years, but never has there been such a comprehensive

survey as the Butterflies for the New Millennium project, which ran from 1995 to 1999. Organised in Britain by Butterfly Conservation, and in the Republic of Ireland by the Dublin Naturalists' Field Club, it was supported by many thousands of volunteer enthusiasts, who recorded insects in the field; and a complete picture of the findings was published as *The Millennium Atlas of Butterflies in Britain and Ireland* – a handsomely produced volume made all the more valuable by the excellence of its colour illustrations.

The survey recorded that although there are about 560 species of butterfly in Europe, only 59 are resident in Britain, and 28 in Ireland, and of these, only 16 occur throughout both countries, the rest being confined to particular areas. Since, in recent years, much concern has been expressed about the general decline of Britain's butterflies, it was a pleasant surprise to find that many of the survey's findings were positive. Although several species, notably those of the fritillaries, *have* been much reduced, others have held their own or even expanded their range. The authors of the *Millennium Atlas* were properly cautious in suggesting reasons for this success, but could not escape the conclusion that global warming is almost certainly one of them.

Butterflies need specific features of habitat in order to reproduce successfully. Adults generally need food such as nectar from flowers or the honeydew produced by aphids. Each species must find particular food-plants on which to lay its eggs, and on which the larvae will hatch and develop into pupae. Besides, the plants must be growing in favourable, warm places – and the necessary combination is by no means always available, especially in an environment as heavily exploited as that of Britain.

Large Copper
Lycaena dispar

A casualty of the nineteenth century, this species went extinct in the 1860s. It was eagerly sought by collectors, but its demise was not caused by their depredations. The trouble was loss of suitable habitat, caused by the draining of wetlands and meres in East Anglia. A similar race found in the Netherlands feeds exclusively on one plant, the water dock, and attempts have been made to reintroduce the species, but so far none has succeeded.

Large Blue
Maculinea arion

In the twentieth century the largest and rarest of our blue butterflies almost became extinct here. This species has a very strange life cycle, in that its larvae feed first on the

BUTTERFLIES, INSECTS AND FLOWERS
(previous pages) PANEL BY JAN VAN
KESSEL, THE ELDER (1626–79).

HEATH FRITILLARY *MELLICTA ATHALIA*
(below) THIS SPECIES HAS BEEN SAVED
FROM THE BRINK OF EXTINCTION.

LARGE BLUE *MACULINEA ARION* (bottom)
THE LARGEST AND RAREST OF BRITISH
BUTTERFLIES WENT EXTINCT IN 1979.

flower-heads of wild thyme, and later in their growth cycle on the grubs in the nests of only one species of red ant, *Myrmica sabuleti*. When the larvae drop off vegetation, they are picked up by foraging ants, which mistake them for grubs of their own kind, and take them into their subterranean brood chambers deep inside the nest. There the butterfly larvae feed on ant grubs and grow until they pupate, after which they have to crawl up to the surface of the ground to open their wings.

Having declined rapidly in the second half of the century, the Large Blue went extinct in 1979. Just too late to save it, research revealed that what it needed was continuous, hard grazing of rough grassland to maintain a high population of the correct species of red ants. If grazing pressure is reduced – as it was when myxomatosis knocked out rabbits in the 1950s – the species of red ant is soon replaced by less suitable species.

More thorough ecological knowledge has enabled experts to reintroduce the Large Blue at four sites in central and southwest England, and the aim is to extend the restoration programme to ten sites by 2005. Early results looked promising, but difficult problems remain, not least that of finding the right kind of grazing animals – sheep, ponies and cattle – and keeping exactly the right pressure on the vegetation.

Heath Fritillary

Mellicta athalia

Another species saved from the brink of extinction, the Heath Fritillary is known as the Woodman's Follower because it has always been associated with the traditional practice of coppicing, and moves into areas in which hazel or other shubs and trees have been cut. Its decline was hastened by the abandonment of coppicing as a means of woodland management, but it also lives on grassland in Devon and Cornwall, and in some of the sheltered combes on Exmoor. Active conservation works – the removal of conifers and the resurrection of coppicing – have given it a new lease of life, but it is present on only a handful of sites in the south-east and far southwest of England.

Holly Blue

Celastrina argiolus

During the last 20 years of the twentieth century the Holly Blue extended its range, colonising new parts of the Midlands and northern England. In spring this species is easily identified, as it is the first of the blue butterflies to emerge, and it generally flies around fairly high in the air, while other grassland blues remain near ground level.

As its name suggests, it feeds principally on the flowerbuds,

HOLLY BLUE *CELASTRINA ARGIOLUS* (below) A BUTTERFLY WHICH HAS EXTENDED ITS RANGE DURING THE LAST TWENTY YEARS.

SMALL TORTOISESHELL *AGLAIS URTICAE* (bottom) NETTLES, WHICH GROW IN ABUNDANCE IN BRITAIN, ARE ITS STAPLE FOOD-PLANT.

PAINTED LADY, *CYNTHIA CARDUI* (right) A MIGRATORY BUTTERFLY THAT VISITS BRITAIN IN LARGE NUMBERS DURING THE SUMMER.

berries and leaves of holly in spring, and of ivy in summer, and it has somehow survived the wholesale removal of hedges from agricultural land. Churchyards, with their heavy evergreen growth, remain one of its favourite habitats, but the reasons for its success are not clear cut. Climate warming may be one of them, and another, the fact that much woodland is now neglected, with the result that ivy is allowed to grow and flower freely on many trees. In Ireland the Holly Blue is widely distributed, but in pockets, and there is no evidence of its range changing much in recent years.

Small Tortoiseshell

Aglais urticae

Another flourishing species, this has remained stable throughout its range, and is found in good numbers from Land's End to John O'Groats and Orkney, as well as from end to end of Ireland, in city centres as well as on mountain tops. One secret of its success is that it has an abundant, and probably increasing, supply of nettles, its staple food-plant, which grow in every nook and cranny of neglected land and have become ever-more luxuriant as farmers scatter fertiliser.

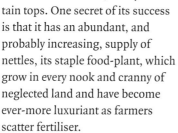

The butterflies lay their eggs on the undersides of nettle leaves, and the larvae grow inside silk webs spun on the tops of nettle plants. In favourable conditions, such as generally persist in the south of England, Small Tortoiseshell females can breed during their first season, thus producing two generations in one year.

Red Admiral

Vanessa atalanta

A regular migrant, which reaches almost every corner of Britain and Ireland, is the gaudy Red Admiral. A few individuals hibernate here through the winter, but the main population is of visitors, which pour in from the south of Europe, even from as far away as Africa. The earliest arrivals settle in the south of the country, then spread farther north. Their main food-plants are nettles, on which they lay their eggs. Reverse migration begins in mid-August: on the coast of County Dublin Red Admirals have been seen flying steadily southwards at heights up to 10 metres. Large numbers build up along the south coast of England, waiting for calm weather or a favourable wind, and some – though by no means all – manage the Channel crossing, to continue their journey to the south.

Painted Lady

Cynthia cardui

Still more spectacular is this migrant, which breeds all year round in Central Asia, North Africa and the Middle East, and sets out every year from those far sources to recolonise Europe. The numbers that reach Britain and Ireland depend largely on the weather: with favourable winds, the total of immigrants can become immense – as happened in 1996, when several million Painted Ladies arrived within a few days. It was clear, moreover, that some of them had flown direct from Africa, covering average distances of 150 km every 24 hours. One curious fact is that no comparable reverse migration has been recorded, and the fate of most of the visitors is not clear.

Large White

Pieris brassicae

It is unfortunate that, lovely as they are, butterflies often inflict serious damage on farms and gardens. The larvae of the Large White are the yellow-and-black caterpillars that eat their way through whole crops of brassicas, protected by their bold colours, which warn potential predators that they contain poisonous mustard oils assimilated from the food-plants.

In spite of this natural defence, mortality among larvae is extremely high, often caused by the attacks of the parasitic ichneumon fly *Apanteles glomeratus*, which lays its eggs inside the caterpillars, so that the growing larvae kill their hosts, eating them away from the inside until only the skins are left. Even with this predation, the Large White is one of the most successful species in Britain, for it is highly mobile, and migrates between the United Kingdom, Ireland and Europe. For gardeners, the best defence against it is to surround brassicas with nasturtiums, which the butterflies favour above all else.

COLLECTING BUTTERFLIES

Long a popular hobby, unlike the taking of birds' eggs, collecting butterflies and moths remains legal, although a few rare species are protected by law. The number of insects taken by collectors is so small that the activity is not seen as a threat – and in any case, most people now prefer to amass photographs of butterflies alive and in their specific habitat, rather than collecting the corpses of beautiful specimens.

The future for butterflies and moths looks reasonably bright. For one thing, interest in these creatures is intense, and many skilled conservationists are working on their behalf. For another, extensive efforts are being made to rebuild the countryside and re-create traditional habitats, by restoring or maintaining rough grassland and woods with plenty of wide rides and open clearings. Experts point out that restored habitats are never as complex or diverse as ancient ones, and warn that it may take hundreds of years to re-establish replicas of what nature created in the first place. But on this front, at least, it can be said that humans are doing their best.

that protrude from her body, and whenever she drops one, a soft, white nymph emerges, hardening and turning brown when exposed to the air.

American Cockroach

Periplaneta americana

Twice the size of the common species – up to 5cm long – and brown, with a yellowish head, the American cockroach has well-developed wings that enable it to fly long distances. It often infests ships and ports, and on land lives outdoors or in dark, heated areas such a boiler rooms. During its adult life of about 18 months a female American cockroach deposits at least 50 egg cases, each containing about 16 eggs.

bursts lasting only a second or so, often three in a row.

Locusts are large grasshoppers which devastate crops when they congregate in huge swarms. They are not much found in Britain, but the **Migratory locust** (*Locusta migratoria*) does rarely appear in the south of England. Males are about 3.5 cm long, usually brown, and screech loudly when in the presence of females, which tend to be green.

Cockroaches Blattodea

Cockroaches are among the most primitive living winged insects: fossil remains show that they have scarcely changed in 300 million years. They have flattened, oval bodies, long, thin antennae and shiny outer skins. They live on the ground, feeding on dead plant matter and remains of food, and, as anybody who has tried to kill one knows, can run at a surprising speed. They flourish most in hot countries, and were once such a menace in ships that boys were paid a penny for every 20 they caught; but with the spread of central heating several species have adapted to colder climates and become a nuisance in houses, bakeries and so on.

Common Cockroach

Blatta orientalis

This is reckoned one of the most unpleasant household pests, as it gives off a disagreeable smell. It is often called, and mistaken for, a black beetle: males are short and squat, about 2–3 cm long, broad in proportion and almost black, females slimmer and browner. The insect is mainly nocturnal, and scuttles for cover if caught in the open when a light is switched on at night. The female carries eggs in cases

True Flies Diptera

In this huge order, comprising over 100,000 species worldwide, the rear pair of wings are no more than pin-shaped balancers known as *halteres*, which act as gyroscopes and help maintain stable flight. Hence the name Diptera meaning 'two wings'. Most flies feed on liquids such as nectar, soaking up fluid with the spongy pads on the tips of their mouthparts, but some, like female mosquitoes, midges and horseflies, live on blood, attacking humans and animals to get it. Female horseflies have blade-like jaws which cut through skin, so that fleshy pads can mop up blood oozing from the wound, whereas a female mosquito has a proboscis like a hypodermic syringe. Houseflies and blowflies subsist entirely on surface liquids, but they constitute a health hazard because they feed on carrion, dung or manure heaps and then regurgitate over food in the house.

Bluebottle

Calliphora vomitoria

Blowflies are large and stocky looking, with a loud buzz, and the commonest species is the bluebottle, which has a metallic, dark-blue sheen on its abdomen, and often comes into houses. Females seek out meat, fish or other kinds of food as hosts on which to lay their eggs. Bluebottles are most in evidence during the summer, and rapidly spoil any

COMMON FIELD GRASSHOPPER
CHORTHIPPUS BRUNNEUS (left) ITS SONG
IS PRODUCED BY DRAWING A WING
ACROSS THE HIND LEG.

BLUEBOTTLE *CALLIPHORA VOMITORIA*
(below) FEMALES SEEK OUT MEAT,
FISH AND OTHER FOODS ON WHICH
TO LAY THEIR EGGS.

COMMON HOUSEFLY *MUSCA DOMESTICA* (below) THESE POSE A HEALTH THREAT TO HUMANS BECAUSE THEY REGURGITATE OVER FOOD.

GIANT CRANE FLY (right) COMMONLY KNOWN AS DADDY-LONG-LEGS, THERE ARE SEVERAL SPECIES OF CRANE FLY IN BRITAIN.

food left in the open. They pose a threat to human health because they land on food and pass on bacteria which can cause problems. In winter they hibernate in crevices, especially the pulley slots at the side of sash windows; dozens often congregate in such places. But on warm, sunny days they come out and fly around.

Common Housefly

Musca domestica

This breeds not only in and around dwellings, but also on farms, rubbish tips and in any decomposing matter. In the autumn it crawls into recesses to hibernate. It is the male lesser house fly (*Fannia canicularis*) that circles incessantly round lightbulbs.

Face Fly

Musca autumnalis

These are the insects that bother horses and cattle, settling thickly round their eyes. They closely resemble houseflies, but are slightly fatter. They tend to sunbathe on walls and wooden fences, and in autumn draw into buildings to hibernate.

Yellow Dung Fly

Scathofaga stercoraria

Swarming on to fresh cowpats and horse-droppings in huge numbers, yellow dung flies take off with a tremendous fizz when disturbed. Females look rather grey, but the reddish fur on males takes on a bright golden tinge in sunlight.

Warble Fly

Hypoderma bovis

The warble fly is one of the insects that uses animals as hosts: it can easily be mistaken for a bee, being hairy, solid-looking and coloured orange and black. Its scientific name, 'under the skin of a cow', gives a clue to its unpleasant method of reproduction: it lays eggs on the legs of cattle and deer, and the grubs work their way up through the body to a position just under the skin of the back. Warble fly grubs spend three months maturing, and when they break out through the skin, they fall to the ground and pupate, leaving exit holes that destroy the hide's commercial value.

Bot-fly

Gasterophilus intestinalis

Another parasite, this lays its eggs on the legs of horses, donkeys and mules; when the animals lick themselves, the larvae pass into their stomachs, where they grow, attached to the lining, until they are passed out of the intestinal tract in droppings, whereupon they pupate in the soil.

Crane Flies

Tipulidae

Commonly known as Daddy-long-legs, these flies vary in size from relative giants with a wingspan of 5 or 6 cm to small species no bigger than mosquitoes. They have slender, translucent wings, and their spindly legs break off with distressing ease if the insects are handled. Several species are common in Britain, damp woods being among their favourite haunts. Adults are harmless, but the larvae of two species, known as leatherjackets, do serious damage to farm crops.

Horseflies

Tabanidae

There are numerous species of these hefty, fast-moving flies, but the commonest and most vexatious in Britain is the cleg-fly (*Haematopota pluvialis*). Damp, muggy weather brings them out, especially in July and August. Males feed on nectar, but females are bloodsuckers and attack large mammals, humans included, with their sharp

10

Insects
True Flies

Common Housefly
Horseflies

mouthparts. One reason for their success is that they approach silently and land so softly that the victim is often unaware of their arrival until a jabbing pain signals a bite, which can cause an uncomfortable swelling.

Myriapods

Neither centipedes nor millipedes are insects, but belong to a group of arthropods (Myriaposia) whose bodies are made up of a certain number of segments, each of which bears one or two pairs of appendages or legs.

Centipedes

Chilopoda

If centipedes were accurately named, they would have exactly one hundred feet. They are indeed equipped with dozens of legs, but numbers vary considerably. *Haplophilus subterraneus*, for instance, which is yellow and lives among leaf litter, has about 80 pairs of legs in its 5 cm length,

whereas the shorter *Cryptops hortensis* has only 21 pairs.

The creatures are mainly nocturnal: having limited or no vision, they emerge at night to attack small invertebrate prey. Although they have poison claws alongside the head to stupefy victims, none of the species found in Britain are harmful to humans – unlike the giant centipede (*Scolopendra gigantea*) of the East Indies, which reaches a length of 280 mm and can inflict a severe bite.

Millipedes

Diplopoda

Literally 'thousand-footers', millipedes have two pairs of legs on each body segment, and the number of segments varies, with the species, from 20 to 60. Most millipedes live in leaf litter on the ground, but some climb trees to eat moss and algae, and several species coil up tightly into a spring-like circle when alarmed. A female builds her nest with fine particles of earth and her own saliva, enclosing a chamber about the size of a marble, then drops an egg through an aperture in the top and closes the hole, leaving the egg to hatch.

WOODLOUSE (below) NOT AN
INSECT BUT A LAND-BASED
CRUSTACEAN, WOODLICE PREFER
DARK, DAMP HABITATS.

CENTIPEDE (bottom) EQUIPPED
WITH NUMEROUS PAIRS OF LEGS,
ATTACHED IN PAIRS ON EACH
SEGMENT OF ITS BODY.

SPIDER'S WEB (below) IS MADE FROM
STRANDS OF SILK EXTRUDED FROM
THREE SETS OF SPINNERETS ON THE
SPIDER'S HIND END.

Ticks Acarina

Ticks form a major group of the great phylum Arachnida and like spiders, centipedes and millipedes, are not insects. They are parasites that cause trouble out of all proportion to their very small size. In general, ticks only irritate large animals, but they are vectors of Lymes disease, which can make humans seriously ill. They are often fatal to grouse because they carry a disease known as louping ill, which can kill 80 per cent of chicks.

Sheep Tick

Ixodes ricinus

This tick lives in grassy places, and particularly in bracken; its larvae fasten on to sheep, deer, dogs, grouse and humans, with the headparts buried in the skin, and the body gradually swells up until it is full of the victim's blood.

If a tick is discovered on a human or a dog, it should not be pulled out immediately, because the head is likely to break of and remain buried in the skin, where it is liable to set up severe irritation. The best policy it to soak the protruding body with insect repellent or disinfectant, and wait for the tick to fall off of its own accord.

Woodlice Isopoda

To the extent that they have numerous pairs of walking legs – seven – and a plate-covered body, woodlice resemble centipedes, but they belong to an entirely different order. In fact, they are land-living crustaceans, being short and stout and covered with plates, and although fully terrestrial, they generally still need damp places in which to live. These curious little creatures have many local names – slaters, cheesy bugs, monkey-peas – and they are often found clustered together in huge numbers under garden pots, rocks or fallen timber. If threatened, a woodlouse rolls into a ball, and its plates form defensive armour, reinforced by the fact that its skin gives out acid secretions when squeezed.

Spiders Araneae

Spiders, like ticks, are members of the phylum Arachnida, although they are not parasites. It seems strange that many people are terrified of spiders. For one thing, all the species found in Britain are harmless; and for another, in legend and folklore the creatures are generally bringers of good luck. In many parts of Britain a spider inside the house is taken as a good sign, foretelling prosperity. If one falls on to someone from the ceiling, that person will soon receive a legacy. For these and other reasons, nobody should kill a spider. In some areas of the Scottish Highlands it is good luck to see a spider out of doors in the morning, but dangerous in the evening. Spiders and their cobwebs were once thought efficacious in curing diseases. The answer to ague was to catch two or three spiders, put them in a bag, and wear it hung round the neck.

No doubt it was the insects' predatory habits, and the skill with which they spin silken webs in order to ensnare victims, that made people both fear and admire them. Cobwebs are wonderfully elaborate, and perfectly formed to fit whatever space is available, the silk threads being extruded through three pairs of spinnerets in the spider's hind end. Droplets of gum on the threads are sticky enough to trap other insects, but the spider itself is protected by waxy hairs on its feet.

While waiting for prey to be caught, spiders normally move off into shelter, but remain in contact by means of a signal- or trip-thread, which tells them the moment any-

thing touches the web. When an insect becomes enmeshed, the resident kills it by stabbing it just behind the head with its poison fangs; and because it can ingest only liquid food, it pumps digestive juices into its victim to dissolve the tissues. Females are much larger than males, and often eat a prospective mate if he makes too rapid an approach during courtship.

Garden Spider

Araneus diadematus

The scientific name refers to the cross of white dotted lines on the spider's back, which makes it easily recognisable. It lives in gardens, often lying up underneath a leaf, and

WOOD ANTS' NEST (below) LARGE
MOUNDS OF LEAVES AND OTHER
LITTER MAKE UP THE NEST IN A PINE
WOOD IN ABERNETHY, SCOTLAND.

BLACK GARDEN ANT *LASIUS NIGER*
(bottom left) NEST UNDER PAVEMENTS
AND GARDEN PATHS AND MATE ON
THE WING.

spins its web on bushes, walls and fences: when it captures
prey, it often does not kill the victim immediately, but rolls
it in silken coils until it is stifled. Like the toad, the creature
was once believed to contain a stone which cured disease.

House Spider

Tegenaria gigantea

The largest indoor spider in Britain has a dark body about
2 cm long and a legspan of at least 5 cm. Females can
survive for months without food or drink, and may live for
several years. They spin triangular webs in corners of sheds
and outbuildings, and become most obvious in autumn,
when males run about looking for mates.

Water Spider

Argyroneta aquatica

Having built a bell-shaped web under water, this spider
fills it with air bubbles, and lives in its miniature dome by
day, occasionally nipping out to snatch a passing insect.
At night it comes out to hunt in the water, and from time to
time it refreshes its oxygen supply by bringing down new
bubbles from the surface.

Crab Spiders

Thomisidae

These spiders lie in wait on flowers or leaves and pounce
when prey comes past. They walk sideways, having two
pairs of front legs longer than the two behind. The **zebra
spider** (*Salticus scenicus*) stalks prey and jumps on it from a
distance. **Money spiders** (*Linyphiidae*) make hundreds of
small sheet webs in the grass, creating wonderful patterns
in meadows on frosty or dewy mornings.

Ants *Formicidae*

In Cornwall, ants – also known as *meryons* or *muryans* – were
once thought to be fairies in the final stage of their earthly
existence. Another belief was that unbaptised children
took the form of ants after death, so that to destroy or even
disturb a nest was extremely unlucky. On the other hand, a
piece of tin placed carefully in a nest while the moon was
new would turn to silver.

Such fanciful ideas perhaps reflected admiration for the
highly organised social systems which ants adopt – for in

antiquity the creatures were considered models of industry and thrift. 'Go to the ant', commands Solomon in the Book of Proverbs. 'Consider her ways and be wise: which, having no guide, overseer or ruler, provideth her meat in the summer, and gathereth her food in the harvest.'

There are over 15,000 known species worldwide, some carnivorous, some herbivorous and some omnivorous, and they live in large colonies, each containing males, females and

neuters, or aborted females, all dominated by a queen. Their nests consist of irregular cells, connected by passages, so that different temperatures prevail in different areas, and the inhabitants keep them scrupulously clean, removing dead bodies and extraneous matter.

Sometimes both males and females have wings, but sometimes winged and wingless live together. The neuters include workers and soldier ants, which guard the colony. Like fertile females, the workers have stings and can eject poisonous formic acid in self-defence. Mating takes place between winged ants in flight, after which the males soon die. Fertilised females shed their wings and make their way to a nest, or are dragged to one by workers, and there they lay their eggs, which the workers carry from one part of the structure to another, to keep them at the optimum temperature. When the larvae hatch, they are fed with semi-digested food by the workers, which continue to look after them in the pupa stage, helping them out of their cases and licking them clean when they are fully formed.

A queen ant may reign for several years, but although workers can survive a winter by hibernating, most ants live for only one summer.

The most abundant species in Britain is probably the **Black garden ant** (*Lasius niger*), which nests under pavements and garden paths, or in crevices at the foot of walls. The dense swarms that fly about in summer and autumn are ants mating on the wing. The **Yellow meadow ant** (*Lasius flavus*) is very similar in shape, but pale yellow-brown instead of black, and builds its ant hills in rough pasture-land with such vigour that it often becomes a nuisance to farmers. Early in the twentieth century yellow meadow ants were imported to Petworth Park in Sussex, for the benefit of pheasants; but they made the pasture so

bumpy that it became impossible to cut the grass, and a bulldozer had to be brought in to level some areas. The ants are now an important source of food for green woodpeckers and other birds.

The **Red ant** (*Myrmica rubra*) often lives in garden soil or under stones. Like black ants, in summer it takes to the air to swarm and mate, the males much smaller than the young queens. Worker females are equipped with stings.

The large mounds of chopped leaves and other litter found in forests are made by the **Wood ant** (*Formica rufa*), which is protected by law in parts of Europe because of its value in destroying woodland pests. Although it has no sting, the wood ant can squirt formic acid from its rear end in self-defence.

Lice Mallophaga; Anoplura

Lice have troubled humans for thousands of years. They have been found in the hair of Egyptian mummies, and nit-combs have been used since at least 1500 BC. Yet they have also had their uses. In the north of England, during the nineteenth century, one remedy for jaundice was to swallow a tablespoonful of live headlice, which were supposed to make their way to the liver and cure it. A similar remedy, popular in the West Country, was to put nine lice on a piece of bread and butter, and eat it.

These minute, wingless parasites feed on mammals and birds. Their bodies are flattened, making them difficult to crush, and they have powerful claws for gripping on to their hosts. Biting species infest cattle and birds, pigeons and poultry especially, feeding on flakes of skin and feather.

HUMAN HEAD LOUSE *PEDICULUS*
HUMANUS (below) EVERY FIFTH
PRIMARY SCHOOLCHILD IN BRITAIN
IS THOUGHT TO BE INFESTED.

BIRD FLEA *CERATOPHYLLUS GALLINAE*
(bottom) THIS FLEA IS SHOWN
MAGNIFIED TEN TIMES, UNDER
POLARISED LIGHT.

Human Louse

Pediculus humanus

This blood-sucker can carry typhus fever, but is unlikely to do so in Britain. It exists in two forms, one that lives on the head, in the hair, and the other, which is larger, on the body. Head lice are so difficult to eliminate that every fifth primary school child in Britain is thought to be infested: children pass them on to one another in school and unwittingly bring them home. Mothers become distraught in trying to get rid of them, for they have grown resistant to most forms of insecticide, and some people try desperate remedies: there is one record of a woman anointing her children's heads with a mixture of dog-shampoo and whisky. Often the only way of eliminating lice is the laborious old-fashioned practice of fine-combing out their eggs when the hair is wet.

It used to be said that lice cannot survive in clean hair – but this was a myth, designed to promote more frequent washing. So long as a louse can suck blood from the scalp, dirt or cleanliness make no difference to it. Like many insects, it reproduces with dismaying facility. A female head louse lays an egg attached to a hair near the scalp. In seven days the egg hatches into a

nymph, and over the next six days this metamorphoses through three stages into an adult already capable of laying eggs. The term 'nit', often incorrectly used of the louse itself, in fact refers to the discarded egg case.

Fleas Siphonaptera

Also wingless parasites, fleas, too, are flattened, but from side to side, rather than from top to bottom, and their extra-long hind legs enable them to jump considerable distances, so giving them a measure of mobility. Different species live on humans, cats, dogs and rabbits, although identification of the various species is almost impossible without a microscope, which reveals differences in the shape of heads and the arrangement of bristles. The commonest household species, which often bites humans, is the **cat flea** (*Ctenocephalides felis*), but the **human flea** (*Pulex irritans*) and **dog flea** (*Ctenocephalides canis*) are also frequently found in houses, often in pets' sleeping quarters. There they scatter white eggs; when the larvae hatch out, they feed on debris. The **rabbit flea** (*Spilopsyllus cuniculi*) breeds in burrows and clusters round the hosts' ears, transmitting myxomatosis (*see page 85*). The most common **bird flea** in Britain is *Ceratophyllus gallinae*, which infests poultry houses.

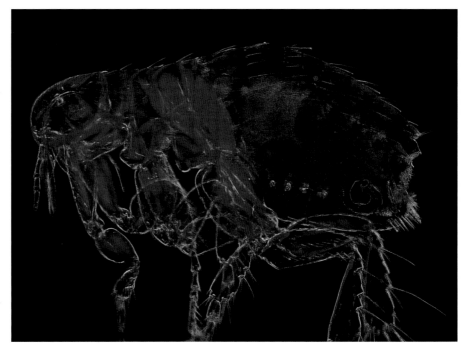

Bees

This large group of insects feed on pollen and nectar, which they carry back to their nests on their hairy back legs or their stomachs.

Honey Bee

Apis mellifera

For humans, this species is the most important bee. There are several strains, some almost black, some yellow, and some with a large orange patch on the base of the abdomen. Dark strains often seem more aggressive than the others.

Honey is one of the best natural sources of energy available to humans, and it has been valued for thousands of years. A celebrated Stone Age cave-painting in Spain shows a man up a tree or perhaps on a cliff-face, robbing a bees' nest, with angry insects swarming behind him. In time such wild honey hunting and gathering gave way to an intermediate process of making artificial hives out of hollow tree trunks or bark, in the hope that insects would occupy them; and from this developed the practice of active bee-keeping, in which the farmer manages colonies and takes off surplus honey as a regular harvest. From a very early date men realised that smoke could be used to stupefy bees temporarily and give some protection to a human raider of nest or hive.

The Romans were dedicated apiarists, and none more so than the poet Virgil, who was brought up on his family's farm near Mantua in the first century BC, and devoted almost the whole of his fourth *Georgic*, or agricultural treatise, to the techniques of bee-keeping. The poem begins with the lovely sentence, 'Next I will tell of heaven's gift, honey from the skies,' and the author's love of his bees shines out in passage after passage, as does his admiration of the insects' organisation and industry. Many of his precepts hold good to this day: he believed that thyme flowers produced the best honey, saw that different bees had different roles, recommended the use of smoke when honey was being taken, and understood that bees must be fed in winter; but along with the rest of his contemporaries he mistook the sex of the insect in charge of a colony, calling it the king instead of the queen.

He also misinterpreted much of the bees' behaviour, believing that swarms, for instance, were set off by the kings going out to do battle with another colony, and taking their troops with them. In trying to account where bees came from, he fell back on the old (and disgusting) story – 'the famous device of the Arcadian master, Aristaeus' – which claimed that the way to create a colony was to bludgeon a

bullock to death in a small enclosure and smash it to pulp, with the skin unbroken, and leave it there until fledgling bees began to emerge from its rotting remains.

In the Middle Ages, as now, bee-keepers regarded their charges with affection and respect. Colonies were neither bought nor sold for sordid money – only exchanged for other goods – and the insects were accorded every civility. A death in the family had to be reported to the inmates of hives immediately, or else they would die themselves, or fly away in umbrage.

To this day, if the owner of a colony sees his bees swarming, he tries to follow them across country, often ringing a bell or banging on a tin can or saucepan with a spoon or hammer. The practice goes right back to Roman times, but the purpose of it seems to have been often misunderstood. The eighteenth-century apiarist John Keys thought that the disturbance 'secures a legal right to follow your swarm upon another person's grounds in order to hive them'. Now, the idea of raising a racket is that if the bees hear sudden, loud noises, they may mistake them for approaching thunder, and quickly coalesce into a solid lump on the branch of a tree, so that the pursuer can take the swarm before it disappears over the horizon.

The social organisation of bees is intricate. Each colony consists of a queen, a huge number of workers – a total of about 10,000 in winter, rising to 50,000 or more in summer. In summer there are also a few hundred drones (males), which are killed off in autumn by being denied access to the hive. Besides these adults, the colony contains numerous immature bees in various stages of development – eggs, larvae and pupae – each sealed in a separate cell.

Wild colonies generally establish their nests in hollow trees or other protected sites, but sometimes they build from scratch in the open, glueing their structure to the branch of a tree. The nest consists of wax combs suspended vertically, each made up of hundreds of hexagonal cells in which young are reared and honey and pollen are stored. In a hive, the bee-keeper provides frames on which the insects draw out their cells.

In summer, while the colony is active, the average life of workers is only about five weeks. For some of the time they guard the hive and perform housekeeping duties, and for the rest, during daylight hours, they ceaselessly forage for pollen, nectar, water and propolis, the gluey substance collected from flowers and used for filling tiny holes or sticking down anything loose inside the hive.

The function of the queen is simply reproduction: she does not work, but is fed and looked after by the rest of her colony. Having hatched from her cell in a hive, she becomes mature in a couple of days, and within two weeks takes off on mating flights, during which she is mated by up to 15

Honey Bee

HONEY BEE *APIS MELLIFERA* (left)
A WORKER BEE GATHERING POLLEN
AND NECTAR.

BUFF-TAILED BUMBLE BEE (below)
LARGER AND THICKER THAN HONEY
BEES, THEY DO NOT STORE HONEY.

HONEY BEE COMB (following pages)
WORKER BEES IN THE COMB ON
HONEY STORAGE CELLS.

drones. Returning to base, she lays eggs at the rate of up to 3000 a day.

As the population of the hive rapidly builds up during the summer, especially in hot weather, part of the colony very often swarms, accompanying the old queen on a mass-flight to find a new home. A swarm departing makes an impressive sight and sound. More and more bees emerge from the hive and form a cloud whirling above the entrance, with their massed wings roaring. As the queen herself comes out, they all lift off and escort her away across country, until suddenly they descend onto the downward hanging branch of a tree or a fence-post, and coalesce into a single, solid lump, with the queen in the centre. Scouts, meanwhile, are searching for new quarters, and when they find somewhere suitable, they lead the swarm to it.

A swarm which has landed is often heart-shaped, and about the size of a rugby football. It looks solid and sticky, because the wings of the insects glisten as they move about. Yet in fact the mass is very light and bone dry: with one sharp twitch of the branch, a keeper can dislodge the whole lot, which falls with a quick rustle into his skep (a special basket) or box. He can then tip the bees out onto a board sloping up to the entrance of an empty hive, and, provided they like the smell of the place, they will march in, closely escorting the queen into her new quarters.

In winter the colony congregates inside the hive in a dense cluster, forming a ball among the combs. The bees at the top of the cluster are in contact with stored honey, and when they eat it, they generate heat, which passes outwards by radiation and convection. This keeps up the temperature of even the outermost bees, and enables the colony to withstand heavy frosts. So efficient is the system of control that a cluster temperature of 31°C has been recorded when the temperature outside the hive was −28°C – a difference of 59°C. Winter bees, and having stored up fat in autumn and being relatively inactive, live much longer than their summer fellows – maybe as much as six months.

Besides producing honey, bees perform the invaluable function of pollinating flowers and blossom. Fruit-growers often pay bee-keepers to bring hives and station them in their orchards during the spring, knowing that the insects will improve the crop; and professional apiarists move their hives around to take advantage of successive flowerings – lime trees, oilseed rape, clover, heather and so on alters the flavour of the final product.

During the 1990s British bee-keepers were much troubled by varroa, a fungal disease spread by mites which weakens or kills whole colonies unless treated with appropriate chemicals.

Like horses, honey bees can sense if a human being is nervous. A keeper who is calm and confident can often handle them without wearing gloves, but anyone apprehensive or frightened is liable to be attacked. A bee's ultimate weapon is its sting: however, when it stings, it sacrifices itself because the sting and its sac of venom are torn away from the abdomen.

Bumble Bees

Bombus

These large, hairy social bees have a more precarious existence than honey bees, for they do not store food. All but the mated queen die off in autumn, and she alone lives through the winter in hibernation, to start a new colony in spring. Bumble bees generally nest in holes in the ground – often in disused mouse holes – and they build their wax cells inside balls of grass and moss.

They are easy to distinguish from honey bees, being much larger and thicker, and their black bodies are banded with bold rings of yellow and orange. Several species have white tails, among them *Bombus jonellus*, which has a prominent yellow collar, and lives mainly on coasts and heathland. Also white-tailed, with collar and second segment of abdomen lemon-yellow, is *Bombus lucorum*, which is abundant in most districts, nests underground, and is out and about early in the year. *Bombus terrestris* is also common in the south of England, with collar and second segment orange.

Cuckoo Bees

Psithyrus

These are social parasites. There are no workers, and females lay in the nests of bumble bees, often killing the resident queen. Bumble bee workers rear the young cuckoos, which generally resemble the species on which they have been imposed. Cuckoo females hibernate through the winter, but arouse later than bumble bees, waiting for host nests to be started.

CABBAGE APHIDS *BREVICORYNE BRASSICAE* (below) FEEDING ON A CABBAGE LEAF.

GREENHOUSE WHITEFLY *TRIAL-EURODES VAPORARIORUM* (bottom) INFESTING TOMATO PLANTS.

VIOLET GROUND BEETLE *CALOSOMA VIOLACEUS* (right) HUNTS SLUGS AND SIMILAR PREY AT NIGHT.

Bugs Hemiptera

The word 'bug' is often used disparagingly, along with 'creepy-crawlie', to describe any insect of which the speaker disapproves. In fact it is the correct name for a whole order of insects, of which there are some 1700 species in Britain. Their variety is enormous – lace bugs, mirid bugs, water bugs, stilt bugs, shield bugs, ground bugs, squash bugs – but all have a pointed beak, called a rostrum, like a tiny hypodermic needle, for penetrating and sucking juices from plants or animals. Many do serious damage to plants, partly by physically injuring them, partly by spreading viral diseases.

Assassin Bugs

Reduviidae

Assassin bugs are powerful enough to pierce the skin if handled: they feed on other insects and often closely resemble their prey, in what is known as aggressive mimicry. If touched, several species stridulate loudly by rubbing the tip of the rostrum over the ridges underneath the thorax. The **bedbug** (*Cimex lectularius*), which can vary in colour from dark brown to bright orange, hides itself away by day, emerging at night to suck blood from humans or animals.

Water Bugs

Among water bugs, one of the most familiar is the common **pond skater** (*Gerris lacustris*), a predator which travels rapidly across the surface, snatching fallen insects with its front legs, prevented from getting wet by its covering of water-repellent hairs. The **water boat-man** (*Notonecta glauca*) – properly named the common backswimmer – swims upside-down, using the keel on its back to steer, with a bubble of air attached to its ventral surface, attacking tadpoles and minnows. In warm weather it often takes to the air.

Aphids

Aphididae

Gardeners need no introduction to aphids, which are sap-sucking bugs, and in spite of their tiny dimensions, cause enormous damage to plants in summer. The most notorious is the **Black bean aphid**, or **blackfly** (*Aphis fabae*), which infests broad beans in particular. Having spent the winter as eggs on spindle bushes or other shrubs, the insects take to the air and cruise across country in huge clouds, descending on host plants such as beans, sugar beet, docks and thistles, and, if left alone, crippling them by sucking out the sap. The **Rose aphid** (*Macrosiphum rosae*), commonly known as **greenfly**, does much the same, and the **Cabbage aphid** (*Brevicoryne brassicae*), which has a black thorax and green abdomen, feeds on brassica in spring and

early summer. Chemical pesticides will control all these species, but organically-minded gardeners prefer to wash the insects off plants with a hose or soapy water. Inside greenhouses, infestations of **Greenhouse whitefly** (*Trialeurodes vaporariorum*) play havoc with tomato and cucumber plants.

Beetles Coleoptera

There are some 4000 species of beetles in Britain, and although the majority can fly, they spend most of their time on the ground or on vegetation. They are easy to distinguish from other insects because their front or main wings, known as elytra, cover the whole abdomen when folded, meeting neatly in the middle and giving the body its characteristic armoured look, often with a metallic sheen. The hind wings are membraneous and transparent, and are kept folded beneath the elytra.

Biting jaws enable beetles to live on mainly solid food. Most species feed on living plants – leaves, fruit, roots and stems – but some can manage on dry food such as grain, animal bones and the mature wood in furniture, and others have hollow mandibles through which they can suck juices from victims. Those species that live in water can generally still fly, so that they have the ability to move from pond to pond; but they have developed paddle-like hind legs for swimming, and various methods of carrying air – often trapped in the space between the elytra and the body – which enable them to spend time under the surface.

GROUND BEETLES (Carabidae) are long-legged, fast-moving predators with powerful jaws. One of the commonest, often found in gardens, is the **Violet ground beetle** (*Calosoma violaceus*), a large insect over 2.5 cm long, which lurks under stones during the day, and comes out at night to hunt slugs or similar prey. Many people mistake these beetles for cockroaches, because from a distance they look almost black: in fact, as their name suggests, they have a dark purple thorax, and the elytra are almost black, with a crimson rim at the outer edges.

Another big black beetle, about 2 cm long, with ribbed elytra that give it an armoured look, and orange clubs on the ends of its antennae, is *Nicrophorus humator*, largest of the BURYING BEETLES (Silphidae). These are also known as **Sexton beetles**, and are carnivorous scavengers, equipped with a keen sense of smell. Other burying species are smaller, and several are boldly banded in black and orange. Often the beetles work in pairs: when they find a small corpse, of a bird or a mouse, they dig a shaft underneath it and pull the body down. The female then lays eggs close to the putrefying remains, on which she and her larvae feed.

Longer and slimmer are ROVE BEETLES (Staphylinidae) which are also scavengers and predators. The strangest-looking is the **Devil's coach-horse** (*Staphylinus olens*), which is all black and covered in fine hair. During the day it hides under stones, sticks or other litter, and at night emerges to hunt slugs and other invertebrates. It is also known as the Cock-tail, because when disturbed it curls its tail upright and opens its jaws wide in a threatening attitude.

Stag beetles are so-called because the male's long jaws are spread apart in a wide V, like the antlers of a red deer. The resemblance is increased by the fact that each jaw has three inward-facing hooks near the end, just like the points on antlers. There are two species of stag beetle in Britain: the Stag beetle (*Lucanus cervus*) and the Lesser stag beetle (*Dorcus parallelipedus*) which is the more common. The Stag beetle is large – over 3 cm long – and almost black, with a fine, dark-purple sheen on the elytra. Males often fight, grappling with their jaws, but not doing each other much harm. **Scarabs**, or **Dung beetles**, of various genera and species, feed on dung and either burrow under cowpats or roll manure into balls and then push them about before eating them.

The **Cockchafer** (*Melolontha melolontha*) also known as the May-bug, is smartly coloured, with bottle-green thorax and orange-bronze abdomen, but is a pest, because it chews the leaves of deciduous trees, and its larvae feed on the roots of plants, causing widespread damage to farm crops. So too do wireworms, which are the larvae of the **Click beetle** (*Agriotes lineatus*). The name derives from the insect's trick, if it falls onto its back, of flipping into the air and landing the right way up with a sharp click.

WOOD-BORING BEETLES are by their very nature destructive, since they scavenge in dry organic matter such as wood. The one with the worst reputation is the **Death-watch beetle** (*Xestobium rufovillosum*), which breeds in old trees and house timbers, preferring hardwoods such as oak, and thriving in damp conditions. Its larvae cause extensive damage in old buildings by tunnelling, and the name of the insect comes from the tapping noises which adults make to attract mates when they come out in the spring. Still more common is the **Furniture beetle** (*Anobium punctatum*), whose larva is the woodworm that bores holes through all kinds of timber. Its presence is usually given away by the small piles of wood-dust which tend to accumulate beneath the places in which it has been tunnelling.

One of the most mysterious beetles is the **Glow-worm** (*Lampyris noctiluca*), which gives out luminous signals to attract potential mates. The creatures have fascinated many a versifier, from Robert Herrick, who in the seventeenth century serenaded his lover, Julia, with lines like 'Her eyes the glow-worm lend thee, / The shooting stars attend thee', to the twentieth-century writer Walter de la Mare, for whom the insects evoked the essence of warm summer nights:

> But dusk would come in the apple boughs,
> The green of the glow-worm's shine …

In fact only the male glow-worm takes to the air, cruising around while the wingless female waits on the ground, seeking to attract attention with her phosphorescence. The soft green glow is produced by a chemical reaction in the rear sections of the abdomen, each illumination lasting only a second.

Anyone who sees a **Colorado beetle** (*Leptinotarsa decemlineata*), which is quite small, but boldly striped in yellow and black from fore to aft, must warn the police or some other suitable authority, for the insect, which originates from North America, is a lethal destroyer of potato and tomato crops.

BEETLE BANKS
Increasing awareness of the need for conservation, coupled with reluctance to scatter chemical

COLORADO BEETLES *LEPTINOTARSA DECEMLINEATA* (bottom left) AN EFFICIENT DESTROYER OF POTATO AND TOMATO CROPS.

WASP (below) ALTHOUGH SOCIAL CREATURES, WASPS DO NOT STORE FOOD SO HAVE A MORE PRECARIOUS EXISTENCE THAN BEES.

pesticides, has led researchers to experiment with the use of predatory insects for pest control, and striking results have been achieved, particularly on the Game Conservancy Trust's farm at Loddington in Leicestershire (*see page 210*). Long, low ridges of earth were heaped up, running across arable fields and planted with coarse grasses to form habitat for predatory beetles – the idea being that after overwintering in cover, the beetles would emerge in spring and and march out to devour pest species of insect in the adjacent cereal crops.

Such beetle-banks have proved extremely successful. Because the grass on them is left rough and thick, it harbours amazing numbers of predators. Polyphagous beetles – those which eat all species of prey, rather than specialising on one – have been recorded at a density of 1500 per square metre during winter, and in early summer – perhaps triggered by the lengthening of daylight hours – they move out into cereal crops, so that they are in position to make a killing the moment any pest species arrive.

The marauders have been found up to 200 metres from the banks, and the beauty of using them is twofold: not only do they obviate the need for toxic chemicals – they are also far cheaper. The cost of establishing and maintaining a bank is no greater than that of one season's application

of pesticide – so that each bank pays for itself in a single year. Before the banks were constructed, very few predatory beetles were present: their rapid build-up shows what can be achieved by simply providing good habitat.

Social Wasps Vespidae

Unlike bees, wasps do not store food, but live an apparently precarious existence, starting afresh every spring. Only mated queens survive from one year to the next, hibernating through the winter in rock crevices or behind flaps of bark on tree trunks.

In spring each queen builds a rudimentary nest, sometimes in a hole in the ground, sometimes in the roof space of a house, and lays several hundred or even a thousand eggs, which develop through a larval stage into young wasps. The female workers then extend the nest, chewing up dry wood from dead trees or fence-posts and mixing it with saliva to form a kind of grey paper. The structures can become enormous, often 50 cm or more across, and they contain combs of hexagonal cells, in which more young are reared, with the workers bringing in small insects to

383

WORKER HORNET *VESPA CRABRO*
(below) HORNETS LIVE ONLY IN THE
SOUTHERN HALF OF BRITAIN.

**MOSQUITO LARVA AND ADULT
EMERGING FROM PUPA** (opposite left
& right) ONLY FEMALES BITE.

feed them. Only in late summer do male wasps appear, and one of them mates in mid-air with the queen. In autumn workers and males die, leaving the nest abandoned.

There are several species of social wasp in Britain, mostly much alike, and differing only in details of colouring. The **Common wasp** (*Vespula vulgaris*) is the most familiar: the paper of its nest tends to have a yellow tinge, and is built into shell-like plates on the outside of the nest. The nests of **Tree wasps** (*Dolichovespula sylvestris*) are round balls, slung in bushes, and those of **Norwegian wasps** (*Dolichovespula norvegica*) are similar but looser-looking.

DIGGER WASPS (Sphecidae), of which some 9000 species are known to exist, tend to have broad, black heads and relatively slender bodies, some black and yellow like social wasps, some with reddish or orange bands. Most species dig burrows and nest in the ground, some build nests of mud. All tend to stock their bases with dead prey insects, paralysed by the stings of females.

Hornet

Vespa crabro

Because they look like (and are) outsized wasps, hornets are often thought to be aggressive and dangerous. In fact they are pacific insects, and do not attack humans unless severely provoked – for instance by someone creating a disturbance right in front of their nest. On the other hand, unlike bees, which can only sting once and then die, hornets, like other wasps, can sting repeatedly and implant a substantial dose of venom.

Hornets live only in the southern half of Britain, and their colonies are smaller than those of wasps, generally numbering only 200–300. Their life cycle is much the same, except that a mated queen often returns to the same nest, year after year, starting a new colony each time, but using the old structure, which can be in a hollow tree, a chimney or wall cavity.

Ladybirds Coccinellidae

Seven-spot Ladybird

Coccinella 7-punctats

With its round shape and bold colours – brilliant-red with black spots – this ladybird is a cheerful-looking beetle, and generally reckoned a bringer of luck. Nevertheless, it is saddled in folklore with a melancholy background: anybody on whom one lands is supposed to let it fly off on its own, or to accelerate it with a gentle puff of breath, at the same time reciting: 'Ladybird, ladybird, fly away home. Your house is on fire, and your children are gone.'

The commonest of the 42 British species is the Seven-spot ladybird, but other species bear spots in varying numbers, from 2 to 24. Not all ladybirds have black spots on red; some have red spots on black or black on yellow. All are carnivorous, and perform a useful service to gardeners by eating aphids such as greenfly and blackfly. In the past, in country districts, the ladybird had a variety of peculiar names: 'cush-cow lady', 'dowdy-cow' and the inexplicable 'Bishop Barnaby'.

Mosquitoes Culicidae

The males of this large family of flies are harmless to man, since they feed on nectar. It is the female, with her long, forward-pointing proboscis, that penetrates the skin to suck blood. Both sexes are mainly nocturnal, and females lay their eggs in water since their larvae are aquatic.

There are two main groups: the *culicines* and the *anophelines*. The first rest with their bodies almost parallel to the surface, the second sharply tipped up. The *anophelines* are the malaria carriers, but they are represented in Britain by only four species, one of which, *Anopheles plumbeus*, lives mainly in woods and often bites humans. Another frequent but relatively harmless biter is *Culiseta annulata*, one of the largest mosquitoes, which has spots on its wings and bold green and black bands on legs and abdomen. *Culex pipiens*, a very small form of mosquito, is generally known as a gnat. All British mosquitoes hibernate in winter, although they may fly in warm weather.

Midge

Culicoides obsoletus

'Often makes life intolerable in northern and upland areas', says the guidebook. 'Too true!' snorts the hiker, camper or fishermen, beset by clouds of midges on a muggy Highland evening, as the wretched little creatures attack with such persistence as to make any intricate activity, like erecting a tent, reading a map or tying a fly, impossible to perform.

Midges are by no means a purely Highland or even British nuisance. More than a thousand species exist, and in places like Florida millions of dollars are spent trying to suppress them, by draining swamps and spraying, so that they do not infuriate tourists. In the western Highlands of Scotland alone there are 50 species, many of them non-biting; the ones that annoy humans, animals and birds are the *Culicoides*, the only kind that feed on mammals. Other species are also carnivorous, but eat fellow insects, and

others again live on fungi. The notorious Highland midge is *Culicoides impunctatus*, the name referring to the light and dark patterns on its wings.

It is little comfort to know that only the females bite. Males have practically no jaws, but a female must get a feed of blood before she can lay her clutch of 50 to 100 eggs – and so, every two or three days throughout her life of about two weeks, she latches on to a deer, cow, rabbit, sheep, human or bird. Her jaws consist of three different pairs of biting, gripping and sucking organs, and her tactic is to puncture the skin with a tiny hole, in which a pool of blood collects. The agent which makes the bite itch and irritate is the anticoagulant in her saliva. Humans, being generally short of protective hair and feathers, offer prime targets. The midge's habit of landing on a victim and crawling make the fringes of one's hair and the cuffs of one's shirt or jacket favourite areas for infiltration.

The eggs are so small that they are only just visible to the naked eye when set out on white paper. In the wild they are laid on wet mud, peat or other choice hosts such as cowpats, and the larvae which hatch from them travel through water with wriggling, snake-like movements. Adults are killed off by autumn frosts, but their offspring survive the winter as mature larvae, buried in the soil. Their

bodies appear to contain some natural antifreeze, and as the weather grows colder, they burrow deeper into the ground for increased protection. In spring they hatch out and lurk in vegetation, waiting for targets to come along.

Minute though they are, midges are extraordinarily complex organisms, equipped all over their bodies with hundreds of receptors for measuring levels of light, temperature, carbon dioxide and so on. In the words of one scientist, Dr Richard Lane, 'Under a microscope, they're really elegant little things. They make a spacecraft look clumsy'.

It is their intricate sensory equipment that enables them to judge weather and atmospheric conditions (and smell humans) so well. They are essentially crepuscular, flying at dawn and dusk, and on days that are overcast. In bright sunlight they stay at home – as they do if the wind is blowing at more than six or seven km/h.

Yet it is also their sensors that give humans a chance to keep mosquitoes and midges at bay, using one of the patent repellents on the market. These are mostly based on chemicals DMP and DEET, which function not by confronting the insects with an unpleasant-smelling barrier, but by confusing their receptors and jamming their radar as they come in to land.

10

Insects
Mosquitoes

Midge

386

Annelids

This order includes earthworms and leeches, both of which have segmented bodies and well-developed vascular and respiratory and nervous systems, but no eyes. There are 1800 species of terrestrial worms and about 300 species of leeches.

Common Earthworm

Lumbricus terrestris

This humble creature contributes immensely to the fertility of soil by digging, ingesting earth and decayed vegetable matter, passing it through its body and casting it out again, thus aerating and draining the ground. A single hectare of good pasture may support 250,000 worms. They grow to a length of about 15 cm, and each body segment is equipped with four pairs of bristles, or *chaetae*, which grip the ground or the walls of tunnels as the owner stretches and contracts its body, thus allowing it to move along.

Although blind, they are sensitive to light and to vibration, and they come to the surface at dusk or after dark on warm evenings. Even then they tend to keep their tails in the entrances of their burrows, so that they can beat a rapid retreat if danger threatens. Their purpose in surfacing is usually to mate, for which purpose they wrap themselves in a coccoon of mucus. Every worm has five hearts, which store blood rather than pulsate.

Medicinal Leech

Hirudo medicinalis

For 2000 years at least doctors have used leeches to drain blood from their patients. The practice was common in ancient Greece, and in 1829–36 some 6 million leeches were used Paris hospitals. Yet only in recent years have scientists come to understand the value of hirudin, the substance which a biting leech releases to stop the blood of its host clotting; now an artificial version of the substance, known as bivalirudin, is used on patients who have suffered heart attacks, to reduce the risk of blood clots and repeated attacks. Hirudin is extracted from leeches on a large scale for medical use and demand is so high that a number of leech farms exist to supply the medical industry. Leeches themselves are still used today in medicine, mainly to remove excess fluid following plastic surgery or swelling after deep-vein thrombosis.

Leeches are worm-like creatures that grow to about 15 cm: their slender, slightly flattened bodies are grey-green on top, with thin orange lines running along it, and brighter green underneath. They swim by undulating their bodies, and on land they advance by hooping their backs and using their suckers, front and rear, to push and pull themselves along. Armed with three tiny serrated teeth sharp enough to penetrate human skin, a leech can ingest five times its weight of blood at one session. In earlier times it was common, but it has now become rare, and is listed for support in the Biodiversity Action Plan.

Gastropod Molluscs

The name gastropod means 'belly-foot', and both slugs and snails move on a flattened, muscular part of their body which acts as a foot, expanding and contracting to draw the creature along. Slow-moving they may be, but they are also surprisingly agile, and can often be found high up trees or vertical walls. In winter they generally hibernate in sheltered hollows, but if the weather warms up they come out to forage. Male and female sexual organs exist in the same individual, and numerous eggs are laid in decaying vegetation. Slugs and snails both have mouths equipped with external fleshy lips and internal teeth.

Slugs

In many respects slugs resemble snails, except that they have no external shell, or, at most, only a small vestigial shell growing under the skin of the back. If disturbed in the open, a slug attempts to defend itself by drawing in its head and tentacles and shrinking to the smallest possible size.

Grey Slug (Field Slug)

Deroceras reticulatum

One of the commonest slugs in Britain, this is the one that does most damage in gardens. By day it tucks itself away in crevices or under stones, but at night it emerges to feed on many kinds of plant. It also comes out after rain. Luckily it also eats dead plant and animal matter, and this minimises damage to some extent. On a muggy night in summer a walk with a torch may reveal that slugs are present in alarming numbers. In one study of a garden in Hertfordshire, a researcher found 200 slugs every half-hour: during the

GREY SLUG *DEROCERAS RETICULATUM* (below left) IS EXTREMELY SOFT AND GIVES OFF A MILKY FLUID IF TOUCHED.

GARDEN SNAIL *HELIX ASPERSA* (below) HIBERNATES AMONG IVY IN WINTER BY RETREATING INSIDE ITS SHELL.

year, he removed 16,000 slugs from the garden, yet at the end of the experiment, there were just as many.

Grey slugs are extremely soft, and give off a milky fluid if touched. The **Large black slug** (*Arion ater*) is more common in fields and along hedges than in gardens, and can grow to a length (extended) of 10–15 cm. The **Garden slug** (*Arion hortensis*) is also black, but much smaller – only 3–4 cm long. In autumn several species eat their way into field mushrooms, leaving them full of holes. They also eat poisionous fungi, without taking harm. Species that live in woodland tend to be larger, the **Great grey slug** (*Limax maximus*) reaching a length (extended) of 20 cm.

Snails

People have been eating snails since the Stone Age, and the creatures were long considered an excellent remedy for coughs, colds and tuberculosis. In Victorian London dairymen used to beat up snails in milk and pass off the frothy white product as cream. Although not much fancied in England, the French still consider escargots a delicacy.

Because all land snails are descended from sea creatures, they need a moist environment, and flourish particularly in typically wet British weather. One characteristic is that, like slugs, they secrete slime as they move, and leave a trail of it behind them. Some kinds of snail have two pairs of retractile tentacles protruding from their heads, with eyes on the ends of the upper pair. Others have one pair of non-retractable tentacles, with eyes at the base. All kinds of snails can withdraw head and foot fully into the shell as a form of defence.

The **Roman snail** (*Helix pomatia*), with its creamy-brown shell, is still the favourite of French gastronomes, and occurs widely in England, often in woods. But the **Garden snail** (*Helix aspersa*) is probably the most familiar. In summer it wreaks havoc on crops such as lettuces, and in winter dozens of the creatures congregate in some snug retreat, often among thick stems of ivy, to hibernate, closing down for the duration by forming membranes across the opening of their shells.

11 FOREIGN BODIES

After some sharp lessons in the past, conservationists are now more responsible and cautious about bringing back animals and birds which were once native to Britain; but enthusiasm for enriching our fauna runs high. Ornithologists have been thrilled by the re-establishment of the osprey, and the more recent return of the red kite and the sea eagle – but these successes have all been the result of careful management.

The folly of introducing exotic species without proper examination of the possible consequences has been brutally demonstrated by the fiasco of the grey squirrel. Earlier sections of this book have described the problems created by the importation and deliberate spread of sika and muntjac deer, both of which are increasing fast and will never be eliminated. Another, though lesser disaster, has been the proliferation of American crayfish, imported for commercial gain. Yet many introductions have been accidental rather than deliberate: our feral mink, for instance, escaped from fur farms, and are here to stay. Another animal which caused enormous damage before it could be brought under control was the coypu.

Persuasive arguments can be advanced for the reintroduction of once indigenous species like the wolf and beaver, but there is no justification for the all-too-prevalent practice of dumping unwanted animals in the countryside and leaving them to their fate. Even a creature as small and apparently harmless as an edible dormouse can become a nuisance in an alien environment.

Coypu (Nutria)

Myocastor coypus

One of the largest rodents in the world, the South American coypu is a relative of the guinea pig: it grows to a length of 60 cm and weighs up to 9 kg. In appearance it is somewhere between a small beaver and an enormous, bloated rat, brownish-yellow on the back and lighter below, with conspicuously bright orange incisor teeth and long, scaly tail. Except that it does not fell trees or build dams, its habits are like those of the beaver: for living quarters, it excavates burrows along the banks of streams and lakes, or builds platform nests in stands of reeds, and it is almost entirely vegetarian, eating leaves and roots of water plants.

The first coypus brought to England were imported in 1929, to be farmed for their soft under-fur, known as nutria, and within three years they had begun to escape. Those that got away into Hampshire, Sussex and Surrey soon died out, but in Norfolk some established themselves in the Broads: with females capable of breeding twice a year, and producing up to nine young in each litter, they increased rapidly, and their descendants spread out through East Anglia.

At first it was hoped they would prove a beneficial addition to the native fauna – that, by eating reeds, they would help keep waterways clear. Soon, however, they proved too powerful for the environment. Not only did they devour garden vegetables, cereal crops, potatoes and above all sugar-beet, and undermine the banks of waterways with their burrows; they also destroyed whole reed-beds, thereby damaging the habitat of rare birds and causing a scarcity of reeds for thatching.

In 1943 the War Agricultural Executive Committee set out to control the pests – and it should have been easy enough, for although good swimmers, coypu are slow and clumsy ashore, and easy to trap. But the first trapping campaign, which ran for two years, proved ineffective, and the feral population built up so fast that by 1960 it was reckoned to be 200,000. The government then enlisted the aid of rabbit-clearance societies, increasing grants so that they could tackle the coypu, and by the autumn of 1962 nearly 100,000 had been

killed, caught in live-capture traps and then shot. Many thousands, however, remained at large, and another major assault was launched. Nobody, at that stage, believed it would be possible to eliminate coypus entirely: rather, the objectives were to stop the animals spreading any farther, and to reduce those on the Broads to tolerable numbers.

During the next three years some 40,000 were killed in the core area; and nature lent a hand, in the form of the bitter winter of 1962–3, during which thousands more animals died of cold. Yet the survivors dispersed even more widely, and an organisation known as Coypu Control was set up to continue culling. Numbers fell during the late 1960s, but then, boosted by a series of mild winters, rocketed away again: by 1972 the average number caught every month rose to 270, and the population was thought to be still 10,000.

With the aim changed to total eradication, a final campaign was launched. Trapping was intensified, especially on the Broads, where traps set on rafts proved most effective, and the population fell rapidly from about 6000 in 1981 to zero in 1987. This last operation alone cost £2.5 million.

Muskrat

Ondatra zibethicus

Another substantial amphibious rodent, twice the size of a water vole but less than half that of a coypu, the muskrat is a native of North America: it was introduced to Europe in 1905 to produce fur (known as musquash), and escapees spread until the animal had colonised much of the Continent. Breakouts from fur farms in England during the 1930s led to the establishment of a large feral colony in

Shropshire, along the Severn Valley, and smaller colonies in Surrey, Sussex and on the borders of Perthshire and Stirlingshire in Scotland.

Intensive trapping campaigns, launched in 1932, quickly eliminated the invaders: within three years nearly 1000 muskrat had been caught in Scotland, almost 3000 in Shropshire, and by 1938 there were none left in the wild. Another infestation, around Loch Derg, on the Shannon in the centre of Ireland, was similarly contained, and nearly 900 muskrat were caught. Unfortunately, because leg-hold traps were used, more than 2000 water voles and 2000 moorhens were also killed in Ireland alone.

Wild Boar

Sus scrofa

After at least four centuries of absence, wild boar are back in England. Reintroduction occurred accidentally: the process started in 1981, when a farmer bought surplus stock from London Zoo and began to breed boar for the meat market. Boar farming expanded rapidly, and at some point, or points, animals escaped, with the result there is now a feral population of at least 100 in the extensive woodland of Kent and East Sussex, with a small separate colony in Dorset. Wild boar are common in many countries of mainland Europe, but Britain is not yet adjusted to having such powerful and destructive creatures at large, and their presence has caused considerable disquiet.

Nobody has owned up to losing any, but the total of potential sources is considerable. Over 40 farms are registered with the British Wild Boar Association, and an unknown number of other establishments are also breeding the animals: stock is thought to number about 2000 sows. At first farmers favoured crossing wild boar with domestic pigs, and in particular with Tamworths, to produce what they called the 'Iron Age pig', the main reason being that hybrid sows would have two litters a year. Soon, however, it became apparent that meat from the cross-breeds lacked the distinctive flavour which makes wild boar so sought-after, and producers once again concentrated on truly wild animals, many of which were imported from Scandinavia.

From examination of shot carcasses, experts are convinced that the animals at large are genuine wild boar, rather than free-living feral pigs (domestic animals that have gone wild) or hybrids – and this indicates that the escapees are breeding among themselves. Wild boar are much rougher and hairier than domestic pigs, with a bristly coat which may be black, grey or brown, but grows thicker and greyer in winter.

Wild boar are among the species listed in the Dangerous Wild Animals Act of 1976; and their reputation for being highly strung and aggressive if frightened, has been confirmed by several incidents in Kent. One farmer was charged by a large male, which forced him to take refuge on the roof of an outbuilding. A deer-stalking friend, summoned by telephone, quickly came and shot the animal in an adjoining field – but only just before it put in a charge at him as well. Another farmer in Kent was harvesting wheat when he disturbed a sow with six piglets. The animal attacked the wheels of the combine before taking her family off into a nearby wood.

Such encounters make it clear that the wild boar could be a hazard to members of the public, walking on footpaths through woods or fields. They have already caused several accidents on roads; but a greater danger is that they may spread diseases like swine fever or foot-and-mouth by breaking into domestic pigs' enclosures

A full-grown boar is a formidable animal, with tremendously powerful head, neck and shoulders, and razor-sharp tusks with which to rip open any opponent. A big male, weighing up to 150 kg, can burst through normal stock fences with ease by pushing his snout under the bottom wire and forcing it up. Stronger barriers, with the lowest section buried 30 cm deep in the soil, are needed to keep such hefty creatures in or out, preferably reinforced by electric wires close to the ground, and set half a metre from the main fence.

They live in small groups known as sounders up to 20 strong, based round a core of two or three mature females and their most recent litters; but outside the breeding

season, males are solitary. Like red or fallow deer, they rut in the autumn: males move into the family groups and fight each other for dominance. After 15 weeks' gestation, sows farrow in a scrape in the ground lined with grass and twigs, producing between four and six piglets, which are strongly striped in brown and white.

Both sexes and all ages are largely nocturnal: the pigs spend most of the day lying up in thick cover, and go out to forage on fields at or after nightfall. They are practically omnivorous: although plant food such as shrubs, roots, bulbs, seeds, grain, nuts and fruit makes up 90 per cent of their diet, they also eat mice, birds, snakes, lizards, worms, beetles and carrion. In arable fields and pastures they cause considerable damage by devouring corn and rooting up the ground, and many farmers are convinced that they take newborn lambs.

Their secretive nature and nocturnal routines make them difficult to cull, especially in summer and autumn, when undergrowth is high. Yet on the Continent wild-boar shooting is a valued sport: in Germany, for instance, over 200,000 animals are killed every year, either in drives or from high seats, by marksmen using high-velocity rifles, and the meat commands high prices. There and in Italy the authorities pay large amounts of compensation for damage to agriculture and forestry. Here, in contrast, there is as yet no organised shooting and no system of compensation:

only 40 wild boar had been shot up to 1998, and culling had been haphazard; but a report compiled by the Central Science Laboratory and published that year concluded that the population – about 100 in 2000 – is likely to go on rising, perhaps to 400 by 2010.

European Beaver

Castor fiber

Four hundred years have passed since beavers were hunted to extinction in Scotland, but now carefully laid plans to bring them back are at last coming to fruition.

In the 1870s several attempts to reintroduce the animals were made by the Marquis of Bute, who walled in four acres of ground in the middle of a pine wood, with a stream running through it, and in 1874 released four beavers into the enclosure. These soon died, but seven more were imported in 1875, and within three years the keeper in charge of them reported that he was 'certain of 16 being alive', and probably more. He was fascinated by the animals' industry, and by the skill with which they built dams to raise the water level. By 1878, when he wrote, they had already felled 185 trees, the biggest 1.5 metres in circumference, and 'done a great amount of underground work, such as cutting channels in their dams and making burrows'.

In the south, also, an attempt at reintroduction was

WILD BOAR *SUS SCROFA* (left) WILD
BOAR WITH YOUNG, KEPT WITHIN
AN ENCLOSURE. HEFTY BARRIERS ARE
NEEDED TO KEEP THEM CONFINED.

EUROPEAN BEAVER *CASTOR FIBER*
(below) AFTER A GAP OF 400 YEARS
THE BEAVER HAS BEEN REINTRO-
DUCED TO KENT.

made in 1869, when beavers were released into Sotherley Park in Suffolk. There, however, their energetic building was appreciated less than in Scotland, and one of their dams was destroyed 'as an eyesore'. Stragglers of the colony, swept downstream, survived for a couple of years, but in the end two were killed and one captured. The natural historian J. E. Harting concluded his account of them with the enigmatic remark, 'Two of the three were sent to London to be stuffed for Lady Gooch, and the headkeeper took the skin of the third.'

Some 130 years on, well-planned experiments should have better chances of success. Wolves still stir atavistic fears in humans; but recent research has shown that on the whole people like the idea of beavers, which they perceive to be industrious, furry vegetarians, harmless to man. The animals are large, amphibious rodents, and the object of their characteristic activity – cutting down trees and building them into dams – is to raise the water level round the lodge in which they live. The process not only gives them security, by flooding the immediate area: it also inundates the land round about, creating waterways into forage areas. The lodge itself, made of branches, is placed so that its entrances are under water but the nest chamber is on a platform above the surface.

Beavers have several unusual physical features, including webbed hind feet and special lobes of tissue in the cheeks which close the mouth behind the incisor teeth, so that they can gnaw underwater without swallowing. They can also close their ear and nasal passages while swimming. In spring and summer they live on a wide variety of grass, twigs and leaves, and in winter they turn to the bark of trees like willow and poplar, storing felled trunks in water to preserve their nutritional value.

They normally live in small family groups, depending on the environment, and mark their territories by spraying castoreum from their scent glands on mounds of earth around the perimeter. After a gestation period of about 15 weeks, up to six young are born in June: pups are fully furred at birth, and learn to swim within a few hours.

The initiative for reintroduction to Scotland came from Scottish Natural Heritage (SNH), which in 1999 issued a consultative document and circulated a questionnaire. Responses showed that an overwhelming majority of ordinary people – 86 per cent – were in favour of beavers returning, and it was decided to stage a limited trial.

Preliminary research was carried out

jointly by the Forestry Commission and SNH. Contact was made with overseas experts, three of whom came from Norway to look at Scottish forests and assess their potential as beaver environment. SNH then asked the Commission to suggest possible sites for a trial, one vital consideration being that the deer population in the area should be fairly low – for if beavers are released into a habitat that is already overgrazed, they can wreck the environment. Their instinctive aim is always to promote the growth of relatively small trees and shrubs, and to manage their surroundings so that they have a good supply of regenerating shoots and foliage on which to feed. If grazing and browsing by deer are too severe to let such shoots come up, the woodland will be eliminated and the beavers will move on.

In due course the choice of site fell on Knapdale, in Argyllshire, where a mixed forest is threaded by burns and dotted with lochans and swamps. To test local opinion SNH invited members of the public to a village on the edge of the forest for two 'drop-in' days, one of which attracted 200 people. SNH emphasised that the experiment would proceed there only if the local majority was behind it – and public opinion came out firmly in favour. The next step was to seek the approval of the Scottish Assembly (Parliament): not until this was forthcoming could any beavers be imported and in the summer of 2002 this was still awaited.

If beavers got out of control, they could cause immense damage, since their gnawing and digging powers are formidable: one animal can fell a tree with a circumference of 25 cm in about four hours, a single family may cut down 300 small trees in one winter, and all ranks constantly excavate burrows and water channels. Yet it should be possible to keep numbers to an optimum level, for the animals are large – almost a metre long, not counting the tail and

weigh up to 155 kg – and if necessary can be culled by marksmen with rifles, as indeed they are in Norway.

In April 2001, while the Scots were still deliberating, the Kent Wildlife Trust stole a march on them by flying in a group of nine beavers, a gift of the Norwegian government. The aim is to carry out a five-year trial, with the animals released into a fenced reserve of about 50 hectares – a former peat bog, with a stream running through it – and to discover how they would modify or influence their environment. It is hoped that the beavers' activity will benefit other wildlife such as otters, water voles and dragonflies.

Big Cats

Are there pumas, black leopards and lynxes at large in Britain, or are there not? Hundreds of people claim to have seen big cats or found their tracks, and give convincing descriptions, yet although fresh sightings keep being reported, the evidence remains inconclusive.

The saga dates at least from 1962, when a hefty carnivore began to be seen in the thickly wooded country south of Godalming in Surrey. First-hand accounts built up so fast that the creature soon became known as the Surrey Puma, and in 1964 the police in Godalming opened a Puma Book in which some 380 incidents were recorded.

Some witnesses were clearly over excited – among them the woman who reported 'exceptionally loud purring' outside her window one night. Others, however, had their feet firmly on the ground. One farmer saw a huge black cat with a small head and long tail sweeping down so that the back half of it was parallel with the ground, stalking up one of his hedges. Having watched it for a minute, he ran in to fetch a gun and buckshot cartridges, but by the time he went out again, it had vanished.

Sheep were killed, bullocks and heifers lacerated by claw marks, and gamekeepers found roe deer with their necks broken. Presumably the killer had been released by an owner who had acquired it as a pet or guard, but found it growing too big and too expensive to keep. But nobody could account for its provenance, and no clue ever emerged about what happened to it in the end.

During the 1970s the main theatre of activity shifted to Exmoor, where sightings and incidents increased steadily, and during 1976 the government introduced the Dangerous Wild Animals Act, largely in response to public disquiet about the keeping of big cats. The Act made it obligatory for anyone wishing to keep a dangerous animal to take out a licence from the local authority, to provide secure accommodation, to hold insurance against any liability caused by the animal, and so on.

Whether or not the Act had any effect on owners in other areas, it seemed to put the wind up somebody in Scotland, where a female puma was trapped in Glen Cannich during 1981. The animal had clearly been a pet, for it was tame, thin and unable to kill even something as small as a rabbit: it was taken to the Highland Wildlife Park at Kincraig, where it was named Felicity, and lived for the rest of its life. Its stuffed form now graces a gallery in the Inverness Museum.

Meanwhile, in Devon, acitivity came to a peak in the spring of 1983: so many sheep were killed on Drewstone Farm, South Molton, that the owner, Eric Ley, called in independent hunters, the police, and finally a detachment of Royal Marines, hoping that professionals would shoot the marauder. Again, although losses of sheep diminished, there was no conclusive result.

In 1989 there appeared *They Stalk by Night*, an 80-page book by Nigel Brierly, a retired biologist living on the southern edge of Exmoor. Years of research, and analysis of numerous sightings, had convinced him that the sheep-killers were big cats, and not, as many people had claimed, half-wild dogs. Everything reported about the elusive hunters was feline, from their round heads, green eyes and long tails to their method of killing, which was to stalk a victim and spring on it, without any of the preliminary coursing and harassment characteristic of dogs. Mr Brierly came to the conclusion that several different species were involved, for his informants had given clear, detailed accounts of pumas both black and brown, and also of lynxes, which have a different shape and are easily identified by the long tufts on their ears.

In 1993 the focus switched to Bodmin Moor, where Rosemary Rhodes, a farmer near Jamaica Inn, caught a large black cat on video. For the previous three years she had been harassed by phantom sheep-killers, and in 1992 she had called in John Lambert, a professional tracker who had been one of the Royal Marines deployed on Exmoor nine years earlier. During this new assignment he had several encounters with big cats, including one with a lynx, which passed under the tree in which he was sitting. Yet still the evidence remained equivocal – until Mrs Rhodes managed to film one of the raiders, which an expert from London Zoo identified as a Southeast Asian leopard.

One persistent puzzle has been the failure of local hunts to pursue the animals. Several times after sightings, foxhounds have been brought in and put on the line, but never with any success. It may be that dogs do not recognise big cats as huntable prey, but on the contrary have a natural fear of them. Many eyewitnesses have described how dogs bristle up and bolt when they come across one of the felines, or even its scent.

By the mid-1990s the beasts of Bodmin and Exmoor

crouching under a hedge. Attempts to net it having failed, the forces of law-and-order cornered it under the steps of a nearby flat, and Mr March sedated it with a dart from a blow-pipe. The creature turned out to be an 18-month-old female lynx, which the Zoo officials named Lara. Obviously someone had released it – and probably not far away – but nobody came forward to own up, and inquiries revealed that the local council (Barnet) had not issued any Dangerous Wild Animals licence.

By the beginning of 2002 Ian Wickison, a wildlife photographer living near Peterborough, had devoted much of the past eight years to the study and tracking of feral big cats. His researches have left him convinced not only that pumas, black leopards and lynxes are at large, but that their numbers run into

were causing farmers serious concern. The sight of two pumas together, both wearing collars, made people fear that animal-rights activists had been making releases; and this, combined with the fact that big cats already on Exmoor had bred cubs, threatened to produce a population of major carnivores larger than the fragile environment would stand. Roe deer and rabbits provide a certain amount of food, but attacks of farm stock seemed bound to increase.

Thereafter the number of attacks dwindled, but sightings continued to be reported. Attempts to analyse the DNA in hair and droppings collected in the West Country yielded no positive results, and at the end of the millennium the mystery of the big cats remained unsolved.

In May 2000, however, sceptics received a further set-back. A woman in Golders Green, north London, telephoned the police to say she had seen a leopard sitting on her garden wall. The head keeper of big cats at London Zoo, Terry March, was immediately driven to the scene with a police escort – and sure enough, he found a substantial animal

hundreds. According to his records, an old male puma has been seen many times near Northampton; black leopards frequently appear in back gardens in Peterborough, and there has been much activity in the country to the south-west of the city.

New legislation introduced during 2000 tightened the regulations on the disposal of surplus animals by zoos; but it was still relatively simple to obtain a big cat on the black market, or through the Internet.

Wolf (Grey Wolf, Common Wolf)

Canis lupis

In recent years several enthusiasts have shown keen interest in reintroducing wolves to the Scottish Highlands. The main arguments for reinstatement are that the carnivores were part of the original fauna, and that there is now a superabundance of natural prey in the form of red, roe and sika deer, which need to be reduced for the good of the

environment. The arguments against are that wolves would attack the easiest targets first – that is, sheep – and would also scare hikers, climbers and tourists in general. Any decision to bring them back would be based more on political than on purely ecological considerations.

Earlier apprehension about wolves seems to have died away: in 2001, when the Mammal Society conducted an Internet survey to find out which animal people would most like to see repatriated to Scotland, 33 per cent of the 1000-odd respondents voted for the wolf. Next came the beaver, with 27 per cent, easily beating the lynx (20 per cent), and leaving the brown bear and wild boar trailing with 10 and 9 per cent respectively.

Most people agree that, even though wolves are timid creatures, and keep out of man's way as much as they can, a general release would not be tolerable. Nevertheless, various schemes have been suggested – for instance, for putting wolves on to an island such as Rhum, which belongs to Scottish Natural Heritage, is self-contained, and has a large deer population of about 1600 head, but no sheep. It has been calculated that surplus animals from the deer herd would sustain two packs of about ten wolves. Another plan was for the establishment of a wolf centre, where a pack of tame animals would be kept in large enclosures, primarily for educational purposes. The idea was that children would visit the centre to learn about wolves and other wildlife, and that the animals themselves would tour schools, spreading useful knowledge.

That scheme foundered for lack of funds. But in the south something almost identical has already proved a great success. Since its foundation in 1995 the UK Wolf Conservation Trust at Beenham in Berkshire, has done much to banish the traditional, storybook image of the animal as a sinister and dangerous creature. The trust now has over 2000 members: it is run largely by dedicated volunteers, who in winter take the wolves for walks through nearby woods, accompanied by up to 30 visitors, and in summer tour schools and country shows.

One ambitious conservationist hopes to bring back not only wolves, but also the other major carnivores which once were present in the Highlands, the brown bear and the lynx. The proposal here is to create a wildlife reserve on the lines of the one at Madikwe in South Africa, where a huge area of derelict farmland has been ring-fenced and stocked with wildlife, including lions, leopards and elephants. In Scotland, the organisers hope to acquire an estate of perhaps 20,000 hectares, fence it securely, and release animals fitted with radio transmitters so that their movements can be monitored. The park would be financed by tourism, with visitors (it is hoped) paying high prices to stay in a luxurious lodge and have the thrill of walking or riding

among major carnivores, thus helping to create jobs and bring money into an impoverished area.

Whether or not this will ever prove feasible, everyone agrees that wolves still exercise a powerful fascination and can be used as magnets to draw people in. At the Highland Wildlife Park near Kingussie the wolves are by far the strongest attraction, easily beating lynxes, bison, beaver and other original denizens of the Scottish mountains.

Reindeer

Rangifer tarandus

Reindeer were once common all over Britain (*see page 26*). Attempts to reintroduce them began in the eighteenth century, when the Duke of Atholl released 14 on his estate in Perthshire. Again, in the nineteenth century, several landowners imported stock – to Orkney, to Aberdeenshire and Northumberland – but all attempts failed, even though the animals were turned out at fairly high altitude, on a type of mossy pasture which seemed to suit them best in their native country.

It was not until 1952 that, in an attempt to set up reindeer-herding as a commercial venture, a herd was firmly established on the Cairngorms. In May that year eight animals were brought from Sweden by Mikel Utsi and his wife Dr Ethel Lindgren. After nearly two months' quarantine, during which one calf died, the remaining seven were released into a 120-hectare, wired-in reserve on the hills of Rothiemurcus estate, in Inverness-shire. In October ten more joined them, later reinforced by two from London Zoo. At first their performance proved disappointing: there were early casualties, and breeding success was poor; but the group kept going, and in 1988, when the herd was about 70-strong, it was bought by Alan and Tilly Smith, who had helped look after it for the previous 10 years.

One of their first decisions was to reduce grazing pressure by splitting the herd in two. They obtained a second site on the Crown estate at Glenlivet, and the reindeer responded so well to fresh management that they now number 150 in all: indeed, the new owners have had to limit breeding. In summer they keep the Cairngorm herd in a 400-hectare enclosure, partly to protect calving females from walkers' dogs, but in winter the deer are loose on the mountain. Unlike sika, they are socially exclusive, and do not associate with the red deer.

The original aim, of furnishing Scotland with a source of good meat, has never been achieved, and no animals are slaughtered for consumption. Yet the Smiths manage to finance their herd by taking members of the public up to see it, by getting people to adopt individual deer (at £28 per head per year), and, in December, by transporting seasoned, castrated bulls to key places such as Harrods, where they star in Christmas displays.

Both sexes of reindeer have antlers, although those of the cows are much smaller. A bull's head, being irregularly branched and asymmetrical, gives the animal an awkward, untidy look. A bull stands about 100 cm at the shoulder – roughly the same as a fallow buck – and is noticeably greyer in the coat than red deer or fallow. While a herd is feeding, cows and calves keep up a continuous low barking, and on the move the animals give out a curious clicking sound, made by tendons in their legs stretching over bony protruberances.

The British animals have adapted well to a form of life quite different from that in Lapland, where reindeer are herded, in a semi-wild state, and moved on by their keepers to ensure that they are on the best form of pasture at each season of the year: although they will eat moss, seaweed and various kinds of grass, as well as woodland fungi, lichens are the most important item in their diet. In their native habitat the animals mass together to migrate huge distances – up to 1000 km – moving as much as 150 km a day on their journey between tundra and woodland. Lapps use reindeer for milk, meat and hides, as well as for transport and draft: they can pull heavy loads on sledges over good snow.

Elk

Alces alces

During the 1970s a Scottish farmer, Hugh Brunton, decided to diversify by breeding moose (American elk) and crossing them with red deer, to produce large hybrids for meat production. He obtained his foundation stock from Chester Zoo, and by the end of the millennium he had expanded his herd to almost 70 individuals, varying from pure elk to quarter-bred.

Hybrid animals are a good proposition for the butcher, as they weigh more than twice as much as red deer, and the joints are much larger. Other farmers have bought pure-bred elk from Mr Brunton, to start similar enterprises, so that after several centuries of absence, the animal (albeit of the American variety) has made a limited and somewhat confined comeback in Britain.

Appendix

Organisations concerned with animals

Advocates for Animals Founded 1912. Membership 12,000. *Leading animal-protection organisation. Campaigns against all forms of abuse, particularly against the use of animals in experiments.* 10 Queensferry Street, Edinburgh EH2 4PG

Animal Aid Founded 1977. Membership 19,000. *Campaigns against cruelty, especially in factory farms and laboratories.* The Old Chapel, Bradford Street, Tonbridge, Kent TN9 1AW

Animals (Scientific Procedures) Inspectorate *Controls experimental and other scientific work on living animals.* Home Office, 50 Queen Anne's Gate, London SW1 9AT

Atlantic Salmon Trust Founded 1967. *Encourages conservation of salmon and sea trout. Campaigns for sound management of wild stocks.* Moulin, Pitlochry, Perthshire PH16 5JQ

Bat Conservation Trust Founded 1990. Membership 4000. *Only British organisation solely devoted to conservation of bats.* 15 Cloisters House, 8 Battersea Park Road, London SW8 4BG

Battersea Dogs' Home *Charity, founded 1860. Aims to rescue, rehabilitate, rehome dogs and cats. Has 140 staff in London and 60 at Old Windsor, Berkshire and Brands Hatch, Kent.* 4 Battersea Park Road, London SW8 4AA **Lost Dogs Line** 0990 477 8477.

Blue Cross *Charity founded in 1897 as Our Dumb Friends' League, an animal welfare organisation. Name changed to Blue Cross in 1950s. Aims to find new homes for unwanted animals; to promote responsible pet ownership and welfare of companion animals.* The Blue Cross, Shilton Road, Burford, Oxon OX18 4PF

Bristol Zoo Gardens Clifton, Bristol BS8 3HA

British Association for Shooting and Conservation Founded 1908. Membership 112,000. *Formerly the Wildfowlers' Association of Great Britain and Ireland, BASC works to ensure highest standards in shooting.* Marford Mill, Rossett, Wrexham LL12 0HL

British Bison Association Founded 1991. Membership 21. *Promotes the keeping of North American bison.* Bush Farm, West Knoyle, Warminster, Wilts BA12 6AE

British Deer Society Founded in 1963, the BDS promotes the welfare and good management of all species of deer. *A private charitable organisation, 6000 members.* The British Deer Society, Burgate Manor, Fordingbridge, Hampshire

British Falconers' Club Founded 1927 by surviving members of the Old Hawking Club. Membership 1000. *Maintains standards in falconry, provides advice.* Home Farm, Hints, Tamworth, Staffordshire B78 3DW

British Goat Society *Aims to circulate information, encourages goat-keeping and improve breeds.* 34–36 Fore Street, Bovey Tracey, Newton Abbot, Devon TQ13 9AD

British Hedgehog Preservation Society Founded 1982. Membership 10,000. *Encourages conservation study and care of hedgehogs.* Knowbury House, Knowbury, Ludlow, Shropshire SY8 3LQ

British Herpetelogical Society Founded 1947. Membership 1000. *Caters for all interested in reptiles. Education, conservation, captive breeding.* c/o Zoological Society, Regent's Park, London NW1 4RY

British Horseracing Board Founded 1993. *Governing authority for horseracing in Great Britain.* 42 Portman Square, London W1H 0EN

British Horse Society Founded 1947. Membership 50,000. *Charity, to improve the welfare, care and use of the horse.* British Equestrian Centre, Stoneleigh Park, Warwickshire CV8 2LR

British Isles Bee Breeders' Association Founded 1964. Membership 480. *Organisation of owners who seek to improve the standard of bee-keeping in the British Isles by promoting restoration of native honeybee, the Dark European.* 11 Thomson Drive, Codnor, Ripley, Derbyshire DE5 9RU

British Mule Society Founded 1978. Membership 150. *Promotes responsible care of mules.* 2 Boscombe Road, Swindon, Wiltshire SN25 3EY.

British Ornithologists' Union Founded 1858. Membership 2000. *Aims to promote ornithology in the scientific and birdwatching communities. Helps finance research into and management of declining species. Publishes quarterly journal Ibis.* Natural History Museum, Akeman Street, Tring, Hertfordshire HP23 6AP

British Rabbit Council Founded 1934. Membership 4000. *Aims to further the interests of all British rabbit breeders and to promote the welfare of rabbits in general.* Purefoy House, 7 Kirkgate, Newark-on-Trent, Nottinghamshire NG24 1AD

British Show Jumping Association Founded 1925. Membership 15,000. *Governing body of show-jumping in Britain. Formulates rules and codes of practice.* British Equestrian Centre, National Agricultural Centre, Stoneleigh Park, Warwickshire CV8 2LR.

British Trust for Ornithology Founded 1933. Membership 12,000. *The leading wild bird research organisation in the UK, concerned with scientific study. Information collected by 10,000 volunteer watchers and analysed by the staff of 75; forms the basis of conservation action in the UK.* The National Centre for Ornithology, The Nunnery, Thetford, Norfolk, IP24 2PU

British Trust for Conservation Volunteers Founded 1959. Membership 83,000. *The UK's largest practical conservation charity. Organises wide range of work opportunities for volunteers.* 36 St Mary's Street, Wallingford, Oxfordshire OX10 0EU

British Veterinary Association Founded 1880. Membership 9000. *National representative body for the veterinary profession.* 7 Mansfield Street, London W1M 0AT

British Waterfowl Association Founded 1872. Membership 1000. *Promotes the keeping of domestic ducks and geese.* Oaklands, Blind Lane, Tamworth in Arden, Solihull B94 5HS

British Wild Boar Association Formed 1989. 42 member farms. *Aims to promote the commercial development of husbanded wild boar.* PO Box 100, London W6 0ZJ.

Butterfly Conservation Founded 1968. Membership 8250. *Dedicated to saving wild butterflies and their habitats.* PO Box 222, Dedham, Colchester, Essex CO7 6EY

Cairngorm Reindeer Centre *Manages the only herd of reindeer in the UK.* Glen More, Aviemore PH22 1QU

Care for the Wild Founded 1984. Membership 20,000. *International charity dedicated to protecting animals from cruelty and exploitation.* 1 Ashfolds, Horsham Road, Rusper, Horsham, West Sussex RH12 4QX

Carnivore Wildlife Trust Founded 1991. Membership 500. *Aims to facilitate introduction of wolves to the Scottish Highlands.* 35 Church Street, Kidlingon, Oxon OX5 2BA

Cat Association of Britain Formed 1983. Membership 600. *The British member of the Fédération Internationale Féline, a non-profit association of worldwide cat fancy organisations. Promotes welfare and reponsible breeding of domestic cats. Holds international shows.* Mill House, Letcombe Regis, Oxon OX12 9JD

Cats' Protection Founded 1927. *The UK's oldest and largest feline charity.* 17 King's Road, Horsham, W. Sussex RH3 5PN

Chester Zoo Caughall Road, Upton-by-Chester, Cheshire CH12 1LH.

Countryside Alliance *Formerly the British Field Sports Society. Founded 1930. Membership 85,000. Defends field sports and rural way of life.* 59 Kennington Road, London SE1 7PZ

Countryside Council for Wales *British government's statutory adviser on Welsh wildlife, countryside and maritime matters. The national wildlife conservation authority. Employs 540 staff.* Plas Penrhos, Ffordd Penrhos, Bangor, Gwynedd LL57 2LQ

Deer Commission, Scotland *Formerly the Red Deer Commission, founded 1959. Statutory body charged with furthering the conservation and control of deer in Scotland.* Knowsley, 82 Fairfield Road, Inverness IV3 5LH

DEFRA – Department of Environment, Food and Rural Affairs *Government department. Responsibilities include wildlife and fisheries.* Nobel House, 17 Smith Street, London SW1P 3JR

Donkey Breed Society *Charity founded as the Donkey Show Society 1967. Membership 900. Aims to encourage the use of donkeys, their protection and general welfare, and the breeding of good quality stock.* The Hermitage, Pootings, Edenbridge, Kent TN8 6SD

Donkey Sanctuary *Established 1969. Became a charity 1973. Aims to prevent donkeys suffering worldwide. Has taken in 8500 donkeys on its 11 farms.* Slade House Farm, Sidmouth, Devon EX10 0NU

Edinburgh Zoo 134 Corstorphine Road, Edinburgh EH12 6TS

English Nature *Government-funded body, promotes conservation of England's wildlife and natural features. Employs 660 permanent staff, and its responsibilities include overseeing 200 National Nature Reserves; 1 Marine Nature Reserve; 4088 Sites of Special Scientific Interest (SSSIs, or Triple SIs); 76 Ramsar Sites – wetlands of international importance; 80 Special Protection Areas; National Office:* Northminster House, Peterborough PE1 1UA

Environment Agency *The Environment Agency for England and Wales was set up in 1995, superseding National Rivers Authority. The Agency employs over 9000 staff. Aims are to protect or enhance the environment, to improve the quality of air, land and water, to encourage the conservation of natural resources, plants and animals, to reduce pollution and generally to manage water resources. The agency encourages measures which will reduce the emission of greenhouse gases.* Rio House, Waterside Drive, Aztec West, Almondsbury, Bristol BS32 4UD

Farms for City Children *Founded 1974 Charity takes inner-city schoolchildren to live and work on farms. Owns farms in Devon, Pembrokeshire and Gloucestershire.* Nethercott House, Iddesleigh, Winkleigh, Devon EX19 8BG

Federation of City Farms and Community Gardens *Organisation of local projects involving people, animals and plants. Some 65 farms and over 500 gardens, ranging in size from 16 hectares to 100 square metres.* The Green House, Hereford Street, Bristol BS3 4NA

Federation of Zoological Gardens of Great Britain and Ireland Zoological Gardens, Regent's Park, London NW1 4RY

Game Conservancy Trust *Independent wildlife conservation charity which conducts research into game and its associated species and habitats. 25,000 members, spends over £2 million a year on research, carried out by 60 scientists based at Fordingbridge and at study centres throughout UK. Head Office:* The Game Conservancy Trust, Fordingbridge, Hampshire SP6 1EF

Governing Council of the Cat Fancy *Founded 1910. 139 affiliated clubs. The feline equivalent of the Kennel Club, the GCCF is the governing body of the Cat Fancy in UK, and licences pedigree cats and shows.* 4–6 Penel Orlieu, Bridgwater, Somerset TA6 3PG

Guide Dogs for the Blind Association *Founded 1934. Charity devoted to breeding and training guide dogs. Employs 1200 professional staff in 18 centres across the UK. Three-quarters of income derives from legacies.* Burghfield Common, Reading RG7 3YG

Hawk and Owl Trust *Founded in 1969 because of concern about the fall in peregrine numbers. Charity works to conserve wild birds of prey and their habitat.* c/o Zoological Society of London, Regent's Park, London NW1 4RY

Heather Trust *Charity which promotes the good management of heather moorland for the benefit of domestic stock, game and other wildlife.* The Cross, Kippen, Stirlingshire FK8 3DS

Herpetological Conservation Trust *Charity set up in 1989 to safeguard British reptiles and amphibians. Aims to protect, improve and manage suitable sites, promote research, education and public awareness. Manages over 60 reserves covering nearly 1500 hectares, and conducts research into conservation techniques.* 655A Christchurch Road, Boscombe, Bournemouth, Dorset BH1 4AP

Highland Wildlife Park *Founded 1976 as a private venture. Now a department of Edinburgh Zoo. Extensive wildlife park containing many animals once native to the Scottish Highlands, including wolf, lynx, bison and beaver.* Kincraig, Kingussie, Inverness-shire PH21 1NL

Howlett's and Port Lympne Wild Animal Parks *Has the largest captive breeding group of gorillas in the world.* Port Lympne, Lympne, Hythe, Kent CT21 4PD

Hurlingham Polo Association *Founded 1874. Membership 2000, through 46 affiliated clubs and 62 pony clubs*

Jersey Zoological Park *Founded by Gerald Durrell, 1959. Headquarters of Durrell Wildlife Conservation Trust.* Les Augrès Manor, Trinity, Jersey JE3 5BP, Channel Islands.

Joint Nature Conservation Committee *British government's wildlife adviser. Undertakes conservation work on behalf of the three national agencies, English Nature, Scottish Natural Heritage and the Countryside Council for Wales.* Monkstone House, City Road, Peterborough PE1 1JY

Kennel Club *Founded 1873. Membership 750. Aims to promote the general improvement of dogs. Classifies and registers pedigree dogs and associated societies. Licences 5000 shows, trials and competitions annually. Promotes responsible dog ownership.* 1 Clarges Street, London W1J 8AB

London Zoo *Founded 1828. Now attracts 1 million visitors a year. Conducts extensive research in Britain and many countries overseas.* Regent's Park, London NW1 4RY

Mammal Society *Dedicated to the study and conservation of British mammals. Publishes books and fact-sheets. Organises national surveys through volunteer members.* 15 Cloisters House, 8 Battersea Park Road, London SW8 4BG

Mammals Trust UK *Founded 2001. Only charity dedicated to raising funds for the conservation of British mammals and their habitat.* 15 Cloisters House, 8 Battersea Park Road, London SW8 4BG

Marwell Zoological Park *Opened 1972.* Golden Common, Winchester, Hampshire SO21 1JH.

Masters of Draghounds and Bloodhounds Association *Represents all the packs in the UK.* Blacklands Farm, Milford Road, Elstead, Surrey GU8 6LA

National Association of Farms for Schools *Organises farm visits for school children. Has more than 200 farms on its books.* PO Box 27, Hebden Bridge, HX7 5YZ

National Birds of Prey Centre *Founded 1967. Aims to conserve birds of prey through education, captive breeding, research and rehabilitation. Has one of the oldest, largest and best-known collections of birds of prey in the world.* Newent, Gloucestershire GL18 1JJ

National Canine Defence League *Founded 1891. Britain's largest charity working for dog welfare runs network of 15 rescue centres.* 17 Wakley Street, London EC1V 7LT

National Cattle Association *Founded 1906. Membership 20,000. Represents the interests of cattle breeders.* 60 Kenilworth Road, Leamington Spa, Warwickshire CV32 6JY

National Fancy Rat Society *Established 1976. Aims to promote domesticated rats as pets and exhibition animals.* PO Box 24207, London SE9 5ZF.

National Federation of Badger Groups *Founded 1986. Membership 14,000. Promotes welfare and conservation of badgers, working through 90 local groups.* 15 Cloisters House, 8 Battersea Park Road, London SW8 4BG

National Foaling Bank *Founded 1965. Membership 1170. Provides an adoption service for orphan foals by matching them with suitable foster mares.* Meretown Stud, Newport, Shropshire TF10 8BX

National Mouse Society *Founded 1895. Membership 120. Promotes the breeding and welfare of fancy mice.* 44 Speeton Avenue, Bradford BD7 4NQ

National Sheep Association *Founded 1892. Membership 11,000. Represents the interests of members in the sheep industry.* The Sheep Centre, Malvern, Worcestershire WR13 6PH

Organisations
concerned
with animals

403

National Trust Founded 1895. Membership 2.8 million. *The Trust is not a government body, but an independent charity which exists primarily to preserve places of historic interest and/or natural beauty.* The National Trust, 36 Queen Anne's Gate, London SW1 9AS General inquiries, including membership and requests for information: National Trust Membership Department, PO Box 39, Bromley, Kent BR1

Naturewatch Founded 1993. Membership 20,000. *Campaigns against animal cruelty, promotes awareness of welfare issues in schools and colleges.* 122 Bath Road, Cheltenham, Gloucestershire GL53 7JX

Otter Trust Founded 1971. Membership 1500. *Registered charity which promotes restoration of otters and their habitat.* Earsham, Bungay, Suffolk NR35 2AF

People's Trust for Endangered Species 15 Cloisters House, 8 Battersea Park Road, London SW8 4BG

Pony Club, UK Founded 1929. Membership 40,000. *Works for young people with an interest in horses and riding.* British Equestrian Centre, Stoneleigh Park, Warwickshire CV8 2LR

Poultry Club of Great Britain Founded 1877. Membership 2000. *Aims to encourage the conservation of 300 pure and rare breeds of poultry.* 30 Grosvenor Road, Frampton, Boston, Lincolnshire PE20 1DB

Racehorse Owners' Association Founded 1945. Membership 4000. *Professional representation in dealings with other bodies in racing.* 42 Portman Square, London W1H 9FF

Rare Breeds Survival Trust Founded 1973. Membership 10,000. *National charity founded to ensure the survival of all endangered rare breeds of British farm livestock. Carries out a regular census of less common breeds and publishes lists of those at greatest risk.* National Agricultural Centre, Stoneleigh Park, Warwickshire CV8 2LG Also: Cotswold Farm Park, Guiting Power, Stow-on-the-Wold, Glos. GL54 5UG

Riding for the Disabled Association Founded 1969. Membership 714 groups. *Aims to enable the disabled to ride and drive.* Lavinia Norfolk House, Avenue R, National Agricultural Centre, Stoneleigh Park, Warwickshire CV8 2LY

Royal Agricultural College Founded 1845. *First agricultural college in English-speaking world. Leader in agricultural education.* Cirencester, Gloucestershire GL7 6JS

Royal Agricultural Society of England Founded 1838. Membership 15,000. *Promotes and develops farming; organises Royal Show and other events.* National Agricultural Centre, Stoneleigh Park, Warwickshire CV8 2LZ

Royal Racing Pigeon Association Founded as the National Homing Union in 1897. Membership 60,000. *Representative body of UK racing pigeon owners. Registers 1.5 million birds every year.* The Reddings, Cheltenham, Glos. GL51 6RN

Royal Society for the Prevention of Cruelty to Animals *Founded in 1824 as the Society for the Prevention of Cruelty to Animals, the RSPCA received its royal charter from Queen Victoria in 1840. A registered charity supported by a volunteer network of 195 branches; it has 50,000 adult members, 38,000 junior members and an annual income of £70 million, more than half of which comes in the form of legacies. Has four animal hospitals and three wildlife hospitals. Has campaigned for the abolition of hunting with hounds and for a ban on mink farming.* Causeway, Horsham, West Sussex RH12 1HG

Scottish Natural Heritage *Statutory body set up by Act of Parliament in 1991, an amalgamation of the former Countryside Commission for Scotland and the Scottish Nature Conservancy Council. Has dual role, to oversee conservation and recreation in the countryside. Employs 600 staff. Owns several large nature reserves, including the Isle of Rhum.* 12 Hope Terrace, Edinburgh EH9 2AS

Sea Watch Foundation Founded 1991. *Charity created to find out more about whales, dolphins and porpoises in British and Irish waters, by involving members of the public in monitoring of living cetaceans. 2000 volunteers from all over Britain help gather information.* 11 Jersey Road, Oxford OX4 4RT

Soil Association *Charity founded 1946. 30,000 members and supporters, over 40 local groups. Aims to protect the environment by promoting sustainable relationships between the soil, plants, animals, people and the biosphere. Campaigns for organic farming and food, and for reduction in use of antibiotics in animals.* Bristol House, 40–56 Victoria Street, Bristol BS1 6BY

Turkey Club UK Founded 2000. Membership 70. *Aims to promote pure, rare breeds of turkey.* Graycots, 4 Kingston Road, Great Eversden, Cambridge CB3 7HT

Royal Society for the Protection of Birds Founded 1889. Granted royal charter 1904. Membership over 1 million. *The largest wildlife conservation organisation in Europe. Manages 161 nature reserves covering 111,500 hectares.* The Lodge, Sandy, Bedfordshire SG19 2DL

UK Wolf Conservation Trust Founded 1995. *Non-profit trust. Aims to enhance conservation, scientific knowledge and public awareness of wolves, and to improve their image.* UK Wolf Centre, Butlers Farm, Beenham, Reading, Berks RG7 5NT

Vincent Wildlife Trust *Private charity, founded 1975 by Vincent Weir. No members; seven field staff. Commissions research into mammals, especially bats, otters and pine martens.* 3 & 4 Bronsil Courtyard, Eastnor, Ledbury, Herefordshire HR8 1EP

Wildfowl and Wetlands Trust Established 1946. Membership 90,000. *Aim is to conserve wetlands and the species that live in them. Some 8 million people have visited Slimbridge, on the bank of the Severn, but the organisation has 8 other reserves.* Slimbridge, Glos. GL2 7BT

Wildlife Trusts *The Wildlife Trusts evolved from the Society for the Promotion of Nature Reserves, founded in 1912 by Charles Rothschild, who compiled a list of 240 sites which he thought worthy of protection. The oldest of the Trusts is Norfolk, inaugurated in 1926 to buy Cley Marshes. With the establishment of the Scottish Wildlife Trust in 1964, 36 trusts covered the whole of UK.*

In 1976, with membership over 100,000, SPNR changed its name to the Society for the Promotion of Nature Conservation, and in 1977 HRH the Prince of Wales became Patron. In 1981 the name changed again to the Royal Society for Nature Conservation. At the end of 2000 the group had a network of 46 independent wildlife charities, over 100 urban wildlife groups and a total of 325,000 members; in all it was managing 2300 nature reserves, which cover some 80,000 hectares. The junior branch of the Wildlife Trusts, Wildlife Watch, has 20,000 members.

On a political level, the organisation has pressed for a radical reform of the Common Agricultural Policy, and a switch from subsidies that encourage production to payments that promote environmental improvement.

Woodland Trust Membership 100,000 *UK's leading woodland conservation charity. Manages over 1100 sites covering 19,000 hectares.* Autumn Park, Grantham, Lincolnshire NG31 6LL

Sources Consulted

AIKIN, Arthur, *Journal of a Tour through North Wales in 1787*. 1797.

ALDERTON, David, *Cats*. Dorling Kindersley Handbook, London, 1992.

ASHER, Jim and others, *The Millennium Atlas of Butterflies in Britain and Ireland*. Oxford, 2001.

BANVILLE, Larry, *The Banville Diaries*. London, 1986.

BLUNT, Wilfrid, *The Ark in the Park*. London, 1976.

BOSTOCK, Stephen St C., *Zoos and Animal Rights*. London, 1993.

BOSWELL, James, *The Life of Samuel Johnson*. London, 1791.

BOVILL, E.W., *English Country Life 1780–1830*. London, 1962.

BRIGHT, Michael, *The Private Life of Birds*. London, 1993.

BUCKLAND, Frank, *Curiosities of Natural History*. Two vols, London, 1866.

BULLER, Fred, and Falkus, Hugh, *Freshwater Fishing*. London, 1975.

CADBURY, Deborah, *The Dinosaur Hunters*. London, 2000.

CAESAR, Julius, *De Bello Gallico*. Translated by S. A. Handford, London, 1963.

CAIUS, Dr Johannes, *De Canibus Britannicis*. Translated by Abraham Fleming as *Of Englishe Dogges*. London, 1576.

CAMDEN, William, *Britannia*, London 1610. Translated by P. Holland, 1611.

CARR, Raymond, *English Fox Hunting*. London, 1976.

CHESTER, Robert, *Love's Martyr*. London, 1601.

CHINERY, Michael, *Collins Guide to the Insects of Britain and Western Europe*, London, 1986.

CLABBY, John, *The Natural History of the Horse*. London, 1976.

CLARK, Michael, *Badgers*. London, 1988.

COOPER, Jilly, *Animals in War*. London, 1983.

CUNLIFFE, Barry and others, *The Penguin Atlas of British and Irish History*. London, 2001.

DANIEL, Rev. William B., *Rural Sports*, Two vols, London, 1801.

DIPPER, Dr Frances, Powell, Dr Anne, and others, *Reader's Digest Field Guide to the Water Life of Britain*. London, 2001.

FAIRLEY, J. S., *An Irish Beast Book*. Belfast, 1975.

FLANNERY, Tim, *The Eternal Frontier*. London, 2001.

FRASER DARLING, Frank, *A Herd of Red Deer*. Oxford, 1937.

GASCOIGNE, Bamber, *Quest for the Golden Hare*. London, 1983.

GEIST, Valerius, *Deer of the World*. Swan Hill, Shrewsbury, 1999.

GREEN, Miranda, *Animals in Celtic Life and Myth*. London, 1992.

HAGENBECK, Carl, *Beasts and Men*. Abridged trans. by Hugh S.R.Elliot and A. G. Thacker. London, 1909.

HALDANE, A.R.B., *The Drove Roads of Scotland*. London, 1952.

HARTING, J.E., *British Animals Extinct Within Historical Times*, London, 1880.

HAWKES, Jacquetta and Christoher, *Prehistoric Britain*. London, 1947.

HAYMAN, Peter, and Hume, Rob, *The Complete Guide to the Birdlife of Britain and Europe*. London, 2001.

HELM, P.J., *Exploring Prehistoric England*. London, 1971.

HOLINSHED, Raphael, *Chronicles, Vol. 1*. London, 1577.

HONE, William, *Every-Day Book or Everlasting Calendar of Popular Amusements*. Three vols. London, 1827.

HOPKINS, Harry, *The Long Affray*. London, 1985.

HOWELL, James, *Familiar Letters*. London, 1624

HOWITT, William, *The Rural Life of England*. Two vols, 1838.

HUBBARD, Clifford L.B., *Dogs in Britain*. London, 1948.

LEVER, Christopher, *The Naturalised Animals of the British Isles*. 1977.

LISTER, Adrian, and Bahn, Paul, *Mammoths: Giants of the Ice Age*. London, 1994.

MACDONALD, David, and Barrett, Priscilla, *The Collins Field Guide: Mammals of Britain and Europe*. London, 1993.

McDONALD, John, *The Origins of Angling, including the text of Dame Juliana Berners' The Treatise of Fishing with an Angle*. New York, 1963.

MACDONALD, David, and Barrett, Priscilla, *The Collins Field Guide: Mammals of Britain and Europe*. London, 1993.

MEAD, Chris, *The State of the Nation's Birds*. British Trust for Ornithology, 2000.

MORSE, Richard, *The Open Book of Wild Life*. London, 1941.

MORTIMER, Roger, *The History of the Derby Stakes*. London, 1962.

MUSGROVE, Andy and colleagues, *The Wetland Bird Survey, 1999–2000*. British Trust for Ornithology, 2001.

NEAL, Ernest, *The Natural History of Badgers*. London, 1986.

NICKERSON, Joseph, *A Shooting Man's Creed*. 1989.

NIMROD (C. J. Apperley), *The Life of John Mytton Esq.*, London, 1835.

PALMER, Roy, *The Folklore of Gloucestershire*. Westcountry Books, Tiverton, 1994.

PARKER, Eric, *English Wild Life*. London, 1929.

PAWSON, H. Cecil, *Robert Bakewell, Pioneer Livestock Breeder*. London, 1957.

PERRINS, Christopher, *Birds of Britain and Europe*. Collins New Generation Guide, London, 1987.

PHIPSON, Emma, *The Animal-Lore of Shakespeare's Time*. London, 1883.

RADFORD, E. & M.A., *Encyclopaedia of Superstitions*. Edited and revised by Christina Hole, London 1961.

RITCHIE, James, *The Influence of Man on Animal Life in Scotland*. Cambridge, 1920

RUDGLEY, R., *Lost Civilisations of the Stone Age*. London, 2000.

ST. JOHN, Charles, *The Wild Sports and Natural History of the Scottish Highlands*. London, 1888.

SMITH, Tilly, *Velvet Antlers, Velvet Noses*. London, 1995.

SPENCE, Lewis, *The Magic Arts of Celtic Britain*. London, 1945.

SPINDLER, Konrad, *The Man in the Ice*. London, 1994.

STREET, Philip, *Mammals in the British Isles*. London, 1961.

TAPLIN, William, *The Sportsman's Cabinet*. Two vols, London, 1803.

TAPPER, Stephen, *Game Heritage*. Joint Nature Conservation Committee, 1992.

TAPPER, Stephen (Editor), *A Question of Balance*. Game Conservancy Trust, 1999.

THOMAS, Keith, *Man and the Natural World*. Penguin, 1987.

TOPSELL, Edward, *Historie of Four-footed Beastes*. London, 1607.

TOPSELL, Edward, *Historie of Serpents*. London, 1608.

YALDEN, D.W., *The History of British Mammals*. London, 1999.

YARRELL, William, *A History of British Birds*. Four vols, London, 1882–84.

VIRGIL, *The Georgics, Book 4*.

WALTON, Izaak, *The Compleat Angler*. First published 1653.

WHITE, Gilbert, *The Natural History and Antiquities of Selborne*. First published 1788.

WHITEHEAD, G. Kenneth, *The Deer of Great Britain and Ireland*. London, 1964

WHITEHEAD, G. Kenneth, *The Whitehead Encyclopedia of Deer*. Swan Hill, Shrewsbury, 1993.

WHITLOCK, Ralph, *Royal Farmers*. London, 1980.

WOOD, Rev. J.G., *Illustrated Natural History, Vol. 1: Mammals*. London, 1865.

WOODFORDE, Rev. James, *The Diary of a Country Parson*. Five vols, 1924–31.

ZEUNER, Frederick E., *A History of Domesticated Animals*. London, 1963.

Index

General Index

Headings in *italics* refer to titles of paintings or books. Numbers in *italics* refer to illustrations.

Index of animals

Page numbers in *italics* refer to illustrations. Where there are three or more text entries the main reference page numbers are in **bold** type.